The Making of Social Theory

ORDER, REASON, AND DESIRE

ANTHONY THOMSON

OXFORD
UNIVERSITY PRESS

OXFORD

UNIVERSITY PRESS

70 Wynford Drive, Don Mills, Ontario M3C 1J9
www.oup.com/ca

Oxford University Press is a department of the University of Oxford.
It furthers the University's objective of excellence in research, scholarship,
and education by publishing worldwide in
Oxford New York

Auckland Cape Town Dar es Salaam Hong Kong Karachi
Kuala Lumpur Madrid Melbourne Mexico City Nairobi
New Delhi Shanghai Taipei Toronto

With offices in
Argentina Austria Brazil Chile Czech Republic France Greece
Guatemala Hungary Italy Japan Poland Portugal Singapore
South Korea Switzerland Thailand Turkey Ukraine Vietnam

Oxford is a trade mark of Oxford University Press
in the UK and in certain other countries

Published in Canada
by Oxford University Press

Library and Archives Canada Cataloguing in Publication

Thomson, Anthony, 1949–

The making of social theory / Anthony Thomson.

Includes bibliographical references and index.

ISBN 13: 9780195419683   ISBN 10: 0-19-541986-3

1. Sociology—Philosophy—Textbooks. I. Title.

HM586.T49 2005   301'.01   C2005-901846-1

Cover design: Brett Miller

1 2 3 4 – 09 08 07 06
This book is printed on permanent (acid-free) paper ⊚.
Printed in Canada

CONTENTS

ACKNOWLEDGEMENTS

The idea to write an introduction to social theory came, initially, through practical necessity. When I was instructing a graduate seminar on British intellectual history in Beijing, there were few resources to use, but I had access to an old computer and a photocopier. That was the origin of the earliest drafts of some of the discussion that follows. I remember quite humbly the comradeship that my family and I shared with my students and our friends, Cao Zhigang, Guo Xueyan, Gu Zhen, Ma Lin, Song Wei Wei, Tan Wu Feng, Xu Xiao, Wang Qiang, Yang Huai En, Yin Xiau Shan, and Zeng Yi. I am anxious for a reunion banquet in one of the backstreet restaurants we had frequented.

Back in North America, the search for material that would reflect the approach to social theory I was adopting led me to begin turning these early drafts into text. The motivation to write one's own material commonly arises among instructors who have been working in a field for some years. The notion that there may be wider interest in my approach to the development of social theory came later. I am indebted to Megan Mueller, who first found some merit in the idea of this text and encouraged me to turn it into a book. I also wish to thank her successor at Oxford University Press Canada, Lisa Meschino, whose enthusiasm helped me complete the process.

I have been greatly assisted by numerous students, too many to mention, who have been obliged to work through this material and who helped shape some of the examples and concerns reflected in it. Over the years a greater proportion of students reading social theory are women. They helped me become aware of the need to incorporate feminist perspectives more consistently in the book. It may not be as inclusive as it should be, but it is better through their inspiration.

Several colleagues obliged me by reading portions of the manuscript. In particular, for their freely given constructive criticisms and encouragement in the writing of this book, I wish to thank Graham Morgan, Herb Gamberg, and Jim Sacouman, who have played various roles in my life as teachers, friends, and colleagues. I was also very fortunate at the editorial stage to have the help of Richard and Laurna Tallman, for whose hard work and critical appreciation for the manuscript I am extremely grateful. It is so much better for having fallen into their dedicated hands. Despite what may sometimes appear to be the case, writing is a highly co-operative process and I am fully aware that the book could not have been written without the efforts of many people who contributed to the process. It is important to point out, of course, that, despite the best efforts of my reviewers and critics, the flaws in the book are my responsibility. If it lives to see a second version, I will undoubtedly have to acknowledge a much longer list of critics.

Finally, I wish to dedicate this book to three people to whom I owe a debt that is immeasurably deep: to Heather for her spontaneity and poetic spirit; to Julia for her many talents and ambitions, and for teaching me about what is important in life; and to Devon for his generous nature and extensive interests, and for keeping us amused.

PREFACE

'[T]o explain is to attach things to each other and to establish relations between them.'
—Émile Durkheim, *The Elementary Forms of the Religious Life* (1912)[1]

The purpose of reading theory is to understand ideas in the context of time and space. Theories relate to the social circumstances and characteristics of the people who produce them and to preceding social thought. They are then consequential in a variety of social forms. This book was written from the perspective of the sociology of knowledge, which is to understand ideas in their social, political, and cultural context. As sociologist Émile Durkheim claimed, 'for the sociologist as for the historian, social facts vary with the social system of which they form a part; they cannot be understood when detached from it.'[2]

Just as every person is, to some measure, a product of her or his society, every thinker stands on the shoulders of those who have gone before. In the words of Thomas Mann, 'A man lives not only his personal life, as an individual, but also, consciously or unconsciously, the life of his epoch and his contemporaries.'[3] The study of social thought is an intellectual exercise. What were the main ideas of a particular theorist or recognizable social movement? How can this theory be related to previously existing ideas and subsequent theoretical positions? Why did an idea arise when it did? Does it reflect the interests or perspectives of certain identifiable social groups? What were the social consequences of the theory? Finally, in addition to understanding and appreciating, the third task of a discussion of ideas is critiquing. Some critique in what follows is explicit; much more is implicit.

This viewpoint derives from my interest in social change and the history of ideas reflected in the conflict theories of Marx and Weber, and the emergence of social movements rooted in unequal gender and race relations. It is structured around a historical framework that includes different or alternative perspectives in time and place, some reflecting marginalized populations. It is intended to reflect a broad sympathy for the objectives of movements for liberation and social equality. This underlying bias shapes the interpretation of social theories and the selection of some of the material. It is not replete with postmodern sensibility. On the contrary, it is a narrative. As such it presents the making of social thought as far less complex, uncertain, and under-determined than it is.

While a systematic framework distorts ideas and channels its audience, it also provides a foundation for constructing meaning out of the progression of ideas. As sociologist Karl Mannheim put it, 'The sociological history of intellectual life is fundamentally nothing more than [a] *post factum* reconstruction . . . through which, even with the help of many intermediate links, we can [attempt to] explain why this or that person was interested in this or that subject and why' from that standpoint she or he 'saw, or distorted, things in such and such a way.'[4] The book is not only about the concepts developed in classical social theory; it reflects a wider sociological interest in the historical processes through which ideas are generated and the forms through which they become consequential in society. Many of the most important nineteenth-century social theorists approached the study of society historically and holistically. Classical social theories deal with grand issues of long-term social importance: the transition from traditional to modern society; the conditions that contributed to the rise of capitalist industrialism; the origin and forms of the state; the types of social inequality that divide societies and the consequences of these divisions; social order and social change; freedom; and equality.

The book offers an introduction to the theoretical analysis of these issues that is broad but often shallow. It is like skating across a very wide lake on ice of varying thickness. It concentrates on what is sometimes called classical social theory, in this case, an era of social theorizing and research that ended in the early decades of the twentieth century. Necessarily, the central ideas of these social theorists are presented in some degree of depth. They are surrounded by a larger cast of minor characters and extras, selected from the pool of thinkers who are significant in the history of ideas. Few of them are treated in detail, though the coverage is uneven. Often, only a preliminary scan of socially significant movements and ideas is presented while the depths under the ice remain unexplored. There is also much open water on the lake; many strands of social thought are ignored or afforded scant mention. Furthermore, as wide as the lake is, it is connected to numerous, even larger bodies of water that are glimpsed only at a distance.

While one of the central concerns of classical sociological theorists was to construct sociology as a distinct, specialized discipline, the narrative approach adopted in this book does not focus exclusively on this tale. In part, this reflects the contemporary fragmentation of sociology to include numerous subdisciplines and specializations, such as black or women's or cultural studies, to name a few. Each subdiscipline has its own theoretical tradition. Pedagogically, this book is designed as a more general introduction to social theory.

The book invades the spaces between conventional disciplines, although it is not multi-disciplinary. Once started down the road of boundary transgression, disciplinary lines disappear at the vanishing point and only chaos theory remains, which is, appropriately, an oxymoron. Academic disciplines have distinctly different focuses. Literature, film, the arts generally are best appreciated in their own right, in terms of form and aesthetics. The ideological implication of content is often of only marginal interest. Nevertheless, in an era when the medium is an important part of the message, form and content are less distinguishable than may have been assumed in the past. In the field of post-colonial literature, for example, cultural products are contextualized by the social and political.

Similarly, the book presents an overview of certain historical developments in order to construct a context in time and place for social theory. It thereby overlaps somewhat with the modern turn to social history. More generally, however, the discipline of history seeks to interpret events, recognizes multiple perspectives in the construction of the historical record, and takes into account personal and idiosyncratic causality. The French Revolution looked considerably different from the perspectives of social classes in Paris and in rural France, and among various social and religious groups. The question here is limited to the ideological implications of events. The Revolution played an important role in the making of social theory with respect to the meanings that some intellectuals attributed to it.

To understand the historical standpoint of marginalized groups, it is necessary to consider the less explicit theoretical forms through which ideas may be expressed, such as the work of women novelists in the nineteenth century. While this book attempts a narrative presentation of social theory, contrary to postmodern sensibilities, it reflects simultaneously an interest in literary and artistic cultural production, which became an important theme in twentieth-century sociology. The cross-disciplinary content, however, is highly selective and primarily illustrative. Wordsworth's Romanticism is pastoral and naturalistic. I am interested in his early identification with the French Revolution. Shelley's magnificent imagery interests me less than his radical concern for the labouring poor. *Robinson Crusoe* represents far more than 'economic individualism', but that is what I sought to emphasize in my discussion of the novel. Art for art's sake was a conscious repudiation of the social, an aspect that makes that late nineteenth-, early twentieth-century movement sociologically interesting in itself, relating it backwards to Romanticism and foreshadowing the trend towards modernism in the twentieth century.

Generally, however, literary or artistic examples are introduced in relation to strands of social thought they reflect. It is not just the generation of a theory or point of view that is sociologically interesting; once it is present to the imagination, the social consequences of a theory are explored through other media, including literature and the arts. It is equally likely that novel ideas and perspectives are explored first by writers and artists. Part of historical analysis is the reconstruction of the past to provide a lineage or genealogy for the interests of the present.

Coverage is highly selective in another sense. The book is Eurocentric (in the wider sense of Western) and is heavily weighted towards Anglo-American social thought, then French and German. Within this narrow space, social thought is understood in terms of the emergence, evolution, and consequence of ideas expressed by recognized social and political theorists, but also as it is reflected in the work of some poets, novelists, and visual artists. The book casts down its bucket into many pools, but draws selectively from them.

While an overview of the development of social thought must include the perspectives of women and racial minorities, the coverage of the book is weighted towards white men. European males had the privilege and power of defining what counted as theory and what ideas and perspectives were deemed academic long before women or people of colour had such access to institutions of higher learning. The ideological context of theory production includes consideration of past or competing theories seen as significant by writers in their own period. White males most often drew positive and negative inspiration from other white males.

One objective of this text is to illustrate the pervasiveness of theoretical ideas in works not normally considered theoretical. Theories shape the thinking of the cultural producers of any age and, through them, help to form the world views of differently situated people. In a few places in the book, I include some contemporary illustrations derived from forms of popular culture such as the cinema, contemporary music, and children's literature. These are partly to enliven the reading but also to suggest that recognizable social ideas can be found in what may be considered unlikely places. The book works, in part, to the extent that it provides a framework that helps to stimulate the discovery of theoretical ideas in a wide variety of cultural products. The book also includes some biographical elements, partly to humanize the theorist, but also to suggest connections between specific aspects of biography and the resulting social theory.

The book does not demand a previous knowledge of history. I have attempted to provide this context. The more information and interpretation can be linked to existing knowledge, the more comprehensible it is and the easier it is to build a framework of time and space within which new information can be situated. As Durkheim put it, knowledge is relational. From the moment when people 'have an idea that there are internal connections between things, science and philosophy become possible.'[5] Learning new things is more effective the more they can be connected to what is already known. That is the basic idea underlying the historical and contextual approach that is incorporated in what follows.

946 Approximate birthdate of Gerbert of Aurillac, Pope Sylvester II (999–1003).

1095 The First Crusade; Crusades continue until 1244.

1225 Birth of Thomas Aquinas, medieval theologian whose scholasticism combined Christianity with Aristotle (d. 1274).

1232 Pope Gregory IX establishes the Court of the Inquisition to root out heresy.

1265 Birth of Dante Alighieri, author of *The Divine Comedy* (d. 1321).

1348 The Black Death strikes Europe, killing one-third of the population in some areas.

1363 Birth of Christine de Pisan, whose prose and verse reflected a woman's standpoint (d.1431).

1381 Peasants' Revolt in England led by Wat Tyler.

1455 Johannes Gutenberg, using innovative movable type, ushers in the era of printing by producing an edition of the Bible.

1503 Michelangelo, a principal artist of the Italian Renaissance (era of the rebirth of classical art and literature), paints the *Mona Lisa*.

1517 Martin Luther (1483–1546) posts his '95 Theses', criticizing the Roman Catholic Church and initiating the Protestant reformation.

1564 Birth of William Shakespeare.

1626 Francis Bacon (b. 1561), British scientist and advocate of the empirical method, dies of illness contracted in the course of an experiment.

1633 Galileo Galilei (1564–1642), Italian astronomer who argued that the sun rather than the earth was the centre of the universe, is condemned for heresy and recants.

1641 The French philosopher René Descartes (1596–1650) publishes his *Meditations*.

1642 The English Revolution begins: Parliament, led by Cromwell, overthrows the monarchy. (Charles II is restored to the throne in 1660.)

1642 Birth of Isaac Newton, British scientist who defined the force of gravity (d. 1727).

1651 Thomas Hobbes (1588–1679) publishes *Leviathan*.

1689 England's 'Glorious Revolution': King James II is deposed and Parliament claims political supremacy.

1690 John Locke (1632–1704) publishes *Two Treatises on Government*.

1719 Daniel Defoe (1660–1731) publishes his novel *Robinson Crusoe*.

1726 Jonathan Swift (1667–1745) publishes his satire *Gulliver's Travels*.

1733 Alexander Pope publishes his *Essay on Man*: 'Whatever is, is right.'

1754 Jean-Jacques Rousseau (1712–78) publishes his *Discourse on Inequality*.

1759 French satirist and *philosophe* Voltaire (1694–1778) publishes his novel *Candide*.

1776 Adam Smith (1723–90), English laissez-faire economist, publishes *The Wealth of Nations*.

1776 American Revolution begins.

1789 French Revolution begins.

1792 Mary Wollstonecraft (1759–97) publishes *A Vindication of the Rights of Women*.

1798 Thomas Malthus (1766–1834) publishes his *Essay on the Principle of Population*.

1799 Napoleon Bonaparte (1769–1821) leads coup in France (crowned Emperor in 1804).

Part I FROM REASON TO REVOLUTION

Catherine: Do you remember Lescoff?
Alice: Our old chemistry teacher?
Catherine: Remember what he said? Life is made up of three essential elements. Only a scientist would think they're hydrogen, oxygen, and carbon.
Alice: What are they—air, fire, and water?
Catherine: Desire, disorder, and danger.
—*Chaos and Desire* (2003), written and directed by Manon Briand

Catherine, the lesbian journalist in Briand's naturalistic film, personifies 'desire, disorder, and danger', her decidedly modern definition of the essential elements of life. She rejects out of hand both the traditional and the scientifically rational world views. In the ancient conception, still believed by some in Shakespeare's time, the material world was composed of the four basic elements: earth, water, air, and fire. When God had created the world out of chaos, he gave it order and stability, but a return to the void was ever possible. In the medieval view, the cosmic order was continually renewed by the active intervention of angels and other heavenly forces, keeping danger at bay since the world, left on its own, would naturally degenerate into disorder. The worm in creation, the source of greatest danger, was desire or sin. It was desire that had thrust Adam and Eve out of the Garden of Eden; it was desire that made human beings resemble the beasts more than the angels.

Humans were in part like angels because of the gift of reason, the engine of free will through which humans could choose good over evil and voluntarily muzzle their desires. They could also choose desire and disorder. Reason, then, was a dangerously edged gift. The spirits that populated the heavens possessed unlimited knowledge, a wholeness they shared with the deity. Human reasoning was an arduous, difficult, and error-prone process that yielded only an approximation of the understanding the angels grasped intuitively. Just how limited were the powers of the human mind?

According to traditional Christianity, which rose to social predominance in the Middle Ages, reason was weak, suspect, and subordinate to that portion of absolute truth that had been revealed to humanity through sacred texts such as the Bible and the pronouncements of the Church. The focus of life should be on death or, what amounted to the same thing, life after death, or salvation. The world was a vale of tears that would deteriorate until the Second Coming when Christ would return and bring justice to the earth. A yawning canyon separates this world view from the modern age of materialism, self-centredness, and Jerry Springer.

Part I of this book begins a narrative of the passage from traditional theories of society to the sharply contrasting scientific and anti-scientific ideologies of the modern age. Whole epochs of history are shaped by dominant world views. Nowhere, however, even in the most absolute state, are the dominant views the only ones. In the traditional society of medieval Europe, Roman Christianity struggled for superiority with a variety of religious perspectives outside the dogma of the Church. It made a difference to the character of the society which specific set of ideas and beliefs succeeded to power and which were suppressed. With a variety of religious beliefs competing with each other for the status of truth, how could these claims be assessed? By their very nature it was difficult for disputants to agree even on a shared basis for judging one truth claim from another, let alone to determine which was correct. We may have a reasonable idea of how many average-sized humans can be squeezed into a Volkswagen; but how many angels can fit in? When it comes to ephemeral questions such as this, truth may simply become the views of those who shout the loudest, or who have the most stamina and can simply argue their opponents into exhaustion and acquiescence. To put it baldly, it might appear that might makes right.

One of the ironies of social theory is that the modern world shares some elements of the traditional view. In the contemporary world, where desire, disorder, and danger are essential elements, truth is relative; good and evil are matters of opinion; yet the powerful, those who would define good and evil for all of society, have their interests inscribed in law and their ideology infiltrates and saturates the media of communication. One of the differences between the traditional and the modern eras is that the former sought to find an absolute truth and searched for the invariable and unbreakable laws of existence in theological speculation. In modern times, spiritual views coexist with a host of alternative conceptions, new age delusions, and plausible alternatives. None of these intellectual styles, however, defines the essential, dominant world view of the post-traditional world.

In between 'air, fire, and water' and 'desire, disorder, and danger' came 'hydrogen, oxygen, and carbon'—the world view of rationalistic science. We live in a world created by the Industrial Revolution and the microchip, a world of global capitalism and its extremes of poverty and wealth, resistance and repression, order and disorder, technological success and emotional despair. It is a world where the most varied beliefs proliferate and the most bizarre desires may be realized. Yet this overflowing abundance of fancy springs from

a mundane foundation. A more grounded and deeply rooted world view dominates Western social life. It is composed of rational science and the technological overabundance in which it is inscribed, the liberal principles of liberty, legal equality, and human rights, and the economic practices of acquisitive capitalism.

If these are the essential ingredients of modern society, they stand in the sharpest contrast to the traditional world of earth, water, air, and fire. The scientific revolution drove traditional society to the precipice from which Christianity had either to leap into pure faith or descend gingerly to the ground and accommodate the secular. The world of trade and commerce, which was disreputable in the ancient world, had to be washed clean of the odour of sin to become the engine of industrial progress. The ideals of liberty and equality were released from the straitjacket of hierarchy and order and fuelled the forces of modernity.

Part I of this narrative of social theory presents an overview of the great transformation of society and social theory from the traditional order of the Middle Ages to the modern world. Economically, traditional society gave way to the rise of commercial capitalism rooted in the theory of liberal economics. Politically, the rule of monarchs and aristocrats was challenged, more successfully in some places than others, by demands for popular rule and the social theory of liberal democracy. Culturally, theological thinking was challenged by modern science. These changes were closely interconnected. Traditional society did not evolve quietly into modernity. The passage from one era to the other was marked by political and social revolution, epitomized by the great revolution in France in 1789.

The basic dichotomy underlying classical sociology distinguishes the modern from the traditional. The first chapter begins with a description of late medieval society as it was being shaped by forces and events that would transform it. This period serves as a foil against which to develop the core ideas of liberalism, laissez-faire, the Enlightenment, and the age of revolution and individual rights. It is also a wellspring of traditional ideas about the social that resurface in post-Enlightenment conservatism and positivist sociology—concepts such as hierarchy, natural inequality, the organic model of society, and specific notions about gender relations.

Chapter One describes the beginning of the intellectual transformation of society that occurred at the end of the first Christian millennium. This conflict was more profound in its implications for society than a disagreement over the correctness of theologies. Newly unearthed or rediscovered manuscripts of Greek and Arabic science and philosophy began to infiltrate through the great wall of Christian doctrine. Not only did these pagan authors possess a wealth of knowledge that cast medieval science into the shadows, but it was created in the absence of Christianity, solely from the exercise of human reason. These new ideas were corrosive agents in an age of faith, even in the hands of Christian scholars. The unenviable task of putting reason in what was believed to be its proper, secondary place was undertaken by Thomas Aquinas. In the process of establishing a doctrine that would solidify the structure and inequalities of traditional society, Aquinas erected fences to divide and confine the open range of human reason. His hope that he had settled this question was pure vanity.

At first, these new ideas fell on barren soil. As Chapter Two describes the situation, by the fifteenth century revolutionary changes were underway in all the institutions that had given traditional society its stability. In social theory, the most important development was the growing dominance of rationality and its use to gain control over the natural world through the application of scientific principles. Theories of society also began to take on a scientific hue. In this early part of the modern era, the perspective known as liberalism grew up simultaneously with the rise of new social classes that challenged the traditional

powers of kings, aristocrats, and clergy. Even when social circumstances change and become linked to changed perspectives, older ideas take new forms and continue to shape the ideas of social minorities, and these older ideas persist more strongly in places that have been less susceptible to change. Liberalism is still the ideological basis of Western society, often existing in opposition to the persistence of traditional attitudes in many parts of the contemporary world.

Liberalism and the social and economic changes that gave rise to it did not come peacefully into the world, nor did it create a social order of peace and harmony. Chapter Three examines the rebellious side of liberal social theory and varieties of opposition to it. Generally, ideologies are linked to social and economic interests in society. A variety of social groups, including women and oppressed nations, grasped the rebellious core of the liberal ideas of equality and justice and applied them to their own situation. The danger to traditional society was greatest when the discontent of the people was channelled into social and political revolution by the new demands of rising classes. Chapter Four examines the emergence of revolutionary theory and its trial by fire in the French Revolution, concluding with the emergence of a feminist critique of the social theories in which modern society rested.

The time had long passed when it was possible to tame the new ideas of reason, criticism, and science and make them serve traditional society. The roots of this transformation extend back to the tenth century, when a young European scholar travelled to the edge of Christian Europe to study the science and philosophy of the ancient world. He was unaware of the chain of circumstances this cross-cultural contact would initiate. By studying the society to which he returned, we can construct a picture of the traditional world that was about to enter a new, dynamic phase of world history.

TRADITIONAL SOCIETY: REASON AND DESIRE UNDER WRAPS

GERBERT AND HIS TIMES

Towards the end of the tenth century Gerbert of Aurillac, a brilliant young scholar, was sent to Spain to study the *quadrivium*—arithmetic, geometry, astronomy, and music. When Gerbert crossed the Pyrenees and descended into northern Spain,[1] he entered what was to him a strange and multicultural intellectual world. It was the first step in an ambitious career that would take Gerbert to the pinnacle of power in the Church. By the close of the first millennium, he had become Pope, calling himself Sylvester II (999–1003). His four-year tenure as head of the Church was brief and tumultuous, made more difficult by charges that he had sold his soul to the devil.

Gerbert was likely born to a poor family in south-central France around 946.[2] For a young man from this background, being admitted to formal schooling was unusual, but he so impressed his teachers that he was recommended for higher study. Cathedral schools provided what formal education there was in Europe. The curriculum consisted of the seven liberal arts, adding grammar, logic, and rhetoric (the *trivium*) to the *quadrivium*. There were very few texts to study and only a handful of authors whose ideas were acceptable to the Church. The most important of these *auctores* or authorities was St Augustine. Their wisdom was to be memorized by students and not questioned.

In Spain, Gerbert experienced the intellectual liberation that is inspired by cultural diversity. Spain was a crossroads, the meeting place of cultures. Arabic-speaking peoples from North Africa had conquered the entire peninsula by AD 711, part of a tidal wave of conquest that had carried Arabic culture and the religion of Islam from the holy city of Mecca eastward into Persia, north into the Balkans, and west into southern France. By Gerbert's time, Moors and their Arabic-speaking, Islamic culture were confined to the southern half of Spain.

Ideas cross borders more readily than armies. While Christian teaching had sunk into repetition and dogma, Arabic scholars in Spain had access to a much wider range of knowledge and texts, from Greece, Egypt, Persia, and North Africa, including works of the Greek philosopher, Aristotle, that were still unavailable in Europe. The Muslims were in touch with the ancient civilizations of China and India through their extensive trading connections. Muslim astronomers, physicians, and mathematicians were far in advance of their Christian counterparts.[3] The challenges of these new ideas filtered into Christian Spain and were imbibed by scholars such as Gerbert. Before long, it would be increasingly difficult to regard the *auctores* with the absolute reverence that the Church expected.

When Gerbert returned to France, he made a great impression because of his exceptional knowledge of mathematics and science.[4] He used Arabic numbers in place of the clumsy Roman numerals and the Chinese abacus, and introduced decimal calculations, enabling scholars to solve complicated calculations. As the Master of the Cathedral School at Rheims in France, Gerbert acquired a large collection of manuscripts of original works on medicine, philosophy, mathematics, and the natural world.

Gerbert brought back to France not only a new library, but also an independent, inquiring mind. He helped to reinvigorate teaching by emphasizing scientific study and the dialectical form of argument. His ideas were more innovative in science than religion. Gerbert did not directly challenge the teachings of the Church—he was making a career within the embrace of the Roman Church. Certainly, he agreed, only Christians understood the truths of theology, such as the resurrection of Christ and the mystery of the Trinity. But Gerbert realized that the *auctores* disagreed with each other even within the Christian tradition and were especially contradictory on matters of science and natural philosophy. Rather than blindly accepting the texts of established authorities, he thought it was up to each student to apply reason to the information available and establish what was true by developing an argument, which could be defended with evidence. It was a potentially revolutionary idea. The generation of scholars he inspired to seek truth through rational argument spread the new knowledge and Gerbert's logical method. Gerbert had no deeper intention than to place Christian doctrine on a more secure foundation. Once unleashed, however, human reason has the capacity to challenge existing knowledge and beliefs.

Gerbert's reputation for knowledge and his dialectical approach to argument singled him out for suspicion, but it was his dabbling in politics that aroused the ire of his rivals. The idea that religion should be kept separate from politics is modern in origin. In medieval Europe, government and religious power were intricately intertwined, and the Church contested with kings and emperors for secular power. Gerbert became the tutor of the young Holy Roman Emperor, who had became Otto III at the age of three.[5] Otto planned to restore the Empire to its previous glory. To further his ambitions, Otto helped Gerbert become the first non-Italian Pope.[6] But Gerbert's time at the pinnacle was short and conflictual, due more to the power struggles of medieval politics than theology. When Gerbert's rivals used his reputation for exotic knowledge against him, they were attempting to undermine Otto III as much as Gerbert himself.

As the world changes, older ideas become increasingly incongruent with people's experiences. When Gerbert returned from Spain, he re-entered a more *traditional* world carrying the seeds of intellectual reawakening. Forces for change were emerging within the traditional social order that, in the long run of history, brought his world to an end. This traditional society can be described by referring to three basic features: economic relations, political power, and ideological control.

Economic Relations

When Gerbert travelled across Christian Europe on his way to become Master of the Cathedral School in Rheims, he passed few large towns and saw little overland trade. Local areas were economically self-sufficient, inward-looking, and seemingly changeless. During the Middle Ages, a great variety of unequal relationships developed between social groups. Economic conditions and social relations were distinctly different, for example, in Southern and Northern Europe. A feudal/manorial system developed in northern France and England, in which most people were rural labourers working under a form of bondage to their local landlord.

The social structure of feudal society included a sharply differentiated social hierarchy—a set of categories of people from high to low. Near the top of the hierarchy was a hereditary aristocracy—the knights, barons, earls, and assorted other titled members of the aristocratic class. A hereditary monarch, the King, stood at the apex of the social system. The monarch granted large portions of land known as fiefs to an aristocracy of nobles. In feudal Europe, most political and economic power was in the hands of these local landlords. In return for the grant of land, the lord of the fief promised to supply the King with a certain number of foot soldiers and mounted knights. The nobles, in turn, granted portions of their land to knights in return for their services. The knight became the lord of numerous peasants who lived on the knight's estate and became his tenants. These titled aristocrats, of various degrees, were given the right to tax their tenants, to extract services and labour from them, and to exercise legal authority over them. While some of the poorest labourers at the bottom of the scale might have been enslaved, most were serfs, bound to their landlords by rigid ties of obligations making them unfree in a different sense. Serfs were somewhat better off than enslaved people, having more rights and protections. Ultimately, the peasants worked the land and paid taxes to their landlord that supported the knights, the rest of the aristocracy, and finally the monarchy. Between the aristocracy and the serfs was a class of labourers known as yeomen, who were independent peasants having some control over their own small farms. The yeomen were a significant class in England, where they were seen as proud and independent—as Mark Twain suggested (Box 1.1), they were the heart and soul of the nation.[7]

Unlike slavery, which compelled labour through brute force, as Karl Mannheim observed, serfs were induced to work to support their families and allowed a share of their labour, providing an emotional attachment to the land. Their ambitions were checked, however, by social regulation and the law that required them to remain on the land.[8] The feudal form of exploitation was directly observable: the serf either paid a certain proportion of her or his produce to the overlord for taxes, or agreed to work on the lord's land for a certain number of days each year. In either case, the amount of surplus they produced (wealth they created but did not receive) was measurable. Unlike slaves, feudal peasants received some basic rights. In return for handing this surplus over to the aristocracy, the peasants were given the hereditary right to remain on the land and use it—they could not be removed from the land by their overlord. They also had the right to use a community-controlled portion of the estate (the common) together with other peasants. These few rights were not much but, at least in good times, they provided some security and enough to eat or take to the local market, providing subsistence for themselves and their families. Property, then, was only partly privately controlled. The nobility could not do as they chose with their land; they could not sell the land, or remove the peasants from it. Everyone had some claim on, or right over, the use of the land. The concept of real private property as we know it did not yet prevail.

These unequal groups were not so much classes in a modern sense, but **estates**—social categories into which people were born and remained

---

Box 1.1

Seven-tenths of the free population of the country were . . . small 'independent' farmers, artisans, etc.; which is to say, they were the nation, the actual Nation; they were about all of it that was useful, or worth saving, or really respect-worthy; and to subtract them would have been to subtract the Nation and leave behind some dregs, some refuse, in the shape of a king, nobility, and gentry, idle, unproductive, acquainted mainly with the arts of wasting and destroying, and of no sort of use or value in any rationally constructed world. And yet, by ingenious contrivance this gilded minority, instead of being in the tail of the procession where it belonged, was marching, head up and banners flying, at the other end of it; had elected itself to be the Nation, and these innumerable claims had permitted it so long that they had come at last to accept it as a truth; and not only that, but to believe it right and as it should be. The priests had told their fathers and themselves that this ironical state of things was ordained of God. . . .

—Mark Twain, *A Connecticut Yankee in King Arthur's Court* (1889)

for their lifetime. There was very little social mobility. People were seldom able to rise from lower to higher estates, stories of princes marrying commoners such as Cinderella to the contrary, although exemplary service during war might lead to a knighthood. The Church was a second avenue for upward mobility. Gerbert had achieved a considerable rise in his private fortune through his intellectual service to both Church and state.

Political Power

Gerbert did not have the advantages of birth that feudal society reserved for the aristocracy. He lived his own Cinderella story, partly through his intellect but ultimately through his connection to secular power. The social structure of feudal society is often symbolized by a pyramid with the single monarch at the top and the powerless majority at the bottom. It more closely resembled a large number of intersecting pyramids, for power was decentralized in feudal Europe. Each local lord held considerable political power and controlled his own army and territory. It was a fractious period as nobles formed alliances and contested for power among themselves. The King was the foremost aristocrat, but in the feudal system, the monarch shared political control with the aristocracy and competed with them for supremacy. The

threat of local warfare perpetually hung over the heads of the people. Over the centuries, in countries such as Spain, Portugal, France, and England, aggressive and domineering monarchs expanded their power at the expense of the feudal nobility and created nations. Members of the aristocracy, including the King, claimed to rule on the traditional basis of their direct relationship with their titled ancestors and all rights to property were handed down to the eldest son.

Parallel to the political uncertainties of life, traditional society was also characterized by considerable social stability. There was also little geographic mobility: people generally lived, worked, and died in the village of their parents, and these small communities changed little from generation to generation even in more recent times, as depicted in the prologue of the movie *Chocolat* (Box 1.2). Traditional authority dominated everyday life: the King ruled the kingdom within traditional limits, the lord ruled the fief, the husband ruled the wife, and the father ruled the household. Compared to today, people knew their place and understood their duties. Conversely, however, lives were unstable because political and military power within the feudal system was decentralized among a variety of titled aristocrats who vied with each other and with the monarch for wealth, power, and prestige.

Box 1.2

Once upon a time, there was a quiet village in the French countryside whose people believed in *tranquilité*—tranquility.

If you lived in this village, you understood what was expected of you. You knew your place in the scheme of things. If you happened to forget, someone would help remind you. . . .

In the village, if you saw something you were not supposed to see, you learned to look the other way. If by chance your hopes had been disappointed, you learned never to ask for more.

So, through good times and bad, through famine and feast, the villagers held fast to their traditions.

—*Chocolat* (2000), directed by Lasse Hallstrom, screenplay by Robert Jacobs

There are several caveats to this simple scheme of pyramids of power in feudal society. It is a picture of the rural social structure. As society began to change from traditional to modern, towns and cities emerged as important centres of commerce. An urban class of crafts workers, dominated by master artisans in each branch of manufacturing, slowly developed. In addition, merchants and traders, who made a living buying, transporting, and selling commodities, emerged as another small but potentially very important urban social class between the aristocracy and the peasantry. At first, this commercial class served the powerful; later they would amass great wealth and acquire political power in their own right. Perhaps the most famous early European trader was Marco Polo (1256–1323), who travelled to China, India, and other empires of the Far East, expanding European horizons and stirring both a sense of adventure and greed.

Christian Europe initially set its sights on the wealth of the eastern Mediterranean. As Europe aroused itself from what later became known as its Dark Age, the sword of conflict between Christianity and Islam was transferred to European hands. European kings and the Roman Church colluded with European monarchs to achieve military domination over its great cultural and economic rival. This time the Christians wore the armour of the aggressor, invading the Middle East in a series of invasions known as the Crusades that were intended to wrest control of the land, riches, and trading routes of the Middle East from the Islamic 'infidels'.

While the military accomplishments of this European aggression were short-lived, the economic and intellectual changes that came in its wake were irreversible. Surviving Crusaders came back into Europe with several kinds of booty. The great wealth they had plundered—which came more from the Eastern Christians at Constantinople than from the Moslems of the Holy Land—raised the status and power of the bankers and merchants in the Italian cities who had financed and supplied the Crusaders. The Italians became the great commercial capitalists, traders, and adventurers of the period.

Ideological Control

Feudal society was dominated by two interconnected institutions of traditional authority: Church and state. The Church acquired considerable land and wealth, creating an aristocracy parallel to the secular government. The two sources of power were closely connected. Younger sons of the nobility who were excluded from inheriting the family title and land routinely sought careers in the Church hierarchy. While the Christian God was believed to be above the feudal pyramid, there was a dispute over who was next in line and represented divine power on earth. Secular and religious authority struggled for supremacy over society. Gerbert, as Pope Sylvester II, had been placed in office by the power of the Holy Roman Emperor, but the papacy had not yet achieved a dominant position as the single, authoritative voice inside the Church. During the eleventh century, and especially under Pope Gregory II (1073–85), the Roman Church was transformed into an autonomous and dominant institution under the rule of a single theological monarch. By the time of Pope Innocent III (1198–1216), the Pope had been elevated to the position of uncontested authority over the Church.

Several changes had been made in the Church to separate it from secular authority. The rule of celibacy for priests was enforced, which meant that a priest would be loyal only to the Church hierarchy and the Church would not lose property through inheritance. Priests were authorized to hear oral confessions, making the clergy an intermediary power between the deity and ordinary people, elevating them above other human beings. Even the King went to confession, and a priest was empowered to remove his sins. To ensure the unity of the Church, successive popes created a hierarchy of ecclesiastical positions modelled after the pyramid-shaped social structure in the rest of society, consisting of cardinals, archbishops, bishops, and the like. The Roman Catholic Church became a monolithic and powerful bureaucracy, the great international institution of ideological control. The whole structure of feudal society as well as people's thinking about the world and their place within it was held in place by a belief in a single deity and 'one true Church'.

The centralization of power to determine truth and falsity was accompanied by a militant intolerance of dissent and **heresy**, ideas that were defined as false and dangerous to true belief. In the centuries prior to the consolidation of papal supremacy in the Church, varieties of Christian beliefs persisted in various places in Europe, mixed with the survivals of paganism and with theological doctrines imported from the Near and Middle East. From being relatively tolerant of differences of opinion, the Church began to suppress heresy as part of its consolidation of power. This was a workable strategy so long as the heretics were relatively few and unprotected.

Dissent within Europe took the form of different interpretations of theological truth. The problems in society were largely defined as ethical issues, of how individuals should act in a fallen, cruel world. Social critics complained about the way individuals performed their duties; they did not think to condemn the unequal power relations in society or imagine structural changes. Individual kings or lords acted unethically when they fought with each other for personal gain or warred on the Church. They sinned when they neglected their secular duties and caused unnecessary suffering. Social criticism consisted of appeals to people in power to act justly, keep to the boundaries of tradition, and perform their Christian duties. Nevertheless, the cornerstone of a more profound social critique had been laid by scholars such as Gerbert, who emphasized the capacity of human reason to achieve knowledge through its own powers.

What in Gerbert's time had been an uncertain trickle of foreign knowledge seeping into Christian Europe became a wide river by the eleventh and twelfth centuries, as returning Crusaders brought with them an intellectual booty more profound than gold. The natural philosophy of the Greeks had been preserved for more than 1,000 years in the Middle East and had been extensively studied, translated, and commented upon by Arabic scholars. A flood of translations of the works of such ancient figures as Aristotle previously unavailable in Europe came into the eager hands of the new masters. They learned the astronomy of Ptolemy, the mathematics of Euclid, and the medicine of Hippocrates. The Crusaders had expected to eliminate a foreign 'heresy'. Ironically, they succeeded in inspiring more dangerous heretical ideas than those they were designed to suppress. European scholars rediscovered the intellectual heritage of ancient Greece and gained a share of the accumulated knowledge Muslims had acquired over the centuries that Europe had remained isolated and inward-looking.

By the eleventh and twelfth centuries, Europe had begun to experience a wide intellectual Renaissance known as the 'new logic'.[9] Outside the existing cathedral schools, a peripatetic breed of masters emerged, modelled after the ancient Greek philosophers. They moved from place to place, teaching avid students by the use of dialectics. Among the first major scholars and teachers who helped spread this new scholarship was Abelard.

ABELARD, HÉLOÏSE, AND THE STATUS OF WOMEN

Pierre Abelard (1079–1142) was a twelfth-century 'original thinker' who was remembered in the nineteenth century primarily as the lover of Héloïse, a brilliant young woman he was hired to tutor. Unlike Gerbert a century earlier, Abelard was downwardly mobile, being born into a knighthood but choosing the life of a scholar. Abelard had an egotistical and quarrelsome personality, although he was reputed to be a popular teacher because he was 'controversial, arrogant, [and] **charismatic**'.[10] He preferred the rational philosophy of Aristotle to the dogma of St Augustine and his lectures were regarded as skeptical and rationalistic. In a book called *Sic et Non* (*Yes and No*), Abelard posed 158 questions and then answered them in conflicting ways from Scripture and the medieval 'authorities' (*auctores*).[11] According to Abelard, 'The first key to wisdom is assiduous and frequent questioning. . . . For by doubting we come to inquiry, and by inquiry we arrive at the truth.'[12]

One of Abelard's works consists of a debate between a Christian and a philosopher about the nature of goodness. The argument does not represent the traditional distinction between reason (philosophy) and faith (Christianity), and neither of the disputants relies on the authority of texts. Instead, reason and logic are the only weapons and the disputants employ only rational arguments.[13] The Roman Church declared some of Abelard's books heretical, and ordered them to be burned. Condemned for heresy again in 1140, Abelard was compelled to take refuge in the monastery at Cluny, where he spent his last years.[14]

The Romantic Era (the early 1800s) remembered Abelard not as a theorist, but as a lover. While in his forties, Abelard became romantically obsessed with Héloïse, a brilliant 17-year-old Parisian woman who could read Latin, Greek, and Hebrew. With seduction in mind, Abelard offered to tutor Héloïse and moved into the house where she lived with her uncle, Fulbert, who was unaware that 'he had entrusted a tender lamb to the care of a ravenous wolf.' Soon, according to Abelard's written confession, 'love drew our eyes together far more than the lesson drew them to the pages of our text.' To avert Fulbert's suspicion, he sometimes struck his lover: 'there were . . . sometimes blows', he wrote. There was much to be suspicious about. According to Abelard, 'No degree in love's progress was left untried by our passion, and if love itself could imagine any wonder as yet unknown, we discovered it.'[15]

This illicit liaison produced the expected result: Héloïse gave birth to a son, who was named Astrolabius after a scientific instrument used in navigation.[16] Abelard agreed to marry Héloïse, but only in secret in order to preserve his teaching post. Romantically, Héloïse argued against marriage because the two should be tied 'only by disinterested love freely given', what Héloïse called the 'chastity of spirit'. She gave in, however, and after the pair were married secretly Abelard enrolled Héloïse in a convent. Furious over the affair, over Abelard's confession that he had planned the seduction, and over the marriage, Héloïse's guardian, Fulbert, conspired to have Abelard attacked. The thugs he hired extracted revenge by cutting off Abelard's testicles.[17]

Like Héloïse in her convent, Abelard ended his life in a monastery. The two continued to correspond. Abelard resumed his publication of sometimes heretical ideas while Héloïse put her many talents into founding religious houses. For the later Romantics, the tale of the lovers' romance exemplified the tragedy of love. In 1817, the bodies of Abelard and Héloïse were re-buried in a single tomb in Paris.[18]

Héloïse was more the exception than the rule in her learning. Generally speaking, the prevailing view in the Middle Ages accorded women low status, although Christian women were restricted less than their Moslem or Jewish counterparts. The daughters of wealthy burghers and gentlefolk received some education in convents or from private tutors, as had Héloïse, although the training was often ornamental.[19] Although one of the major poets of the age was Mary of France, the dominant social institutions of the day, feudalism and the Church, tightly constricted the potential of women.

Much of the traditional thinking of the time could be traced back to the age of Aristotle. Aristotle had believed that biological males were the normal human being and that women were imperfect men, errors of nature.[20] The organs of both genders were the same, but women's were hidden inside their bodies. Consequently, women were naturally passive and occupied a lower social status than men. Similar ideas have stubbornly persisted throughout social history, surfacing in one guise or another to the present day. Male writers in the medieval period complained that it was a waste of time to educate women who would spend their lives in domestic duties. What was worse from the male point of view was that 'learning inclined women toward insubordination.'[21]

Christine de Pisan (c. 1364–c. 1431) was one of these insubordinate women. The first professional woman writer, in the Cité des Dames de Pisan imagined a community of independent women.

She disproved the inferiority of women by situating in her city the most accomplished women, including many of her contemporaries.[22] De Pisan reflected a distinctly feminine standpoint by opposing the warfare that was nearly continuous during her lifetime. Her world view, shaped by the horrors of the Hundred Years War, as McDonald notes, deglorified warfare and was rooted in domesticity, in the bonds of motherhood and family that she saw being destroyed by civil war.[23] She spoke on behalf of the widows and of those deprived of kin, appealing to the Queen, herself a mother, to exert her public influence in the interests of peace. There was no glory or honour in a civil war, de Pisan said, and no real victory. There was only death to your own kin, destruction of your homes, and devastating famine. Appealing to the self-interest of the powerful, she argued that civil war would inspire the people to revolt because they 'have been too often robbed, deprived and oppressed', forced to pay outrageous taxes, and 'had their food stolen by soldiers'. French women were not powerless in their efforts to bring peace, de Pisan counselled. They should imitate the actions of the legendary Sabine women who threw themselves 'with hair dishevelled into the battlefield', their children in their arms, shouting: ' "Have pity on our dear loved ones! Make peace!" '[24]

This sentiment represented the voice of the most obvious victims of war. De Pisan was exceptional not in her viewpoint but in having the opportunity to present her arguments publicly. The main source of autonomy for an aristocratic woman in the Middle Ages was to gain control of a nunnery, such as that founded by Héloïse. A few women were able to exercise influence over their sons who inherited positions of power in their youth. When their husbands were absent, upper-class women managed their estates. Although women's legal and civil rights were generally circumscribed in the Middle Ages, there were some exceptions and the boundary between public and private spheres was permeable. Lower- and middle-class women frequently worked in the family business or independently. Some crafts, by definition, were women's domain; in addition, many widows acquired the control of their

husbands' craft and, simultaneously, their citizenship rights. As the urban economy grew in the later Middle Ages, women were integrated more fully into the economic life of the towns. The Wife of Bath in Chaucer's *Canterbury Tales* possessed civil rights equal to men.[25] The status of women, however, was susceptible to changes wrought by the power of patriarchy. As craft guilds monopolized trades, women were confined to gender-specific work in the home. Inheritance laws discriminated against wives, so widows often suffered severe poverty and, at worst, were forced into prostitution.[26] At the bottom of the social scale, peasant women married relatively young and were under the customary authority of their husbands.[27] Their only hope for escape from a life of complete subordination, Rowbotham claims,[28] was to join the band of whores who followed behind the armies—though this is hardly a model of female liberation.

Nothing symbolizes medieval patriarchal authority more succinctly than the locking up of women's sexuality by the chastity belt, forced on some wives by men before setting off on the Crusades. This cruel, iron body cage, along with the powers of legal marriage, ensured that property was inherited by children born legitimately. It also implied that men were never secure in their control over women and that resistance could take many forms. Shakespeare had an inkling of women's sexual appetites, as Desdemona's maidservant, Emilia, explained in *Othello* (Box 1.3).[29] Middle-class men, such as independent peasant landowners and town merchants, were also concerned with controlling women. In some jurisdictions, Mundy observes, town officials established houses of prostitution. In this way, he claims, the middle class 'took seriously [St] Augustine's celebrated observation that whores were necessary lest men fall into even worse vices.'[30]

Ultimately, the reality of gender inequality was rooted in the absence of control over childbearing and the social institutions of religious and secular society that buttressed the patriarchal family. While the Hebrew Old Testament has been interpreted by many contemporary feminists as unrelentingly patriarchal and androcentric,[31]

Box 1.3

Emilia: Let husbands know
Their wives have sense like them: they see and smell
And have their palates both for sweet and sour,
As husbands have. What is it that they do
When they change us for others? Is it sport?
I think it is: and doth affection breed it?
I think it doth: is't frailty that thus errs?
It is so too: and have not we affections,
Desires for sport, and frailty, as men have?
Then let them use us well: else let them know,
The ills we do, their ills instruct us so.

—William Shakespeare, *Othello*, IV, iii

---

strong women appear in extra-Biblical literature. One is Judith, in the Apocrypha, a pious widow who plays the harlot to gain entrance to the tent of Holofernes, the Assyrian general, and then decapitates him.[32] In the early years of Christianity, women were not denied a voice, and women in the New Testament are shown in a variety of social roles. The status of women changed with the institutionalization of Christianity, especially through the doctrinal and organizational work of St Paul. By the twelfth century, the Church was reiterating Paul's injunction on the subordination of women, as the Dominican, Humbert of Romans (Box 1.4), made explicit.[33] The Christian image of women as it was constructed through the Middle Ages was distinctly bipolar, either represented by the evil seductress, Eve, or by the pure and chaste Madonna, the Virgin Mary.

There was an ideal of equality between men and women, Mundy suggests, in the medieval love literature,[34] which derived originally from Muslim Spain and incited the passions with legends of love, adventure, and chivalry. The courtly love rituals of southern France, in which women were idealized as virtuous and were worshipped from afar on pedestals of poetry and song, elevated the perception of women as ornamental property and reduced their brutalization.[35] For Rowbotham, however, courtly love was little more than an elaborate ritual that masked women's real powerlessness.

Box 1.4

I do not permit a woman to teach for four reasons. The first is her lack of intelligence which women have in smaller quantity than men; the second is the subjection imposed upon her [by the Bible]; the third the fact that, if she does preach, her appearance will provoke lust . . . ; and the fourth because of the memory of the first woman [Eve] who . . . taught but once and turned the whole world upside down.

—Humbert of Romans, *De eruditione praedictatorum* (*On the Learning of Preachers*) (c. 1240)

Aristocratic women accepted the security that their position offered them and did not rebel against the ever tighter constraint of patriarchy.[36] The dilemma of occupying a somewhat comfortable and privileged yet ultimately restricted and disrespected position haunts the subsequent efforts of upper- and middle-class women over many centuries to achieve independence and equality.

THE INTELLECTUAL REVOLUTION

By the twelfth century, a more confident and prosperous European society was taking shape. A merchant class of traders had emerged in the cities, particularly in the Italian ports of Genoa and Venice. The new prosperity was obvious in the construction of the great Gothic cathedrals in every major city, such as Notre Dame in Paris. These cathedrals stood as massive monuments to the wealth and power of the Christian Church.

The other characteristically medieval institution was the university, where the new, critical learning, symbolized by Abelard's appeal to the evidence of reason, challenged traditional thought. As students assembled around popular scholars, paying them directly for their teaching, independent bodies of teachers organized in guilds to establish universities and protect their independence. Abelard was a leading intellectual figure at the University of Paris. Other universities were founded, for example, in Oxford and Cambridge, as well as Bologna and Padua in Italy. In Bologna, students were free to elect their own teachers. Paris developed the model curriculum, established around logic, followed by theology, law, and medicine. Degrees were introduced to indicate the stage of scholarship achieved, and masters from any university were eligible to teach at any other.[37] The early universities were still largely theological. All learning was linked to religion, including the study of nature. Even then, however, universities provided a refuge for radical thought. There were different versions of Christianity, departing in small or large ways from the official dogma of Rome, and these views were debated and even propagated by some teachers in the universities.

More dangerous to the Roman Church than other religions, such as Islam and Judaism, were deviations of doctrine that arose within Christianity to challenge its established dogmas. Heresies usually originated in other religions and the number and importance of these new doctrines were proliferating in the twelfth century as new ideas poured into Europe. The ironically named Pope Innocent III launched a 'crusade' in 1209 against the Albigensian heresy in Languedoc, in southwestern France, drowning this challenge to papal authority in blood and destruction. The Albigensians practised a religion according to which the material world, including the Catholic Church, represented the forces of evil. When the papal armies battered their way into Languedoc, according to later legends, they wondered how to avoid killing Catholics and slaughter only Albigensian heretics, since the two were indistinguishable by race or language. The papal representative reportedly said, 'Kill them all, the Lord will know his own.'[38]

Military conquest and massacre were one way to re-establish Church dominance. The Church devised a second, more institutional, strategy in the thirteenth century by establishing two new orders of friars, the Dominicans (founded by the Spanish priest St Dominic in 1215) and the Franciscans (founded by the Italian St Francis of Assisi in 1209). They were charged with the task of identifying heretics and bringing them back into the Church if possible or, if necessary, persecuting them. These new orders proved to be a two-edged sword for the Church. Some of the radical followers of Francis of Assisi argued that Christ had been a poor carpenter and, to follow in his footsteps, they took vows of poverty. They lived simply and helped the poor. Meanwhile, the Roman Church was becoming increasingly wealthy and even opulent. The Franciscan doctrine of Christ's poverty would later be condemned in 1323 by Pope John XXII. The Church subsequently rewrote the early life of St Francis to 'tone down' his potentially radical social views.[39] More ominously, the Roman Church established the infamous Inquisition to identify, torture, and execute heretics and others whose ideas were deemed dangerous.

The operation of the Inquisition paralleled the introduction of the new heresy of reason. The rediscovery of previously unknown works by classical authors such as Aristotle and access to the wide scholarship possessed by the Islamic world wrought a revolution in traditional social theory. An alternative, self-contained system of knowledge, pre-Christian in origin and created in a pagan culture without the benefit of God's **revelation**, became available to scholars. The contrast between the two systems of knowledge was considerable. For Aristotle, the universe was infinite, not newly created; humans were creatures like any others, not possessed of immortal souls; God or the Gods were completely inaccessible and unconcerned about the world, rather than actively intervening in its workings.

According to the dominant Christian theology, since Adam, the first human male, was made in God's image, God was masculine. He had revealed truth to humans through the Bible or by speaking directly to people, the only two sources of absolute truth. Knowledge was through 'revelation'—the view that God had allowed portions of his absolute wisdom to become known to human beings. Christian doctrine taught that the earth was newly created; that humans possessed immortal souls and would have life after death in either heaven or hell; that God was all-knowing and all-powerful, and performed great miracles in the world and small ones when he directly answered prayers.

Most fundamentally for social theory, the received wisdom of the Middle Ages distrusted human reason. God had given people the ability to think so they could freely choose to be good and to worship God. Otherwise, the ability to reason that every individual possessed was a dangerous thing. Human reason was weak, prone to error and mistake, and tainted by original sin. It was dangerous because humans could be tempted into evil, even into doubt about the truths of the Christian religion. Reason had to be guided by the truths of the Bible and the Church, and not left open to speculation.

The alternative view—that knowledge derived from human reason—offered a new appreciation of the powers of the human mind to reason and find truth even if it contradicted the Bible. At its most extreme, a form of atheism emerged that sought to replace all religious beliefs with truths determined solely by human reason. In the long run, this was a more profound alternative belief system than a competing religion.

Since it is easier to kill believers than to kill beliefs, the new ideas had to be fought ideologically. Christian theologians developed two strategies to neutralize and weaken the influence of the new rationalism. One strategy was to deny that religion could be understood rationally. The religious experience was something that one felt, or experienced internally, but it could not be explained or understood. Religious truths were deeper and more profound than mere human reason; they were knowable only spiritually. Faith and reason were two different or dual principles coexisting in humanity, and one could not be reduced to the other.

This solution did not satisfy all Christian theologians. Rather than separating faith and reason as irreconcilable, they proposed an alternative solution by incorporating human rationality into religion. Reason was to be surrounded and captured for religion, not eliminated by burning heretics or ignored by asserting the irreconcilable duality of faith and reason. Thomas Aquinas (1225–74) undertook this difficult task.

THOMAS AQUINAS

Aquinas was born near Naples, Italy, to an aristocratic family. Educated in a monastery and then at the University of Naples, his family expected him to become an abbot of a rich monastic estate. Aquinas dashed these expectations at the age of 19 when he joined the Dominicans. The Dominican order had been created to combat heresy more by persuasion than by force and sought well-educated teachers suited to proselytizing Christian beliefs. While abbots held secure and powerful positions in the feudal hierarchy, friars were mendicant—they preached to ordinary people and lived solely from charity.

Aquinas's family did not give up without a fight. On his way to Paris, his elder brother forcibly seized him and he was confined in a family castle for over a year. Despite the pressure, Aquinas remained fixed on his chosen vocation.[40] According to one story, while he was being held prisoner in his room, his brother sent a young woman to seduce him. Grasping a glowing brand from the fire, Aquinas drove her away, later dreaming that angels had bound him in 'perpetual chastity'. The temptation must have been almost overwhelming because, according to Kenny, from that day 'it was his custom always to avoid the sight and company of women—except in case of necessity or utility—as a man avoids snakes.'[41]

Aquinas was exposed to the breadth of Aristotle's writings in Cologne, where he was recognized as a brilliant student despite a deliberate, plodding style and body shape that earned him the nickname 'Dumb Ox'. While still in his twenties, Aquinas went to the University of Paris to study, engage in disputations, and lecture on philosophy and theology.[42] Years later, in 1268, he returned to Paris where an extreme form of rationalism derived from Aristotle was being debated. The new rationalists argued that knowledge required only physical senses (such as sight, sound, touch) to experience the world and a mind to understand these sensations. Truth, in short, was independent of revelation. This was a direct challenge to Christianity, a belief system Aquinas proceeded to defend.

To combat the new **rationalism**, Aquinas sought to reconcile pagan learning with Christian beliefs. Reason could be harnessed by the Church and used to help maintain the faithful. The result was a body of doctrine that still shapes much Catholic doctrine. Aquinas's contributions to social theory can be understood by outlining some of the general principles underlying his ideas, especially the concept of natural hierarchy and the organic model of society. Second, a number of specific aspects of the social theory he inspired reflected the social and political conditions of his time.

Finally, Aquinas's solutions to the problems posed by the new rationalism also reflected the emergence of new forces in society. What Aquinas thought to be the final resolution of questions of knowledge actually opened the door for the further evolution of social theory, away from faith and towards unrestricted rationalism.

The Principle of Hierarchy

Aquinas was born in a very rigid, feudal system of social stratification that shaped both secular and religious institutions. The principle of hierarchy underlies much of his social theorizing. For Aquinas, a hierarchy contains different orders 'based on different duties and functions' existing 'under the government of one ruler'.[43] Since the world and everything in it was divinely created, hierarchy was assumed to be God's basic principle of organization. The great diversity of living creatures had been created exactly as they presently appeared[44] and existed in a great hierarchy that reflected 'a deliberate intention of God to make the created universe as hierarchically perfect as possible'.[45] In this great Chain of Being, the lowest forms of life were at the bottom and the highest at the top.

While humanity stood at the top of this ladder of life, even in a naturally innocent state there were inequalities of sex, age, and physical ability.[46] In society, Aquinas said, two stable hierarchies of inequality had developed. In the country were 'judges', soldiers, and those 'who labor in the fields'. In the cities were the nobles, 'the respectable people' in the middle, and the common people.[47] Aquinas argued that 'people cannot live in society unless someone is in authority to look after the common good, for the many as such seek different objectives, while one person seeks only one.'[48] Since people were naturally unequal in their 'knowledge and justice', the judges and nobles were obligated to exercise their superiority and rule 'for the benefit of the others'. Ultimately, hierarchy implied not just a differentiated order, but government by a single ruler.

To the principle of hierarchy, Aquinas attached an organic conception of social order. For Aquinas, society was like a living organism. It was composed of different parts, some more essential than others, but all part of a single whole. Each group of people occupied a specific place in the feudal structure. The 1848 hymn by Cecil Alexander, 'All things bright and beautiful', described the social structure this way:

> The rich man at his castle,
> The poor man at his gate;
> God made them high and lowly,
> He ordered their estate.

Each received unequal rewards and possessed unequal rights and was bound by duty to perform whatever tasks corresponded to this social placement. If the monarchy was the head and the Church the heart, the serfs were the feet, the hands, the arms and legs. Society worked best— part of God's design—when all performed the tasks to which a higher power had consigned them, as the German folktale, 'Eve's Various Children', demonstrates (Box 1.5).[49]

Christian thinking simultaneously contained the kernel of an alternative idea. In essence, humans were equal. Every individual was born equal in the sight of God and possessed an individual soul that could be saved. In heaven, earthly distinctions would be erased. Medieval art pictured the grim reaper cutting down clergymen, nobles, and peasants without distinction. In addition, to be wealthy was to be unholy. The more one renounced worldly goods the closer one was to God. The renunciation of wealth by Francis of Assisi reflected the original attraction of Christianity to the poor and oppressed in the Roman Empire. Passages in both the Old and the New Testaments have been interpreted to suggest God favours the poor over the rich. After children were brought to Jesus for blessing, one disciple asked what good deed he must do to gain eternal life. He had assiduously kept the Ten Commandments, but what did he still lack? 'Jesus said to him, "If you would be perfect, go, sell what you possess

---

Box 1.5

When Adam and Eve were driven out of Paradise . . . [e]very year Eve brought a child into the world; but the children were unlike each other, some pretty, and some ugly. . . . God . . . announce[d] that he was coming to inspect their household. Eve . . . brought in her children, but only the beautiful ones. . . . The ugly children were . . . not to let themselves be seen. . . . The Lord . . . began to bless them: 'Thou shalt be a powerful King. . . . Thou a prince . . . a count . . . a knight . . . a nobleman . . . a merchant . . . a learned man. . . .'

When Eve saw that the Lord was so . . . gracious, she thought, 'I will bring hither my ill-favoured children. . . . Then came the whole coarse, dirty, shabby, sooty band. The Lord . . . said . . . 'Thou shalt be a peasant . . . a fisherman . . . a smith . . . a weaver . . . a shoemaker . . . a tailor . . . a potter . . . a sailor . . . an errand boy . . . Thou a scullion all the days of your life.'

When Eve heard all this she said, 'Lord, how unequally thou dividest thou gifts. . . . [T]hy favours should be given to all alike.' But God answered . . . 'It is right and necessary that the entire world should be supplied from thy children; if they were all princes and lords, who would . . . be blacksmiths, weavers, carpenters. . . . Each shall have his own place, so that one shall support the other, and all shall be fed like the limbs of one body.'

—'Eve's Various Children', *Grimm's Fairy Tales* (1812–15)

and give to the poor, and you will have treasure in heaven . . . ." And Jesus said to his disciples, "Truly, I say to you, it will be hard for a rich man to enter the kingdom of heaven." '50 The belief that 'many that are first will be last, and the last first' inspired generations of social rebels and Christian socialists who were not willing to await the treasures of heaven and, instead, sought to bring paradise down to earth.

The subversive undercurrent of this radical, levelling, and selective reading of the Bible entered popular culture, as another German folktale suggests. In this story, collected by the Grimm brothers, a poor but pious peasant dies and stands at the gate of heaven behind an extremely wealthy lord. St Peter admits the lord but doesn't see the peasant, who patiently waits outside, listening to the music and singing as the angels joyously welcome the rich lord to heaven. After all is quiet, St Peter admits the peasant and the angels greet him affectionately, but there is no celebration or singing. The peasant, taken aback, questions St Peter about the difference between the welcome he had received compared to that for the rich lord 'and said that it seemed to him that there in Heaven things were done with as much partiality as on earth.' In reply, St Peter assures the peasant that everyone would receive the benefits of heaven equally, 'but poor fellows like thee come to Heaven every day, but a rich man like this does not come more than once in a hundred years.'51 In the late nineteenth century, the German philosopher, Friedrich Nietzsche, would denigrate the Christian ideal of equality and the exalting of the meek at the expense of the proud.

Aquinas argued that all humans had been equal before the original sin of Adam and Eve had thrust them out of Paradise.52 Inequality resulted from sin. In society after the 'fall' of humanity, all people were guilty of sinning, but some sinned more than others. Subjection and inferiority, including enslavement, were 'the result of sin', Aquinas claimed. Whereas Aristotle had believed that some people were naturally slaves because they were servile by birth, Aquinas said that slavery was the result of sin, since 'this

kind of domination could only be a punishment for those subject to it.' Although the slaves' situation was painful because they were used for the benefit of their owner and were forced to 'yield to the decisions of another' when these decisions 'should be one's own', enslavement was not morally wrong. The slave deserved to be dominated and to suffer.53

Aquinas's theory of hierarchy legitimated the traditional, feudal society. He was living in a time of change, of cultural conflict and intellectual turmoil. Unlike some defenders of the Roman Catholic faith, who simply reiterated the old doctrines about the weakness of human reason and the importance of irrational faith, Aquinas sought a place for rationality in the traditional social order.

Rationality

As St Augustine54 had said, 'no institution of human society can remain stable once we have decided to believe in nothing which we cannot grasp with our senses.' To accomplish this, Aquinas utilized once again the basic principle of hierarchy. Like everything else in divine creation, reason itself existed in a hierarchy. At the top was absolute reason, possessed only by God, who was all-knowing. Some small part of God's infinite wisdom had been revealed to human beings through revelation, principally in the Bible. God had also given humans the capacity for 'natural reason'. They could not fathom all the secrets of the universe—only *absolute reason* could do that— but human reason could be used to prove things that could not be perceived, such as the existence of God and the 'immortal soul'. Aquinas argued that there were five reasonable 'proofs' for the existence of God. Most people, however, do not possess sufficient 'natural reason' to understand these proofs. Some are not 'disposed to learning' and cannot 'attain the highest level of human knowledge'; others are too busy in practical affairs, while laziness prevents others. In practice, then, such people must believe solely on the basis of faith. Finally, asserted Aquinas, 'There are some truths . . . that exceed the capacity of human reason' itself. These 'truths' could only be accepted on faith, such as the belief in the resurrection of Christ, or the conception of the Trinity, that God is three in one.[55]

Given the vast scientific knowledge discovered in such pagan authors as Aristotle, it was clear that human reason could independently discover much of the workings of the world, about which revelation was silent. Human reason was a powerful instrument but, being only human, it was not infallible. Human reason, Aquinas asserted, was inferior to absolute reason—it existed on a lower plane of the hierarchy and was prone to error. Humans could be led astray into untruths. The main test regarding the truth or falsity of knowledge derived from human reason alone was whether it agreed with or contradicted 'the self-evident first principles'. If scientific knowledge confirmed the Bible and revelation, then it was true. If it had no relationship at all to revelation, then it might be true and the further application of human reason would be able to determine whether it was true or not. If, however, humans arrived at a belief based on their reason that contradicted scripture or disagreed with revelation, then it was obviously wrong. For Aquinas, 'any arguments made against the doctrines of faith are incorrect.'[56]

The principle of the hierarchy of reason had further uses for Aquinas. It was obvious to him that the social elite of the Church and the aristocracy possessed the greatest amount of reason, while the lowly serf possessed only enough to be able to understand and obey religious and secular authority. Furthermore, as between the authority of the Church and the monarch, since the Church was charged with receiving and interpreting revelation, then the Church was the superior institution. Aquinas may have been born a noble, but he had chosen his vocation and he was determined to establish the Church in a position of social dominance. It is a natural law that one man rules in any hierarchy, he claimed, and the Pope in Rome was the 'one person' who ruled 'over the whole church'.[57]

If some men were more rational than others, all humans were more rational than animals, while animals themselves existed in a hierarchy of mental abilities. It was also obvious to Aquinas that, among human beings, children were inferior in their reason to adults. Similarly, women were naturally inferior to men 'because by nature man possesses more discernment of the reason.'[58] At the same time, Aquinas challenged Aristotle's claim that a 'woman is a misbegotten man.' This implied that God had made an error in the act of creation, an argument Aquinas could not accept. Perhaps, if you looked at woman's 'particular nature', he said, a woman was 'somewhat deficient and misbegotten' compared to the active power of the 'perfect male', but with respect to 'nature in general, a woman is not something misbegotten but intended by nature to be directed to the work of procreation.'[59] What we would regard as gender roles were, for Aquinas, part of the natural division of tasks. The human nature of each sex was suited for the task God had ordained for it. Women were excluded from formal education in the cathedral schools and universities.[60] Although they were inferior to men in rationality and power, women were created with a specific function in mind.

Aquinas was not arguing that the two genders were different in a complementary and otherwise equal way. It was in the nature of women to be subject to men. Unlike slaves, who were used only for the good of their master, the subjugation of women was 'for their benefit or good'. The view that women's nature was essentially different from that of men and, in particular, that women were less rational persisted throughout the centuries, becoming part of both the later conservative and Romantic ideologies.

Women's inferiority was apparent in sexual intercourse, where 'the active principle is in the male and the passive in the female.' In the state of innocence, Aquinas agreed, sexual intercourse for the purpose of procreation was natural and in accordance with God's will. In this natural condition, passion would not rule people's actions; rather, 'the lower powers would have been subordinated to reason.' The pleasure of sexual intercourse would have been moderated in its use by reason, and specifically limited to the purposes of procreation.

The experience of sexual intercourse, though not its natural purpose, changed after the 'fall': 'When man engages in sexual intercourse he becomes like a beast because the reason cannot moderate the pleasure of sexual intercourse and the heat of desire.' Medieval Christianity linked the doctrine of 'original sin', which originated in the wilful disobedience of Adam contrary to the instructions of God, with sexual desire (lust). This argument had been popularized in the previous century by the influential theologian, Peter Lombard (c. 1100–60), who had declared: 'The cause of original sin lies in the manifold defects of the flesh, especially in a pollution which the body, when it is conceived, contracts from the parents in the heat of intercourse and sexual concupiscence [lust].'[61]

The result of the fall of Adam was 'lust', an obsession with sexual pleasure as a glutton overindulges in the pleasure of eating.[62] Lust leads to lecherous acts that violate 'the natural order of the sex act', such as when 'orgasm is induced for the sake of sexual pleasure without intercourse', when intercourse is carried out with a different species, when 'intercourse is with a person of the same sex', and 'when the natural method of intercourse is not observed either as to the proper organ or using monstrous or bestial techniques'.[63] In medieval Christian doctrine, sexual desire and sin were closely related, if not identical. The Catholic Church has persistently resisted efforts to change its doctrines on sexuality, particularly as they have affected women and same-sex couples.

Trade and Commerce

Aquinas moved to adapt Church teachings to the new climate of commercial capitalism and private ownership of land. The return to prosperity in Europe during the twelfth century created a market for more exotic goods, such as spices, sugar, silk, and jewellery. These goods were obtained from the Far and Middle East, which required lengthy sea and overland trading voyages. This trade was controlled by Islamic merchants in the Middle East and North Africa, and then by merchants in Italian cities such as Venice and Genoa.

The merchant class had benefited more than any other group from the Crusades, acting as middlemen, carriers, and suppliers. They were becoming self-conscious as a new 'middle class' in between the labourers and the aristocrats. The accumulation of wealth would soon thrust them onto the wider political stage. Yet, traditional Christianity regarded the poor to be closer than the rich to God. Using property privately for personal gain, profit-making, and charging interest on loans were morally suspect practices.

The fundamental feudal principle was that the land was 'common' in the sense that no one possessed rights over it exclusive of the rights of others to enjoy it. In practice, however, individuals exercised exclusive rights over the agricultural and commercial property they controlled. The Church itself was increasingly involved in commerce, financing, and the monopolization of land. Aristotle had justified private property in his assertion that 'the possession of external things is natural to man.'[64] Real private property, the exclusive ownership of a thing vested in an individual, was a necessary part of life. This view appealed to the new middle class of merchants and traders as well as those who controlled the financial fortunes of the Church.

Aquinas attempted to devise a compromise position. He agreed with the traditional Christian view that, in principle, all of creation was actually 'common'. Adam and Eve in the Garden of Eden had no private property, so initially all of nature belonged to humanity as a whole, and 'the possession of all things in common and universal freedom' were both part of 'natural law'.[65] But this had changed after the fall of humanity. In the sinful world, 'it is legitimate for a man to possess private property; indeed it is necessary for human life.' It provided individuals with an incentive to look after and improve the things that were theirs, since property held in common was often neglected. One of the Ten Commandments was not to steal; however, if all property was really 'common', was stealing actually possible? Aquinas interpreted the commandment to be proof that someone was entitled to the 'use' of their property and that any other individual who unlawfully appropriated it had committed a sin. Private property was recognized in the Bible.

For Aquinas, this was not an absolute right because 'a man should not possess external things as his alone but for the community, so that he is ready to share them with others.'[66] In dire circumstances, private property someone was using for his or her private 'use' could be confiscated by the monarchy or the Church temporarily until the dire straits had passed, when property would revert to its habitual users. Since in its essence all property was common, a person in desperate need was justified in taking the property of another. Strictly speaking, this was neither theft nor a sin. It was understandable and forgivable. What was not forgivable was to withhold something from another in desperate need—such an act reflected the sin of greed or avarice. The sanction of private property became the Church's prevailing doctrine by the thirteenth century. Although neither 'separate possessions nor slavery resulted from nature', Aquinas argued, both had been 'produced by human reason for the benefit of human life.'[67]

Property might be private, but making a profit from it smacked of indulging in the sin of greed. According to the orthodox Christian principle, exchanges should be equal—I give you a loaf of bread and you give me a chicken. What we each have now is different but equal in value to what we had before. No one has achieved a 'profit' unless the goods exchanged were not equal; that is, either you had bought it too cheaply, thereby cheating the seller, or you sold it too dearly, cheating the buyer. By its nature, then, profit from trade has an element of moral baseness.[68]

The merchant class was growing in a society that did not necessarily respect its occupation—buying and selling for profit. This is true generally of traditional societies, as otherwise distinct as ancient China and feudal Europe. There was no honour in commerce. For Aristotle,[69] the simple household economy with its one-on-one bartering of goods between families constituted the natural economy. Trading one good for another was a purely functional act. The real goal of living was to lead a good, moral life. With the introduction of money, Aristotle had said, rather than trying to lead an ethical life, the goal of human activity became the acquisition of wealth, a pursuit that is endless, as is the exploitation of other people to achieve it. Profit was hardly distinguishable from the Christian sin of **usury**—charging interest on a loan—which Aristotle found to be particularly unethical.

In Aquinas's time the question of money-making raised practical as well as moral questions for the Church. The traditional doctrine that profit was unethical left the lucrative trade markets in the hands of Moslems and Jews and drove Christian merchants away from the Church. As commercial capitalism expanded in the Italian cities after the Crusades, the prosperous merchants cared more for their pocketbooks than for the salvation of their souls.[70] Aquinas sought to make profit-taking and charging interest on loans ethical practices.

Aristotle had already added the qualification that however much merchants may be a social evil, they were a necessary evil. They performed an essential function, similar to prostitutes according to St Augustine. Similarly, Aquinas put aside his hostility to merchants by finding a place for profit, which was not necessarily 'contrary to virtue'. It was perfectly moral, Aquinas believed, to make 'a moderate profit through trade' if you had done some social good, such as supporting the poor or even your own household, or had contributed to public welfare. You could also receive profit 'as a recompense' for your labour,[71] perhaps by transporting goods from one place to another. The 'just price', then, would include a certain percentage profit. Nevertheless, he concluded, the 'things anyone has in superabundance ought to be used to support the poor.'[72]

Finally, Aquinas examined the sin of usury. In traditional society the moneylender was a social pariah. As sociologist Karl Mannheim argued early in the twentieth century, the prohibition on usury presupposes a small, closely knit community. At first, the Catholic Church assimilated this ethic and formalized it in its system of morality. To 'receive interest for lending money is unjust in itself'[73] because you are profiting unfairly from another's dire necessity. After the rise of capitalism, the Church used the doctrine against 'the emergent economic force of capitalism'. As the structure of society changed, however, this doctrine was increasingly violated in practice until even the Church had to discard it.[74] As Aquinas asserted, usury might also be one of those necessary sins. By lending money, you deny yourself the pleasure of spending it. The interest simply compensates you for the temporary loss of the use of your property: '[H]uman law allows usury not because it considers it just but to avoid interference with the useful activities of many people.'[75]

Of course, not all profit and interest were moral. It was still sinful to hoard a good in order to artificially drive up its price. This led to excessive profit and was unethical. Similarly, it was wrong to charge too much interest because then you would be taking unfair advantage of someone else's need. It was possible for human reason to arrive at what would, in any circumstance, be a 'just price' and a just rate of interest. Aquinas did not champion dog-eat-dog competition, yet his compromise on profit and interest opened the door of Christian acceptability for these business practices, placing the commercial actions of the rising class of merchants and traders on a moral rather than an immoral plane.

Political Authority

Aquinas opened one other door in his attempt to compromise the results of human reason with orthodox religion: the question of the rights of the citizens against the monarch. Traditional authority would assume that it was the right of the monarch to rule and the duty of subjects to obey. '[I]n human affairs inferiors are bound to obey their superiors according to the order contained in the natural and divine law', Aquinas believed. Without this duty to obey, 'stability . . . could not be maintained in human affairs.' Nevertheless, there were limits to this duty to obey. '[B]y nature all men are equal', Aquinas recognized, so even slaves were right to refuse to obey their master in areas of human nature, such as procreation or marriage. Duty was owed to a superior only in areas where superiority is legitimate, as a soldier obeys an officer or 'a slave his master in what pertains to his work as a slave'.[76]

In his political theory, elaborated in *On Kingship* (1265–7), Aquinas argued that humanity is by nature political and social, and was not meant by nature to be solitary. People live naturally in association but, since their private, individual needs are not the same as the needs of the group, there must be government to meet the needs of everyone. 'Private concerns divide the community while common concerns unite it.'[77]

Government by one person was the best. In fact, asserting the argument that kings rule by divine right, Aquinas claimed that a king 'has been appointed to exercise judgement over the kingdom in God's place.'[78] A single ruler would be most likely to achieve unity and peace, the fundamental objectives of government. In a country ruled by the many—a democracy—dissension would soon make government impossible and inevitably lead to the rule of a tyrant. A mild tyranny should be tolerated by the people because attempts to overthrow it would lead only to worse tyrannies.[79]

In his later writings, Aquinas came to a more liberal conclusion. The best form of constitution, he later concluded, 'is a judicious combination of kingship—rule by one man, aristocracy—rule by many in accordance with virtue, and democracy—i.e., popular rule in that the rulers can be chosen from the people and the people have the right to choose their rulers.' In this balanced government, everyone would play some part in the government 'because they are all eligible to govern and those who govern are chosen by all.'[80] Would it follow that people have a right to choose new rulers, to replace one government with another?

If the tyranny is extreme and unbearable, Aquinas said, it is still better to submit than for an individual or a few individuals to attempt to overthrow the tyrant. The only solution, Aquinas said, would be to proceed 'through public authority'.[81] If ordinary people were not fully rational, since they existed on a lower plane in the hierarchy of reason than the aristocrats, then they were incapable of judging when authority was unjust. They must seek the guidance of the Church. They were wrong unless their rebellion was directed against secular authority (the monarchy or aristocracy) and unless it was sanctioned and led by the clergy.

Aquinas's solution appeared to allow some appeal against tyranny, though it was restricted to the bounds of traditional authority. Nevertheless, it suggested a more radical interpretation than Aquinas intended, the doctrine of popular sovereignty—that real political authority lay with the people and the monarch ruled only so long as he or she had the confidence of the people. Aquinas did not intend this radically democratic interpretation. By the seventeenth century, however, it would become increasingly popular.

In his social and political arguments, Aquinas did not simply represent traditional society; rather, he straddled the past and the future. His ideas represent an early step that would take social thought in a direction Aquinas would have neither appreciated nor desired. Some theorists would later argue that human reason was the *only* source of knowledge, that the belief in God was simply a creation of the *human* imagination. Economic theorists would eventually assume that giving individuals absolute control to use their private property to obtain the highest profit possible would lead, inevitably, to the greatest good for all. Aquinas did not foresee that he was clearing some of the underbrush leading to these constructions.

Aquinas wrote prodigiously in his later years, finishing the second part of his major treatise, the *Summation of Theology* (*Summa theologiae*), Sigmund claims, by 'dictating to as many as three or four secretaries at a time, even, it was said, continuing to dictate in his sleep.'[82] Aquinas began to suffer from serious bouts of complete distraction, becoming so absorbed in his own mind that he forgot his surroundings and had to be recalled to his present circumstances. On the sixth of December 1273 Aquinas had a 'mysterious experience', a late-life crisis. He announced quite suddenly that he could write no longer since 'All that I have written seems like straw to me.' His contemporaries believed he had a mystical experience of the divine. It was possibly a stroke, or a mental breakdown from overwork. Aquinas died a few months later.[83]

The compromise Aquinas sought between orthodox Church ideology and the new rationalism then entering Europe would eventually become a standard element of Church doctrine. Initially, however, many Church leaders found his teachings too radical. By emphasizing the importance of human reason as an independent source of knowledge for natural philosophy, Aquinas had unintentionally charted a course for intellectual history that would undermine any non-rational claims about knowledge. Even in his lifetime, some Church leaders feared that opening the door to human reason at all would be dangerous to faith. In this view, religious beliefs should be based on faith, on the non-rational. This duality of reason and non-reason would be played out in different ways in much of the social theory that followed Aquinas.

THE DECLINE OF THE WEST

Aquinas died in 1274, at the height of medieval power. For about two centuries thereafter, Europe went into a decline that was exacerbated by the loss of population caused by the Black Death. The controversies over reason, knowledge, faith, economic change, and political authority slumbered until the fifteenth century, when many of the more radical implications of Aquinas's theory began to re-emerge.

The towering intellectual figure of the next generation was not a churchman, but a poet who was intimately involved in the political and financial wrangling of his native Florence. Dante Alighieri (1265–1321) was a humanist whose romantic poetry was first inspired by his youthful, though chaste and distant love of Beatrice. Dante faced a moral crisis, '[m]idway in . . . life's journey', when he realized he had gone astray from the 'straight road' to salvation by being overly concerned with worldly affairs.[84] In *The Divine Comedy*, a term that implied a happy ending, Dante imagined the journey of his soul through Hell, Purgatory, and finally Paradise, every Christian's ultimate goal. In this allegorical poem, Dante expounds his ideas on morality and sin through conversations with well-known people who were long dead. Hell or the 'Inferno' (see Box 1.6)[85] was structured hierarchically and rationally, with appropriate punishments imposed for specific types of sin.

Dante's guide through Hell and Purgatory is the Roman poet, Virgil, who represents human reason. Virgil died a pagan, so his unbaptized soul is spending eternity between Hell and Paradise. For Dante, reason could help one recognize sin and lead to repentance, but it was not capable of appreciating the divine. Ultimately, with his soul finally purged of sin, Dante glimpses Paradise: 'the truth I wished for came / cleaving my mind in a great flash of light.' In his final salvation,

Dante says, the great duality of human nature was reconciled, his 'instinct and intellect [were] balanced equally.'[86] *The Divine Comedy* expresses the traditional Christian concern with eternity, but by writing in the vernacular Italian Dante reached a wide audience and contributed to the birth of humanism.

By the fourteenth century, the Church had largely triumphed over its internal enemies in Europe, although in the Holy Land the Crusades had failed. The initial flurry of European aggression and expansion was temporarily halted. Europe was a chastened and temporarily weakened continent, having sunk into financial chaos. The Black Death had struck Europe in 1347, carrying off about one person in three and severely depopulating the continent.

These natural and social disasters sharpened conflict between the aristocracy, the peasantry, and the urban classes. One response to social and economic crisis was to lay blame on a scapegoat. The most visible ethnic minority in Europe was the Jews, a group that occupied an important place as moneylenders and merchants in the medieval cities, yet they were defined as a pariah people,

---

Box 1.6

In Dante's poem, Hell is an abyss composed of a series of concentric ledges (or Circles) on which reside different classifications of sinners, each with an appropriate punishment. The Roman poet Virgil was in Limbo, Circle 1 of Hell, where all virtuous pagans spend eternity since they lived before Christianity and 'lacked Baptism's grace'. A glorious, green meadow, Circle 1 was the final resting place of 'Aristotle, the master of those who know'. He was 'ringed by the great souls of philosophy', pagans who suffer 'without hope [but] live on in desire'. Reaching Circle 2, Dante passed from light to 'eternal night' where 'the voice of the damned rose in a bestial moan'. Circle 2 punishes the souls 'of those who sinned in the flesh, the carnal and lusty / who betrayed reason to their appetite'. In Circle 4 Dante found hoarders and wasters who 'were so skewed and squinteyed in their minds / their misering or extravagance mocked all reason'. The 'weed of avarice sows its rankest seed' among popes and cardinals. At Circle 6, where 'the arch-heretics of all cults' are punished, is a great wall separating upper from lower Hell. The deepest circle, save only where Satan dwelled, was for those who were treacherous to their kings and masters.

—Dante Alighieri, *The Inferno* (c. 1314)

ghettoized and isolated. In the context of economic and social distress, the friars fanned the flames of anti-Semitism and Jews were expelled from England in 1292.[87] Massacres of Jews preceded the many Crusades, particularly in advance of the so-called People's Crusade when thousands were slaughtered. Additional **pogroms** (the systematic murdering of Jews and expropriation of their property) were carried out on a large scale in the mid-fourteenth century as Jews were blamed for the Black Plague. Anti-Semitism became systematic and entrenched in Europe.

The shortage of labour caused by the plague contributed to the breakdown of feudalism, as many peasants were able to buy their freedom and establish themselves as independent farmers (yeomen) or migrate to the newly expanding towns. Where the authorities tried to re-establish the old conditions of servitude and increase exploitation, peasants and crafts workers revolted. The weavers were especially radical. In England, John Ball preached human equality and, in 1381, Wat Tyler led a large but unsuccessful revolt. According to the eighteenth-century Scottish historian and philosopher, David Hume, John Ball was 'a seditious preacher' who 'inculcated on his audience the principles of the first origin of mankind from one common stock, their equal right to liberty, and to all the goods of nature, the tyranny of artificial distinctions, and the abuses that had arisen from the degradation of the more considerable part of the species, and the aggrandizement of a few insolent rulers.'[88]

As the poverty of Christ was downplayed, the Church itself grew richer and more powerful. By the later Middle Ages, monasteries had acquired large tracts of property and considerable wealth. Social criticism of the licentious lifestyle of many clergy began to appear in written form. The bitter and critical fourteenth-century poem *Piers Plowman* documented the general discontent in England and expressed sympathy for the conditions of the common people. The allegorical poem tells the story of the Dreamer, Will, who recounts sharply critical stories that include churchmen who are parasitical upon the common folk.

Most medieval intellectuals did not imagine that the hierarchical structure of power in society could be changed. The peasant rebellions were the periodic cries of the wretched and oppressed driven to violence by their circumstances. The suggestion that the state of equality, which Christians imagined in the Garden of Eden and heaven, could be created on earth by human will was far in advance of the age, though in later centuries it would help inspire the most profound social revolutions.

Conclusion

'Traditional' is a loaded and problematic word. It makes sense to call a set of ideas traditional the more a particular world view, deeply rooted in the past, dominates the consciousness of the era. By the time the Middle Ages reached its apex, the exact content and meaning of revelation, which had been debated over the centuries, was finally solidifying into Church dogma through numerous councils and encyclicals. Even then, a dominant view did not monopolize human understanding. In a society fractured by social distinctions and inequalities, beliefs, ideas, and practices come into conflict. Aquinas lived at a time when world views were in contention. Christianity had not yet been constructed into the dogmatic truths of the medieval papacy. Versions of Christian theology commingled with exotic Eastern religions and the survival of pagan rituals. Many of the latter were disarmed through their identification with Christian practices, as, for example, Easter was read into and displaced pagan fertility cults.

Similarly, Aquinas sought to surround and absorb much of the knowledge and beliefs of the ancient world and Arabic scholarship, relegating them to a subordinate position. Aquinas's writings on social and political thought represent a fraction of his scholarship. Many, though not all, of his beliefs were typically traditional—ideas that dominated society and competed with other views that, in historical hindsight, would come to predominate in the future. His absolute belief in revelation, the principle of a natural hierarchy, the importance of fulfilling one's duties within this structure, and the conception of society as functioning like an organism were initially or became traditional views.

In his theorizing about economics and politics Aquinas approached what, in historical hindsight, has the potential for modern, liberal views. While property was in essence common, those who exercised the customary right to the use of property possessed, in unexceptional times, rights of ownership. In commerce, both profit from trade and interest from moneylending, within set limits, were just rewards for hard work and sacrifice, and fit employment for Christians.

As the Middle Ages plodded unknowingly towards the modern world, it appeared that society had achieved its highest potential under the rule of the medieval popes. Thereafter, convulsed by periodic social rebellions, devastated by disease and epidemic, threatened by the breakdown of traditions and social conventions, Europe appeared destined for another age of retraction and stagnation. If Europeans had possessed a global perspective, the destiny of the world would have appeared to rest in the hands of the vast Chinese empire, then under the domination of the great Ming dynasty. Yet within 100 years the trend of world history would be reversed. A small, hitherto insignificant part of the globe—Western Europe—would begin its rapid ascent to world domination. Christianity may have failed in the Crusades, but riding on the tail of colonial conquest, European ideologies—secular as well as religious—began a long period of global influence and economic dominance. The new social theory that the intellectual revolution of the late medieval age had unintentionally spawned evolved into modern liberalism.

2 THE REVOLUTION IN NATURAL AND SOCIAL SCIENCE

The medieval conception of society as part of a divinely ordained hierarchy was decisively squeezed out of Western social theory by the relentless pressure of social change. In its place, liberalism has achieved ideological dominance. Liberalism was first advocated by a progressive minority of intellectuals in the face of stubborn resistance from traditionalists. It was incompatible with some of the most entrenched institutions found in traditional society, especially autocratic monarchy and the aristocratic privileges held by secular and religious authorities.

Liberalism emerged in a world that legalized slavery, gave absolute power to kings and princes, gave some groups legal rights that were denied others, and maintained patriarchal dominance over women and children. The fundamental principle of liberalism is that each individual has a natural right to liberty, a claim that is far-reaching and radical in its implications. The demand for liberty echoed in the hearts of all who felt oppressed and unjustly treated, from every group whose interests were smothered by the traditional world order.

In the medieval world view, the stability of the universe was potentially insecure because the celestial bodies required continual intervention by supernatural powers. Angels pushed the planets along their circular orbits; they did not move on their own accord. An absence of movement and change was the normal state of affairs. The threat of immanent chaos should the angels relinquish their role made people suspicious and fearful of change.

What proved precarious was the stability of this traditional world view itself. Liberalism

embodied a fundamental reorientation of Western thought because it included a dynamic element of perpetual movement and progress. The normal form of matter was motion, not rest, implying constant change. Liberalism reflected the world that was coming to be. Economic change, propelled by the emerging business class, had been underway throughout the late medieval period. The transition to the modern era was punctuated by religious protests and institutional changes, and by the revolution in science that was fuelled by a belief in the unlimited potential of human rationality to obtain knowledge about the world and change it for the better.

The rebirth of the knowledge of the ancient world, which had lain dormant since the thirteenth century, burst forth in new bloom in fifteenth-century Italy and stimulated a flourishing change in culture and science. A dress rehearsal for the Renaissance had occurred in the time of Aquinas, but it had no permanent effect on European culture. The **Renaissance** stimulated a much higher appreciation of humanity and human potential than the limited medieval view. Rather than people being taught to accept the social order as it was, to perform the duties of their station in life, to obey their earthly rulers and await the Second Coming, there was a new belief that social life could be improved by the application of human reason. According to the new doctrine of humanism, the individual was potentially perfectible, not fallen or awash in original sin as in Christian dogma. Just as the Renaissance gave recognition to the ancient geniuses of classical antiquity, a new cult of genius was emerging in early modern

Europe. As art historian Whitney Chadwick argues, the creativity of the artist was parallel to the creativity of God.[1] The ideal Renaissance figure, exemplified by Leonardo da Vinci, embraced all forms of knowledge. In some instances, the Renaissance restored the limited degree of equality many urban and upper-class women had lost in the later Middle Ages. The new economy, however, promoted the privatization of women's role, exemplified by the Renaissance Italian essay *On the Family* (1435), which described the ideal woman as modest, pure, and chaste, and properly excluded from the public world of business and government.[2] While women were freer in Northern Europe than in Southern Europe, as some of Shakespeare's strong female characters demonstrate, the Renaissance initiated the long process of confining women to the domestic tasks of the nurturing wife and mother that would dominate social thought in the eighteenth and nineteenth centuries.

THE SCIENTIFIC REVOLUTION

And new philosophy calls all in doubt,
The element of fire is quite put out.
—John Donne, 'An anatomy of the world'
(1611)

The Renaissance scientists sought truth from their observations of the natural world, not from mere authority, whether it was the authority of Aristotle, some other ancient sage, or the Bible. Careful astronomical observations suggested to Nicholas Copernicus (1473–1543) and Galileo Galilei (1564–1642) that the sun, not the earth, was the centre of the solar system. According to the traditional outlook, the heavens, unlike the earth, had no imperfections. Through the use of telescopes he constructed, Galileo demonstrated that the moon had craters and mountains, that the sun had 'blemish' spots, and that there were alternative centres of rotation in the universe demonstrated by the existence of Jupiter's moons.[3]

These heretical claims contradicted scripture and made humanity insignificant in the universe.

In his 1936 play about Galileo, the German playwright Bertolt Brecht imagined the reaction of a tradition-bound, elderly cardinal to the modern conception of the universe:

> I won't be a nobody on an inconsequential star briefly twirling hither and thither. I tread the earth, and the earth is firm beneath my feet, and there is not motion to the earth, and the earth is the center of all things, and I am the center of the earth, and the eye of the Creator is upon me.[4]

Galileo's sin was not only in degrading creation, humanity, and the earth, but he popularized his conclusions by writing books in his native Italian to make them accessible to a larger audience.[5] On two occasions Galileo was summoned before the Inquisition, his ideas were condemned, he was confined in prison, and his books were burned. So vehement were the inquisitors that Galileo was forced to agree publicly he had been mistaken, although he is alleged to have muttered, 'And yet it moves', after finally being released—into house arrest on his estate for the final eight years of his life—by the Inquisition. Some rationalists, such as the playwright Brecht, would later condemn Galileo for recanting and living when he could have died and joined Socrates as a martyr for the cause of human reason and scientific investigation (see Box 2.1).[6] Three centuries would pass before the Roman Catholic Church acknowledged it had made a mistake in condemning Galileo.

Galileo also made many mistakes. The method he used advanced science further than some of his findings. While Galileo modelled the ability of the new science to combine technology and observation with human reason, he was unable to rise above some of the theoretical assumptions he had inherited. Galileo overturned the ancient conception that the moon, sun, planets, and stars were all fixed in place in a series of concentric spheres above the earth, but he still attempted to fit his observations of planetary orbits into the traditional view that they followed absolutely circular paths, since that was the most

---

Box 2.1

Galileo: 'For two thousand years man has chosen to believe that the sun and all the host of stars revolve around him. Well. The Pope, the cardinals, the princes, the scholars, captains, merchants, housewives, have pictured themselves squarely in the middle. . . . [But a] new age was coming. . . . There was a group of masons arguing. They had to raise a block of granite. It was hot. To help matters, one of them wanted to try a new arrangement of ropes. After five minutes discussion, out went a method which had been employed for a thousand years. The millennium of faith is ended, said I, this is the millennium of doubt. . . . The sayings of the wise men won't wash any more. Everybody, at last, is getting nosy. . . . [Soon] they will be learning that the earth rolls around the sun, and that [all of us] . . . are rolling with it.'

—Bertolt Brecht, *Galileo* (1936)

---

perfect shape and the one God surely would have planned. More ironically, perhaps, while Galileo was opposed to the supernatural explanations of astrologers who believed the moon and stars had a causal influence on earthly events, a scientifically progressive position, it caused him to reject the conclusion that the moon exerts a force causing the ocean tides.[7] Creating the modern distinction between science and mythology was a slow process.

Ultimately, the Church was fighting a losing battle by challenging scientific evidence on the grounds of theological truths. European theory prior to the sixteenth century had been rooted in **deductive reasoning**. Beginning with a priori assumptions—statements believed to be true, which therefore required no proof—theorists deduced conclusions logically from them. At the foundation of the scientific revolution was a new appreciation for the ability of human reason to construct knowledge derived from sensory experience. In place of authority, whether secular or religious, the scientists of the new age combined rational thought with careful observation and experimentation, a process known as **inductive reasoning**.

In England, Francis Bacon (1561–1626) was an early propagandist for this new **empirical method** of knowledge acquisition. For Bacon, scientific knowledge was acquired inductively, from the data derived from observation. General scientific principles could be understood over time through the careful accumulation of observations of the natural world, appropriately guided by the use of human reason. Science would usher in a new age for humanity. For Bacon, Patterson argues,[8] the systematic application of reason would eliminate custom and superstition, allowing humanity to conquer nature and improve social institutions. The superior civilization was the one where reason was the most fully developed; the uncivilized society was still dominated by traditional values, beliefs, and customs. The growth of reason was the engine of progress and was behind the rapid development of technology in England and the conquest of the 'uncivilized' regions of the globe.[9]

According to Mies, Bacon asserted humanity's right to exploit nature, which was a vast treasure of wealth to be subdued and controlled. The goals of science were to subject nature to human will and improve daily life for people. Bacon taught that the earth had to be probed and violated in order to reveal its secrets. He employed the imagery of the witch hunt to describe his scientific method as the inquisition of nature. In Mies's words, Bacon used the same method to extract information from nature as 'the witch-persecutioners used to extract the secrets from the witches, namely torture, destruction, violence.'[10]

In the end, nature had the last laugh on Bacon's use of the inductive method. On a snowy day in April 1626 he undertook an experiment to see whether cold could preserve meat as efficiently as salt. He purchased a hen, cleaned it, and then stuffed it with snow. Shortly afterwards, Bacon became ill from the chill. Writing from his sickbed, Bacon said: 'As for the experiment itself, it succeeded excellently well', but he sensed the research would kill him as well as the hen. Bronchitis developed rapidly and Bacon died a short time later.[11]

The model scientist of the time was Isaac Newton (1642–1727), who claimed that, while all knowledge derived from sensory experience, natural phenomena were to be explained in the language of complex mathematics. For Newton, the universe was orderly and understandable, functioning according to causes and effects that were mechanically linked together. Observations guided reason to a comprehension of the basic laws underlying physical phenomena, such as the universal law of gravity.

The transition from the older natural philosophy to empirical science was not straightforward. It was seen as a 'scientific revolution' only in hindsight. Newton confined his work to the natural world, calling himself an 'experimental philosopher', and refused to speculate about such concepts as the 'human soul'.[12] The boundaries of this new science were, nevertheless, extremely porous and a specifically 'scientific' discourse took time to develop. So intent was Newton to produce 'philosopher's mercury', the substance that was thought capable of turning base metals into gold, that he often stayed up all night in his lab, barely eating and sleeping.[13] Although Newton spent a considerable amount of his time fruitlessly trying to create gold, his view that the universe was driven by unchanging and discoverable laws of direct cause and effect dominated the scientific imagination until the twentieth century.

Alchemist John Dee perhaps best typifies the hybrid beginnings of the scientific method. Dee 'wanted to discover nothing less than the secrets of the universe and humankind's place within it.'

In this quest, he treated astrology, magic, and alchemy as equivalent ways to discover truths. Dee approached this indiscriminate search for knowledge in a way that would be recognized as scientific, making careful observations and recording his results, whether he was investigating magic, the influence of the stars, his wife's menstruation, or his own sexuality. At one point he attempted to discover the most effective form of séance, concluding that one should abstain from sex for three days before trying to contact the spirits.[14] Modern science gradually disavowed the old search for the mercury of life and the philosopher's stone and, as Mary Shelley put it, plodded along the slow and careful road of the modern scientific method to accumulate a fortune in practical knowledge (see Box 2.2).[15]

Eventually, scientists would make an absolute distinction between material facts, which could be studied scientifically and for which truths could be determined, and non-material forms of speculation—magic, religion, astrology, and so on—for which no truths could be proven. Science was the key to unlocking the secrets of the physical universe. For Newton, the universe was 'a cryptogram set by the Almighty'.[16] The early scientists wanted to eat from the tree of God's secrets.

While the search for hitherto forbidden knowledge did not bring immediately an almighty curse, the more science advanced, the more it came into conflict with the established Church. A skeptical attitude began to creep into the cracks that science was opening in religious beliefs. By the early 1700s, the Bible and Christianity had been discredited for many intellectuals who professed the theology of deism in the place of organized religion. Deists did not deny the existence of God but held that the deity was only a 'first cause', the great watchmaker who had created the universe as a machine that ran automatically. The deity had devised the inherent laws upon which this mechanical universe operated, set it in motion, and had then retired to allow his creation to operate on its own. The universe moved perpetually according to principles that were written in the language of mathematics and were

---

Box 2.2

'The ancient teachers of this science', said M. Waldman, 'promised impossibilities, and performed nothing. The modern masters promise very little; they know that metals cannot be transmuted [into gold], and that the elixir of life is a chimera. But these philosophers, whose hands seem only made to dabble in dirt, and their eyes to pore over the microscope or crucible, have indeed performed miracles. They penetrate into the recesses of nature, and shew how she works in her hiding-places. They ascend into the heavens; they have discovered how the blood circulates, and the nature of the air we breathe. They have acquired new and almost unlimited powers; they can command the thunders of heaven, mimic the earthquake, and even mock the invisible world with its own shadows.'

—Mary Shelley, *Frankenstein* (1818)

---

discoverable by human reason.[17] The deity was remote from human affairs and no longer intervened with the mechanism that had been created.

ECONOMIC AND SOCIAL CHANGE

The scientific revolution was the handmaiden of three parallel developments in European society that combined to undermine the tottering feudal structure and erect the foundations of modern society. In religion, the unity of Western Christianity was broken through the Protestant **Reformation**. In economics, the rise of **commercial capitalism** was replacing the agrarian system of feudal estates. In culture, a wholesale revival of ancient learning stimulated a cultural explosion that placed humanity squarely on the pedestal of admiration. The core idea that unified these diverse movements was an appreciation for the power and capability of the individual.

By the sixteenth century, the theological unity the Church had established was broken, not by deism, which was confined to philosophers and scientists, but from within the Church itself. The old challenges to the Roman Catholic Church that Aquinas had faced were revived and multiplied manyfold. The stream of protests against the numerous and varied abuses of the clergy became a flood. Rebellious clergy began to demand the reconstitution of Christianity on a simpler basis,

founded more directly on the New Testament. The result was the Protestant Reformation, the great split in Western Christianity between the Catholic Church and various dissenting denominations.

The essential idea of the Reformation was that each individual was alone before the deity. Each individual was responsible for his or her own soul and salvation and for developing a direct relationship with God. Individuals possessed sufficient reason to understand the Bible, which had been translated from Latin into various European languages. There was no need for an intermediary, such as a priest or pope, between the individual and the single, all-powerful deity. With the Reformation, the unity of a shared ideology based on a single religious interpretation was shattered. The Reformation greatly simplified the traditional medieval image of society as a natural hierarchy. In the Protestant view, individuals were either saved or damned and, among the saved, all were essentially equal.

Commercial capitalism also focused on an individual's rational calculation, not of her or his state of grace, but of the pocketbook. There was a close and essential connection between the growth of capitalism and the emergence of the new social theory of liberalism. In England, where feudalism was in rapid decline, the birth of the modern world could plainly be heard in the jubilation of the prosperous middle class and the lamentations of villagers displaced from their ancestral property. The right of rural peasants to security of tenure was rapidly eroded as the rural gentry transferred the land their tenants traditionally had the 'use' of to private property. In place of the old subsistence farming, the land was converted into commercial farms to produce cash crops or was enclosed as pasture for raising sheep, the produce being sold in the market or exported abroad. The modernizing rural gentry and the class of commercial capitalists in port cities such as London and Bristol developed close economic and personal connections.

In government, the propertied middle classes were represented in the House of Commons, which entered into competition with the monarchy and the House of Lords for political power in England. Over the course of centuries, the House of Commons had gradually emerged as a significant political force, at first representing only the best-heeled property owners who had the right to vote and sit in Parliament. The highlight of this long conflict between Commons and King came during the English Revolution, 1640–60, when war broke out between the supporters of the King and those who championed the supremacy of and democratic notion represented by Parliament. The civil war culminated in the capture, trial, and execution of King Charles I. The claim of English monarchs to absolute power met a violent end on the executioner's block. For a decade and a half, England recognized no king and commoners ruled under Oliver Cromwell, the leader of the Parliamentary Army. When he died and a new King was invited to take the throne once again, the restored monarchy was weakened, and the propertied classes, acting through the House of Commons, exercised considerable power.

This evolution of political power was not duplicated elsewhere in Europe at the same time. In France the monarch was all-powerful until the late 1700s. Louis XIV of France, for example, referred to himself as the 'Sun King', a reference to his absolute power on earth, as a single God was omniscient in the heavens. Absolutism persisted in France despite the growth of a prosperous class of merchants and traders that had no permanent political representation. Other types of modified feudal relations continued to prevail elsewhere in Europe.

England was the exception, and it was in England undergoing transition that social theorists developed the new liberal ideology in opposition to the traditional, orthodox views represented by the elites of feudal society. The social theory of liberalism can be summarized by contrasting it with certain elements of traditional social theory.

Liberalism replaced the idea of divine order with the belief that society was a human creation. Whereas the traditional concept held that society originated in a plan devised by a deity, liberal thinkers argued that society had been a conscious human creation. Rather than people being mere cogs in the machine of a divine plan, humans were seen as free and independent individuals who possessed rationality, and who had constructed 'society' by agreeing to a rational '**social contract**'. Just as one person contracted with another to supply certain goods for an agreed-upon price, so, too, liberal social theorists posited, humans entered into a contract to set up social rules for the safety of all.

Second, liberalism undermined the traditional, feudal economy in favour of **free enterprise**. The traditional economy was hampered by numerous obligations and restrictions. The right to practise certain crafts was restricted in the guild system; the landlord was required to allow his tenants peaceful use of the land; the richest trade routes were in the hands of a few monopolies granted by the English monarch. Economic activity and trade were tightly controlled and benefited only a few politically favoured courtiers.

Fundamentally, the 'freedom' expressed in liberal economic demands was the right to do with your property as you saw fit. Land should be bought and sold on the market, labour contracts should be entered into freely, prices should be determined by supply and demand, and the government ought to remove all restrictions on the economy. The role of the government in liberal theory was minimal: to maintain internal law and order and to protect the nation from external enemies.

Finally, liberalism endorsed individual rights rather than collective rights. According to traditional values, feudal society was seen as organic; individuals were unequal and occupied different stations in life that were predetermined by the deity. In these various stations they had specific duties to perform and received specific rewards or privileges according to their status. There were no human rights, only those rights associated with the individual's particular status. Liberal theory, in contrast, was individualistic, arguing that all people were equal in rights by virtue of being human. The watchword of liberalism, then, was liberty: the right to do what you wanted provided you did not infringe on the rights of others.

Liberal theory did not emerge all in one piece. The ideology of liberalism would have a long and convoluted career. In 1651, the English theorist Thomas Hobbes published a lengthy essay defending the necessity for government to be under an absolute power. On the surface, this sounds like a reiteration of traditional authority, a viewpoint strengthened by Hobbes's portrait of human nature that he copied from the school of original sin. While Hobbes wrote with one hand resting in the absolutism of traditional society, he lived during an age of transition, and his other hand rested squarely on an individualistic view of human society.

THOMAS HOBBES

In 1588 Philip II, the Catholic monarch of Spain, launched a large-scale invasion of England, hoping to overthrow England's Protestant Queen Elizabeth and restore Roman Catholicism as the state religion. As Philip's Spanish Armada approached the English Channel, according to Alan Ryan, in a village in North Wiltshire a pregnant woman was so afraid of the invasion that she went into labour, giving birth to a son, Thomas Hobbes, who later remarked that 'fear and he were born twins into the world.'[18]

She needn't have worried. Bad weather and the English fleet routed the Armada. Thomas Hobbes (1588–1679) was born into a fairly stable and secure society under the popular, effective, and sometimes harsh rule of Elizabeth I. Beneath the calm surface of a thriving artistic and commercial community, however, religious conflict continued to seethe between Catholics, dissident Protestants, and the Anglican Church. Religious differences in the sixteenth and seventeenth centuries were not merely a matter of private opinion and worship. They had serious political implications and reflected the deep divisions in English society that Elizabeth was successful in controlling. Although Hobbes experienced the stability of a strong ruler during his early lifetime, by 1640 the social, religious, and economic fractures of English society had propelled the nation into the destruction and violence of civil war. Hobbes's lifelong search was to discover the basis of social stability and order.

Although members of Hobbes's extended family had become prosperous in the cloth-making business, the earliest large-scale capitalist industry in England, his father was a poor, ill-educated parish priest who, Malcolm claims, likely spent more time in the alehouse than the pulpit. The wayward elder Hobbes was eventually excommunicated for slandering a local vicar and then attacking him in the churchyard. While his older brother was expected to enter the family cloth-making business, Thomas was sent to the University of Oxford in his early teens to train for the clergy. He did not become a cleric; instead, Hobbes spent his life as a tutor and secretary for a few wealthy aristocratic families in southwest England. Under this secure patronage, Hobbes was able to spend most of his life in academic pursuits, travelling abroad, corresponding with the leading scientists of his day, and writing extensively. His wide interests included mathematics, the sciences, and moral and political philosophy.[19] In this Renaissance period, Hobbes was conscious of being part of an international intellectual revolution. Indeed, he was an early and influential exponent of the application of the scientific method to the study of society,[20] although his method was more deductive than inductive. He was essentially a rationalist, moving from first principles or theorems to explanations of general laws.

The first important expression of Hobbes's social theory was *The Elements of Law*, written in the late 1630s in the context of the sharpening conflict between King Charles I and Parliament. Charles was attempting to rule as by divine right, and for many years he did not allow Parliament to meet. Grievances against his rule mounted along with the debate about whether the King's powers were absolute or were limited by the rights of Parliament. At this juncture, Hobbes elaborated the traditional conclusion that the powers of the sovereign were absolute, although he did not deduce his conclusion from the traditional belief in the divine right of kings. When Parliament was finally recalled in 1640, Hobbes was vilified by the anti-Royalists. With English society perched on the precipice of civil war and with his life at risk, Hobbes took flight. He collected his savings and went into exile in Paris.[21]

The Parliamentary Army routed the Royalists and, after Charles I was executed in 1649, England was ruled as a republic under the authority of Parliament. During his lengthy stay in France, Hobbes experienced the chaos of the civil war from his close contact with the Royalist émigrés who sought safety in France. He was engaged as a mathematical tutor for the Prince of Wales, who had been forced into exile but would be restored to the English throne in 1660 as Charles II. Hobbes also continued to write, completing *Leviathan*, his theory of politics and society, in 1651. While still a Royalist at heart, Hobbes returned to republican England in that year, arguing that *Leviathan* demonstrated the necessity for the rule of a strong sovereign power, which need not be exercised only by a king.[22]

Besides being drawn back to England, Hobbes found it convenient to flee from Paris. His writings were often critical of, indeed hostile to, organized religion, particularly the Catholic Church. In *Leviathan*, Hobbes called the hierarchy of the Roman Catholic Church the 'Kingdome of Darknesse' and compared it 'not unfitly to the *Kingdome of Fairies*; that is, to the old wives *Fables*

in England, concerning *Ghosts* and *Spirits*, and the feats they play in the night.'[23]

MacPherson says that Hobbes was then left undisturbed in England until the disastrous Great Plague and Great Fire struck London in 1666. Acting on the traditional superstition that calamities were caused by sin, the House of Commons passed a bill to stamp out 'atheism and profanity'. A parliamentary committee compiled a list of books 'tending to atheism, blasphemy, and profaneness', which included *Leviathan*.[24] Hobbes spent much of his later years defending his writings from these charges. Malcolm notes that Hobbes's fear of being burned as a heretic caused him to consign some of his own manuscripts to the fire,[25] though he continued to be intellectually active until his death in 1679, at the age of 90.

The Natural State of Humanity

For Hobbes, all objects in the universe, including human beings, were bodies in motion that were independent of each other and subject only to the laws of nature. He derived this theorem from Galileo, whom he met in the mid-1630s. Galileo had reversed the ancient belief that objects were naturally in a state of rest by asserting, in his doctrine of inertia, that movement was perpetual unless another force prevented it.[26] Starting from this scientific theorem, Hobbes believed he could explain the development of human society and the necessity for a sovereign, all-powerful state.

Unlike Aquinas, Hobbes did not begin his theory of society with the assumption that the structure of the social world had existed in the mind of the creator even before there were any people to populate it. His deductive method was to assume that humans existed first in a state of nature without any society and to explain the development of society and government from this original condition. The powerful state was an organ of control and regulation that limited elementary freedom but permitted, in its place, peace and security. Humanity, as the 'rationall and most excellent worke of Nature', has itself constructed society and government.

The state of nature was populated by iso-lated, individual human beings who were in per-petual motion, like elements in nature, and had only incidental contact with one another.[27] The natural state of humanity was freedom of motion, freedom from constraint. In a state of nature there were only natural and unavoidable con-straints that restricted the absolute freedom of individuals. There were no artificial constraints, such as government, created by humans them-selves. By placing individuals at the centre of his theory, Hobbes adopted a perspective consistent with liberalism.

To understand this human act, it was neces-sary to understand the nature of humanity as a whole. Hobbes distinguished between vital motion, such as breathing and heartbeat, which is internal to a body and continues throughout its existence, and voluntary motion, which Hobbes called 'endeavour'. Endeavour is either towards something desirable and is called appetite (or desire), or away from something undesirable, called aversion. A few appetites and aversions are innate in humanity: passions such as '*desire, feare, hope, &c*' are the same for everyone.[28] The rest result from experience. While the objects of appetite or aversion differ from time to time and person to person, for any individual the object of his or her desire is called 'good' while the object of aversion is 'evil'. Good and evil, then, are rela-tive to time and place and are not rooted in the nature of the objects themselves.[29] This was a rad-ically relativist conclusion in a world dominated by absolute morality.

Before we begin an action or an endeavour, we deliberate, as various appetites and aversions alternate in the mind. Deliberation ends when we act, after which we are no longer free not to do the action. The last appetite or aversion before we act Hobbes called the 'will', following which deliberation begins again. There is no end to motion because, 'Life it selfe is but Motion, and can never be without desire, nor without Feare.' The object of this perpetual motion is 'continuall prospering' or '*successe* in obtaining those things which a man . . . desireth'.[30]

People can use various means to obtain their desired ends, although they have unequal access to these means. The greater their 'present means, to obtain some future apparent Good',[31] the greater their power. Individual humans differed, one from another, in size and strength. In their motion they collided with one another, from which derived the domination of some individu-als and the subordination of others. Some people are naturally pre-eminent over others in the state of nature, having more natural sources of power, such as strength, prudence, or eloquence. Once society is created, humans acquire additional 'instrumental' means or powers derived initially from their natural powers, such as riches, reputa-tion, and friends, which they can also use to attain their goals.[32] The sum total of an individual's power is that person's value, which Hobbes also calls her or his 'price'. Employing the language of capitalism, Hobbes claims that 'not the seller, but the buyer determines the price.'[33]

In this life, Hobbes asserts, there is no such thing as complete satisfaction because desires cease only with death. Happiness is nothing but continuous, progressive desire, from one thing attained to the next not yet attained. The real object of human action is not to enjoy something desired and then obtained, but to ensure that future desires will be met. This would be difficult enough for a solitary human who had to contend only with the forces of nature. It is much more difficult because individuals compete with each other to achieve their ends, and they cannot rest once they have achieved any goal for fear that they might not be able to preserve it. An individ-ual continually endeavours 'to secure himselfe against the evil he feares, and procure the good he desireth'.

In this natural state, Hobbes assumed, humans possess natural liberty, which, simply understood, is the power to act on your will with-out impediment. In the state of nature, Hobbes declared, every one 'has a Right to every thing; even to one anothers body', so that 'there can be no security' of life for anyone.[34] In addition, how-ever, all people have the right to do whatever is necessary to preserve themselves from harm, but this does not amount to much in a world where others have an equal right to take your life. Clearly in this natural state, there is no law and hence no concept of justice. All that counts is the ability to use force or fraud to secure your interests.

For Hobbes, there was no conception of private property in a state of nature, 'no *Mine* and *Thine* distinct' in the sense of a right recognized by others to your possessions. There was only what you could manage to get, for as long as you could keep it.[35] Humans were egotistically self-centred and acted in a state of nature solely for their own selfish purpose, not for the good of the group, or for any other wider purpose. Hobbes argued that no one gives anything to another without intending good for him or herself. The objective of every voluntary act is to achieve your own desires, your own good.[36]

While humans are not identical in their natural abilities, 'when all is reckoned together', Hobbes asserts, the difference between individuals is not very great, making people essentially equal 'in the faculties of body, and mind'. The weakest human has enough strength to kill the strongest either by stealth or by joining together with others. People are perhaps even more equal to each other in their ability to reason.[37] Unlike Aristotle and Aquinas, Hobbes argued that no one is by nature more worthy to rule, or obliged by their inferiority to serve others. In fact, Hobbes said, it was a natural law that everyone must acknowledge others as equals by nature, from which it followed that social inequalities were developed only in society.[38]

Because humans are also equal in their hopes and desires, natural equality does not lead to peaceful coexistence but, rather, to its opposite. The competition for 'Riches, Honour, Command, or other power' leads 'to Contention, Enmity, and War'. When any two people 'desire the same thing . . . they become enemies' and, to preserve themselves, endeavour to destroy, or 'kill, subdue, supplant, or repell the other.'[39] Feeling thus endangered, there is no way for an individual to be secure other than 'by force, or wiles, to master

the person' of everyone he or she can. They are obliged not just to defend themselves, but to go on the offensive against others, increasing their domination over them as the surest way to lessen their own insecurity.[40] So, Hobbes asserts:

> in the first place, I put for a generall inclination of all mankind, a perpetual and restlesse desire of Power after power, that ceaseth onley in Death. And the cause of this, is . . . because he cannot assure the power and means to live well, which he hath [at] present, without the acquisition of more.[41]

Ironically, for Hobbes (anticipating George Orwell), seeking peace while still in a state of nature means perpetuating war.

With an unlimited appetite to acquire goods and an insatiable need to secure as much power as possible, no one was safe from his or her neighbour. In the natural state, all people had a natural disposition to violence and no assurance of peace; so it follows that people found themselves 'in that condition that is called Warre; and such a warre, as is' everyone against everyone, all against all. In such a time there is no culture, no commerce, 'no Arts; no Letters; no Society; and which is worst of all, continuall feare, and danger of violent death'; and the life of humanity is 'solitary, poore, nasty, brutish, and short'.[42]

Hobbes's natural human was like a capitalist driven to accumulate power and wealth at any cost to others. The view that human nature is rooted in a natural self-interest would become the foundation of liberal, capitalist economics, and the prevalence of this view measures the degree of social and economic change that had taken place during the 400 years since Aquinas. The individual pursuit of profit, which had been exceptional and morally suspect in traditional society, had become normal by the seventeenth century.

While it may be doubted that Hobbes considered the 'state of nature' about which he theorized to be an actual era in the history of humankind, 'generally so, over all the world', he did think it probable that some North American

Aboriginals were 'savage people' with no government and lived 'at this day in that brutish manner'. Similarly, the kings of European nations, who were equal in their powers, related to each other like competitive individuals in a state of nature, threatening wars of nation against nation. Finally, as the English civil war had demonstrated to Hobbes, it was possible for a people who had 'formerly lived under a peacefull government . . . to degenerate into' a civil war.[43] In short, in its pursuit of its unlimited desires, humanity was potentially perched on the verge of chaos.

Social Contract

For thinkers such as Aquinas, God had implanted a natural sociability in humanity that could account for the existence of human society. Hobbes rejected this conclusion. In his view, social organization was a human construction, developed by rational beings who were nevertheless egotistical. The individual and society existed in a powerful contradiction. What needed explanation was how such individualistic beings, naturally free of any obligations or duties, had come voluntarily to construct a society that restricted their natural freedom. Being asocial (without society) was not the same as being by nature anti-social. Since society must at least be consistent with human nature, Hobbes postulated a further 'natural law' that there was in humanity an 'aptnesse to Society' by which everyone must strive to accommodate himself or herself to the rest, to be sociable.[44]

While people employ their powers to attain their desired ends, Hobbes assumed that underlying their action is the fundamental human desire to have a 'contented life', to live together 'in Peace and Unity'. The ability to reason makes it difficult for humans to achieve a state of contentment. Like beasts, humans are aware of their present fears. Because they alone possess reason, humans are also conscious of the dangers that lurk in the future. Only humans are aware they will die. Looking beyond the present produces further anxiety because a person's 'heart all the day long, [is] gnawed on by the feare of death, poverty, or other

calamity', and respite from this anxiety occurs only in sleep.[45]

Formulating a number of 'laws of nature' was consistent with Hobbes's purpose, to write a 'science' of society. These laws, however, were not like the laws of nature that scientists had discovered, such as the law of gravity, because the motions of the universe were not dependent on human will. Hobbes's natural laws of society, however, were not an explanation of things that had to be. Humans could live in a state of war, although they did not have to; there was a natural law that humans desired peace, but that did not make order inevitable. The problem was in the dual nature of humanity. The laws of nature 'are contrary to our naturall Passions, that carry us to Partiality, Pride, Revenge, and the like.'[46] Our innate human nature threatens us always with a return to the war of all against all.

People naturally desired peace, Hobbes argued, but in a natural state of equality, each individual had unlimited desires and a natural right to everything. These two claims existed in a powerful contradiction since to act on the second right, to acquire anything even at the cost of conflict with others who have the identical right, leads to perpetual war rather than peace. Given the assumption of a natural desire for peace, however, Hobbes proposed that an individual would be willing to abandon his or her right to all things if (and this is an important qualification) others were equally willing to likewise abandon their right.[47] If you give up your right to kill me, then I must be willing to give up my right to kill you. People must be satisfied with having no more freedom in their dealings with others than they would be willing to grant others in dealings with them. As Hobbes recognized, this reflected the religious injunction to do unto others as you wish them to do unto you.

Humans would have continued in the state of natural warfare with each other without escape had it not been for the possession of reason, which raised them above other animals, and for their concern with self-preservation, which may be interpreted as an instinctual fear of death. With any ability to reason at all, it would have become clear to humans that the condition of life Hobbes assumed to be natural would not be a desirable place to live. In a state of nature, the right to everything is really the right to nothing because you can never be secure in your possessions, even in your life. If you actually recognized what was in your interest, you would be willing to surrender your right to harm others as long as it was reciprocated. How could humans escape from this natural state so that they could preserve their security?

The answer, for Hobbes, was the creation of a society and the establishment of a government or state through a mutual 'social contract'. Contracts were mutual agreements between people that involved promises of future action. In a state of nature, people might make such promises to each other, but the contracts were insecure and easily betrayed, since 'nothing is more easily broken than' a person's word. People will keep their promises only 'from Feare of some evill consequence upon the rupture'.[48] A contract between two people will be kept only if both are under the thumb of a 'coercive Power' that is 'set over them both . . . to keep them in awe, and tye them by feare of punishment to the performance of their' contracts.[49] In the words of the Italian political philsopher, Niccolò Machiavelli (1469–1527), a king should be feared more than loved (Box 2.3).[50]

Hobbes claimed that people are obligated by natural law to fulfill their part of any contracts they have voluntarily made; however, since a contract involves a promise of future action, it is impossible to keep in a natural state. There is a compelling contradiction between the existence of a natural law and the impossibility of complying with this law in a state of nature. In the war of all against all, this natural law will always be overridden by pressing immediate needs for self-preservation. The 'natural law' that people must perform the contracts they have made cannot exist in nature, but only in a society with a coercive power. Society is not contrary to natural law; rather, it is its logical outcome. The only solution is to move beyond this natural state. We are obliged, wrote Hobbes, 'to transferre to another, such Rights, as being retained, hinder the peace of Mankind'.[51]

The social contract is the rational agreement among humans in their mutual interest to establish a single authority and hence a society to create order out of chaos. Since humans naturally, more or less by instinct, desired to maximize their power and their acquisitions, the social contract without power to enforce it would be flimsy. What would prevent some humans from deciding to violate the social contract, to grasp for more power and steal the property of their murdered neighbours? At any time, humans could be thrust back

---

Box 2.3

[A] prince must not concern himself with the infamy of cruelty when it comes to keeping his subjects united and obedient; for, with just a few displays of cruelty, he will turn out to be more compassionate than those who, through excessive compassion, allow disorders to arise from which spring forth murder and ravaging; because these usually hurt the community in general, while those executions that come from the prince hurt one in particular. . . .

[I]t is much safer to be feared than loved, if one of the two must be lacking. For . . . men . . . are ungrateful, fickle, liars and deceivers, avoiders of danger, greedy for profit. . . . [L]ove is held by a link of obligation, which, since men are wretched creatures, is broken every time their own interests are involved; but fear is held by a dread of punishment which will never leave you.

—Niccolò Machiavelli, *The Prince* (1532)

into the state of nature and lose everything. Human contracts, Hobbes believed, would only be kept if there existed a 'Common Power, to keep them in awe, and to direct their actions to the Common Benefit'. The only way such a common power could be erected would be for everyone 'to conferre all their power and strength upon one Man, or upon one Assembly of men, that may reduce all their Wills . . . unto one Will.' This act of mutual contract creates a sovereign power. Everyone must submit their wills and judgement to the common power. Thus is constructed the Commonwealth, 'that great LEVIATHAN' or 'Mortall God' under the immortal one.[52]

Leviathan

The creation of a **Leviathan** (single sovereign power) was the beginning of society. It meant renouncing your individual rights to be sovereign of yourself more than conferring additional rights on the monarch, because these rights already existed for the king or queen as an individual. The monarch was the only one to retain his or her natural right to do anything.[53] Consequently, the so-called social contract is not, for Hobbes, a mutual agreement between two equal parties, the people and the sovereign; even less does it imply that individuals retain any of their original sovereign rights. Hobbes rejected the claim that the ultimate power in a society rested with the people.

The powers of the sovereign were absolute. In Hobbes's conception, the purpose of this contract was to empower the sovereign 'to do whatsoever he shall think necessary to be done' to preserve security for all. The sovereign had the authority to censor books and teachings that were conducive to discord, to make laws on ownership, to decide all controversies, to choose all ministers and other officials, and to reward and punish in accordance with these laws. Only the sovereign could declare war on another nation. It was imperative that power be completely centralized, a lesson Hobbes believed the English had learned the hard way. In Hobbes's interpretation of history, if it had not been for the pernicious doctrine of the separation

of powers between the King, and the Lords, and the House of Commons, 'the people had never been divided, and fallen into this Civill Warre'. Hobbes called the separation of powers 'mixt government' and likened it to conjoined triplets—in his mind a monstrous creation.[54]

The sovereign power of the state could take other possible forms besides a central, absolute monarchy, such as democracy or rule by an aristocracy. For Hobbes, the disadvantages of these forms made them undesirable. The question was which form of government would be most conducive to producing peace and security. It is difficult to come to a single resolution in a democracy or aristocracy when individuals disagree with each other for reasons such as envy or self-interest. Aristocrats would compete with each other for power; democracy, which spreads power more widely, would be even more likely to produce only social instability. Even in a democracy, Hobbes said, it is usually the wealthy who have the right to be heard rather than the knowledgeable, and they excite people to action, stirring 'the flame of the Passions' while obscuring the light of reason.[55]

The only real opportunity for social peace was to grant a monopoly of power to a single sovereign authority, preferably to a monarch. This common power must be separated from and placed above the rest of society. The mandate of the sovereign power was to enact laws that protected society as a whole. In Hobbes's view, the state embodied everyone's interest, not only the interests of the rich. Everyone needed protection. The state had been created when people were in a situation of equality and it expressed the mutual interests of all. No one desired to return to the state of nature, which, given what Hobbes assumes human nature to be, was the only alternative to an absolute sovereign state.

Only within this social contract can humans achieve anything beyond their own survival. Civilization itself rested on the basis of social order established by the sovereign. The social contract did not abolish human nature. People in society still competed for honour and dignity, and 'Envy and Hatred, and finally, Warre'[56] would inevitably arise. It was not possible for the sovereign to suppress these natural passions since people relish most being superior to others. The object of the state was to construct a framework of rules that would allow individuals to acquire goods, to accumulate private property, to compete peacefully with other human beings—and to be secure in their possessions. These laws would provide the minimum framework of security within which human freedom could operate. Within these guidelines, backed up by the threat of the use of force by the state, people 'have the Liberty of doing what their own reason shall suggest, for the most profitable to themselves . . . such as . . . the Liberty to buy, and sell, and otherwise contract with one another'.[57] Economic freedom in society would coexist with political powerlessness.

Granting all political power to a central, absolute monarch is not without problems, Hobbes recognized. A monarch stood for the whole people and should act for the common good, but also possessed his or her 'own naturall Person'. Individuals with sovereign power would naturally seek to procure their 'private good' and that of their family and friends. When a contradiction arises between a sovereign's private interest and the public interests, Hobbes reasoned, he or she 'prefers the private' because an individual's 'Passions . . . are commonly more potent than their Reason.'[58] Hobbes did not assume that God has somehow chosen the best, or wisest, or most just individual to be the sovereign. The monarch is subject to the same desires, the same instincts, as any other human, but the social contract gives this single individual a monopoly of power. What is to prevent the monarch from abusing this position, from stealing from and murdering his or her own subjects?

For Hobbes it would seem to be very little. Everything the sovereign does is, by definition, just. Once people have consented to be governed, they are obliged to continue in the observance of the duty they have undertaken. For Hobbes, the people did not give their powers to the monarch; they simply agreed to renounce them. The monarch, surprisingly, was the only one who was not a party to the social contract since he or she simply retained the natural rights originally possessed. By this reasoning, the people were not ultimately sovereign, and they had no right to rebel against authority they considered unjust.

As long as the sovereign retains power, people must obey. A strong sovereign will oblige them to obey if they don't want to. A strong sovereign is essential for social stability; people will want to obey or will be afraid to disobey. The situation would be entirely different if the sovereign power were weak. A weak sovereign would be unable to control his or her subjects; natural greed and violence would get out of control and people would lose their peace and security. The obligations subjects have to their sovereign lasts 'no longer, than the power lasteth, by which he is able to protect them'.[59]

For Hobbes, a weak sovereign will bring destruction down on her or his own head and on the heads of the people. As society disintegrates into a state of nature, only the re-establishment of a new Leviathan can secure order and peace. This is not a matter of rights, or of justice according to which the sovereign is accountable to the people. The sovereign's obligation, derived from natural law, is to procure the safety of the people, and he or she is liable 'to render an account thereof to God, the Author of that Law, and to none but him.'[60] The sovereign is subject to the laws of nature; it is his or her duty, but also in his or her interest, to govern well, for to do otherwise is to violate natural law and, consequently, suffer the fate of eternal death.[61]

Hobbes was absolutely opposed to the doctrine of popular sovereignty, that is, that the monarch is part of and not above the social contract. He was not willing to grant any right of popular rebellion even if the sovereign was a tyrant. The sovereign is not subject to the civil laws.[62] Hobbes recognized that sovereign powers may do much harm 'in pursuit of their passions'. This is a breach of trust, he asserted, but 'this is not enough to authorise any subject, either to make warre upon, or so much as to accuse of Injustice, or any way to speak evil of their Sovereign.'[63] In fact,

Hobbes went so far as to assert that even people who do no more than 'reforme the Common-wealth' are also guilty of disobedience because 'they do thereby destroy it.'[64] People guilty of trea-son cannot look to the law to protect them but are at the mercy of the sovereign. Rebels, who have descended into the state of nature and make war on the sovereign, must suffer the vengeance of the sovereign, which is, Hobbes emphatically claimed, 'lawfully extended, not onely to the Fathers, but also to the third and fourth genera-tion not yet in being, and consequently innocent of the fact, for which they are afflicted.'[65] This was Hobbes's version of original sin.

Hobbes likened political problems to sick-nesses in the body. One such harmful illness was caused by dividing power or relinquishing part of it (as King John had done by signing the Magna Carta). Another illness was caused by allowing to be taught the doctrine that people have the right to depose a tyrant. Books by such 'Democraticall writers' contain a poisonous venom, which is like being bitten by a mad dog. They suffer from '*Tyrannophobia*', Hobbes said: the 'feare of being strongly governed'.[66]

Despite his conclusion that society needed a central, absolute authority, Hobbes's theory was attacked by traditional monarchists in his own time. They argued there was virtually no place for God in Hobbes's theory, making it a heretical and dangerous doctrine. Hobbes was accused of athe-ism. He openly distinguished between science and religion, for example, attacking superstition, magic, and the ritual of priests. Underneath his anticlericalism, however, lurked Hobbes's actual conservatism. The 'true religion', Hobbes claimed, is whatever the sovereign says is the 'true religion'. The point was not the truth of the theology, but the necessity to have a single belief for unity and strength. In the end, one state religion was neces-sary to maintain social order.[67]

Second, there was no place for morality in Hobbes's theory. Reason can establish scientific laws that can be accepted as truth by everyone because they do not conflict with anyone's indi-vidual, material interest. This is not the case with

claims about morality or justice. For Hobbes, people dispute moral truths because they involve their material interests, and their lust, ambition, and greed.[68] As with the 'true religion', one moral-ity must be imposed from above. People obey the law only through the fear of naked power. What is right is what power determines is right.

Similarly, Rogers argues, Hobbes's theory pro-vided a reinvigoration of patriarchal theory. Hobbes inherited the traditional notion that the Cosmos was gendered and 'two great Sexes ani-mate the world'.[69] This conception of duality, of yin and yang, could imply a variety of interpreta-tions. Difference did not necessarily imply domi-nation and subordination but, potentially, could be interpreted as establishing a complementary division of labour. Hobbes, on the contrary, pro-vided support for the patriarchal interpretation of the sexual division in his mechanistic theory of atoms in motion, which was applied to individu-als in nature. In this motion, the stronger atoms (or individuals) thrust aside the weaker, pursuing 'a course of perpetual conquest and self-aggran-dizement'. Men were stronger and more active than women and therefore, through the natural processes of motion, became the dominant, patri-archal, and authoritarian sex.[70]

In contemporary sociology, Hobbes is por-trayed as a theorist who advocated the thesis that human nature is inherently evil. Civilization is a thin veneer stretched precariously over the beast within human beings. Once authority is removed, people will revert to their natural barbarity. This perspective, which was later given a more scien-tific pedigree by Charles Darwin, underlies William Golding's 1954 allegorical novel, *Lord of the Flies*. A group of English schoolboys are stranded on a deserted island after their plane crashes. In the absence of any authority, they quickly degenerate to what Golding suggests is their natural state: primitive (Hobbesian) savagery. For Golding, the source of humanity's 'essential ill-ness' is rooted in 'the darkness of man's heart', a highly pessimistic conclusion suggesting that humanity's higher aspirations for equality and democracy are forever unrealizable.[71]

Hobbes's theory included a number of innovative features. Rather than starting with the assumption that society had been created by God and was itself 'natural', Hobbes claimed that society was the rational creation of human beings. Individuals existed first, and society was their special creation. Government was not part of God's plan, but was a structure that humans had invented. The monarch's right to rule was guaranteed only so long as he or she maintained peace and stability, though Hobbes resisted the conclusion that subjects had a right of sovereignty and could rightfully replace one monarch with another. In a state of nature, everyone was equal and possessed equal rights, and everyone continued to be legally equal in society (with the exception of the monarch). Within the structure of society that humans had created, people were free to pursue their selfish interests within legal limits. Their property was protected as well as their lives.

Hobbes's conception of the state of nature was a metaphor that allowed him to distinguish between chaos and order, making the latter a human rather than a divine creation. Society was always under the threat of disorder, whether it took the form of war between territorial sovereigns or rebellion from within.

While Hobbes's theory emerged from the particular historical background of social anarchy and civil war within which it was written, his ideas reflected a wider social canvas. He was living in a transitional age, between traditional and modern society. The individualistic starting point of his theory, the concept of natural rights, and the endorsement of private property and individual economic competition represented the world that was becoming, the world of modern capitalism. For Hobbes, 'the Businesse of the world . . . consisteth almost in nothing else but a perpetuall contention for Honour, Riches, and Authority.'[72] His limited view of popular sovereignty and his support for autocratic rule also reflected the era of absolute monarchy in which he lived. The 'Sun King' was an idea originating in the Protestant Reformation as well as in the scientific revolution.[73]

While traditionalists feared the consequences of the radical ideas given concrete expression by the Levellers and Diggers (see below), these movements were repressed and driven underground. They also found dangerous ideas in Hobbes's social theory. Once the principles of human equality, natural rights, and popular sovereignty were let out of their cages, they had the potential to challenge the hierarchical, undemocratic, and greatly unequal society that had given these ideas birth.

SOCIAL CHANGE AND RADICALISM IN ENGLAND

If traditionalists did not side with Hobbes's method and line of argument, his theory was also contrary to more radical thought developing in England in the context of the clash between Parliament and the monarchy. Challenges to traditional authority appeared in politics, in economics, and in the question of the natural subordination of women.

As capitalism spread to agriculture, Hill argues, landlords sought to raise what had been customary rents and then to evict peasants from their small properties when they could not pay. Tenants were forced to sign precise and limited contracts that they could not meet or that lasted for a specific term, after which they could be evicted legally. The peasants rested their argument on their traditional, customary rights that had existed for centuries but had never been formally written down. As the poet John Milton said, they wanted 'but a moderate and beseeming share' (Box 2.4).[74] Hobbes sided squarely with this new capitalist class of gentry farmers, claiming that justice was served when contracts were honoured and that, if there was no precise and legal contract, there was no injustice in expropriating the tenant.[75]

In the context of open revolution in the 1640s, two radical social movements, the Levellers and the Diggers, emerged to voice the struggle of the dispossessed. The Levellers spoke on behalf of small independent farmers, merchants, and crafts workers. The Leveller document, *The Agreement of the People*, demanded political rights

Box 2.4

If every just man that now pines with want
Had but a moderate and beseeming share
Of that which lewdly-pampered Luxury
Now heaps upon some few with vast excess,
Nature's full blessings would be well dispensed
In unsuperfluous even proportion,
And she no whit encumbered with her store;

—Milton, 'Comus' (1633)

for the common man, including giving all adult males the vote regardless of property ownership.[76] Equally prescient were the Diggers, who urged the nationalization of all Church and state land and the return of all land that had been enclosed by large landowners. The Diggers practised an agrarian socialism that became known as Bible Communism, since it reflected a religious rather than a secular view of the world. Led by Gerrard Winstanley, the Diggers projected a radical interpretation of Christianity emphasizing equality and the sinfulness of riches (see Box 2.5)[77] and applied the injunction to love thy neighbour as thyself to experiments in communal living.

The Puritan spirit of the English revolutionaries was less susceptible to notions of gender equality. The oppression of women crossed class and religious lines. Like the democracy of the Levellers and the communalism of the Diggers, the feminist sentiments of Margaret Cavendish, though often confused and contradictory, were equally prescient. An *emigré* in Paris during the civil war, where she married a Royalist general, William Cavendish, Margaret Cavendish was a Renaissance thinker, expressing her ideas in poems, letters, prose, philosophical writing, and scientific inquiries. Her advantageous marriage and scientific interests prompted the all-male Royal Society, the scientific elite in Britain, to invite her in 1667 to a private exhibition of the most advanced experiments of the day.[78]

In her many prefaces to her works of poetry and prose, Cavendish speculated on the position of women and the origin of the differences between the sexes. She argued that the intellectual inequality of women was socially fashioned by the

Box 2.5

Is not buying and selling a righteous law? No, it is the law of the Conqueror. . . .

When Mankinde began to buy and sell, then did he fall from his Innocency, for then they began to oppress and cozen one another of the Creation Birth-right. . . .

But all rich men live at ease, feeding and clothing themselves by the labours of other men, not by their own; which is their shame and not their Nobility; for it is a more blessed thing to give than to receive: But rich men receive all they have from the labourer's hand, and what they give, they give away other men's labours, not their own.

—Gerrard Winstanley (1652)

rules of exclusion that forbid higher education to women. Consequently, Cavendish wrote, while 'many of our Sex may have as much wit, and be capable of Learning as well as men; but since they want Instructions, it is not possible they should attain to it.' Women were confined to a much narrower range of motion and action than men. Women were too closely confined in the home, she complained—'we are kept like birds in cages to hop up and down in our houses.' This circumscribed motion prevented women from intellectual progress. Without access to natural experience from which they could be self-taught, and barred from formal knowledge and understanding through their exclusion from the universities, Cavendish hyperbolized, 'in time we should grow irrational idiots.'[79]

Yet the aristocratic Cavendish was not consistent in this sociological view that women's inequality was rooted in the sexual discrimination practised in society. While 'many women' were capable of the highest intellectual achievements, she believed there was a great, natural difference between the male and female body and brain. Men's physically greater strength was complemented by their different brain, which was constructed for understanding: 'Women can never have so strong Judgment nor clear Understanding' as men.[80] Cultural discrimination exaggerated these natural differences, Cavendish thought. Just as access to education would narrow the intellectual differences, she argued, 'let us Hawk, Hunt, Race, and do like exercises as Men'. As women imitate men, 'so will our Bodies and Minds appear more Masculine, and our Powers will Increase by our Actions.' Nevertheless, cultural practices could never fully overcome the essential distinctiveness of women rooted in their different nature.[81] This refrain would often be echoed by later male theorists, even the most liberal ones.

The **Commonwealth** created in England after the revolution was a political innovation; no government like it had existed. Oliver Cromwell had ruled England much like Hobbes's absolute sovereign, taking the title 'Lord Protector' in 1653. He did not, however, preside over a peaceful nation.

Cromwell led his English Protestants into the conquest of Catholic Ireland, an adventure that would have centuries of repercussions. England chafed under the restrictive yoke of **Puritan** rule. On the right, the Royalists, who had never been reconciled to republican government, pined for a new king. By suppressing the Levellers and denying the extension of popular sovereignty, Cromwell had alienated support from below.

The principal political weakness of the Commonwealth government was the absence of any provision for the succession of power. Who would rule after Cromwell died? One solution was to make him King, from which a new hereditary dynasty would spring. Before he died in 1658, the Puritan leader had been offered the Crown, but refused it. Cromwell objected to the old title, not the principle of inheriting political power, since he hoped to secure the succession of his son, Richard, as the new 'Lord Protector'. This attempt to create a new hereditary title failed quickly. Parliament then offered the Crown to Charles, the son of the executed king, the Prince who had been tutored by Hobbes during his exile in Paris.

When Charles II ascended the throne in the Restoration of 1660, he was not the absolute monarch his father had tried to become. The new King's sovereignty was limited because power was shared with the House of Lords and the House of Commons. From Hobbes's perspective, this monstrous separation of power ensured only further social conflict, and England was poised for another bout of anarchy and civil war.

As usual, Hobbes was in a minority. Most political theorists supported the Restoration and the mixed sovereignty represented by the separation of powers. Included in this company was John Locke (1632–1704), a member of the lower gentry represented in the House of Commons. Although Hobbes may have been right that England was headed for another rebellion, it was not caused by the separation of powers but, rather, by the King's attempt to rule without Parliament. When Parliament deposed one king in 1689 and invited another to the throne, it appeared that sovereignty rested with the citizens.

The rising commercial capitalist class wanted political as well as economic power for themselves and therefore opposed an absolute monarchy. In *Leviathan*, Hobbes had very carefully defined sovereign power to include a monarch or an 'Assembly of men', which suggests that a body such as Parliament might exercise state power. However, as MacPherson argues, Hobbes opposed an elected Parliament. In his view, every sovereign must alone determine who succeeded to power. Otherwise power wasn't really sovereign.[82] To say that those below the sovereign should decide who represented them would actually grant *them* sovereign power, a system that was overly democratic and would lead to civil war. So the new middle class turned from Hobbes to two theorists who were more committed to the new principles of liberalism. In economic theory, Adam Smith's laissez-faire doctrine expressed the material interests of the rising merchant class. In politics, the spokesperson for this middle class was John Locke, who formulated the principles underlying this claim for popular sovereignty and limited democracy.

JOHN LOCKE

Locke was born in 1632 into a rural gentry family with Puritan sympathies. His father served as a captain in a parliamentary army during the civil war,[83] when Locke was a youth, and he grew to adulthood in Cromwell's Commonwealth. At the University of Oxford, Locke unhappily endured the traditional education for young men destined for occupations in the Anglican Church, labouring through philosophical and theological studies in formal logic and metaphysics. Locke passed his time reading plays and romances while his professional interests shifted to medicine and science. According to historian J.R. Milton, Locke's political ideas during his young adulthood were mildly conservative. When he became a college tutor in his twenties, he replicated for his students the educational experience he had found so unsatisfying.[84]

For most of the next decade, Locke's studies were devoted to medicine and science. He realized that most of the common theories of disease lacked any basis in experimental science. It was necessary to take a scientific approach to health and illness, to develop a base of knowledge from empirical principles related to careful observation, experimentation, and generalization from observable facts.[85] Locke's speculations about the sources of knowledge led him to write *An Essay Concerning Human Understanding*.

Locke sought to develop an empirical theory of knowledge based on a novel conception of **human nature**. Assumptions about human nature are crucial determinants of a social theory. Aquinas had accepted human nature as 'fallen' and naturally hierarchical. For Hobbes, while everyone was naturally equal, human nature was asocial and bleak, precipitating society into a perpetual struggle for power. Locke adopted a more neutral assumption about human nature. In his *Essay Concerning Human Understanding* Locke claimed an individual's mind is originally a blank sheet, a 'white paper, void of all characters, without any ideas'.

This argument directly challenged the traditional view that ideas were innate, having been embedded in the human mind by a deity. In the place of theology, some scientists had advocated a scientific and rational explanation for human knowledge, arguing that knowledge derives directly and only from sense experience. In this entirely empirical view of knowledge, the world humans perceived through their senses provided an accurate reflection of actual, externally existing reality. Knowledge derived directly from the accumulation of sense experiences.

Locke did not accept the view that the brain is merely a repository of sense experiences from which knowledge automatically arises. He agreed that the source of the raw materials of reason and knowledge is experience, the accumulated perceptions by the senses, but argued that these experiences are not identical with knowledge. All creatures capable of perception experienced sensations, but only humans were capable of assimilating and connecting the impressions derived from experience into knowledge through the use of their reason. Our ideas of the world emerge from 'the internal operations of our minds, perceived and reflected on by ourselves'.[86]

For Locke, humans were limited in their mental abilities. Our ignorance, he wrote, is 'infinitely larger than our knowledge'. Compared to other intellectual beings—Locke meant supernatural ones—humans were mediocre, finite creatures, 'inconsiderable, mean, and impotent'.[87] There was a vast and unlimited body of things to know, some of which were beyond human capacity, and knowledge of them rested solely on belief.[88] Even in science, where human reason was most capable, there were limits to our abilities. Newton's law of gravity was understood as a force, but what caused gravity—the essence of this force—remained a mystery. Locke never pushed his argument to the conclusion that you could never be certain of knowing anything, although a group of philosophers did reach that skeptical conclusion.

From the point of view of social theory, Locke's theory of knowledge had radical social implications. A neutral view of human nature coupled with an emphasis on experience as the fundamental source of knowledge implied that human conduct is a matter of environmental influence rather than instincts (as for Hobbes) or innate knowledge (as for Aquinas). For Locke, humans possess the capacity for both good and evil, but they are not naturally one or the other. Most importantly, however, they are potentially good in the best circumstances. With this assumption, it becomes possible to theorize about the type of environment that would cultivate positive and minimize negative human abilities. In its high regard for human potential, liberal doctrine was fundamentally revolutionary.

Natural Law

The crucial task of social theory was to uncover the **natural laws** that shaped human society and actions. First, humans were limited by the physical laws of the universe. They could not, for example, defy the natural law of gravity. In addition, there were natural laws of society.[89] Just as the laws of nature were discoverable by human reason, so, too,

were God's laws for the proper ordering of social life. Earlier philosophers were wrong to suggest that people were created unequally, in a divinely inspired hierarchy. Locke inferred that humans were born free and equal—they were naturally 'free of each other . . . and equal to each other'.

Natural rights were fundamental to the essence of humanity, and they were to be respected in society and written into social laws. To achieve correct knowledge, it was crucial to understand natural law and the rights derived from it. To be wrong in one's claims about natural law would lead to serious errors. Some Diggers had used a natural law argument to justify their belief that people were not only equal, but that property was naturally held in common. It followed that any human laws protecting private property must be contrary to natural law. The conservatives, who had rejected this claim because it led to social anarchy, denied there were any 'natural rights'. Locke disagreed with both positions. His theory was rooted in natural law arguments, but he rejected the view that property ought to be held in common. On the contrary, he argued that the right to own private property was itself based on natural law.

In a state of nature, Locke said, people were created in a state of equality in which no one had more power or rights to anything than any other. Individuals were in 'a *State of perfect Freedom* to order their Actions, and dispose of their Possessions, and Persons as they think fit, within the bounds of the Law of Nature, without asking leave, or depending upon the Will of any other Man.'[90] From a similar beginning, Hobbes had argued that everyone had an equal right to everything, including the freedom to subjugate others.

In Locke's formulation, freedom was not the same as 'licence', which implied the freedom to do whatever you wanted regardless of the consequences for others. Natural law established boundaries around this state of freedom and equality. Even a state of nature had laws to govern human action, which were derived from the creator. The laws of nature were not innate in the mind; rather, the deity had endowed humanity with reason to discover these boundaries. Newton had discovered the law of gravity; liberal theorists believed that when individuals used their reason, they could rationally determine the laws by which the deity intended human society to be ordered.

For Locke, the laws of nature included the obvious right of self-preservation, but this was necessary only in extreme circumstances. Ordinarily, when their 'own Preservation comes not in competition' with others, individuals ought to help preserve the rest of mankind.[91] In the state of nature, which Hobbes had perceived to be red in tooth and claw, people actually lived 'together according to reason', making it 'a state of Peace, Good Will, Mutual Assistance, and Preservation'. Locke was aware that people did not actually live in a world of peace and goodwill. Natural laws were not written on the mind, like instincts. They were discovered only by the arduous task of reasoning and, even if known, they could only explain how humans ought to act, not compel them to act lawfully. The moon had no choice but to orbit the earth; humans possessed the freedom to live their lives according to natural law or in opposition to it.

Some human laws, then, could be contrary to natural law. The Diggers had drawn the conclusion that inequalities of property violated natural law and therefore caused the absence of peace and goodwill in society. Locke believed that inequalities in wealth were consistent with natural law, not contrary to it. He argued that individuals had an obvious right to their person, which might be considered the original private property, from which it followed that no one 'ought to harm another in his Life, Health, Liberty, or Possessions.'[92] The controversial point was Locke's extension of this argument beyond the individual person to include that person's 'possessions', his or her tangible private property.

According to Locke, when the deity created humanity in a state of nature, the earth as a whole was given 'to Mankind in common'. Humans were created by a God and were 'sent into the World by his order and about his Business'.[93] The goods of the earth 'are produced by the spontaneous hand of Nature' and no individual has any right to any particular one of them while they are in their natural state, such as apples lying on the ground. These apples are there for the use of all as common property. It is obvious, however, that everyone cannot eat each apple, nor can anyone eat all of them. One individual will pick up an apple in order to consume it, an act that appropriates that particular apple. By so doing, the individual has exerted his or her labour on that apple and, 'by this labour' of picking it up, has joined that apple to her or his body, which is the original 'property' of the individual. No other person now has any right over that apple, which has become 'the unquestionable Property of the Labourer'.[94]

Locke's basic assumption was that, in the state of nature, the fruits of the earth were bounteous and the human population relatively small. Any object of nature that an individual appropriates, becoming thereby her or his private property, did not leave any other person poorer because there was a great surplus of equally desirable and available goods for all. Everyone has the right to the use of those things that were necessary for subsistence. But, Locke asked, does this natural right to private property allow individuals to grasp any amount of nature's goods? Locke had asserted that the earth was given to humankind as a whole to enjoy, from which it followed that an individual has the right to convert to private property '[a]s much as any one can make use of . . . before it spoils'. Anything beyond the amount needed for immediate use 'is more than his share, and belongs to others.'[95]

Locke extended this principle beyond the ownership of the beasts and the objects that grow on the earth to the ownership of the land itself. Although 'God gave the World to Men in Common . . . for their benefit, and the Greatest conveniences of Life they were capable to draw from it', Locke claimed, 'it cannot be supposed he meant it should always remain common and uncultivated.'[96] Just as a person may appropriate an apple, so, too, may a person 'inclose . . . from the common' a portion of land. By expending labour on the land, as in agriculture, people are carrying out the divine injunction to subdue the earth. This enclosed land becomes the individual's private property when that person's labour is spent to make of it something that it had not been before. Enclosing land does not interfere with anyone else's rights, any more than taking a big drink out of a river deprives anyone else of water to quench thirst. Cultivable land was plentiful and sufficient for all. People had no business meddling in the property being improved by another's labour; 'If he did, 'tis plain he desired the benefit of another's Pains, which he had no right to.'[97]

As with property generally, under the law of nature the ownership of land was limited to as much as someone 'Tills, Plants, Improves, Cultivates, and can use the product of', industriously and rationally. Natural law confined 'Possession, to a very moderate Proportion', such as you might appropriate for yourself, 'without Injury to any Body'.[98] If you appropriated more than you could use and allowed it to sit unused, as it must over time, you would have unjustly 'invaded' your 'Neighbour's share'.[99]

Ownership of an excess of a certain good would be theft from the common, Locke says, only if it was allowed to spoil. The sin was not possessing more than you need; it was allowing something to perish uselessly in your hands when someone else could have used it. Locke had in mind the situation of small, independent property holders, none greatly richer or poorer than any other, with no need to amass more property from nature's vast storehouse than they could use, and having no inclination to contest anyone's right to any particular modest amount of property.

The world could have stayed at this peaceable stage if people had not invented money and agreed to put a value on it. By consenting to use money for exchange, people have found a way that some may 'fairly possess more land' than they themselves 'can use the product of' and thus they are able to accumulate greater possessions. So, 'it is plain, that Men have agreed to disproportionate and unequal Possession of the Earth.'[100] Not everything provided by nature rots or spoils. If you acquired an excess of apples and traded them

for durable goods, such as building material, you could begin to accumulate private property of a non-perishable kind that would be reasonable under natural law. What about bartering for a good that has no intrinsic use? Locke said that an individual who otherwise had enough to live could acquire excess property and then barter it for a durable good such as a diamond or a piece of gold. Even if the individual then hoarded this wealth 'all his Life, he invaded not the Right of others, [and] he might heap up as much of these durable things as he pleased.' The bounds of what was just did not depend on how much you possessed, but whether anything perished uselessly in your possession.

In this new exchange-based economy, Locke said, trade and the total amount of social wealth grew, so that the poorest members of society were better off than anyone in the subsistence state of nature, such as the North American Aboriginals. Society, then, had grown from its origins in a state of nature in accordance with an evolution that was consistent with natural law, and this was beneficial for all.

The first step beyond the state of nature was a small, yet unequal society, in which there was no need for a strong, central government. As population increased, however, and as people 'settled themselves together, and built Cities', disputes over property ownership occurred more frequently. It became necessary to establish the boundaries of each family's distinct territory and that of their neighbours.[101] It was necessary to institute laws regulating exchange and property ownership in order to resolve disputes and secure everyone in their rightful possession.[102] In short, Locke supposed that people built a society composed of mutually accepted rules before they erected, on top of the society already constructed, a government or state to settle the disputes that arose in society.

For Locke, humans were not free to follow their passions or their will in any circumstances; rather, they should act according to the dictates of reason.[103] If social rules were consistent with reason and 'natural law', individuals were bound to obey them and should freely choose to act consistent with reason. If they refused, Locke added, they could be compelled to obey. For Locke, unreasonable conduct made humans 'beasts' and they were to be treated as such.[104] This assumes, however, that humans could all come to agree on what was 'reasonable'. To whom would the power fall to determine what was reasonable? Should a person wilfully reject what was taught as reasonable, who shall compel obedience? Locke did not trust a single monarch to arrive at a just determination of what laws were reasonable. The chief target of Locke's criticism was absolute authority—Hobbes's Leviathan—that imposed the will of one person on everyone else. Just such a political problem had arisen once again in England.

Political Theory

By 1679, England faced another political crisis. King Charles II did not have a legitimate child to inherit the throne, which, on his death, would pass to his brother, James. James was a Catholic, however, and Parliament attempted several times to exclude him from the line of succession to the throne. In response, Charles II dissolved Parliament permanently and began to rule in an increasingly absolutist fashion. English politics became embroiled in a confusing mix of political crisis, religious dispute, and social conflict. The situation could have degenerated into another civil war, although most men of property had no wish to return to the chaos of war or to military rule. Locke was deeply embroiled in the rebellion against Charles II and, when an insurrection fizzled in 1683, he escaped to Protestant Holland. Locke's *Two Treatises of Government* was written during these years of political conflict and instability.

When James II inherited the throne from his brother, he faced immediate opposition. When the army deserted him, he was forced to abdicate. The question of what form of government was to replace the old regime was settled when a new king, William III, accepted Parliament's invitation to become the constitutional monarch, sharing political power with Parliament.

Locke's political theory was inspired by the need to justify rebellion against a monarch turned tyrant. Initially, Locke considered the same question faced by Hobbes: given free, equal individuals, how did the state arise? Humans possess 'natural rights', such as the right to life, liberty, and the enjoyment of private property. In the state of nature, Locke reasoned, the enjoyment of a person's rights was 'very uncertain, and constantly exposed to the Invasion of others.' People may have a natural right to the property they acquire through their labour, but no one was under any obligation to respect this ownership other than through fear of the owner. However, people often violate the natural rights of others, out of motivations of jealousy, or revenge, or greed, potentially plunging society into a state of war. Society required a social contract to establish a 'common superior' capable of protecting private property and social peace. The principal purpose of creating a government, Locke asserts, was 'the Preservation of their Property'.[105]

In the state of nature, executive power resided in individuals; that is, individuals had the right to protect themselves with force and assert their individual rights against others.[106] When the majority of individuals agree to a social contract and create the institution of government, they give up their 'Natural Liberty', including that right to exercise executive power over others. They put 'on the bonds of Civil Society . . . by agreeing with other Men to joyn and unite into a Community, for their comfortable, safe, and peaceable living one amongst another, in a secure Enjoyment of their Properties'.[107] By this contract, people in a certain territory gave their natural right to legislate and enforce laws to a sovereign authority who agrees to act for the public good. The main functions of government are to judge the disputes of citizens fairly and equally and to enforce the laws on everyone.[108]

Hobbes had argued that the absolute monarch existed in a state of nature vis-à-vis the people, who were bound by the original contract to obey no matter how oppressive the ruler was. Locke denied that in such a situation there is any obligation to obey. On the contrary, such a government does not reflect a genuine civil society. A monarch is party to and not above the social contract. Everyone is subject to the rule of law, which rests on a majority of the people since a consensus of all individuals is not possible.

Government was the result of the social contract between free and equal parties, based on their mutual interest.[109] The powers of constitutional government were contractually granted by the majority of free men, in whose hands ultimately lay sovereign power. The community of people could legitimately dissolve the existing government, and construct another, when it acted contrary to the trust they had placed in it. The people had the right to resist arbitrary authority because the rule of law must rest on the will of the citizens. Locke's *Treatise* justified the rebellion of 1689 when James was forced to abdicate and William III was invited to become the monarch of England.

Andrew argues that Locke agreed that people had a right to 'rebellion' but not a right to 'revolution'. They had the right to change the personnel who occupied positions of power in the government, but they did not have the right to overturn the social order and its underlying property rights that had emerged under natural law before people had contracted together to form the government.[110] This conception of a rational, contractual community of citizens held together by each person's calculation of his or her interests contrasted sharply with the feudal assumption of an organic, hierarchical society held together by tradition and custom.

Limited Democracy and Social Inequality

Full citizenship, however, was very limited in Locke's conception. Who comprised this 'community' of citizens? For Locke, humans were born free, equal in rights, and competent to understand each other and co-operate. They were also born unequally with respect to talent and reason—'Locke often spoke harshly of the dull minds of the common people', Aarsleff notes—and individuals also had unequal opportunities for communication

and acquiring knowledge.[111] While Locke championed the idea of popular sovereignty, he held a gloomy view of the actual rational capacity of most people.[112] Like most members of the upper middle class, he feared the 'rule of the mob'. The best type of government was a constitutional monarchy, with power being shared by the monarch and the representatives of those who held a substantial property stake in the nation.

The number and definition of eligible voters in England—how to distinguish substantial property holdings from minimal holdings—were matters of struggle and debate at different times and places. A conservative position demanded a narrowly restricted franchise, and the Levellers would have extended the vote to all adult males. Actual voting practices were somewhere in between. According to Ashcraft, a statute written in 1429 restricted the English electorate to men who were freeholders with full legal title to land valued at no less than 40 shillings. By 1680, this attempt to limit the number of electors had been substantially undermined by inflation, and the franchise had come to include thousands of 'shopkeepers, artisans, tradesmen, and small farmers'. Furthermore, in actual practice, the vote was often more widespread than the letter of the law allowed.[113]

Locke's argument was not simply that the wealthy ought to be represented in Parliament. For Locke, it was a question of an individual's degree of rationality. Only those men with a fully developed ability to reason had a right to be distinctly represented in Parliament. The sign of the ability to exercise reason, however, was successful property ownership. The right of any group to political representation existed 'in proportion to the assistance, which it affords to the publick', that is, to the extent that it pays taxes to the government.[114] Ashcraft argues that, while Locke's conception of democracy was limited, it was not narrowly elitist. His political writings were not addressed to the aristocracy and the rich landed class, 'but rather to the urban merchants, tradesmen, artisans, and independent small gentry' who formed the social foundations 'for any radical political theory' in the seventeenth century.[115]

There were important limitations on Locke's radicalism. As Andrew notes, 'If Locke is held to be the progenitor of liberalism, it is to be remembered that "Our Father" profited from the slave trade, justified slavery in his writings . . . advocated colonial conquest and denied the right to rebel against the colonial power, lobbied for the destruction of Irish industry, and denied the utility of education for labourers.'[116] He had become a wealthy property owner from investments in the silk trade and from interest from loans and mortgages. He invested heavily in the Bank of England in the 1690s and became a member of the Board of Trade. In that capacity, Locke entered the debate about what should be done for the poor in England. He recommended that the Poor Laws of England ensure that every person receives the subsistence minimum to which they were entitled under the law of nature.[117] As much as possible, however, the poor had to earn this charity through hard work. According to Zinn, Locke 'regretted that the labor of poor children "is generally lost to the public till they are twelve or fourteen years old"' and he suggested that children over three who came from families receiving charity, should be sent to 'working schools' so that, from infancy, they would be 'inured to work'.[118]

Although Locke's proposals for the English poor were lacking in Christian charity, Andrew asserts, they were consistent with his times. He held that poverty was a punishment for idleness, drunkenness, and lack of discipline (the result of sin, in Aquinas's terms). Able-bodied beggars were to be conscripted into the navy; the elderly or maimed were to be confined at hard labour in the workhouse. The children of poor women were to be taken from them, so the women could find work, while the children were to be placed in working schools where, Andrew claims, Locke would have them '"soundly whipt" if their dawn-to-dusk work does not earn a profit.'[119]

The immoral poor had been born free and with equal rights, but either because of their innate inferiority or because of unfortunate experiences, they had allowed their passions to overrule their reason and had sunk into idle dis-

solution. Just as capacities for rationality differed between one individual and another, Locke believed, differences in the ability to reason also occurred among larger groups of people and particularly among the various races, which were unequal by their nature. When Locke asserted that people were equal, he really meant white, propertied males.

According to Patterson,[120] Aristotle had claimed that certain groups of people had an inner essence that naturally made them inferior, and this made them subject to enslavement. Locke agreed that different races did have a different inner essence, but thought that the methods of science, which were based on the experiences of our senses, could not penetrate beneath the surface appearances to understand this 'essence'. It was scientifically unknowable. Only the external appearance could be appreciated empirically. Was 'appearance' an accurate reflection of 'essence' or, rather, could you really not tell a book by its cover?

For Locke, it was also an empirical fact, according to his Eurocentric view, that Europeans had developed an advanced civilization, while other races continued to live in a state of barbarity. The actual conditions of life of certain races, such as the Africans, were empirical proof of their inferiority, claimed Locke. In addition to their different inner essences, each race also had a 'nominal' or observable essence that was reflected in their surface appearance. Scientists, then, could define a surface appearance as representing the inner essence of different races.[121] It wasn't just that different races had different skin colours; it was that the different coloured skins were an outward appearance that gave scientists an insight into the unequal 'inner essences' of the races. The 'black' skin of the African, for Locke, was an indication of inferiority relative to the superior 'white' race. Enslavement was therefore justifiable, although on grounds only slightly different from Aristotle.

Patterson adds[122] that Locke's rationale can be explained by his social context. Not only was he employed as an administrator for the British colonies, he was a founding member and stockholder in the slave-trading Royal African Company, which made its profits in the slave trade. Locke would have a material interest in a theory that claimed Africans were inferior to whites and, hence, subject to enslavement.

The essence of Locke's radical thinking is his doctrine of popular sovereignty—people have the right to choose their government—and the corollary that there is a right to rebellion against a sovereign who has violated the social contract. These positions were considerably in advance of Hobbes and would be used to justify the American and French revolutions in the next century. In particular, Locke said that there were limits to the right of the government to tax property owners, which amounted to converting some private property back to common ownership. This issue would surface during the American Revolution, which was, essentially, an anti-colonial struggle led by a nationalist elite of prosperous property owners who wanted to wrest the mantle of political power from the British and devise their own form of constitutional government.

CONCLUSION

The seeds of rationalism sown in the age of Aquinas produced a deluge several centuries later. Gradually the principles of modern science emerged from the medieval search for the philosopher's stone and the elixir of life. When Isaac Newton wasn't labouring to turn lead into gold, he was imagining the law of gravity and trying to understand the natural laws of the universe that kept it in motion. Galileo, who wrote that the earth travelled around the sun, narrowly missed being burned at the stake but revolutionized humanity's conception of the universe. Science promised humanity the power to dominate nature, not to be mere stewards. The rebirth of the ancient belief that people were perfectible, rather than sinful and fallen, revolutionized humanity's conception of itself.

In economic relations, commercial capitalism slowly transformed traditional economic practices

and principles. In the early modern period, the merchants of the Italian peninsula dominated the foreign trade, banking establishments, and municipal governments of their city-states. At least nominally Catholic, they had been appeased by the ideological changes in the Roman Church that had bestowed blessings on trade and commerce, profit-making, and usury. Italian traders were the indispensable middlemen of European commerce. As the Muslims monopolized the slow and dangerous caravan routes from China and India, the Italians dominated the sea lanes of the Mediterranean. The prevailing wind, however, changed in 1492 when the newly powerful nations of Spain and Portugal broke the monopoly of the Italian city-states.

The great commercial expeditions of Columbus and other European explorers exposed new worlds to exploitation and fed the emergence of a rich and aspiring new middle class of bourgeois merchants. They provided a willing market for the technological advances that were the fruits of the new sciences, and for a new ideology that condemned the wastefulness, luxury, and idleness of the traditional economic system and championed, instead, economic and political liberty. Following its detour through the ambiguous mind of Thomas Hobbes, the voice of the new middle class reverberated in the political doctrine of John Locke.

Liberalism is a theory that, in its origins, is peculiar to Western thought. When Eastern philosophies such as Buddhism began to intrude into the fabric of Western culture in the nineteenth century, they came fully developed with a complex set of principles and an independent history. Liberalism did not emerge as a consequence of this type of cultural diffusion; it evolved out of the soil of European culture. There was a symbiotic relationship between the rise of the new capitalist class and the development and ascendancy of liberal theory. Nevertheless, commercial trade is not automatically associated with ideas of legal equality, liberty, and representative government. When the principles of liberalism were elaborated in England and America, they reflected the economic and political changes of the early modern era.

Locke has remained the great theoretician of the propertied classes. At the core of his theory of 'natural law' and 'natural right' was a proposition that put private ownership of property beyond interference or attack. For Locke, the chief purpose served by the uniting of people into a society under a government was the preservation of their property. While this original social contract necessitated the agreement of the majority of men, only a propertied minority were fit to influence legislative power directly by voting or being eligible for election to Parliament. In the context of the times, however, political liberalism was radical in its opposition to absolute authority and in its demand for popular sovereignty and government that was representative and accountable to the people.

The economic socialism of Winstanley and the Diggers, the radical liberalism of the Levellers, and the early feminism of women such as Margaret Cavendish would inspire future generations in England and elsewhere to advance these democratic beginnings. These alternative voices, however, were quickly eclipsed. The elitism of Locke and the principle that property ownership implied the right to monopolize political power dominated English liberalism. Locke's theory of property justified unequal possessions, but not the granting of a freedom that amounted to licence in the use of this wealth. When liberal principles were applied to economics, not only was the unequal distribution of property considered just and proper, but those with the most property were given full power to do with their property as they desired. Liberal economists assured everyone that allowing the rich unfettered rights to make economic decisions based solely on the profit motive—what was best for their own fortune—would actually benefit everyone. More than any other theorist, Adam Smith popularized this justification for unequal property ownership and unrestrained economic freedom.

3 REASON AND REBELLION

By the fifteenth century, conceptions of individualism and rationalism coexisted symbiotically in religious, cultural, and economic spheres, heralding the beginning of a new, modern era in Europe. The orientation of Protestantism reflected what sociologist Max Weber termed the spirit of commercial capitalism. As capitalism grew throughout Europe, the new principles of commercial profit-making came into conflict with the traditional economic organization of the feudal community. Feudal ideology had restricted the free pursuit of an individual's economic interests. The concept of a reasonable or just price was giving way to the principle of supply and demand—it became acceptable to charge as much as the market would allow. As the merchant class prospered, the old feudal economy became untenable, and the pursuit of profit was anointed as moral and ethical. Above all, the new capitalist morality asserted that individuals should be free to do with their property whatever they deem most advantageous for their private enrichment. While feudal society had emphasized religion, hierarchy, and the organic interconnection of the various parts of society, the emerging new age emphasized science, liberty, and the rights of the individual, a set of ideas at the heart of liberal ideology.

During the two centuries following the first voyage of Columbus to the New World, the economic centre of gravity in Europe moved first towards the Iberian Peninsula in the west, then north to Holland, eventually coming to rest in France and England. The economic backdrop for the rise of political liberalism in England was the spread of commercial capitalism and the rise of a new middle class consisting of rural gentry, who revolutionized farming through the introduction of new techniques and by consolidating their property, and an urban bourgeoisie evolving from retailer to manufacturer. The trade in wool, England's first great export industry, dramatized the unity of interests among the countryside manufacturers and the port-city merchants.

Behind the walls of **economic protectionism**, European nations sought to develop strong national economies. As political power was centralized in the hands of absolute or constitutional monarchs, governments sought to create a unified national market. This meant protecting local industry from international competition while, simultaneously, encouraging the export of cheap manufactured goods to other markets. The principle underlying this early economic policy was simple. What made one individual richer than another was the amount of gold and silver she or he possessed. A nation's wealth could be similarly calculated.[1] Following this reasoning, Spain had an early advantage when its conquest of the Aztec and Inca empires resulted in a massive importation of New World gold and silver. Not all these riches stayed in Spain. Pirates such as Francis Drake, under licence from the Queen of England, hijacked many Spanish gold shipments, diverting Aztec gold to England. Exporting English goods abroad and exchanging them for gold provided an even more profitable source of precious metal.

Through these and other measures under the doctrine of **mercantilism**, which were stimulated and controlled by the national governments, prosperous economies grew in Britain and France.

Their colonial conquests in North America and Asia became the arms and legs of a single national economy. The purpose of colonialism was to contribute to the prosperity of the 'mother country'. Typically, this meant passing laws prohibiting certain types of manufacturing enterprises in the colonies, requiring finished goods to be bought only from merchants licensed by the colonial power, and confining the colonial economy to the supply of raw materials. Locke had endorsed the principle that the object of economic policy ought to be to multiply the amount of gold and silver in a nation. Accordingly, nations passed laws forbidding the exporting of precious metals, restricting foreign trade, imposing taxes on imports, and hindering the transportation of goods.[2] Privileged merchants with influence at Court would be granted the sole right or monopoly to trade in a colony, such as India, while other merchants were simply excluded from this commerce and from the large profits it generated.

To the critics of mercantilism, the economic system of the eighteenth century was top-heavy with government rules. Other members of the new middle class, the *bourgeoisie*, wanted the freedom to decide for themselves what to do with their money—to calculate and then act on what was in their best financial interests, and not be closed off from profitable ventures by government policies. It was against this policy, in part, that the Americans had revolted. By 1776 the mercantilist system appeared to liberal thinkers to be detrimental to the expansion of the national economy. The hoarding of gold and silver may have made governments appear to be rich, but it had unforeseen consequences, such as severe inflation—more money in circulation caused higher prices. Mercantilism did not stimulate the growth of the economy, liberals believed, as rapidly as the alternative policy of allowing nations to trade freely, specializing in the goods for which they had a national advantage.

In France, economists known as the Physiocrats argued that France would benefit from liberalizing trade and removing the barriers that prevented the free movement of goods from one country to another—the doctrine of free trade. The most prominent early English theorist who advocated economic liberalism was Adam Smith (1723–90), who provided a blueprint for an alternative, pure capitalist economic system in which everyone would be expected to calculate his or her own business interests and act on them with no restrictions from government.

ADAM SMITH

Smith published his groundbreaking book, *An Inquiry into the Wealth of Nations*, in 1776. Appropriately, it was a year of revolution. As the American colonists fought against the economic and political restrictions imposed by the English government, Adam Smith's *Wealth of Nations* criticized government regulations on economic trade and endorsed economic freedom.

For Smith, humans were essentially economic animals, endowed with a natural 'propensity to truck, barter, and exchange one thing for another',[3] a tendency found only in humanity. Unlike animals that are self-sufficient, humans in society need help from others to attain all they require. Only in the most backward societies, with the poorest standards of living, would people provide all their necessities by their own labour. In more prosperous countries, people seek the goods they don't make from others willing to trade for them, using their reason to strike the deal that is most advantageous. In business, Smith said, you must show that what you require is actually to the advantage of the other contracting party:

> It is not from the benevolence of the butcher, the brewer, or the baker, that we expect our dinner, but from their regard to their own interest. We address ourselves, not to their humanity but to their self-love; and never talk to them of our own necessities, but of their advantages.[4]

Defoe had his fictional character Robinson Crusoe put the argument in virtually identical words: '[G]ratitude was no[t] inherent virtue in the nature of man; nor did men always square their dealings by the obligations they had received, so much as they did by the advantages they expected.'⁵ The economic system was run on the engine of individual calculations of personal benefit and private profit. Where did profit come from, however, and how could it be justified? Locke had argued almost a century earlier that you were entitled to the ownership of anything upon which you had laboured. According to Smith's **labour theory of value**, the value of any good produced, its 'real or natural price', was the amount of labour it embodied.⁶ If the value of a commodity is equal to the labour expended on it, it would seem to follow that a labourer should receive the full value of the sale of the good. This is only the case, Smith says, in the simple stage of independent commodity production, when labourers worked for themselves alone and fashioned an article from beginning to end. The economic system had evolved beyond this early beginning.

Once some individuals had accumulated enough 'stock' (raw materials, machinery, workshops, and so on), they began to hire other labourers, setting them to work on their stock. This hired labour added value to the stock by converting it into commodities for sale. For Smith, 'The value which the workmen add to the materials . . . resolves itself' into three parts. One portion goes to the payment of rent, a second pays the labourers' wages, while the third pays 'the profits of their employer'. This profit is the capitalist's motivation for employing labourers and setting them to work to add value to the original stock.

If labour alone adds value, how is profit justified? Logically, profit could be a wage paid to the capitalist for 'a particular sort of labour, the labour of inspection and direction'. In Smith's view, however, profits are 'altogether different' and do not relate to 'the quantity, the hardship, or the ingenuity of this supposed labour of inspection and direction', which, in any case, could be performed by some principal clerk.⁷ Profits were simply rewards for having advanced the capital. In a capitalist society, most labourers need a 'master' to

provide them with employment. Consequently, they must share the produce of their labour and the value that they add to the materials upon which they labour with the owner of the stock who employs them, 'and in this consists his profit.'⁸ Capitalists do not need to work; the labourer supplies the capitalist with her or his 'just reward' in the form of profit. While perhaps being spared from the necessity to labour, unlike the idle aristocrats, capitalists are obliged by the law of competition to be frugal, to save as much as possible, and to plow as much profit as they can back into their business. Unlike the idle aristocrats, capitalists are forced to be virtuous. Capital accumulates by thrift, Smith argues, by the capitalist saving rather than spending his or her share of the value created that is taken as profit.

The saved portion is employed as capital and is consumed by labourers 'who reproduce with a profit the value of their annual consumption'.⁹ The capitalist uplifts the moral standards of the entire community. Where large capital is employed, the 'inferior ranks of people' are also generally 'industrious, sober, and thriving'.¹⁰

Unlike the parsimonious capitalist, the example of the wasteful aristocrat encouraged the inferior sort of people to be 'idle, dissolute, and poor'.¹¹ You grow rich by employing many productive labourers; you grow 'poor by maintaining a multitude of menial servants' and idle guests. Like Monseigneur's four lackeys in Dickens's *A Tale of Two Cities*, their work is unproductive and 'adds to the value of nothing' (Box 3.1).¹² By Smith's reckoning, some unproductive work is socially useful, such as the work of the sovereign, the officers of justice, the armed forces, and the Church. Smith's point is that, whether useful or not, unproductive labourers of all types are 'maintained by the annual produce of the land and labour of the country'.¹³ They are a drain on the stock that could be employed as capital and detract from the wealth of the nation. For a country, the more capital, the more industry, the greater the number of 'productive hands', the greater the value of the goods produced, and the higher 'the real wealth and revenue of all its inhabitants'.

> **Box 3.1**
>
> Monseigneur, one of the great lords in power at the Court . . . was about to take his chocolate. Monseigneur could swallow a great many things with ease, and was by some few sullen minds supposed to be rather rapidly swallowing France; but his morning's chocolate could not so much as get into the throat of Monseigneur without the aid of four strong men besides the Cook.
>
> Yes. It took four men, all four ablaze with gorgeous decoration . . . to conduct the happy chocolate to Monseigneur's lips. One lacquey carried the chocolate pot into the sacred presence; a second, middled and frothed the chocolate with the little instrument he bore for that function; a third, presented the favoured napkin; a fourth . . . poured the chocolate out. It was impossible for Monseigneur to dispense with one of these attendants on the chocolate and hold his high place under the admiring heavens. Deep would have been the blot on his escutcheon [coat of arms] if his chocolate had been ignobly waited on by only three men; he must have died of two.
>
> —Charles Dickens, *A Tale of Two Cities* (1859)

Free Trade and Laissez-Faire

> Thus God and Nature linked the general frame,
> And bade self-love and social be the same.
> —Alexander Pope, *Essay on Man* (1733)

Profits were limited because governments were interfering in the natural laws of economics by acting according to the prevailing mercantile (or commercial) system of economics. For Smith, this obsession with hoarding gold made trade with other countries more difficult by disallowing the most convenient medium of exchange.[14] Nations resembled misers who wanted to count their money rather than invest it as capital. The 'contrivers of this whole mercantile system' were principally 'merchants and manufacturers' for whose benefit the interest of the consumers has been sacrificed.[15] Even attempts by governments to protect basic food supplies in their countries to ensure against famine were harmful to the overall good of the country, said Smith. Government regulations on basic necessities such as food often contributed to rather than helped to prevent famine. However, Smith assured his readers, if all countries allowed free trade in grains, these harmful consequences could be minimized.[16]

The interests of the nation must be calculated in the same way a capitalist makes her or his business decisions. Individuals make what they are best at and buy from others those things they need but cannot supply as advantageously through their own efforts. This is the prudent course for every person's private affairs and no different for a nation. It is better to buy a good from another country if its price is cheaper than the cost of producing it at home. A country ought to direct its capital to making those things for which it has a natural advantage. To refuse to buy cheaply from abroad means that capital will be forced to enter an unprofitable industry rather than be directed towards the most profitable alternative. Any industry that has to be artificially expanded is not naturally suitable for investment and it will stagnate, simultaneously preventing capital investment in an industry with a natural advantage for growth. The total economic value created in the society is thereby diminished rather than increased. Capital and industry must be 'left to find out their natural employments'.[17]

By advancing these arguments, Adam Smith attacked old-fashioned economic logic. According to the traditional, conservative view, since the objective of trade was to export the most while importing the least, the way to accomplish this was to have government restrictions on what could be imported. The problem with this logic, Smith and other liberal economists reasoned, was that other governments could adopt identical measures against goods made in England. In the end, all trade could be frozen. It was better, Smith argued, to allow free trade, to remove all regulations, restrictions, and tariffs, provided that other countries did the same. Free trade would benefit all, Smith believed, because it creates markets for what otherwise would be the 'superfluities' of home production and allows the importation of 'other useful commodities, which the freedom of trade, without any such [government] attention, never fails to supply in the proper quantity.'[18] It also allows the division of labour in the industry to expand to its maximum, rather than being restricted by the boundaries of the home market. All countries engaged in foreign trade 'derive great benefit from it'.[19]

The French term 'laissez-faire', which translates as 'let us alone', best expressed this liberal view that the most appropriate economic policy was to abolish all government restrictions and to allow individuals the maximum freedom to use their wealth in any way they chose. The proper functions of government were national defence, the administration of impartial justice, and the support of those public institutions—such as the prison and the workhouse—which had to be maintained from government taxation because the expenses of these establishments were always greater than the profit that could be derived from them.[20]

Otherwise, the poor had to be sustained from charity, unless like Charles Dickens's character, Scrooge, you preferred to be left alone in that area as well. The money needed to support this limited government role had to come from taxation, but government revenue should not be derived from profit, which, Smith declares, 'is evidently not taxable directly'. Scrooge would have agreed (Box 3.2).[21]

Smith had several arguments to justify exempting profits from taxation. Profit, he argues, is in most cases 'no more than a moderate compensation, for the risk and trouble of employing the stock'. If government threatens to reduce the reward for investment, capital will not be put into employment. In addition, if the manufacturer was taxed directly 'in proportion to the whole profit', it would simply be passed on to consumers as higher costs, affecting negatively the national wealth.[22] Taxing profit would require the government to inquire into the private circumstances of

---

Box 3.2

'[A] few of us are endeavouring to raise a fund to buy the Poor some meat and drink, and means of warmth.... What shall I put you down for?'

'Nothing!' Scrooge replied.... 'I wish to be left alone.... I don't make merry myself at Christmas, and I can't afford to make idle people merry. I help to support the establishments [prisons and workhouses] I have mentioned: they cost enough: and those who are badly off must go there.'

'Many can't go there; and many would rather die.'

'If they would rather die,' said Scrooge, 'they had better do it, and decrease the surplus population. Besides.... It's not my business,' Scrooge returned. 'It's enough for a man to understand his own business, and not to interfere with other people's. Mine occupies me constantly. Good afternoon, gentlemen!'

—Charles Dickens, *A Christmas Carol* (1843)

every capitalist, which no one could support. In addition, since capital is removable, if profit were 'assessed a burdensome tax', the capitalist would 'be apt to abandon the country . . . and would remove his stock to some other country where he could either carry on his business, or enjoy his fortune at his ease.'[23]

Smith and the other liberal economists believed that government regulation of the economy was not only harmful but was unnecessary. In their view, they had uncovered the 'laws of the market'—capitalism would operate automatically according to basic laws that were 'natural' rather than humanly imposed. By the law of supply and demand, for example, the best-quality goods would be produced for the lowest possible price. For Smith, if each individual pursued his or her personal interest, then he or she would promote the good of the whole society.[24]

Capitalists direct their capital to develop domestic industry and ensure that the greatest value is produced; in doing so they intend only their own security and their own gain. But in so doing, they promote the interests of all. A capitalist is 'led by an invisible hand to promote an end which was no part of his intention.' Every individual is the best judge of the type of domestic industry in which to employ capital, and better than any meddlesome politician.[25] This argument rationalizes the pursuit of selfish interests, regardless of the effect on others, and expresses the fundamental individualism at the heart of laissez-faire economics.

For Smith, the 'wealth' of a nation was determined by how large a market there was for the goods it produced. In his view, free trade created the opportunity for the widest possible market. While the middle-class merchants would benefit most from the profits made, if the economy grew larger, more jobs would be created, wages would rise, and there would be more money to buy goods—in short, everyone would benefit. As Smith argued, real wages had increased during the eighteenth century in England: 'The common complaint that luxury extends itself even to the lowest ranks of the people, and that the labouring poor will not now be contented with the same food, clothing, and lodging which satisfied them in former times' was proof, he claimed, that the benefits of capitalist industry extended to all classes.[26] Late in the twentieth century, when laissez-faire ideas had again become popular, this became known as the 'trickle-down' argument. When the rich are prosperous and happy, the system runs smoothly and benefits 'trickle down' to the poor. It is the argument of those who have vastly more than others.

The Division of Labour

Capitalism contained within itself the dynamic principle of competition that forced capitalists to innovate and introduce new technologies in their enterprises. When many producers of a good competed with each other for a share of the market, the one who could manufacture an item most cheaply had a competitive advantage. This drove capitalists to reduce their costs of production. Lowering wages was an obvious way to do this. While wages might be driven to rock bottom, capitalists would simply chase each other to the wage basement and none would have a competitive advantage for long. This policy also directly incited rebellion among the labouring classes.

A second way to increase the productive powers of labour was to divide the various tasks in the manufacturing process.[27] In the early manufacturing economy, a crafts worker produced finished products, from start to finish. A master shoemaker, for example, would acquire the leather, design the shoe, cut the leather and sew the pieces, add the eyeholes, the heel, and the insole, and then display the final product for sale. Under laissez-faire competition, however, more shoes could be produced in the same time if the various separate tasks were divided and workers were forced to specialize in only one of these tasks. Instead of 20 workers each producing shoes individually, the process of shoemaking could be divided into 20 different steps. One worker could be assigned to specialize in a single task (it would not be accurate any more to call it a 'skill'), passing on the unfinished shoe to the next station. The result would be far more efficient production, in the sense that the division of labour would allow more shoes to be made by the same number of people in the same time.[28] Dividing the labour in this way provided the capitalist with a competitive advantage.

The division of tasks facilitated the introduction of machinery into the factory since it was easier to mechanize simple, repetitive jobs than complex, differentiated ones. Once a source of power, such as steam, was added to drive the machinery, the Industrial Revolution was well underway. For Smith, the consequences for profit of this division of labour were obvious. Critics, however, were quick to point out that the world of laissez-faire capitalism was harmful to crafts workers, who, along with their special skills, became redundant, and to factory workers who suffered the indignities of mind-numbing repetitive labour. Conservatives deplored the destruction of the traditional small farm and the rural village community that depended on it. Villages were depopulated and destroyed as fast as dirty, noisy, polluted, and slum-ridden cities arose.

The theory of free trade also assumed that all nations would benefit from abolishing government restrictions and tariffs. However, some countries would benefit more than others. England was in the position to benefit the most from free trade. Being the first country to experience the Industrial Revolution, England was able to produce large quantities of manufactured goods at the lowest possible price. English goods could compete successfully anywhere in the world, especially in places where goods were still handmade.

It was not necessarily good for the American, or German, or Italian bourgeoisie, who could not produce the same quantity of cheap goods. With free competition, they would be driven out of business and their national industries would collapse. This implied that highly capitalized industries in one country could destroy the less-developed industries in others. Ultimately, free competition with England would mean that other countries would have difficulty industrializing

and would be obliged to import manufactured goods. Consequently, many other nations, such as the United States, Canada, and Germany, adopted a protectionist policy by not removing their taxes on imports. They protected their national economies so that their business class would have a chance to develop manufacturing industries and, later, be able to compete internationally.

THOMAS MALTHUS

Even where national governments refused to embrace laissez-faire wholeheartedly in their industrial policy, they endorsed the social implications of the liberal doctrine, which were clearly explained by the British economist, Thomas Malthus. In his *Essay on the Principles of Population*, Malthus took issue with the Enlightenment doctrine that humanity was eventually perfectible. Tremendous and insurmountable obstacles, in his view, stood in the way. His argument rested on two postulates: that food was necessary to human existence and that the instinctual passion between the sexes was also necessary and would 'remain nearly in its present state.'[29] These two laws were fixed in our nature by God and neither may be extinguished as long as humanity exists. From these two statements, Malthus drew the conclusion that the power of population growth is indefinitely greater than the power of the earth to produce subsistence. When population growth is unchecked, it increases geometrically while the means of subsistence increases only arithmetically.[30] Thus, while the human population could quickly double in number, it was much more difficult to expand the production of food.

If the earth does not provide enough sustenance while humans reproduce rapidly, not everyone will have enough to eat and some must die. Nature in vegetable and animal life produces far more seeds and offspring than can survive, and humanity cannot escape from this fate. The tendency to overpopulation necessarily produces misery, as well as vice and immorality. Famine and its associated deaths, then, were natural occurrences in society. In the ideology of **Malthusianism,** however, famine, disaster, and war were actually beneficial for society. Not only did these natural and social disasters have the tendency (and socially positive function) of reducing the size of the population, they also eliminated, above all, the weak, the ill, and the poor—the socially disadvantaged generally. Only the fittest survived. That was a law of nature and a law of society as well. This argument, Malthus claimed, is a conclusive proof against the perfectibility of society.

The poet, William Blake, exposed the hard-heartedness and self-interest behind this doctrine:

> When a man looks pale
> With labour & abstinence, say he looks
>   healthy and happy;
> And when his children sicken, let them die,
>   there are enough
> Born, even too many, & our earth will
>   be overrun
> Without these arts.
> Preach temperance; say he is over grog'd &
>   drowns his wit
> In strong drink, tho you know that
>   bread & water are all
> He can afford.[31]

Malthus argued that it was socially harmful to give charity to the poor because they would simply survive and produce more offspring who would be poor and hungry. You would end up with more starvation and suffering than before. Even if the land was made more productive so that more people could be fed, the supply of people would expand until there were again too many and the society would enter another period of misery and starvation. While it might appear to be cruel and harsh not to give the poor money, the most humane thing would be to let nature take its course and allow laissez-faire to operate in the control of population. Let natural selection weed out the weak and inferior from the population and increase the number and vitality of the strong. Given this view, it is no wonder that liberal economics became known as the 'dismal science'.

The theory of economic liberalism was suited to the new capitalist middle-class that was becoming increasingly numerous, wealthy, and literate, providing a large potential market for cultural goods such as novels, paintings, music, poetry, and theatre. The demands of the new class affected the content as well as the development of distinctive styles of art and literature.

The new middle class had arisen in a society dominated by traditional authority and elite culture. The aristocracy defined good taste and used part of their wealth to sponsor arts such as painting, music, and architecture. They looked down their cultural noses at the bourgeoisie, who were eminently practical people. With their middle-class noses to the grindstone of hard work, abstinence, and thrift, there appeared to be little room for ornamentation and diversion among the daily calculations of their profits and losses. They were '**philistines**', interested only in crass, mundane, materialistic pursuits, and went 'about joking and making money and filling their bellies'.[32] As Dabydeen points outs, some authors accommodated their writing to the mercenary attitude that nature was there to be exploited for private profit. Forests were beautiful because they could be fashioned into masts for British schooners; flowers existed for their commercial potential.[33] Many early eighteenth-century English writers wholeheartedly supported the rise of modern commerce, urbanism, and rural decay.

Over time, however, as the bourgeoisie settled comfortably into prosperity and acquired the dominant share of political power, they wanted to display their superior style, creating a growing market for new literary and artistic products. The bourgeoisie saw themselves as morally superior to the decadent aristocracy, and more serious-minded. They wanted to be entertained, but also educated. They read journals and newspapers that commented on the affairs of the day. They enjoyed literature that was critical, even satirical, towards the frivolous fops of so-called high society.

Once the middle class had become firmly established within Parliament, thus solidifying its political power, and once English trade and prosperity brought world dominance, the general attitude among the educated classes turned to contentment and smugness. In this 'Age of Reason', progress was being made apparently on all fronts. The literature of the time reflected the assurance that the basic foundations, the institutional structures of society, were sound. The new middle class and their spokespersons were supremely confident that the world was better than ever before, that progress was bound to continue. Society might not be perfect, but their world was the best of all possible worlds. It was a waste of time to dream about ideal societies; things were pretty much as good as they should and could get. Even things people couldn't understand were actually for the best, as the English poet, Alexander Pope, wrote in his *Essay on Man* (1733):

> All nature is but Art unknown to thee;
> All chance direction, which thou canst not see;
> All discord, harmony not understood;
> All partial evil, universal good;
> And spite of Pride, in erring Reason's spite,
> One truth is clear, *Whatever is, is right*.[34]

A more self-satisfied and confident expression about social life would be difficult to find. Pope did not actually mean everything was right. Many things needed to be corrected; above all, good taste had to be reinforced. The literary masters of the age propagated the rules of taste, of manners and propriety, enforcing this 'social correctness' (to adapt a contemporary phrase) on others. Their literary weapons of choice were the essay and the satire. A satire was a form of exaggeration of general ideas and conventional tendencies meant to point out and ridicule what the dominant writers believed to be poor taste or lack of reason. As a style, however, social satire could also raise public awareness about more serious injustices and wrongs.

The chief paradox of the new culture was that everything wasn't right. The middle class was, in many respects, rebellious. In a traditional society, demands for freedom, legal equality, and greater democracy were radical. English liberal ideas about the rights of 'man' had inspired the American Revolution. Adam Smith's political economy, which demanded economic freedom, was a challenge to the tradition-based economy of the time.

In a literary world dominated by the reasoned essay and the satirical poem, a literary innovation was taking shape. The most important contribution made by the new middle class to literary forms was the novel. While they also set their stamp on other cultural forms—from painting to drama and poetry—the novel was the special creation of the time. The eighteenth-century English novel portrayed common types of people and drew accurate pictures of social life and manners. Among the earliest and most innovative novelists was Daniel Defoe (1660–1731). Henry Fielding, in *The History and Adventures of Joseph Andrews* (1742) and *Tom Jones* (1749), developed the novel to high art.

DANIEL DEFOE

In various respects, Defoe was both typical and atypical of his age. He sought to make his fortune in business and trade, which were expanding rapidly towards the end of the 1600s in England. During periods of rapid capitalist expansion, business opportunities proliferate and it is possible to enter new lines of trade and make a fortune quickly. For Defoe, the feudal economy had been like a stagnant pond; in contrast, free trade was a bubbling spring—the capitalist's wealth flowed continually. The economy moves and expands, creating new wealth. The 'nouveaux riches' merchants and business owners 'grew immensely rich'. Many merchants 'lived in more real splendour and spent more money than most of the noblemen in England could singly expend'.[35] New possibilities for amassing wealth appear in any period of capitalist expansion—for example, the microchip revolution of the last decades of the twentieth century.

Such periods are also especially volatile—business failures are as common as business successes. Over the course of his life, Defoe established successful businesses, suffered business failures, and faced debtors' prison. Defoe's politics were never stable, at a time when political parties were just beginning to form, though in many respects Defoe represents the most progressive attitudes of his time. He championed the liberal freedoms of religion, of the press, and of the rights of citizens over their representatives in Parliament. He was an early advocate of the equal education of women and of more liberal divorce laws. Defoe's economic writings were ahead of his time—decades before Adam Smith he anticipated many of his ideas. His political writings and demands for religious toleration were punished by periods of imprisonment and time in the public stocks.[36]

Like the dynamism of trade itself, individual lives have their own saga. Stories of people rising from poverty and obscurity to riches and fame had a large public market. Among the most popular of early English novels was Defoe's *Robinson Crusoe* (1719). The story was inspired by the adventures of Alexander Selkirk, who had been marooned on an island similar to the one Defoe imagined. Defoe incorporated realistic detail and moralizing into his novel, two elements of content favoured by the new capitalist class.

The principal part of the narrative of *Robinson Crusoe* offers a detailed description of Crusoe's 28-year exile off the coast of South America, a world that possessed natural wealth in abundance. As the bourgeois traders built their individual fortunes in a volatile but rapidly expanding world of trade, Crusoe's self-portrait was an image the bourgeoisie fancied of themselves.

Defoe did not plunge his imaginary Crusoe into an absolute state of nature. Crusoe retained his cultural knowledge and spiritual beliefs along with the material he salvaged from the shipwreck. Defoe illustrated the labour theory of value in this simplest of all economies. Crusoe's labour was the sole source of value, embodied in the goods he fashioned and directly measurable in units of time.[37] He learned the basics of horticulture and animal husbandry, made pottery and baskets, hewed a boat from one log and planks from others. His crowning achievement was designing and constructing an umbrella. As he carved a simple replica of European society out of the raw materials of nature, Crusoe demonstrated the middle-class virtues of ingenuity, self-reliance, skill, hard work, and perseverance, which created for himself a prosperous life: 'I seldom gave anything over without accomplishing it, when I once had it in my head enough to begin it.'[38] Ironically, as an artisan, Crusoe's self-made individual was soon to be made obsolete in the factory system spawned by the Industrial Revolution.

In *The Fortunes and Misfortunes of Moll Flanders* (1722), Defoe told the story of a female counterpart to Robinson Crusoe. Moll Flanders was a castaway from society, not on a deserted island but in the city of London. In this urban wilderness she had nothing but her own resources to make her way and her fortune. Where Crusoe's misfortunes had been caused by fate and his prosperity resulted from hard work, the misfortunes of Moll Flanders were social in origin. Since women could not own property, they could prosper only indirectly, through their relations with men. Poverty and necessity drove her to find innovative ways to survive, from prostitution and theft, to marriage, and eventually to high social standing as a wife in the colonies. Marriage opened the best opportunities for women. According to Moll Flanders, 'a woman should never be kept for a mistress that had money to make herself a wife.'[39]

RURAL NOSTALGIA AND SOCIAL SATIRE

[C]riticism is the beginning of progress and enlightenment.
—Thomas Mann, *The Magic Mountain* (1924)

The new middle class in England quickly developed an ambivalent attitude to the aristocracy. On the one hand, they condemned the waste and ostentation of the upper-class lifestyle. On the other hand, they sought to enter the old ruling class through marriage, combining new money with ancient prestige. As the bourgeoisie rose to the position of social dominance in English society, they would, of necessity, become conservative rather than radical. Once out in the open, however, their initial radical ideas had stimulated demands from the great majority of people for equality and freedom. The socially critical literature that developed during the Age of Reason similarly would not be confined to the boundaries of middle-class 'good taste'.

While Defoe represented progressive liberal thinking in the early eighteenth century, most social critics of the time were **Tories**. The liberals were acutely critical of the fashionable excesses of the old feudal aristocracy. But the capitalist economic revolution, which was making many people rich, was also causing unprecedented hardship among the small property owners and the urban poor. Large landowners were enclosing the common land with fences, evicting peasants from their traditional landholdings, and converting their traditional estates to capitalist agricultural enterprises. The socially conservative Tories, who saw the growing social misery of the poor, blamed these evils on the new people of power (landowning capitalists and merchants) and on the new regime of capitalism. Instead, they remained wedded to the rural, feudal way of life, which was deemed moral and healthy. The growth of capitalism was destroying these traditions and simultaneously creating urban jungles of dirt, disease, pollution, poverty, and despair.

In his poem *The Deserted Village* (1770), Oliver Goldsmith condemned the harsh effects of the enclosure movement on the lovely 'Sweet-smiling village' of the English countryside, which was becoming a desolate place.[40] Once a vigorous and independent peasant class had worked the land in 'innocence and health'. Now 'times are altered.' The land is being usurped by 'the sons of wealth' and the peasantry dispossessed: 'One only master grasps the whole domain.' In a world 'Where wealth accumulates, and men decay', the countryside had become home to 'Unwieldy wealth' that was even 'beyond the miser's wish'.

As the 'rich man's joys increase, the poor's decay.' The proud country family could seek employment only in the mushrooming cities; but, Goldsmith wondered:

> If to the city sped, what waits him there?
> To see profusion that he must not share;
> To see the thousand baneful arts combine
> To pamper luxury, and thin mankind;
> To see each joy the sons of pleasure know
> Extorted from his fellow-creatures' woe.

Jonathan Swift

The most savage satires of the eighteenth century were written by Jonathan Swift (1667–1745), an Irish clergyman. Swift's main cause was independence, and his satires exposed the oppression of the Irish by their English conquerors. Swift argued that to be governed without their consent, as the Irish were by the English, was slavery:

> For, *in reason*, all government without the consent of the governed, is the very definition of slavery. . . . A people long used to hardships lose by degrees the very notion of liberty; they look upon themselves as creatures at mercy, and that all impositions laid on them by a stronger hand are . . . legal and obligatory. Hence proceed [derives] that poverty and lowness of spirit, to which a kingdom may be subject, as well as a particular person.[41]

Swift's *Gulliver's Travels* (1726) is a savage satire on the English government and monarchy. Swift recounts Gulliver's fantastic voyages to four imaginary lands, including Lilliput with its miniature human beings, and Brobdingnag, peopled by a race of giants.

Little escaped Swift's caustic pen. He dismissed most of what passed for 'academic learning' in Part III of *Gulliver's Travels*, in which the Laputans were so wrapped up in the speculations of their own minds, they had to be reminded to speak and listen to others.[42] In the Grand Academy of the city of Lagado, inventors were at work on large numbers of absurd projects, such as reducing human excrement to its original food and softening marble for pillows. In one room, a professor demonstrated a machine that generated random sequences of words, which were then read and, 'where they found three or four words together that might make part of a sentence', they were written down. This procedure was repeated many times and several volumes of broken sentences had been compiled, which, one day, might be pieced together. 'By this contrivance,' Swift concludes, 'the most ignorant person at a reasonable charge, and with little bodily labour, may write books in philosophy, poetry, law, mathematics and theology, without the least assistance from genius or study.'[43]

Gulliver's visit to the land of the Houyhnhnms, a race of highly intelligent, peaceful horses, is particularly insightful and critical. These horse-like beings lived among another species of animals, the Yahoos, who were primitive, nasty, and vicious in their habits. Gulliver had never before seen 'so disagreeable an animal'. When he was later brought face-to-face with a Yahoo, he was horrified and astonished to observe, 'in this abominable animal, a perfect human figure'. Naturally, Gulliver was taken to be a Yahoo at first, but he surprised the Houyhnhnms by his ability to talk and reason. When they asked Gulliver to describe European culture, he told them, in great detail, about lying, the vices of crime, drink, and gambling, and about the many wars and ingenious devices for killing people invented by Europeans.[44] The more he talked, however, the more Gulliver revealed that human beings were, essentially, nothing but Yahoos. In fact, they were worse. Yahoos were incapable of reason and could not be blamed for their ignorance and violent behaviour. Humans possessed reason, making them blameworthy for the abuses Gulliver revealed. In fact, the Houyhnhnms conclude, humans don't possess true reason; by some accident they had come to possess 'some small pittance of reason', the effect of which was only 'to increase' their 'natural vices'. Finally, Gulliver comes to understand his own society 'in a very different light'.[45]

Swift's most biting satire was his *A Modest Proposal* (1729), on the liberal theories of laissez-faire and overpopulation. Essentially, Swift proposes that the problems in Ireland of poverty, starvation, and overpopulation could be solved by a simple measure that would simultaneously reduce the Irish population and feed the people. Swift suggests that the Irish eat their poor children. As a satire, Swift writes his *A Modest Proposal* in a mock-serious vein, after the fashion of the liberal political economist who would not, Swift implies, debate the morality of raising children like cattle, but merely the financial costs and benefits to be realized.

Opposition to laissez-faire and the ideology of free enterprise has always come from a number of quarters. Those privileged under the mercantile system condemned the new system as much as the more genuine victims who were being displaced from their traditional landholdings and means of livelihood. Poets such as Oliver Goldsmith lamented the passing of traditional society and compared the present circumstances unfavourably with the past. The painter and engraver Hogarth put on display for all classes his view of the impoverished world of the underclass—of gin-soaked mothers, neglected children, moral degenerates—where cruelty was commonplace. Swift's satires expressed the resentments and anti-colonialism of the oppressed Irish. Rather than celebrating their society or challenging people to live by the standards of divine morality, these artists distanced themselves from the social world to comment ironically about it. However outraged the criticism, as sociologist Karl Mannheim points out, the critic had not broken with the social order as a whole.[46]

The general ideas of liberal theory were not confined to the English-speaking world. Similar developments in social thought were emerging on the Continent, particularly in France where the social structure was more rigid than in England and where the traditional monarchy and Church continued to exercise absolute authority. Just as its structure of authority was more rigid and unbending, so too the opposition to it was more extensive and extreme. This intellectual movement of opposition in France became known as the Enlightenment. It prepared the way for the French Revolution, one of the great turning points in history and in social theory.

THE ENLIGHTENMENT

Feudalism was a decentralized political structure from which it was at least as logical to derive the separation of state power as the centralization of power in the hands of an absolute monarch. Medieval guilds and incorporated towns exercised limited self-management of common affairs. In a number of countries, including England and France, representative bodies or parliaments emerged from within feudalism. However limited they were in conception or function, they embodied a potential for popular power that was greatly in advance of their original, advisory role. Even in Christianity, despite its history of hierarchy and ideological control, notions of equality (if only in death), of the simple yet ethical life, and of peace made liberal doctrines appear palatable. More than one potential future coexisted within the institutional structure of medieval Europe, and the historical path taken by each nation reflected the changing balance of forces over time.

The gradual assumption of power in England by a commercial class of landowners and merchants took several centuries. In Continental Europe, similar battles erupted within the old regime. While England was undergoing the social and political violence that reflected the birth pangs of the modern social order, France was consolidating central power in the hands of an absolute monarchy and a powerful Church. France developed as a single nation through its Hundred Years War with England, inspired by the heroism and sacrifice of a common-born woman, Jeanne d'Arc. By the time of the Restoration in England (1660), France was under the autocratic rule of Louis XIV. Underneath the splendour of the French court at Versailles, the rapid growth of the French economy under the doctrine of mercantilism (the target of Adam Smith's laissez-faire attack), and the flowering of French culture,

numerous social conflicts festered and erupted periodically in violence. The landed aristocracy contended with the Crown for political power, peasants groaned under heavy taxation and sometimes rose in rebellion, and clashes between French Protestants and the Roman Catholic majority were particularly violent and vicious.

Economic prosperity in the eighteenth century stimulated an economic revolution on the French side of the Channel, precipitating the types of social changes that had engulfed England. As new sources of conflict jostled with the old ones, the intellectual atmosphere became volatile and critical of the social order. The conflict between the autocratic powers and the upstart social classes was reflected in ideas of freedom, equality, and natural law. This ideological revolt against the old regime is known as the 'Enlightenment'.

What liberalism was to seventeenth-century England, the **Enlightenment** was to eighteenth-century Continental Europe. The major thinkers of the Enlightenment era, known as *philosophes*, drew their inspiration from Renaissance humanism. What set some humans above others, and humanity above all the rest of 'creation', was the possession of reason and the potential for perfection through the capacity for rational thought. The *philosophes* worshipped the cult of human reason. The dominant Enlightenment philosopher was René Descartes, who drew an absolute separation between humanity and nature. For Descartes, 'reason or sense . . . is the only thing that constitutes us men and distinguishes us from the beasts.'[47] The underlying substance that is the essence of humanity is simultaneously reason, mind, and soul, drawing Descartes's theory closer to traditional thinking. Since this essence was found in all of humanity, however, Descartes added the modernist claim that rationality 'is by nature equal in all':

> Good sense is of all things in the world the most equally distributed. . . . [T]he power of forming a good judgment and of distinguishing the true from the false, which is properly speaking what is called good sense or reason, is by nature equal in all men. . . .

For myself I have never ventured to presume that my mind was in any way more perfect than that of the ordinary man.[48]

In *The Discourse on Method*, Descartes began his search for philosophical truth by rejecting as false everything for which he could imagine the least ground for doubt. 'Knowledge' must begin with one belief that was entirely certain. Consequently, Descartes rejected knowledge from the senses because they sometimes deceive us, as a straight stick appears bent in water or, as the poet Tennyson put it:

Law is God, say some;
No God at all, says the fool,
For all we have power to see
Is a straight staff bent in a pool.[49]

Descartes also discarded mathematical proofs that he could not be absolutely certain were free from error. Chasing truth to its rock bottom, Descartes concluded that 'everything that ever entered into my mind was no more true than the illusion of my dreams.' All that was left, he said, was his thinking mind itself, leading him to the one truth of which he could be certain, the proposition 'I am, I exist, is necessarily true'.[50] Descartes expressed this in his famous maxim, '*I think, therefore I am.*'[51]

Descartes's **skeptical** method resulted in pulling down the philosophical 'house which we inhabit'. Beginning with the belief that you could be certain only of your own, individual existence and that everything else might be an illusion, Descartes intended to construct a theory of existence that was objectively true and that all reasonable people would accept; in his words, to 'provide materials and an architect' for rebuilding knowledge.[52] If you can't trust your senses, but only your mind, how can you be certain that matter exists at all? From his initial supposition of an existing individual mind, Descartes jumped to the abstraction of a universal mind: the second cornerstone of Descartes's theory is the existence of God. He premised the existence of an all-knowing and benevolent God and then proceeded to the proposition that matter exists as emanating from this omniscient Being. The world is objectively as we perceive it to be because God is infinitely good and would not deceive us. In this fashion, Descartes charts a subjective or idealistic course for social theory, focusing first on the human mind and then on an Absolute Mind from which reality derives.

As for Newton, for Descartes all objects in nature, including the behaviour of living things, can be explained by the laws of mathematics and physics. Bodies are essentially machines that can be dissected and their mechanisms studied and understood by the sciences. Human actions, however, are of an entirely different character because of the individual's mind, which is a prime mover of each person. For Descartes, humans possess a soul and freedom of the will.

Descartes postulated a fundamental **duality** between mind and matter. His rationalism was different from English liberalism in the relationship that was assumed to exist between mind and body. The English empiricists, such as Bacon and Locke, regarded mind as being derived from reality, an argument that emphasized the material world as the source of knowledge. As science developed beyond Bacon and Descartes, some theorists would come to doubt that thinking had anything to do with an underlying soul and was, rather, a function of brain chemistry and physics. What was called 'mind' was, in the scientific view, another form of matter, and its functioning could be explained according to physical laws. This materialist view was a leap beyond Descartes, and it denied the duality of mind and matter.

The Catholic Church condemned Descartes's rationalist philosophy and added his name to the list of forbidden authors. His immediate impact on social thought was to focus attention on rationality and the need to begin inquiry by assuming radical doubt. Church doctrine rested on faith, not reason. In a world dominated by traditional institutions, autocratic government, and religious dogma, doubt acted as an especially caustic acid.

THE *PHILOSOPHES*

> It is dangerous to be right when the government is wrong.
> —Voltaire (attributed)

The **philosophes** contended that God had given humanity the ability to reason for a purpose. These social theorists of the Enlightenment adapted the methodology of doubt to the examination of all existing social rules and arrangements. By applying the measuring rod of reason to their society, the *philosophes* believed they could distinguish those aspects that were reasonable and good from those that were not and thereby devise better social arrangements that would be in harmony with the laws of nature. If you simply 'dared to know', harmful social practices could be exposed and reasonable remedies applied. All previous knowledge was suspect; all that was believed to be true was to be challenged; all traditional social institutions were to be subjected to the test of reason. For the *philosophes*, the problems of the world resulted from ignorance, which rested on religious superstition and unreasonable traditions, blinding people to the truth. As Friedrich Engels argued, the *philosophes* 'recognised no external authority of any kind whatsoever. Religion, natural science, society, political institutions, everything, was subject to the most unsparing criticism; everything must justify its existence before the judgment seat of reason, or give up existence. Reason became the sole measure of everything.'[53]

The most influential intellectual project of the Enlightenment was the publication of the great *Encyclopédie*, a massive undertaking of several volumes meant to represent the most advanced knowledge drawn from the best minds in France. These 'best minds', however, tended to be highly critical of traditional knowledge, which they termed 'fanaticism' (religion) and 'tyranny' (unenlightened monarchs).[54] The purpose of the *Encyclopédie*, Denis Diderot explained, was to overturn the 'rubbishy edifice' of existing prejudices, replacing this 'futile dustheap' with evidence that established the contrary truths and was sufficient to convince reasonable minds.[55] The *Encyclopédie* was subversive of established authority, and the police authorities struck back. The *philosophes* were charged with violating the censorship laws; such heretical ideas would give support 'to materialism, subvert religion, spread licentiousness, and promote moral depravity'.[56]

The most important institutions to bear the brunt of their withering scrutiny were the twin foundations of authority sustaining the Old Regime: the Church and the unenlightened State. François-Marie Arouet (1694–1778), who used the pseudonym 'Voltaire', was a leading *philosophe* who understood where this criticism was leading: 'Everything I see around me', he wrote, 'is sowing the seeds of a revolution, which will infallibly take place.' More colourfully, according to later legends, Voltaire asserted that, before freedom of inquiry could be certain, 'the last king would have to be strangled with the guts of the last priest.'[57]

Voltaire used satire to lampoon his opponents and criticize ignorance and gullibility. He studied Newtonian science and developed a skeptical attitude to religion, though he remained a Deist, believing in God as a first cause. Satire is designed to challenge the reader's ideas and beliefs, and stimulate change. Voltaire's principal target was blind, **optimistic** faith in the essential goodness of the universe as created by God, which was expressed in the poetry of Alexander Pope and the philosophy of Leibniz, for both of whom all was best in this best of all possible worlds. From this fundamental optimism, theorists deduced that what appeared to be evil was actually part of universal goodness that humans were incapable of understanding. Voltaire's doubts about this doctrine, which suggested it was useless to attempt to improve life, became overwhelming after the 1755 Lisbon earthquake that killed 10,000 men, women, and children. He couldn't believe in a God who would allow such suffering or accept Alexander Pope's irrational faith that if something appears to be partially evil, it is actually for the best if rightly understood.[58]

Voltaire proceeded to demolish the false optimism of Pope and Leibniz in his satirical story, *Candide or Optimism*. Voltaire's method is to understand society from outside, as if the earth were viewed from the stars, so that what is thought to be normal can appear in a new, skeptical light. In his story, Candide was brought up by a noble family and was tutored by Dr Pangloss, the world's greatest philosopher, in metaphysico-theologo-cosmolonigology, which taught that 'things cannot be otherwise' and 'everything is necessarily for the best.' Kicked and thrust out of his original earthly paradise, Candide embarks on a tumultuous voyage of discovery seeking to understand the cause of evil in the world, 'to reason about effects and causes', and debate the Hobbesian view of humanity as inherently evil (Box 3.3).[59]

Shanghaied into the army, Candide witnesses the brutality of warfare—the disembowelled girls, murdered wives, and scattered brains—all done, however, 'in accordance with international law'. In Lisbon after the earthquake, the wisest men condemn three people to be executed, having decided 'that the sight of several persons being slowly burned in great ceremony is an infallible secret for preventing earthquakes.' In Paraguay, where the rulers 'have everything and the people have nothing', government claims to be a 'masterpiece of reason and justice'. In Surinam, Candide encounters a slave who lost a hand in the sugar mill and a leg, which was amputated for escaping. He tells Candide: 'This is the price paid for the sugar you eat in Europe.'[60]

After surviving innumerable hardships and witnessing dreadful barbarities, Candide renounces his optimism, which he calls 'the mania of maintaining that everything is well when we are wretched'.[61] Eventually, he learns that the secret to a life of contentment is simple farm labour, which 'keeps at bay three great evils: boredom, vice and need.' Candide and his few companions settle down co-operatively to cultivate their own garden and eat candied citrons and pistachios, working 'without theorizing', because ''tis the only way to make life endurable.'[62]

Most Enlightenment *philosophes* did not agree with Voltaire that questions such as why evil existed were unanswerable. Instead, they sought to discover new absolute truths. They replaced the dogmas of religious belief with a dogma of reason, implying that everyone who was willing to reason about things would, by the quality of argument and evidence, eventually arrive at a shared agreement. In a greatly unequal world, especially when considering ideas of the social world, this was wishful thinking. The model Enlightenment thinkers were empirical scientists and the model method was the inductive and rationalist scientific method.

If the *philosophes* were generally united in their attacks on the Church and religious authority, they were less united in their views on the other main subject of controversy: politics. Certainly, they opposed unenlightened, arbitrary rule. The greatest

---

Box 3.3

'Do you think,' said Candide, 'that men have always massacred each other, as they do today? Have they always been liars, cheats, traitors, weak, flighty, cowardly, envious, gluttonous, drunken, grasping, and vicious, bloody, backbiting, debauched, fanatical, hypocritical, and silly?'

'Do you think,' said Martin, 'that sparrow hawks have always eaten the pigeons they came across?'

'Yes, of course,' said Candide.

'Well,' said Martin, 'if sparrow hawks have always possessed the same nature, why should you expect men to change theirs?'

'Oh!' said Candide, 'there is a great difference; free will.'

—Voltaire, *Candide* (1759)

political theorist among them was Montesquieu, who supported the **separation of powers** between the executive, legislative, and judicial branches of government. For other *philosophes*, the form that government should take was less important than the specific, enlightened policies that the state should rationally pursue. *Philosophes* such as Voltaire were considerably less democratic than the English liberals. Voltaire believed in the natural superiority of the cultured elite and preferred the rule of an enlightened king who would rule wisely and justly in accordance with reason. He certainly eschewed any experiment with popular forms of democracy. The *philosophes* advocated many liberal reforms, such as greater freedom of speech, an end to torture to extract confessions, and equality before the law. These civil liberties, they claimed, could be granted by any enlightened form of government, from the British House of Commons and the American House of Assembly to the enlightened but still absolute monarchs of Europe.

Most of the *philosophes* were unwilling to accept Descartes's belief in the equal rationality of all human beings. While they affirmed reason was a human attribute, the *philosophes* argued that did not mean that all humanity possessed it in equal amounts. The job of the intellectual elite was to uncover truth and then present reasonable arguments to the political elite who were empowered to make changes. The *philosophes* trusted that the so-called enlightened monarchs could be persuaded to bring social progress by rational arguments. The model Enlightenment king was Frederick the Great of Prussia, a favourite of Voltaire. Frederick's court sheltered many French theorists who, to avoid being imprisoned, fled that country's harsh censorship laws.

THE AMERICAN REVOLUTION

> The cause of America is in a great measure the cause of all mankind.
> —Thomas Paine, *Common Sense* (1776)

The expectation of the *philosophes* that social change could proceed rationally and incrementally did not take into account the intransigence of powerful vested interests. The grievances leading to the insurrection that became the American Revolution were rooted in domination by the British monarchy and ruling class. The economic policies that benefited the British Empire were largely detrimental to the interests of the American elite, who had come to feel they would be better served in a sovereign nation under their own control.

The American situation was complicated by its colonial status. The American Revolution was a national or anti-colonial revolution, with the objective of dissolving the strings of domination held by the British and establishing a government based on the sovereignty of American citizens. It was also a republican revolution intent on establishing a popularly chosen centralized government that in certain respects would also be democratic. While Locke argued against the rights of colonialists to rebel, his arguments about popular sovereignty would be used against him.

As British oppression of the 13 colonies intensified after the Seven Years War the American elite found itself in a dilemma. Gaining independence from Britain required channelling the protest of the lower orders against the British elite rather than against large property owners in general. According to Zinn, this task was performed exquisitely well by Thomas Paine.[63]

Thomas Paine had been a poor immigrant to Philadelphia from England in 1774. Two years later he was in the thick of the insurgency, publishing a widely read pamphlet called *Common Sense* that enumerated the many complaints of the colonists against the British government, attacked the principles of absolute monarchy and hereditary privilege, and called for a war of national independence. Paine took Locke's limited democracy several logical steps further; in fact, in his injunction that government is merely a necessary evil his views were more characteristically American than British.

> Some writers have so confounded society with government, as to leave little or no distinction between them; whereas they are not only different, but have different origins.

Society is produced by our wants, and government by our wickedness; the former promotes our happiness *positively* by uniting our affections, the latter *negatively* by restraining our vices. The one encourages intercourse, the other creates distinctions. The first is a patron, the last a punisher.

Society in every state is a blessing, but government even in its best state is but a necessary evil; in its worst state an intolerable one. . . . For were the impulses of conscience clear, uniform, and irresistibly obeyed, man would need no other lawgiver; but that not being the case, he finds it necessary to surrender up a part of his property to furnish means for the protection of the rest. . . .[64]

The American revolutionaries wanted a republic—a type of government without even a constitutionally limited monarchy. Paine argued, essentially, for all power to be held by representative bodies that were to be elected by the people—a President and Congress. No one should be born into government, as in the British House of Lords, or appointed to government. Paine's argument went well beyond Locke's cautious constitutional monarchy and democracy for the conventionally propertied. For Paine, if Locke was right and the most fundamental form of property was a person's own body and abilities, then even the wage worker performing labour for a livelihood owned 'property'. Paine asserted: 'It is property to him; he has acquired it; and it is as much the object of his protection as exterior property.'[65]

When the American Constitution was ratified in 1787, Jefferson's phrase 'Life, Liberty and the Pursuit of Happiness' from the Declaration of Independence was replaced by 'Life, Liberty, and Property' in the Fifth Amendment of the Constitution:

We hold these truths to be self-evident, that all men are created equal, that they are endowed by their Creator with certain unalienable Rights, that among these are Life, Liberty and the pursuit of Happiness. That to secure these rights, Governments are instituted among Men, deriving their just powers from the consent of the governed, that whenever any Form of Government becomes destructive of these ends, it is the Right of the People to alter or to abolish it, and to institute new Government. . . . [From the American Declaration of Independence, 1776]

No person shall be held to answer for a capital, or otherwise infamous crime, unless on a presentment or indictment of a Grand Jury, except in cases arising in the land or naval forces, or in the Militia, when in actual service in time of War or public danger; nor shall any person be subject for the same offence to be twice put in jeopardy of life or limb; nor shall be compelled in any criminal case to be a witness against himself, nor be deprived of life, liberty, or property, without due process of law; nor shall private property be taken for public use, without just compensation. [Amendment V, from 'The Bill of Rights', the first 10 Amendments to the Constitution of the United States of America]

The altered phrase, however, represented more than the interests of the small elite who owned considerable wealth. A wide stratum of small property holders existed in the United States, consisting of independent farmers in the countryside and crafts workers, merchants, and artisans in the cities. As Zinn notes, 'This was a larger base of support for government than anywhere in the world at the end of the eighteenth century.'[66]

The American government subsequently broadened the popular appeal of the Constitution when the first Congress passed a series of amendments known as the 'Bill of Rights' extending people's liberties to free speech, a free press, freedom to assemble, and so on. Predictably, American democracy was still fundamentally limited. Property qualifications generally circumscribed the right of many men to vote. In addition, women, African Americans held as slaves, and Native Americans all were excluded from government.

THE STATUS OF WOMEN

Political liberalism in the United States surpassed its modest beginnings in England. As this list of excluded groups demonstrates, however, traditional ideas about women tended to persist even while the position of women in society was changing. In new times, traditional arguments have to be couched in different terms. Locke speculated that a man should not be in the position of an absolute monarch in the household and women should be, 'in many cases', at 'Liberty to separate from him'. Nevertheless, he left no doubt where authority resided. While wives could have different understandings and different wills from their husbands, like a nation, a household should have a single purpose and viewpoint. Consequently, he reasoned, since it was 'necessary, that the last determination, *i.e.* the Rule, should be placed somewhere, it naturally falls to the Man's share, as the abler and the stronger'.[67]

Medieval views on gender differences persisted into the eighteenth century and beyond. The place of women in this universe was clearly secondary, as the Biblical story of the creation of Eve from Adam's rib exemplified. This medieval view was structured around a set of permanent dualisms, a gendered *ying* and *yang*. The male form had been conceived in the image of the deity. Like God, the male was one, unique, and universal. Man was 'mind' and 'spirit', represented by reason, judgement, self-control, and order; woman was 'matter', flesh, the body, and appetite, represented by emotion, mercy, lust, desire, and disorder. The female principle was associated with detail, accessory, ornament, and style; the male with intelligence, abstraction, logic, and philosophy. As Bloch asserted, 'form and matter, activity and passivity, soul and flesh' were 'gendered male and female from the beginning'.[68] These dualisms persisted from the ancient to the modern world, as the distrust of the senses was linked to distrust of the feminine.[69]

The mind and body were not simply a duality but a hierarchy, a view derived from Plato. The body was the seat of the passions or appetites. As on the great chain of being, higher placement implied superiority. Hence the brain was located above the heart, and the sexual passions originated low in the body. In their possession of appetites, humans were not different from animals whose behaviour was controlled by their natural drives. In her lamentation on 'the evils of the civil war', the early anti-war social theorist, Christine de Pisan, asked rhetorically how the human heart could 'make men revert to the nature of a voracious and cruel beast?' Men had been transformed into serpents and had become 'the enemy of humankind'. Unlike animals, humans had the potential to be rational[70] and restrain their passions. In Iago's words, the rational mind should be able to 'cool our raging motions' (Box 3.4). Ironically, Iago used his power of reason to inflame rather than cool Othello's passion until he was blinded by jealousy. Humans were differentiated from 'natural agents' such as the beasts because they possessed free will, but this made them capable equally of good or evil.

From this ideological foundation, it was assumed that women were unfit for political and public roles, and were naturally confined to the private, domestic sphere. Rubinstein argues that, by the age of liberalism, the position of women—especially upper- and middle-class women—had actually deteriorated from the times of Chaucer and Shakespeare. Women's economic independence had been greatly eroded. Feminist scholarship has concluded that the subordination of women in the early modern era may be attributed in part to the persecution of strong, independent women as 'witches'.[71]

As the status of women declined, their occupation was reduced to preparing for marriage, guarding their reputation for chastity, and attempting to make the most advantageous match possible.[72] To exemplify this attitude, Rubinstein cited a passage from the essayist Addison, for whom women were 'beautiful romantic animal[s]' whose chief employment in life was 'the right adjustment of their hair'. The proper sphere for women was the private household; their virtues were entirely domestic. Women were to distinguish themselves as 'tender mothers and faithful wives'.[73] Addison's contemporary, the early social theorist Mary Astell,

> **Box 3.4**
>
> Shakespeare foreshadows Othello's tragedy in an ironic modality, putting these words in the mouth of the character who would later destroy his beloved Desdemona and hence himself by inciting his jealousy, causing him to abandon his own power to reason.
>
> *Iago*: 'Our bodies are our gardens, to the which our wills are gardeners; so that if we will plant nettles, or sow lettuce ... either to have it sterile with idleness, or manured with industry, why, the power and corrigible authority of this lies in our wills. If the balance of our lives had not one scale of reason to poise another of sensuality, the blood and baseness of our natures would conduct us to most preposterous conclusions: but we have reason to cool our raging motions, our carnal stings, our unbitted lusts. . . .'
>
> —William Shakespeare, *Othello*, I, iii

repudiated the 'contemptible opinion' men held about women. Men looked down on women, she said, 'as void of understanding, full of ignorance and passion, so that folly and a woman are equivalent terms'. Astell wanted husbands to respect their wives rather than treat them as slaves to their will, assuming they had 'no higher end than to serve and obey' them. It was no wonder, she said, that women did not respond to their husbands with gratitude but, rather, resentment.[74] For an independent and intellectual woman like Astell, the assumption of intellectual inferiority and servitude was particularly galling.

These traditional ideas about women would persist in various forms into the twentieth century. However, much earlier there were alternative, liberal voices, among men and women. Various forms of radicalism emerge in revolutionary situations. Ideas of insubordination, Rowbotham asserts,[75] aroused women to express demands publicly in the seventeenth century. 'Impudent lasses' petitioned Parliament for the release of the Leveller leader, Lilburne, who had been imprisoned for publishing pamphlets demanding greater liberty. The 'lasses' asserted that women were not so stupid as to just 'sit and keep at home' when their peace and welfare were being 'trod underfoot by force or arbitrary power'. Their rebellion, however, was largely moral and few made any claims

to equal the political power of men. Their most radical demand was for the right to be educated, a liberal demand that was endorsed by some men.

Daniel Defoe, for example, argued towards the end of the seventeenth century that the difference between men and women was largely one of education:

> I have often thought of it as one of the most barbarous customs in the world considering us as a civilized and a Christian country, that we deny the advantages of learning to women. We reproach the sex every day with folly and impertinence, while I am confident that, had they the advantages of education equal to us, they would be guilty of less than ourselves.
>
> One would wonder, indeed, how it should happen that women are conversible at all, since they are only beholding to natural parts for their knowledge [denied formal education]. Their youth is spent to teach them to stitch and sew, or make baubles. They are taught to read, indeed, and perhaps to write their names, or so; and this is the height of a woman's education. And I would but ask any who slight the sex for their understanding, what is a man (a gentleman, I mean) good for, that is taught no more?[76]

Women's perspective, as exemplified by the views of Christine de Pisan (see Chapter Two), were shaped by the overwhelmingly domestic role assigned to women and the varying degrees of legal restraint imposed on their actions and their bodies. Thomas Jefferson praised American women, who confined themselves to domestic duties, as angels in contrast to the Amazon women in Paris, who were too involved in politics (Box 3.5).[77]

When eighteenth-century women did adopt a social theory, McDonald argues, their views were rooted in mutual obligations, love, and empathy, reflecting their domestic and familial roles. The early liberals, in contrast, postulated an original, asocial, solitary, and individualistic human nature that acted on the basis of self-interest and created society from fear.[78]

Most women who wrote during the English Revolution and the period of the Restoration (1660–89) were conservative and royalist in their opinions, reflecting their upper-class origins. Traditional theorists emphasized the importance of obligations and the duties owed by subordinates to authority, and justified social inequalities as reflecting the divine principle of hierarchy. The social theory of Mary Astell (1668–1721), however, voiced the conservative principles of religion and monarchy, but also drew from Christian ideology the fundamental tenets of justice and essential equality.

Mary Astell

The demand for women's equality in the public sphere, which culminated in the twentieth century with women's success in winning the vote, was beyond the horizon of most women in the early eighteenth century. If a woman's social perspective was shaped by her domestic role, she was unlikely to perceive that women could shoulder a full share of the public role monopolized by men, although the author of *Women Not Inferior* made this claim anonymously in 1739.[79] Even if women's inferior position was not in itself unjust, the conditions of women's subordinate role could be made less unjust. The wrongs that were done to women within their domestic role could be challenged without calling into question the whole framework of authority that had, as its justification, the weight of tradition as well as the laws of government and religion. The socially unequal position of women could be reformed, if not overthrown.

Astell accepted as natural and right that some should be placed in positions of authority over others, 'from the throne to every private family'. For Christians, it is 'unnatural . . . to disobey those whom Christ instituted to *have rule over them*'. In her view, it was better to submit to injustice than rebel against authority. Seeing this arrangement from the point of view of the subordinate, Astell asserted that, although the powerful were placed

---

Box 3.5

Men, women, children talk nothing else [in Paris but politics]. . . . But our good ladies, I trust, have been too wise to wrinkle their foreheads with politics. They are contented to soothe & calm the minds of their husbands returning ruffled from political debate. They have the good sense to value domestic happiness above all others. . . . Recollect the women of this capital [Paris] . . . hunting pleasure in the streets, in routs & assemblies, and forgetting that they have left it behind them in their nurseries; compare them with our own countrywomen occupied in the tender and tranquil amusements of domestic life, and confess that it is a comparison of Amazons and Angels.

—Thomas Jefferson, letter to Anne Willing Bingham, 1788

in their exalted position by the grace of the deity, they owed 'brotherly affection' to their social inferiors. If the powerful conferred equity and justice on those beneath them rather than fulfilling their own pleasures or will, the governed would 'respect their governors as placed in God's stead' and offer a 'cheerful and ready compliance'.[80] Astell appealed to the powerful on the basis of morality and religious sentiments, hoping they would voluntarily change their own behaviour.

Consistent with women's domestic role, Astell did not theorize from the vantage point of individuals. Her Christian principles suggested to her that she was part of a great whole and that the interests of society were paramount. It was morally good 'to pursue . . . that which is the most public, universal and greatest good' 'without regarding any particular or separate interest'. For Astell, 'the good of the *many* is preferable to the good of a *few* or of *one* . . . the public before the private', from which principle she derived the conclusion that it was right to submit to authority even if it resulted in injustice for yourself. The individual should never put her or his interests ahead of the good of the community.

> [I]t is better that I endure the unreasonableness, injustice or oppression of a parent, a master etc. than that the established rule of order and good government should be superseded on my account. . . . It is better that I should submit to an unjust sentence . . . and that these private persons though ever so innocent should suffer than that the majesty of government, and herein the divine authority, should be violated and the public should be disturbed. . . . [I]t is fit that . . . I should suffer some real wants than that, by invading my neighbour's property, the laws of society and good government should be broken.[81]

In privileging the society over the individual, Astell reflected her conservative, royalist inclinations.

Astell's principle—that morality implied seeking the good of the greatest number—would later be adopted by liberal theorists under the doctrine of utilitarianism. However, Astell added a more critical twist to this doctrine. Basing her argument once again on Christian principles, she asserted that the rights of her neighbour were more important than her own desires or appetites. 'It is much better that I should want [go without] some of the conveniences of life than that any of my neighbours should want the necessities.'[82] Even so, this merely implied that the rich ought to offer Christian charity to the poor. Only extreme inequalities did Astell find immoral. She accepted the traditional belief that social distinctions of rank were natural and in accordance with the divine plan. The rich had necessities about which the poor couldn't even be aware. For some upper-class people, what might appear to others as a luxury was a necessity. The social rank in which the deity has placed us affords unequal 'necessities and moderate conveniences'. If you hold a position of authority, it is required that you demonstrate the 'trappings' of 'splendour and show . . . to raise a veneration in the vulgar [common people] who won't be moved by better reasons.' Astell was not a social leveller. Nevertheless, she argued it is not 'charity but justice that requires' us to give to our neighbours that which we cannot use. In a later, revolutionary age, Mary Wollstonecraft would take up this refrain.

Abigail Adams

The liberal demand for the formal recognition of the rights of women, which would be made forcefully during the French Revolution late in the eighteenth century, had been voiced earlier (1739) by Sophia in *Women Not Inferior*:

> [T]here is no *science, office* or *dignity* which women do not have an equal right to share in with the *men*. Since there can be no superiority but that of brutal strength shown in the latter to entitle them to engross all *power* and *prerogative* to themselves, nor any incapacity proved in the *former* to disqualify them of their right but what is owing to the unjust oppression of the men, and might be easily removed.[83]

Women formulated clearly the demand for political equality during the American Revolution. While some women were dramatically active in battle during the revolutionary war, women's resistance to British authority took other forms, such as smuggling food to guerrilla rebels and spying on the enemy. As in any war, women maintained the home—at a time when much of the national economy was centred in the household—through seven years of warfare.[84]

Among the talented women who managed the family farm, raised children, and supported the revolutionary cause was Abigail Adams. Hampered by a lack of formal education, Adams nevertheless aspired to exercise some political authority—a right that was denied to all women. Her husband, John Adams, was a member of the Convention that drew up the new Constitution of the American Republic. Writing to him in 1776, Abigail Adams asked that the Convention include the rights of women. Among other revolutionary slogans, the American rebels were arguing that they should not be governed by laws they did not have a voice in making: there should be 'no taxation without representation'. It was obvious to Abigail Adams that women were in the same position vis-à-vis men as were the Americans vis-à-vis the British. In a letter to John Adams in the revolutionary year of 1776, using the very arguments of the American revolutionary men, Abigail Adams asked:

> in the new code of laws which I suppose it will be necessary for you to make, I desire you would remember the ladies and be more generous and favourable to them than your ancestors! Do not put such unlimited power in the hands of husbands. Remember all men would be tyrants if they could. If particular care and attention is not paid to the ladies, we are determined to foment a rebellion, and will not hold ourselves bound by any laws in which we have no voice or representation.[85]

As the British tried to lord it over the Americans, Abigail Adams concluded—linking one struggle with the other—men were tyrants in their rule over women.

John Adams considered his wife's request 'extraordinary'. He replied that the example of the American Revolution 'had loosened the bonds of government everywhere'—that even 'children and apprentices . . . Indians and Negroes grow insolent.' And now, this 'insolence' had grown among women. However, he flatly declared, men were not about to repeal their 'masculine systems'. John Adams concluded with a final statement that twisted the argument in favour of men: wives were the real tyrants over their husbands. Women exercised their power behind the scenes, in the private sphere, where they influenced their husbands. This was the 'despotism of the petticoat', in John Adams's words. Giving women equal political power as citizens in addition to their supposed personal influence would not be in the interests of men.[86]

NATURAL LAW AND SLAVERY

Among the controversial practices that capitalists either created or transformed to suit their purposes, one of the most vicious was the slave trade. The real test for liberalism comes when groups espousing its principles achieve social power. Principle is sacrificed for expediency when the interest of the dominant group is incompatible with the demands for liberty from those beneath them. The survival of liberalism over the centuries is a tribute to its flexibility. It was compatible with religion, as long as church and state were separated. Monarchy was acceptable, provided that the interests of property owners were paramount. The oppression of women, minorities, and foreign nations was tolerable as long as domination could be rationalized as being in their best interest.

The commercial bourgeoisie in the English ports benefited substantially from the North Atlantic slave trade and tended to oppose any government plan to limit, regulate, or eliminate this trade in 'human resources' (to use a contemporary phrase). Even so, the issue of slavery was not ideologically polarized. Locke had claimed that captives who were taken in a 'just war' were 'by the

Right of Nature' under the absolute and arbitrary power of their master. They had 'forfeited their Lives, and with it their Liberties, and lost their Estates' and were then bound 'in the *State of Slavery*' and were not to be considered part of civil society.[87] Many other liberal theorists had argued the anti-slavery cause, including Montesquieu in the *Spirit of the Laws* (1748) and Adam Smith in *Theory of Moral Sentiments* (1764). In addition, many of the most determined opponents of slavery were Christians, although others selectively used religious arguments to support the practice.

Rubinstein shows that the Tory Samuel Johnson believed Africans had a 'natural right . . . to liberty and independence'. Johnson didn't wish to hear news of new geographical discoveries because, he said, 'I am always afraid they will end in conquest and robbery.' In his ironic way, Johnson pointed out the hypocrisy of the liberals who were making demands for ever greater 'freedom' for themselves while they were buying and selling slaves: 'How is it we hear the loudest yelps for liberty among the drivers of the Negroes?'[88]

The liberal Boswell responded to Johnson's attacks on the slave trade by offering the most basic rationalizations for it: slavery was the will of God, Africans were better off under European domination, the slaves were the *property* of the English bourgeoisie, and therefore the government must protect a person's property:

> To abolish a status which in all ages GOD has sanctioned and man has continued would not only be robbery to an innumerable class of our fellow subjects; but it would be an extreme cruelty to the African savages, a large portion of whom it saves from massacre, or intolerable bondage in their own country, and introduces into a much happier state of life . . . to abolish that trade would be to shut the gates of mercy on mankind.[89]

Much social thought in the eighteenth century (of sometimes a liberal and other times a Tory stripe) tended to justify the slave trade and colonialism, which were of great economic importance to the European elites. In England, the revenue from the slave trade was generally regarded as benefiting the nation as a whole. While he was not a consistent advocate of enslavement, Daniel Defoe made the common argument that the slave trade was both highly profitable as well as being necessary and beneficial for English commerce generally and for the employment of the poor in England in particular.[90] West Indian historian Eric Williams claims that the profits from the slave trade formed the foundation for the Industrial Revolution.[91]

A variety of grounds were used to support the argument that races were inherently unequal, including the authority of the Bible. Locke had argued that the dark skin and other physical characteristics of Africans and Aboriginal Americans were external signs of their innate inferiority. One theoretical justification for slavery denied that Africans were fully human, a position that undermined even the civilizing impulse.

In his very popular novel *Robinson Crusoe*, Daniel Defoe argued a modern, relativist position on slavery and the nature of Native society. The fictional Crusoe had several close encounters with enslavement. On an early voyage to the coast of Guinea, Crusoe was captured and made a 'miserable slave' by a Moor—a considerable reversal of fortune for the English merchant, although realistically the fate of thousands of Europeans who were captured in raids and sold into slavery in northern Africa.

Following his escape, Crusoe becomes the owner of a small tobacco plantation in Brazil and quickly prospers. Knowing that for 'trifles' it was possible to purchase 'Negroes, for the service of the Brasils, in great numbers', he embarks with a crew for the Guinea coast, the ill-fated voyage on which Crusoe was marooned. The evil that God punished by this disaster, Crusoe reasons, was not the buying of slaves; he had failed to act as a prudent, cautious businessman. Rather than investing with his partners in a 'supra-cargo to Guinea, to fetch Negroes, . . . patience and time would so have increased our stock at home, that we could have bought them at our own door, from those whose business it was to fetch them.'[92]

Making the distinction between civilization and savagery more relative than absolute was one of the liberal social themes Defoe elaborated in *Robinson Crusoe*. Although the Natives who visit periodically his deserted island are cannibals, Crusoe realizes their habits are 'customary among the people of their nation' and best left to God to judge.[93] They were no more murderers than those Christians who 'put to death the prisoners taken in battle', and no worse than the Spaniards who committed atrocities against the Native people of the New World. The destruction of millions 'of these people' was 'a meer butchery, a bloody and unnatural piece of cruelty, unjustifiable either to God or man.'[94] In extreme circumstances, Christians also had resorted to cannibalism.

The differences in culture between Europeans and the American 'savages' did not reflect a different human nature; each had the same capacity for rationality and goodness. The Native Americans possessed 'the same powers, the same reason, the same affections, the same sentiments of kindness and obligation, the same passions and resentments of wrongs, the same sense of gratitude, sincerity, fidelity, and all the capacities of doing good and receiving good' that Europeans claimed.[95] The problem, Defoe believed, was that Natives were culturally inferior, giving Europeans an obligation to bring civilization to them. When, after more than two decades on the island, he rescued the Native man he called Friday, Crusoe endeavoured to be a benevolent and lenient master, undertaking the civilizing mission of instructing Friday in Protestantism and practical training. While Defoe rejected any claims that Native Americans were essentially inferior by nature, the similarity between his sympathetic portrayal of the Native population and Boswell's blunt justifications for slavery is that both assumed that Europeans ought to undertake what came to be called the 'white man's burden' to bring the Native population under the domination of the Christian Church and the white plantation owner. Africans would be safer and happier under English law and the Gospel.[96]

Among the supporters of slavery there was a minority sentiment that suggested the 'civilizing mission' of Europeans was better undertaken by way of education and charity than enslavement and exploitation. This more radical view was bolstered by Rousseau's conception of the 'noble savage'. For Rousseau, civilization had brought destruction to natural humanity—the Native populations had been better off without European 'help'.

The liberal economist Adam Smith, on the other hand, provided a rational, economic argument against slavery, claiming that it was inefficient. Although the work done by slaves, Smith asserts, appears to be inexpensive since they are given nothing other than bare subsistence, slavery 'is in the end the dearest of any' system of labour. 'A person who can acquire no property, can have no other interest but to eat as much and labour as little as possible.'[97] Under the rationalist interpretation that Smith usually employs, slavery should not exist at all if it is an inefficient form of production. As the root cause of slavery, however, Smith posited the existence of a non-economic human trait that sometimes overshadows the natural propensity to 'truck, barter, and exchange'. For Smith, human pride 'makes him love to domineer'. Nothing 'mortifies him so much as to be obliged to condescend to persuade his inferiors. Wherever the law allows it, and the nature of the work can afford it, therefore, he will generally prefer the service of slaves to that of free men.'[98]

The apparent exception to Smith's assertion was the colony of Pennsylvania, where the Quakers had emancipated their slaves. Smith attributed this act, not to their religious charity, but to a rational, economic motive. They were largely independent farmers who grew grain on small landholdings, unsuitable for a large amount of slave labour. Had the number of slaves represented 'any considerable part of their property', they would not have been freed. On the large sugar and tobacco estates in the West Indies, where slaves did all or most of the work, the profits were much higher and there was no movement towards the emancipation of slaves.[99] As long as slavery was efficient, as it was in the West Indies where the slave trade procured a sufficient supply of coerced labour, there were no economic arguments that could be successfully advanced against it.

Early American Abolitionism

Not simply arguments, but a vigorous movement to end the degrading practice of human slavery arose during the anti-colonial struggle in North America. Many social theorists of the time were aware of the deep contradiction between the colonists' fight for freedom from tyranny and the theory of natural rights that supported it, and the existence of slavery. Radical sentiments during an age of revolution are not confined to the narrow causes that give them birth. In addition to moral arguments, support for black emancipation as a 'natural right' was predicated on the belief that the degraded condition of Africans in America resulted from environmental causes and social conditioning, and not innate racial inferiority.[100] Many religious leaders added their voice to the call for emancipation. While the Quakers were the only organized religious body to forbid the ownership of slaves among its members, in other denominations some leaders debated the issues and advocated an end to the 'communal sin'.[101]

Nash argues that the anti-slavery feeling was widespread during the revolutionary era in the North and also in the key southern states of Virginia and Maryland. The Continental Congress held a debate on slavery and the slave trade, recommending the suppression of the trade.[102] It was easier to gain approval of measures to stop the importation of slaves, even though many northern merchants grew rich from the slave trade, because it did not challenge the immediate interests of slave owners. In 1776, Thomas Jefferson drafted a bill in Virginia that would have emancipated all slaves who were born after his new law was enacted. The bill included a provision for the education of ex-slaves at state expense and a proposal to remove them to a new land.[103] It was a curious mixture of enlightened humanitarianism and racism. Jefferson was a slave owner who believed that blacks were innately inferior.

From the point of view of many African Americans, emancipation was not a gift to be bestowed on a passive people. Revolutionary ideology, in its widest application, necessarily implies the equality of races. Black **abolitionists**, such as Phyllis Wheatley, actively pursued the cause of emancipation during the upheavals of the revolutionary war.

> God has implanted a Principle, which we call love of freedom; it is impatient of Oppression. And pants for Deliverance; and by the leave of our modern Egyptians I will assert, that the same principle lives in us.[104]

Thousands of slaves, especially the more physically able, accepted the British offer of freedom and ran away from the plantations, settling in eastern and central Canada. Others adopted the language of natural rights and enlightenment, and petitioned state legislatures for their freedom on the grounds of both reason and personal revelation. By 1787, political expediency had gained the upper hand over anti-slavery idealism. The Constitutional Convention ensured the lawfulness of slave ownership in the new United States and protected the slave trade for 20 years.[105] The American political system rested on a coalition of northern business leaders and the southern, slaveholding planter class—a new aristocracy of wealth and an aristocracy of landed gentry.

Among the most eloquent spokespersons for black equality was the mathematician and surveyor, Benjamin Banneker, who was appointed to survey the new city of Washington.[106] Writing to Thomas Jefferson, among the more liberal of the American revolutionaries despite his published race prejudices, Banneker 'freely and cheerfully acknowledged' that he was 'of the African race, and in that color which is natural to them of the deepest dye.' Banneker said that he belonged to 'a race of beings, who have long labored under the abuse and censure of the world; . . . long been looked upon with an eye of contempt; and . . . long been considered rather as brutish than human, and scarcely capable of mental endowments.'

Despite these 'absurd and false ideas and opinions' that prevailed about African Americans, Banneker believed that Jefferson was more flexible in his opinions. He would agree that both races had been made of one flesh by a single universal God who had endowed both with the same sensations and 'the same facilities'.[107]

Banneker appealed to Jefferson on the grounds of natural right, as reflected in the principles of the American Declaration of Independence, and on the grounds of morality. Once weaned away from his 'narrow prejudices', Banneker hoped he would bring justice and Christian relief to African Americans who were under 'groaning captivity and cruel oppression'. Pricking his personal conscience, Banneker reminded Jefferson that he was a member of a class that had 'been found guilty of the most criminal act, which you professedly detested in others, with respect to yourselves.'[108] Like many in the elite minority he represented, Jefferson was a slave owner and fathered a line of interracial descendants.

However much Jefferson's sentiments may have been 'concurrent' with Banneker's, practical judgement led Jefferson to allow the historical opportunity to embed racial equality in the American Constitution to pass him by. Nash notes, however, that Jefferson replied graciously to Banneker, reiterating the liberal argument that environment caused racial inequalities and acknowledging that 'nature has given to our black brethren talents equal to those' of other colours.[109] Appealing to the elite on the basis of reason had met the predictable result. As a political leader in a time of crisis, Jefferson had been concerned more with white solidarity in the face of England's intransigence and North–South unity than with the future of black slaves. Liberals were more comfortable with pious hopes than concerted action. Since the tide of public opinion appeared to be turning in favour of emancipation, they pragmatically hoped that individual slave owners would succumb to an enlightened view and voluntarily manumit their slaves.[110]

Despite the stirrings of abolitionism in the United States during the American Revolution and the acceleration, for a time, of the individual manumission of many African Americans, the conditions of African Americans did not improve in the new republic. The political and social elite that emerged from the war for independence represented a compromise between a merchant class in the North and the slave-owning plantation owners in the South. Both slavery and the slave trade were guaranteed to continue in the new nation.

Outside the United States, a more receptive group was inspired by the demands for equality emanating from the North. The call to liberation would be answered by enslaved Africans toiling under the harsh regime of French colonialism in the West Indies, as Haiti followed the example of the 13 colonies, fighting a successful war for independence and establishing the first black republic.

As cotton became king in the southern United States, slavery became institutionalized in custom and law. This fundamental and absolute inequality is the foundation of all subsequent race relations in the United States. The existence of slavery in America violently flaunted the liberal principles of the new republic. One of the logical consequences of the liberal doctrine of natural law was the condemnation of slavery. If all people were essentially equal according to a natural right, then this doctrine should be applied equally to black as well as white. The black abolitionist Frederick Douglass expressed in his Fourth of July oration in 1852 the essential incompatibility of the principles of American republicanism, enshrined in the Constitution, with the existence of legal slavery:

> What, to the American slave, is your 4th of July? I answer; a day that reveals to him, more than all other days in the year, the gross injustice and cruelty to which he is the constant victim. To him, your celebration is a sham; your boasted liberty, an unholy license; your national greatness, swelling vanity; your sounds of rejoicing are empty and heartless; your denunciation of tyrants, brass-fronted impudence; your shouts of liberty and equality, hollow mockery; your prayers and hymns,

. . . mere bombast, fraud, deception, impiety, and hypocrisy—a thin veil to cover up crimes which would disgrace a nation of savages. There is not a nation on the earth guilty of practices, more shocking and bloody, than are the people of these United States, at this very hour.[111]

The early abolitionist movement that had sprung from the ideals of the American Revolution withered in the face of southern opposition and northern self-interest. Many northern abolitionists could not part with their slaves and the abolition acts passed in the North were steeped in hypocritical gradualism, often postponing manumission to future generations. Nash argues that two concrete and thorny problems accounted for the failure of emancipation in the North during the revolutionary era. The first was economic. Throughout its birth and evolution, liberalism embraced the rights of property as inextricably linked with human rights more generally. This was the heart of the contradiction between republican ideology and the persistence of slavery. If a government deprived a person of her or his property, this violation of human rights could be just in principle only if it was accompanied by monetary compensation equal in value to the property lost. Although practicable schemes for federal funding existed, Nash argues, the cause of emancipation was abandoned by northerners and slavery remained a matter of the right of individual states.[112]

Even if African Americans were emancipated and slave owners generously compensated for their economic losses, the second horn of the dilemma pricked even deeper. What was to become of the freed blacks? The abolitionist sentiment, Nash argues, went beyond the desire to be 'quit of slavery' and wished as well to be 'quit of blacks'. Emancipation would be predicated on returning Africans to their homeland or finding some alternative form of segregation, a position that Jefferson had endorsed earlier. Whites' fears of blacks were sharply intensified by the slave revolt and revolution in Saint Domingue, in the West Indies, which erupted in 1791. The Virginia abolitionist St George Tucker warned white Americans that 'if something is not done, and done soon, we shall be the murderers of our own children . . .; the revolutionary storm, now sweeping the globe, will be upon us.'[113]

Fear fostered prejudice and violence, directed particularly against the free black population who lived in communities alongside those of whites and who were included in the proposed schemes of forced emigration. As slavery was further institutionalized in the South by the rise of the cotton industry, made possible by Whitney's invention and by northern investment, in the North, Nash writes, the embers of abolitionism 'ceased to glow', being replaced by 'a belligerent **white supremacism**' that quickly became violent. Following the War of 1812, white mobs attacked black neighbourhoods and burned black churches. Social theory went hand in hand with discrimination, as a new spate of racist essays were published in the North asserting that both African Americans and Native Americans were not 'genetically endowed for citizenship'.[114]

In the end, however, principle was sacrificed to expediency and slavery persisted and spread. By the early decades of the nineteenth century, slavery was deeply institutionalized in the South and, despite the evolution of legal emancipation in the North, white prejudice and discrimination brought about a de facto segregation of African Americans and perpetuated their second-class conditions and opportunities.

The domination and exploitation of non-European peoples were extremely profitable. The Atlantic slave trade and the West Indian plantation economy it supported were crucial components of the early expansion of capitalism. In brief, powerful vested interests wished to continue slavery. While Africans may be human beings, they argued, they were nevertheless inferior. Authorities such as Aristotle, who believed in natural inequality, and passages from the Bible were invoked to support the contention of natural inequality. Locke had argued that non-whites were essentially inferior and that external appearances were indications of this otherwise invisible condition.

In England, many of the pro-capitalist writers also justified the slave trade as profitable, or necessary, or even beneficial for the Africans. Many of the authors who minimized the inhumanity of slavery, claiming that it taught Africans the benefits of hard labour, directly or indirectly profited from the trade.[115] Madame Jeanne-Marie Roland, however, saw that slaves and slaveholders were equally degraded, if for differing reasons:

> Slavery and virtue are incompatible. Slavery breaks all the ties that connect man with his fellow creature. It releases and destroys the two springs that contribute most to the development of our faculties: self-esteem and glory. . . . It lets nothing subsist but odious force and degrading fear.
>
> Tyranny degrades equally the one who exercises it and the one who is enslaved by it; by it all lose the sentiments of truth, the idea of justice and the taste of good.[116]

In this context, applying the doctrine of natural rights to African people was socially progressive.

CONCLUSION

Voltaire is at once one of the principal spokesmen of the Enlightenment and, at the same time, expresses pessimism about the prospects of rationalism. We should abandon social theory, he concludes, and merely cultivate our gardens, perhaps doing what we can to improve our immediate environment and elevate humanity one person at a time. A more general disillusionment with the Enlightenment would alight half a century later, when the revolutionary implications of the rationalist perspective were clear. The new Age of Reason, however, promised a great deal. As Thomas Mann described these claims: 'the powers of reason and enlightenment will in the end set humanity wholly free and lead it in the path of progress and civilization toward an ever brighter, milder, and purer light.'[117]

Already in the eighteenth century, with the Industrial Revolution barely underway, social critics were decrying the social consequences and attacking the new economic doctrines of liberalism. The star of laissez-faire was rising, though more slowly than some would have wished. It was obvious to the business class in emerging nations such as the United States that they would be better off with an interventionist government that was motivated to assist national industry as much as possible. While free trade may have remained a blueprint for a future economy, the most fundamental lesson of Smith's economics was written on the banner of free enterprise. Adam Smith was the *guru* of the rising capitalist class and his *Wealth of Nations*, frequently reprinted, was both fashionable and powerfully influential in shaping the ideology and class awareness of the capitalists.

The laws of economics developed by economists such as Smith were premised on an individualistic view of the world. People were assumed to act on the basis of rational choice to maximize their interests or utilities. As individuals made choices and acted on them, the patterns of economic life emerged, such as the price structure and the growth or decline of investment in certain industries. The social world was the sum of the independent actions of a multitude of freely acting individuals. This highly individualized and rationalistic model of human action would later be applied to social phenomena more generally.

Smith's model of laissez-faire capitalism dominated economic policy in capitalist nations until the Great Depression of the twentieth century demonstrated the self-destructive tendencies of free-enterprise capitalism. In place of laissez-faire a new model of economic policy known as 'welfare state capitalism' became the dominant form. With increased state intervention and regulation, some redistribution of income through taxation, and government-operated services such as socialized medicine, the new policy was an economic reversal of the principles advocated by Smith.

Since about 1980 and into the beginning of the twenty-first century, however, there has been a revival of laissez-faire economic policy, marked by the collapse of government welfare policies, deregulation of businesses, increasing free trade, and an emphasis on individualism and entrepreneurship. The modern prophets of laissez-faire, such as Milton Friedman and Michael Walker, champion the return of the dog-eat-dog world of competitive capitalism, now extended into globalization, where the gap between the rich and the poor grows locally and globally, and national governments find it more and more difficult to protect their communities and citizens from the domination of powerful, global oligopolies.

4 ROUSSEAU, RIGHTS, AND REVOLUTION

At the beginning of the Enlightenment, there was a considerable distinction between 'high' (aristocratic) and 'low' (common) culture. The arts, such as music, painting, and architecture, catered to the expensive tastes of the upper class. Only the aristocrats had the time to cultivate what Voltaire regarded as genuine, refined taste[1] and the inclination to spend large sums of money on luxury consumption. This arrangement was fine for most of the master artists who sought sponsorship from individually rich patrons. The intellectuals of the age believed that the arts and literature could be reconstructed on the ideal basis of reason. The English poet, Alexander Pope, expressed several of the main tenets of the Enlightenment in his *Essay on Man*, endorsing modern humanism in the following couplet:

> Know then thyself, presume not God to scan;
> The proper study of Mankind is Man.

As painters and writers revived classical styles, many endowed their art with the weightier moral purposes of instruction and education. In contrast to aristocratic art, which was designed primarily for pleasure and **aesthetic** enjoyment, Enlightenment artists added a social purpose: to expose the vices and frivolous nature of the life of the upper class. Alexander Pope's lengthy satirical poem, *The Rape of the Lock*, ridiculed pompous, affected, and shallow aristocratic values. Art should represent social values and inspire people to virtue and effort.

The attempt to apply rationality to art was a common characteristic of the artistic style called **neo-classicism**. Certain literary or artistic conventions were propagated as the standards of correct form. In drama, plays were to be of a specific type, a tragedy or a comedy, for example, and each was to imitate a designated structure and form divided into acts and scenes, building to a climax and followed by a resolution. Writers were to compose specific types of poems, such as odes or sonnets, each with its own rules. Many neo-classical writers adopted the rhyming couplet: two lines of poetry, each written in iambic pentameter (lines of five pairs of syllables, each of the vocal pattern: unstressed-stressed). The couplet, such as the one above from Pope, was to introduce a thought on the first line and then complete it on the second line. This form of neo-classical poetry was symmetrical, orderly, balanced, and avoided undisciplined emotion and imagination.[2]

Parallel standards of rational structure were imposed on the other arts, such as architecture, music, and painting. Neo-classical architecture was characterized by the use of Greek columns and symmetrical, proportional designs in such public buildings as museums and churches, and in private homes, exemplified by the Georgian-style row houses of the Circus in the city of Bath. These elegant row houses were designed for the new gentry. The movement to improve nature that developed in the Renaissance was also reflected in the further evolution of formal 'gardens'—carefully planned collections of plants symmetrically arranged outside the houses on the estates of the upper class, and imitated by the middle class. Nature itself was to be reshaped and reorganized according to rational principles of beauty.

The defining concepts of neo-classicism in France were order, balance, and proportion, producing, in Kennedy's view, an art of ideals, principles, and fixed rules. Reason applied to painting declared that the purpose was to portray ideas, such as ideal beauty or truth, through the use of symbols or idealized portraits. The aristocratic culture of eighteenth-century France was condemned for its 'artifice, sensation, and pleasure' and derided as particularly 'feminine', as distinct from the masculine values of action, virtue, and progress. In the Enlightenment, the courtly culture was criticized for producing 'effeminized' men.[3]

The most famous painter identified with the neo-classical style in France was Jacques Louis David (1748–1825). With David, the critical side of the Enlightenment is apparent in such works as *The Oath of the Horatii* (1785) and *Brutus* (1789). The first illustrated the classical Roman story of three sons vowing an oath to defend the Roman republic with their lives; the second recounted the return of Brutus's sons who were about to be executed on their father's orders for betraying the republic. Neo-classical art was inspired by republican sentiments when the monarchy of Louis XVI and the Old Regime were still intact.[4]

For David, as Kennedy shows, the purpose of art was to penetrate the soul and make 'a profound impression on the mind'. By depicting heroism and civil virtues for the public gaze, the artist stimulates 'the passions of glory, of devotion for the welfare' of the nation.[5] In his *Death of Socrates* (1787), David portrays the moment when the great Greek educator, seen as the founder of reason, is about to drink poison. From the point of view of Enlightenment thinkers, Socrates had been convicted of impiety—disbelief in the gods—and of corrupting youth. He died a martyr for the cause of reason in opposition to superstition and arbitrary, corrupt authority. No more fitting subject could have been found for a pre-revolutionary, Enlightenment painting.

One exception to this stream of rationalism emerged as a school of painting that celebrated everyday life, honouring the heroism and reflecting the natural taste of common people. According to

this view, which may be regarded as pre-Romantic, intellectuals should produce art for the common folk that expressed their true sentiments.[6] The major inspiration for a more naturalistic art and social theory emerged from the writings of Jean-Jacques Rousseau (1712–78). Rousseau did not share the Enlightenment emphasis on reason. He condemned rather than celebrated the growth of civilization, praising instead the natural virtues of primitive humanity and the noble savage. Rousseau believed that society caused corruption. The most virtuous humans were the most natural and least 'civilized', those who trusted more to instinct than to rationality. In the aftermath of revolution, Rousseau would inspire the movement known as Romanticism.

JEAN-JACQUES ROUSSEAU

> Man was born free, and everywhere he is in chains.
> —Rousseau, *The Social Contract* (1762)

Jean-Jacques Rousseau died in 1778, on the eve of the French Revolution his ideas helped to bring about. But Rousseau had not been a violent revolutionist. His ideas had an enormous and varied appeal in the eighteenth century. A **deist** in the Enlightenment tradition, Rousseau worshipped the spirit of nature. In his view, both the natural world and the natural human being were essentially good. His discussion of the cause of social inequality, conflict, and the emergence of government inspired later revolutionaries and socialists. Rationalists of all kinds admired many of his progressive ideas on education and the educability of ordinary people. In his views on human nature, Rousseau was Romantic and anarchistic.

Rousseau was born in 1712 to a lower-middle-class family in the Swiss city of Geneva, at that time a city-state with its own government. His birthing killed his mother, so Jean-Jacques was raised by his father, 'a footloose, irresponsible, and tearful watchmaker',[7] who shared his love of reading with his son.[8] Throughout his life, Rousseau would be self-taught. He made his living as a tutor for wealthy families, became the lover of several upper-class, usually older, women, and found employment as a diplomatic secretary. Drawn to Paris at the age of 19, Rousseau's strongest impression was disgust for the 'dirty stinking little streets, ugly black houses, and aura of uncleanliness, poverty, beggars'.[9] As he matured, he deplored the extreme contrast he encountered in Paris between the ostentatious residences of the wealthy and the miserable hovels of the poor.

In the 1740s, Rousseau joined a circle of *philosophes* that included Voltaire and contributed entries to the great *Encyclopédie* project. He lived with Thérèse Levasseur, a young, uneducated woman with whom he had five children, all of whom were 'turned over to a foundling home'.[10] Rousseau's reputation, formed by his unusual lifestyle, was compounded by unorthodox ideas he expressed, for example, in his *Discourse on the Arts and Sciences* (1750), where he argued that the sciences and arts had contributed to the corruption rather than the purification of morals. Rousseau self-consciously defended this unpopular argument, stating he did not 'care about pleasing either the witty or the fashionable'. He was writing for posterity, for those beyond his century.[11] In the prize-winning *Discourse*, Rousseau developed his central thesis that humans were naturally good and became evil as a consequence of social institutions.[12] This unpopular argument did not make Rousseau sufficiently notorious to prevent King Louis XV from offering him a pension in 1752, as a reward for writing an opera the King had greatly admired. This income smacked so much of royal patronage that Rousseau claimed to be ill and left Paris. He preferred to repudiate the reward rather than, in his words, say 'farewell [to] truth, courage, liberty'.[13]

Over the next decades, Rousseau quarrelled with the leading *philosophes*. His notoriety was increased by his novel, *Julie* (1761), which included frank discussions of sexuality. In his autobiography (the *Confessions*), Rousseau exposed his troubled side—his affairs, his sado-masochism, and masturbation, as well as the sorry fate of his own children. His books were burned in Paris and

Geneva.[14] Rousseau's ideas escaped the conflagration, inspiring revolutions in and beyond his century in political ideology, education, and society.

The Origins of Inequality

Rousseau's *Discourse on the Origin and Foundations of Inequality Among Men* (1754) did not win a prize, but it solidified the author's reputation as a radical social theorist. Typical of a natural law argument, Rousseau began his theory by imagining humans living in a primitive condition as they were formed by nature, equal among themselves.[15] Humans in a natural state were endowed with two fundamental principles, the first of which was self-preservation. Humans were saved from the Hobbesian war of all against all because they also possessed a second impulse of compassion or natural pity, which Rousseau defined as 'a natural repugnance to seeing any sentient being, especially our fellow man, perish or suffer.'[16]

For Rousseau, the **state of nature** was a reasonable inference about what humans might have been if left to themselves.[17] Without instincts, humans learned what they needed to survive from their observations of nature, and had all their needs satisfied. Strong, robust, and self-confident, the original humans lived a simple, regular, and solitary lifestyle in which their desires did not extend beyond their physical needs.[18] Primitive humans would not have lived in nature simply as beasts, however. While animals follow their instincts when they feel the demands of nature, humans knew they were free to go along or to resist these natural impulses. Nevertheless, their horizon was limited to the here and now. They lacked imagination, had no conception of a future or of death, and had neither foresight nor curiosity. There was also no stable family life. Reproduction was a matter of brief and impermanent 'chance encounters, occasions and desire'.[19]

Solitary humans in a state of nature would have expressed the virtues of simplicity, modesty, and essential goodness. They 'knew neither vanity, nor deference, nor esteem, nor contempt'; they 'had not the slightest notion of mine and thine';

they had no true idea of justice and did not even dream of vengeance. Nor was their peaceful nature clouded by the strongest passions of sexual desire. In Rousseau's view, humans in a natural state would be satisfied solely by the physical acts of reproduction. They would neither experience love, as this term was understood in society, nor its counterpart, jealousy.[20] Individual, solitary, and indifferent to one another, they would not have possessed language. At this stage, 'love of well-being is the sole motive of human action.'[21] For Rousseau, 'Man is born free.' The more natural the human group, the less they were civilized, the less corrupt they were.

Ideally, they would have lived in a world where their simple needs would be satisfied by the resources of nature. The mythology of the Garden of Eden represented this hypothetical state. Unlike Eden, for Rousseau, the state of nature was permanent. There was no reason to wish for anything more and no possibility of imagining a different life: 'everything seems to remove savage man from the temptation and the means of ceasing to be a savage.'[22] In their primitive state, people had no vices, but neither could they develop virtue. Humans were potentially perfectible, but this potential was forever closed off; they were stuck in the sands of time.

Whence society, then? Rousseau suggests that two conditions were necessary to move humans from their original state. The first was communication that developed through relationships. As they learned to manipulate nature, people became self-conscious of their superiority over other animals, engendering the first stirrings of pride or vanity. Then, as humanity began to spread into new territories, there were occasions when mutual assistance was necessary and some occasions for competition.[23]

Rousseau located the origins of the family—the first important social institution at this early stage—as the only natural form of society.[24] Rousseau makes a considerable leap from the world of asocial mating, which he initially assumed, to the formation of relatively stable families, associated with common habitation in primitive huts. 'This was the period of a first revolution', which led to 'the distinction among families and introduced a kind of property', a distinction between yours and mine. The more humans interacted with each other, the more they learned to differentiate among themselves as being lesser or greater; they learned the ideas of merit and beauty. In this more settled, familial life, humans also would have experienced the first developments of the heart, by which Rousseau meant 'the sweetest sentiments' of 'conjugal love and paternal love'. From this developed the sexual division of labour and the beginning of the domestication of humanity. With slightly softer lives, humans began to lose their ferocity and vigour while simultaneously increasing their need for co-operative protection.[25]

From these simple, familial beginnings came bands, established rules of behaviour and customs, and eventually different national groups. As families and communities developed, people experienced love for one another as well as understanding and empathy. On the other hand, humans would also have felt envy of others, as 'jealousy awakens with love' and 'the sweetest passion receives sacrifices of human blood.'[26]

In these simple, communal villages, the first step towards inequality appeared as humans began to compete with each other over who was the most beautiful, who was the most accomplished, or the stronger, or most adroit. Some were esteemed more than others. From this competitive inequality grew vanity or shame about the self, and contempt or envy for others, the first human vices, which eventually 'produced compounds fatal to happiness and innocence.'[27]

Still, Rousseau argued, this small, simple society was perhaps the best for humanity. It was a middle position between the indolence of our primitive, original life and the egocentrism of civilization. When humans lived largely by their individual efforts, in a simple society, 'they lived as free, healthy, good and happy as they could.' With the emergence of society, however, 'equality disappeared, property came into existence, labor became necessary', and soon 'slavery and misery' followed. This great revolution was produced by the invention of agriculture and metallurgy.[28] From cultivation came the division of land and the exercise of a person's labour to produce a harvest. When this right was recognized from year to year, it became the concept of private property, a right that was social and not part of natural law. Social development led to the 'perfection of the individual' but, simultaneously, to the 'decay of the species'.

The first man who, having enclosed a piece of ground, to whom it occurred to say *this is mine*, and found people sufficiently simple to believe him, was the true founder of civil society. How many crimes, wars, murders, how many miseries and horrors Mankind would have been spared by him who, pulling up the stakes or filling in the ditch, had cried out to his kind: Beware of listening to this impostor; You are lost if you forget that the fruits are everyone's and the Earth no one's.[29]

A second condition was necessary for the emergence of civilization. As long as nature was bounteous and there was no shortage of resources, families could be relatively equal in the amount of property they controlled. Human needs could be met by nature's vast storehouse, and society could still be quite peaceful and harmonious. It would not be equal, however, because people are naturally unequal in such traits as strength, adroitness, and perseverance. Competition and rivalry grew between people, motivated by 'the hidden desire to profit at the expense of someone else'. Inequalities emerged and become more permanent over time. At the same time, individuals become increasingly dependent on others because the rich require the services of the poor; the poor need the help of the rich.[30]

Inequalities were exacerbated when an increase in the population caused an imbalance between people's needs and the available natural resources. In the ensuing struggles, some families were better able to control resources than others and accumulated considerable private property; others possessed no property. From this social inequality grew relationships of domination and subjugation; the rich 'thought of nothing but the subjugation and enslavement of their neighbours'. On the other hand, the poor coveted the property of the rich, expressing their own right of property through theft and brigandage. Finally, Rousseau claims, 'Emerging society gave way to the most horrible state of war, since the human race, vilified and desolated, was no longer able to retrace its steps or give up the unfortunate acquisitions it had made.'[31] Private property gave rise to selfishness, social inequality, competition, conflict, and war. For Rousseau, these vices were not originally part of human nature and would not have existed in a state of nature; rather, they were the products of the growth of civilization.

The State and the General Will

Having arrived in his theorizing at a stage similar to that of Hobbes, Rousseau imagined that people would rescue themselves from this state of 'perpetual war' in which all were in danger of their lives. The rich, however, had more at stake since they also risked losing their accumulation of personal goods. Unable to protect themselves or their property, 'the rich, pressed by necessity, finally conceived the most thought-out project that ever entered the human mind': the creation of law and government—the state. The calculated proposal was presented as being advantageous for everyone. Creating one supreme power would protect the property of the rich; in addition, it would 'protect the weak from oppression, restrain the ambitious, and assure everyone of possessing what belongs to him.' This new state would create rules of justice and peace for all, and make exceptions for no one.

For both Hobbes and Rousseau, the state was created to prevent social conflict. But there is a significant difference in their conceptions. For Hobbes, although humans were equal in a state of nature, life was a continuous round of uncertainty and violence because of human nature. The state was created to meet the common interests of everyone in society. The only alternative to centralized and absolute power was anarchy. Society was held together by a mutual agreement in a social contract. For Rousseau, social inequality came first and was the cause of social conflict. The state was created in a condition of inequality at the behest of the rich to protect their property and to tie the hands of the poor. The state embodies the interests of the dominant class.

As civilization developed further, government became the absolute power in society and kings claimed to be above the law, treating the nation as their private property. They called 'themselves equals of the gods' and their fellow citizens their slaves, even counting 'them like cattle'. Society was held together by force against the interests of the majority of the people; the state subjected them to labour, servitude, and misery. As the number of states proliferated across the world, wars grew more terrible and 'men were seen massacring one another by the thousands without knowing why.'[32]

Finally, kingship becomes absolute and degenerates into **tyranny** and despotism, 'trampling underfoot the laws and the people'. Under absolute power, everyone is plunged into a new equality, an equality of servitude and fear under the power of the strongest, a corrupted state of nature. As soon as sovereign power is usurped by a tyrant, the social contract is broken.[33] In this situation, force alone can keep the tyrant in power or bring the tyrant down. For Rousseau, an uprising that ends in the strangulation of a tyrant is no more unlawful than the tyrant's cruel rule had been.[34]

Rousseau's interpretation of the origins of inequality and the state represents his radical side. In the place of a centralized and repressive authority, Rousseau believed people ideally should live in a small, democratic state with a genuine social contract under which they would be bound by rules that were mutually agreeable. It would not be a social contract between the people and a ruler, setting some limitations on the power of the ruler (as with Locke), but a contract between free and equal individuals who would alienate their rights to the entire community, with no one in a position of power or authority over anyone else.[35]

For Rousseau, the greatest good for all can be expressed in two words: equality and liberty, and the latter cannot exist without equality (Box 4.1).[36] By equality in society, however, Rousseau did not mean absolutely equal possessions; rather, he advocated moderation in the amount of goods possessed by the rich and, in turn, moderation in the covetousness of the lowly. As long as it wasn't excessive, some inequality was necessary and acceptable. Since inequality naturally grows larger over time, Rousseau concluded, it is necessary for laws to regulate this moderate inequality. Furthermore, while Rousseau's *Discourse on Inequality* bristled with the evils that result from private property, in his later work, *The Social Contract*, Rousseau accepts that property ownership was

---

Box 4.1

I know that enslaved peoples do nothing but boast of the peace and tranquility they enjoy in their chains and that *they give the name 'peace' to the most miserable slavery*. But when I see free peoples sacrificing pleasures, tranquility, wealth, power, and life itself for the preservation of this sole good [liberty] which is regarded so disdainfully by those who have lost it; when I see animals born free and abhorring captivity break their heads against the bars of their prison; when I see multitudes of utterly naked savages scorn European pleasures and brave hunger, fire, sword and death, simply to preserve their independence, I sense that it is inappropriate for slaves to reason without liberty.

—Rousseau, *Discourse on Inequality* (1754)

both inevitable and acceptable, provided no one claimed title to more than he or she needed for subsistence or could actively cultivate,[37] a position that in this respect was similar to Locke's view of natural property rights in a state of nature.

By liberty, Rousseau did not mean the freedom of asocial individuals in the state of nature. In society, people could not be free to act any way they pleased according to their individual wills. They were bound to follow the mutually agreed-upon rules, termed by Rousseau the **general will**. The social contract specifies the rights of a citizen but it also imposes the duties of a subject. Individuals have their own private interests, which are the most immediate to them and tend always towards their own advantage. In society, the interests of a single individual will often conflict with the common interest of the society as a whole. Consequently, the whole society may legitimately apply force to compel an individual to obey the general will, which is the basis of the social contract. 'This means merely that he will be forced to be free', Rousseau claims,[38] since maintaining the social contract is the necessary foundation for everyone's freedom.

Rousseau's doctrine of the general will illustrates the influence of Enlightenment rationality on his social theory. In the state of nature, Rousseau argued, an individual has natural liberty but is a slave to her or his appetites and cannot rise above them. In society, the individual has civil liberty, which restricts individual freedom but provides the opportunity for personal development and perfectibility. Under the social contract, humans consult their reason before blindly following their passions and inclinations.[39]

Rousseau's ideas about the general will are complex and controversial. The concept does not necessarily represent mere majority opinion but, rather, the best interests of all. This poses the difficult question of who decides what is the general will. Somehow, each individual must make up her or his own mind, and decide on the basis of what is good for all.[40] Unfortunately, people may not understand the general interest, or groups of individuals within the state may put forward their own private or group interests as being the general will, thereby coming to dominate the state and using it for their own advantage.

Later, 'the general will' was applied in ways Rousseau had not intended. On the one hand, it was used to justify dictatorship—the domination of one individual who enforces what he or she interprets as the general will. Rousseau argued that, when the safety of the nation is at stake, it is necessary to suspend the laws and name a supreme leader, who represents the general will nevertheless since no population would wish to lose its national independence. Such a dictatorship must be limited to the short duration of the crisis; otherwise it would degenerate into tyranny.[41] On the other hand, the general will could be interpreted to endorse mob violence, on the assumption that mass action best expresses the will of the people. Both of these interpretations were applied during the French Revolution to justify various political acts.

Rousseau's depiction of a society run according to a contract between free and equal people expressing their general will was an image of a hypothetical society. It was used negatively and critically to demonstrate the difference between the present state of civilization—which was oppressive and unfree—and a potential state of democracy and freedom. In fact, in *Social Contract*, Rousseau doubted that a genuinely democratic government was possible or desirable. 'It is contrary to the natural order', Rousseau wrote, 'that the majority govern and the minority is governed.'[42] Any people capable of complete self-government would not need government at all.

This image was idealistic in that Rousseau did not create a social movement with the aim of securing such a future. Consistent with liberal and Enlightenment thought, reforms were to be brought about rationally, by means of education. Since human nature was powerfully shaped by parenting practices, Rousseau turned his attention to the family and the proper upbringing of children. Among the enlightened middle classes of Europe, Rousseau's views on the education of children became temporarily popular.

The Education of Men

Like most liberals, Rousseau believed that social change occurred gradually, over time, and that education was the appropriate way to bring about change. This view can have radical implications. If people are the way they are because of their education, then if we educate them in new ways, people can be very different from the way they are. For Rousseau, the first step in analysis is to imagine humans in a state of nature—what they were naturally. In his *Discourse on Inequality*, he had condemned the development of civilization because it had created more evil than good. For Rousseau, a child's education ought to recreate as much as possible the experience of nature to provide a sound foundation for becoming a member of society.

At least for men, Rousseau declared, 'Life is not just breathing; it is action.' The one 'who gets most out of life is not the one who has lived longest, but the one who has felt life most deeply.' Contrary to the customs of the time, Rousseau condemned the practice of tightly swaddling infants, leaving them unnaturally immobilized, and said they ought to be breast-fed by their mothers rather than handing them over to wet nurses. It is the duty of the father to educate his son to manhood, to help him become a social being and a fit citizen. 'A child will be better brought up by a wise father however limited, than by the cleverest teacher in the world.'[43]

To better illustrate his educational principles, Rousseau presented readers with an 'imaginary pupil' in his treatise, *Émile* (1762). In the education of Émile, however, Rousseau violates two of his cardinal principles. He imagines the boy to be an orphan. In the absence of his mother, he should be brought up by a nurse in a village 'away from the disease and vice of the man-devouring town'. With no father, Émile was educated by a tutor who would apply Rousseau's principles. The object of early childhood education was to prepare Émile for an independent life. The stages of early development, such as weaning, talking, and walking, are natural and will develop on their own if neither

frustrated nor encouraged beyond their capacity. As a boy, Émile must learn courage and endurance in the face of the small injuries that are natural for childhood. The duty of the parent is to be humane, Rousseau counsels: 'Love childhood.'[44]

The supreme good, Rousseau asserts, is freedom. As much as possible, the child must be independent of other people; 'He should have no consciousness of obedience when he acts'; as much as possible, Émile must be free from any yoke. On the other hand, he should not feel a sense of mastery when someone does something for him; he must not become 'a dictatorial headstrong child'.[45] He is taught his place, suitable for his age, and kept firmly in it. Denial must be firm and absolute and, while he is young, not accompanied by reason. It is a mistake to try to reason with children. 'If children appreciated reason they would not need to be educated.' Therefore Émile won't be taught to read until he is an adolescent. 'Reading is the greatest plague of childhood.' Above all, Rousseau said, the tutor must avoid the common ways that parents attempt to direct their children, by 'emulation, jealousy, envy, vanity, greed or base fear', all dangerous passions sure to corrupt youth.[46]

The first idea that a child should learn, Rousseau claims, is private property because from this will spring the first sense of justice. If he breaks a window, Rousseau says, let him be cold, even catch a fever, so that he can learn respect for property.[47] While still a child, Émile must perform physical exercise and be taught the use of his senses. Émile knows by experience, not by memorization; he cannot read a book, but reads nature, and so arrives at the last stage of childhood. By being introduced to the various trades, Émile learns that humans are not self-sufficient; they depend on others for what they do not make. He must learn the basics of several trades, including carpentry, to instill the honour of labour and the appreciation of human skills. He is not to be confined to a single trade, however; his real education is to be a man. Adam Smith's division of labour, where humans are directed to perform routine, monotonous, and simple repetitive tasks, would be immoral and unnatural in Rousseau's view. The importance attached by Rousseau to independence reflects the pre-factory age. Rousseau's model of work is craftsmanship, although this form of production was slowly disappearing in the Europe of the 1700s.

In adolescence, Émile must acquire the social virtues; from being a solitary person, he must develop relationships with others. The child's first sentiment was self-love. As social relationships multiply, Émile learns the concepts of duty and preference. He develops self-esteem by comparing himself with others, and must learn compassion or pity for them, which is elicited by becoming aware of their sufferings.[48]

The final step in Émile's moral education is to show him the whole social order. At this point it is not possible that Émile learn from experience directly; he cannot know first-hand the life of those who live at different social levels. Émile has his first need for book-learning, for understanding history. Still, Émile must be given only facts and be allowed to judge for himself, beginning with individual biographies, which are the most concrete and to which he can relate most closely. Finally, Émile requires a mate, though perhaps he can be diverted from this preoccupation for a time by hunting, though Rousseau generally considered 'the slaughter of animals' a 'cruel passion'.[49] The woman who is to be Émile's soulmate, however, must be brought up in an entirely different fashion.

Sophie, or Rousseau's 'Ideal Woman'

Rousseau presents Sophie as the female counterpart to Émile, his ideal mate who represents the other half of human nature. Unlike Émile, Sophie is brought up by her parents, most importantly by her mother because she has to be socialized into the feminine role. The view that women's nature was essentially distinct from men's was deeply rooted in classical, medieval, and Renaissance thought. If women, by nature, are passive, quiet, and uninterested in world affairs, then women's education should properly be directed towards goals that are different from those appropriate for

men. By the Enlightenment, it was taken for granted that two distinct natures were anchored in biological and anatomical differences. The sexes were opposites, and these differences were intellectual and moral, as well as physical.

Rousseau's point of departure from this existing body of thought was his insistence that it was wrong to consider women inferior to men. Women were not imperfect males, as Aristotle proposed; rather, both sexes were equally perfect, but essentially different, forms of humanity. Each had strengths independent of the other. Consequently, the worst thing a parent could do would be to attempt 'to bring up your daughter to be like a good man'. By trying to be the same as a man, a woman would clearly become inferior, Rousseau suggests.[50] Women, rather, should be taught to be superior in those areas where nature has given them an advantage over men.[51]

For Rousseau, social **customs** (the 'bonds of convention') always develop on the basis of nature. 'Everything that characterizes sex should be respected as established by nature.'[52] Hence, any social arrangement that violated this view of natural man and natural woman was in error. Consequently, while his approach to the education of men contained many progressive elements, he did not overcome the biases of his time regarding the natural role of women.

For Rousseau, men were naturally active and strong while women were naturally passive and weak, from which it followed, he extrapolated, 'that woman is intended to please man . . . and to be dominated'. This domination, however, is partly reciprocal since women's special talents have armed them to subjugate the strong. Women have the ability to stimulate greater desire in men than can be satisfied. Consequently, a man must seek to please a woman and is dependent on her favour. By her resistance, his esteem for her grows as strong as his desire.[53] In its moral aspect, Rousseau argued, 'love is an artificial sentiment born of social custom, and extolled by women with so much skill and care in order to establish their hegemony and make dominant the sex that ought to obey.'[54]

Rousseau's notions about female human nature shape his advice on educating male and female children as expounded in *Émile*. Education 'ought to be in conformity with . . . original inclinations', Rousseau believed. He appeared to challenge the contemporary prejudice that women were not capable of sound reasoning,[55] arguing that women should not 'be brought up in utter ignorance and confined to domestic tasks'. Nature has 'endowed women with quick pleasing minds' with the intent that they think, judge, and 'cultivate the mind as well as the countenance'. The proper gardeners for this cultivation were not women themselves, but men. These natural gifts were not intended for women's independent use, Rousseau asserts, but were designed to cement a woman's relationship with a man, since women are more dependent on men than vice versa. Having a quick mind gives her a peculiar charm that makes a wife a companion rather than a servant. The proper education of women is essential for the happiness of men.[56]

> For this reason their education must be wholly directed to their relations with men. To give them pleasure, to be useful to them, to win their love and esteem, to train them in their childhood, to care for them when they grow up, to give them counsel and consolation, to make life sweet and agreeable for them: those are the tasks of women in all times for which they should be trained from childhood.[57]

Women possess reason for a second purpose: to develop an inner conscience that is, in general, in agreement with public opinion. Since public opinion may be based on prejudice and not reason, a woman must cultivate her mind to better guide both her conscience and her actions. Sophie's mind, then, 'is pleasing but not brilliant, solid but not deep.'

'From the beginning', Rousseau asserts, 'little girls are fond of dress.' They want to be noticed and, when they learn speech, they can be controlled by telling them what people think of them.

Women's self-esteem depends on others' opinions; men's sense of self comes from their independence and strength. Dressing up dolls is the first expression of women's coquetry. It is a fact, says Rousseau, that 'nearly all little girls greatly dislike learning to read and write but they are always willing to use the needle', the better to adorn themselves when they are older. By the age of 15, Sophie knows all the details about running a household, including the keeping of accounts.[58]

The most dangerous faults that women potentially have are idleness and indocility—simultaneously being idle but insufficiently docile. To prevent these vices, women 'should be kept under control from an early age', a condition that 'is inseparable from their sex.' Women are strictly subject to social proprieties and must learn to take them as a matter of course; they must automatically bow to authority for dependence is their natural state. Girls are made for obedience and must learn sweetness. Since men are imperfect and often have many vices, for her own sake 'she must learn to submit uncomplainingly to unjust treatment and marital wrongs.'[59] Rousseau had opposed swaddling children. Yet, Rousseau's argument about the appropriate education for women suggests that they should, in fact, be swaddled because this would provide appropriate training in docility. Chadwick argues that Rousseau's injunction against swaddling was inappropriate for working women, who needed to immobilize their infants in order to have hands free for labour. For middle- and upper-class women, however, it was part of the movement, thoroughly endorsed by Rousseau, to remove women from the public and confine them to the private, domestic sphere, supposedly their natural destiny.[60]

When she reaches a proper marriageable age, Sophie's mind is still vacant; she has a pleasing ignorance, though she knows how to learn. Contrary to the custom of the time, according to which a girl's parents chose a husband, consulting their daughter only as a matter of form, Sophie is to exercise her right to choose freely, leaving only to the parents the final approval.[61] At marriage, Émile becomes her teacher; she becomes his disciple and learns to share her husband's taste. She is capable of being instructed, and with her husband as her teacher she will become his companion in mind as well as body. Although Émile teaches Sophie about mathematics, science, philosophy, and history, there are natural limits to how much she is able to learn. She has only a vague understanding of logic, the general laws of physics and the universe, and of **metaphysics**. 'Sophie forms some idea of everything, but most of what she learns is soon forgotten.' She is best at learning right conduct and proper taste.[62]

Many of Rousseau's ideas were liberal for the time. Women were not inferior to men, just as an apple is not inferior to an orange; they are merely different. Marriages should not be arranged by parents but should be based on the choice of the youths, with parental approval. Women have an ability to reason, however limited their abilities to understand the more abstract subjects. Nevertheless, his account is saturated with the prejudices and prevailing customs of his age. Once the assumption is made that women's nature is essentially different and that this accounts for the differences between the sexes, then only harm can come from educating women in ways that contradict the natural pathways. In the end, for Rousseau women remain unequal and inferior. Their presumed place in the world is the sphere of domesticity and their life work is to marry, have and raise children, and be their husbands' helpmates.

It is ironic that a man who gave up his own children for adoption should write a tract on parenting or make suggestions about marriage. Towards the end of his life, Rousseau married his long-time mistress, just in time for her to nurse his various illnesses. He died in 1778, at the age of 66.[63]

Rousseau died before the outbreak of the French Revolution, but in an important way he helped prepare the ideological ground for this revolt. More than any of the other *philosophes*, Rousseau's writing on inequality, the state, and popular sovereignty inspired the revolutionary leaders of France, particularly the more radical Jacobins.

Rousseau's radical ideas had other legacies. His theory that government was an invention of the rich to protect their own property and interests against the threats from classes below influenced Marx in the next century. Rousseau uncovered the root of social inequality in the development of private property, but he concluded that some amount of ownership is inevitable, necessary, and socially beneficial. He did not conclude that it was necessary to recreate a system of communal, rather than private, ownership of productive property. Many people could own a small piece of property and make a living at it—property ownership was relatively equal and not, in itself, the source of great inequality and injustice it would become under the factory system. For Rousseau, the owners should be permitted to do as they please with their property. Socialists would later conclude that justice and private property were contradictory concepts.

Rousseau's worshipping of nature and the natural human being inspired the post-French Revolution generation of artists and political rebels who participated in the movement known as Romanticism. His image of a state of equality, in which people surrender their power to the democratic majority but nevertheless live in liberty and peace, is at the heart of the political philosophy of anarchism, the doctrine that any exercise of authority of one human being over another is a form of tyranny. Finally, Rousseau's attack on civilization—in more modern terms, on technology and bureaucracy—in favour of a simpler and more genuine life is reflected in a host of lifestyle rebellions, from nineteenth-century bohemians to twentieth-century 'hippies'.

In one important way Rousseau differed from the other *philosophes*: he was not a champion of human reason. For Rousseau, human goodness was natural; in many ways, the society that had been constructed by human reason was the chief evil that humans faced. The human virtues of simplicity, modesty, and goodness were natural and it was only necessary to create more natural conditions for these virtues to surface. This was contrary to the dominant thrust of the Enlightenment —the construction of social rules on the basis of reason. Rousseau's naturalism was the inspiration for a new appreciation of untamed nature. In lieu of the neo-classical manicured garden, nineteenth-century Romantics would worship nature in its wild, untamed, emotionally raw state. The appreciation for real nature or the ordinary beauty of the natural world was paralleled by the development of an appreciation for ordinary humanity. If the worshipping of the natural world would eventually inspire the Romantic movement, the discovery of the dignity and high potential of the ordinary person would inspire revolution.

THE FRENCH REVOLUTION

The *philosophes* attacked the Old Regime on the basis of reason and declared it to be unjust and tyrannical. The old had to be destroyed and then the new had to be created, guided by human reason. The French Revolution expressed the faith of the revolutionaries that a new social order founded on liberty, equality, and fraternity could be rationally constructed. But the revolutionaries differed on how to construct this new society. The more prosperous rebels were inspired by Rousseau's rational arguments. The radical Jacobins would rule in the name of the democracy of the masses and the 'general will'.

In Paris in 1789, however, the cult of reason was about to be brought from the heavens down to earth—some would say at the time, down to the netherworld. Out of the disorder of the French Revolution would come a reaction to Enlightenment rationalism as a flawed and dangerous model of humanity. To the unrepentant rationalists, however, this implied a retreat to medieval spirituality or traditionalism. For them, the way forward was not to go backward, but to perfect a scientific method that would be applicable to society. Before this irrevocable split in social theory occurred, the Enlightenment had given birth to its legitimate offspring, the French Revolution.

Towards the end of the eighteenth century, France was careening towards collapse. Political power was centralized in the hands of an absolute monarch and a strong, traditional Church. A hereditary nobility continued to exercise special legal privileges in a social world that did not recognize equality before the law. The middle class of merchants and businessmen were largely excluded from direct political power. Many of the peasants, who comprised the majority of the population, were still serfs and continued to pay various dues to the nobility.[64] When the English poet Robert Southey complained that the 'nobly born' had no natural right to oppress the poor, since all were born of Adam and Eve (Box 4.2),[65] these sentiments were even more sharply felt in France. The common people, whether artisans, merchants, or peasants, had numerous grievances and no way to have them resolved satisfactorily.

Ideas have an effect on persons. By 1788 Louis XVI's government was in a financial crisis and the King found it necessary to call for an election for a sitting of the French parliament (the *Estates General*), a body that had not met since 1614. In this deepening social and political crisis, radical views emerged and grew stronger, inspired by the practical example of the new American republic, a liberal and relatively democratic government that recognized neither a king nor nobility.

Acting on Rousseau's principle of popular sovereignty (Box 4.3),[66] the representatives of the common people declared the formation of a new **National Assembly**, claiming the right to make laws and set tax rates for all of France. Most members of the National Assembly expected to create a constitutional monarchy similar to the system in England. Even this change, however, was too much for Louis XVI. For him, the existence of the new National Assembly was an act of treason.

Fearing that the King would try to dissolve the National Assembly by force, people rebelled openly in the streets and succeeded on 14 July 1789 in capturing the Bastille, a fortress used as a royal prison and a powerful symbol of the Old Regime. Bastille Day is now celebrated as the national day in France. The politicized and self-conscious market women of Paris participated in the assault on the Bastille and led a procession of ordinary citizens to the palace of Versailles in October, when the King and Queen were arrested and brought back to Paris.[67] Ordinary people, men as

Box 4.2

'When Adam delv'd, and Eve span,
Who was then the gentleman?'
Wretched is the infant's lot,
Born within the straw-roof'd cot!
Be he generous, wise, or brave,
He must only be a slave.
Long, long labour, little rest,
Still to toil, to be oppress'd;
Drain'd by taxes of his store,
Punish'd next for being poor:
This is the poor wretch's lot,
Born within the straw-roof'd cot.
While the peasant works—to sleep,
What the peasant sows—to reap,
On the couch of ease to lie,
Rioting in revelry;
Be he villain, be he fool,
Still to hold despotic rule,
Trampling on his slaves with scorn;
This is to be nobly born.
'When Adam delv'd, and Eve span,
Who was then the gentleman?'

—'Song', by Robert Southey, *Wat Tyler* (1794)

Box 4.3

Once the populace is legitimately assembled as a sovereign body, all jurisdiction of the government ceases; the executive power is suspended, and the person of the humblest citizen is as sacred and inviolable as that of the first magistrate [king].

—Rousseau, *On the Social Contract* (1762)

well as women, joined in the spontaneous acts of the social revolution in France. Fearing for their lives, the conservative nobility fled France and sought refuge in countries such as Germany, Austria, and Italy. They became known as the *émigrés*. A new dawn of freedom and equality seemed about to break and liberal intellectuals welcomed it.

To usher in this new, promised era when, in Wordsworth's phrase, 'joy of one / is joy of tens of millions' (Box 4.4),[68] the National Assembly began to take revolutionary measures. The revolutionary government disbanded the army, established a militia or army of citizens, abolished feudal duties, permitted civil marriages and

Box 4.4

> ... 'twas a time when Europe was rejoiced,
> France standing on the top of golden hours,
> And human nature seeming born again.
> Bound, as I said, to the Alps, it was our lot
> To land at Calais on the very eve
> Of that great federal Day; and there we saw,
> In a mean City, and among a few,
> How bright a face is worn when joy of one
> Is joy of tens of millions. . . .
>
> —William Wordsworth, 'The Prelude, Book VI:
> Cambridge and the Alps' (1805)
>
> ... festivals of new-born Liberty:
> A homeless sound of joy was in the Sky;
> The antiquated earth, as one might say,
> Beat like the heart of Man: songs, garlands, play,
> Banners, and happy faces, far and nigh!
>
> —William Wordsworth, 'To a Friend, Composed
> Near Calais' (1802)

divorces, and created new local governments. The National Assembly opened debate on a new Constitution for France, increasingly under pressure from a radical citizenry known as *sans culottes*—those who wore ordinary pants rather than the breeches favoured by the wealthy—who wanted radical changes in society and government. Church lands were confiscated. Land from clerical and secular estates was redistributed, some to the middle class and some to the peasantry, enlarging the class of small landholders. The new National Assembly also made changes that were purely symbolic, such as renaming the months on the French calendar and changing the date, so that Year One celebrated a new age for humankind. The powers of the King, the aristocracy, and the Church were severely curtailed. The new Constitution (1791) began with the famous 'Declaration of the Rights of Man and the Citizen' and enshrined the revolutionary goals of *liberté, égalité, et fraternité*.

Conflict, however, was inevitable. The leaders of the Revolution had been united in their opposition to the Old Regime. Once it had been overturned, they disagreed over what type of government should replace it. The National Assembly was divided into several factions, which represented distinct interests in French society.

The *philosophes* had expected social change to be directed from above, by enlightened rulers acting on the basis of reason. They had been content to allow ideas to wage battle in the safe environment of the salons and cafés. Revolution, in contrast, was emotional, bloody, and frenetic, rather than reasonable, polite, and dispassionate. There were real interests at stake—the interests of power and wealth, and the interests of those who wanted little more than bread and land.

On the right were the royalists and monarchists, who wanted to bring back an absolute monarchy and restore conditions as they had been in 1788. They were supported by the French *émigrés* abroad and by foreign monarchs who feared the spread of revolution to their own countries.

The **Girondin** faction in the Revolution, Stromberg claims, was anticlerical, anti-aristocratic, and liberal in ideology.[69] They admired the limited constitutional democracy of Locke, the anticlericalism of Voltaire, and the republicanism of the United States. They recognized their class interests as 'the upper bourgeoisie' when they prohibited workers from forming associations or trade unions in 1791. Something of this spirit of the Girondists is reflected in the speech by M. Homais, the apothecary in Gustave Flaubert's novel, *Madame Bovary*:

> Homais: 'I do have a religion—my religion; and it's even deeper than all of theirs with their mummery and their tricks! On the contrary, I worship God, I believe in a Supreme Being, in a Creator, whoever He is, it doesn't matter, who placed us here below . . . but I don't need to go into a church to kiss silver plates and fatten up a bunch of fakers who eat better than we do! . . . God for me, is the God of Socrates, [Benjamin] Franklin, Voltaire. . . . I am for the . . . immortal principles of eighty-nine! So I cannot accept a doddering deity who parades around in his garden with a cane in his hand . . . dies with a shriek, and is resurrected three days later. These things are obviously absurd, and besides, they're completely opposed to the laws of physics.'[70]

The **Jacobins**, who sat on the left of the National Assembly, considered themselves direct descendants of Rousseau and claimed to speak for the *sans culottes*, the radicalized urban poor who wanted a more egalitarian system of popular sovereignty. Democrats of a more radical kind than the Girondists, the Jacobins were the spokespersons of the masses, ruling on behalf of the common workers; in fact, they claimed to represent the 'general will' of the people, a concept taken from Rousseau. Political power was to be wielded by a dictatorship on behalf of the masses—it

would be a 'democratic dictatorship'. Stromberg[71] described Jacobin ideology as combining a paradoxical disregard for individual liberty and parliamentary rules with a deep sense of democracy. They had 'a feeling for the common man *en masse* . . . a passion for equality', and wanted to involve the people more directly in government.

In England as in Europe generally, intellectuals at first, almost without exception, welcomed the Revolution and were caught up in its excitement, its proclaimed ideals, and its promise for a better future for humanity. Among them was the first generation of English Romantics—William Wordsworth, Helen Maria Williams, Samuel Taylor Coleridge, and William Blake. A politically active circle of radical Jacobins, as these English democrats and republicans also were called, revolved around the writer, William Godwin, an enthusiastic supporter of Rousseau. Godwin's book, *An Enquiry Concerning Social Justice*, presented a Utopian picture of an ideal state of equality and rationality, based on the natural goodness of humanity.[72]

By 1792, the revolution was being progressively radicalized and was increasingly under attack. Wherever the French *émigrés* alighted, they persuaded the European upper classes that the Revolution in France had to be stopped by force. When the liberal Girondists achieved power in the French National Assembly in 1792, they declared war on Austria, intending to spread the Revolution to other countries.

At first, the revolutionary war against Prussia and Austria did not go well for France. As the situation in France became more desperate, the population of Paris was further radicalized, and the leadership of the Revolution was wrested from the Girondists by the more radical Jacobins, who became increasingly dictatorial. They ignored the Declaration of the **Rights of Man** and put the security of the Revolution first. Between 1793 and 1794, thousands of people were condemned as counter-revolutionaries and sent to the guillotine, among them King Louis XVI and Queen Marie Antoinette, along with many aristocrats, royalists, and Girondists.

Among the influential Girondists who were executed was Marie-Jeanne Roland, the centre of a revolutionary intellectual circle. When the Jacobins arrested and interrogated her in 1793, Hesse asserts, the eloquence and evasiveness of her replies forced the inquisitors to restrict her to 'yes' and 'no' answers. At her public trial, she was again silenced by the judiciary and by the Jacobin supporters in the public galleries who denounced her as a traitor to both her nation and her sex.[73]

The Jacobins also imprisoned the English poet, Helen Williams, who had been drawn to the magnet of Paris in revolution, where 'the peasant knows / Those equal rights impartial heaven bestows'. Williams, who was attracted to the Girondist cause, as were most English radicals, was left wondering whether she would be 'dragged to the scaffold, with the illustrious members of the Gironde, the martyrs of their country'.[74] This period of the Revolution became known as the Reign of Terror.

No memory of the revolution is more familiar than the **Reign of Terror**; no symbol more potent than the guillotine. This selective memory reflects, above all, that the history of an event is written by the victors. In his nineteenth-century novel *A Connecticut Yankee in King Arthur's Court*, the American author Mark Twain traced the origins of the 'glorious French Revolution' to the oppression the French peasants and urban poor experienced under the Old Regime. In his view, the people had suffered a much worse and bloodier reign of terror that had lasted for centuries. The Revolution had 'swept a thousand years of villainy away in one swift tidal wave of blood'. What was called the Reign of Terror was a settlement of the debt the aristocracy owed to the people who had been squeezed by slow torture over a thousand years:

There were two 'Reigns of Terror,' if we would but remember it and consider it: the one wrought murder in hot passion, the other in heartless cold blood; the one lasted mere months, the other had lasted a thousand years; the one inflicted death upon ten thousand persons, the other upon a hundred millions; but our shudders are all for the 'horrors' of the minor Terror, the momentary Terror, so to speak; whereas, what is the horror of swift death by the axe, compared with life-long death from hunger, cold, insult, cruelty and heart-break? What is swift death by lightning, compared with death by slow fire at the stake? A city cemetery could contain the coffins filled by that brief Terror which we have all been so diligently taught to shiver at and mourn over; but all France could hardly contain the coffins filled by that older and real Terror—that unspeakably bitter and awful Terror which none of us has been taught to see in its vastness or pity as it deserves.[75]

The Jacobins had no clear vision of the needs of post-revolutionary society beyond a belief that they represented the 'general will' of the urban masses. The *sans culottes* themselves had no consciousness of any longer-term revolutionary objectives; neither did they create any movement to identify and realize them. The radicalized poor knew only that they had received few of the benefits the French Revolution promised and that they were in danger of losing what little they had gained. The Jacobins were trying to cope with an economic collapse and the resulting rise of speculators, fraud, corruption, and internal rebellion as well as foreign war. But the Jacobins had only the most rudimentary understanding of the causes of counter-revolution and conceived only the crudest means to resist it.

Eventually, the Jacobins were undermined. Even Jacobin leaders were suspected of working against the Revolution and were condemned to death. As it was said, the revolution began to devour its children. As the Reign of Terror continued and as the war with Austria and Prussia began to turn in favour of France, opposition to the Jacobins increased. French politics was fractured among factions. On the left a minority of Jacobins wanted to take the Revolution in the direction of communal ownership and radical democracy. On the right, monarchists wanted to restore the Old Regime. As violence continued, the National Assembly eventually acquiesced in the concentration of power in the hands of a few men and, finally, of one man—Napoleon Bonaparte, who led a *coup d'état* in 1799. By the revolutionary calendar, the *coup* occurred on the 18th Brumaire, Year VIII. Five years later, Napoleon crowned himself Emperor. History appeared to have come full circle from one autocratic form of government to another.

Napoleon rolled back most of the radical and democratic measures that had been taken by the French Revolution. Under the Napoleonic law code, employees were forbidden to unionize and were placed squarely under the powerful thumb of their employers, who could fire them at will. Employees were issued work cards attesting to their employment and good conduct. The loss of this card branded the unfortunate ex-worker a vagabond subject to imprisonment in a workhouse.[76] Napoleon revived and expanded the role of the police in his authoritarian regime. He restored much of the power of the Catholic Church, and his Code of Laws confirmed the second-class status of women. Not every social change was undone. Napoleon strengthened the economic reforms of the Revolution. He opened his regime to men of talent and ambition from the middle classes, thereby consolidating the position of the new propertied groups in France and creating a new nobility, a legion of honour consisting of the old and the newly wealthy.

Replacing a King with an Emperor was not sufficient for the royalists, however, nor for those European countries still at war with France. For the European conservatives, Napoleon still represented many of the ideas of the Revolution. For more than a decade Napoleon was supreme in France. His armies conquered much of Europe and even extended French control into Egypt and Russia. Everywhere French troops went, some of the radical and democratic ideas of the Revolution stayed behind, a long-lasting legacy that outlived Napoleon and stimulated other rebellions and revolutions well into the nineteenth century.

In 1814–15, however, a coalition of European forces finally defeated Napoleon, forcing him to abdicate and sending him into exile. The monarchists then had their day. Louis XVIII was restored to the French throne, though only as a constitutional monarch, the head of a government that included a National Assembly for which only substantial property owners could vote. A limited monarchy was still not enough for the more extreme royalists. Post-revolutionary politics in France was dominated by conflict between the liberals, who were middle-class democrats wishing to restore some of the reforms of the Revolution, and the royalists, representing the extreme wing of a new conservatism.

Under the roof of the **constitutional monarchy** and the fractious National Assembly, a new revolutionary generation was to emerge in France. Inspired by the legends of the Revolution, these new rebels lived in a considerably different atmosphere and time, influenced by Romanticism, a literary, political, and lifestyle movement that flowered in the first half of the nineteenth century.

WOMEN, ENLIGHTENMENT, AND REVOLUTION

Enlightenment social theorists intended to hammer all previous custom and superstition on the anvil of reason. Half of the population were women, traditionally assumed to be inferior to men and incompetent to understand abstract thought. While this prejudice proved extremely durable, once ajar, the door to civil liberties cannot be barred against the demands of excluded groups. Some liberal thinkers in the early 1700s, such as Mary Astell and Daniel Defoe, believed that women should be educated equally. Most men could not be easily persuaded about a matter that closely affected their personal as well as their public interest. Traditional views about the nature of women persisted into the eighteenth and nineteenth centuries, although they were underwritten by different theoretical rationalizations.

While the new scientific age helped undermine the belief that rebellious women were evil 'witches', it reiterated the definition of women as deficient in reason—a worse sin in the eyes of the *philosophes*. Men, the argument went, were able to assert rational control over their emotions, a necessary precondition for political involvement. As sociologist Karl Mannheim observed, the Enlightenment foreshadowed 'a new social economy in the control of impulses and a new self-conscious . . . restraint'.[77] Men had a duty to dominate nature, which included women. Women were still considered closer to the animal and the natural world than men. Women were governed by the forces of the moon and the tides, and tended towards irrational and inconstant, often extreme, actions.

The Renaissance initiated the movement to domesticate women by defining the public space of politics and business as masculine and confining women to the private space of the home. In the Republic of Florence, the powerful Medici princes consolidated state power and patriarchal domination over property and male succession. Leon Battista Alberti's *On the Family* (1435), the 'major Renaissance statement on the bourgeois domestication of women', rigidly prescribed women's virtues to be 'chastity and motherhood' exclusive of any public role.[78]

Restrictions of status and privilege elicit resistance. Intellectual women were forced to choose between marriage and learning. Choosing the latter meant seclusion at home or in a cloister. Women who were favourably patronized, either in their family or through the Church, had more opportunities for independent development and expression. Among the Renaissance artists were several prominent women who reflected a woman's standpoint in their painting. Many turned to the Bible rather than classical mythology for legends of powerful women. The artist Artemisia Gentileschi (*c.* 1593–1652) was raped when she was 19 by her private tutor. Although the famous trial of 1612 was essentially a question of the wrong done to her father's property, the experience sharpened Gentileschi's standpoint on the female heroine and victim in her paintings. In her early work *Susanna and the Elders* (1610), which depicted the Biblical story of the attempted seduction of Susanna by two Jewish elders, Gentileschi presciently blamed the elders and showed

Susanna to be vulnerable and distressed by the clearly unwanted sexual advances.[79]

Women artists also brought an alternative perspective to the depiction of female heroes, another of the common interests of the period. Elisabetta Sirani (1638–65) painted *Portia Wounding her Thigh* (1664), which both reflected and critiqued the patriarchal prejudice and distrust that separated women from public power and discourse. Portia was the wife of Brutus, a Roman senator who was implicated in the plot to assassinate Julius Caesar. In order to prove herself worthy of sharing her husband's trust, Portia deliberately wounded herself in the thigh with a dagger to demonstrate that her character was as brave and steadfast as a man's.[80] Shakespeare includes the legend in his play, *Julius Caesar*, where Portia must prove that she is stronger than her sex (Box 4.5).[81] In Shakespeare's *Macbeth*, Lady Macbeth understood that female and male natures were different. To play her part in the murder of Duncan, she called on the nether spirits to 'unsex' her so that the naturally feminine emotions of pity, conscience, and remorse could be transformed into manly cruelty.[82]

Even the liberal argument about the need to educate women was part of the Enlightenment attempt to dominate them, Mack claims. Education would replace those traits that were regarded as 'feminine', such as their tendency towards passionate enthusiasm, with a masculine ideal of calm rationality. As men used reason to dominate nature, so, too, masculine science would penetrate and define passive, feminine nature. Women were to be reformed by modelling them after men.[83]

This implies that women had the potential to become more like men. If the female mind was not inferior, women should be recognized as the rational equals of men. A new generation of radical women, caught up in the passionate enthusiasm of the French Revolution, would apply Enlightenment theories to their own sex. An alternative viewpoint agreed that women and men were essentially different, but argued for the superiority rather then the inferiority of the feminine. Women were naturally different from men in their

Box 4.5

Portia: Within the bond of marriage, tell me, Brutus,
Is it excepted I should know no secrets
That appertain to you? Am I yourself
But, as it were, in sort or limitation,
To keep with you at meals, comfort your bed,
And talk to you sometimes? Dwell I but in the suburbs
Of your good pleasure? If it be no more,
Portia is Brutus' harlot, not his wife.

. . .

I grant I am a woman; but withal
A woman that Lord Brutus took to wife:
I grant I am a woman, but withal
A woman well-reputed, Cato's daughter.
Think you I am no stronger than my sex,
Being so father'd and husbanded?
Tell me your counsels, I will not disclose 'em:
I have made strong proof of my constancy,
Giving myself a voluntary wound
Here, in the thigh: can I bear that with patience,
And not my husband's secrets?

—William Shakespeare, *Julius Caesar*, II, i

sensitivity, their intuitive understanding, and their passions. They possessed deeper, more spiritual ways of knowing and were ethically superior to men, a theme that would persist as a thread through nineteenth- and twentieth-century feminism. The male Romantic poets would later claim that men, too, possessed these feminine qualities.

While the Enlightenment perspective emphasized the superiority of reason and the necessity for the rational mind to dominate human passions and appetites, humans also possessed 'sensibility', thought of as the seat of morality or ethics. In the truly enlightened person, there would be no contradiction between sense and **sensibility**, between what was felt to be true and just, and what reason said was true and just. For most Enlightenment theorists, however, the mind was the best guide to truth. Since sense was thought to be primarily masculine, men were superior to women in their greater ability to see beyond the details of the present and to reason abstractly. Men produced abstract social theory; women maintained the practical social networks of family and *salon*, where men were sustained physically and provided with a comfortable, civilized forum to debate public matters.

Inevitably, intellectual women joined the debates and sought recognition as theorists in their own right. The English historian, Catherine Macaulay, travelled to France in the 1770s and the United States in the 1780s, meeting and corresponding with the leading reformers of the day. Her most scathing theoretical writing was in opposition to Hobbes. If government derived from a social contract, she reasoned, it was absurd to think that such a contract was binding on future generations or empowered the monarch to rule at will. Contracts were mutual obligations; both parties were obligated to meet the conditions of the contract. The people reserved the right to revoke any contract that had been broken, a key principle endorsing the right to rebel against tyranny.[84] When humans abandon their right to rule themselves by handing over absolute power to a monarch, Macaulay continued, they surrender their power to an individual man who is subject to the same passions and appetites as other men. With no earthly power to fear, such absolute monarchs 'must be inclined to abuse in the grossest manner their trust . . . because to act by selfish considerations is in the very constitution of our nature.'[85]

Rather than conceiving of society as originating in a social contract, Macaulay and other women writers of the Enlightenment argued that the fundamental bond in humanity was the natural feeling of sympathy for others, a bond that was strongest between a mother and her child. The instinct of sympathy, which requires systematic training to develop fully, is the foundation of virtue and of the idea of equality. Hobbes had said that a type of primitive equality had existed in the hypothetical state of nature, but that the establishment of effective government required the development of social inequality. For Macaulay, equality would lead to peace, the opposite of Hobbes's perpetual war of all against all, and was the cornerstone of good government.[86]

For Enlightenment theorists, social change was not a matter of passion, violence, or real conflict; it was about scientific evidence, carefully and rationally weighed, and the application of knowledge to the construction of a reasonable, ordered, and balanced world. As for the common people, they were ignorant and superstitious, and had to be controlled. If religion had any social purpose at all, it was to help keep the masses in check. Voltaire commented ironically that if God did not exist, it would be necessary to invent him. Certainly, the *philosophes* would have detested the French Revolution when it burst upon the nation. They were champions neither of the masses (whom they held in contempt) nor of violent change.

Revolutionary movements awaken the spirit of revolt in all oppressed people. Women were among the most oppressed persons in Europe. Some upper-class women carved a space of influence and power for themselves by providing *salons*, which were venues for artists, philosophers, and other intellectuals to debate ideas. The *salon* produced an intermediate space between the bourgeois private home and the public sphere of the court. While they were mostly attended by men, women were able to participate in the debate and influence intellectual trends. By the middle of the century, however, the *salons* were being criticized by Enlightenment rationalists as sharing in the artifice, manners, and frivolity of the aristocratic courts. Rousseau, for example, attacked the *salons* as a place where men were subject, unnaturally, to the authority of women. The women *salonières* were usurping male authority and public power and abandoning their natural, private, and domestic sphere, which must consequently become corrupted.[87]

Working-class women actively fought in the French Revolution. Market women in Paris had a long tradition of activism in support of basic demands for reasonably priced flour and bread. Women contributed to the mass action that liberated the Bastille and, as we have seen, led the capture of the royal family at the palace of Versailles in October 1789.[88] Some prosperous middle-class women actively supported the *philosophes* in the clubs and drawing rooms where new ideas were debated. Inevitably, radical thinking took root among a new generation of women, such as Madame Roland, one of the most prominent Girondists to be condemned during the Reign of Terror. Censer and Hunt add that women were active in such political groups (or clubs) as the Jacobins and then formed their own Society of Revolutionary Republican Women in 1793. Adequate food supplies were a common concern of these radical women, but they also pressed for more liberal divorce laws and for the right to inherit property, both granted by the National Assembly by 1793.[89]

For most revolutionary men, however, the goals of liberty, equality, and fraternity did not include women. Although women actively took part in revolutionary actions, even the most radical of the male Jacobins were opposed to granting rights for women equal to the rights of men. Many French women, however, actively championed the rights of women in the revolutionary movement, demanding that the Revolution should champion their liberty and equality. As Rowbotham points out, women of the time were not silent on the issue. They petitioned the National Assembly in 1789 with the argument that 'You have destroyed all the prejudices of the past, but you allow the oldest and the most pervasive to remain, which excludes from office, position and honour, and above all from the right of sitting amongst you, half of the inhabitants of the kingdom.'[90] These revolutionary men had read their Rousseau and justified the exclusion of women, Rowbotham asserts, not on the prejudices of the past, but on the prejudices of their time. Rousseau had asserted that women were naturally different, intellectually inferior, suited to be only wives and mothers.

As in the American Constitution, women were excluded from the Declaration of the Rights of Man. Louis-Marie Prudhomme, the editor of the radical Parisian paper *Révolution de Paris*, justified this omission in the name of nature, which had assigned to both sexes their respective functions. When the father leaves his home to defend property and liberty, the mother must focus on her domestic duties; she 'must make order and cleanliness, ease and peace reign at home.' For Prudhomme, 'political liberty is in a manner of speaking useless to women and in consequence must be foreign to them.' Women need know no more about public affairs than their fathers or husbands deem fit to teach them.[91] Eventually, Rowbotham concludes, upper- and middle-class women would come to accept, and to perpetuate among new generations of women, the role of 'helpless, emotional, hysterical angel in the house'. Whether she studied, prayed, or worked, 'she was still man's object. . . . She saw herself through his eyes. She defined herself in relation to his needs, his achievements. In return, she was pampered and cared for.'[92]

This became the dominant ideology that survived the Revolution. In 1793, even women who owned property were denied political rights. According to Patterson, by 1795 with the anti-Jacobin forces in power, women's political clubs were outlawed. Women were forbidden to congregate in public and could attend a meeting of the National Convention only if they were accompanied by a male citizen. The new government moved to establish a new moral code in society, establishing a system of public education that included separate primary schools for boys and girls designed to educate the two sexes in appropriate social roles: as homemakers or breadwinners. Women were excluded from higher learning.[93] Napoleon's **Civil Code** of laws was designed to complete the task of putting women back in their customary place. Making women by definition the second sex, the Code was heavily paternalistic, re-establishing the authority of fathers, giving husbands the exclusive right to manage property, severely restricting divorce, and confirming the absence of political rights for women. The Code enshrined the sexual double standard in law. A wife convicted of adultery could be imprisoned for two years. A wife could petition for divorce from an adulterous husband, but only if he brought his mistress to live in the family home.[94]

For both the revolutionary and the Napoleonic regimes, independent, forceful, and active women were regarded as anomalies and threats to male dominance. Marie the Girondist Roland and Charlotte Corday—who assassinated the Jacobin leader Marat—were silenced by the guillotine. The demands from women for political and social equality were the least successful during the Revolution. There had been, nonetheless, a minority revolutionary view that demanded that the Enlightenment principles of equality and liberty be extended to women. The *philosophe* most consistently in favour of the rights of women was Marie-Jean Condorcet, a Girondist supporter. After his arrest in 1794, Condorcet died in prison, likely by suicide.

Condorcet's progressive stance on women's rights was influenced by his wife, Sophie de Condorcet, who challenged the Enlightenment belief in the paramount importance of reason. Most *philosophes* accepted without question the ancient belief that rationality was superior to passion and that civilized life meant to subdue passion in the name of reason. Sophie de Condorcet argued that the cornerstone of society was morality, which derived from a feeling of sympathy for others and was later developed by reason. The idea of justice, she wrote, is 'the necessary work of sensibility and reason' together. Marie Roland made a similar argument: 'The highest degree of virtue is to do good with enthusiasm because it is honourable and delightful. . . . Exact calculation and cold reasoning never make us capable of it; feeling alone inspires us.'[95] This argument would recur in a variety of social theories developed by women.

For most male theorists, however, males were superior to females in their higher ability to reason abstractly. Consequently, women should not have equal political and social rights. Olympe de Gouges and Mary Wollstonecraft were two early feminists who directly challenged these patriarchal views and argued for women's equality.

Olympe de Gouges

Olympe de Gouges was a French playwright who welcomed the coming of the Revolution. In 1791, when it had become clear that the new French government would not extend equal rights to women, de Gouges published the *Declaration of the Rights of Women and the Citizen*. De Gouges argued on the basis of natural rights that the principles of the Revolution ought to be extended to women. Nowhere in nature, de Gouges claimed, does one sex oppress the other; rather, 'everywhere they cooperate in harmonious togetherness.' In this century of enlightenment, however, men have become 'bloated with science and degenerated . . . into the crassest ignorance'. Men want 'to command as a despot a sex which is in full possession of its intellectual faculties'. The Revolution may have freed men, but women have

received only scorn and disdain. Women must wake up and use reason to oppose 'the empty pretensions of superiority. . . . [I]t is in your power to free yourselves; you have only to want to.'[96]

De Gouges's document was a feminist tract that went beyond the claim of women to equal rationality with men. She identified the source of the oppression of women in patriarchy, arguing that male tyranny limited women in the exercise of their natural rights. In fact, for de Gouges, women were superior in beauty and in courage, which they demonstrated during the sufferings of childbirth.

The challenge of de Gouges's *Declaration* extended into very private areas of patriarchal control, including male succession rights. By law, only children of marriage were legitimate; illegitimate children were unrecognized in law or in inheritance, as she complained:

> Marriage is the tomb of trust and love. The married woman can with impunity give bastards to her husband, and also give them the wealth which does not belong to them. The woman who is unmarried has only one feeble right; ancient and inhuman laws refuse to her for her children the right to the name and the wealth of their father; no new laws have been made in this matter.[97]

De Gouges demanded the precious right of the 'free communication of thoughts and opinions . . . since that liberty assures recognition of children by their fathers. Any female citizen thus may say freely, I am the mother of a child which belongs to you, without being forced by a barbarous prejudice to hide the truth.' Fathers of so-called illegitimate children would be publicly identified and forced to give their names and wealth to their children. Her challenge went directly to the foundation of male control of the family.

At the beginning of the Revolution, de Gouges supported a constitutional monarchy, dedicating her *Declaration of the Rights of Women* to Queen Marie-Antoinette. After the execution of the King and Queen, de Gouges became a vociferous critic of the National Assembly and was arrested and charged with sedition. The Jacobins said her ideas originated from a delirious imagination rather than from nature; she had 'forgotten the virtues that belong to her sex'. In 1793, even women who owned property were denied political rights.[98] Her specific crime was publishing a pamphlet opposing Robespierre, under the pseudonym 'an amphibious animal'—by which she meant neither male nor female, but combining the traits of both sexes.[99] Undoubtedly, her feminism was her principal crime in the eyes of the male revolutionaries.

In her *Declaration*, de Gouges had argued that, since a woman has the right to 'mount the rostrum' (attain political power), so, too, she 'has the right to mount the scaffold.' Ironically, the Jacobins accepted this argument in favour of women's equality. De Gouges was condemned and sent to the guillotine in November 1793, the same month that Marie-Jeanne Roland was executed. Both Girondin women, Censer and Hunt note, challenged the dominance of patriarchy. They were outspoken women who were denounced as being 'women-men' for defying the gender role that was supposedly natural for their sex.[100] They were silenced by the Revolution.

Germaine de Staël

Not even the powerful Napoleon succeeded in silencing Germaine de Staël (1766–1817). Born in Paris but the daughter of a Swiss banker, de Staël was declared a foreigner in 1796 and exiled from Napoleonic France. For feminist writers such as de Staël, the novel was a form of philosophical discussion suitable for women. The protagonist of her romantic novel *Corinne* (1807), which achieved international fame in Europe, was a tragic figure because she was unable to reconcile her genius and demand for autonomous selfhood with the social requirements of the traditional wife. The real villain of the novel was unjust social convention that doomed an independent woman.[101] Social conventions did not intimidate de Staël. She was a free-spirited woman who quickly abandoned a disastrous arranged marriage to Baron de Staël, took a variety of lovers, and gave birth to five children by different partners.[102]

De Staël was the chief feminist thorn in Napoleon's side. With her books banned by Napoleon's censors and forced into exile, de Staël became one of France's sharpest critics. In 1818, in the face of the Restoration of the Bourbon monarchy, de Staël's *Considerations on the French Revolution* was published posthumously. While deploring the Reign of Terror, de Staël blamed the Revolution on the narrow-minded intransigence of the aristocracy and clergy who failed to carry through the demands for reform.[103]

De Staël wished to restore balance between emotion and reason, tilted precipitously by the *philosophes* towards rationality. The *philosophes* had generally consigned women to the side of passion while men claimed the higher ground of reason and civilization. De Staël countered with the feminist argument that the Revolution had been driven by negative passions in men, such as revenge, ambition, and fanaticism. The real impulse to civilization was in the emotion of pity, a natural passion associated with sacrifice, selflessness, and love, and existing most absolutely in the instinct of motherhood. Pity, which was primarily but not exclusively a female sensibility, was implanted in the nature of humanity, becoming the source of virtue just as the existence of private property was the practical foundation of society.[104] According to these French feminists, it was not women's ability to reason that alone led them to insist on political equality for women. Cold reasoning, as Marie Roland put it, cannot inspire anyone to virtue. Adding women's distinctive standpoint would bring balance to society and government.

None of these intellectual women wanted to disparage the importance of cultivating women's reason along with their sensibility. A central feminist theme during the Enlightenment was the equal education for women. In Mary Hamilton's novel *Munster Village* (1778), described by Mellor as a feminist Utopian fantasy, Frances Munster founds an academy for the coeducation of men and women in all subjects, works as an accomplished artist, and develops a keen sense for business deal-ings and technical matters.[105]

Hamilton's fantasy did not reflect the actual direction of change. Women certainly achieved the right to be educated during the Enlighten-ment, but it was the right to a different education. Women were to be trained in such pleasing accomplishments as painting or music, which were thought to be consistent with their status as decorations that represented the power and wealth of their patriarchal husbands. Going against the grain of these accepted practices, Mary Wollstonecraft demanded that women be recog-nized as independent, rational human beings in their own right.

MARY WOLLSTONECRAFT

> It is justice, not charity, that is wanting in the world!
> —Mary Wollstonecraft, *Vindication of the Rights of Women* (1792)

Mary Wollstonecraft (1759–97) was the grand-daughter of an English manufacturer. Her father, who inherited the family fortune, drank, bullied his wife, and gradually sank into dissolution, dragging the family downward in society. What money the family had left was inherited by the eldest son, leaving Wollstonecraft to find work as a paid companion to a wealthy woman. The wretched life of her sister, Eliza, who married early to escape misery at home only to suffer abuse in her marriage, is described in Wollstonecraft's *Wrongs of Women*. For a time, Wollstonecraft was a governess for an aristocratic family in Ireland, but she was soon dismissed.[106] These experiences taught her life's hard lessons about the injustices of **patriarchy** and authority. Coming to intellec-tual maturity in radical times, Wollstonecraft became sympathetic to the French Revolution and the writings of Rousseau.

In 1789 Wollstonecraft was a member of a radical, republican intellectual circle in London that included Thomas Paine, William Godwin,

William Blake, and Richard Price. That year, Price spoke before the London Revolution Society, attacking the English monarchy and the privileges of the aristocratic classes and calling for a new English Revolution. While most English intellec-tuals were sympathetic to the Revolution in France, the conservative, Edmund Burke, was not. Challenged by Price's call for revolt, Burke pub-lished his *Reflections on the Revolution in France*. Wollstonecraft then wrote a rejoinder called *Vin-dication of the Rights of Men* in 1790.

Burke had argued that the rights the liberals and *philosophes* claimed to be natural actually originated in social conventions that had devel-oped historically and were expressed in the law of a given nation. As products of the history of nations, they varied in place and time. According to Burke, any seeming injustice that had persisted over time would become legitimate: 'time sancti-fies crimes'. Wollstonecraft asserts, on the con-trary, that humanity possesses universal, natural rights as rational creatures, which are inherited at birth. These rights are not merely handed down by their forefathers but derive directly from God.[107] She was outraged by Burke's dismissal of women as 'but an animal, and an animal not of the highest order'.

Rather than being the disinterested writer that Burke had proclaimed in his *Reflections*, Woll-stonecraft charged him with being the champion of property who tried to make power and right identical. Burke's argument elevated sensibility above the sovereignty of reason, Wollstonecraft argued, asserting that instinct was more truthful than reason: 'A kind of mysterious instinct is *sup-posed* to reside in the soul, that instantaneously discerns truth, without the tedious labour of' rea-soning.[108] Such a claim is open to no refutation; on the basis of sensibility alone, anything could be held up as truth or falsehood.

Wollstonecraft wrote from the point of view of the industrious middle class. For her and for the middle class, the aristocrats Burke regarded as noble were 'monsters in human shape' who ate sumptuously each day and were habitually pampered by the flattery of sycophants. It was only among the industrious middle class, whose inventiveness was sharpened by necessity, that a person's true talents would emerge. Wollstonecraft was indignant about Burke's contempt for the poor, although she admitted there is 'something disgusting in the distresses of poverty'. The poor work out of necessity and face unemployment and ruin when the economy and trade stagnate. It is in such necessitous circumstances that the poor succumb to those vices that Burke attributes to their nature.[109]

From Rousseau, Wollstonecraft derived the argument that the evils and vices of the world derive from 'the respect paid to property'. While people naturally seek the respect of their fellows, she argued, respect was accorded only to wealth and 'personal charms', and not talent and virtue— an argument that would be echoed by Jane Austen. By castigating the idle rich and endorsing the virtues of hard work, exertion, and self-denial, Wollstonecraft reflected the perspective of the middle class, which 'appear[s] to be in the most natural state'. While her sympathies were with the 'numerous class of hard working mechanics, who pay for the support of royalty when they can scarcely stop their children's mouths with bread',[110] poor women were confined by their circumstances, she said, and could not be lifted from drudgery to enlightenment.

There is no need in nature for there to be such poverty, distress, and vice, Wollstonecraft argued. Virtue could only flourish among people who were equal. Large estates could be divided into small farms; industrious peasants could be allowed to fence off a small parcel of land from the vacant and unused land. The result would be 'a garden more inviting than Eden', where the common people would breathe a 'bracing air, far from the diseases and vices of cities'.[111] Wollstonecraft, like Rousseau, held a romantic and positive conception of human nature, believing that a person's character was formed by experience and was, therefore, educable towards perfection. Political authority should not be based on tradition or custom, but on reason and justice, key Enlightenment values.

Wollstonecraft was part of a radical circle that believed people should express their political beliefs in the way they live their lives. At one point she attempted to have a rational sexual relationship with a married man, but this predictably fell through. She went to France, where the Revolution had become increasingly polarized, violent, and less romantic, and began to question her ideals and the potential for revolutionary change. She lived for a time in France with an American sea captain, Gilbert Imlay, while resuming her radical writing on the Revolution. Although Wollstonecraft gave birth to a daughter in 1794, this relationship with Imlay was disastrous for her mental well-being. Back in England in 1795, the combination of her personal troubles with Imlay and her political doubts made her distraught and led to two suicide attempts.[112] As Rowbotham explained her situation, 'To have an illegitimate child, to be a revolutionary, to write the *Vindication*, was in England in the 1790s to be desperately alone and cut off, socially, politically and emotionally.'[113]

In 1797, Wollstonecraft married William Godwin, with whom she had been living, although they both disapproved of the institution of marriage. Godwin had been brought up a strict Puritan and had become a Calvinist minister. His religious beliefs were undermined by his study of the French *philosophes*. Godwin associated with English radicals and supported the French Revolution. When he married Mary Wollstonecraft, the two maintained separate apartments in conformity with the view that too much intimacy would result in mutual weariness. Wollstonecraft died in 1797 shortly after giving birth to a second child, also named Mary. In 1813, their daughter, Mary Godwin, eloped with the Romantic poet Shelley. As Mary Shelley, she wrote the novel *Frankenstein*. As conservative times settled over Europe after 1815, Wollstonecraft's ideas were largely ignored. Her name was associated with immorality, and her tragic death was interpreted as the logical outcome of her dangerous and disordered life.

Vindication of the Rights of Women

> Rousseau exerts himself to prove that all *was* right originally; a crowd of authors that all *is* right now; and I that all will *be* right.
> —Mary Wollstonecraft, *Vindication of the Rights of Women* (1792)

In 1791 the revolutionary French government (at the time dominated by the Girondists) proposed a state-supported educational system to provide free public education for men, but excluded women. Wollstonecraft responded in 1792 with *A Vindication of the Rights of Women*, an early feminist document based on the conviction that women were capable of the highest human rationality and demanding equality for women. By this law, Wollstonecraft charged, half of humanity was excluded from any participation in government by the other half. The rights of men were justified on the principle that men were rational. Since woman were equally endowed with the gift of reason, Wollstonecraft argued, it was logical that women, as fully human, embodied these inalienable and universal rights as well as men. Men were granted the freedom to judge their own happiness, and it was inconsistent and unjust to subjugate women and deny them this freedom.

For Wollstonecraft, 'tyrants of every denomination, from the weak king to the weak father . . . are all eager to crush reason' in the hopes that women can be kept in their place. Yet, argues Wollstonecraft, this traditional place, where women were merely convenient slaves, was detrimental to women, degrading to men, and damaging to the nation. It was only because women were denied any access to power that they were forced, by circumstances, to seek power indirectly through flattery, coquetry, and undue attention to their appearance. Only through full participation in public life and equal educational opportunities could women lead genuinely virtuous lives and would women and men be mutually content in their companionship.[114]

The grand source of misery was the false system of education that was particularly harmful to women, who were defined as though they were entirely a separate category from men rather than as human creatures. Women were kept in a state of 'perpetual childhood', dependency, and weakness, which led them ultimately to 'become objects of contempt'. Women were taught to seek and inspire men's love 'when they ought to aspire to a nobler ambition and by their abilities and virtues exact respect.'

This nobler ambition was to be a virtuous mother and wife. Wollstonecraft's objective was to help women become affectionate wives and rational mothers; they should be taught to govern a family with sound judgement and take proper care of the education of their children.[115] The ideal home she imagined replicated the public/private split in gender roles, with both sexes fulfilling their respective duties, the man active in the world and the woman nursing her children and 'discharging the duties of her station with, perhaps, merely a servant maid to take off her hands the servile part of the household business.'[116] For Wollstonecraft, middle-class women lived in the most natural state.[117] Only for such women were independence and rational education possible.

Wollstonecraft insists, nevertheless, that husbands and wives ought to be independent of each other and that the first duty of a woman is to herself as a rational creature, though she adds that, as a citizen, her second duty is to 'manage her family, educate her children, and assist her neighbours.' In this sense, she does not attack gender roles and women's domesticity directly. She does, however, object to this role being forced on all women. Some women should be physicians as well as nurses, study politics, or pursue various businesses. To fulfill this larger role, women should be educated to think for themselves, an argument that leads directly to a demand for a role in government for the better-educated women. She laments that 'women of a superior cast' are not allowed to pursue a more useful and independent road, 'for I really think that women ought to have representatives, instead of being arbitrarily governed without having any direct share allowed them in the deliberations of government.'[118]

For male theorists, whether radicals such as Rousseau or conservatives such as Burke, women were not merely different from men in degree, but different in essence.[119] In an essay on 'the sublime and beautiful', Burke had claimed that women were designed by nature to be small and weak, traits which defined natural beauty. These *'little, smooth, delicate, fair creatures'*, Burke declared, should exacerbate their natural weaknesses by learning to lisp and by tottering in their walk, thereby becoming even more desirable as pleasing sensations to inspire men's love. Women were not designed by nature to exercise their reason, to seek the supposedly manly virtues of truth, justice, and wisdom. For Burke, they were to be loved but not respected as equals in mind and, therefore, Wollstonecraft concludes, not really loved at all.[120]

Burke's extreme prejudices were easily exposed to those with an open mind. Rousseau was another matter. Rousseau's progressive ideas about child-rearing and education (expounded in *Émile*) were widely admired by English radicals such as Godwin and Wollstonecraft. While she found much to praise in Rousseau, Wollstonecraft rejected some key elements of his theory, including his cornerstone assumptions about the state of nature—that humans were originally solitary and asocial and that all evil came from civilization. On the contrary, Wollstonecraft believed, adopting a **feminist standpoint**, the lengthy dependency of childhood and the resulting need for care and love provided the foundation for civilization. Furthermore, by granting people the ability to reason, the deity had given them the potential and the responsibility to achieve virtue (goodness), a potential they had so far squandered. Human rationality allowed them the opportunity to achieve perfection and, although they had not yet succeeded, they would in the future: 'all will *be* right', Wollstonecraft optimistically asserted. Rousseau sought only a 'flight back to the night of . . . ignorance' rather than moving forward to true civilization.[121]

It was Rousseau's patriarchal ideas about women's nature and education that most raised Wollstonecraft's ire. She found them puerile, ridiculous, and below contempt. Rousseau believed women should be to be trained for obedience, Wollstonecraft claimed, for '[g]entleness, docility, and a spaniel-like affection'. For Rousseau, she said, woman 'was created to be the toy of man, his rattle, and it must jingle in his ears whenever . . . he chooses to be amused.'[122] Women were trained to be like useless and insipid aristocrats, who were vain and helpless, and lived only to amuse themselves; or like soldiers indoctrinated to obey commands and submit blindly to authority.

Wollstonecraft agreed with much Rousseau had said about educating men and sought only to extend it to women, not, she insists, to give them power over men but to have power over themselves. The wise mother would raise her daughter diametrically opposite to Rousseau's prescriptions. Women were being miseducated to cultivate feminine beauty and to seek indirect influence by playing up to men. Women's real nature was being distorted by society. In this situation, it was not possible to prove directly that women were naturally the rational equal of men; but it could also not be proved that they weren't. In her view, only in a situation in which hereditary distinctions between people had disappeared and the education of women was based on rational principles—and women still persisted in their degraded condition—could it be 'prove[d] that they have *less* mind than men.'[123]

Mellor claims that Wollstonecraft's **gender politics** contained an unresolved tension between women's sexuality and the practicalities of marriage. Most women would get married and Wollstonecraft pictured an egalitarian marriage between two mutually respectful adults that would be based on rationality rather than passion or sexuality.[124] For Wollstonecraft, true love, as well as 'beauty and grace must arise from the play of the mind', not the passions. She championed the liberation of women's rationality, but not sexual liberation as feminists would later understand the term. While men were deemed to be the more rational of the two sexes, they were also, Wollstonecraft thought, 'more under the influence of their appetites than women', whether overindulgence referred to eating or to sexuality.[125]

Wollstonecraft distinguished between mere coquetry and love; with a lover a woman is led by her emotions to gratify her heart. Love is natural and genuine, expressing 'the artless impulse of nature'. She warned, however, against intemperate love, sexual licentiousness, and overindulgence in animal appetite. After marriage, a couple 'ought not to continue to love each other with passion' or indulge 'those emotions which disturb the order of society'. Reason must subdue passion and restrain emotions; sense must channel sensibility. Love must be dignified, purified, and delicate, and should subside 'into friendship, or companionate tenderness'.[126]

As Wollstonecraft explained the situation, women were taught literary and artistic accomplishments to please men; they were taught to be concerned with their appearance and dress to incite men's sexual passions, which they then had to resist while simultaneously repressing their own passions, lest they become fallen. The result corrupted both women and men. It was time, Wollstonecraft said, 'to effect a revolution in female manners'.[127] The nature of women and men must both change in order for this liberal feminist ideal to be realized.

Numerous women novelists of the early nineteenth century embraced Wollstonecraft's image of the rational woman in their writing. They advocated 'the revolutionary idea that women must think as well as feel', Mellor claims.[128] Consistent with the socially constructed need to restrain and repress their sexuality, she argues, the heroes of women's fiction during this period had to 'act with prudence, avoid the pitfalls of sexual desire, and learn from their mistakes'.[129] In the novel *Julia* (1790) by Helen Maria Williams, unrestrained sexual passion destroys everyone; peace is not restored to the family unit until there is no longer any opportunity for unrestrained emotions. Rational affection is more permanent and sustaining then short-lived, frenzied passion, a position, Mellor asserts, Wollstonecraft would have endorsed.[130]

According to literary critic Loraine Fletcher in her examination of four Jacobin women writers, the novel *A Simple Story* (1791) by Elizabeth Inchbald similarly reflects the classic narrative of the evil or virtuous woman. In Fletcher's modern interpretation, the hero of *A Simple Story*, Miss Milner, who exhibits a 'free, **transgressive** personality', is confined by the powerful forces of the Church and social custom.[131] A bad woman 'asserts herself, is disobedient to patriarchal authority and comes to a miserable end', while the good heroine suppresses her individuality, assents to male guidance, and marries happily.[132]

In her later novel, *Nature and Art* (1796), Fletcher points out,[133] Inchbald depicts a fallen woman's plight more realistically and critically. Agnes is a victim of cruel men and the social system. When Agnes is seduced and left pregnant by William, the seduction produces neither social stigma nor a barrier to his successful career as a lawyer and judge. To support herself and her son, the abandoned Agnes is forced into prostitution in the underworld of London's outcasts, a fate that reflected the life experience of many women, including Inchbald's sister. Brought to court for her crimes, Agnes appears before William and is condemned to death, as the story comes full circle, from private humiliation to public condemnation.

JANE AUSTEN

The rational and moral woman championed by Wollstonecraft in her *Vindication of the Rights of Women* was reflected in the female heroes depicted by the English novelist, Jane Austen (1775–1817). Austen began writing fiction in 1787 but it remained unpublished until 1811, when *Sense and Sensibility* appeared in print. Austen was younger than Mary Wollstonecraft and, although she spent her adolescence and young adulthood during the turbulent years of the French Revolution, her political views shrank from the agnosticism and apparent immorality of the radical women novelists of her time. Austen wrote about the more complacent and conservative world of the rural gentry, a life she understood intimately. Within the constraints of her religious beliefs, which prejudiced her to conservatism, Austen exposed the aristocracy to ridicule and challenged the assumption that women were intellectually inferior to men.

Like many late eighteenth-century English writers, Austen was critical of the exaggerated deference extended to the titled nobility who neglected their economic and social duties. Her perspective on the English class structure is readily apparent in *Persuasion*, published posthumously in 1818, which depicts three levels of social status. The minor aristocrat Walter Elliott paid more attention to his own comforts and status than to the management of his estate or the duties he owed to his tenants. As a baronet, Elliott stood higher in the ladder of prestige than the rural gentry, but he was ranked beneath the titled nobility, represented by the snobbish and deplorable Lady Dalrymple, who had nothing of substance to recommend her, 'no superiority of manner, accomplishment, or understanding'.[134] Elliott's middle position among the upper class made him hypersensitive to status differences and deferential to unworthy people. Austen believed people should be judged on their personal qualities and how they act in the world, rather than because of their social status. In this respect, Austen self-consciously reflected 'the unfeudal tone' of her day.[135]

Austen admired the modernizing rural gentry who managed their property on practical business lines rather than squandering their wealth and neglecting their social duties. The youngest of the Elliott daughters in *Persuasion* married beneath her station to Charles Musgrove, the son of an enterprising gentry family 'of respectability and large fortune'. She had 'given all the honour, and received none'.[136] The hard-working Musgroves improved the land and prospered while the Elliotts sank deeper in debt until they were humbly obliged to rent their estate. When Walter Elliott handed over the management of his estate to Admiral Croft, it 'passed into better hands than its owners'.[137] Rather than being born into social rank, talented and hard-working individuals

could achieve honour and promotion in the Navy, a moderately liberal view endorsed by Austen.

As Sutherland points out, Austen was also sympathetic to the cause of the abolition of slavery. In *Mansfield Park*, the aristocratic Thomas Bertram owned an estate in the British colony of Antigua, implying that his fortune came from the labour of African slaves. Only once is the subject of slavery brought into the novel, when Bertram's niece, Fanny, asks him 'about the slave trade' but then does not pursue the question because 'there was such a dead silence!'[138] With this cautious reference, Austen allows her critique of slavery to remain implied rather than direct. *Mansfield Park* was written during the anti-slavery campaign in England inspired by the reformer, William Wilberforce.[139]

Neither did Austen comment directly on the parallel oppression of African slaves and European women, a common theme in the feminist literature of the period. However, Bertram was described as 'so . . . infamously tyrannical' that he made a disagreeable father and an arbitrary uncle. His advice was 'the advice of absolute power'.[140] Under his patriarchal influence, one of his two daughters married unhappily for social position while another rebelled, escaping into a ruinous though initially romantic attachment. Reflecting on his failures as a parent, Bertram concluded that his daughters had been taught female accomplishments and appropriate manners, but not to think beyond their own feelings.

Austen's main contribution to social thought is her depiction of the position of women, which was determined first by their birth and, second, by the social status into which they married. This theme is established in the opening sentence of *Mansfield Park* when we learn that, 'Miss Maria Ward of Huntington, with only seven thousand pounds, had the good luck to captivate Sir Thomas Bertram, of Mansfield Park, . . . [and] be thereby raised to the rank of a baronet's lady, with all the comforts and consequences of an handsome home and large income.' Her two equally handsome sisters did not make such elevated matches. One married a clergyman who had 'scarcely any private fortune', while the other, Frances, married a lieutenant 'without education, fortune, or connections', the three routes to upward mobility for a man.[141] When Frances's eldest daughter, Fanny, is taken in by the Bertrams, the nine-year-old is made painfully aware of the elaborate pecking order of the upper class. Her station was below her cousins and she was taught her 'rank, fortune, rights, and expectations' would always be different.[142]

The social process of selecting a marriage partner is a predominant theme in Austen's fiction. Anne Elliott, the protagonist of *Persuasion*, was 'a most extraordinary young woman; in her temper, manners, mind, a model of female excellence.'[143] She is one of Austen's typically unblemished female heroes, who were usually insufferably and improbably virtuous. At the age of 29, Anne was unmarried, having been persuaded as a young woman to reject marriage with Captain Frederick Wentworth despite their deep and mutual love. Anne's father considered the class differences made it 'a very degrading alliance' since Wentworth had neither personal fortune nor aristocratic family connections to secure rapid promotion.

Similarly, Fanny Price in *Mansfield Park* was obviously very bright and observant, although, repressed by her stepdaughter status in the Bertrams' mansion, she learned to be 'properly submissive and indifferent'. From the traditional point of view, this made her a desirable marriage prospect since her apparent malleability was suitable for 'a sweet little wife; all gratitude and devotion'.[144] Faced with her refusal to marry Harry Crawford, a match that her uncle favoured because it would be financially advantageous for his niece, Bertram expressed the patriarchal ideology of his age when he fumed to the intransigent Fanny: 'I thought you peculiarly free from wilfulness of temper, self-conceit, and every tendency to that independence of spirit which prevails so much in modern days, even in young women, and which in young women is offensive and disgusting beyond all common offence.'[145]

For Austen, character and personality were partially inborn and partially constructed by experiences—continuing Inchbald's debate about art and nature. Although a person could be improved through education and experience, nature set limits to how much improvement was possible.[146] Fanny's poor sister, Susan, who had been brought up in the poverty from which Fanny had been elevated, 'had an innate taste for the genteel and well-appointed'.[147] If Susan had remained uneducated under her parents' confining roof, she would have felt forever dissatisfied without understanding why; had she lacked the natural potential to be improved, no amount of education could have changed Susan's natural inclinations.

On the question of women's rationality, Austen's gender politics were especially anti-feudal. Women should not be treated as if they 'were all fine ladies, instead of rational creatures.'[148] Anne Elliott's superiority in *Persuasion* comes as much from her mind as from her typically feminine sensitivity. In her discussion with Captain Benwick about poetry, Anne was the one giving advice, 'feeling in herself the right of seniority of mind'.[149] She realized that most books prove nothing about women since they were written by men, as her argument with Captain Harville shows (Box 4.6).[150] Not rank, or wealth, or sex determine superiority, but strength of mind and character.

Because social conventions confined women to traditional domestic occupations, they had little scope for expressing their rationality. Austen's early novels, *Sense and Sensibility* (1811) and *Pride and Prejudice* (1813), were concerned with the difficult business of choosing marriage partners. Only a marriage could save a woman from the poverty of spinsterhood, but a woman did not have the option of initiating a marriage proposal. As Austen wrote, 'Single Women have a dreadful propensity for being poor—which is one very strong argument in favour of Matrimony.'[151] A woman was dependent on a man to propose; at most, she could refuse, as Elizabeth Bennett, the intelligent and independent hero of Jane Austen's *Pride and Prejudice* does. For Austen, marriage should be the wedding of sensibility and rationality; it involved both

---

Box 4.6

Captain Harville: 'Well Miss Elliot . . . as I was saying, we shall never agree I suppose upon this point. No man and woman would, probably. But let me observe that all histories are against you, all stories, prose and verse. . . . I could bring you fifty quotations in a moment on my side [of] the argument. . . . Songs and proverbs, all talk of woman's fickleness. But perhaps you will say, these were all written by men.'

    'Perhaps I shall.—Yes, yes, if you please, no reference to examples in books. Men have had every advantage of us in telling their own story. Education has been theirs in so much higher a degree; the pen has been in their hands. I will not allow books to prove any thing.'

—Jane Austen, *Persuasion* (1818)

---

the heart and the mind. Elizabeth Bennett is courted by Mr Collins, for whom marriage is a very practical and pecuniary matter deserving careful consideration, such as he would give to any business venture. When Elizabeth rejects him despite his excellent economic situation and social connections, Collins assumes she is playing the traditional coquette, so her refusal 'is merely words of course'.[152] Elizabeth then speaks plainly, making the assertion that her rejection was based both on her reason and her feelings:

> I would rather be paid the compliment of being believed sincere. I thank you again and again for the honour you have done me in your proposals, but to accept them is absolutely impossible. My feelings in every respect forbid it. Can I speak plainer? Do not consider me now as an elegant female, intending to plague you, but as a rational creature, speaking the truth from her heart.[153]

Marriage required sensibility as well as sense, mutual love and mutual respect. When Elizabeth's mother attempted to bring her to reason and accept Collins, she said Elizabeth was a very 'headstrong foolish girl' who didn't 'know her own interest'. This was precisely what Collins did not want to hear. To be headstrong and independent was a defect in women and would not make her 'a very desirable wife'.[154]

In the end, Elizabeth married Mr Darcy, though not because of material calculations or parental authority. Their mutual affection and respect grew slowly, almost imperceptibly, beginning in what is now a literary convention of initial misunderstanding and dislike. Darcy loved Elizabeth but he also appreciated her intellectual qualities: 'I knew enough of your disposition to be certain, that, had you been absolutely, irrevocably decided against me, you would have acknowledged it . . . frankly and openly.'[155]

Austen was no radical. Love naturally flowed along the proper social channels. Freedom of choice in relationships would not find an upper-class lady in the arms of a gamekeeper. Austen learned mostly negative lessons from the earlier female voices who had demanded equality and power in the revolutionary period, and who had been silenced for their impudence. Despite her social conservatism, Austen's novels continued the genre of middle-class realism, depicting in minute detail the actual life and circumstances of women among the rural gentry while inserting their claims for respect, recognition, and independence.

CONCLUSION

The French Revolution was a momentous and complicated social movement. Its initial liberating effect on both social theory and the arts produced an exuberance and radicalism that would survive the collapse of the Revolution. In social theory, what the French Revolution was taken to mean, how it was understood, is more important than the events it precipitated, the personalities involved, or the practical changes that were made. The Revolution shaped the perception of theorists and writers for generations to come. No event was comparable in significance to the French Revolution until war and revolution erupted in the early decades of the twentieth century.

In the Marxist interpretation, the events in France amounted to a bourgeois revolution, in which the new, rising class of capitalists had replaced the old aristocratic elite. The transformation from one era to another is not usually precipitated by a single event, even as dramatic as revolution. The old elite had not been shattered; a new amalgamated elite emerged under Napoleon, which included members of the old aristocracy who could adapt themselves to the new world of commercial capitalism.

The French Revolution, however, was not an unqualified victory for the rising bourgeoisie. From an economic point of view, as in England, changes did not occur quickly. The independent peasantry continued to be a strong force in French society throughout the nineteenth century. The persistence of small landholdings and the traditionalist ideology of the rural priests slowed economic change in the countryside and, simultaneously, the Industrial Revolution in France. France's quick military defeat in 1870 by newly industrializing Prussia revealed the extent to which the economic revolution in France lagged behind its neighbours and competitors.

Four powerful intellectual movements emerged from the French Revolution. Radical ideas had a very long taproot, certainly extending back to the Diggers and the Levellers of the English Revolution. While the crushing defeat of the Revolution drove radicalism underground, the demands for equality, democracy, and justice can be repressed only for a time. They continued to reappear in new forms to suit new conditions in the nineteenth century.

Revolutionary movements inspire other revolts. Conscious of their oppression, African Americans and women drew inspiration from the ideologies of the French Revolution and the Enlightenment that preceded it. There were many parallels between the social statuses of the two groups, not the least of which was that both were devalued by the assumption that they were naturally inferior in their ability to reason. Two streams of feminist thought emerged from the rejection of this prejudice. Feminist thought demanded recognition of women's equal rationality, reflected in their educational, occupational, and political rights. An alternative feminist standpoint stressed the maternal bond, women's superior sensibilities, and their natural desire for peace and order. The family, not government, was the basic building block of society and women were at the heart of the family. Men should be more like women. With some exceptions, early feminism was not extended to sexual liberation. Many practical obstacles stood in the way of a woman's independent decision-making about personal matters.

The immediate response to the defeat of the Revolution, however, was to strengthen the ideology of conservatism, which also had long roots in the Middle Ages. Slavery was reinstituted in France, the Code Napoleon tried to put women back in their pre-revolutionary place, and political reaction undermined liberties in England and led to a restored monarchy in France.

The fourth great intellectual movement fertilized by the Revolution combined certain elements of both radicalism and conservatism. Less directly political than either of these polar standpoints, **Romanticism** was concerned more with ideas and lifestyles, and was expressed primarily in the arts and literature. It is to the conservative and Romantic movements that we next turn.

1689 English political philosopher John Locke (1632–1704) publishes *An Essay on Human Understanding*: at birth the mind is an 'empty cabinet'.

1710 Bishop George Berkeley (1685–1753) criticizes empiricism: 'To be is to be perceived.'

1774 Johann von Goethe (1749–1832) publishes *The Sorrows of Young Werther*.

1781 Immanuel Kant (1724–1804) publishes *Critique of Pure Reason*.

1789 Jeremy Bentham (1748–1832) establishes the English school of utilitarianism.

1790 Edmund Burke (1729–97) publishes his conservative *Reflections* on the French Revolution.

1794 Girondin-led faction overthrows the Jacobins in France, ends the Reign of Terror, and precipitates a 'White Terror'.

1797 Joseph de Maistre (1753–1821) publishes a reactionary attack on the French Revolution.

1818 Mary Shelley (1797–1851) publishes her Gothic novel *Frankenstein*.

1818 G.W.F. Hegel (1770–1831), idealist philosopher, accepts the Chair of Philosophy at Berlin.

1821 French social philosopher Saint-Simon (1760–1825) publishes his sociological study *On the Industrial System*.

1824 English Romantic poet George Gordon, Lord Byron (b. 1788), dies.

1830 Auguste Comte (1798–1857), founder of positivism, begins publishing his *Positive Philosophy*.

1830 Revolution in France ends with 'Citizen King' Louis-Philippe on the throne.

1831 Alexis de Tocqueville (1805–59) begins tour of the US; publishes *Democracy in America* in 1835.

1837 Harriet Martineau (1802–76) publishes her sociological study *Society in America*.

1841 Critical Young Hegelian Ludwig Feuerbach (1804–72) publishes *The Essence of Christianity*: God is the projected essence of humanity.

1845 Author, orator, and ex–slave Frederick Douglass (c.1817–95) publishes his autobiography.

1848 Urban revolutions erupt in Europe; Karl Marx (1818–83) and Friedrich Engels publish *The Communist Manifesto*.

1848 Women's convention at Seneca Falls, NY, produces historic declaration on women's rights.

1849 US Transcendentalist Henry David Thoreau (1817–62) writes *Essay on Civil Disobedience*.

1851 Harriet Taylor Mill (1807–58) publishes 'The Enfranchisement of Women'.

1852 Military coup in France ends the Second Republic; Second Empire established under Napoleon III.

1854 Charles Dickens (1812–70) publishes *Hard Times*, his attack on utilitarianism.

1857 Gustave Flaubert (1821–80) publishes his anti–Romantic novel *Madame Bovary*.

1859 English social liberal John Stuart Mill (1806–73) publishes *On Liberty*.

1861 The American Civil War begins; Lincoln issues 'Emancipation Proclamation' in 1863.

1864 Marx helps to establish the (first) International Workingman's Association.

1867 Marx publishes Vol. 1 of *Das Kapital*, his detailed critique of capitalism.

1867 UK Parliament passes Reform Bill, widens the franchise to include working-class men.

1871 Revolutionary Paris Commune established; after three months, the communards are massacred by French troops.

1871–2 English novelist George Eliot (Mary Ann Evans; 1819–80) publishes *Middlemarch*.

Part II FROM CONSERVATISM TO SOCIALISM

After Napoleon was defeated a second time and exiled to the island of St Helena, European politicians set about trying to put the historical clock back to pre-revolutionary times. The basic goal of the victorious powers, principally Prussia and Austria, was to erect a permanent bulwark against any further revolution in Europe. The more conservative politicians tried to restore the Old Regime in France and recreate the rule of aristocracy, monarchy, and church, the more they alienated the middle class, the shopkeepers, merchants, lawyers, and other professionals. The middle classes had gained a share of power in England and America, where liberalism flourished. In France, the middle classes had fought for the Revolution and then succeeded to office and influence under the regime of Napoleon, who opened recruitment to public office for talented individuals from below. Under the Restoration, however, liberalism was deemed revolutionary and social stability appeared to require only liberal doses of repression and authority.

Chapter Five examines the development of two opposing social theories that emerged following the French Revolution. One was the theory of conservatism, developed in reaction to the Revolution by a breed of theorists bent on restoring the traditional order. At first, they encountered opposition, but soon they found that the mainstream flowed with them. Conservatives in England and France attempted to uproot a large piece of the Western heritage, anchored in Enlightenment rationality. Conservative theory substituted for liberalism the belief that the duty an individual owed to the preservation of the society as it was greatly outweighed any individual rights, which had been granted to people by society in the first place. Conservatism was the theory of reaction, of restoration. Conservatives worshipped history, though not recent history. The Revolution had been a perversion. Civilization had reached its highest point in the Middle Ages. A generation of novelists created a new mythology of medieval chivalry and honour. If the past hadn't really been this rosy, it ought to have been.

The forced march back through time was resisted in France by the middle classes, who felt betrayed and abandoned by the new regime of the right. The second type of post-Revolution social theory was Romanticism. Grasping the revolutionary concept of liberty, many Romantics found themselves forced underground, sharing space with the liberal middle class. Romantics and liberals made common cause in their opposition to the right as political conflict seethed in France and was openly taking to the streets in 1830 and 1848 to secure a return to republican, perhaps even radical republican, government. This revolt of the people was led by students and professionals, such as journalists and lawyers, and the ever-radical independent artisans. Their inspiration, in part, came from Romanticism, a movement of rebellion that took as its watchword 'liberty'. Ultimately, however, it wasn't the ideals of political liberalism that drove the middle class into rebellion as much as their economic interests. Prosperity did not require republican government, and the middle classes soon settled comfortably under the rule of another autocrat, Napoleon III, who held power in France from 1851 to 1870. As the hopes of the Romantic rebels were dashed, Romanticism was given a new, anti-science twist. From that moment, modern social thought was split between a dominant, rationalist ideology and an oppositional Romanticism that rejected social convention and, absolutely, any idea that human beings could be understood rationally.

The anti-rational Romantics had a lot to complain about. Out of the mix of social theory that had developed before and after the Revolution grew the notion of creating a science of society. As Chapter Six explains, sociology was conceived during the post-Napoleonic age as a scientific approach to the understanding of society. The sociological approach grew out of a curious mixture of Enlightenment rationalism and conservative theory. The course of human history could be analyzed in terms of an evolutionary sequence of stages, propelled by a logic of development that was subject to laws analogous to those that determined physical phenomena. Society was like an organism, composed of many necessary and interrelated parts functioning as a whole, as the conservatives believed. The social structure was held together by irrational factors such as custom, tradition, and religious beliefs, but these could be understood rationally. Social science could account for the predominance of non-rational elements. France had experienced a revolving door of right-wing and left-wing governments. A stable and secure government could rest only on the rule of the few over the many, but the old aristocratic elite was passé. Modern governments had to be run by the most active and inventive people, the new elite of intellectuals and industrialists who would govern the nation, guide it to prosperity, and spread the benefits of industrialization to all classes.

American society, born of a nationalist revolution, existed through a contradictory mixture of liberty and authority. The United States proved to be particularly fertile ground for the spread of liberal individualism. In the early decades of the nineteenth century, frontier democracy competed for power with an eastern establishment based on mercantile trade and a southern aristocracy that survived from slave labour. The most liberal government coexisted with the most oppressive tyranny. In some cases, foreign observers perceived this monstrous juxtaposition more clearly than Americans. The American republic, these observers feared, faced dangers from both of its extremes. The fundamental flaw in American democracy, they claimed, was the danger that the majority could act tyrannically against the interest of the minority. Rule by a majority was no guarantee against the oppression of government. The other danger to the new republic came from the potential revolt of the oppressed Africans. Keeping Africans in bondage would not be possible for long, but emancipation would not solve the racial strife in America.

Early French sociology found a sympathetic audience in England. The dominant liberal ideology in England opposed government limitations on the economic freedom of individuals. For most Anglo-American intellectuals, government intervention meant limitations on freedom and smacked of tyranny. Yet, as Chapter Seven demonstrates, as the laissez-faire doctrine was manoeuvred into an ascendant position in England, and as negative social effects resulted, a cautious reformism developed despite the English predilection for smaller rather than interventionist government. Soon a number of reform ideologies, termed 'social liberalism', buffeted nineteenth-century English society, from demands for limited democracy that could be extended to women to a proposal for state-controlled medical care.

In England, and especially in America, parallels were noticed between the condition of slavery and the constraints and absence of rights imposed on women. The modern movement for women's right was sparked in the 1840s by American women whose intellectual independence and organizational abilities had been honed through their abolitionist work. For women's groups, however, getting involved in other causes has often meant shelving their own battles, temporarily at first and more permanently later.

One of these radical movements was social-ism, to which some women as well as men committed their energies and lives. The develop-ment of radical social theory in Germany is the subject of Chapter Eight. The socialist movement in Europe had survived the repression of the post-Revolution reaction, although it was disunited and often contradictory in its aims and tactics. Co-operative and union movements existed precari-ously as either alternatives to the existing social and economic system or a component of it. In con-trast, the Marxists looked for fundamental social change to come from below, from the collective political activities of the masses or the property-less workers. Marxism synthesized the scientific observations in British political economy, the rad-icalism of Rousseau, and the critical elements from the Romantic socialist movement, in the terms of a philosophical heritage rooted in German idealist philosophy.

5 THE CONSERVATIVE REACTION AND ROMANTICISM

The revolutionary upsurge persisted for close to half a century until 1818, when it was temporarily run to ground. Many who still clung to the dreams of revolutionary change had greeted Napoleon as the hero who would salvage the liberal aspects of the French Revolution and spread them to the rest of Europe. This sentiment soon was buried under the pomp and ceremony of Napoleon's self-coronation as Emperor. This act so disillusioned the composer Ludwig van Beethoven that he scratched out the dedication he had penned initially for Napoleon on his *Eroica* symphony. Napoleon's transformation into an 'Emperor' and his compromises with the Old Regime left little reason for optimism about the possibilities of making the world a better place through revolutionary politics.

When Napoleon was finally defeated and exiled to the small island of St Helena off the west coast of Africa, European elites relaxed in the restoration of the traditional social order and the contemplation of a new social theory that legitimated their rule. Conservatism was a reaction against the spectre of the French Revolution and the philosophy of the Enlightenment, and had its roots in tradition, feudal society, and the ideas of thinkers such as Aquinas.

The immediate forerunners of conservatism had appeared in the eighteenth century, when the traditional social order was being undermined by the slow erosion of economic change and the tidal wave of political revolution. What was called 'Tory' opinion (later a synonym for conservatism) had long protested the inroads that commercial capitalism and the Industrial Revolution were

making into traditional society, and had extolled instead the apparent virtues of the simple, rural community. When democratic sentiments had emerged during the American Revolution, **conservatives** denounced them as dangerous and impractical. John Adams complained that Paine's call for a single, popularly elected body of representatives was 'so democratical, without any restraint or even any attempt at any equilibrium or counter-poise, that it must produce confusion and every evil work.' Giving an elected body the sole power to make laws would lead to 'hasty results and absurd judgments', Adams thought.[1] This view, historian Zinn adds, was later echoed by Alexander Hamilton, who claimed:

> All communities divide themselves into the few and the many. The first are the rich and well-born, the other the mass of the people. The voice of the people has been said to be the voice of God; and however generally this maxim has been quoted and believed, it is not true in fact. The people are turbulent and changing; they seldom judge or determine right. Give therefore to the first class a distinct permanent share in the government. . . . Can a democratic assembly who annually revolve in the mass of the people be supposed steadily to pursue the public good? Nothing but a permanent body can check the imprudence of democracy.[2]

The Revolution in France crystallized opposition to political liberalism and fostered the development of conservatism. The governing elite in England regarded support for the Revolution to be an act of treason because it threatened the constitutional monarchy and limited democracy. In their fear of revolution, the English government tightened the censorship laws and prosecuted dissidents. The poet William Blake was tried for sedition in 1804 and the radical scientist Joseph Priestly was attacked by a conservative mob who wrecked his home, library, and laboratory. Liberal theorist Thomas Paine was forced to flee to France to avoid a likely conviction for treason.

As England and other European countries went to war against revolutionary or, later, Napoleonic France, most intellectuals dropped their radical posture and became conservative in their opinions. Radicalism had become unpatriotic. In 1794, while in the enthusiasm of his early twenties, playwright Robert Southey had written the play, *Wat Tyler*, which proclaimed the equality of men and denounced nobility and kingship. This subversive drama was not published until 1817 when a pirated version first appeared. Southey was greatly embarrassed by this publicity because, by then, he had become conservative and was the official poet laureate of England. The unauthorized publication was timely, however, because once again English liberties had been suspended by the government, not from the dangers of foreign invasion, but through fear of rebellion from below.[3]

The youthful radicalism of only a few of the English Girondins survived as a well-spring of revolt into their old age. Most intellectuals who had been initially sympathetic to the French Revolution were repulsed by the Reign of Terror and the wars that followed. The English Romantics, one by one, succumbed to the disillusionment of ideals gone wrong and the repression of dissent. Wordsworth and Coleridge, who had once believed that revolution was idealistic and romantic,[4] hastily trod Southey's political path from left to right.

One English intellectual, Edmund Burke, hardly strayed from the right-wing path. An early opponent of the French Revolution and the social theory that had given it birth, Burke advocated a new conservative outlook on society. In France, two **reactionary** theorists, Louis de Bonald and Joseph de Maistre, hoped the return of the monarchy would be the prelude to the restoration of the entire fabric of medieval society. The conservatives challenged the political philosophy of liberalism, from its emphasis on individualism and the fiction of a social contract to the inhumane and unjust ethics of laissez-faire capitalism.

Not every intellectual who was disillusioned by the unfolding of historical events fell back into conservatism. Many abandoned any concern with political change altogether, steering English Romanticism away from its concern with social injustice and plunging instead into the beauties of nature, or the harmonious myths of the past, or the imagination. The only real opportunity for change appeared to be the reform of individuals, and only through the actions of individuals could society as a whole be improved. The road to this Romanticism of withdrawal that focused on the role of the personal, individual subject had been prepared by the groundbreaking philosophy of Immanuel Kant.

PHILOSOPHICAL FOUNDATION

'What the eye doesn't see and the mind doesn't know, doesn't exist.'
D.H. Lawrence, *Lady Chatterley's Lover* (1928)

The early liberal view of how humans found knowledge was based on English empiricism. In this view, the individual mind was empty at birth. Knowledge came from outside, entering the brain as numerous and discrete sense experiences, which, in a simple cause-and-effect relationship, produced ideas. According to empiricism, our mind is like soft wax. We perceive the real world through our senses and each perception leaves its imprint on the mind. Over time, the repetition of perception and impressions leads to true knowledge about the world. Empiricism begins with matter, which is experienced by sensations, is absorbed into the mind, and then is converted into knowledge. This view of knowledge is related to the theory of **materialism**, which arose in opposition to the traditional view that knowledge was innate in the mind. For materialists, knowledge came only from our perceptions of the real world, which existed apart from and independent of our minds.

The empirical view that the mind reflected the fundamental qualities of existing things was soon challenged by social thinkers. Some wanted to go back to the traditional view that knowledge was embedded at birth by an all-powerful deity. In contrast, Bishop George Berkeley (1685–1753) took empiricism one step further. Perceptions would not exist, he said, without a mind to record them. If we had no mind, things would not exist for us. Colour does not exist for a blind person. If we were all blind, the idea of colour, let alone the classification of light into numerous colours, would not have been conceived. For Berkeley, 'to be is to be perceived'. The physical world only exists when it is perceived as an idea by a mind, ultimately, by the mind of God.

With Berkeley, the objective world becomes essentially subjective. David Hume (1711–76) took this argument to its conclusion, coming to doubt the possibility of any 'true' knowledge whatsoever. Hume began his *A Treatise of Human Nature* (1739–40) with Locke's empiricism, the view that knowledge derived from sense experiences. Fundamental to knowledge was the principle that every effect resulted from a cause. Causality, however, was purely an inductive matter—two connected events were experienced so frequently or strongly that the mind inferred that one was the cause of the other. This was a mental construct that resulted from habit; it was always possible that the two facts might not be connected. There was a probability they would be, but not a certainty. Knowledge rested on what we were accustomed to, so nothing could be certain. Hume became the essential skeptic; it was never possible to know beyond doubt what was true. For Hume, even our individual sense of 'self' was the result of our experiences with others. This reasoning led Hume to the study of history, since it was through the accumulation of experiences over time that

individuals come to understand the connections between things and regard them as necessary and true. Hume became the philosophical parent of conservative social theory, which regarded the present as the consequence of a slow evolution of customs and habits.

Philosophical speculation appeared to be a powerfully self-destroying acid. No knowledge was certain. It was impossible to prove, using reason, that objects existed independent of mind. Following this proposition, philosophers argued that no objective standard could prove the existence of mind, either. Nothing was left but subjective tautology: I know my mind exists because my mind tells me so. As pure reason chased its tail and, like the self-devouring serpent, swallowed itself, philosophers searched for a new, more secure foundation for knowledge and religion. Perhaps the mind was not simply Locke's white piece of paper but an active participant in creating knowledge. Empiricism assumes that knowledge derives from an objectively existing external reality, though, like Locke, objects were unknowable in their essence. Some things, however, were true at all times and places, but were not empirically observable. The new philosophy was soon to be associated with the name Immanuel Kant. Knowledge was constructed subjectively, by each individual's mind, though in accordance with embedded and universal imperatives.

IMMANUEL KANT

Romanticism and conservatism both are underwritten by the idealistic philosophy of Immanuel Kant (1724–1804). Kant was born in 1724 in Königsberg, in eastern Prussia. His father was a hard-working master harness-maker, a member of one of the less prosperous artisan guilds. His mother, Anna Reuter, was a harness-maker's daughter who was better educated than most women of her class and a devout Pietist, an evangelical Christian sect.[5] Because business competition was intense and the guild system was in crisis, Kant's family faced a slow but inevitable descent into poverty.[6] Despite these difficulties, at the age of eight Kant was offered a place in a Pietist school, where he was struck by the fanaticism of his teachers and the slavery of the discipline they imposed. He complained about the coercion, 'mechanism, and the shuttle of rules [that] . . . often robs people of all the courage to think for themselves'.[7]

At the age of 16, Kant began to study at the University of Königsberg. He pursued his studies autonomously and independently, and became quickly controversial. In 1755, Kant speculated that the universe was formed through the opposite principles of repulsion and attraction over millions of years, and speculated that intelligent life existed on other planets.[8] Singularly attached to Königsberg and determined to make his living there, Kant first became an unsalaried lecturer, finally becoming a professor of metaphysics and logic in 1770, having turned down prestigious offers to teach elsewhere. Kant lived a fastidiously disciplined bachelor's life that replicated his precise and methodical approach to philosophy.[9] He followed a routine that was almost as completely a pure life of the intellect as was possible outside a monastery or a desert hermitage.

With his first major publication, *The Critique of Pure Reason* (1781), Kant's theory of knowledge became the touchstone of Enlightenment philosophy. His *Theory of Practical Reason* (1788) expounded his equally influential theory of morals. According to Richard Rorty, Kant argued that fundamental distinctions existed among science (epistemology), morals (ethics), and art (aesthetics): 'Truth', 'morality', and 'beauty' represented three separate qualities and one could not be reduced to either of the others.[10]

Kant sought to develop a philosophy that combined empiricism and rationalism. From the empirical point of view, we achieve knowledge of things directly from our sense experiences. The problem is that understanding requires more than the perception of individual objects. Our perceptions have to fit into a framework of the intellect in order for the person to make sense of them. Understanding was a different kind of knowledge from sensory experience. This framework consists

of what sociologist Émile Durkheim, following Kant, called 'the categories of the understanding . . . ideas of time, space, class, number, cause, substance, personality, etc.' For the empiricists, these general concepts result simply from the sum total of sense experiences. On the contrary, Kant had argued, 'we can see certain relations in things which the examination of these things cannot reveal to us.'[11] What, then, is the source of the categories of the understanding?

Kant had argued that sense experience derived from specific objects was not sufficient to explain the creation in the human mind of general ideas. Rather than being a blank sheet upon which is written the results of experience, the human mind is active and creative, and plays a decisive role in interpreting and assigning meaning to sensory experience. There are universal elements in all knowledge, in Kant's words **a prioris** that inhere in the mind. The mind contains at birth the structures that organize the millions of sense experiences or perceptions that we have every day. They would all be a meaningless jumble if the mind were not equipped at birth with the ability to select, classify, and assign meaning. Concepts such as time, space, cause and effect, for example, were built into the structure of the individual mind and did not derive from sense experience. They were subjective 'intuitions' that were prior to experience and necessary to make sense of it.

In Durkheim's terms, Kant's a prioris are 'simple and irreducible data, imminent in the human mind by virtue of its inborn constitution'. Hence, they must be 'purely and absolutely homogeneous'.[12] This presupposed that all minds were identically structured. While Durkheim agrees that the mind has a power to transcend, or go beyond experience, he argues that Kant fails to explain the origin of this ability, since 'it is no explanation to say that it is inherent in the nature of the human intellect.' What, then, is the source of the generalized categories of knowledge that exist in the mind prior to, and help to organize, the endless number of sense experiences we perceive? For the Kantians, who recognize but fail to account for the power of the mind, Durkheim said, the origin of these general categories must be outside nature and science. In the absence of a scientific explanation, they must ultimately derive from God, or divine reason, 'a superior and perfect reason from which the others emanate'.[13] Durkheim would later argue that the source of these concepts was in the human experience of society; they derived from collective experience and not from individual experience (empiricism) or divine creation (a priori).[14]

In Kant's social philosophy, science cannot attain absolutely true knowledge because the world of sensation cannot penetrate to the inner essence of a thing. You could perceive only the surface appearance of objects. Similarly, you cannot prove theological truths beyond any doubt. Kant, however, was not content to remain in the depths of this skepticism. There were truths that were absolute, he believed, truths that people would realize were universal regardless of any doubts that reason might suggest. These were felt to be true; by intuition you knew that certain things were right or moral, and others were wrong or immoral. Your conscience did not derive from sense experience; it was the normal reaction of your mind's recognition of wrong. In Durkheim's view, rational thinking for Kant meant 'thinking according to the laws which are imposed upon all reasonable beings'. Everyone ought to think alike. In turn, acting morally meant making your actions conform to those universally valid rules and maxims that impersonal reasoning can deduce. In the highest form of reason, individuals are able to raise themselves above their own particular point of view and understand universal truths.[15]

In this sense, absolutely true ethical and moral laws were innate in the mind; they were not mere social conventions or the product of experience, but categorical. Kant held, for example, that the golden rule—do unto others as you would have them do unto you—was hard-wired (to use a contemporary colloquialism) into the brain. Any person could discover the universal truth of this proposition by using his or her mind. It followed from the golden rule, Kant argued, that we would deprive no one of something that we would not

willingly deprive ourselves. People's freedom, for example, should be limited only by the exercise of freedom of others. Freedom must be compatible with everyone else having the same freedom. This was an obvious, intuitive truth that was as valid as a rule of mathematics. As Kant developed his arguments, there were other innate truths, such as the existence of an immortal soul.

If people intuitively knew right from wrong, the perpetration of evil posed a problem Kant had to face. Why did people act wrongly even when they should know, intuitively, that it was wrong? Evil was caused by the freedom of will, another fact the individual would know intuitively. People make choices to act in one way or another, in some cases in their own selfish interests, other times in accordance with universal ethics. Human reason had the power to rise above the perspective and interests of the individual and arrive at universal truths. When the will was guided by this generalized human reason, people would act morally. Kant was skeptical, however, whether people, in general, were capable of achieving this moral life. Humans were partly animal in nature, causing a powerful duality in humanity that limited the capacity of reason. People were rational beings and animals simultaneously, Kant believed, and it was very doubtful that they could actually achieve a society based on the rational and mutual exercise of freedom.

Kant distinguished what he considered to be rational beliefs in God and immortality from the specific dogmas of various religions. Not all the practices of Christianity derived from the laws of universal reason. His arguments seemed more compatible with Deism than with any specific religious ideology. Like Descartes before him, Kant was accused of undermining organized religion, and the Prussian authorities at first attempted to suppress his *Critique*.

There was a rebellious side to Kant's eccentric character that emerged late in his life. For most of his career, Kant taught and wrote under the protection of the absolute Prussian monarch, Frederick the Great, who encouraged intellectual debate and religious tolerance. Frederick had sheltered the *philosophe* Voltaire from persecution in France. When the Prussian King died in 1786, this liberal atmosphere expired along with him. The new ruler, Frederick William II, imposed religious and moral orthodoxy on Prussia, a public decree that was contradicted by his sordid private life.[16] Official edicts prohibiting rationalist teaching threatened Kant's cherished liberal principles of freedom of thought and speech. After the French Revolution of 1789, the state censorship that Frederick had imposed to stifle religious and political dissent became even more intolerant.

Like most intellectuals, Kant welcomed the French Revolution as 'the glory of the world' and became a convinced republican.[17] He did not, however, champion the right to rebel against authority. People were free and rational; they could recognize the existence of categorical rules and should freely choose to obey them. While this meant people had a categorical duty to 'Obey Authority!', they also had the right and the duty to question authorities who imposed laws contrary to reason,[18] but this right was confined to freedom of speech.

Kant espoused other liberal principles. He declared slavery cruel and criminal and refuted the argument that Africans were a distinct human species.[19] He was more conservative, however, with respect to gender and class inequalities. While he believed each partner in marriage had a duty to treat the other as a moral individual and not merely as an object, women's sphere was properly confined to the domestic.[20] Kant had been attracted to several women early in his career, but the initial poverty of his life as a scholar and his tendency to procrastinate ensured that he remained a bachelor. His biographer, Manfred Kuehn, claims that Kant never had sex, consistent with his definition of 'morality as freedom from affection and desire'.[21]

Kant assumed that individuals must express their essential freedom and be equal in terms of rights. This implied the principle that aristocrats ought to have no special privileges.[22] Women and children, however, did not have sufficient mental capacity to reach the stage of autonomous self-determination and should, therefore, be excluded from government. Like women, servants should similarly be disqualified. The interests of excluded groups were supposedly represented by their husbands, fathers, or masters, respectively.[23] For Kant, progress did not come '*from bottom to top*, but *from top to bottom*'.[24]

For a time, Kant evaded state censorship and continued to criticize the King's religious and political intolerance. In 1794 he was given a direct edict prohibiting him from discussing theological questions. Kant obeyed the authority of the monarch until he outlived Frederick William II and, on the King's death, resumed publication of his liberal views. Soon afterwards, Kant's physical and mental health began to decline. His mind deteriorated to the point where he had no wish that his body continue to live. Near the end, in 1804, a visitor sadly remarked he had not seen Kant, but only 'Kant's husk'.[25]

Kant's philosophy had a dual legacy in the nineteenth century arising from his emphasis on subjectivity—the construction of knowledge by the individual mind. Kant's belief in the existence of such universally valid truths as 'doing one's duty' completely, for its own sake, became central to the claims of the conservatives. The fundamental truths of God, immortality, social duties, and morality existed innately in the mind. They were felt by intuition and were, in principle, discoverable by reason. Upon this platform the new breed of post-revolutionary conservative theorists in France and England, such as Burke, constructed a social theory based on the evolution of traditions and customs that originated in the mind. In contrast to materialism, the philosophy of **idealism** stressed the creation by the mind of an individual's sense of reality.

As sociologist Georg Simmel asserted, Kant claims that what we know of the objective world is the product of the individual, 'creative, unchangeable ego'. Kantian idealism assumes '*one* truth, of *one objective* world', from which 'it follows that in all men the ego which forms . . . this world, must always be identical.'[26] Kant presupposed a universal human mind and absolute standards of morality that did not differ in time and space. But if feeling and intuition are the fundamental grounds for the recognition of truth, it doesn't follow that everyone will feel the same or recognize the same truths. Kant was living in an oppressive society and his assumed universally valid laws of morality, such as obeying the law, helped maintain the repressive status quo. What seems reasonable in an ideal society is unreasonable in an oppressive one. Similarly, not everyone feels the same about moral rules and duties. Kant's belief that moral rules were absolute and universal reflected a fundamentally ethnocentric view of other cultures with different values and of minority viewpoints within his own society.

The modern reorientation of social philosophy from the objective world to the individual mind inspired the Romantic imagination. To Descarte's egoistic 'I' was added Kant's subjectivity, shorn of its universalism. If you strip away the universalistic assumptions, what is left are individual egos constructing, each alone through subjectivity, a world perceived as objective. If reality was essentially subjective, and there were no embedded structures of understanding, then what is taken for knowledge and truth becomes radically individuated. Kant's second theoretical legacy was his contribution to Romanticism or, rather, the Romantic movement as a whole, since it was as diverse as subjectivity could devise.

It would appear that the likely outcome of pure **subjectivity** as a guide to knowledge is the fragmentation of accepted truths and beliefs, rather than the confirmation of universal truths. Philosophical certainty seemed to have dissolved in relativity. On the other hand, no yardstick was left to measure veracity, confirming Hume's skepticism but ironically sheltering fundamentalism from critique since no objective standard remained to judge any truth claim. One response to this dilemma is to assert that truth is historical; it is the sum of the social heritage of the past, embodied in national traditions and customs passed down from generation to generation. This was the direction taken by conservative social theorists.

CONSERVATISM IN FRANCE

In France, where the revolutionaries had attempted to remake society from the top to the bottom in conformity with reason, the conservative response was equally extreme. Conservatives interpreted the Revolution as the evil consequence of original sin and the depravity of human nature acting in the absence of organized religion, the only force capable of obliging people to be moral.[27] Theorists such as Louis de Bonald and Joseph de Maistre wanted to restore the institutional pillars of French society, particularly the monarchy and the Catholic Church.

Joseph de Maistre (1753–1821) was born in Savoy, a French-speaking principality near the Swiss border. In the 1760s, two decades before the Revolution, Savoy had taken the unusual step of abolishing feudal dues, minimizing an important grievance between the rich and poor that had divided many French provinces. De Maistre's father was a jurist who had been newly raised to the lower aristocracy; his mother was exceptionally devout. Joseph was given a tranquil, religious, and reasonably privileged upbringing. His counterpart, Louis de Bonald (1754–1840) also came from a privileged background and was, for a time, a member of the elite royal guard known as the Musketeers.[28]

The chief anomaly in de Maistre's background was his membership in the Sincerity Freemason Lodge. **Freemasons** were members of a secret society, which had its roots in the skills and rituals of medieval stonemasons. As an elitist, private, and self-selecting club, Freemasonry exhibited a strange combination of ideas and rituals that included Eastern mysticism and Enlightenment theory. Many prominent revolutionaries, such as George Washington, Benjamin Franklin, Georges Jacques Danton, and the Italian, Giuseppe Garibaldi, adhered to an enlightened and democratic version of Freemasonry. Although de Maistre adhered to the more mystical, Catholic, and conservative version, as a young man he had been attracted to some of the ideas of limited democracy.[29]

Neither de Maistre nor Bonald had been immediately opposed to the early developments of the French Revolution, supporting the abolition of feudalism and the demand for a constitutional monarchy. For de Maistre, the Declaration of the Rights of Man and of the Citizen and the attacks on the clergy proved that the Revolution had gone too far, a view that was confirmed by reading Edmund Burke's conservative critique. He was surprised and disappointed when the majority of the people in Savoy were willing to give up their independence and join the revolutionary French Republic. De Maistre went into voluntary exile in Switzerland, where he helped French *émigrés* and actively worked to support counter-revolution in Savoy.[30]

In 1796, both the exiled aristocrats de Maistre and Bonald, each independent of the other, published theoretical books calling for a counter-revolution in France to restore the power of the monarchy and Catholic Church. Feudal society, they reasoned, had been unified under God and through the power of the Church. This profound social solidarity had been disrupted first by the Protestant Reformation, which had divided the Church, and then by the secular Enlightenment, which had attacked religion as a whole. In the face of these attacks, the Old Regime had proved incapable of holding society together and failed in its duty to maintain order, thus allowing the spread of moral and religious decadence, culminating in rebellion. De Maistre claimed that the French Revolution was God's punishment for religious and ideological wickedness, and he believed that counter-revolution would triumph, restoring the lost religious and political authority of the Middle Ages.[31]

In the conservative view, the liberals and the *philosophes* were socially corrupting. No society could be based on the doctrine of freedom or liberty; on the contrary, people had the right to be governed, not the right to rule themselves. The basis of government was not a 'social contract'. The natural form of rule was absolute monarchy and a hereditary, privileged aristocracy, which was the foundation of honour. Human nature was both social and religious. The doctrine of **individualism**, that society was composed of mere grains of sand, was completely false and led automatically to the dissolution of social order. Society was rooted in the traditions of the family and the laws of the Church. Faith, not reason, was the fountainhead of truth and order.

In conservative theory, society is the product of slow, historical evolution, dominated by customs, traditions, and prejudices. Any attempt to construct society anew by writing a constitution is absurd and will lead only to disunity, discord, and distress. In the end, the will of God would prevail and a new regime would be established in France. A new social pyramid would be constructed under the deity and united by the truths of the Catholic Church. At the top would be a hereditary, 'royal monarch', absolute in his power under the laws of the nation. Between the king and his subjects, the aristocracy would provide a council of advisers who would ensure that the monarch's actions would be consistent with the ancient traditions and laws of society.[32] Rights had their origin not in natural law but in the specific historical traditions of a nation, from which they derived their legitimacy. This idea was at the centre of Burke's social theory and, through him, of contemporary conservatism.

EDMUND BURKE

Edmund Burke (1729–97), a determined opponent of the French Revolution, became the principal spokesperson of early British conservatism. Although Burke had influenced de Maistre and Bonald, English conservatism was based on a historical tradition different from that of France. England did not have a written constitution, but it did have an implicit and established set of precedents that had been handed down from the past. Conservatism found fertile soil in the Tory tradition in England. For the Tories, England was the best of possible worlds and, where it fell short of what might be desired, the unwritten constitution provided the necessary means for peaceful, slow reform. In the absence of a social revolution, English conservatism was content to preserve what was; it was not necessary to restore what had been.

Burke was born in Dublin, Ireland, then under the boot of English colonialism. Early in his career, Burke spoke out against British abuses in colonial India and gave some qualified support for the rights of the American colonists to have a voice in government. From Burke's point of view, the American colonists were British subjects and, as such, ought to have representation. By imposing taxation without representation on the colonists, the British government had violated the customary, traditional rights of its citizens in America. More pragmatically, Burke advocated making concessions to the Americans in order to prevent a revolution that he feared would undermine the British Empire and possibly inspire an Irish uprising.[33] In the long run, as British conservatism evolved, it would abandon any hint of Burke's reformed colonialism and stand, instead, unwaveringly on the side of British imperialism and patriotism.

Burke was born a commoner but, in the England of the eighteenth century, he was able to rise in the social scale by placing his considerable talents as a speaker and pamphleteer at the service of the aristocratic class. While never becoming one of the great landed proprietors himself, as F.P. Lock points out, Burke defended their interests more eloquently and effectively than they could themselves.[34] As an ideal servant to the upper class, he did more than merely flatter their beliefs about their superiority, impeccable taste, and perfect manners; he believed them. Burke was proud to be admitted to the perimeters of high society and grasped at the recognition he received, which was more considerable than any wealth the elite afforded him.

The French Revolution erupted late in Burke's life. He hated and feared any uprising from below. In 1790 Burke published his conservative *Reflections on the Revolution in France*, following which he received a comfortable government pension. For Burke, the revolutionaries represented the worst human types and acted on the basest of human instincts. The French mob was a 'swinish multitude', driven by criminal desires to murder, rape, loot, and rob their betters. The revolutionaries were like savages or fierce Maroon slaves, a 'band of cruel ruffians and assassins' and 'the vilest of women'.[35] France had become 'a nation of gross, stupid, ferocious, and at the same time, poor and sordid barbarians, destitute of religion, honour, or manly pride, possessing nothing at present, and hoping for nothing hereafter'.[36] Burke's hostility represented a minority position initially, but it became increasingly fashionable among the English intellectuals as the Revolution in France became more radical. Burke had simply blazed this trail considerably earlier.

While revolutionaries based their theories on human reason and materialism, conservatives focused instead on tradition and religion. For Burke, truth was not fully discoverable by scientific methods, and truths could emerge from emotions, intuition, and spirituality—from the irrational side of humanity, which the *philosophes* had ignored. These truths were not open to scientific investigation, but they were even more important to human life than cold, calculating reason. For Burke, the results of human reason were 'fallible and feeble' compared to nature and 'her unerring and powerful instincts'.[37] Most people were not primarily rational beings: each person's 'private stock of reason . . . is small', he wrote.[38]

The *philosophes* had railed against tradition and ancient **prejudices**. Burke declared, on the contrary, people should embrace their prejudices and 'cherish them because they are prejudices; and the longer they have lasted, and the more generally they have prevailed, the more we cherish them.' It is 'natural', for example, to be reverential to authority. The reasoning ability of the individual was nothing compared to the wisdom of the ages. Rather than attempt to undermine traditions and prejudices, the proper task of reason was to discover the latent wisdom that prevailed in them. Prejudice provides a steady guide to doing our duty, and leads us to wisdom and virtue:

We have real hearts of flesh and blood beating in our bosoms. We fear God; we look up with awe to kings; with affection to parliaments; with duty to magistrates; with reverence to priests; and with respect to nobility. Why? Because when such ideas are brought before our minds, it is *natural* to be so affected; because all other feelings are false and spurious, and tend to corrupt our minds, to vitiate our primary morals, to render us unfit for rational liberty; and by teaching us a servile licentiousness, and abandoned insolence, to be our low sport for a few holidays, to make us perfectly fit for, and justly deserving of slavery, through the whole course of our lives.[39]

Nothing better exemplified the dangerous and false notions of Enlightenment thinking than Rousseau's attack on the sacred institution of property. In Burke's social theory, private property was the basis of all civilization. Government was instituted for the purpose of protecting property.[40] Burke was not so conservative as 'to confine power, authority, and distinction to blood, and names, and titles.'[41] There was a place in government for representatives of the people, at least some of them. The two things that must be represented were ability and property. By ability, Burke meant people such as himself, who had climbed the social ladder through their talent and hard work. They were properly represented in the House of Commons. By property he meant the traditional, wealthy, landed elite—those who had inherited land, titles, and authority from their ancestors. They were the source of a nation's stability and order, and held their seats by heredity in the House of Lords.

The two Houses of Parliament must be unequal in power. Since landed property is 'sluggish, inert, and timid' while ability is the most 'vigorous and active principle', property must be represented disproportionately in government in order to make it 'safe from the invasions of ability'. Hence, the House of Commons must be the weakest component of the government. The best form of government was the one England then possessed: a constitutional monarchy, combined with a substantial aristocracy and a Parliament in which were represented the people who owned substantial property. The two threats to stability were from the monarch, who might become dictatorial, and from the people, who could threaten to overturn the status quo. Burke had no faith in the political abilities of the common woman or man, arguing that absolute democracy was no more a legitimate form of government than absolute monarchy. A democracy is similar to tyranny since 'the majority of the citizens is capable of exercising the most cruel oppressions upon the minority', worse than any single ruler could carry out.[42] For Burke, people did not have the right of consent over who governed them.

Burke's *Reflections* was written in response to a sermon by the **Nonconformist** minister, Richard Price, in which he asserted that all monarchs were illegitimate with the exception of the British king, who owed his crown to the choice of his people. Price asserted that there was an implicit Bill of Rights in England according to which the people had a right to choose their own government and to replace a government guilty of misconduct. According to Price, the absence of popular representation, as in France, was a fundamental grievance that rendered the entire government illegitimate and justified revolution.[43]

Price's doctrine, Burke claimed, was both **seditious** and unconstitutional. On the contrary, Burke asserts, the laws that frame the British Constitution established the principle that hereditary monarchy was alone conducive to 'the unity, peace, and tranquillity' of the nation. Parliament had deliberately renounced any intention to claim a right to elect kings.[44] Social institutions were legitimate simply because they existed; they were the heritage from the past. Any claim that they were not legitimate, whether made on the grounds that they were unreasonable, as the *philosophes* had said, or that they were inefficient, as the English liberals maintained, was rejected by Burke.

In France before 1789, Burke wrote, the foundation and walls of society had been sound. He denied 'that the nobility had any considerable share in the oppression of the people', while admitting they did have a number of faults and errors. They were habitually dissolute in their manners, which was excusable when they were young but had continued beyond the period of life when such conduct was pardonable. The French nobles had made the mistake of not raising the richest commoners to higher ranks, bringing them into the ruling class in some capacity, as Burke had been elevated in England. By keeping them separate, they were incited to jealousy and opposition. Their gravest error had been not suppressing the *philosophes* and their dangerous ideas; they tolerated 'too much that licentious philosophy which has helped to bring on their ruin.' The *philosophes'* attack on the nobility was unjustified, Burke declared; it was merely a work of art, a fiction: 'Nobility is a graceful ornament to the civil order. It is the Corinthian capital of polished society.'[45]

Similarly, the clergy had not been abusive; the atheistic *philosophes* had merely dredged up some of the wrongs from the past and exaggerated them. Similarly, Burke asserted, Louis XVI was a mild and lawful monarch whose hand was 'holding out graces, favours, and immunities'. Louis had made concessions, relaxed his authority, granted his people a share of freedom, and did not deserve the treatment he had received from the Parisian mob. The resulting revolution was not just unnecessary but unnatural. The age of chivalry, Burke complained, had given way to the rule of opportunists, 'economists, and calculators . . . and the glory of Europe is extinguished forever.' In Burke's rhetoric, all the 'decent drapery of life' had been 'rudely torn off'. All that reason, morality, and compassion had procured 'to cover the defects of our naked shivering nature, and to raise it to dignity' had been 'exploded as a ridiculous, absurd, and antiquated fashion'. According to this scheme of things, 'a king is but a man; a queen is but a woman.'[46]

Instead of looking back into the past and finding the conservative principles of moderation and compromise, the *philosophes* chose to believe that everything had to begin anew; and they began by despising everything that belonged to them. Burke's objective, on the contrary, was to preserve and reform, to keep the useful parts of the old establishment and fit what should be added to what is best left unchanged.[47] For conservatives such as Burke, society was like a living organism. All the parts were connected together and most were fundamental to the organism's survival.

The conservative approach, at least in its origins with Burke, does not necessarily oppose all changes, although conservatives want to preserve society fundamentally the way it is. In England, if not in France, conservatives recognized that the status quo had changed irrevocably from the feudal past. While such liberal notions as **popular democracy** and republicanism were dangerous and must be suppressed, conservatives were willing to make small adjustments or reforms to make the organism of society work better; inheritance did not preclude improvement, Burke said.[48]

Just as he took the political status quo in England for granted, so, too, Burke justified the economic system of small-scale capitalism, private pursuit of profit, and the right to use private property as the owners saw fit. Burke's class prejudices were clear. For Burke, the poor were in a state of natural subordination, and 'They must respect that property of which they cannot partake.' When they realize that no matter how hard they work they can never succeed, 'they must be taught their consolation in the final proportions of eternal justice'; that is, that they will reap their rewards for hard work not on earth, but in heaven.[49]

Andrew argues that, in most respects, Burke adopts Smith's laissez-faire economics. In his 'Thoughts and Details on Scarcity', Burke agreed that markets should always be unregulated even in times of shortages. The government should not provide any special provisions for labourers 'in calamitous seasons, under accidental illness, in declining life, and with the pressure of a numerous offspring' because that would violate the law of demand that determines the proper level of wages. Even in times of famine, governments should not tamper with the buying and selling of food. For

Burke, 'the laws of commerce . . . are the laws of nature, and consequently the laws of God.'[50]

With Burke, conservatism took a step away from defending the feudal economy, as French reactionary theory was wont to do, and several steps towards accepting capitalism as the natural form of economy. Tory opinion in England had reconciled itself to commercial capitalism, if not the practices of greedy, rapacious capitalists. As much as anything, this difference between Burke and the French conservatives reflected the historical differences between England and France at the time.

The Conservative Attitude to History

'Don't think; feel. . . . Your hand is wiser than your head is ever going to be.'
—*The Legend of Bagger Vance* (2000), directed by Robert Redford, screenplay by Jeremy Leven

The conservatives tried to refocus social theory away from its focus on the individual, which was dominant in liberalism, and back to the collective, to society. In doing so, they emphasized the importance of taking a historical attitude to society. They applied the idea of **evolution**—slow, gradual, small changes—to the development of social institutions. More extreme conservatives might still assert, with Bonald, that society was **providentially** arranged, i.e., by a supreme deity. However, this creationist assumption is unnecessary for conservative thought. Just as it is possible for a theorist to bracket (or put aside and not deal with) theological questions, so, too, it can be claimed that the origins of society are so far in the distant past that no certain knowledge can be formulated. Certainly, for Burke, the liberal postulate of a social contract was purely ideological and had no foundation in historical fact, either in the past or the present.

Bracketing the question of social origins, however, does not mean also **bracketing** history. On the contrary, conservatism emphasizes the continuity of the past in the present. The present is not irrational, as the *philosophes* claimed; rather, the present is the sum of all past rationality. What

is, is rational. As Hobsbawm puts it, 'Above all [humans] lived together, in tight networks of social and personal relationships, guided by the clear map of custom, social institutions, and obligations.'[51] The social institutions that exist are the best that human beings have to pass on to future generations. The nation, the community, society as a whole are the result of slow, historical growth, with each generation progressing slightly over the preceding one. The aristocratic poet, Tennyson, celebrated England's 'settled government' and the slow evolution of ideas that remained consistent with its precedents thus:

> A land of settled government,
> A land of just and old renown,
> Where freedom slowly broadens down
> From precedent to precedent.
> Where faction seldom gathers head,
> But by degrees to fullness wrought,
> The strength of some diffusive thought
> Hath time and space to work and spread.[52]

Throughout history, society develops necessary social institutions that are combined in an organic whole. The present, then, is our heritage from the past, the sum total of all past reasoning. For Burke, 'The very idea of the fabrication of a new government is enough to fill us with disgust and horror.' All that people possess, he said, is an inheritance from our forefathers to which no alien addition should be introduced. Just as property is passed from one generation to the next, the whole 'body and stock of inheritance', including social privileges and government, are 'to be transmitted to our posterity'.[53]

Conservatives attacked the assumption held by the *philosophes* that anything irrational was bad. On the contrary, knowledge derived from reason was no better than any other knowledge; rather, it was usually worse because one person's reason was inferior to the collective wisdom of all the preceding generations, summed up in custom and tradition. There were other, equally good or better sources of knowledge than mere reason, such as nature and 'her unerring and powerful instincts'—

the hand and the heart were wiser than the head.[54] Some conservatives, such as Bonald, returned to a belief in revelation and Church doctrine as knowledge. For Burke, as well, religion was the basis of civil society, a fact that we 'know, and what is better we feel inwardly'. The vast majority of people are convinced, he believed, that religion is the source of all good and all comfort, and that Christianity has been the 'one great source of civilization amongst us'. He far preferred the absurdities of superstition to the dangers of impiety. 'We know, and it is our pride to know, that man is by his constitution a religious animal; that atheism is against, not only our reason but our instincts; and that it cannot prevail long.'[55]

The assumption by the liberals that society derived from a social contract was false. The idea of a social contract was a dangerous fiction because it led people to believe that the social structure was the result of rationality and that humans had the ability to understand society and the right to change it. Society is indeed a contract, Burke argues, but it is not a business contract, which could be dissolved at anyone's pleasure as 'in a trade of pepper and coffee, calico or tobacco, or some other such low concern'. It is a partnership in everything, 'not only between those who are living, but between those who are dead, and those who are to be born.' More than that, society exists as part of a great original contract with God, 'linking the lower with the higher natures, connecting the visible and invisible works', and fixing all physical and moral life 'each in their appointed place'. Society and the state are institutions willed into existence by a deity.[56]

People did not have natural rights, but they did have social rights, which they had inherited from their community, such as rights to 'the unhindered possession of their goods and labour, to order, justice and security'.[57] The most damaging liberal and Enlightenment ideas were that all people were created equal and had natural rights that should not be violated. For Burke, the idea of social equality was a 'monstrous fiction, which, by inspiring false ideas and vain expectations' in people who were 'destined to travel in the obscure walk of laborious life', served only to aggravate and embitter them, making them feel unjustly treated (Box 5.1).[58] In place of this false notion of equality, the true equality of humankind is moral equality; that is, the potential each person had of being moral and virtuous, a quality that was possible in any station in society.

That society should consist of different and unequal ranks was natural; this was a real inequality that could never be removed. In fact, the natural order of civil life establishes this inequality 'as much for the benefit of those whom it must leave in an humble state' as for those more privileged ranks, 'whom it is able to exalt to a condition more splendid, but not more happy.'[59] Each rank in society had its naturally ordained place. Common working people, Burke argued, should not be permitted to rule. Such a democratic doctrine is at

---

Box 5.1

Believe me, Sir, those who attempt to level, never equalize. In all societies, consisting of various descriptions of citizens, some descriptions must be uppermost. The levellers therefore only change and pervert the natural order of things; they load the edifice of society, by setting up in the air what the solidity of the structure requires to be on the ground. The associations of tailors and carpenters, of which the republic (of Paris, for example) is composed, cannot be equal to the situation, into which by . . . an usurpation on the prerogatives of nature, you attempt to force them.

—Edmund Burke, *Reflections on the Revolution in France* (1790)

war with nature, contrary to the Bible and to common sense.[60] Burke emphatically denies that each individual has a direct, original (state of nature) right to a 'share of power, authority, and direction . . . in the management of the state'. Rather, people only had those rights that society had given them, rights that had slowly evolved over time by the hard struggles of previous generations.

Burke endorsed what he called the real rights of humanity. They have a 'right to justice . . . to the fruits of their industry', and the right to inherit from their parents. Furthermore, all people have 'a right to a fair portion of all which society . . . can do in' their favour. A fair share is by no means an identical amount for all, an equal distribution of goods. Society may be a partnership in which everyone has 'equal rights; but they don't have a right to equal things.' Burke suggests that society is like a joint stock company in which one person owns five shillings of stock while another owns five hundred shillings. Each has a right to a share of the dividend, but only in exact proportion to her or his stock. The person with five shillings has no right to a dividend equal to the person who owns 100 times more stock. By this analogy, the common person owns no stock at all and, therefore, has no right to influence politics.[61]

Despite these assertions, Burke's conservatism was not dogmatic; he acknowledged no rights other than social rights. Over time, as social traditions changed, conservatives have adapted to relatively more democratic forms of rule. A right is not derived from reason but from history; it is an idea that has matured over time.

ROMANTIC CONSERVATISM

The historical frame of mind that inspired conservative social theory merged with the philosophical focus on individual subjectivity to produce a new, Romantic movement in the arts that was part of a broader but complex and differentiated intellectual movement known as Romanticism.

Romanticism in its many forms developed parallel to the dominant Enlightenment rationalism in the last half of the eighteenth century. The two ideologies were conjoined twins. At first Romantic subjectivity was overshadowed by the dominance of reason and did not come into its inheritance until rationalism appeared to fail during the French Revolution. While the *philosophes* had focused attention on reason or sense, the Romantics believed the dominant element in humanity was an emotional energy that drove people to aspire to the good, the just, and the true. More generally, Romantics referred to the passionate, emotional side of human nature, the side that the medieval mind feared and the Enlightenment tried to subdue under the restraint of reason. Emotion or sensibility could focus on fear, death, melancholy, grossness, and terror as well as virtue.[62]

Romantic conservatives, like their Tory correlates, held an idealized view of the feudal past, admiring chivalry, the love of honour, loyalty to one's monarch or nation, and bravery. Idealizations of the Middle Ages filled the expanding market for popular romance novellas. The novelist Walter Scott (1771–1832) popularized the historical novel and revived an interest in medieval times and institutions. Scott's *Ivanhoe* (1820), which was set during the reign of Richard I, idealized the medieval knight in shining armour and resistance to foreign conquest. In Germany, the new, spiked helmet designed for the Prussian cavalry, 'With the point of steel as the topper', recalled the knights of the Middle Ages. The German poet and critic Heinrich Heine wondered whether this absurd decoration from 'the printless age of faith' would actually function as a lightning rod.[63]

A similar medieval revival occurred in architecture. The German plan to complete the magnificent Cologne Cathedral reflected the wish to mimic the medieval Catholic Church. As Stromberg pointed out,[64] the Enlightenment had despised the grand **Gothic** cathedrals of the Middle Ages, partly because of their religious themes, partly because of their exuberant and ornate architecture, and partly because they were built on the backs of the poor. French revolutionaries had wanted to destroy the cathedrals as monuments to superstition. In the Romantic era, however, a Gothic revival entirely reversed this view. The term 'Gothic' suggested that art should be inspired by the great works of the past. The twelfth- and thirteenth-century cathedrals were restored, and the neo-Gothic style, a revival and exaggeration of the ornate, decorated art from the Middle Ages, became fashionable in new public buildings and private homes. Above all, Gothic meant a rejection of the calm, ordered, carefully proportioned architecture of neo-classicism, with its heavy columns and rectangularity. In painting, the new style was expressed in an interest in spirituality and mysticism, as in the engravings William Blake created to illustrate his poems.

The term 'Gothic' was also given to a new form of the novel, which was inspired by medieval mystery and superstition. In his groundbreaking novel, *The Castle of Otranto* (1764), Horace Walpole told a tale of chivalry, castles, hidden passages, graveyards, revenge, the supernatural, and the grotesque.[65] From the vantage point of contemporary society, this early Gothic novel presented a template for a now-familiar formula, and the genre continued into the next two centuries with, for example, the tales of Edger Allan Poe and Bram Stoker's *Dracula* (1890). When conservative Romantics turned their interests inward, to the imagination, they gave expression to one of the defining characteristics of Romanticism. There was also a critical element in the Romantic movement that inspired the young Wordsworth and his contemporaries and would shape a new version of radicalism in nineteenth-century France.

ROMANTICISM

[I]n the last two hundred years . . . Rationalism and romanticism fought for the heart of humankind and between them pretty much divided up the spoils.[66]
—Eugene H. Peterson, *Subversive Spirituality* (1997)

The conservative reaction to the French Revolution and the Industrial Revolution was characterized by a dethroning of reason in favour of the non-rational. It was not possible, however, to reassert traditional theology as the dominant world view of Western society. The economic changes at the very foundation of modern liberalism had permeated the larger culture. The juggernaut of industrial capitalism had been set in motion and nothing in its path could remain unchanged. While traditional Christian views persisted, they were confined narrowly to the private sphere, as the separations between religion and politics and religion and the economy became entrenched.

As society changed, so did social theories. Laissez-faire liberals claimèd that the dreadful social conditions that early capitalism brought in its train were temporary, or the fault of the victims themselves, or weren't really so terrible after all. Critics were outraged at the social costs of capitalism, including the devastation of rural life and the rapid spread of urban squalor. The Romantic conservatives had responded by idealizing the lost medieval world of chivalry, custom, and community, but as capitalism changed society permanently their literature became more obviously mere fantasy. In addition, a more cosmopolitan irrationality emerged as the Western world was affected by spiritual ideologies diffused from the East, and as secular, and therefore modern, forms of anti-rationality developed to challenge the dominant materialism. The fusion of these counter-rational elements produced more radical forms of Romanticism.

Romanticism was a very complex movement. The simplest way to approach it is to recognize that the Romantics shared many ideas with the conservatives but had much in common with the liberals. Unlike the conservatives, they drew inspiration from the rebellious spirit of the Enlightenment while rejecting what they saw as its overemphasis on rationality. Unlike the liberals, they detested the base materialism of bourgeois society while endorsing its core value of individual freedom. In the Romantic view, the modern capitalists sought to make money for the purpose of making more money. Only those things that could be bought and sold at a profit were valuable. They were the modern Philistines: their

interests were narrowly materialistic and their culture was limited to double-entry bookkeeping and
the sharp deal. For the bourgeois, critics charged,
the ideals of truth, beauty, goodness, and justice
could be reduced to the economic laws of supply
and demand.

The Romantics were primarily intellectuals
who expressed their values in culture, in their
poetry, painting, and music. They comprised the
first artistic counterculture. Artists in the past had
been primarily self-conscious exponents of the status quo. Medieval art had depicted religious
themes. The masters of the Renaissance and the
rise of capitalism painted portraits of kings, aristocrats, and wealthy burghers because art was subsi-
dized by the wealthy and powerful. The Romantics
idealized artistic creativity, beauty, and truth for its
own sake. Commercial considerations were not
supposed to be foremost in the artist's mind, but
they could not be ignored. A compromise between
artistic integrity and the necessity to sell their art
was possible because the Romantics had wedged
their way between the old dichotomy of elite art,
commissioned and paid for by the wealthy, and the
people's or folk art, produced by the masses for
themselves. Nineteenth-century novelists were the
first to make an independent livelihood writing
and selling to a wide, increasingly literate audience. As Stromberg pointed out,[67] one major factor that was distinct about the generation of poets
in the Romantic age was that they 'brought poetry
to the people', exerting an influence on millions
and moulding the consciousness of the first half of
the nineteenth century.

While our concern is with Romanticism as an
important and influential post-revolutionary intellectual movement, like any type of social theory it
has long roots in the past and inspired a long line of
progeny. The term arose from the tales of medieval
romance that represented an early form of popular
literature. Many of the themes that the Romantics
would embrace already were apparent in the pre-
revolutionary environment, especially in the writings of Rousseau in France and Goethe in Germany.
The Romantic movement would evolve through
several generations, resurfacing in different forms

in various places and times down to the present. The
first generation of English poets and theorists—
Wordsworth, Coleridge, Wollstonecraft, Godwin—
initially had been enamoured of the great
transformation promised by the French Revolution.
Once the conservative reaction had achieved dominance following the fall of Napoleon, a new generation of Romantics emerged in England and France.
While not all of these artists and writers were
engaged in the social problems and politics of their
day, many of them were. In France, where politics
was, as always, sharply divided, Romantics were
deeply involved in social change until the revolutionary failures of 1848–51.

Romanticism grasped the spirit of rebellion
from the Enlightenment and the critique of bourgeois society from conservatism, and wedded it to
subjectivity and individualism. The social theorists of the Enlightenment had assumed that truth
could be discovered by reason and that human
rationality also could determine 'beauty', although
these two qualities rested on distinct foundations.
Under the principle of rationalism embodied in
neo-classicism, Enlightenment painters had
devised what they thought were the rules of good
painting. There were rules for poetry exemplified
by the rhyming couplet, correct styles of architecture and sculpture derived from ancient Greece
and Rome, and rules about the purpose of art. The
Romantics rebelled against the constraints of these
rules. They were critical of bourgeois society while
being, simultaneously, a product of that society.

While the conservatives focused on the last
element, 'fraternity', of the revolutionary slogan,
by which they meant one's loyalty to the nation,
and the socialists would later endorse 'equality',
the radical Romantics took 'liberty' as their first
principle. The link between Romanticism and
political involvement is tenuous because they seek
individual freedom and personal rather then institutional change. They are more likely to withdraw
from rather than to engage in collective movements for social transformation.

The roots of Romanticism can be traced to the
years before the French Revolution when intellectuals of an independent mind were rebelling

against the chains of neo-classicism. The chief individualist of the era was the German dramatist, novelist, and poet, Johann Wolfgang von Goethe (1749–1832). Shortly after a broken romance of his own, Goethe wrote the novel *The Sorrows of Young Werther* (1774) about a young man who possessed great sensitivity—whose personality was formed essentially on his emotions. Werther falls into a totally self-absorbed and infinite love with Charlotte, who already is engaged and utterly unattainable. Over a few short months, Werther becomes increasingly isolated from society, sinks into a solitary existence, and is rejected by aristocratic society. Increasingly immersed in himself, Werther finds it difficult to act, complaining that his 'active spirits have degenerated into contented indolence.'[68] Werther's goal, which is to be one with his love, with nature, and with the infinite, is not possible in this world. He longs to surrender his whole being to the final wholeness, to 'be filled with the complete and perfect bliss of one glorious emotion' (Box 5.2). But even if we attain that moment when our desires are fulfilled, it is not enough because 'our souls still languish for unattainable happiness.'[69] Werther's conclusion is that his sensibility can be fully realized only through death. He borrows two pistols from Charlotte's husband and shoots himself in the head.

The novel's individualism and subjective focus (on the inner feelings of the protagonist) created a sensation at the time. Swales argues that *Werther* became a cult book that resulted in 'Werther fever'.[70] Huge numbers of young men adopted Werther's style, dressing conspicuously in the Werther costume of 'blue frock-coat, buff waistcoat and trousers, and boots'—and thousands committed suicide.[71] In Mary Shelley's famous Gothic novel, the soulless 'creature' that Frankenstein brought to life studied Goethe's *Werther* to learn about 'lofty sentiments and feelings'. The creature 'inclined towards the opinions of the hero, whose extinction' made him weep 'without precisely understanding it'.[72] Werther's death was not meant to be precisely understood but, rather, to be felt, so that the creature's response reflected his humanity. Goethe was a Romantic in his individualism and in his belief that the only true freedom was personally rather than socially political.

In art, Romanticism was a rebellion against the straitjacket of neo-classical rules, formulas, and conventions that had been dictated in the Age of Reason. During the neo-classical period, nature had been deemed obscene, irregular, and, at best, something to be tamed by human action. The age was aptly symbolized by the great garden with its

---

Box 5.2

A wonderful serenity has taken possession of my entire soul, like these sweet mornings of spring which I enjoy with my whole heart. I am alone, and feel the charm of existence in this spot, which was created for the bliss of souls like mine.... When, while the lovely valley teems with vapour around me, and the meridian sun strikes the upper surface of the impenetrable foliage of my trees, and but a few stray gleams steal into the inner sanctuary, I throw myself down among the tall grass by the trickling stream; ... then I feel the presence of the Almighty, who formed us in his own image, and the breath of that universal love which bears and sustains us, as it floats around us in an eternity of bliss; and then ... I often think with longing ... that it might be the mirror of my soul, as my soul is the mirror of the infinite God! O my friend—but it is too much for my strength—I sink under the weight of the splendour of these visions!

—Goethe, *The Sorrows of Young Werther* (1774)

orderly arrangements of flowers, shrubs, trees, walkways, and ornamental grass lawn. When reason was applied to nature, it became symmetrical, orderly, and artfully arranged. It was, neo-classicists argued, surely the way the deity had created the Garden of Eden. But after the fall of humankind, with Adam and Eve cast out of the Garden, nature had become wild, irregular, and irrational and it was the duty of humankind to bring order to nature and dominate it.

The Romantics, on the other hand, worshipped untamed nature where they could feel at one with their conception of the divine and experience the soul, as young Werther does in Goethe's novel.[73] In the Romantic view, the artist and the poet were gifted with the ability to experience this wholeness and able to render the experience in symbolic words or paintings, reaching down to the deeper reality inside things, beyond their mere outward appearances. In Gustave Flaubert's *Madame Bovary* (1857), in speaking about the Swiss Alps, Leon tells Emma Bovary:

[Y]ou can't imagine the poetry of the lakes, the charm of the waterfalls, the gigantic effect of the glaciers. You see evergreens of an unbelievable size spanning the torrents, cabins jutting out over precipices, and there are entire valleys a thousand feet below you, when the clouds part. Sights such as these overwhelm you, dispose you toward prayer and ecstasy![74]

In the view of Edmund Burke, mountains were not merely beautiful, which was delicate and feminine. They were sublime, awe-inspiring, and reflected masculine power and strength.

The critique of neo-classicism and the worshipping of untamed nature were connected to a more explicitly individualistic type of Romanticism, which extolled the freedom of the individual, particularly the freedom of individual genius, and proclaimed the need to 'release creativity' from social convention. In his seduction of Emma in *Madame Bovary*, Rodolphe expresses his disdain for any notion of:

. . . respect for law and the fulfillment of duty. . . . I'm fed up with these words. They're a bunch of old fogies in flannel waistcoats, bigoted old ladies with foot warmers and beads, who keep singing into our ears, 'Duty! Duty!' Our duty is to discern the great and cherish the beautiful and not to accept all those conventions of society with the ignominies it imposes on us.[75]

For Rodolphe, the Romantic, there were two moralities, the 'petty conventional morality' and 'the eternal morality, [which] is all around and above us like the . . . blue sky that sends down its light.' He is revolted by the 'conspiracy of society' that condemns every ounce of a person's deepest feelings. In the straitjacket of society, 'The most noble instincts, the purest emotions, are persecuted and slandered.'[76] Passions are 'the only beautiful thing on the earth, the inspiration for heroism, enthusiasm, poetry, music, art, for everything'. Of all the Romantic passions, romantic love is the fullest expression, but 'if two poor souls finally meet, everything is organized so they cannot unite. But they will keep trying [and] . . . sooner or later . . . they will reunite and love each other because destiny demands it and they were born for each other.' The concept is distilled in Flaubert's profession that 'You've already met in your dreams'[77] and is echoed in contemporary popular culture (Box 5.3).

In effect, these Romantics followed the Enlightenment proclivity to rebel. They had, however, abandoned any notion that the world could be understood rationally. In fact, the attempt to remake the social order according to the principles of rationality had led to disaster. Consistent with the conservative view, humans should be seen as primarily non-rational. Unlike the conservatives, however, the Romantics did not want to replace reason with tradition, custom, the established church, and the monarchy. The radical Romantics were in rebellion against all of these. No single person of the period expressed his individual rebellion against all social convention more thoroughly or controversially than the Marquis de Sade.

Box 5.3

I knew I loved you before I met you;
I think I dreamed you into life.

—'I Knew I Loved You', Savage Garden, *Affirmation* (1999)

'You look so familiar; have I seen you before somewhere?'
'Only in my dreams.'

—*Femme Fatale* (2003), written and directed by Brian da Palma

La Agrada: 'You are more authentic the more you resemble what you dreamed you are.'

—*All About My Mother* (1999), written and directed by Pedro Almodovar

Marquis de Sade

What is it men in women do require?
    The lineaments of Gratified Desire.
What is it women in men do require?
    The lineaments of Gratified Desire.
—William Blake, 'The Question Answered'
(*c.* 1793)

One form of Romantic liberation from an oppressive reality, however limited, is individual rebellion. Perhaps no one epitomizes the complete rejection of all social morals and the substitution of their opposites more than Donatien François, known by his aristocratic title, the Marquis de Sade (1740–1814). De Sade was an artist, a poet, and a playwright who was condemned as sexually immoral in both his writings and lifestyle. Although he was born an aristocrat, de Sade was imprisoned for 'sexual excesses' by the Old Regime. He was released during the French Revolution, but he was not permitted to stage any of his plays during his period of freedom.

In Peckham's interpretation[78] of de Sade, the Christian conception of a loving and just God is a shield humans have erected to protect themselves from the truth. Actual life is full of suffering

and injustice. As an all-powerful God able to do anything, he must have wanted the world to be this way. The real purpose of creation, then, was to allow God to experience pleasure from human suffering. According to Christian doctrine, most people would suffer eternal punishment because they would be condemned to hell after death. This must be pleasing to God, de Sade reasoned. Pleasure, then, was to be found in the infliction of suffering on others (now termed '**sadism**'), in watching others suffer, and in experiencing pain oneself (masochism).

While de Sade's passions were gross and cruel, Kennedy argues, his excesses represented the extreme on a scale of libertarianism, one that flourished among the upper aristocracy beneath their 'reasonable' exterior of polite, enlightened society. In the libertarian perspective, good and evil were purely relative—socially constructed concepts. That which is real fundamentally is passion, and passions exist only to be indulged. 'The good' was simply that which gave pleasure. Anything could be indulged in private. In his novel *Justine* (1791), de Sade vividly portrayed sexual violence perpetrated in a monastery against an innocent woman. Justine's world was dominated by the insatiable passions of cruel men who lived in a world where morality and virtue were meaningless abstractions next to the concrete pleasures of unbridled power.[79] Although de Sade's personal indulgence in sexual exploitation could not compete with his depraved imagination, he demonstrated the addictive nature of the abuse of vulnerable women that was prevalent among the aristocracy. De Sade revealed, even celebrated, his debauchery publicly and it exposed the decadence of his class. His imprisonment for immorality, however, was linked to wider political and personal motives, including the power wielded by enemies of his family and his influential, vengeful mother-in-law.[80] Authorities were more likely to prosecute his sacrilegious behaviour and the buggery with his valet than his sexual abuse of women.

After Napoleon had brought the more radical aspects of the Revolution to an end, de Sade was again imprisoned, this time at the asylum of Charenton along with lunatics, criminals, and political radicals. At Charenton he produced and acted in plays, using the inmates of the asylum as actors— a stratagem regarded by the director of the asylum as therapeutic for the patients. In 1964, playwright Peter Weiss set one of his dramas, *Marat/Sade*, in the asylum of Charenton in the year 1808, and made the historical de Sade one of the characters in his play. Weiss used this device to present a debate between the ideas of political revolution espoused by the Jacobin leader, Jean-Paul Marat, and the ideas of individualism and sexual licence pursued by de Sade.[81]

De Sade represents the search for extreme experience, the belief in the supremacy of the individual will, the rejection of conventional morality—all elements of the individualistic forms of rebellion that have emerged from time to time in the last two centuries. In his own words, he was 'uncontrolled, extreme in everything, with an unbridled imagination as far as morals are concerned which has never been paralleled.'[82] This is the perspective with which Weiss has invested de Sade's view of the world. In *Marat/Sade*, Weiss has de Sade ask the revolutionary, Marat:

[W]hy should you care about the world
  outside
For me the only reality is imagination
the world inside myself . . .
I don't believe in idealists
Who charge down blind alleys
I don't believe in any of the sacrifices
That have been made for any cause
I believe only in myself[83]

In more recent years, de Sade has been reinterpreted as a Romantic genius who was despised during his lifetime, to be belatedly recognized by contemporary writers and social theorists. The French poet, Guillaume Apollinaire, began the rehabilitation of de Sade's reputation in 1909, claiming he was an early modernist who revealed the roots of human behaviour in erotic desire.[84] Writing in 1946 in a foreword to his **dystopia**, *Brave New World*, Aldous Huxley argued that, during the French Revolution, Robespierre had created merely 'the most superficial kind of revolution, the political'. In turn, the communistic Conspiracy of Equals had been somewhat deeper in its attempt at an economic revolution, but this, too, had been incomplete. De Sade, however:

regarded himself as the apostle of the truly revolutionary revolution, beyond mere politics and economics—the revolution of individual men, women, and children, whose bodies were henceforward to become the common sexual property of all and whose minds were to be purged of all the natural decencies, all the laboriously acquired inhibitions of traditional civilization.[85]

For de Sade, the only truth was pleasure and self-assertion, the only reality, the individual. In many respects de Sade epitomizes the brutality of his age—the religious inquisitors, judicial torturers, and slave traders. What is particularly modern is that de Sade rejects all of the moral or rational justifications for this brutality, justifying it simply as the gratification of desire. In the contemporary world of desire, disorder, and danger, de Sade has become something of an icon. His type is not unusual.

ENGLISH ROMANTICISM

> Negative Capability, that is when man is capable of being in uncertainties, mysteries, doubts, without any irritable reaching after fact and reason.
> —John Keats, letter to George and Thomas Keats, 13 January 1818

In less unconventional terms, Romanticism meant immersing oneself in the extraordinary, the exotic and foreign, the occult and spiritual, the ancient. Romantic artists depicted the fury of action; they pictured the brave, but doomed, hero. Above all, Romanticism was a movement of radical individualism, of people who chose to isolate themselves from society and seek the inaccessible, the extreme. The result was a host of interconnected artistic movements in the late nineteenth and early twentieth centuries, including **Impressionism, Expressionism**, and **symbolism**.

In their search for extreme experience the Romantics travelled to North Africa and the Middle East, where they experienced first-hand tremendous cultural diversity. The realization that people elsewhere live very different lives proved to be liberating. The old rules of their own society were revealed even more surely to be simply rules. It wasn't necessary to imagine living according to other, even opposite, social standards—one could experience it by travel. The Romantics were in search of the exotic. Romantic paintings often depicted Arabian culture. Some Romantics, such as Samuel Taylor Coleridge, experimented with opium to expand the intensity of their experiences. A great many more people were experimented *on* with opium by a medical profession that did not understand its effects. An opium derivative was also the main ingredient of laudanum, a sedative drug that was widely prescribed for nervous disorders among nineteenth-century upper- and middle-class women.

The Romantics also continued attempts to revolutionize moral standards. George Gordon, Lord Byron, was a notoriously profligate lover. Those most committed to Romantic rebellion would, like Mary Wollstonecraft, reject marriage as bourgeois, have children out of wedlock (an interesting term), experiment with sexuality, and attempt to establish relations of equality between men and women. This was a lifestyle rebellion, an attempt to create new social relationships by example. The Romantics dressed outlandishly and acted out their eccentricities in conscious rejection of social conventions.[86] Many of the most famous Romantics led fast, short lives. Byron died in 1824 at the age of 36, the consummate Romantic hero, dying on his way to help the people of Greece achieve independence; two years earlier, Percy Bysshe Shelley had died at age 29; John Keats, dead at 26 in 1821, was the first of this trio to die.

Byron was esteemed the embodiment of the Romantic ideal—aristocratic by birth, sexually promiscuous, his life dissipated in the passionate pursuit of his own pleasures. Although aristocratic men were given wide latitude for promiscuity, sexual experimentation, and lifestyle eccentricities, Byron suffered social ostracism after rumours of an affair with his half-sister put him **beyond the pale** of even aristocratic moral negligence. This fall from social favour, however, did not affect the wide popularity of his poetry. His poems were often ironic and satirical, sexually suggestive, and set in exotic, Oriental locations. As in painting, the contemporary audience was more likely to accept sexual explicitness in poetry if the settings were foreign or otherworldly. Byron's heroes were tall, dark, handsome, melancholy and moody, and frequently doomed—a type that became known as **Byronic**, although these heroes sometimes professed loftier sentiments than the satisfaction of personal desire, such as martyrdom in the cause of national freedom, as expressed by Byron in 'Sonnet on Chillon' (1816):

> Eternal Spirit of the chainless Mind!
> Brightest in dungeons, Liberty! Thou art:
> For there thy habitation is the heart—

The heart which love of thee alone can bind;
And when thy sons to fetters are consigned—
To fetters, and the damp vault's dayless gloom,
Their country conquers with their martyrdom,
And Freedom's fame finds wings on every
   wind.[87]

Byron carried his Romanticism into political action, becoming involved in the Italian movement for national liberation, and then, determined to be his own Byronic hero, rushing to help the Greeks achieve independence from the Ottoman Empire. Like 'Brunswick's fated chieftain' in *Childe Harold's Pilgrimage*, who 'rushed into the field and, foremost fighting, fell',[88] Byron died, but not fighting; he died from malaria in Greece before seeing any action. His death, nevertheless, was seen as a consummation of his Romantic character.

In their demand for erotic love, many of the later Romantics imagined a condition of equality in erotic love—free love, equally for men and women—rather than being restricted by the traditional or Christian rules of marriage. As Mellor points out, however, this erotic ideal was not realizable at that time for women, who had to face the physical consequences of pregnancy and childbirth outside the security of marriage and the social consequences of disrepute and ostracism this entailed. Romantic politics was male-centred. A similar sort of contradiction would emerge in the free-love movement of the 1960s.

During the Enlightenment, a natural duality was assumed between male and female, masculine and feminine. Even the Romantics supposed that only men possessed the higher forms of reason. As Mellor explains, in the mythical past, humanity and nature were one. Following the loss of this golden age, however, humanity became alienated from nature. This was particularly true for men. Women, however, remained closer to nature. They gave birth to new life; their menstruation followed the cycles of the moon; they possessed a spiritual, intuitive knowledge. Women represented the realms of emotion, feelings, intuition, and sensibility.[89] For the philosopher Immanuel Kant, women had better access than men to genuine truths about ethics and morality. In this way, Romanticism helped keep women—at least women assumed to be pure and virtuous—'on a pedestal', a condition of exaggerated admiration that could only lead to disappointment, and hence, actually constituted a form of disrespect.

In the imagery of this duality, the natural world was 'female'—'she' was Mother Nature—mysterious, unpredictable, beautiful, but potentially dangerous. If the ideal man could think logically and clearly, and act rationally, the ideal woman 'could love passionately, faithfully, purely'.[90] Mellor finds this exemplified by the female voice in Byron's epic poem, *Don Juan*, who states:

Man's love is of his life a thing apart,
'Tis a woman's whole existence; . . .
Man has resources, we but one,
To love again, and be again undone.

According to Mellor, the English Romantic poets claimed to overcome this duality. Alone among men, the male poets could experience the ultimate harmony between their minds and nature, love, sensibility, and beauty. Their self-proclaimed achievement was to effect a marriage between their mind and nature (the female). Mellor interprets this as theft, or **colonization**. The Romantic poets 'stole from women their primary cultural authority as the experts in delicate, tender feelings and, by extension, moral purity and goodness.' For Shelley, the male poet becomes a mother giving birth to poetry representing 'the highest wisdom, pleasure, virtue, and glory'.[91]

For Mellor, the principal feminine emotion colonized by the male Romantics was romantic love, defined by Byron, Shelley, and Keats as fully erotic, not merely platonic. Essentially, Mellor argues, they were in love with themselves and the ideal woman actually was their mirror image. Women did not exist as independent beings. In fact, women who demonstrated independence, intelligence, and will power[92] were still defined as evil, as *femmes fatales*.

The Shelleys

One of the most important Romantic writers, Mary Shelley, sought to reverse this argument about the source of evil, tracing its roots, rather, to male rationalism and science instead of to female passion. Mary Shelley's *Frankenstein, or the Modern Prometheus* (1818),[93] which depicts the monstrous possibilities of modern science, is probably the best-known Gothic novel. Victor Frankenstein, the scientist whose creation became the 'monster', was motivated by his vanity to 'pioneer a new way, explore unknown powers, and unfold to the world the deepest mysteries of creation'—to go where no man had gone before. His early wish to study **natural philosophy** (science) was driven by the 'glory [that] would attend the discovery, if I could banish disease from the human frame, and render man invulnerable to any but a violent death!' After years of studying chemistry and physiology, Frankenstein 'succeeded in discovering the cause of generation and life' and became 'capable of bestowing animation upon lifeless matter'.[94] Frankenstein applied his genesis formula to the reconstructed human form he stitched together from cadaver parts. Then:

> I collected the instruments of life around me, that I might infuse a spark of being into the lifeless thing that lay at my feet. It was already one in the morning; the rain pattered dismally against the panes, and my candle was nearly burnt out, when, by the glimmer of the half-extinguished light, I saw the dull yellow eye of the creature open; it breathed hard, and a convulsive motion agitated its limbs.[95]

Filled with 'breathless horror and disgust', Frankenstein fled from the creature who stretched out its hands to its creator. The creature was as helpless as a **feral child**, with only nature as its guide. Like the noble savage in the Romantic imagination, the creature naturally felt 'the love of virtue, the feelings of happiness and affection' with which his 'whole being overflowed'. At first, his 'thoughts were . . . filled with sublime and transcendent visions of the beauty and the majesty of goodness.'[96]

For everyone with eyes to see, however, the creature was perceived to be a monster. In response to his natural acts of kindness, the creature was shunned and received only violence at the hands of a frightened humanity. As **labelling theory** would now predict, the creature came to perceive himself as others did; his innate sense of morality and goodness was perverted by experience. His 'heart was fashioned to be susceptible of love and sympathy', and only 'when wrenched by misery' did he turn 'to vice and hatred'.[97] He became the monster that civilization had said he was.

After several years, the self-taught creature confronted Frankenstein, related his miseries, and demanded a companion, a woman of the same species and with the same defects as himself. In 'the remotest of the Orkney' islands, Frankenstein prepared a second animation—a bride for his first creation. Yet, consistent with the sexist ideology of the time, Frankenstein feared that the female of his newly created species 'might become ten thousand times more malignant than her mate, and delight, for its own sake, in murder and wretchedness.'[98] Rather than generate a malignant race, Frankenstein 'tore to pieces the thing' he was creating. Deprived of a companion for his misery and with no feelings left except revenge, the creature stalked Frankenstein and strangled his creator's bride on their wedding night. The creature completed the circle linking creation and destruction, leaving her body 'lifeless and inanimate, thrown across the bed'.[99]

The underlying sociological theme conventionally drawn from Shelley's novel is that by pursuing 'nature to her hiding-places', humankind is dabbling with forces that cannot be controlled. Scientific creations can, ultimately, be destructive, a point especially pertinent in the modern age. As Frankenstein pursues his wife's murderer to the Arctic wastes, he is rescued by a group of scientific explorers whose ship is trapped in the Arctic ice. Their fate is symbolic of the weakness of humanity in the face of the awful powers of nature. Held fast in the frozen grip of mountains of ice, Frankenstein continued to proclaim the superiority of humanity to nature. The dangers of untamed nature, he declared to the ship's crew, 'are mole-hills which will vanish before the resolutions of man.' He tells them that ice 'is mutable' and 'cannot withstand you, if you say that it shall not.'[100] He asserts the ultimate arrogance of humanity in the face of nature; the more dangerous and full of terror a task, the more glorious and honourable it is. Shelley's novel was an exotic parable about the fall of humanity. The theme of rationality gone mad has become a staple of the science fiction **genre**.

Percy Shelley, Mary's husband, was the most radical, socially, of the English Romantics. From the point of view of social theory, **social Romanticism** embraced an explicitly critical politics. For Shelley, poets were 'the unacknowledged legislators of the world'.[101] They had a responsibility to expose wrongs and incite reform. William Blake, better known for his mystic verse and spirituality, had been moved by the 'eternal winter' of the poor and oppressed in his own society (Box 5.4),[102] where:

> . . . souls of men are bought and sold
> And milk-fed infancy for gold;
> And youth to slaughterhouses led,
> And beauty for a bit of bread.[103]

Shelley's radical side had surfaced early in his life. He was expelled from Oxford University allegedly for writing the pamphlet *The Necessity of Atheism*, which had been sent to the masters of the colleges as well as to high-ranking clergy. Shelley's reputation in England never approached the adulation heaped on Byron. In fact, Shelley's short and tragic life was remembered at the time for being anti-Christian and for what was deemed its immorality. He abandoned his first wife to elope in 1814 with Mary, the daughter of Mary Wollstonecraft and William Godwin. Shelley assumed that his first marriage had been a free-love union,

---

Box 5.4

Is this a holy thing to see,
In a rich and fruitful land:
Babes reduced to misery,
Fed with cold and usurous hand?

Is that trembling cry a song?
Can it be a song of joy?
And so many children poor?
It is a land of poverty!

And their sun does never shine,
And their fields are bleak and bare,
And their ways are filled with thorns;
It is eternal winter there.

For where'er the sun does shine,
And where'er the rain does fall—
Babe can never hunger there,
Nor poverty the mind appal.

—William Blake, 'Holy Thursday' (1789)

from which either party could make a rational decision to leave; his first wife, however, felt differently and, after her suicide, Shelley was driven out of England by scandalized public opinion. Mary agreed to marry him, after his first wife's death, perhaps because of the social condemnation her own mother had endured as a result of her unorthodox lifestyle. For both mother and daughter, however, their chosen lives demanded a great deal of sacrifice punctuated by the travails of child-bearing. Mary's mother had died shortly after bringing her into the world. By the age of 20, following her elopement with Shelley, Mary had been pregnant three times. Two children survived; their first child, a daughter, died shortly after her birth in 1815.[104]

Shelley is remembered for his evocative and naturalistic lyrics and his honed sensibilities. He also wrote about the misery and oppression of English labourers, where he expressed socialist ideas early for his time. In 1819, while living in Italy with Mary, Shelley was driven to write two political poems upon hearing news of a bloody massacre in England. Several working men, who were demonstrating for basic, liberal democratic rights, had been murdered by government troops. The following excerpt from 'Mask of Anarchy' demonstrates Shelley's spirited rebelliousness and his appreciation for the plight and the potential of the working masses. Shelley told the working 'Men of England' that their labour went to support tyrants and 'ungrateful drones':

> Men of England, wherefore plough
> For the lords who lay ye low?
> Wherefore weave with toil and care
> The rich robes your tyrants wear?
> Wherefore feed, and clothe, and save,
> From the cradle to the grave,
> Those ungrateful drones who would
> Drain your sweat—nay, drink your blood?
> . . .
> Have ye leisure, comfort, calm,
> Shelter, food, love's gentle balm?
> Or what is it ye buy so dear
> With your pain and with your fear?

> The seed you sew, another reaps;
> The wealth ye find, another keeps;
> The robes ye weave, another wears;
> The arms ye forge, another bears. . . .[105]

Shelley cultivated his 'delicate sensibilities' in his **lifestyle** choices. He became a vegetarian, although he would nevertheless allow his guests to be fed what he termed 'a murdered chicken'.[106] With Shelley, Rowbotham argues,[107] the personal and the political were connected. Shelley claimed that love relationships should be 'freely contracted, and freely dissolved'—'Love withers under constraint.' Being a revolutionary meant you had to change your life as much as you had to criticize social institutions. Lifestyle change eventually became the essential component of Romantic rebellion.

When Shelley drowned in Italy, his body was cremated with the exception of his heart, which Mary kept with her thereafter, wrapped in a silken shroud.[108] Later, Karl Marx had the following observation to make about the early deaths of both Byron and Shelley:

> The real difference between Byron and Shelley is this: those who understand them and love them rejoice that Byron died at thirty-six, because if he had lived he would have become a reactionary bourgeois; they grieve that Shelley died at twenty-nine because he was essentially a revolutionist and would always have been one of the advanced guard of socialism.[109]

Emily Brontë

Romanticism, as an ideology and literary form, did not disappear with the death of the second generation of Romantics in England. In 1847, an astonishing and unique Romantic novel, *Wuthering Heights*, was published in England. Clearly in a direct line of descent from the English Romantics, overflowing with passion, nature, eroticism, and death, *Wuthering Heights* was written (at first under the androgynous pseudonym Ellis Bell) by Emily Brontë (1818–48), an unmarried daughter of a clergyman living in rural isolation in York-shire. *Wuthering Heights* was published one year before the author's death at the age of 30. Brontë replicated the short life of the English Romantic poets she admired. In one sense, Brontë was con-nected to the Romantic past. She had lived their lives in her imagination and in her own close rela-tionship with nature.

Brontë also was connected with the future of Romanticism. Many of the English Romantic poets of the second generation had been involved in political causes—with national independence and the labouring poor. The failure of Romantic rebel-lion to effect social change, however, caused wider political aspirations to wither and personal ones to sprout as Romanticism became increasingly subjective. Brontë had no ambition to challenge the social order, even in the 1840s when the storm clouds of revolution continued to gather on the Continent and in England. The wild, apolitical Romanticism of *Wuthering Heights* foreshadowed the literary turn to private and personal subjec-tivity. While the Brontë sisters—Charlotte, Emily, and Anne—experienced the world through their imaginations in the Yorkshire countryside, the generation of 1848 in France, where the Roman-tic movement was more immediately involved in political battles, was about to throw itself onto the barricades. Their disillusionment with politics would come later and be based more on their experiences than on their imagination.

FRENCH ROMANTICISM

The French Revolution, which had begun in 1789, was basically over by 1794 when the rad-ical Jacobins were driven from power and their authoritarian rule in the name of popular democ-racy was abandoned. With the National Assem-bly safely in the hands of the prosperous middle class, a new Constitution was adopted for the French Republic that made property ownership secure and abolished any measures that hinted at **socialism**.[110] From the day of its creation, this new French Republic was politically unstable, threatened by the radicals on the left and the

restorationists on the right, who were eager to restore the King to the throne. Political instability and social chaos were not good for business. Only the army appeared strong enough to put an end to the social strife and secure the interests of the propertied classes. The *coup d'état* that placed Napoleon in power in France brought the First French Republic to a close.

For many French Romantics, Napoleon was the model of the strong, independent hero; he was idolized by the people and carried on his shoul-ders the pride and honour of the nation. The French painter Jacques Louis David contributed importantly in the myth-making surrounding Napoleon. David was a revolutionary whose famous painting, *The Death of Marat* (1793), paid homage to the martyred hero of the Revolution. David later became Napoleon's leading painter, commemorating his rule and helping inspire the cult of Napoleon as a Romantic hero. Under David's brush, neo-classicism was traversed and harnessed to the causes of revolution, Romanti-cism, and the glorification of the heroic.

The more traditionalists hated Napoleon and the more foreign monarchs vied to overthrow him, the more heroic and modern he appeared. Napoleon's success in France depended as much on compromise as on charisma. The millions of agricultural labourers—peasants—were the real foundation of the nation, and many of them had benefited from land redistribution during the Revolution. While Napoleon was successful, he was admired. After his final defeat, the wider democratic demands of the population were tem-porarily smothered by the pomp and ceremony of the restoration.

One important voice that could not be stilled belonged to women. Napoleon's female nemesis had been Germaine de Staël, a popular writer and social critic around whom swirled the currents of revolutionary ideas from the days of the Old Regime to the era of Napoleon. For women, de Staël claimed, autonomy required separating from men, particularly from husbands. This conclusion held equally true for the next generation of rebel-lious women who influenced the mid-century

Parisian revolutions. The novelist George Sand (1804–76), the pseudonym of Aurore Dudevant, left her aristocratic husband in 1831, establishing herself in Paris as the centre of another counter-culture of literary and philosophical debate. In her novels, Sand depicted the tragedy of women who could seek autonomy from male possession only in a hidden, inner self.[111]

When Napoleon was defeated in 1814, the victorious powers demanded that Louis XVIII, a brother of the executed King Louis XVI, be crowned King of France; the restorationists had achieved their wish. Just how thoroughly they and the returning émigrés were going to be able to reverse the tide of history was uncertain. What was clear was that any government would be insecure and be caught in the conflict between the liberal democrats, who wanted to protect and extend the gains of the Revolution, and the right-wing monarchists, who sought a return to autocracy and aristocratic control.

Political lines were paralleled by economic divisions. Napoleon's war economy had been good for French business, not only in the market it created for army supplies, but because of the English blockade. Behind this providential protective barrier, French commerce and industry expanded rapidly, large enterprises were built, and steam engines introduced. At the behest of the large-scale industrialists and landowners, protective tariffs to restrict imports were kept in place after the restoration of the monarchy. This self-interested economic policy divided the upper class from the small owners and crafts workers, who complained of artificially high prices, lack of opportunities, and the tyranny of the French government.[112]

A decade after the defeat of Napoleon, the prospect of social change again began to energize young artists and intellectuals. Their conscience was aroused by the struggles for national independence in Greece and Italy and, in France, by the miseries of the industrial age, which materialized as poverty, destitution, and criminality. Victor Hugo's monumental novel *Les Misérables* moralized about the sufferings of the poor in Paris, reflecting a new social Romanticism, which exposed atrocities while offering no solutions other than Christian charity.

Artistic rebellion stimulated actual rebellion. According to Gillis,[113] Victor Hugo's play, *Hernani*, repudiated everything the neo-classical school of theatre had represented. Performed in 1830, the play ended with a near-riot inside the theatre as the rebellious artists shouted insults at the upper-class audience. It was a prelude to the actual revolution of that year. In Belgium later in the same year, a performance of a play with a revolutionary theme so stirred the emotions of the audience that they left the theatre and proclaimed the independence of Belgium from Holland. In Germany, as well, Heinrich Heine called on artists to 'speak with sabres' rather than 'idyllic-spirit stuff' and make their verses 'strong and biting' (Box 5.5).[114]

Political conflict nurtured by economic crises simmered over the ensuing decade and came to the boiling point in 1830 when a liberal majority was elected to the National Assembly and clashed with the right-wing King, who was determined to limit political and economic freedoms. The battle escalated until the revolution of July 1830 broke out in a few days of furious fighting in the streets of Paris. Led by radical students and workers and inspired by the ideas of republicanism and democracy, barricades and bullets drove the King out of the country. The wave of violent overthrow subsided quickly, leaving in its wake the fundamental question: What kind of regime would replace the old? To the disappointment of the more radical street-fighters, another King, Louis Philippe d'Orleans, was put on the throne. A political compromise, more defeat than victory, Louis Philippe did promise, to grant some democratic reforms and modestly widened the electoral franchise.

Romanticism has always been two-faced. During the restoration, when progress and perfectibility were discredited dogmas, the Romantics sought to revive the past or dwelt in their own private and subjective worlds. In post-1830 France, however, Romanticism regained a political and social edge, supporting republicans and democrats, who were resisting the return to traditional, autocratic rule. Social revolt was expressed in such art as Delacroix's

Box 5.5

German bard, come sing the praises
Of our German freedom till
Song becomes an inspiration
For great deeds to serve the nation
As the rousing Marseillaise is.

Do not coo like Werther, labours
Wastes on a Lotto's sighs.
What the bells are pealing loudly
Speak it to the people proudly,
Speak with daggers, speak with sabres!

No soft fluting, no more quarter,
No idyllic-spirit stuff!
Be the battle drum or thump it,
Be the cannon, be the trumpet,
Blare out, bellow, thunder, slaughter!

Blare out, bellow, thunder, man—
Till the last oppressor flees!
Make your verses strong and biting . . .
But make sure you keep your writing
Just as general as you can.

—Heinrich Heine, 'For the Cause' (1842)

painting, *Liberty Leading the People* (1831), which commemorated the 1830 revolution. Inspired by painters Delacroix and Gericault, novelists Victor Hugo and George Sand, and led by French socialists and anarchists, the new generation of Romantics took an active part in the Paris rebellions.

Among the most active republicans was the French novelist, Alexandre Dumas (1802–70), who took part in the 1830 street-fighting in his twenties and later in the 1848 revolution. When Dumas turned 60, he fought with the Italian revolutionary, Garibaldi. Dumas's rebelliousness was reflected in his turbulent lifestyle, but not in his prose. The most prolific and popular author in France during his lifetime, he published hundreds of novels, mostly in the style of historical romance such as *Les Trois Mousquetaires* and *Le Comte de* *Monte Cristo*. Most of his books were written in what became known as the industrial style, serialized in popular magazines and paid for by the line. Dumas's popularity with the people was not shared by literary critics, who objected to the emergence of mass culture represented by serialized literature.[115]

Dumas was reviled by his critics for the more personal reason of racism. His grandmother was born in Gabon, where she was captured by slave traders and taken to Haiti. She had four children fathered by her white 'master', including Alexandre Dumas's father, who later entered France illegally. Alexandre Dumas was born in 1802, the year that Napoleon reinstituted slavery in the French colonies. The critics who later attacked his novels resorted to racial epithets, focusing on Dumas's physical appearance and alleging that a savage character lurked beneath his only skin-deep layer of civilization. In his early novel *Georges*, Dumas's title character is a half-caste who suffers the indignities of racism that Dumas knew only too well.[116]

Radicals as well as liberal democrats such as Dumas were soon disillusioned with their 'citizen king', an alienation sparked by an economic depression that flared again to rebellion in 1848. The rebels overthrew the constitutional monarchy of Louis Philippe and proclaimed the Second Republic, a victory that was secured at the cost of thousands of lives during heavy street-fighting in Paris. Universal male suffrage followed as a tangible symbol of victory, although there was no noticeable change in the class composition of the French National Assembly. The rebellion in France of 1848 inspired similar revolts in such cities as Vienna, Milan, Prague, Budapest, and Venice. There was even a militant workers' movement in England known as the Chartists, who held a massive demonstration in London.

Again, political factions fought for control of the Second Republic. Radical democrats and republicans representing the voice of the lower-middle and working classes demanded significant political and social reforms. The urban masses who had fought on the barricades in 1830 and again in 1848 remained a powerful opposition in the National Assembly. Workers' voices were heard in the streets, but they lacked organization and had no clear program or leadership.

In the face of this articulate but diffused threat 'from below', conservative forces once again pushed the army into action in a replay of recent French history. In 1851, Louis Napoleon Bonaparte, a nephew of the First Emperor, following in his uncle's footsteps, overthrew the Second French Republic and, in the following year, crowned himself Emperor Napoleon III. The Second French Empire extracted a terrible price in bloodshed from the French people and, once in power, suppressed the demands of the working class and radical republicans. Under dictatorship once again, France saw Louis Napoleon restore the conditions for further capitalist expansion.

Throughout this long period of turbulent history, the revolutionary spirit of 1789 had resurged in 1830 and again in 1848, although both times the rebellions were crushed and the working-class radicals and middle-class youth massacred. Against this volatile political background Romanticism inspired the rebels on the barricades until, with their death, it was also pronounced dead. French Romantics flirted with politics until failure drove many of them to a pervasive disillusionment with humankind. For some, a purely private rebellion remained intact, a freeing of the consciousness towards the movement of art for art's sake.

While Romantic melodrama has survived as a popular form into the twenty-first century, Romanticism as an artistic movement of social revolt was temporarily eclipsed following the defeats of 1848. Delacroix refused to paint a picture commemorating the revolution of that year, to be called 'Equality Leading the People', because he had lost hope for the future.[117] Like the earlier generation of English radicals, such as Wordsworth and Coleridge, the middle-class generation of the 1830s and 1840s abandoned any hopes for political and social reform, developing instead a new experimental, avant-garde style complemented by a bohemian life. Bohemianism meant a purely individualistic lifestyle rebellion that defied social conventions and was fascinated by the occult, sensuality, and the violation of sexual taboos. It initiated a pattern that was to be repeated many times over the next century and a half.

Two important artistic strands survived: realism and art for art's sake. The art for art's sake movement was the resort of the post-Romantic artist whose search for liberty became entirely subjective. Art was nothing more, and nothing less, than the expression of an artist's inner visions and feelings. It had no lofty social goal; it was not to be a mirror for people or nature; it certainly was not art for the masses. Art for art's sake was Romanticism shorn of any wider social or political purpose. The Romantic poet, John Keats, reflected this apolitical orientation while also disavowing Kant's qualitative distinction between the true and the beautiful in the famous final lines from his 'Ode on a Grecian Urn' (1819):

'Beauty is truth, truth beauty,'—that is all
Ye know on earth, and all ye need to know.[118]

Many artists of the later nineteenth-century avant-garde privileged aesthetics over ideology and form over content. They saw their art as revolutionary in a new sense, liberating the artist from the constraints imposed by society. In this respect, they represented the mirror image of social science.

Avant-garde artists engaged in a micro-politics of resistance rooted in the individual but that was apolitical in the wider, social sense. As such, it was the consequence not of victory but of disillusionment and defeat. In politics, the revolutionary torch was passed to the socialists and anarchists, who contended for predominance among the members of the growing working class. In art, the revival of realism made concrete the role of the artist as social critic and reformer.

The origins of realism in literature had been closely associated with the rise of the bourgeoisie, or middle class, and reflected its conflict with the aristocracy. When realism was reinvented in the nineteenth century it emerged as a critique of bourgeois society and of Romanticism, most savagely by Gustave Flaubert in *Madame Bovary* (1857) and *Sentimental Education* (1869).

Emma Bovary, the anti-heroine of Flaubert's realistic novel, *Madame Bovary*, is led to suicidal self-destruction by the contrast between what she defines as her boring, conventional, and provincial existence with her dull but devoted husband and the Romantic images of what life should be, drawn from the popular novels she read. With 'Walter Scott, she grew enamoured of historic events, dreamed of travelling chests, guardrooms, and minstrels. She wished that she had lived on some old manor . . . watching a cavalier with a white feather emerge from the horizon on a galloping black charger.' Bovary dreamed of 'sultans with long pipes, swooning with delight in bowers in the arms of dancing girls!' There were 'tigers to the right, lions to the left, Tartar minarets against

the horizon, Roman ruins in the foreground, and camels crouching'. Above all, Emma yearned for romantic love: 'Love, she believed, should arrive all at once with thunder and lightning—a whirlwind from the skies that affects life, turns it every which way, wrests resolutions away like leaves, and plunges the entire heart into an abyss.' Inevitably, she was sorely disappointed by her extramarital affairs and, in the end, committed suicide, the victim of her fantasies.[119]

Madame Bovary was an anti-Romantic novel. Flaubert portrayed Emma as the victim of an unrealistic, destructive, and unprecedented mass culture. In place of the Romantic imagination and the fascination with the exotic and foreign, the realist authors were concerned with depicting the everyday with a critical edge. Realism continued the intellectual tradition of exposing the hypocrisy and injustices of the new bourgeois world that was rapidly growing up around them.

ROMANTIC SUBJECTIVISM

I wonder who it was defined man as a rational animal. It was the most premature definition ever given. Man is many things, but he is not rational. I am glad he is not, after all.
—Oscar Wilde, *The Picture of Dorian Gray* (1891)

Literary, artistic, and theoretical movements may depart in important ways from the social circumstances in which they arose. Once artists felt themselves alienated from their own society, they experienced 'the great liberation' of subjectivity. Genres emerge, persist, or evolve in the most varied of circumstances, making generalizations about them particularly fragile.

From the perspective of social theory, both realism and Romanticism were born in eras of radical change. Initially, realism celebrated bourgeois individualism and joined the crusade of the new middle class against the remnants of feudal privilege and aristocratic waste. Liberal ideology itself was, at first, radical and rebellious. Bourgeois thinkers challenged arbitrary authority in the name of human freedom. At first social thinkers sought to discover the 'natural laws' of reason that were embedded in nature and derived, ultimately, from divinity. Over time, however, reason became radically individuated and subjective. Freedom came to mean liberation from constraint.

Liberalism remained an ideology of rebellion only so long as the bourgeoisie was not dominant. Once the new moneyed interests were firmly in power, liberalism was muted and tamed to the interests of the new ruling class. Capitalism and limited liberal democracy became the new status quo. The English bourgeoisie cozied up to the aristocracy in marriage and proclaimed the rigid principles, if not always the practice, of morality, religion, and custom. Liberal principles were fine for laissez-faire economics but certainly not for politics (only male property owners should vote), or for the family, or for women, or for lifestyle choices. Rousseau's comment that people were born free but lived everywhere in chains seemed to sum up this oppressive society.

In early nineteenth-century capitalism, the contrasts between the liberal promises of freedom and equality and the realities of a class-divided nation were patently obvious. In this sense, as Hobsbawm says, Romanticism was the instinctive enemy of bourgeois society.[120] To a degree, it is the enemy of society in general. Once out of its cage, human freedom is hypothetically boundless. Romanticism emphasizes the contradiction between the individual and society, and endorses an extreme individualism.

Radical Romantics rejected the whole edifice of bourgeois morality, ethics, and institutions. Capitalism was cold, calculating, and inhumane. Bourgeois society was mechanical, materialistic, and, above all else, stultifying and repressive—in all ways contrary to nature, beauty, novelty, and excitement. Like the conservatives, they rejected science, empiricism, and the world of Newton, because these provided the methodology of capitalism, the intellectual basis of the world the radical Romantics opposed. Subjectivism implies focusing on the mind, on consciousness. Over

time it became radically individuated as social theorists asked: Whose mind? Whose perceptions? To simplify, it becomes Romantic especially when it focuses on the non-rational origins of human motivations. It becomes conservative particularly when it abandons individualism and enthrones such non-rational foundations as nationality, language, or race.

In its individualistic form, Romanticism is often a product of youthful idealism. For Hobsbawm,[121] the Romantics were, above all, youth, 'displaced young men' with no solid roots in the class structure and relatively free of social obligations. For them, bourgeois society represented a 'prison house' of convention, marriage, career, and materialism, all of which they consciously rejected. They had a highly developed sense of their own importance and talent, yet they were at first largely ignored or reviled by dominant social groups. Here was born the intellectual counterculture, consciously alienated from the conventional rules of society. Romantics expressed their rebellion in their art and their lifestyles, flaunting conventions such as marriage and religion, and developing 'bohemian' countercultures. Esler adds that hair styles in 1830s France became visible signs of one's politics. The monarchists wore a slight beard; the Bonapartists, a flamboyant, military moustache; republican youth grew full beards; while both radical socialists and the bohemians grew shoulder-length hair as well as beards.[122] You displayed your personal politics in your dress and style. Bohemia is the vestige of the nonconformist Romantic movement minus its wider political inclinations.

The rebellious generation lived in an age when established figures and conventions dominated the arts and letters, and well-heeled artists provided the aristocratic and bourgeois patrons of the arts with conventional forms and styles. Shut out from lucrative markets, the isolated Romantic artist cultivated the myth of the 'genius'—not merely an intelligent and skilful artist, but one who is unconventional, uncompromising, and egotistical, self-consciously believing in his or her own importance. For the Romantics, the French

Revolution still stood for the promise of liberty and symbolized the individual's boundless potential for change and betterment. From this emerged a vision of 'the revolutionary', someone who was always and everywhere in rebellion against the status quo. Rejecting bourgeois conventions and adopting nonconformism, they envisioned a way of being revolutionary that would define the European anarchist. While the flames of revolution had been snuffed out, the ideals that inspired the radical Romantics continued to smoulder, surfacing in the mid-nineteenth century in the socialist and, particularly, the anarchist movements.

CONCLUSION

The conservatives directed social theory away from the speculations about natural law towards history, which was a construction of human beings. Theorists such as Burke saw England as a model of slow, peaceful change and social progress. Existing rights and duties were the products of the slow evolution of society, the sum of all past reason. Change was right if it was in line with the past and did not challenge the existing social institutions. Nature established limits to the scope of historical change. Only a minority of men possessed sufficient rationality to own property and rule society. Inequalities of class and gender were part of the natural order. People could imagine a different, more egalitarian arrangement, but such thinking was Utopian and was especially dangerous and destructive when the flights of imaginative fancy were imposed by force on an existing society, as they had been in France in 1789. The structure of social institutions inherited from our ancestors resembled a single organism; all parts were necessary to the well-being of the whole and everyone played a role or fulfilled a necessary function, however humble, in maintaining social order. The image of society in terms of structure, inequality, and function linked eighteenth-century conservatism backwards to traditional social theory and forward to nineteenth-century social science.

Conservative social theory and both conservative and radical versions of Romanticism reject human reason as a privileged route to secure knowledge. All three theoretical offshoots have a similar philosophical parent in Kant's subjectivism, although their perspectives are different. Radical Romanticism, like the Enlightenment, rejects what is most important to the conservatives: custom, tradition, the whole weight of past conventions and institutions. The Enlightenment thinkers were the first largely secular body of social theorists to stand in opposition to the status quo ('the intellectual as rebel') and the radical Romantics were rebellious in some of the same ways.

For conservatives and their Romantic cousins, meaning and knowledge are fundamentally subjective. Truths claimed from science based on empirical evidence are no more valid than truths claimed from faith, tradition, or religion; in fact, in the areas of morality and ethics, nonrational sources of truth are the only reliable guides. Rather than being a passive sponge soaking up sense experiences, for Kant and the conservatives and the Romantics who followed him, the 'mind partly creates the external reality it grasps.'[123] The conservatives regarded society as an organism consisting of various parts, which functioned together to maintain social stability. The glue that holds the various parts together is composed of moral consensus, shared values, and common beliefs and sentiments. Traditions and customs, although seemingly irrational, formed part of the consensus of beliefs that were absolutely necessary for social stability. People shared a similar view of the world, followed the same moral code, and felt a sense of belonging.

The conservative critique of liberalism and Enlightenment rationality represented the ideology of the old upper class that was being displaced more than it did the rising bourgeoisie that was replacing it, although in the long run they would become ideologically indistinguishable. Unlike the French aristocracy, the English 'upper crust' survived into the twenty-first century. They did so, however, by making peace with the new capitalist class, joining them economically and socially through marriage. Conservative ideology would slowly evolve in the nineteenth century, combining the elements of old-fashioned religion and veneration of the monarchy with nationalism, patriotism, and support for the paramount place in the world of Empire and nation. In the process, modern conservatives would shed their original Tory distrust of industrial capitalism.

The Romantics inherited the older conservatives' dislike of the objectionable practices of modern, capitalist society. If the Middle Ages were about loyalty, honour, and chivalry, the new age of capitalism could not be more opposite. In the modern laissez-faire world, it was every person for him or herself. Profit was the only object of worship and money was the only god. Society was grossly materialistic, in the sense that things were deemed more important than people. The capitalist owed to the labourer no more than the agreed-upon wage; her or his welfare was of no concern. The conservative Romantics believed that under feudalism the landlord had been concerned about the welfare of his peasants. The modern, industrialized world, then, had debased humanity and the Romantics rejected this world economically, by opposing the Industrial Revolution and its goal of material progress. In one of its extreme manifestations, Romanticism represented a rejection of the world politically, by limiting the humanistic goals of the liberal age to the free expression of individual desires.

If the dominant, modern ideology, rooted in Enlightenment rationalism, had practical consequences in the economy, in politics, and in technology, the alternative, Romantic subjectivism became an influential, parallel discourse. Both ideologies are reflected in the self-centred principles of the modern business economy that have now been promulgated globally, as Jefferson's 'life, liberty, and the pursuit of happiness' has become the rationalization for every form of profligacy.

In the arts and the politics it supports, the Romantic movement had a complex legacy. On the one hand, social Romanticism embraced the revolutionary emphasis on liberty and inspired a social movement based on a moral and idealistic

critique of the bourgeois present. Romanticism reached back to the English liberal emphasis on individualism and freedom. More fundamentally, however, Romantics rejected social order and dethroned reason. What was really important—beauty, self-expression, and, above all, freedom—could never be understood by rational science. Art is the expression of the artist's feelings—her or his mind, emotions, and imagination. This expression has to be spontaneous and not created in accordance with previous traditions of art or conventional rules. While concerned often with everyday things, the object of art is to show the mystery, the natural, and the non-rational.

On the other hand, the Romantic view that individuals were not primarily rational, but were motivated by emotions and feelings and understood things intuitively, had conservative, even authoritarian, consequences. When the elite notion of the individual genius or historical hero is married to the mythical Nation and its people's (or *volks*) culture, a dangerous political dynamic is set in motion, realized in its most extreme form in Nazi Germany. Romanticism could be turned to a number of political purposes, even to contradictory purposes. The Nazi regime, like Shakespeare's Iago writ large, consciously manipulated public passions for explicitly racist and authoritarian ends. Modern Western political 'machines' do the same thing, though generally for less malignant purposes.

The libertarian strand of the Romantic movement led to anarchism because it stood for opposition to all authority. Anarchism is the furthest extension of the will to give humans the maximum freedom. This also has been a persistent movement in the West. In one respect, anarchism does not reflect the Romantic criticism of modernist, Enlightenment ideology: anarchists assumed that all humans were rational enough to live in a society without authority, although they did not assume that rationality alone was enough. While anarchism has resurfaced in the contemporary anti-globalization movement, it is ironic that the multinational corporate world and modern terrorism have both defined themselves largely as beyond the law.

Another strand was reflected in the psychologically penetrating literature of the time. For the Romantics, the rational part of the brain was secondary to the intuitive, emotional essence, which included the most basic and primitive impulses, particularly sexuality. Human rationality in this light amounted to little more than rationalizations—explanations for things that merely excuse or justify actions, which actually spring from deep, unconscious processes. The Enlightenment emphasis on rational thought, then, was wholly mistaken. People were motivated primarily by non-rational factors. This explained the hold that religion and custom had on so many people. This mode of theorizing would be reflected in early twentieth-century psychology and psychoanalysis, as well as microsociology.

In contemporary society, subjectivism has been widely influential beyond the fine arts, penetrating such practices as medicine, journalism, education, religion, and politics. Enlightenment rationalism and Romantic subjectivism are both products of modern, European society. One is the necessary concomitant of the other and, in contemporary times, both are rejected by fundamentalists and traditionalists around the globe, at least, with respect to Romanticism, of the more individualistic ideals of the liberation of desire and rebellion against traditional order.

Among sociologists, as Karl Mannheim observed, both conservatism and Romanticism represented more than a modern counter-current to the bourgeois-rationalistic world view. Both schools of thought reiterated the importance of qualitative knowledge and reoriented social theory by presenting a holistic perspective on society.[124] Conservative Romantics opposed the abstract, mechanical thought of the Enlightenment and reiterated the older, organic view.[125] Sociology entered what is often termed its classical period between 1890 and 1920, founded on the conservative and Romantic evaluations of the non-rational basis of human behaviour and their attempts to grasp the 'whole' of experience. The 'new' science addressed the historically produced structure of customs, traditions, and institutions within which social order was maintained. If Durkheim and Weber are the fathers of contemporary sociology, the respectable conservatives and outcast Romantics were its most prolific grandparents. As much as the late nineteenth-century sociologists felt the threat of social anarchy in laissez-faire economics, they also responded to the chaos of the individualist rebellion of their time.

Romantics regarded themselves as the antithesis of sociology. The entire enterprise of developing a science of society with the intention of being able to control human behaviour was anathema to the Romantics. The search for a social science had motivated Hobbes, Hume, and some of the *philosophes*. In the early decades of the nineteenth century, the social theorists Henri de Saint-Simon and Auguste Comte thought they had realized this rationalist vision.

6 POSITIVISM AND DEMOCRACY

The idea of a science of society has been a goal of social thought at least since Hobbes imagined people to be like single atoms in perpetual motion. Hobbes actually produced a treatise on society that began with assumed first principles and deduced natural laws of society from them. He may have been inspired by Bacon's empiricism, but his theory was heavy on supposition and light on historical fact. The subsequent search for natural social laws in liberal and Enlightenment theory had generally followed Hobbes's path of speculative, deductive reason.

In the southern Italian city of Naples in 1725 Giovanni Vico outlined an alternative to philosophical speculation that was well in advance of Hobbes. In *Principles of a New Science Dealing With the Nature of Nations [and] . . . the Natural Law of Peoples*, Vico sought to make generalizations about the history of groups, connecting common causes and effects. Charles Louis Montesquieu was an exception among the *philosophes* when he adopted Vico's social historical attitude. Montesquieu examined the relationship between climate and geography and the national character of a people in *The Spirit of Laws* (1748). History was not the work of supernatural agents or of single individuals, but the creation of people acting within their environment. History revealed the story of the social construction of humanity.[1]

Conservative social theorists also had argued that the institutions of each national society had been slowly constructed through the work of succeeding generations. But they had not intended to create a science of society; that was too much an Enlightenment project. The legitimate heir of Vico

and Montesquieu was Claude Henri de Saint-Simon (1760–1825), who sought to elaborate the law-like rules he believed governed society. He knew that the Industrial Revolution was here to stay and sought a scientific understanding of the evolution of society towards the golden age that industrialism promised.

SAINT-SIMON

> The Golden Age of mankind does not lie behind us, but before; it lies in the perfection of the social order. Our forefathers did not see it; one day our children will reach it. It is for us to clear the way.
> —Henri Saint-Simon, *On the Reorganization of European Society* (1814)

Born to an aristocratic family in Paris, Saint-Simon's early career was spent in the army. He saw action in the American War of Independence on the American side, which the French government actively supported, and became sympathetic to the principles of democracy, liberty, and legal equality. During the French Revolution, Saint-Simon's liberal preferences led him to renounce his title and he became active in revolutionary politics. He stepped out of the robes of the French nobility into the breeches of the rising bourgeoisie, speculating heavily in land that had been nationalized and could be purchased at a fraction of its value.[2] In 1793, Saint-Simon was arrested. To be on trial during the Reign of Terror was an unhappy prospect for an ex-noble and he was fortunate to outlive Robespierre, finally being released after the fall of the Jacobins. During the next few years, Saint-Simon prospered as a **nouveau riche** gentleman, buying property, establishing industrial and commercial businesses, and becoming involved in the politics of the Directorate.[3]

By 1799, however, Saint-Simon was broke. His passion was not for the details of business organization or diplomacy—nor for marriage. Saint-Simon married a young writer and musician in 1801 in order to have a cultured hostess for entertaining at home. This unromantic match was ill-fated and ended in less than a year. He was attracted to Germaine de Staël, who had conceived of a science of society that she called 'positive', but this liaison remained intellectual. A more pressing concern was money, a problem solved temporarily with the help of a wealthy patron and, after he experienced a nervous breakdown, by modest support from his family.[4]

Saint-Simon's genuine passion was for science and its application to improve human life. The discovery of the famous Wild Boy of Avignon in 1800—a feral child who was abandoned and grew up in the absence of normal socialization—convinced Saint-Simon that the boy was a living reminder of the nature of primitive humanity. Far from being a 'noble savage', the boy lacked language and culture, which convinced Saint Simon that the earliest humans were close to animals and that only the civilizing mission of society created the modern human being.[5] By 1801, Saint-Simon was fully occupied with scientific studies, finding physiology most exciting, because the study of living organisms seemed to him to provide the most appropriate model for understanding society—a theory he began to think of as 'social physiology'. By 1803, Saint-Simon had published an essay in which he outlined his fundamental ideas about social reorganization. Four years later he began to synthesize scientific knowledge, attempting to create intellectual order out of the increasingly specialized and distinct scientific disciplines.[6]

Saint-Simon supported the liberal cause in France. He advocated a political party of big business, the adoption of utilitarian economics, and a business-friendly, representative government. He posed as the spokesperson of the active industrialists, voicing the liberal theme of opposition to the idle classes—the nobles, clergy, and military officers. Arrested in 1820 on a charge of subversion for his published attacks on members of the Bourbon royal family, Saint-Simon barely avoided conviction.

With the collaboration of Auguste Comte (1798–1857), his young assistant from 1818 to 1824, Saint-Simon attempted to convince diverse sections of French society—from the King to manual workers—that society had to be reorganized along scientific and industrial lines. The lack of public appreciation threw him into such despair that in 1823 he attempted suicide by shooting himself in the head. He lost an eye—but survived to finalize a break with Comte, who left to pursue his own writings on positive sociology. When Saint-Simon died in 1825 of a stomach ailment, he left behind a complex legacy that owed much to liberalism, endorsed a conservative image of the organic nature of society, and inspired an early socialist movement aimed at reforming French capitalism.[7]

The Industrial Regime

Like his German contemporary, Georg Hegel, Saint-Simon intended to uncover the general path of history and the principles according to which social life developed and changed, to better understand its future course. The fundamental motive forces of history derived from the nature of humanity, Saint-Simon argued, according to which '*All men, every group of men, whatever their nature, aspire to increase their power.*' The principal tool that humanity uses in this quest is mind, or intelligence, expressed in a succession of general ideas. Understanding the evolution of society meant discovering the law guiding the sequence of ideas and the orderly change from one general conception to another.

In the ancient world, ideas had been at first philosophical and speculative until Plato and Aristotle gave them a scientific character. With the advent of Christianity, however, the 'general idea' became religious and superstitious. During the scientific revolution, systematized by Bacon and Descartes, belief was replaced 'by reasoning and observation', the new general idea of the modern world. Theological beliefs about the natural world were overturned by empirical science, an ideological revolution that had not yet reached fulfilment. The social structure of feudalism had rested on the older foundation of religious ideology. The revolution in society that had occurred since 1789 was the necessary consequence of the revolution in ideas that had been initiated by empirical science.[8]

The present age was an age of transition, from the theological to the scientific (or positive) age. It was necessary to construct a new social order based on the principles of science. The religious, political, and industrial revolutions of the eighteenth century had so undermined the old ecclesiastical and feudal power that these forces no longer possessed 'enough strength and credibility to bind society together'.[9] But the conservatives were wrong if they thought it was possible to return to the pre-industrial age. The old organization 'which still encumbers Europe with its useless ruins' could not be raised from the dust: 'the nineteenth century is too far removed from the thirteenth.'[10] Society, argued Saint-Simon, was evolving into a new and higher stage and there was no going back.

Protestantism and then the Enlightenment undermined the old institutions, but 'nothing new was built up in their place.'[11] The eighteenth century had been revolutionary, critical, and destructive; the nineteenth would be inventive and constructive.[12] Society needed a new 'vital and organic binding force', which could only be found in 'the most advantageous organization for industry'. The progress of industry was sluggish, however, because the industrial class was slow to develop political principles of its own. This had changed with the publication of Adam Smith's *Wealth of Nations*, which enunciated the principles of **political economy**.[13]

In place of the ruined institutions of feudalism, in his work *L'Industrie* (1816–18) Saint-Simon championed the growth of commercial and industrial capitalism. He had first embraced these ideas when he was in the American colonies 'fighting for the cause of industrial freedom'. He hoped he could 'help a plant from the New World blossom in France'. In *L'Industrie*, Saint-Simon adopted the liberal view that the new men of industry needed freedom 'to produce and to be unmolested in the enjoyment of what they have produced'. The most important law was the one establishing and regulating the ownership of property, which was the true basis of the social structure. This law must be exercised 'in the way most favourable to the growth of the wealth and the liberties of *industry*'. 'No progress would be possible without this legal framework because people are naturally lazy', Saint-Simon said, and are 'only really subject to one law, that of self-interest.'[14] They work only to meet the necessities of life or to provide for their pleasures.

In his early social and political writings, Saint-Simon wrote favourably about laissez-faire liberalism. As he matured, he modified his thinking about the role that private capital should play, free from public control. He decided that society required some social and economic reforms directed by an interventionist state, and a new, universal morality well beyond the principle of self-interest. By discussing industry rather than individual industrialists, Saint-Simon took a step beyond the atomistic individualism of liberal economics to an understanding of the role economic groups played in society.

In general, Saint-Simon believed, most classes in modern society were separated only by slight differences.[15] The bourgeoisie and the working class were both productive and had arisen as the natural products of modern society. Their interests were fundamentally the same—to prosper—and each was dependent on the other for success. A large gulf separated these two industrial classes from the class of drones, leftovers from the old feudal elite. The population of France, he said, consisted of twenty-nine and a half million producers and a half million non-producers—'the gentlemen, the public officials, the jurists and the idle landowners'. The class of industrious producers,

Saint-Simon complained, was surrounded by a host of parasites, idlers, and thieves who had the same degree of wants and desires but 'have been unable to overcome their natural laziness' and must live off the work of the industrious.[16]

Another class of people existed in the institutions of government. Created to protect the industrious from the idle, the legitimate task of the governing class was to guard the interests of the producers. If government activity expands beyond this task, it becomes arbitrary and tyrannical, promoting the evil it was designed to prevent. People work for themselves and want to work in their own way. Whenever an action from above, external to industry, interferes with it and claims to rule it, industry is hampered and discouraged. Industrial activity ceases in proportion to the constraint it suffers. Government intervention in the past had lacked the scientific principles to guide social change successfully. In short, 'Industry needs as little government as possible.'[17] The Americans had come closest to establishing such a liberal government. In Saint-Simon's view, the American government was small in principle, promoted industry, guaranteed individual liberty and full property rights, and taxed people as little as possible.[18] In contrast to the old feudal classes, the Americans also did not possess a militaristic, national spirit.

The main source of conflict in industrial society was the contradiction between the interests of the industrious class (the bourgeoisie and workers) and the governing class. While the government had been created to represent the general interest, the class in charge of the state had developed a specific interest of its own. Industry wants as little government as possible, while 'those who govern, inevitably, want to govern as much as possible.' Government officials interfered where they did not properly belong. Government should be the servant of society, not its master. Because there was no longer an inevitable conflict between classes, social evolution had undermined the privileges of the aristocracy and, as a result, in France 'classes are only distinguished by slight differences.' The interests of the scientists, artists, and

industrial leaders were essentially the same as those of the mass of people. They were part of the same industrial class and the intellectuals were its 'natural leaders'.[19] It was their profession to think about the general interest of society, which necessarily kept them in touch with the government. The way forward towards the industrial regime was to unite the manufacturing and commercial producers (the 'empirical industrialists') with the literary and scientific intellectuals (the 'theoretical industrialists'). Saint-Simon's intellectual leaders have evolved into the variety of experts who, in the present era, offer their varied and contradictory prescriptions for changing social life.

People must organize themselves, not to dominate each other, but to work towards the positive aim of dominating nature. That was the promise of the emerging industrial regime. If the wonders of the machine age were the fruits of modern science, so, too, would modern science be the instrument for constructing the best of all possible worlds. In *De l'Organisation Sociale* (1825), Saint-Simon stated that genuine social change must be brought in 'all at once and through a radical change of principles' rather than 'slowly through a succession of measures', as **monotheism** replaced polytheism and slavery was abolished with one decree. The French Revolution had adopted only half-measures so that, in short order, it was 'refeudalized'. The French Revolution had 'placed power in different hands, but did not change the nature of power.'[20] As German poet Heinrich Heine believed, it was time to build heaven now, on earth (Box 6.1).[21]

The industrial regime would also gradually transform the institution of government. The military/feudal system had wasted its resources through the efforts of the minority to dominate the majority, and in the resistance of the latter. For the first time since government was created, collective sovereignty would be possible. Government would be turned from an instrument of domination to a tool of administration, a change that must occur in one step. A nation's government should be modelled after the administration of an industrial enterprise and seek to increase prosperity at

Box 6.1

A newer song, a better song,
My friends, let's bring to birth now!
We shall proceed right here to build
The Kingdom of Heaven on earth now.

We wish to be happy here on earth,
All want eradicated;
The idler's belly shall not consume
What toilers' hands have created.

The soil produces bread enough
For all mankind's nutrition,
Plus role and myrtle, beauty and joy,
And sugar peas in addition.

Yes, sugar peas for everyone
Piled high upon the barrows!
The heavens we can safely leave
To the angels and the sparrows.

—Heinrich Heine, 'Germany: A Winter's Tale' (1844)

the least cost. These questions, Saint-Simon said, were positive and answerable. Those who performed public functions could solve problems by applying scientific knowledge. Decisions would be independent of human will and 'be discussed by all those educated enough to understand them.'[22]

The working people in France, he claimed, were the most highly civilized in Europe. In England, the proletariat was inclined 'to commence the war of the poor against the rich as soon as the right circumstances arise, whereas the attitude of the French proletariat toward the wealthy industrials is generally one of attachment and goodwill.'[23] This judgement seems to fly in the face of the revolutionary character of the *sans culottes* and the industrial strife that accompanied France's industrialization. Arguably, however, at a time when conservative royalists continued to dominate the French government after the restoration, the bourgeoisie and workers alike had a common interest in democratic and republican rule.

Although government was to be controlled 'by the men who are most capable in administration, that is, the most important industrials', Saint-Simon's model of the business-like government was not entirely laissez-faire. It had to perform the function of elevating the common majority of the population. Government money was required to ensure full employment and reasonable standards of subsistence for working people. The state was to provide education and instruction for the masses, and ensure that they developed leisure interests that would develop their intelligence.

Later in his life Saint-Simon believed that the governing elite (scientists, intellectuals, and industrialists) should plan economic change rather than leaving economics in the hands of private entrepreneurs; they should become 'the managing directors of the human race'.[24] At first, Saint-Simon thought, it would be necessary to promote his doctrine among the rich, to assure them it was not opposed to their interests. He argued that improving 'the moral and physical existence of the poor . . . would tend to increase the enjoyment of the rich.' The rich had to be convinced that 'the only reward worthy of their glorious endeavours' was the approval of the people for the services they received.[25]

As this new industrial regime became consolidated, people would become more reasonable, and reasonable people would understand the benefits and limitations of the social organization. '[T]hen there will no longer be any fear of insurrections.' There would be no need of a police force and no need to maintain an expensive army since a real citizens' militia would protect the nation. It would be a society in which the vast majority would be interested in maintaining the established order.[26] In the industrial society, a division of labour would still exist because it was a fundamental requirement of an advanced, organic social structure. However, all would be united in the single interest of advancing prosperity, to the benefit of all, and all would find their own niche in the division of labour. The advantages of birth would be replaced by the advantages of talent. In the industrial regime, all social tasks would have a 'positive character and a clearly determined object' so that it would be clear which specific ability is required to fulfill each position, with the result that 'every citizen must naturally tend to confine himself to the role for which he is most suited.'[27]

The new industrial order, however, would not succeed if it were adopted by only one country. Ultimately, such a model could only be global, Saint-Simon argued. The first practical step was to create a union between British and French industry.[28] The interests of business were worldwide, not narrowly nationalistic, so the spirit of nationalism would gradually dissipate in the industrial regime, which would usher in a long era of peace. In 1814, Saint-Simon proposed what at the time appeared to be his most Utopian scheme: that a pan-European parliament should be constructed from the ashes of Napoleon's Empire, uniting Europe in an era of peace and progress. Saint-Simon died before he could undertake this project, but his schemes earned him the epithet 'Utopian', and today, almost 200 years later, the European Union and its Parliament have drawn the nations of Europe together as a major trading bloc and potentially a unified political actor, and 'globalization', for better or worse, is an established fact.

New Christianity

There still remained the question of establishing a sound, moral foundation for industrial society. As a product of the Enlightenment, Saint-Simon held anticlerical views throughout most of his life, asserting that humanity had invented God. He later concluded that religion had a social and political purpose, which meant it would persist for a long time. In 1825, Saint-Simon published *The New Christianity* in which he advocated replacing the existing Christian schism with a simplified new form of Christianity.

Until the fifteenth century, Saint-Simon argued, the Catholic Church had played a positive and unifying role in Europe, promoting peace and the interests of the community against the nobility. By the early modern era, however, the Church had been transformed into a seat of power, privilege, and wealth, abandoning its mission to look after the interests of the poor. Martin Luther diagnosed the corruption in the Church and initiated a Reformation that divided Christian Europe into two competing and antagonistic halves. By returning the Church through Protestantism to the model of the original Christians, Luther took a backward step, focusing on the afterlife and neglecting the social side of religion, what the true Christian message in the new times, according to Saint-Simon, required: 'True Christianity should make men happy, not only in Heaven but upon earth.' In addition, Luther's belief that people should be free to interpret the Bible their own way caused unintended 'political motives that were contrary to the public welfare' because Bible study encouraged people to work towards equality in society, which was absolutely impossible.[29]

Saint-Simon intended to purify Christianity 'of all superstitious or useless beliefs and practices'.[30] The only true and useful religious doctrine was the teaching of moral precepts. For Saint-Simon, any truth must be reducible to an irrefutable first principle. Christ had delivered the sublime essence of his faith in the form suitable to his age by declaring that all people 'should treat others as brothers'. To put this into practice, the divine principle of Christian action was to organize society so that it was 'most advantageous to the greatest number', which meant seeking *the most rapid improvement possible in the lot of the poorest class*.[31] Scientific truths could best be taught to children and the illiterate by clothing them 'in forms that make them sacred'.[32] By the time he wrote *New Christianity*, Saint-Simon had revised his earlier opinion, coming to believe that Christ's message was divine and that an afterlife was possible. In some of his rhetoric, Saint-Simon declared himself the contemporary messenger of God.

Saint-Simon's new religion was not a rational celebration of humanity or scientific genius, as imagined by the revolutionaries of 1789. He conceived it to be a religion focused on an afterlife, complete with ritual, dogma, and worship, propagated by its own clergy and leaders. 'The intellectual forces of man are very small; it is only by forcing them to unite towards a single end, it is only by directing them towards the same point, that one can successfully produce a great effect and obtain an important result.'[33]

Unlike those who saw in the modern world only the evils of laissez-faire capitalism, Saint-Simon embraced modern industry. The evils of the modern age, Saint-Simon reasoned, were not caused by industry itself, but by the survival of pre-industrial ideas, institutions, and politics. They were also caused by the failure to build positive institutions on the ruins of the old. Society needed a new ethical unity that required a new Church to propagate Christian morality and the interests of the community in place of the new egoism that had become dominant in all classes and individuals. 'It is to this egoism that we must attribute the political malady' of the age.[34]

After Saint-Simon's death, differences among his many followers emerged almost immediately.[35] Like Rousseau before him, Saint-Simon inspired a number of contradictory legacies. A reformist version of Saint-Simonism focused on the expansion of industrialization in France by establishing large financial institutions and funding massive infrastructural programs such as railways and canals. This was the fruit of an alliance between the French state and business interests. Saint-Simon's intellectuals became handmaidens, not guiding partners, in this movement towards increased state involvement in the economy. More radical followers modified Saint-Simon's liberal economic principles to reflect Rousseau's attacks on private property, a position absent from Saint-Simon's writings. This interpretation influenced the socialist movement that was emerging among European workers.

In the 1830s, Prosper Enfantin was spreading his version of **Saint-Simonism** as a new religion. For a time, Enfantin presented himself as the son of God searching for his soulmate, a female Messiah. His sect attracted thousands of adherents, including many eminent intellectuals. The first major crack in the new sect occurred over the issue of women's role in the movement. Enfantin had expanded Saint-Simon's original doctrine to embrace female emancipation and free love, conclusions not found in the original theory. Explaining his views, Enfantin said, 'We may see men and women . . . giving themselves to several without causing to be united as a couple; whose love . . . will be like a divine banquet increasing in magnificence, in proportion to the number and choice of the guests.'[36] This vision of the future of sexual desire as a banquet was not to everyone's taste. It challenged entrenched values in France and contributed to opposition against the sect. Concerned about its political influence, the new French government declared it an illegal organization in 1832 and Enfantin, among others, was imprisoned. After his release, Enfantin dropped his religious mantle and took Saint-Simonism into economic development projects, such as the Suez Canal.[37]

While he enunciated the need for a 'social physiology', Saint-Simon's ideas were unsystematic, often impractical, and saturated with the hues of Romanticism. In its narrowest formulation, positivism implies that it is possible to derive laws of social organization that are analogous to the laws scientists have discovered to understand the physical sciences. When Saint-Simonism splintered into a variety of sects and political tendencies, one social theorist, Auguste Comte (1798–1857), undertook the task of developing this new science of society he would call sociology.

Auguste Comte and Positivism

Auguste Comte attempted to realize Saint-Simon's goal of founding a science of society. Born in 1798 into a petite bourgeois family, Comte's childhood was spent in Napoleonic France where liberal education policies provided opportunities for bright, industrious scholars from poor backgrounds to study at the best institutions. In this environment, the young Comte adopted republican and secular ideas that caused trouble at home, since his parents were royalists and conservatives. Entangled in family conflicts, Comte developed an emotional and rebellious temperament. French politics was in an equally anarchic state, swinging in Comte's lifetime from the despotism of Napoleon to the restoration of the monarchy, and then repeating itself through the rise and fall of Romanticism.[38]

Comte's rebelliousness continued in school. At his *lycée*, Comte excelled particularly in mathematics and the sciences. Admitted to the prestigious *École Polytechnique* in 1814, Comte studied engineering, but he was forced to leave two years later after being involved in a student rebellion. The new, monarchist regime took the opportunity to purge and discipline its youthful liberal critics. Expulsion excluded Comte from a public career.[39] Instead, he found occasional work as a tutor and secretary, living in great poverty, the very model of the starving intellectual whose work happened to be philosophy rather than painting or music. Comte's most important intellectual influence came from his association with Saint-Simon, whose ideas he embraced and expanded, and with whom he worked as a personal secretary until they separated in 'bitter animosity'.[40]

Comte's private life was as conflictive as his professional one. He lived a youthful, bohemian existence in Paris, falling in love at 19 with Pauline, a married Italian pianist. She became his mistress and they had a daughter, Louise, in 1818. Early on it was evident that the anarchy and absence of order Comte saw in the world at large was painfully echoed in his mental illness. By the time he was 20, Comte was suffering a deep depression exacerbated by unemployment and poverty. In 1825, Comte married Caroline Massin, a match he later regarded as an 'irreparable mistake'. The details of Comte's relationship with Massin are highly ambiguous. She was a poor seamstress, the mistress of an acquaintance of Comte. She moved in with Comte in 1824 and they soon married for a variety of reasons, including romantic ones.[41] Massin, Andreski says, was attractive and intelligent. She was interested in Comte's writings and frequently attended his lectures. For Comte, this was a disadvantage in a wife. Men of merit, such as himself, required a woman with a 'certain intellectual mediocrity'; a wife should be attached and devoted to her husband, and sweet in character. Above all, she should not be his equal. Massin's strong, intelligent character was a threat to Comte's fundamentally patriarchal attitude, and he denigrated independent, emancipated women by attacking their morality.[42]

By 1826, Comte's mental instability was becoming recognizable as mania and he lapsed for a time into a state of psychosis. His parents, who had disapproved of his marriage, now blamed Massin for their son's illness, believing and propagating the damaging gossip that she had worked as a prostitute. By the end of the year, Comte was declared incurable and released to his family. He was violent and verbally abusive. In a state of paranoia, he accused Massin of infidelity, a charge he would frequently repeat. Showing great strength and fortitude in the most difficult of domestic situations, Massin tended to Comte during this illness, helping him recover his sanity.[43] She soon separated from Comte, the first of four occasions; thrice she returned despite the obvious difficulties and their increasing estrangement.

During his cohabitation with Massin, Comte wrote his first influential work, the volumes of the *Course of Positive Philosophy* (1830–42), which proclaimed the founding of the science of society, which he named '**sociology**'. This work so impressed the liberals in England that John Stuart Mill organized a donation of money to help support Comte financially. In 1838, during the writing of the *Course*, Comte suffered another mental breakdown characterized by an apparent bipolarity, and he was again confined for a time in an asylum. He was also suffering from impotence. The final break with Massin occurred in 1842, after almost 18 years of marriage, though she still desired reconciliation. The final conflict was over Comte's intention to publish the sixth and final volume of his *Course*, in which he vented his anger towards French academics who had denied him recognition and position. Turned down for academic reappointment, and with his scholarly work dismissed or ignored, Comte detected a conspiracy of silence and ostracism. Convinced that he possessed the intellectual genius and the moral energy to save society from its illnesses, Comte's final break with most of his intellectual contemporaries, as well as with his wife, was a conscious act of martyrdom.[44] In a secret addendum to his will, revealed after his death, Comte repeated the most scandalous allegations about Massin's early prostitution, charged her with extramarital infidelities, and claimed her loyalty as a wife was motivated by her wish to inherit Comte's money and manuscripts. For a long time, his version of their marriage was accepted as truth.

At the age of 45, Comte fell in love with Clothilde de Vaux, a young, middle-class woman whose husband had deserted her. According to Andreski, she insisted that their relationship should be strictly platonic following an 'unsuccessful sexual encounter'. Within a year, the object of Comte's great and passionate love had died of tuberculosis. In death, Clothilde became his muse, as the chaste Beatrice had been for the medieval poet, Dante. At this point in his life, Comte emphasized the importance of spirituality and emotions, as opposed to the excessively rational

and masculine side of social life. Before his death at the age of 59, Comte wrote the *System of Positive Polity or Treatise on Sociology* (1851–4), which described his conception of an ideal society and proclaimed the need for a new secular religion. At the height of his intellectual megalomania, Comte declared himself the high priest of the new Religion of Humanity.[45] Comte's theory appears to have evolved from positivism (science) to theology—exactly the opposite direction he theorized for society as a whole.

Three Stages of Knowledge

Comte believed he had discovered a fundamental law to which the development both of society and of thought, or ideas, was subject: 'each branch of our knowledge passes in sequence through three different theoretical states.' In this he was developing his positivist approach to the study of society: he was finding—or imposing—system upon it. In the first, 'theological or fictitious' stage, humans believe that all phenomena are controlled by the actions of supernatural agents or gods and, ultimately, by a single divine power. In this stage, people seek answers to essentially unanswerable questions, such as the purpose of the universe and the first cause and final end of existence, or they try to understand the invisible essence inside things that make them what they are.

The theological stage eventually gives rise to a transitional stage, which he labelled the 'metaphysical or abstract' stage, during which people still seek to discover the hidden essence of all phenomena, but for a supernatural deity they substitute an abstraction such as 'nature'. This transitory stage prepares the ground for the development of the third and highest stage of knowledge, the 'scientific or positive' stage. He held that this final stage, foreshadowed by the works of Aristotle and the medieval Arabic scholars, began to supplant the first two stages during the revolution in natural science led by Newton and Galileo. Positive science was based on concrete observations of phenomena, seeking the regularities and therefore the laws of cause and effect in each area of physical science.

Scientists make progress in the different branches of knowledge at varying speeds, so each science is not at an identical stage. The first branch of knowledge to make the leap to **positivism** had been astronomy; the last branch, still in need of a thorough scientific grounding, was the realm of social phenomena, where theological or metaphysical theories still predominated. The most pressing need of the time, Comte concluded, was to develop a science of human society to fill this large and most difficult gap in knowledge. Comte termed this application of positivism to society 'social physics'[46] and later 'sociology'.

According to Comte, society ultimately rests on ideas, which 'govern and revolutionize the world'. A genuine social order must be constructed on the foundation of a common social doctrine. For the previous half-century, however, a profound divergence of minds had produced intellectual anarchy in Europe while three opposed and incompatible philosophies—theology, political philosophy (the metaphysical), and scientific positivism—coexisted and struggled for supremacy. Theology represented 'order', the older, universally dominant philosophy. But this order had been irreparably dissolved in the schisms that divided Christianity into numerous denominations and sects, and Europe into distinct nations.[47]

Political philosophy, which represented the idea of progress (derived from the *philosophes*, Rousseau, Locke, and Paine), attacked the *ancien régime* in a 'revolutionary fever' but was unable to achieve any positive reorganization of society, being purely critical and only the simple negation of the first stage. In this second stage, the place held by a deity in the theological period was replaced by a notion of nature that was metaphysical, exemplified by Rousseau, who would 'preach the superiority of the life of savages' and call into question any need for a state. The Enlightenment was destructive of the old order, but proved incapable of building a new one. The abstract principles of liberalism—such as human rights, freedom, and equality—were unscientific and speculative, and had led naturally to anarchy rather than social order.

Comte viewed the result of Enlightenment ideas as social chaos, but decided this violent disruption of order was inevitable in history to destroy the theological system. While the progressive school was responsible for all the reforms of the previous three centuries, Comte was unwilling to see these as positive developments towards a new and better society; rather, he considered liberal and democratic reforms merely as negating the order that had existed previously. He thought that only by developing the knowledge of society to the third and scientific stage, positivism, would it be possible to achieve agreement on scientific principles, a homogeneity of doctrine that would enable a return to a 'normal' social condition.[48] Comte saw it as his task to lay the conceptual foundation for such a social physics.

Social 'Statics' and 'Dynamics'

Comte contended that the two basic principles, order and progress, had become poles between which intellectuals fought and society was pulled, achieving a chaotic stalemate. Conservatives demanded the restoration of the regressive political system and the return to absolute order; the critical school demanded that 'all regulative authority should be suppressed', enshrining a doctrine of change. Comte argued that although order and change appear to be absolutely contradictory, each could be understood as having a particular relation to the other. His chief metaphor for society was drawn from biology. 'Order' in society is represented in the anatomy or structure of an organism—its internal organs and parts. 'Change' in society is represented by the organism's life or physiology—the processes of growth, maturation, and reproduction. Applying this order/change dichotomy to society, Comte distinguished between 'the conditions of existence of a society and the laws of its movement', which he termed '*static and dynamic*' states.[49]

Comte's analogy was notable for its methodical and detailed exploration of these two states in society. The anatomy of the social system was composed of various parts, each of which should be understood in its interrelationship with all other parts 'to which it is bound in fundamental solidarity'. Comte found this fundamental solidarity or basic 'philosophic principle' of the social system to be a general consensus, 'which social life manifests in the highest degree'; this 'consensus' was the principle of **social statics**. The positive conception of consensus or solidarity is extremely important in social systems because of the generally greater complexity of organic systems of which the social is the most complex, therefore necessitating a correspondingly higher degree of consensus.

The complementary principle, that of social movement or change, Comte continued, must be based on the principle of **social dynamics**.[50] The two principles were not in contradiction to each other. In nature, the dynamic state is necessary for continuing and reproducing life. Similarly, social change, 'if rationally conceived must have the continual intention of preserving' the social order. From these principles, Comte concluded that authority is by definition legitimate:

> Any power whatsoever is constituted by the assent, spontaneous or considered, explicit or implicit, of the various individual wills which have decided in accordance with certain convictions, to co-operate in a common action. . . . Thus authority derives really from co-operation, and not co-operation from authority. . . . [B]y their correlation government and society emphasize the fundamental consensus of the social organism, which is the philosophic principle of static sociology.[51]

By positing that it is impossible for social harmony 'not to establish itself in the natural course of events, without any calculated intervention', Comte caught his social theory in the same sort of loop (tautological argument) we observed in Alexander Pope, whose poem stated that 'all that is, is right.' Comte, however, was at pains to point out that it would be wrong to confuse 'the scientific notion of order with the systematic apology for existing order'. If society, by some invisible hand, automatically found its own equilibrium and progressed on

its own, there would be little need for social engineers and sociologists. Positive philosophy asserts only that a particular order will assert itself according to natural laws. This social order, however, will contain disadvantages that can be modified within limits by wise human intervention.

According to Comte's view, in its slow but dynamic change, society follows the law of increasing complexity according to which the parts of society become increasingly diverse and specialized—progress is built into the stages of social evolution. Simultaneously, however, the imperfections in the social institutions increase. Social phenomena are the most modifiable of all and the most in need of being modified by positive philosophers according to rational, scientific prescriptions.[52] Comte's system allows for human interventions in the social and political organization of life, but they remain subordinate to the static and dynamic laws that regulate society. In order to exist, social life must reflect the law of harmony of the various parts, which social action cannot violate.

Neither can human intervention make society deviate from the law of sequence, which means that each stage in social evolution must follow the full development of the previous ones. There can be no skipping of stages in historical evolution: 'the evolution of humanity must be regarded as modifiable to a predetermined degree, as far as its speed is concerned, but without any possible reversal of the order of development, and without any important intermediate stage being completely omitted.' Society evolves through a set of necessary social stages in a definite order, each the necessary result of the one that precedes it and the necessary cause of the one that follows it. Intervention in past societies had been directed by fanciful intellectual speculation and by moral codes developed in the mind and then imposed on social organization. When individuals attempt to pursue social reforms prematurely and opposite to the general laws of motion of civilization, they are effective only temporarily and will fail in the long run. Lasting influences result from timeliness; individuals who succeed do so by being the instruments of social forces ripe for development. Individual or group political actions are effective when they are in harmony with historical tendencies.[53]

If social change is spontaneous and proceeds by natural laws, the effect of this knowledge might induce passivity and inhibit intervention, another charge Comte is at pains to refute. With social physics, he argues, intervention will cease being arbitrary and impulsive and instead become scientific. In order for intervention to assist spontaneous development the scientist must know the laws of harmony and sequence 'that determine in every epoch and for every aspect of society what human evolution is ready to produce, and even indicate the principal obstacles to be removed.' The development of society is not linear; it oscillates between the poles of progress and reaction. Positive science can predict the consequences of change and modify the spontaneous development, though science cannot govern social phenomena. The art of politics would always be concrete, practical, and day-to-day, but positive theory would be included in any political consideration as a guide to what was practically possible.[54]

According to Comte's historical method, sociological knowledge depends on the comparative and historical study of social systems and is designed, not to uncover facts as close to reality as possible, but to abstract from facts the general laws of historical social development.[55] This entails studying the most advanced people, which would reveal the future of the more backward peoples and the laws of development for all societies. On the basis of this knowledge, the people of Western Europe would be able to extend civilization, benevolently, to the rest of humanity. The result would be the creation of a spiritual association, a collective 'intellectual and moral communion more complete, more extensive and more stable than any religious communion.' In the long run, once positive science was enshrined as the theoretical guide for the practical activity of sociology, decisions would be guided by a universal morality that would reflect the harmony of the social organism and the intellectual unity of society.[56] Social stability depends on the ascendancy

of a new moral consensus that in the modern world could be based only on reason and science.

Establishing this Utopian new morality would require a revolution in ideological institutions as profound as those Comte contemplated in economics and politics, because traditional religion has no place in the age of positivism. The Enlightenment had seriously undermined organized religion but, as the conservative and Romantic reaction had demonstrated, there were wider claims to spirituality and supernaturalism, which had resurfaced in religious revivals, such as evangelicalism, or took alternative forms, such as Eastern mysticism. Even if religion might ultimately disappear in the rationalistic, industrial regime, it was a potent force for instilling public morality and was already deeply rooted in the consciousness and practices of the people.

Like Saint-Simon had before him, Comte sought to transform religious ideology from supernatural mythology to a celebration of human potential and achievements. In this he was a forerunner of contemporary secular humanism. The revolutionaries in France had attempted to replace religion with the celebration of reason and the veneration of heroes, complete with festivals, parades, and holidays. Churches could be destroyed or converted into museums to celebrate human progress, but social customs and traditions are not as easy to replace as physical buildings and statues. Comte's solution was to retain the rituals, the buildings, the priesthood, the festivals, but to convert them into a Religion of Humanity. Positivism was the heir of Renaissance humanism, for which humanity was the highest being, suitable at its best to be worshipped. It wasn't necessary to invent a God, as Voltaire had suggested; the new society had to recognize the god-like quality of humanity. The Catholic saints should be replaced by secular geniuses and Church dogma stripped bare of supernatural elements. The essential function of religion, Comte said, was not the belief in an unscientific afterlife but the propagation of morality necessary for this life. Comte wanted the social function of religion to continue, but without the theology.

Comte's positivism followed Saint-Simon's later social theory by asserting the need to create a modern aristocracy—a scientific and industrial/business elite that guided political policy in the interests of society as a whole. Positivism was both conservative—in its view of the essential harmony of the parts that comprised society—and progressive—in advocating the need for social reforms to smooth out the oscillations between progress and reaction. In its rationalism, positivism was an Enlightenment project. It was similar in many respects to English utilitarianism, which developed simultaneously. Positivism grew out of Napoleon's rational administration and proved to be compatible with a modern type of enlightened **despotism**, the tool of a new breed of European autocrats bent on industrial development and national power—the later Napoleons of European industry. Liberty and equality yielded to elitism. The novelist Gustave Flaubert, in looking back at the idealism (his own included) of the 1840s from the perspective of the 1860s, detected in the early French movement, inspired by Saint-Simon and Comte, an exaggerated discipline and tendency to worship the state in a way that made individuals insignificant (Box 6.2).[57]

French intellectuals had to turn to America to find a country that proudly trumpeted the spirit of democracy and rapid industrial growth. In the 1820s and 1830s, American society was of great interest to European intellectuals, chafing under the return of conservative monarchies. Among the most influential commentators on things American were the English positivist Harriet Martineau (1802–76) and the French historian Alexis de Tocqueville (1805–59).

HARRIET MARTINEAU

A social reformer and advocate of positivism, Harriet Martineau was one of the advanced thinkers in a social group that included the novelist George Eliot and the laissez-faire sociologist Herbert Spencer. Martineau's family originally was French. Being Protestant in a predominantly Catholic nation, they migrated to Norwich, England, to escape persecution. Martineau was brought up in a strict Unitarian home with a distant and domineering mother and a bourgeois father, whose textile business was being supplanted by the Industrial Revolution. In the face of tyranny at home, Martineau developed an apparently

---

Box 6.2

Every evening, when his work was over, he regained his attic and searched in books for a justification for his dream. He had annotated the *Contract Social*. . . . He was familiar with . . . Fourier, Saint-Simon, Comte, Cabet, Louis Blanc—the whole weighty procession of Socialist writers—those who would like to reduce mankind to the level of the barrack-room, those who would make them find forgetfulness in brothels, or tie them to the [factory] bench; and out of this mixture he had evolved for himself an ideally virtuous democracy, combining the characteristics of the farm and the factory—a sort of American Sparta, in which the individual existed solely in order to serve the State, which was more powerful, more absolute, more infallible, and more divine than Nebuchadnezzar. . . . He did not doubt that this idea would soon be realized; and, with the logic of a mathematician and the faith of an inquisitor, he bitterly attacked everything that seemed to oppose it. He was shocked by titles, decorations, plumes, liveries—even by excess of fame; for each day his sufferings and his studies revived within him his hatred of every sort of distinction and pre-eminence.

—Gustave Flaubert, *Sentimental Education* (1869)

submissive demeanour that masked her interior rebelliousness[58]—a real-life version of Jane Austen's submissive Fanny Price of *Mansfield Park*.

An imaginative plunge into religion compensated for Martineau's sterile home life. So did the discovery of her musical talent. Unfortunately, in her early teens, she began to lose her hearing. Hearing required a conscious effort even with the use of an ear trumpet, which she acquired when she was 28. She was more fortunate in her parent's advanced views on educating girls. Well-educated women were an exception for the times. Women were usually excluded from formal education, and intellectual work was considered unsuitable for women's temperament and nature. Because middle- and upper-class women were expected to work only in the domestic sphere, exposing them to a liberal education, it was commonly claimed, would induce an unnecessary and unrealistic dissatisfaction with their daily lives. Harriet Martineau's bourgeois background, however, allowed her the opportunity to study privately.[59]

When her fiancé collapsed in insanity, Martineau quickly moved on, passing up the chance of devoting her life to the kind of martyrdom that Comte's wife had demonstrated. Instead, she decided to focus her energy on studying and writing, remaining unattached to a man for the rest of her life. Although she wrote some reviews, novels, and stories, the more typical path for socially conscious women, Martineau tackled what were then thought to be men's subjects and achieved both fame and, inevitably, notoriety. In the economically turbulent 1830s, Martineau studied and wrote about political economy. Two strands of liberalism influenced her perspective and she became a champion of laissez-faire, the principal economic doctrine of her formative years. In her *Illustrations of Political Economy* (1832), she simplified and popularized the economic ideas of Smith and Malthus, advocating free trade and the suppression of trade unions.[60] The second influential doctrine, utilitarianism, held that the objective of social activity was to secure the greatest good for the greatest number. At first, Martineau reconciled both doctrines.

Smith's notion of the 'invisible hand' meant that economic laws naturally secured the best interests of the nation and the individual within it. Over time, however, Martineau concluded that the best interests of the majority would not automatically be served by the maximum of economic liberty.

The most important underlying theme of Martineau's writing was the search for the conditions that would allow morality to flourish. Her most passionate causes would be moral crusades, for the abolition of slavery and in opposition to the Contagious Diseases Act that, in the guise of preserving the health of prostitutes and their clients, enshrined the sexual double standard in English law. Martineau's most sociological book, *Society in America* (1837), resulted from her two years of travelling in the United States. Her aim was to provide an objective account of American politics, religion, and social relations that would be free of the prejudices that coloured the descriptions and judgements of other writers, though she found some American habits, such as chewing tobacco and spitting, to be unpleasant.[61]

Experiencing new cultures with an open mind forces a reappraisal of old habits and prejudices. The United States provided a most impressive laboratory in which to study economic growth. The American business class, with the support of a compliant and active state, had created the freest and most open economic system. Martineau's sociological objectivity, however, led her to reconsider the individualism at the heart of laissez-faire. Americans, she believed, were excessively materialistic and overworked. At the heart of their economic affairs, Americans felt driven and discontented. The competitive system was not delivering on the promise of providing the greatest good for the greatest number. Martineau began to speculate whether there was a fundamental contradiction between democracy and the dominance of private property. This might appear to be a surprisingly radical sentiment for a theorist who advocated the principles of laissez-faire.[62] Martineau's doubts reflected her utilitarian inclination—if the good of the majority was not automatically furthered by free competition, then it was up to intellectuals such as herself to educate the public differently.

Martineau's intellectual contributions were exceptional. She travelled widely, wrote perceptive accounts of other societies, and wrote novels, children's stories, and a history of the early nineteenth century. Throughout this time she was physically and mentally troubled. She suffered a loss of faith in organized religion, which she felt had failed to meet the important moral and spiritual needs of society. Disillusionment led her to the positivism of Auguste Comte, who offered a substitute faith: morality founded on a scientific rather than a theological understanding of society. Comte's work was known in Martineau's intellectual circle. She translated Comte's six-volume *Cours* into English in 1853, introducing a wider spectrum of British intellectuals to Comte's sociology and theory of positivism. For Martineau, the early Comte provided the intellectual framework for developing a science of society, which she sought to condense and popularize. She dismissed his final return to a form of religion (of humanity) as an unimportant aberration.[63]

Martineau's influence was not just literary; she was also an activist. Her visit to the United States stimulated her involvement in the abolitionist cause. She witnessed the enslavement of blacks in the United States and became personally acquainted with the abolitionists in that country, such as Angelina and Sarah Grimke. Slavery was a clear and odious type of oppression that was deeply rooted in American society.[64]

During the American Civil War, the British government and much public opinion were sympathetic to the cause of the southern Confederacy. There were close commercial ties between English merchants and southern plantation owners. Racist attitudes towards Africans permeated these views. Martineau believed that 'Slavery is as thoroughly interwoven with American institutions, ramifies as extensively through American society, as the aristocratic spirit pervades Great Britain.'[65] While 'people of colour' were citizens, Martineau declared:

their houses and schools are pulled down, and they can obtain no remedy in law. They are thrust out of offices, and excluded from the most honourable employments, and stripped of all the best benefits of society by fellow-citizens who, once a year, solemnly lay their hands on their hearts, and declare that all men are born free and equal, and that rulers derive their just powers from the consent of the governed.[66]

Martineau's writing and activism against slavery helped arouse public opinion in Britain in favour of abolition. She also drew a connection between the ideological justification for the subordination of both women and blacks: both were assumed to be unsuited by nature for intellectual work.

Although English writers voiced fears of fire and slaughter should the slaves win **emancipation**, Martineau turned these arguments around: the risk of violence 'is not when an oppressed people obtain what they want, but when they are disappointed of it.' The longer it takes to achieve emancipation, the more lives will be lost.[67] With the American Civil War, change was inevitable and the emancipation of African Americans could not be reversed. The former slaves were 'practised in arms, accustomed to wages, introduced to letters, awakened in mind, cheered in heart and encouraged by the sympathy of all good citizens. . . . [I]t can never be possible to remand them to bondage.'[68]

Emancipation was the first step in social integration, but equality was not immanent, Martineau argued. African Americans still required 'discipline and training' to raise them to a level where they might 'obtain a free social position'. The state of Massachusetts had taken an important step in 1857 by opening schools 'unconditionally to all the children in the state'. With the subsequent integration of Harvard University, 'free people of colour' were able 'to have educated men and women of their own race. There was wealth among them before, now they had physicians, clergymen, tutors and schoolmasters, engineers and men of business' and among women, 'a considerable number of well-cultivated school mistresses, governesses, music teachers and artists'.[69]

Martineau's progressive activism included a campaign to oppose the Contagious Diseases Act in England, by which law women who worked as prostitutes could be forcibly detained, examined for disease, and then confined for treatment. As with laws prohibiting prostitution, it was assumed to be necessary to protect men's health 'from the consequences of their own passions'.[70] According to the double standard of Victorian sexual politics, men were unable to control their urges and required a class of women who worked as prostitutes and could be regarded as common property. As McDonald explains, the women who fought the Contagious Diseases Act argued, on ethical and Christian grounds, that the same moral standards ought to apply to men as to women. Martineau suggested that some practical diversions should be created to alleviate the necessity of soldiers and sailors resorting to sexual vice. Some opponents thought it possible to abolish prostitution altogether, though none suggested mandatory medical treatment for men who had venereal diseases.[71]

Over time, Martineau softened her earlier laissez-faire liberalism in the direction of greater social intervention, consistent with Comte's positivism and with the evolution of utilitarianism. She did not go as far as Florence Nightingale, whose medical heroics in the Crimean War made her a household name, but she collaborated with Nightingale's work on the reform of health and sanitation.[72]

Inevitably, Martineau was drawn into the nineteenth-century feminist movement. In *Society in America* she had linked the subjugation of slaves with that of women. Women were rational beings and, as such, democratic principles demanded their equal political representation. How can obedience to the law be asked of women 'when no woman has, either actually or virtually, given any assent to any law'?[73] As Yates observed, so also for Martineau, a woman (like a slave) 'is not free until she speaks and acts on her own behalf.'[74] Despite their claims to democracy, Americans maintain the 'political non-existence of women'. The American Constitution, Martineau pointed out, stated boldly 'that governments derive their just powers from the consent of the governed', yet the laws affecting women 'are not derived from the consent of the women thus governed.'[75] Ironically:

> While women's intellect is confined, her morals crushed, her health ruined, her weaknesses encouraged, and her strength punished, she is told that her lot is cast in the paradise of women: and there is no country in the world where there is so much boasting of the 'chivalrous' treatment that she enjoys.[76]

Upper- and middle-class women may feel that they reside in a gilded cage, but the indulgences they receive are still a form of confinement and a denial of justice. Martineau did not resolve the fatal contradiction between seeking equality in education and employment, and fulfilling women's traditional child-rearing and homemaking roles. By the positivistic law of progress, however, she believed optimistically that women's opportunities would gradually expand.[77] Martineau sought to help this future realize itself by propagating her ideals of social justice through her academic translations and summaries, and her progressive journalism.

ALEXIS DE TOCQUEVILLE AND AMERICAN DEMOCRACY

> Democracy is coming to the USA.
> —Leonard Cohen, 'Democracy' (1992)

Harriet Martineau had employed a sociological view of the world in her description of the government and society in the United States. Many of her observations on the limitations of American democracy, the oppression of public opinion, and the race relations tinderbox in both slave and free states had been diagnosed in 1835 by Alexis de Tocqueville (1805–59), whose visit had been earlier than Martineau's but comparatively brief. Since French troops helped win the War of Independence, a close connection had developed between France and the new Republic, symbolized most concretely in the Louisiana Purchase, by which the US acquired the vast western territory that drained through the Mississippi River. In 1831, Tocqueville travelled to the United States to report on the American prison system. On his return to France he published a sweeping account of American politics and society called *Democracy in America*.

Tocqueville's observations were made while the United States was beginning the transition to an industrial nation. Coming from Europe, what impressed him most was the relative egalitarianism in the new society. America lacked a hereditary aristocracy. Members of the new elite had, in many cases, risen from social backgrounds that had been considerably more humble than their present circumstances.

When Tocqueville came to America, Andrew Jackson was President. Jackson had been a military leader of the relatively short War of 1812 with Britain and the much longer war on Native Americans, as the new nation expanded into Aboriginal territory, west to the Rockies, south to Florida, and later into Texas and California. Riding on the crest of Jackson's popularity, the Democratic Party made an electoral pitch in the name of democracy to the common man, to the independent farmer in the new territories west of the Appalachians, and to the crafts workers and small merchants in the burgeoning urban centres of the East. Jackson widened the male franchise and appealed to voters on a platform of economic growth and equal competition. The result was the appearance of mass democracy, behind which professional politicians with close connections to the industrial elite competed for public office and the accompanying spoils. Corruption in urban politics may not have reached the excesses of *Gangs of New York* (2002, directed by Martin Scorsese), but votes were bought, voters were intimidated, the polls were manipulated by electoral machines, and to the victor went the spoils of office.

Foundations of Democracy

Tocqueville left France for America soon after the revolution of 1830 had deposed the Bourbon monarchy and revived the spirit of optimism, progress, and democracy that the conservatives in France had thought to bury. In the United States, which was undergoing the turbulence of **Jacksonian democracy**, these sentiments defined the national character. In both countries, Tocqueville believed, a great democratic revolution was underway that had reached its extreme limit in the United States. In America, this social revolution had occurred easily and simply. Americans had reaped 'the fruits of the democratic revolution . . . without having had the revolution itself'. In the United States, public power proceeded through elections; in France it was no less real but it had to proceed through revolutions. This movement towards a general equality of condition, which had reached its extreme limit in America and was advancing in Europe, was irresistibly directed by the hand of Providence.[78]

In Europe, democracy had advanced the farthest in France, but political and economic equality had been imposed from below and the cultural changes necessary to make democracy beneficial and permanent were absent. Like a child abandoned to its natural instincts, democracy had brought to France more vice and wretchedness than morality and prosperity. Democracy was artificial; it had been neither gradually introduced nor peaceably established. Liberty required morality, and morality rested on the rock of faith.[79] Liberty and religion were seen as opposing principles in France, whereas they coexisted in America.

Tocqueville argued that democracy succeeded in the New World because the spirits of liberty, equality, and religion and the doctrine of the sovereignty of the people had been planted by the first English settlers. They became the foundation for established customs that were more deeply rooted than laws. Democracy had sprung full-blown from the head of an aristocratic society. The colonists shared poverty and misfortune, and had no notion of superiority. Since the land in the North was unsuitable for a plantation economy, it was divided among smallholders, preventing the development of a landed aristocracy.[80]

New England was settled by strong-minded and moral Puritans of the middle and lower classes for reasons of intellectual craving rather than quick enrichment, making the colony socially homogeneous. The Puritans were ardent sectarians, harsh in their enforcement of the laws of morality but also daring innovators, liberal in their assertion of self-rule and the political rights of citizens, who quickly established political self-rule. Americans pursued, simultaneously, 'heaven in the world beyond, and well-being and liberty in this world'.[81]

The United States was divided geographically and culturally into three regions. In the South, settlement had originated by adventurers who introduced slavery and, along with it, 'idleness, ignorance and pride, luxury and distress'. Something like an aristocracy arose in the southern plantations founded on slave labour. The South competed with the North over material interests. The North demanded restrictions on commerce to protect its manufacturing community; the South favoured free trade because it was agricultural and sought markets abroad.[82] In the third region, the West and Southwest, which had been settled more recently by bold adventurers, there was neither the natural aristocracy of virtue and knowledge found in the North, nor the aristocracy of wealth of the South. Tocqueville equated grassroots democracy with the existence of social and economic equality. In the new states west of the Appalachians, 'society has no existence' and 'democracy [had] arrived at its utmost limits'.[83] Democracy was stable in America because of the favourable geographical situation and the existence of a boundless continent full of vast amounts of booty, which Americans avidly rushed to secure. It was from the western states, where equality of condition was greatest, that Jacksonian democracy had sprung, intending to weaken the powers of the federal government and protect regional and state interests.

Nevertheless, the appearance of democracy did not always reflect the actual social relationships. Despite democratic forms, the essence of power necessarily remained in the hands of the dominant elite. In New England, he argued, equality was more fiction than fact, giving 'American society . . . a surface covering of democracy,

beneath which the old aristocratic colors sometimes peep out.' Americans hold in the deepest contempt, Tocqueville commented, any notion of the permanent equality of property: 'I know of no country . . . where the love of money has taken stronger hold.' Nevertheless, levelling tendencies existed. There was a wealthy and powerful minority, but wealth circulated so rapidly and often that the fortune of one generation did not pass directly to the next. Furthermore, in place of the rule of primogeniture, where an estate was handed down to a single heir, the American tendency to divide inheritance among a number of children was conducive to greater equality of condition. The new wealthy were likely to be unrelated to the old and to have been formerly poor, making an aristocracy of wealth slow to form.[84]

Religious mores in America also favoured democracy. Church and state were separated and the clergy refrained from politics even in their preaching. Americans practised freedom of religion, which was a school of liberty. Even Catholicism, Tocqueville said, is conducive to equality: not only were most Catholics poor, but Church doctrine declared that all below the priest were equal and all must observe the sacraments. In America the most highly developed freedom coexisted peacefully with a highly cherished religion—a combination the *philosophes* would have regarded as impossible—although religion was pursued more by habit than conviction. Americans were eminently practical people, who preferred the stability of religious morality to the shifting winds of politics. They valued experience over theory and the 'practical knowledge of business to the impatience of their desires'.[85]

The Tyranny of the Majority

Two political consequences can arise from a condition of social equality, Tocqueville argued: 'the sovereignty of all or the absolute power of one'. In France, attempts to impose democracy by the rule of law had led to tyranny. Everywhere, he believed, democracy debases culture and lowers social standards. Human nature contains a passion for equality that incites everyone to seek power and honour. Americans also possessed a more depraved view of equality that induced people to lower the powerful to their level. Such people prefer to impose equality in slavery rather than have inequality with freedom. Equality, not liberty, is their idol.[86]

At the root of the problem that beset democracy was the imperfection of human nature. While human nature was constant in all political societies, **aristocratic cultures** had developed customs of taste and manners that controlled, within certain bounds, people's passions and appetites.[87] Democracy, however, allowed the most extensive flowering of the passions and vices of the masses.

Tocqueville also pointed out natural defects in the representative democratic process. Democracy is unstable because laws can be made and unmade with great ease. Laws passed in a democracy sometimes attack vested rights or prove to be dangerous to the whole community. While democratic laws logically promote the welfare of the greatest number of people in the society, they may attack vested interests. Furthermore, no political form is equally favourable to the prosperity of all the distinct communities and classes that form in the same nation. It is dangerous to place the fate of any one class in the hands of another: 'When the rich alone govern, the interest of the poor is always endangered; and when the poor make the laws, that of the rich incurs very serious risks.' So democracy does not favour the prosperity of the whole community.[88]

Selecting inadequate representatives is another of the dangerous tendencies of democracy. The closer the candidate comes to being elected by popular vote, the less able the representation. Ordinary people don't have sufficiently sound judgement to select genuinely able people and don't have the desire to find them. In America, few able men placed themselves for election. Although ordinary Americans did not hate the higher classes, they were unfavourably inclined towards them and excluded them from power. While the House of Representatives was elected by the people directly, members of the Senate were elected by individuals who were appointed from elected bodies, making them one step removed from popular power. Hence, the Senate enjoyed 'a monopoly of intelligence and talent' while the House was 'remarkable for its vulgar elements'.[89] In addition, democratic institutions promote the feeling of envy not because they give everyone the means of rising but because they disappoint many of those who use them. Democratic institutions awaken a passion for equality that cannot be satisfied. At first the lower classes are 'agitated by the chance of success' but they often reap only 'the acrimony of disappointment'.[90]

Wealthy American citizens, Tocqueville found, had a hearty dislike of their democratic institutions. In public, the rich conversed amiably with the common person, 'But beneath this artificial enthusiasm and these obsequious attentions' the rich fear and despise what Tocqueville called the preponderant power of the people in a democracy. Consequently, the rich were anxious to conceal their wealth. While they dressed plainly, the interior of their houses, to which only a few were admitted, glittered with luxury. They were exclusive in their pleasures and jealous to preserve the advantages of their privileged station.[91]

Unlike Europe, where the turbulent multitude regarded 'the law as their natural enemy, [and] look upon it with fear and distrust', in America the opulent classes viewed the law with suspicion. Since the poor ruled, the rich feared the abuse of their power. The American system of frequent direct elections and short terms of office rendered the power of the majority preponderant and irresistible, but also capricious; the legislature could become the slave of the passion of the majority.[92] French novelist Stendhal's worry about the tyranny of public opinion (Box 6.3)[93] was magnified when this opinion was responsible for law-making, which would be harmful and dangerous for the future.

Tocqueville feared the **tyranny of the majority**, though he did not go so far as to advocate, instead, an aristocracy of the intelligent, the logical counterpart to the incompetence of the masses,

---

Box 6.3

As a matter of fact, these wise folk [who determine respect] exercise the most burdensome *despotism* there; it is because of that ugly word that a visit in such small towns is insupportable to anyone who has lived in the great Republic called Paris. Tyranny of opinion—and such opinion!—is as stupid in the small towns of France as in the United States of America.

—Stendhal, *The Red and the Black* (1830)

---

as suggested by playwright Henrik Ibsen (Box 6.4).[94] Tocqueville argued that all authority has its origin in the will of the majority, but that the people should not have a right to do anything. Above the sovereignty of the majority or even of the people as a whole was the sovereignty of mankind and natural law, making it right to refuse to obey an unjust law. 'Unlimited power is in itself a bad and dangerous thing' and any absolute command 'is the germ of tyranny'. Tocqueville feared the tyranny of the majority might end in political despotism as the majority might use its power to crush minorities in its path. Tyranny may come to the United States, he warned, when the omniscience of the majority becomes so despotic that it forces the minority to desperation and physical force, bringing anarchy.[95]

The institutions of government in America were democratic in principle and the people elected their representatives directly and, in many cases, annually. Yet it was not the people as a whole who rule; rather, the majority governed in the name of the people, which was a different thing. In the American form of representative government, it was evident that no permanent obstacles hindered 'the opinions, the prejudices, the interests, and even the passions of the people . . . from exercising a perpetual influence on the daily conduct of affairs'. To make matters worse, the majority was manipulated by the incessant agitation of

---

Box 6.4

Dr Stockman: [T]his is the great discovery I've made today. The most dangerous enemies of truth and freedom are the majority! Yes, the solid, liberal, bloody majority—they're the ones we have to fear. . . .

The majority is never right! Never, I tell you! That's one of those community lies that free, thinking men have got to rebel against! Who form the majority—in any country? The wise or the fools? I think that we'd all have to agree that the fools are in a terrifying overwhelming majority all over the world! But in the name of God it can't be right that the fools should rule the wise. . . . The majority has the power—unfortunately—but the majority is not right! The ones who are right are a few isolated individuals like me! The minority is always right! . . .

[O]ne acknowledged truth which is really a damned lie . . . the doctrine . . . that the common man, all those ignorant and incompetent millions, have the same right to sanction and condemn, to advise and to govern, as the few individuals who are intellectually aristocrats.

—Henrik Ibsen, *An Enemy of the People* (1882)

political parties having no high principles or ideas. Political parties proclaimed their concern for the public good, but these pronouncements merely veiled selfish and private interests.[96]

The liberty of the press was fundamental to democracy and, in America, the power of the press was second only to the people. American journalists, however, were open and coarse, appealed to the passions of their readers, and attacked the private lives and vices of public individuals. Tocqueville deplored this abuse of the powers of thought that produced the paradox that in a land of a free press, 'I know of no country where there is so little independence of mind and real freedom of discussion as in America.'[97] Democracy debases the character of the people, the most serious reproach that could be addressed to democratic republics. In the throngs and the crowd, few men display 'manly candor and masculine independence of thought'. They may complain, but only to one ear at a time 'and a bird of passage'. Formerly, people submitted to authority out of fear—'I don't like it, but I have to do it.' Now, like lackeys, people feign their agreement—'I don't like it but I'll do it and pretend to like it.' This tendency to curry favour was being introduced into all classes.[98]

Race Relations

Given Tocqueville's concerns about the tyranny of democracy, it is logical that he did not advocate a wider enfranchisement. Male suffrage in the United States excluded slaves, servants, paupers, and Native Americans. In the final section of the first volume of *Democracy in America*, Tocqueville wrote sympathetically, yet pessimistically, about the prospects of blacks and Natives in America. Race constituted a fundamental division in the United States. Unlike Europe, where the scattered groups of human beings all form many branches of the same stock, in America three naturally distinct races were separated by almost insurmountable barriers and distinct destinies (Box 6.5).[99] Europeans stand to these two races, Tocqueville wrote, as humanity does to lesser animals; it makes them subservient, and what they cannot subdue is destroyed.[100]

Tocqueville saw the condition and fate of Native Americans as different from those of the Africans. At the time of contact, the Aboriginal people 'lived quietly in their woods . . . practicing the virtues and vices common to savage nations.' They were 'ignorant and poor . . . equal and free'.[101] As European artifacts were introduced into Native cultures, they undermined traditional livelihoods. European goods could only be bartered for furs, so Native tribes abandoned their traditional economy to hunt, increasing the wants of their community and simultaneously diminishing their resources. As Europeans moved into their territory and drove away the game, Native Americans were forced by famine reluctantly to disperse, facing enemies everywhere. They receded before the invasion of Europeans into their territories, or they were destroyed.[102]

Through the violence of conquest, Native Americans lost their lands and the sentiments attaching them to the land. With their families

---

Box 6.5

[T]he first . . . the superior in intelligence, in power, and in enjoyment, is the white, or European, the MAN pre-eminently so called; below him appear the Negro and the Indian. These two unhappy races have nothing in common [other than] . . . their misfortunes. Both of them occupy an equally inferior position in the country they inhabit; both suffer from tyranny; and if their wrongs are not the same, they originate from the same authors.

—Alexis de Tocqueville, *Democracy in America* (1835)

dispersed, traditions obscured, and the 'chain of their recollections broken', their habits changed, their wants increased, and their conditions became more wretched. They became less civilized, more barbarous. Despite these tragedies, their character remained unchanged; Europe could neither subdue nor 'civilize' them. Growing up independent even of parental authority and in the absence of law, to be free for a Native American signified escaping 'from all the shackles of society'. Independence was delightful and death was preferable to its sacrifice. To civilize Natives, according to Tocqueville, would have required making them accustomed to agriculture—settling down over generations in the same territory. But since they regarded such labour as a disgrace, their pride blocked this path to civilization. Unlike the African, the Indian imagined himself noble and lived in these 'dreams of pride'. While Africans were 'doomed to servility', the pride of the Indians doomed them to death.[103]

These were great evils, Tocqueville agreed, but they were irremediable since Native nations were destined to perish. Ironically, he noted, although the American government lacked good faith when it negotiated treaties with Native tribes that compelled and convinced them to sign over their lands, the Americans had accomplished the destruction of the Native tribes legally: 'It is impossible to destroy men with more respect for the laws.'[104] It was a clear demonstration of the tyranny of the majority in a democracy.

This observation was not applicable to Africans, whether free or in slavery. 'The most formidable of all the ills that threaten the future of the Union arises from the presence of a black population upon its territory.' In Tocqueville's view, oppression had denied to African Americans virtually all the privileges of humanity. The habit of servitude deformed the enslaved person's thoughts and desires: the slave 'admires his tyrants more than he hates them, and finds his joy and his pride in the servile imitation of those who oppress him.' Tocqueville believed that the slave's understanding was degraded to the point where the power of thought seemed a useless gift. Unable

to obey the dictates of reason, freedom became 'a heavier burden than slavery' because the ex-slaves merely serve a new master, their unrestrained passions. While 'servitude brutalizes, liberty destroys'. The African has been told from infancy 'that his race is naturally inferior . . . he assents to the proposition and is ashamed of his own nature.'[105]

When slavery was abolished in some states, Tocqueville observed, it was not for the good of the blacks, but for the benefit of the whites. To keep slaves was more costly and less productive in the long run than to employ free labour. In part, this was caused by the effects of slavery on the character, taste, and ideas of the white southern aristocracy. In place of the heroic avidity in the pursuit of gain of the northern entrepreneur, the southern master scorned labour and coveted pleasure and excitement above wealth. Slavery was not a commercial and manufacturing question as it was in the North; in the South, it was a question of the life and death of a social fabric. While disclaiming any intention of justifying the principle of slavery, Tocqueville recognized that the South would be forced to defend slavery as the foundation of southern society, despite its economic drawbacks.[106]

It was evident to Tocqueville that the social problems caused by African slavery would persist beyond emancipation. Natural prejudice causes people to despise those who had been their inferiors long after they become their equals. Altering laws is easier than modifying customs. Legal inequality implants an imaginary inequality in the manners of the people. The root of this dilemma is the dovetailing of slavery and race: The 'abstract and transient fact of slavery is fatally united with the physical and permanent fact of color.' Visible and indelible, colour becomes 'the eternal mark of . . . ignominy' that the African American transmits to his or her descendants.[107]

In Tocqueville's perception, the wish for amalgamation of the races rested on a delusion. Where slavery had been abolished, he felt that blacks had in no way drawn closer to whites. Furthermore, and paradoxically, he thought race prejudice was 'stronger in the states that have abolished slavery than in those where it still exists; and nowhere is it so intolerant as in those states where servitude has never been known.' Blacks were segregated in the schools, theatres, hospitals, and churches. In states where blacks could legally marry whites, the stigma was so severe that almost no interracial marriages occurred. Blacks could legally vote but to actually cast a ballot put their lives in danger. They might bring civil actions to court, but once there they faced all-white juries.[108]

Thus, for Tocqueville, the future of race relations in the United States was bleak. If slavery were to be abolished in the South and the ex-slaves raised to the level of freemen, they would again rebel against the continuing deprivation of their civil rights. Since it was impossible that blacks could become the equal of whites, they would soon become their enemies. Following emancipation in the South, two foreign communities would face each other, with only two possible remedies: full separation or full intermingling. Emigration to Liberia might be a means of bringing Western civilization to that continent, but it could not solve the racial problem in the South.

With Jefferson, Tocqueville believed that nature, habit, and opinion prevented the second solution—integration. White pride of race blocked intermingling. The abolition of slavery in the South would 'increase the repugnance of the white population for the blacks'. Americans in the southern states had two powerful passions that would keep the races separate: 'the first is the fear of being **assimilated** to the Negroes, their former slaves; and the second, the dread of sinking below the whites, their neighbors.'[109]

Since the black population was increasing in the South absolutely and in proportion to the whites and the barriers to intermingling were insurmountable, it was inevitable that the two races would come into open strife. Generally, Tocqueville believed, the blacks would be subdued, as the minority white population in the Caribbean would be overwhelmed by the black majority. The danger of racial conflict 'perpetually haunts the imagination of the Americans', openly in the North and tacitly in the South.[110]

In the end, Tocqueville's observations on race relations in the United States proved more perceptive than some of his arguments about democracy. For Tocqueville, the key principle of effective government in the era of democratization was to structure the institutions of the state so that the rule of the majority was tempered and controlled by an elitist principle of property. In this way the effects of legislation would be to reinforce social stability in the interests of the dominant group. Effective government required a compromise between popular and aristocratic rule.

THOREAU AND CIVIL DISOBEDIENCE

America has hitherto produced very few writers of distinction; it possesses no great historians and not a single eminent poet.
—Alexis de Tocqueville, *Democracy in America* (1835)

Tocqueville was perceptive about many of the contradictions in American society, but he was wrong about the paucity of American literary genius.[111] About the time he was making his notes about democracy in the United States, the great American Romantic, Ralph Waldo Emerson (1803–82), was keeping company with the English poets Wordsworth and Coleridge. Inspired by their Romantic ideals and subjective search for meaning, Emerson pursued a philosophy of **transcendentalism**, first proposed by Kant, according to which all nature was infused with spirituality and the task of the poet was to infuse this spirit among individuals. Standing on the fringes of a vast, new continent, Emerson was characteristically American in his reverence for the beauty and bounty of the natural world. Transcendentalists sought spiritual wholeness in their relationship with nature and rejected the rationalism and crass materialism that diverted people into the blind alleys of technology and urbanization.

Transcendentalism was to America what Romanticism was to France. While realism in Europe sprang from the conflict of political and social movements and fought to liberate itself from Romantic illusions, literary styles in America were less sharply differentiated. Both Romanticism and realism, Alfred Kazin argues, expressed the 'bewilderment . . . of a generation suddenly brought face to face with the pervasive materialism of industrial capitalism.'[112] American Romanticism was inspired by the contrast between the vast wilderness, which had attracted the Utopian reformers, such as Coleridge, and the depredations of advancing capitalism. Ralph Waldo Emerson's idealism reflected the former; the essayist Henry David Thoreau's individualistic embrace of nature expressed his intense dislike for the materialistic machine age. Realism developed later in America. The nineteenth-century novel in America grew to maturity in an intellectual world in which indigenous American literature crossed paths with influences from abroad. The American novels of Nathaniel Hawthorne and Herman Melville and the stories of Edgar Allan Poe were a melding of frontier Romanticism, Gothic sensibility, and complex allegory. By the time Jack London was writing his naturalistic novels at the turn of the century, the frontier had moved north to Alaska.

Henry David Thoreau (1817–62) was the most strikingly original American individualist of the mid-nineteenth century. Thoreau put into practice his ideal of the simple, natural life by spending two years as self-sufficiently as possible and writing about them in *Walden, or Life in the Woods* (1854). Thoreau's 'Essay on Civil Disobedience' (1849) continues to have an impact on social theory and on movements to resist unjust authority. Like Tocqueville, Thoreau distrusted the power of the majority, which was not necessarily right or fair. Majority opinion could suggest the most expedient means to achieve a simple goal, but it could determine neither what is right nor how to realize it. In Thoreau's view, it is undesirable to cultivate a respect for law: 'The only obligation which I have a right to assume is to do at any time what I think is right.'[113]

Thoreau's individualistic orientation led him to endorse laissez-faire economics and the least government interference in anyone's affairs. The

legal obstacles legislators used to interfere with laissez-faire, he said, were like 'those mischievous persons who put obstructions on the railroads.'[114] In his hands, however, individualism was tuned to social criticism and the need to rebel against unjust authority. Two specific injustices infuriated Thoreau so much that he refused to pay his poll tax and was jailed for his act of individual rebellion; the issues were the abomination of slavery and the unjust war unleashed by the United States on the people of Mexico.

Too often, Thoreau complained, people abandon the difficult chore of determining what is right and wrong according to their own consciences and follow the dictates of governments, acting like objects rather than human beings. Thousands of people may oppose slavery in their beliefs or opinions, he said, but they do nothing about it: 'There are nine hundred and ninety-nine patrons of virtue to every one virtuous man.'[115] In his view, even casting a strip of paper in a vote *'for the right is doing nothing'*. At the very least, a person ought to avoid giving practical support to the wrong cause. Those who refused to serve in the Mexican war but still paid taxes to the government were compromising with evil because the state hired substitute soldiers with their money.[116] You must break the law if, by following it, you are compelled to become the agent of wrong done to another.

If a government imprisons anyone unjustly, the only honourable place for a truly just person is in prison, 'that separate, but more free and honourable, ground, where the State places those who are not *with* her, but *against* her.' The government must be forced to choose between continuing to allow slavery and war, and imprisoning all just people. Bound together by the truth, an imprisoned 'minority . . . is irresistible when it clogs by its whole weight.'[117] Good will triumph when honest people act according to their consciences. With this image of a 'peaceable revolution', Thoreau's writing on **civil disobedience** would help to inspire Gandhi's non-violent resistance to British imperialism a century later and would become essential reading for Martin Luther King Jr during the civil rights movement of the 1950s and 1960s in America. The strain of opposition to government would recur in varieties of American populism through the twentieth century and into the anti-globalization of the next, although an essential difference is that contemporary radicalism is opposed in principle to free enterprise, one of the foundations of American populism.

CONCLUSION

From one point of view, the nineteenth century was a golden age of prosperity. The Industrial Revolution maintained England at the apex of global power, although the up-and-coming national powers increasingly challenged for domination. No country was poised for greater future promise than the United States. Immigrants poured into the vast territories newly wrested from the Native peoples and began to populate the country, bound together by ribbons of railroads and social mobility.

The rapidity of American growth did not, at first, exhibit many of the social problems that accompanied the transition to industrial capitalism elsewhere. Dissatisfaction with the new society helped propel Western expansion. A culture developed that prized freedom and individualism. In the northern states, America pursued capitalism unhindered by a tradition of elite paternalism. Even political and economic solutions to social problems embraced the fundamental individualism of the American way or sprang from the resilience of organized religion, paradoxical in a thoroughly materialistic culture. American democracy was rooted in a society that was the most egalitarian in history. If, for some, it was too democratic and tended to anarchy, for libertarians such as Thoreau it was not democratic enough. History proved to be on the side of the conservatives. As the American economy accelerated into the Industrial Revolution, the power of the elite grew and free enterprise in the industrial core turned into oligopoly—the domination of a few, large, family-based corporations.

In Europe, the movement towards democracy was hindered by the persistence of aristocracy and conservative social theory. Saint-Simon's goal had been to create a theory that would combine the social stability of traditional society with the material advantages of industrialism. His theory did not survive the collapse of the movement to establish Utopian communities and the misdirections of Prosper Enfantin, but it retains importance because of the variety of theories and movements it spawned.

One of the most important theoretical consequences of the doctrine of Saint-Simon was positivism, expounded in elaborate detail in the writings of Auguste Comte, his one-time secretary and co-author. Comte eschewed the revolutionary, socialist interpretation of Saint-Simon. The most important intellectual task he saw was the elaboration of that science of society Saint-Simon had envisaged. In the middle to late nineteenth century, science seemed to promise both a thorough understanding of society and a set of guidelines for making social improvements. Just as engineers were needed to solve technical problems on the basis of the Newtonian science of physics, so social engineers were needed to solve social problems by uncovering the laws of society.

Comte founded the study of society, which he called sociology, the discipline he believed to be the most fundamental of the sciences. His sociology was inspired by the Enlightenment belief that society could be understood and controlled through the application of reason and the scientific method. Comte's conception of society was grounded in the traditional and conservative belief that society was like an organism and had evolved to its present state through a series of logical and necessary stages. He analyzed society as a functional whole consisting of mutually interrelated parts. Social change, however, was not uniform across all aspects of society. In particular, economic change had accelerated beyond the moral capacity of society. The science of society would enable social engineers to diagnose social ills and reform them in a way that would be consistent with the best interests of all. Comte inspired a movement in social theory towards positivism, the belief that social life could be reduced to a number of laws that would make history predictable and subject to human control. Comte's social system appears in retrospect to be more idiosyncratic and speculative than empirical and scientific. He did, however, inspire later generations of theorists to develop systematic and empirically grounded sociology.

Like the positivists who would follow Comte, English liberals took a long, hard look at their own society and perceived the drift at mid-century towards revolution. They sought reforms from above, based on the enlightened self-interest of the propertied and governing elite. Comte's positivism was congenial to a branch of English liberalism known as utilitarianism, which, in the hands of John Stuart Mill, would begin its own migration from laissez-faire to reform.

7 SOCIAL LIBERALISM

Laissez-faire has had a bumpy ride as one of the main wheels of the capitalist juggernaut. In economic policy, it has had to jostle for position with protectionism as various capitalist interests have competed with each other over which form of government policy was in their best interests. Strong nations, and powerful economic groups within them, endorse trade policies that are to their particular advantage. In Smith's time, when the economic battle was against economic irrationality and aristocratic monopolies, capitalists were extricating themselves from the chains of traditional society. While England was moving to free trade in the middle of the nineteenth century, its major rivals, the United States and Germany, were protecting their industry behind tariff walls.

Even in England, the heyday of laissez-faire was short-lived as the nation experienced the disastrous social effects of unrestrained capitalism. Social liberalism emerged in a world that appeared to be on the verge of revolution. The social consequences of the Industrial Revolution were readily apparent in the newly industrialized cities in England, growing uncontrollably in the middle of the country in mushrooming cities such as Manchester, some distance from the traditional centres of power in London and the port cities. Everywhere **industrial capitalism** emerged, the new structure of class relations revealed a breach between the rich and poor that led to conflict. Skilled crafts workers who had lost their independence to the new machines of the factory system found themselves the natural leaders of a mass of unskilled labourers newly arrived from the doldrums of country life and thrown into the drone-like repetitions of factory work. As the devastation of economic depression descended on the vulnerable working class in the 1840s, radicalism was revived—as socialism in Europe and as Chartism in England—culminating in the revolutions of 1848.

It was in the interests of the propertied class that government policies should divert the flow of socialist and reformist demands coming from the working and lower-middle classes into acceptable channels. Social theories evolve in accordance with changed circumstances. By the middle of the nineteenth century, the liberalism of John Locke and Adam Smith had begun to evolve into social liberalism, the forerunner of the modern welfare state. The doctrine of **utilitarianism**, devised initially by the brilliant and single-minded Jeremy Bentham (1748–1832), linked (albeit somewhat ambiguously) early liberalism with later nineteenth-century reformism.

JEREMY BENTHAM AND UTILITARIANISM

Bentham was a child prodigy. He read serious works by the age of three, studied Latin and Greek at six, and entered the University of Oxford at 12, from which he graduated with a degree in law. An eccentric, Bentham directed that, after his death, his body would undergo biological dissection in the presence of his friends. His skeleton was put on display, clothed and with a waxen head, in University College, London. His mummified head was placed at his feet.

Before this gruesome denouement, Bentham had been the leader of a group of social reformers called the **Philosophical Radicals**. In his *Introduction to the Principles of Morals and Legislation* (1789), Bentham outlined the cornerstone of his doctrine of utilitarianism. Bentham subjected English political institutions to the test of reason and found legal practices, from the operation of the courts to the English Constitution itself, to be irrational and harmful. There was a critical and iconoclastic sheen to Bentham's theory, which illuminated the way to a reform movement that ultimately modified the harsh principles of English laissez-faire. Many of those who had initially opposed unrestrained capitalism had been Tories and rural landlords. The Benthamites channelled the demands for reform in new directions because they took the capitalist economy for granted and were more in tune with materialism and individualism.

Bentham took the model of the economic individual imagined in laissez-faire economics and generalized it to human nature as a whole. People were motivated by self-interest to achieve the maximum pleasure and suffer the least pain. Bentham believed that such abstract generalizations as morality or conscience were simply names behind which people acted out their selfish goals. People calculated their actions according to a mathematical formula by which they would weigh their anticipated profit and loss—their pleasure or pain—and determined how they would most benefit. Bentham termed this process moral arithmetic.[1]

Bentham was sympathetic to the idea of Smith's **invisible hand**, according to which the greatest good for all would result automatically if all were free to act in accordance with their personal interests. This was hypothetically correct, Bentham agreed, but his more practical mind knew that the invisible hand would not miraculously produce the best society for all. Too many people made unwise and ignorant decisions—they were deficient in moral mathematics. Uneducated people would be unable to foresee the longer-term social consequences of their short-term selfish acts. Perhaps in the future, when all were educated and able to understand the longer-term calculations of pleasure and pain, the invisible hand might work. In the meantime, however,

it was necessary to guide this hand in its choices. Decisions on social policy had to be based on practical and realistic considerations, not wishful thinking. Rather than allowing people to act on immediate expediency, the goal of society must be to promote the greatest good for the greatest number—the maximum of happiness possible.

Although the greatest good for all was exactly what the doctrine of the invisible hand promised, Bentham believed that the selfish actions of the rich and poor sometimes harmed society as a whole. The fundamental question was the form that the very visible hand of government intervention should take. Conservatives argued that government must act paternalistically to protect the weak and unfortunate, a doctrine consistent with the traditional Tory notion of noblesse oblige—that social superiors had some responsibility for the less fortunate. For many Tories, laissez-faire social policies lacked Christian charity; capitalists had buried morality under the cold calculation of the accounting office. Reforms ostensibly meant providing opportunities for the unfortunate to improve themselves, often through the construction of institutions such as the poorhouse, orphanage, and **workhouse**. Laissez-faire liberals complained that these institutions cost the government large sums of money. They were inconsistent with the interests of private wealth since the poor and the criminal classes were being supported out of government revenue, which ultimately came from taxing the wealthy.

Strict laissez-faire allowed government the narrowest of stages on which to act. Prisons were costly and less effective than capital punishment or exiling convicts abroad. The discipline of the marketplace should be sufficient to lower the birth rate and oblige people to labour rather than starve. While the Benthamites also blamed the poor for their conditions, they argued that the poor should not be left to make their own decisions, because their selfish acts led to overpopulation and crimes against property. The marketplace alone was insufficient for disciplining the working class. The utilitarian solution was not to dismantle the old Tory institutions but to streamline them. As children, the poor ought to be subject to the discipline and authority of the schoolmaster. As destitute vagabonds, they should be confined in workhouses and inured to labour. As adult criminals they should be placed under constant surveillance and put to hard labour. While these institutions required financial support from local or national governments, they provided their unfortunate inmates with only a bare subsistence—no child should ever expect more soup. Under the strict principles of utilitarianism, the conditions of life in the workhouse and prison must be worse than the meanest livelihood that could be earned in the capitalist marketplace in order to deter the poor from their laziness and profligate ways.

For Bentham, continual social progress required positive rather than only negative correction. Society needed a vast network of control to supervise the paupers and criminals. Bentham designed a penitentiary style he called the Panopticon, an architectural plan that would permit authorities the maximum surveillance of the unfortunate inmates.[2] Early intervention was better for the society and the individual. Bentham argued that children required discipline, control, and basic training. Besides the strict discipline that a proper school could instill in the habits of working-class children, they needed to be literate and numerate. Because mass education violated the principle of a do-nothing government, Bentham preferred privately owned over state-run schools.

Charles Dickens satirized utilitarianism and its inhumane practices savagely in his novels, in none more directly than *Hard Times* (Box 7.1).[3] The principal representative of Bentham's doctrine in the novel was Thomas Gradgrind, a retired merchant and the owner of a model school, whose face was 'unbending, utilitarian, [and] matter-of-fact'. Gradgrind was a man of realities, of facts and calculations. He had 'a rule and a pair of scales, and the multiplication tables always in his pocket . . . ready to weigh and measure any parcel of human nature, and tell you exactly what it comes to. It is a mere question of figures, a case of simple arithmetic.'[4]

The typical product of this utilitarian school was Bitzer, the bank clerk, whose mind 'was so exactly regulated that he had no affectations or passions. All his proceedings were the result of the nicest and coldest calculation.'[5] The only ideal he espoused was to buy for as little as possible and sell for as much as you can possibly get, 'it having been clearly ascertained by philosophers that in this is comprised the whole duty of man—not a part of man's duty, but the whole.'[6] Gradgrind's educational philosophy is summed up in the word 'facts'.[7]

Box 7.1

Gradgrind: 'Now, what I want is Facts. Teach these boys and girls nothing but Facts. Facts alone are wanted in life. Plant nothing else, and root out everything else. You can only form the minds of reasoning animals upon Facts: nothing else will ever be of any service to them. This is the principle on which I bring up my own children, and this is the principle on which I bring up these children. Stick to the Facts, sir.' . . .

'You are to be in all things regulated and governed . . . by fact. We hope to have, before long, a board of fact, composed of commissioners of fact, who will force the people to be a people of fact, and of nothing but fact. You must discard the word Fancy altogether.' . . .

The girl [Sissy Jupe] curtseyed, and sat down. She was very young, and she looked as if she were frightened by the matter-of-fact prospect the world afforded.

—Charles Dickens, *Hard Times* (1854)

For Dickens, while political economy was capable of exactly measuring material objects, such as the effect a single pound weight will have on the performance of a steam engine, human nature was incomprehensible by the scientific method: 'not all the calculators of the National Debt can tell me the capacity for good or evil, for love or hatred, for patriotism or discontent, for the decomposition of virtue into vice, or the reverse, at any single moment in the soul of one of these its quiet servants.' There is no mystery in mechanics; 'there is an unfathomable mystery in the meanest of' humanity.[8]

By Dickens's time in the middle of the nineteenth century, when laissez-faire was in the ascendancy in England, it was increasingly apparent that the results were socially disastrous. The moral reformers, Dickens among them, were horrified at the excesses of unrestrained capitalism—14-hour days, poverty wages, child labour, massive urbanization, slum housing, rising crime, and unemployment—an endless litany of sorrow, anger, and human suffering, which was the flip side of economic progress and growth. Society seemed to be dividing into two hostile camps—'two nations' in the words of Benjamin Disraeli in his novel, Sybil (Box 7,2).[9] More and more, British society seemed polarized into the two classes that Marx would theorize, and the gap between the classes widened as the century advanced. It

seemed clear to many that the system, as it was, was not producing the greatest good for the greatest number. Nevertheless, the powerful were seldom moved by arguments of charity. With their faith placed squarely on laissez-faire economic relations and individualism, the elite believed that what happened to people was their own fault and that government welfare was morally wrong and socially harmful.

Working-class revolt had never seemed closer in England than during the hungry 1840s. The spirit of revolt, which had been quiescent since the restoration of the monarchy in France, had been revived by the revolution of July 1830 that deposed one monarch and placed a reforming king on the throne. In England, too, reformers had organized, protested, and published, raising the spectre of social revolution. The result of this agitation and hand-wringing was the Reform Bill of 1832, which modestly increased the number of eligible male voters, while still leaving five of every six British men legally without a vote.[10]

Later in the decade, the threat from below appeared to be more serious as working people organized to win real social reforms and political rights. In their six-point 'People's Charter' the members of the Chartist movement demanded full voting rights for males, the use of secret ballots, and the elimination of property qualifications to run for Parliament. These demands seem relatively

---

Box 7.2

'Well, society may be in its infancy,' said Egremont slightly smiling, 'but, say what you like, our Queen reigns over the greatest nation that ever existed.'

'Which nation?' asked the younger stranger, 'for she reigns over two.'...

'Yes ... Two nations; between whom there is no intercourse and no sympathy; who are as ignorant of each other's habits, thoughts, and feelings, as if they were dwellers in different zones, or inhabitants of different planets; who are formed by a different breeding, are fed by a different food, are ordered by different manners, and are not governed by the same laws.'

'You speak of—' said Egremont, hesitatingly.

'THE RICH AND THE POOR.'

—Benjamin Disraeli, Sybil (1845)

moderate now, but ordinary working men would not win the right to vote for representatives in Parliament and be candidates for office for several more decades.

Serious social rebellions erupted in Europe in 1848.[11] In the shadow of the European upheaval, London's working class held a mass demonstration in favour of Chartist demands in 1848. A radical labour movement was a great threat to the rights and privileges of people with property. In this situation, a potential rebellion by the working class could be handled by repression or by reform. The enlightened members of the English elite became convinced that their long-term interest—maintaining their wealth and power—was more important than the short-term interest of keeping wages low, hours long, and exploitation severe. For their own self-interest, the elite needed social reforms, and there was no shortage of religious and moral reformers to point them in a safe direction.

There were several responses to the perceived threat against social order.[12] Two of these opposed the spread of laissez-faire capitalism and free trade. Socialists wanted a new form of co-operation and collective ownership emphasizing economic and social equality. The second was conservatism, the desire to return to or recreate previous conditions and times when everyone knew his or her place and society was orderly and peaceful, an idealistic more than realistic image of the past. Benjamin Disraeli, the Romantic Tory who twice became Prime Minister, hoped that England could produce a new, enlightened, and reform-minded aristocracy that would rule benevolently and paternalistically, within a hierarchical social order held together by religion. Disraeli's model captain of industry was an enlightened capitalist who provided workers with all the necessary amenities of life.[13]

A third response, **social liberalism**, sought to save capitalism while curing it of its vices. Social liberals, who could occasionally make common cause with the Tories, wanted to reform capitalism so that it would be stronger as well as more moral. If laissez-faire produced social misery and a spirit of revolt among the workers, social liberalism would bring reforms to make the life of workers better while still leaving the economy largely in private hands. For social liberals, the poor were not solely to blame for their destitution. Selfish decisions by capitalists played an important role as well. The state was the only force capable of obliging the elite to exercise restraint. Urged on by pressures from below, the government actively imposed economic reforms on often unwilling capitalists, shortened the normal hours of work, provided for the regulation of factory employment, and offered some relief for the unemployed.

Even as the more socially minded liberals attacked the rapaciousness of laissez-faire capitalism, they did not soften the blows against the idle rich. Essayist Thomas Carlyle, for example, likened the aristocracy in nineteenth-century England to a tree planted on the edge of a cliff, with no soil to sustain its roots, but living off the hard work of others (Box 7.3).[14] As playwright Oscar Wilde commented in 1891, the heirs of the English nobility had time for little more than 'the serious study of the great aristocratic art of doing absolutely nothing'.[15]

The sufferings of those at the bottom of the social scale equally drew Carlyle's attention, as they did a number of other essay writers of the period. Carlyle wrote passionately about the injustices of a social system that produced hunger and overwork at one pole and idleness and overindulgence at the other. In *The French Revolution* (1837), he expressed sympathy for the poor in France whose wretched conditions had driven them to extreme radicalism. For Carlyle, society required guidance by a great man and by an aristocracy of talent that would use their abilities and powers to solve social ills.

Charles Kingsley (1819–75) was inspired by the radicalism of the English Chartists, the democratic working-class movement of the 1840s. He championed the rights of labour and criticized capitalism for destroying the health, life, and morality of a stratum of disinherited workers. For Kingsley, salvation was to be found in a revolution

Box 7.3

Is there a man who pretends to live luxuriously housed up; screened from all work, from want, danger, hardship ... he himself to sit serene ... and have all his work and battling done by other men? And such man calls himself a *noble*-man? His fathers worked for him, he says; or successfully gambled for him: here *he* sits; professes, not in sorrow but in pride, that he and his have done no work, time out of mind. It is the law of the land; and is thought to be the law of the Universe, that he, alone of recorded men, shall have no task laid on him, except that of eating his cooked victuals, and not flinging himself out of window. Once more I will say, there was no stranger spectacle ever shown under the Sun.

—Thomas Carlyle, *Past and Present* (1843)

of morals, making humans 'better' people. Finally, there was John Ruskin (1819–1900), whose views on the economic system inspired English socialism. Rather than a political solution, however, he proposed reforming the educational system as the best means for alleviating social problems and social revolution.[16]

The crowning achievement of nineteenth-century social liberalism was widening the franchise so that all adult males, regardless of property ownership, could vote for representatives to Parliament, measures enacted by the 1867 Reform Bill of Prime Minister Disraeli. To many members of the elite, this was a tremendous gamble. The working class was numerous—what would they do with their votes? How much would their voting power threaten private property? Having the vote gave the working class sufficient political power, during the middle years of the twentieth century, to bring about socialized medicine, social assistance, unemployment insurance, a graduated income tax, and other measures of reform. In the long run, liberalism violated some of the most basic principles of its original laissez-faire doctrine. It was a slow evolution for an ideology that had been founded on the principle of individual liberty in opposition to arbitrary government authority.[17] The utilitarian, John Stuart Mill (1806–73), and his partner, Harriet Taylor (later Harriet Taylor Mill), took some early, tentative steps in the direction of social reform.

JOHN STUART MILL

John Stuart Mill was the son of James Mill, a dour Scottish political economist and disciple of Bentham. It was in many ways an unfortunate legacy for the younger Mill. James Mill subjected his son to a thoroughly rational and materialistic education. John and his father worked together in the same room, James Mill on his *History of British India*, John on a strict and difficult home-schooling regimen. He began studying Greek at the age of three, had read Plato by age 10, and was immersed in political economy by 13.[18] By the time he was 21, John Mill was employed in London as a colonial administrator at the India House, where his father worked. William Thomas comments that J.S. Mill must have appeared to be a replica of his father.[19]

Mill emerged from this training in classical scholarship and political economy as the champion of his father's utilitarianism. In 1826, under the pressures of overwork, Mill suffered a serious mental crisis through which he re-evaluated his dogmatic acceptance of utilitarianism. Through this crisis of faith, Mill emerged, in the 1830s, as a more complex thinker. While still attached to the doctrine of his upbringing, he was drawn to the conservative perspective of respect for tradition, concern for order, and a belief that human nature was as much rooted in emotion and feelings as in reason and materialism. Mill discovered much to admire in the later conservative writings of Wordsworth and Coleridge,[20] although he remained in the shadows of his strict upbringing until his father died in 1836. In 1838, Mill published an evaluation of Bentham's theory in which he concluded that utilitarianism, by itself, could do very little for the individual or for society. It was a settling of accounts with his past.

Mill admired Bentham's analytical assault on ancient institutions, calling him the 'great subversive . . . the great *critical* thinker of his age and country'.[21] In particular, Bentham had attacked and led a reform movement to correct English law and legal practices, which were mired in feudal traditions. Nevertheless, Bentham ultimately failed in his wider analysis, Mill concluded, because he had excluded from his calculations a crucial component of human nature. Bentham's method was empirical, yet the storehouse of human experiences from which his social theory drew was very limited. His rational conclusions were frequently invalid—they were merely half or fractional truths—because of his singular and narrow focus on mere utility as the measure of human action. In Mill's words, 'In many of the most natural and strongest feelings of human nature he [Bentham] had no sympathy; from many of its graver experiences he was altogether cut off; and the faculty by which one mind understands a mind different from itself, and throws itself into the feelings of that other mind, was denied him by his deficiency of imagination.'[22]

The novelist Charles Dickens would have agreed. It was just this contrast between narrow rationalism and imagination that Dickens had satirized in his novel *Hard Times*. Dickens sharply contrasted the inhumanity of the economic system with the human spirit, represented by the imaginative exuberance of young Cecelia Jupe, the daughter of a circus performer. Gradgrind, the utilitarian teacher, was unable to obliterate Jupe's independent imagination and sense of wonder despite enrolling her (out of uncharacteristic charity) in his model school. To Grandgrind, students were merely 'little pitchers . . . to be filled . . . full of facts'.[23] Sissy Jupe, however, was incorrigible.

After eight weeks of being drilled in the principles of political economy, she still believed that the first principle of this social science was, 'To do unto others as I would that they should do unto me.'[24] This maxim was some distance from the utilitarian calculation of profit and loss and expressed the essential qualities of human nature that Dickens and Mill believed utilitarian science could not fathom.

Mill concluded his denunciation of the limits of Bentham's utilitarianism by arguing that the best that this social theory could achieve was to 'teach the means of organizing and regulating the merely *business* part of the social arrangements'. Bentham had 'committed the mistake of supposing that the business part of human affairs was the whole of them'.[25]

What Mill found most compelling about conservative social theorists was their focus on the need for stability and solidarity. Society is held together by the discipline imposed by the educational system, by feelings of allegiance and loyalty, and by 'a strong and active principle of cohesion among the members of the same community or state'. This last requirement was not blind, prejudiced nationalism—as the English Tories would later endorse—but a feeling of common interest, of being one people in a single state.[26] The great shortcoming of the Enlightenment *philosophes* had been to ignore these foundations of any society; the great contribution of the conservatives who followed was to establish in theory these fundamental prerequisites of all societies.

Bentham's radicalism was epitomized by his support for majority (male) rule and for abolishing the monarchy and the House of Lords. Economically, Bentham proposed a minimum wage and the nationalization of the Bank of England.[27] Mill was unwilling to go this far. He believed in representative democracy but, certainly for his own time, not in granting power to the people. In Mill's view, while majority rule was in principle less unjust than any other system, to implement male suffrage immediately would introduce a new form of bad government. Manual labourers comprised the numerical majority of men in England. Granting this majority the power of government would make 'one, narrow, mean type of human nature universal and perpetual'. It would 'crush every influence which tends to the further improvement' of the individual's 'intellectual and moral nature'. Mill feared that majority rule would threaten freedom of thought, individuality of character, and the 'superiority of cultivated intelligence'.[28] With Coleridge, he agreed that government required a balance of power between the landed proprietors, who represented stability and permanence in the House of Lords, and those who possessed personal property and intellectual ability, who were represented in the House of Commons.[29]

Although Mill believed that voting rights should be extended to a broader proportion of the population, he said that those who were educationally incompetent (could not read or write, for example) should be excluded. In 1859, shortly after his wife's death, Mill published *Thoughts on Parliamentary Reform* in which he argued that, while everyone had a right to participate in government, not everyone had an equal right. Mill put so much emphasis on the importance of a person's mental capacity to vote that he advocated giving more than one vote to individuals believed to be mentally superior.[30] Such a scheme would help preserve elite rule, while accommodating some of the demands for reform from below. Mill acquiesced with the cause of giving the vote to working people on the grounds that they, too, must be included in the system. He wanted to avoid allowing the majority to dominate government, but believed exclusion forced them into greater opposition than necessary. Mill developed this theme further in 1861, declaring the House of Commons 'radically unfit' for the 'function of governing'.

Mill was more genuinely radical in his views on women. Long before he stood in Parliament in 1867 and made the first official speech in favour of granting the vote to women, Mill had been involved in women's causes.[31] According to Rowbotham,[32] he had been arrested at the age of 17 for handing out pamphlets on birth control. This reflected more than a concern with overpopulation, since an article he published in 1824 indicates a progressiveness in his thinking about the position of women.[33] Mill's ideas on women's rights were elaborated in 1869 in his book, *On the Subjection of Women*. His stepdaughter, Helen Taylor, had suggested that he write about the beliefs in women's equality he had shared with his wife, Harriet Taylor.[34]

The childless Mill was a reluctant father of social and economic reform. Arguments for greater state control came from various sources. The utilitarian perspective had assumed a role for government in the reform of economic and social conditions. On the other hand, Mill's emphasis on individual liberty inclined him to be wary of government interference with the freedom of individuals. His essay *On Liberty* has been read as endorsing only the most minimal interference on this freedom.[35] Mill played a modest role in moving liberalism along the path of social reform.

In his early essay on Coleridge, Mill had claimed that laissez-faire was half right and half wrong. In matters of economics, Mill agreed, governments do more harm than good when they 'attempt to chain up the free agency of individuals'. In his judgement, however, the let-alone doctrine had been generated in opposition to the opposite extreme: the narrow monopolies and incompetence of European governments. Government ought to exercise its own free agency, employing its powers and finances 'in promoting the public welfare by a thousand means that individuals would never think of', would have no motivation to attempt, and not enough powers to accomplish. Like a great insurance company, the state should assist 'that large proportion of its members who cannot help themselves'.[36]

On Liberty

Government was more than a grand insurance company. Historically, the state had been the gravest threat to individual liberty. To demand freedom was straightforward when governments were arbitrary and despotic. In *On Liberty*, Mill said that the democracies erected in the place of absolute monarchy should equally be subject to analytical critique. While the democratic states proclaimed the principles of self-government or rule by the people, they did not live up to this doctrine. This was not because a minority elite continued to rule in each nation, which would later be Karl Marx's argument. On this question, Mill agreed with Tocqueville. In practice, he said, self-government meant rule by the majority or, at least, 'the most active *part* of the people . . . who succeed in making themselves accepted as the majority'. This was not the same as rule by the whole people. In such a society, the gravest danger to individual liberty came from 'the tyranny of the majority'. This tyranny could be exercised in two ways. Society in general may become a collective tyrant when it represses dissident individuals, exercising the soul-enslaving 'tyranny of the prevailing opinion and feeling'. The second form was the 'tyranny of the magistrate', that is, repression by the government itself. It was this form of injustice that Thoreau had experienced when he was jailed for deliberately breaking the law. Neither the liberal principle of individual independence nor the conservative principle of social control was absolute. The issue, for Mill, was to understand 'where to place the limit—how to make the fitting adjustment' between these two principles.[37]

The social control of public opinion and the direct control of the state could be employed legitimately against an individual only to prevent harm to others. Individuals were not accountable to society for actions that concerned only themselves.[38] The problem, Mill argued, was the growing tendency to expand the power of society over the individual by the forces of public opinion and government legislation. In *On Liberty*, Mill warned that this tendency would spontaneously grow more formidable unless it was consciously checked.[39]

There already existed, Mill said, 'gross usurpations upon the liberty of private life'. Among the most fundamental of liberties were freedom of thought and the right to express opinions—as the poet Alfred, Lord Tennyson, in 'You ask me why', worried that, in England, a time might come when a person could no longer 'speak the thing he wills':

It is the land that freemen till,
That sober-suited Freedom chose,
The land, where girt with friends or foes
A man may speak the thing he wills.
. . .
Should banded unions persecute
Opinion, and induce a time
When single thought is civil crime,
And individual freedom mute,
. . .
waft me from the harbour-mouth,
Wild wind! I seek a warmer sky,
And I will see before I die
The palms and temples of the south.[40]

An opinion claiming that private property is robbery, Mill argued, ought to be permitted if it was simply circulated through the press. A majority of working men in many trades, he realized, hold the socialist opinion that no individual ought to own more property than a small amount and should earn no income except by manual labour. No one should be punished for holding such views or for publicly proclaiming them in the press. There was an essential difference, however, between declaring your opinions openly and acting on them. Punishment should follow only if an opinion is acted on that causes damage or a definite risk of damage to an individual property owner.[41] Many socialists, for example, went too far and harmed their fellow workers. They not only believed that all workers should receive equal wages, regardless of how productive they were, but they actively interfered with the liberty of their fellow workers by preventing them from receiving more than the average wage, in order to reduce competition within their class.[42] Mill knew that competition presupposes losers as well as winners; the interest of society was merely that such competition occurs within the legal rules.[43]

The fundamental social question Mill faced was whether governments ought to restrain freedom of trade and commerce. The principle that everyone ought to be left alone to make economic decisions conflicted with the need to protect the most vulnerable people from severe exploitation.

While government restraint was generally evil, Mill agreed, society had an undeniable right to protect workers employed in dangerous occupations.[44] From his experience in colonial administration, Mill knew that economic development in less industrial nations required the government to play a more direct role in the economy. In such countries, even the state ownership of industries might be necessary. Anywhere that private enterprise was not capable of undertaking the great task of building industry, as the 'lesser of two great evils', the state may 'take upon itself the business of . . . joint-stock companies.'[45]

It was not the job of the government to interfere with the decisions of consumers. That would interfere with the important regulatory power of supply and demand. Although certain economic practices need to be regulated, to prevent serious consumer fraud and the adulteration of food, the government should generally do no more than provide information about any potential harm, so that buyers may make informed decisions. To take a contemporary example, it might be acceptable to warn consumers about the health effects of cigarettes, but it is an objectionable infringement on individual liberty to tax such products excessively with the intention of obliging people to limit their consumption.

But, how far should individuals be allowed to go in creating harmful situations for others? A difficulty arose because numerous individual actions, such as gambling, prostitution, and the consumption of alcohol, are potentially harmful. These dangerous acts, Mill believed, weaken and demoralize society. When an individual's actions cause actual or potential harm to others, the issue becomes one of public morality and law.[46] Given these choices, however, Mill greatly preferred moral persuasion to restrictive law. Creating dangers for others appears to infringe what might be called other people's '**social rights**', a new concept, Mill said, 'the like of which probably never before found its way into . . . language'. The doctrine of social rights, Mill emphatically declares, is a 'monstrous' principle because 'there is no violation of liberty which it would not justify.' The

doctrine of social rights would be the strongest arm in promoting the tyranny of the majority because every individual would define social rights according to her or his own opinion and interest.[47] It is far better, Mill thought, to attempt to educate people about their social duties than to limit the freedom of individual action even in cases where social harm results.

What about state education? For liberals such as Mill, educational experiences were crucial determinants of personal character, abilities, and opinions. Much of the argument about equality of the sexes rested on the provision of equal education. Mill argued that it was the parents' obligation to provide instruction and training for the minds of their children. Should they fail this obligation, the state ought to see it fulfilled. The role of the state, however, was not to provide this education but to require that parents provide a good education for their children, leaving it to the liberty of each parent to determine how this was best accomplished. A variety of educational options would encourage 'individuality of character' as well as 'diversity in opinions and modes of conduct'. State-run schools, on the contrary, inculcated a single standard acceptable to those who control the government, 'moulding people to be exactly like one another'. At most, a government-run school should compete with private educational institutions and lead by example, ensuring high standards by setting early and frequent national examinations.[48]

In this great historical battle between liberty and authority, Mill held the government to have the greatest potential for evil. In principle, individuals alone or in voluntary combination with others ought to provide all necessary and desirable social services. Even where a professional, national bureaucracy could provide better or more efficient services, Mill thought they should still be left in private hands because such institutions as local government and voluntary charities provide for persons the training in citizenship that is essential for developing the sense of moral duty to the community and for equipping citizens to fulfill these requirements. To allow the national government to control these affairs produces the 'great evil of adding unnecessarily to its power'. If all enterprises became mere branches of the government, if all local governments and boards became mere departments of a central administration, if all employees were appointed and paid by the state, then individual freedom would be doomed. The more efficient, the more professional, the more expert the members of this enormous government bureaucracy, the more individual citizens would look for direction from the government and the less able they would be to manage their own affairs or the affairs of the country—the more complete would be 'the bondage of all'. Citizens would be increasingly unable to criticize or to check the operations of the bureaucracy, and no change could be introduced that was against the interests of the state administration.[49]

In the end, Mill acknowledges that there are some advantages to 'centralized power and intelligence' and that it is sometimes necessary for the state to intervene in the social interest.[50] His concern in *On Liberty* was to circumscribe the arena for state control as much as possible in order to reduce the great evil of social power over the individual. In general, power ought to devolve to the lowest level closest to individuals or their voluntary associations consistent with the interests of society as a whole.

Mill's concern about the tyranny of the majority reflected, in part, his worry that you should not allow a majority to determine the rights of a minority. Democratic principles necessarily implied protection for minorities. In economic matters, Mill's notion of appropriate liberty was consistent with small-scale capitalism. In economics, the tyranny of the majority as an independent force threatening liberty proved to be more fantasy than fact. Conservative social theory had recognized the threat posed by the masses to established wealth and power. Mill was concerned about the power the majority had, through elected governments, to threaten the 'liberty' of the laissez-faire business class. The more important source of tyranny was actually the reverse. As large-scale, private corporations evolved towards the end of the nineteenth century, the actual tyranny of powerful, wealthy minorities became the real threat to individual and social interests. It was the growth of centralized economic power in Britain, the United States, and other European powers that caused the role of the state to expand simultaneously.

Mill was a reluctant social reformer. In many ways, his reformulation of utilitarianism undercut some of the arguments in favour of state intervention that Bentham had advanced. Mill hints of progressive reform in proposing limited regulations on employment and salesmanship. He was most progressive in his advocacy of women's political rights, a position he developed under the influence of his strong, independent wife, Harriet Taylor. Other than through the influence of the English socialist and working-class tradition,[51] the evolution of social liberalism towards reform in England was advanced by women and by such positivists as Harriet Martineau.

GENDER POLITICS

The experiences of women in the Victorian age varied considerably by social class. Poor women worked hard, in the home and in the factories, and were the most oppressed group of any class. Among the middle class, early Victorianism represented a trough between two periods of economic participation. As Altick argues, in the eighteenth century upper-class women had managed estates and middle-class women had undertaken a host of social activities that later became monopolized in male-dominated professions. By the time of Queen Victoria, however, aristocratic women were conspicuously idle and members of the middle class aspired to emulate their refined lifestyle. In Britain, industrialization had expanded the numbers, wealth, and power of middle-class men. Their aspirations to be taken for gentlemen depended, in part, on their ability to provide an income capable of keeping their wives from paid employment. As the domestic sphere became the single realm deemed appropriate for middle-class women, the doctrine of motherhood gave them an important, if restricted role. It also reinforced their exclusion from the expanding public sphere, which middle-class men saw as their own preserve.[52]

Stereotypical prejudices about women reinforced their status: 'Man to command and women to obey'; women had a shallower brain, lacked sexual passion, and were inferior in all ways except those specifically feminine.[53] As playwright Oscar Wilde put this idea later in the century, no woman could be a genius: 'Women are a decorative sex. They never have anything to say, but they say it charmingly. Women represent the triumph of matter over mind.'[54] Similarly, business was a male domain for which the female brain was not well suited. Women's education, Altick concludes, was devoid of intellectual content and challenge.[55] Mary Wollstonecraft and her ideological sisters had been written out of historical consciousness.

Under the Victorian cult of True Womanhood, Chadwick argues, middle-class women were excluded from all production except childbirth. As Florence Nightingale wrote:

> As long as you steal from a man his own labour, his power of production, where and how he likes, you can't call him a free man. All your political liberties are a farce. As long as your legislator can find no legislative remedy against the tyranny of [those] . . . who that superior quality of work shall not be paid for—the first element of liberty is wanting. . . . Who steals my purse steals trash, but who steals my power of production steals all I have. I was interfered with in my power of production when I was a girl—so are all women.[56]

Proper women managed the home and refrained from business and politics, while unmarried women were stigmatized as deviant.[57] Beneath the placid surface of Victorian propriety seethed the aspirations of women for change. In *Our Mutual Friend*, Dickens expressed this aspiration through his character, Bella Rokesmith, who informed her husband: 'I want to be something so much worthier than the doll in the doll's house.'[58]

The 'woman question' continued to be debated in England in the 1820s and 1830s. As Caine argues, at that time many of the most prominent voices on behalf of women belonged to men who were reform-minded liberals or were associated with early socialism. Even Harriet Martineau at first wrote mostly under a masculine pseudonym.[59] Feminist arguments and causes have taken many forms historically and been adapted to conditions and ideologies of the times. The Malthusian concern about population growth justified the spread of birth control. While accepting the gendered division between feminine domesticity and male public worldliness, nineteenth-century evangelicals believed that women could use their moral superiority to transform their home and childhood education and extend their 'mission' into the world at large, transforming it.[60]

The argument that women were more moral, 'more chaste, compassionate, virtuous and dutiful' than men, was also used to support women's demand for a greater role in political and economic affairs.[61] A middle-class women's movement emerged in the 1850s and 1860s in England and America with the objective of persuading male legislators to extend political rights to women. A militant form of feminism as a mass social movement of organized women had to await later Victorian times. As Caine demonstrates, however, the concerns of women were not confined to politics and the vote. The oppression of women in marriage, the discriminatory divorce, property, and child custody laws, the exclusion of women from higher education and employment, as well as the sexual double standard were all on the mid-century feminist agenda. Shut out from political polls, many women voted with their personal lives. It was in the 1850s that the novelist Mary Ann Evans (who used the pseudonym George Eliot) openly lived with her lover, George Lewes. She wasn't alone, although unconventional lifestyles were generally kept behind closed doors.[62]

Mid-Victorian women spoke out on issues, such as rape and domestic brutality, that still cry out for reform. Florence Nightingale (1820–1910) advocated socialized medicine. Nightingale is most widely remembered for her pioneering work as a nurse in army hospitals during the Crimean

War. As McDonald demonstrates, she was also a passionate social reformer (see the quotation above), particularly around fundamental issues of health and medical treatment, formulating in 1860 a conception of state-funded medical care. People who were infirm from disease, mentally deficient, or suffering from mental illness were not the same as able-bodied vagabonds, yet the law locked them all away in the workhouse where there was no specialized medical care or nursing. Society owes them every necessary care to ensure their recovery, Nightingale said. 'The treatment of those who are poor and in affliction should be centrally and uniformly administered, and at the expense of society. . . . Sickness is not parochial; it is general and human and its cost ought to be borne by all.'[63] Beyond health care, Nightingale advocated government intervention in employment, suggesting that 'at least in exceptional times of distress the state' could 'give productive work at remunerative prices'.[64]

Both Nightingale and Martineau argued for the reform of British rule in India, especially after the Indian Mutiny of 1857, which initiated the Indian struggle for independence. The two social reformers differed in their response to the issue of the vote for women. While Martineau campaigned actively for women's political rights, Nightingale was only nominally a member of the suffrage movement. What was needed first, Nightingale argued, was economic help from government to end the tyranny that robs workers of their power of production. Rather than focusing the struggle on political rights, she wrote, 'I want my bread first and then you may give me my votes.'[65]

This was a tactical difference. Nightingale's social reformism was more explicit than the views expressed by John Stuart Mill, the most prominent male spokesperson for women's suffrage in the mid-Victorian period. McDonald argues that Nightingale helped push Mill to the political left on the issue of health and sanitation.[66] It is highly probable that Mill also did not come alone to his later, more advanced gender politics. Rather, he was indebted to the influence of his partner, Harriet Taylor, an important feminist theorist.

Harriet Taylor Mill

Harriet Taylor Mill (1807–58) was a member of a radical, religiously **dissenting** social circle that included Harriet Martineau. At the age of 23, having been married for four years and become the mother of two sons and soon a daughter, Harriet Taylor first met John Stuart Mill socially. Mill later recounted in his *Autobiography*, Rossi notes, that their mutual attraction was based on their similar views on the rights of women. From the time of Mary Wollstonecraft, women's rights had been a consistent theme of discussion and writing among members of their intellectual circle.[67] Taylor and Mill soon became intimate. They carried on a long, intellectual, and emotional relationship for 20 years that was scandalous in Victorian eyes, but which Mill claimed was not sexual until 1851, after John Taylor, Harriet's husband, had been dead for two years and she and John Mill were married. Biographers have debated the claim of celibacy of their premarital intimacy, which, if genuine, is almost a caricature of the Victorian attitudes to sexuality. One of the worst forms of tyranny over a wife, Mill claimed, was the tyrant's right to enforce from his wife 'the lowest degradation of a human being, that of being made the instrument of an animal function contrary to her inclinations'.[68] More is implied in this assertion than the need for consent in sexuality. Propriety for women in Victorian times meant, above all, subjecting sexual passion to rational control. Men were allowed to be animals extramaritally, but only low women had similarly beastly passions. In an age when pregnancy could not be controlled, repressing sexuality served at least one practical function.

The ideas that Mill incorporated in his works were developed in close collaboration with Harriet Taylor. Taylor had a strong personality and exercised great influence over Mill during her lifetime. Inspired by the first Women's Rights Convention organized in Seneca Falls, New York, in 1848 and by revolution in France in the same year, Taylor became inclined to socialist ideas and pushed Mill's reformist sympathies in that direction. In the 1850s, her health rapidly deteriorated.

She had contracted tuberculosis from her husband. Less than a month following Taylor's death in 1858, Mill published *On Liberty*, claiming Taylor had been his principal inspiration. Taylor's influence, Himmelfarb argues, was clearly apparent in Mill's warnings about the tyranny of the majority and the stifling effects of public opinion, ideas Taylor had expressed as early as 1832.[69] No group felt the oppressiveness of Victorian public opinion more than women who sought to advance the cause of female emancipation.

Early unpublished essays written by Taylor and Mill, shortly after they met, indicate the mutual sympathy for the cause of women but also, Rossi argues, the differences initially in their views. Taylor was more radical, disavowing the need for any laws on marriage and asserting the right of women to be financially independent and to enter any occupational field. Mill sought a reform in marriage laws, including a more liberal divorce policy. On the issue of women's employment, however, he endorsed the traditional role separation of men and women. Household management and child-rearing were women's contribution to the household and, in marriage, a wife ought to share her husband's interests and discuss issues intelligently with him.[70]

Harriet Taylor persisted in her advocacy of occupational independence for women in an article on the 'Enfranchisement of Women' published anonymously in 1851 shortly after her marriage to Mill and in response to the principles of the women's suffrage movement in the United States. In addition to demanding for women the right to vote and be eligible for political office, the Massachusetts Women's Rights Convention of 1850 advanced the slogan, 'equality before the law, without distinction of sex or colour'.[71]

In opposition to the 'nature' argument of people as diverse as Rousseau, Burke, and Darwin, Mill and Taylor adopted the environmental argument, endorsed by Wollstonecraft and Martineau, that women were subjugated by society. Mill refuted the long-held prejudice that the subjugation of women was so ancient that it was natural, claiming that history had demonstrated 'the

extraordinary susceptibility of human nature to external influences' and its 'extreme variableness'. It was not in their nature but through their social relationships that women were made unequal to men, particularly through their education. The proper education for a Victorian woman was ornamental, as the dialogue from the movie *Cold Mountain* (directed and written by Anthony Minghella, 2003) demonstrates. Surviving on their farm alone during the Civil War, the upper-class Ada is obliged by necessity to learn to labour. She quickly recognizes how ill-prepared for survival she was rendered by her impractical education. When she claims that fence construction was her first useful work, however, her companion, Ruby, suggests slyly that women have a uniquely reproductive role in child-bearing:

Ruby: Where's north?
Ada: North? Ah . . .
Ruby: Name me three herbs that grow wild on this farm.
Ada: I can't. I can't—all right? I can talk about farming in Latin. I can . . . I can read French. I know how to lace up a corset, God knows. I can name the principal rivers of Europe, but don't ask me to name one stream in this county. I can embroider, but I can't darn. I can arrange cut flowers, but I can't grow them. If a thing has a function, if I might do something with it, then it wasn't considered suitable.
Ruby: Why?
Ada: Ruby, you can ask 'why' about pretty much everything to do with me. This fence is about the first thing I've ever done that may produce an actual result.
Ruby: You never wrapped your legs around this Inman?

While, in *Subjection of Women*, Mill acknowledged the disservice women experience from their education, he also spoke more conservatively on the question of natural versus artificial differences between the sexes. On the one hand, he claimed that even the 'least contestable' of the differences 'may well have been produced merely by circumstances'. He observed equally that the general bent of women's talents is towards the practical (darning and child-rearing, not fence-building) rather then the abstract and speculative,[72] reiterating a long-standing distinction with its roots securely in traditional thought.

As had Wollstonecraft, Taylor knew that women were the intellectual equals of men. Similar as well to Wollstonecraft, Taylor asserted that it is not possible to tell what women could actually achieve without complete liberty of choice. Only in a situation of perfect freedom, in which any occupation is open to all, regardless of sex, would each individual be able to prove her or his abilities through experience, giving society 'the benefit of the best faculties of all its inhabitants'.[73]

Taylor rooted her arguments in the parallel oppressions of Africans and European women, as well as in the conceptions men applied to themselves but denied to women. In the United States, she noted, those who advocated the enfranchisement of women were also prominent in the kindred cause of African-American freedom. In Taylor's terms, this attack on the aristocracy of colour had spread to protest against the aristocracy of sex.[74] The American Declaration of Independence, like other male-centred documents of liberation, claimed that all men were equal; all men, Taylor argued, meant all human beings.

The dominant group had seized upon such virtuous ideas as liberty and equality. At one time these rebellious men had challenged the view that 'the supreme virtue of subjects was loyalty to kings.' Now, Taylor argued, their self-interest led them to apply the opposite logic to women, believing 'that the paramount virtue of womanhood is loyalty to men'. Men had overthrown the tyranny of custom except where it applied to women, where women were still expected to be subservient to arbitrary authority. In Europe, men were made tyrants in their own household—'domineering, exacting, self-worshipping' and sometimes 'brutally tyrannical'.[75]

The wrongs done to women are obvious in some circumstances, Taylor says, such as situations of gross brutality, or financial exploitation, or the absence of a right to divorce. More importantly, she adds, in the average marriage, the inequality of domination and subordination is demoralizing to the character of both the man and woman. In men this inequality produces the vices of power, for even the most insignificant man—in Mill's words, from the clodhopper to the noble (Box 7.4)—'finds one place where he is chief and head' and becomes the 'despot of the household'.[76] In women, subordination produces the vice of '**artifice**, obliging women to seek their will indirectly, by artful and dissembling means'.[77]

The glimmer of a new future had already appeared in the United States; in England, as well, women in Sheffield had petitioned for the electoral franchise. These women, Taylor said, demand full equality straightforwardly, by appealing 'to men's sense of justice'. It would seem that equality was to be granted by the powerful, on the strength of logic and argument, rather than being won by the subordinate. In the meantime, the rational liberation of women was an individual

---

Box 7.4

Whatever gratification of pride there is in the possession of power ... is ... common to the whole male sex.... The clodhopper exercises ... his share of the power equally with the highest nobleman ... for everyone who desires power, desires it most over those who are nearest to him, with whom his life is passed ... and in whom any independence of his authority is oftenest likely to interfere with his individual preferences.

—John Stuart Mill, *On the Subjection of Women* (1869)

affair, between a woman and a man. It was not merely a matter of strong affection, or habitual kindness and pleasure in each other's company; the most 'durable and happy attachment' could be found only in a genuine friendship between equals in their mental abilities and their privileges[78]— such a relationship, Taylor implied, as between herself and John Stuart Mill.

Nevertheless, it appeared to her that, with few exceptions, women did not desire their own liberation; most no longer possessed 'either strong wishes or active minds'. For Taylor, these women were made servile-minded by custom and the habits of submission. Only women possessed of unusual moral courage would commit a 'flagrant act of insubordination' by protesting this injustice.[79] She undoubtedly possessed this moral courage.

So did her daughter, Helen Taylor (1831–1907), who continued her mother's work after her death in 1858. She pursued her mother's attack on the traditional idea that women and men should have separate spheres of work, commenting that 'men are, generally speaking, only struck with the unsuitability of work for women when it may lead to profit and honour, and with the unsuitability of work to themselves when there is nothing much worth having to be got by it.'[80] During the debate on the Second Reform Bill, which promised male suffrage, Helen Taylor argued in favour of extending the franchise to the working class and for the nationalization of the land—both causes championed by her stepfather, John Stuart Mill—but took her politics further to the left by joining a moderate socialist group. Writing in support of the 1867 Reform Act, Helen Taylor said that 'the interest of the majority of the nation must surely be the interest of the nation itself.' In her view, a working-class majority would be no 'more fatal to the future prosperity of the country than the continued preponderance in our government of the idle and frivolous men whom our present system has a tendency to bring to the top.' They were too ignorant, prejudiced, and indolent to care about the sufferings of their fellow countrymen. In the limited mental powers of these men, the working class is 'to them like women, not exactly fellow creatures but a kind of animal whom they have never dreamt of considering as on a level with themselves, nor, therefore, as altogether human.'[81] Helen Taylor stood for Parliament in 1885, putting on a lively, radical campaign at a time when women did not have the vote.[82] Few women of her time were willing to be so openly public about their cause, although that was quickly about to change.

As the women's movement became organized in England in the 1860s, it tended to follow John Stuart Mill's advice, focusing energies into demands for the vote. This meant being increasingly public and visible, contrary to proper Victorian etiquette. Many other intellectual women in the nineteenth century expressed their views in more socially acceptable ways, as novelists or poets, such as Elizabeth Barrett Browning. In 1851, Harriet Taylor had dismissed these literary women who, she said, rejected any desire for equality because they 'depend on men's opinion for their literary as well as their feminine successes.' In a later decade, Mill noted that women were becoming more freely spoken in their writing although, he added, their chief deficiency was the narrow circumference bounding their observations and associations, within which their consciousness was developed.[83]

For less politically explicit authors—women as well as men—the novel was the preferred platform for advocating social reform. The social-problem novel continued the realist genre in the mid-nineteenth century. Particularly in England, where feudal relations continued to define part of the social landscape, the idle aristocracy made a convenient target well into the twentieth century. As laissez-faire capitalism exposed its true face, however, **realism** meant exposing the wrongs of bourgeois society, linking the critical or satirical novel with reformist liberalism or socialism.

SOCIAL LIBERALISM AND REALISM

Socialist and positivist ideas are reflected in art in particularly volatile periods of history. In France, both movements inspired a rejection of Romanticism in favour of realism. In an earlier epoch, social criticism had been expressed in the literary world by realism and satire. As the proletariat expanded on the social landscape, a new stage of literary and artistic critique took its place. French novelists such as Gustave Flaubert and Stendhal wrote in a realistic style that, as before, provided the artistic form to expose the problems of modern society. The paintings and lithographs of Honoré Daumier depicted the harsh life of working-class women and commemorated the 1830 people's revolution in France (*The Uprising*).

The most explicitly socialist and realist painter was Gustave Courbet, who sought to portray the 'heroism of modern life'. In the revolutionary fervour of 1848, Courbet had come to reject the world of Romantic imagination as merely a form of escapism from the task of social change. In Jansen's view, Courbet's radical socialism was evident principally in his choice of subject. In *The Stone Breakers* (1849), Courbet depicted one aged and one young workman engaged in back-breaking labour, unsuitable for either of them. It is a realistic, unsentimental painting showing the dignity and independence of labour.[84]

In England, social liberalism in literature reached a mass audience by combining realistic portraits with sentimentality and melodrama, most conspicuously in the popular novels of Charles Dickens. By the middle of the nineteenth century, the novel had undergone a considerable revival. The novel was still the best medium to express realism—the depiction of social life as it actually was. If social liberalism was the political response to the serious failings of laissez-faire capitalism, the new novelists expressed this response in fiction. Novelists who wrote in a realistic style most successfully portrayed the bleakness and inhumanity of the Industrial Revolution—somewhat later in America than in England.

By being realistic, a work of art need imply nothing more than that it faithfully reproduces nature. When a member of the bourgeoisie, or a royal family, commissioned an artist to paint a portrait, they expected to appear more or less as they were, with perhaps only the most obvious blemishes removed. As an artistic movement, however, realism encompassed more than style. It surpassed technique and included as subject matter the depiction of the everyday, of common people going about the business of their lives. Early realism had been consistent with the emerging middle-class position and rebellious interests of the bourgeoisie. By the mid-nineteenth century, Western art had been diverted away from Romanticism back towards realism, but it was newly inspired by the scientific spirit of the age and the more practical perspective of business.

When realism also embraces a social purpose—to instruct, or critique, or expose social ills—it is termed **social realism**. Clarence Darrow recognized the critical, radical element of realism:

> The true realist cannot worship at the shrine of power nor prostitute his gifts for gold. With an artist's eye he sees the world exactly as it is, and he tells the story faithfully to life. . . .
>
> The artists of the realist school have a sense so fine that they cannot help catching the inspiration that is filling all the world's best minds with the hope of greater justice and more equal social life. With the vision of the seer they feel the coming dawn, when true equality shall reign upon the earth—the time when democracy . . . will be a part of human life.
>
> The greatest artists of the world today are telling facts and painting scenes that cause humanity to stop and think, and ask why one shall be a master and another a serf—why a portion of the world should toil and spin, should wear away their strengths and lives, that the rest may live in idleness and ease.[85]

Equally important in this era of free-market writing was a growing audience eager to purchase and buy this new literature. It was not only the educated middle class who could afford to purchase books. There was also a growing body of literate working people for whom social criticism in a popularized form was welcome both as entertainment and as edification. Novelists such as Dickens sold their works packaged piecemeal in serialized periodicals. The Victorian age popularized a literary genre known as the social-problem novel, which elaborated on Disraeli's description of England as divided between 'two nations': the rich and the poor. George Eliot and Charles Dickens were among the most significant authors of this genre in England.

George Eliot (Mary Ann Evans)

> I hold it blasphemy to say that a man ought not to fight against authority: there is no great religion and no great freedom that has not done it, in the beginning.
> —George Eliot, *Felix Holt* (1866)

Within the social conventions of the Victorian age, literature was a relatively safe outlet for the re-emergence of feminist thinking. Since women were excluded from both politics and business, they had to find a socially acceptable outlet for their talents. Harriet Taylor Mill's dismissal of literary women should not have extended to Mary Ann Evans (1819–80), the brilliant Victorian essayist who, as a novelist, wrote under the masculine pseudonym, George Eliot. She wished to be anonymous in the hope that her gender and her cohabitation with a man legally married to another woman would not prejudice the reception of her fiction.

As a youth, Eliot had fallen under the spell of evangelical Christianity but, by her early twenties, she rebelled against her strict religious upbringing. Like other intellectuals, she found the path to liberation by reading rationalist and socially critical literature, history, and philosophy. She translated Feuerbach's *The Essence of Christianity* into English. In her thirties, as an editor of a progressive literary review, Eliot began a stimulating association with influential thinkers such as John Stuart Mill, Harriet Taylor, Herbert Spencer, and Harriet Martineau. Within this circle she became romantically involved with George Lewes. Unable to divorce his wife legally, Lewes lived with Eliot in a warm and productive relationship until Lewes's death in 1878. For Eliot, the illegality of their relationship was a necessity rather than a

lifestyle rebellion, as it had been for the Romantics. She believed that relationships 'formed in the maturity of thought and feeling, and grounded only on inherent fitness and mutual attraction, tended to bring women into more intelligent sympathy with men.'[86]

By 1856, Eliot had begun to write fiction. Like Jane Austen's female heroes, Eliot reasserted women's claim to equal rationality. The hero of *Middlemarch* (1872), Dorothea Brooke, was a rational woman who was capable of abstract thought, contrary to the prejudice of John Stuart Mill. As described by Eliot, 'Her mind was theoretic and yearned by its nature after some lofty conception of the world . . . ; she was enamoured of intensity and greatness and rash in embracing whatever seemed to her to have those aspects.' Like Elizabeth in Austen's *Pride and Prejudice*, Dorothea's feisty character in a 'marriageable girl' made it difficult for her to find a partner, marriage ordinarily being determined by custom, good looks, 'vanity, and merely canine affection'.[87]

The extensive research that went into the detailed backgrounds of Eliot's novels, as well as her approach, which she described as learning 'how ideas lie in other minds than my own',[88] was sociological. Her novels revealed an understanding of the social situation of many classes of people, not just the provincial upper class, which most women novelists knew best. Her characters, however, were complex, psychological, and multi-dimensional. In addition to social circumstances, life was a matter of the hard choices that people made.

Eliot's most engaging and realistic character in *Felix Holt*, one of her lesser-known novels, is Mrs Transome, the wife of the insipid and weak owner of the estate called Transome Court. Because her husband was a half-witted fool, Mrs Transome managed the affairs of the property: '*she* was master' and sat 'in the saddle two or three hours every day'. When her son, Harold, returned home to take over the reins of estate management, Mrs Transome was thrust into irrelevance. Harold told her she no longer 'had to worry . . . about things that don't properly belong to a woman. . . . We'll set all that right. You shall have nothing to do now but to be grandmamma on satin cushions.' For upper-class men, Eliot commented, to be good to women meant giving cushions and carriages to them, promising to have their house redone, and expecting them to be content with the formalities of affection that masked contempt for their independence.[89] For Eliot, authentic love meant that a man and woman must share a genuine partnership in their ideals. Perhaps that is how she viewed her own rejection of the conventions of Victorian propriety in her deeply romantic, yet socially illicit attachment to George Lewes.

Charles Dickens

> In the little world in which children have their existence . . . there is nothing so finely perceived and so finely felt as injustice.
> —Charles Dickens, *Great Expectations* (1860–1)

In his socially conscious writing, which reached an international audience, novelist Charles Dickens (1812–70) exposed the evils and hypocrisy of mid-nineteenth-century Victorian England. He described the scandalous conditions in workhouses, boarding schools, and debtors' prisons; satirized lawyers, magistrates, religious hypocrites, and utilitarian businessmen; condemned the death penalty; called the law 'a ass—a idiot'; and championed the honesty and virtues of the poor and the working class. His social criticism condemned the system of industrial capitalism that dehumanized common people and thrust them into the chaos of the grey and grimy industrial ghettos such as 'Coketown' in *Hard Times*:

> This . . . was among the fictions of Coketown. Any capitalist there who had made sixty thousand pounds out of sixpence always professed to wonder why the sixty thousand nearest Hands didn't each make sixty thousand pounds out of sixpence, and more or less reproached them every one for not accomplishing the little feat. What I did you can do. Why don't you go and do it?[90]

Dickens was a popular author who made an independent living from the sale of his writing. He had no aristocratic or bourgeois patron. Dickens's works were popular among a wide range of the literate classes. On the one hand, his novels were realistic in their portrayal of the grim lives of working people in the heyday of laissez-faire capitalism, appealing to reform sentiments among the working and middle classes. On the other hand, Dickens's novels were popular because they were entertaining, **melodramatic**, and sentimental. In many of his novels, the plight of the disadvantaged was emphasized by describing the victimization of children, the most vulnerable members of society.[91] If his depictions of the conditions of life of the poor were realistic, Dickens's characters were often caricatures of real life. His writing about persons was not usually psychologically complex.

In *Little Dorrit*, Dickens pillories the materialism of the capitalist ethos and paints a savage account of the larger prison house that, critics charged, England itself had become. In his next novel, *Hard Times*, Dickens's satirical account of the brutal culture of utilitarian capitalism, he contrasts the inhumanity of the utilitarian system with the fundamental decency and humanity of the average working hand. For Dickens, workers possessed an essential nobility of spirit, an innate intelligence, and a basic, underlying decency. Their honour and 'honesty in the main no competent observer free from bias could doubt'.[92] Wealth and power were more likely to degrade a person's character than poverty and squalor. Human nature, for Dickens, held potential for good in every economic class—even Ebenezer Scrooge could be reformed with supernatural help—although it had been terribly distorted by the institutions and ideologies of industrial capitalism. Dickens did not appeal only to the conscience or morality of the factory-owning class. He also had this warning and advice for the 'Utilitarian economists, skeletons of schoolmasters, Commissioners of Fact': when romance was utterly driven out of the souls of the poor, 'and they and a bare existence stand face to face, Reality will take a wolfish turn and make an end of you.'[93]

This was a dire warning, something Karl Marx might have written. Liberalism, however, demanded an appearance of even-handedness, of finding wrongs on both sides of the class divide. Dickens was a perceptive enough social critic to know that the poor were not largely to blame for their plight; however, he shied away from violence or agitators who would advocate *any* means to change social reality. Dickens believed that in trade unions, as well as in the satanic capitalist mills, working people lose their individuality. Both institutions cause suffering and hardship to befall honest individuals. Dickens is unsympathetic to trade union leaders, such as Slackbridge in *Hard Times*, who wiped his brow 'always from left to right, and never the reverse way'.[94] To criticize social problems, especially in a satire, was socially acceptable. To suggest radical solutions was not. Dickens may have been more radical in his own opinions than he demonstrated in his novels, but this gap reflected a new dilemma of the modern age: how far do you sacrifice your aesthetic or political views in the interests of achieving popularity or prosperity?

CONCLUSION

From one point of view, the nineteenth century was a golden age of prosperity for many. The Industrial Revolution maintained England at the apex of global power, although the up-and-coming new national powers increasingly challenged that domination. No country was poised for greater future promise than the United States. Immigrants poured into the vast territories newly wrested from the Native peoples and began to populate the half-continent with small property owners.

The rapidity of American industrialization exacerbated the social problems that accompanied the transition to industrial capitalism everywhere. America embraced capitalism unhindered by a tradition of elite paternalism. Even political and economic solutions to social problems encompassed the fundamental individualism of the American way or sprang from the resilience of organized religion, which seemed so paradoxical in a thoroughly materialistic culture. Laissez-faire competed with varieties of Christian reformism. Collective ideologies, which had their origin in the Old World, were carried to the new by those immigrants who had experienced the socialist and anarchist movements in their European homelands. In this cultural mosaic, American social scientists in the late nineteenth century would take one of two diverging paths. One road explored the persistence of the Old World cultural heritage and the unique, multinational culture that was emerging in the urban centres of America. The second followed the individualistic and subjective path into social psychology.

English liberals, after taking a long, hard look at their own society and perceiving the drift at mid-century towards revolution, sought reforms from above, based on the enlightened self-interest of the propertied and governing elite. Comte's positivism was congenial to a branch of English liberalism known as utilitarianism, which, in the hands of John Stuart Mill, would begin its own migration from laissez-faire to reform. Just as liberalism began to take the first tentative steps away from laissez-faire individualism and the dog-eat-dog philosophy of early capitalism and moved towards a theory of social reform, conservatism also underwent a transformation in the nineteenth century. As capitalism became consolidated, as English power spread around the globe, the conservatives dropped their moral outrage about the excesses of early capitalism. They became the party of the Empire, of strong nationalism and British chauvinism. The more obviously reformist the liberals became, the more conservatives championed the new status quo. In the twentieth century, the business elite would abandon the Liberal Party and identify with the Conservative Party in Britain. Meanwhile, the banner of social reform would be hoisted by the Labour Party in Britain and by the Progressive Movement in the United States. Caught between the hammer of the socialists and the anvil of the conservatives, the Liberal Party in Britain would shrivel into insignificance while Progressivism would be unable to generate a third alternative to the established American dual-party system.

During the dawn of liberalism, when the bourgeoisie began to displace the traditional landed aristocracy, the fundamental social question was whether laissez-faire should be reined in by some government protection. Utilitarianism and social liberalism nudged liberal ideology in the direction of reform, simultaneously encouraging the oppressed groups—principally women and blacks—to identify and struggle for their own emancipation. The social liberals were assisted in popular culture by writers who adopted a new realism that exposed the wrongs of industrial society.

This style was the choice of a new breed of critical novelists who were drawn to the needs of the poor and oppressed. From being its special creation, realism became a useful weapon against the dominant capitalist class. The working class, however, needed another weapon. In the works discussed above, the social-problem novelists wrote about working-class organization and politics. In Germany, Karl Marx, a young radical, was coming to the conclusion that organization alone was not enough. The working class also needed a theory of their place in capitalist society and their future beyond it. For Marx, elaborating this idea first required a thorough critique of the philosophical heritage of Germany, principally the dominant ideas of Georg Hegel.

8 HEGEL, FEUERBACH, AND MARX

Social theorists develop new ideas during times of social change. Theories of laissez-faire coincided with the multiple transformations wrought by industrial capitalism. French society rotated through successive bouts of revolution and reaction, expressed in social theory by versions of liberalism, radicalism, conservatism, and Romanticism. Social conditions were different in Germany and beyond to the east. As a generalization, the farther east you went in Europe in the nineteenth century, the more traditional the social and political conditions that persisted. The Russian Empire was strengthening its semi-feudal social structure. The majority of peasants in Russia were bound under the yoke of serfdom, and the Empire was ruled by an aristocracy closely tied to the Czar. The economy was still largely pre-industrial, lacking a large and influential class of capitalists, and the country had only a small industrial working class. In many respects Russia resembled pre-Revolution France.

In Central Europe, between France and Russia, a multitude of small states and principalities were all that remained of the Holy Roman Empire that had been founded at the beginning of the ninth century by Charlemagne. The Holy Roman Empire included, in part, as many as 300 principalities, each a small, independent state dominated by a local prince. As England and France developed into prosperous nation-states under strong central governments, the local rulers in Germany reinstated serfdom, revoked the freedom of the towns, and attempted to eliminate feelings of German nationalism. The Empire was dismantled and Germany disunified.[1]

No European country underwent more rapid and fundamental social change in the middle decades of the nineteenth century than those German states forged by the military power of Prussia into the new state of Germany. By 1870, its industrial and military power had grown to the point where Germany was the most powerful nation on the continent, and German colonial expansion would soon make it a global rival of Britain.

In the turmoil of monumental social changes that rocked the German states from Napoleon's conquest to the 1870s, equally consequential developments occurred in social theory. Germany produced many prominent social theorists, among whom were G.W. Hegel and Karl Marx. Hegel primarily was a philosopher. Marx's life work was an attempt to synthesize and transcend Western social thought and create a theory that would both explain and transform capitalist society. Placing these German theorists in context requires some attention to the economic and social conditions of their time.

GERMAN SOCIETY AND POLITICS

The social structure of the German-speaking states in Central Europe in 1800 varied considerably depending on their geography and history. Many regions were still, in their general outline, what has been described as traditional. About 80 per cent of the population lived in the countryside. In the small towns and their surrounding farming regions, according to social historian Morazé, both tradition and the laws of local princes fixed the class and occupation of the inhabitants. Private ownership in the countryside was making headway in the western regions, although the small class of commercial capitalists found themselves confined by the traditions of the closely knit society. As German nobles expanded to the east, they created large estates on which peasants worked under semi-feudal regulations. The urban economy was still pre-industrial.[2]

The multitude of German-speaking small principalities jealously guarded their limited independence. These remnants of the Holy Roman Empire were rich plums on an ancient and tottering tree. In the powerful German state of Prussia, the class of land-owning aristocrats—**Junkers**—comprised the dominant class in politics, economics, and the military. From its capital in Berlin, the Prussian ruling class controlled the rural estates and the growing trading ports of the Baltic Sea.

The Enlightenment made a significant impact on Germany. German intellectuals sought to convert their rulers to the political doctrine of reason and good government. The dominant culture of the region was German, although no composite German nation had yet been forged. Most German intellectuals did not embrace wholeheartedly the Age of Reason. German traditions included mystical and spiritual elements that tended more towards Romantic influences. The great genius of eighteenth-century German literature, Johann Wolfgang von Goethe, in *The Sorrows of Young Werther*, gave the world the model of the sad, self-absorbed, thoroughly subjective, and extremely sentimental modern anti-hero. *Werther* was a forerunner of Romanticism, although it is difficult to shoehorn Goethe into any single literary tradition. Most importantly, Goethe was the spokesman of a specifically German culture and language, a lightning rod for German nationalism.

Early nineteenth-century nationalism was often liberal and progressive, particularly among people, such as Italians, Hungarians, and Poles, who were oppressed by other countries. In Germany an indigenous, conservative nationalism expressed in mysticism, folk stories, heroes, and emotionalism had been aroused by the Prussian, Johann von Herder (1744–1803). Travel had

impressed on Herder the great diversity among different peoples. Yet, the Enlightenment rationalists seemed to assume a single human nature and a single type of rationality such that—given sufficient powers of reasoning—all humans would think alike. Although the *philosophes* had rejected the idea of a single truth achieved through the agency of revelation, they expected to find a single truth through the use of reason. As Sophie de Condorcet had argued, 'every reasonable and sensitive being will have the same ideas . . . everyone who reasons well will have a common notion of justice.'[3]

Herder thought this was a mistaken assumption. Germans were different in fundamental ways from other people, the French distinct from the English, and so on. Each nation was characterized by a particular and unique spirit, or **Volksgeist**, providing every nationality with a different character or spirit. Herder, as Godechot argues, saw each nation having a fixed destiny arising from certain basic imperatives, such as race. This national spirit originated in the mysterious past and evolved over time. A nation's *Volksgeist* 'is singular, marvellous, inexplicable, ineffable'. It courses through language, mythology, religion, and customs—all that would be part of a national culture. Each person had a duty to protect and serve the fatherland.[4]

When Napoleon invaded the German principalities, the German fatherland was in need of all the protection it could muster. Napoleon's conquest of the German states rekindled feelings of national identity among the German-speaking people who were swept into Napoleon's vast European empire. Occupation by a foreign power unites all classes in a common struggle. In Germany, the voice of resurgent nationalism was enunciated, most dramatically by Johann Fichte, who held the Chair of Philosophy at the University of Berlin. Fichte's 'Addresses to the German Nation', Shirer declared, 'rallied a divided, defeated people'. A German national identity, Fichte believed, could be created by reflecting on what distinguished Germans from others, particularly Jews and Latin-speaking people such as the French, who belonged to 'decadent' races. Under the Germans, whose language was the purest and most original, 'a new era in history would blossom' that 'would reflect the order of the cosmos'.[5]

Napoleon stimulated a nationalistic drive among German intellectuals, who sought to define what it meant to be German. The question of the distinctiveness of national identity arises in any new nation, particularly so in Germany where, prior to German unification, cultural identity had to substitute for political identity. Romanticism in art and literature, particularly the more conservative and nationalistic versions, flowed easily through German culture, where subjective tendencies were never far from the surface.

As the conservatives had argued, the meaning and spirit of the nation could be revived through the rediscovery of past cultural glory. A nation that had once been great could be powerful again. Part of the rediscovery of nationhood was the reconstruction of ancient myths and legends that were uniquely German. Jacob and Wilhelm Grimm undertook an investigation into the roots of German culture, collecting oral folktales and publishing them in *Nursery and Household Tales* in 1812. These fantastic folk stories and ancient Germanic legends reflected a trend towards Romantic conservatism.

Napoleon's invasion also had important economic implications for the German states. His armies swept all before him and did not grind to a halt until they reached Moscow and the devastating Russian winter. The shock of defeat thrust the German ruling class into the modern world, compelling them under the threat of extinction to catch up and surpass the French, to overcome the weakness of division, and to industrialize the economy. The Prussian *Junkers*, an aristocratic class of landlords and soldiers, grasped the political initiative. From this class emerged the founder of the modern nation of Germany, Otto von Bismarck. In 1862, Bismarck declared that 'the great questions of the day . . . will not be settled by resolutions and majority votes—that was the mistake of the men of 1848 and 1849—but by blood and iron.'[6] Under Bismarck's iron fist, Germany was industrialized as the *Junker* class transformed society from above,

becoming in the process the ruling class of a modern, authoritarian, and expansionary state. German nationalism was a potent unifying force. A sense of national destiny was created as the German nation was forged in the fires of war with Austria and France. The quick German defeat of France in the Franco-Prussian war (1870–1) inflated German pride and avenged Napoleon's invasion earlier in the century. Some German-speaking provinces that had been under French control were incorporated into Germany. The victory symbolized how far German industrial power had come in half a century. It was this unified German state that the *Junker* class led into World War I.

The economic transformation of Germany 'from above' (that is, by the actions of the old elite) was both economic and social. Ideological change was more complicated. In France and England, the bourgeoisie fought with the aristocracy and monarchy for dominance and political power, developing the ideology of individual freedom, limited democracy, and laissez-faire economics. In Germany, social transformation did not spring from below. The members of the traditional ruling class remained in power and transformed the economy themselves. The *Junkers* became class-conscious. They intended to develop German industry and catch up with the more advanced capitalist nations. Wanting a strong, central government to create the conditions necessary for industrialization, they preserved an authoritarian style of politics that was distinct from the limited democracy established in France, England, and the United States. The German ruling class demonstrated that you could have industrial capitalism without political liberalism or laissez-faire.

Once firmly established on the road to industrialization by the late nineteenth century, the strong German state was able to introduce social and even some political reforms. The German government eventually adopted policies that, in England, were called 'social liberalism' such as a government-sponsored pension scheme for workers, laws limiting the hours of work, and the legalization of unions. A form of representative democracy emerged late in Germany and male workers were granted the franchise. Even the socialist Marxist party eventually was legalized and allowed to run candidates for election. In sum, the economic gains were substantial. German workers won a share of the increased productivity brought about by German industrialization. With respect to democracy, the political gains were more modest and when it was created, the elected parliament in Germany had little actual power.

Not all German intellectuals embraced the type of nationalism imposed by Prussia. There was an undercurrent of liberty and laissez-faire in the alienation of some young artists from social traditions, as liberal ideas infiltrated into the German universities. When German Romanticism took on a political flavour, the personal was preferred to the public. The theme of the new literary rebellion, *Sturm und Drang*, meaning '**storm and stress**'—at first, the title of a play—expressed a style that emphasized individual rebellion and subjective introspection. Many of these Romantics interpreted freedom to be more an inner, spiritual phenomenon than a movement for political rights.[7]

Nevertheless, Romanticism in the early nineteenth century also had a political dimension. Inspired by the 1830 Revolution in France, a new generation of German intellectuals, who were identified as **Young Germany**, wrote in opposition to feudalism and absolutism. The death of the poet Goethe in 1832 severed the symbolic chain tying the new generation to the age of classicism. Young German writers were inspired by the social side of Romanticism to chart a more political course for German declarative art, demanding democracy, republicanism, and national unification. Many followed the logic of their radicalism to support the cause of women's rights and expose the exploitation of the German working class in the early days of industrialization. In his poem, 'The Silesian Weavers', Heinrich Heine condemned the Prussian military for their violent suppression of weavers in 1844, the first mass revolt of the German working class.

Heine had been active in the 1830 political revolt in Berlin. Following its failure, he went into exile in Paris, where he became acquainted with the French socialists. Heine was committed to German nationalism, but only in its liberal form. He would respect the colours of the new nationalist flag—red, black, and gold—when it no longer symbolized the blind patriotism of the *Junker* class and the philistinism of the bourgeoisie, and represented instead a modern, liberal Germany, which would become a beacon of freedom for all humanity (Box 8.1).[8]

Before Bismarck forged the unity of the German states, the idea of a German nation embracing all the German-speaking peoples in Central Europe existed only in theory. German nationalism was an important theme in the social thought of Georg Hegel (1770–1831), the most influential social theorist of early nineteenth-century Germany. Hegel attempted to synthesize the many strands of European philosophy. After his death, his theory unwound, inspiring both a right-wing movement for German nationalism under a strong state, and a left-wing revolutionary socialism.

G.W.F. HEGEL

Hegel was born in Stuttgart, the eldest child of a civil servant. His mother was well educated and came from a prominent family. His younger brother, Georg Ludwig, became a soldier and died at a young age fighting in Napoleon's Russian campaign. His sister, Christiane, suffered a mental breakdown and committed suicide in 1832 shortly after her eldest brother's death. Hegel intended to study theology and become a clergyman, entering a seminary at the University of Tübingen in 1788. As a university student, as Wiedmann describes him, Hegel was less than brilliant, avoided physical exercise, was sloppy in his appearance, and appeared to be older than his years. Hegel balked at the strict discipline of the seminary and enjoyed wine, snuff, and the delights of the tavern.[9]

Box 8.1

I shall respect and honor your colors when they deserve it, when they are no longer a pointless and servile triviality. Plant the black-red-gold flag on the heights of German thought, make it the banner of a free humanity, and I will give my heart's blood for it.... I love the Fatherland just as much as you do.

Mankind will rally to the cause of Germany if we complete what the French have begun; if we surpass them in deeds as we have already done in the realm of thought; if we rise to the heights required by the farthest consequences of that thought; if we destroy servitude down to its last hideaway, Heaven; if we save the god that dwells within people on earth from his own degradation; ... if we restore to their proper dignity the poor people disinherited of happiness, genius scorned, and beauty ravished.... [Then] the whole world will become German! Of this mission of Germany and its universal sway I often dream when I walk under oak trees. This is *my* patriotism.

—Heinrich Heine, 'Germany: A Winter's Tale' (1844)

The French Revolution overshadowed all other social issues, and Hegel caught the spirit of revolt, delving deeply into the writings of Rousseau. He adopted a rebellious attitude, paying homage to human rights and the spirit of liberty. Rather than joining the clergy, Hegel continued to study philosophy at Tübingen until 1793 and then found work as a private tutor.

Benefiting from an inheritance after his father's death in 1799, Hegel became financially independent and ready to begin the new century as a professor of philosophy at the University of Jena where, in 1806, he began the publication of his first major work, *The Phenomenology of Mind*. This writing was interrupted by war. In October 1806, the city of Jena fell to Napoleon, who personally led his troops into the captured city. It was an impressive spectacle—Hegel in 1806 called Napoleon a 'world-soul'—and made a profound impression on the young philosopher:

> I saw the Emperor [Napoleon]—that world-soul—riding out to reconnoiter the city; it is truly a wonderful sensation to see such an individual . . . astride a single horse, yet reaching across the world and ruling it. . . .

To make such progress . . . is possible only for this extraordinary man, whom it is impossible not to admire.[10]

The ransacking the French army gave his house, an act that initiated another difficult period in Hegel's life, left at least an equal impression, and this was further punctuated by the birth in 1807 of his illegitimate son by his landlord's wife. Christened Ludwig, Hegel's son was her third illegitimate child. In 1811, Hegel married Marie von Tucher, who was just 20 to Hegel's 41.[11]

In 1812, Hegel published his complex *The Science of Logic*, a work in which he said he had 'demonstrated "God's thoughts prior to creation"'. It was a preposterous claim. In 1816, he resumed his career as a professor of philosophy at the University of Heidelberg, a beautiful city on the banks of the Rhine River. Hegel quickly acquired a reputation for absent-mindedness, Wiedmann claims. According to one anecdote, while walking across campus in a heavy rain, Hegel lost a shoe in the mud but continued to walk, deeply lost in thought and unaware of the missing footwear.[12] Two years later, Hegel's career reached its zenith when he succeeded Fichte as Chair of Philosophy at the

University of Berlin, a part of Germany dominated by the powerful state of Prussia. Hegel proceeded to teach and publish his complex and influential social theory.

Quantitative and Qualitative Changes in Nature

[A]ll small children are potential old men, all sucklings have death within them.
—Hermann Hesse, *Siddhartha* (1922)

For Hegel, **Spirit** (a concept that might be considered analogous to a deity) was a 'being-in-itself' that existed in the absence of time and space; that is, everywhere and always. In a sense, though, this pure mind was also nowhere and nothing. Mind can be conceived in actuality only in opposition to matter. Consequently, Spirit embodied itself in the physical world, which was nature, made to exist in time and space—for Hegel, mind was made real in the objective world.[13] Absolute Spirit and material nature existed separately, in alienation from each other. The only way to overcome this new mode of existence that had been split into two opposites—spirit (mind) and physical existence—was through a being that combined in itself these two opposites. This being was humanity, the unique part of nature that possessed a mind and was capable of developing self-consciousness. Thus began the long process through which the human mind strives to attain full self-awareness or knowledge and overcome the alienation of mind and matter. Spirit seeks to return to itself, to become in Hegel's terms a 'being-in-and-for-itself', through the agency of human consciousness.[14] Having discovered to his own satisfaction the secret of existence, Hegel proceeded to elaborate the 'essence of the universe'.

Hegel intended his theory to apply to all matter, natural as well as social. Reality is, for Hegel, dynamic and ever-changing, driven by an 'inner-directed self movement'[15] to fulfill its destiny. Things are always becoming something other than what they are. In order to understand his evolutionary view of society, we must first consider nature. For Hegel, 'the germ [seed] bears in itself the whole nature of the tree, and the taste and form of its fruits.'[16] You should not simply see something for what it is because within its outward appearance is also what it will become, its potential—a seed is also, ultimately, a tree. To use another example, a tadpole is essentially the immature form of a frog. The frog is inside, inherent within the tadpole. Given the necessary conditions, a tadpole will slowly grow (develop, change) into a specific type of frog and into no other kind of animal or thing. A natural object expands itself in 'a direct, unopposed, unhindered manner', becoming *actually* 'what it was always *potentially*'.[17] What it *will be* may be thought of as being programmed into it as it *is* at a specific time.

While everything changes, there are two kinds of change. Everything changes in small ways, gradually accumulating small differences. Despite these small changes, the thing is still essentially itself. A child, for example, changes daily, however imperceptibly. For years she or he is still a 'child'. These changes within a thing are called **quantitative changes**. Over time, however, the slow accumulation of changes proceeds to the point where the thing is no longer fundamentally the same. The child, for example, becomes an adolescent—hitherto, the adolescent was simply a potential, inherent within the child. The recognition that something has changed fundamentally, from one thing or stage into another thing or stage, is called a **qualitative change**; for example, from the tadpole into a young, immature frog.

When a qualitative change occurs, Hegel says that the previous stage has been 'negated'—it has been transformed into its potential. The frog, then, is a negation of the tadpole. The tadpole, however, was once an embryo—becoming a tadpole was a qualitative change, a **negation** of the embryo (which was once an egg cell and a sperm cell). A frog, then, is a negation of a negation, since the tadpole was itself a negation of the embryo. The sequence of negations, like change, is endless. All of nature follows a pre-programmed plan in an endless cycle of repetition, which unfolds naturally and automatically, guided by Absolute Mind or Spirit.

This process of change is often represented by the process by which a thesis generates an antithesis and produces a synthesis. As things strive to realize their potential, Hegel suggests, there is opposition and conflict. Something is what it is, but it also contains within it the potential to be something else, and the qualitative change is always the result of a conflict between the old and the new. For example, a child is a child but she/he is also potentially an adult. What something is initially may be termed a **thesis**.

The thesis (in the above example, the child) undergoes quantitative changes, growing bigger and stronger, developing a greater capacity to reason, and so on, all attributes that are slowly changing the child in the direction of adulthood. Developing in the child (in the thesis) are attributes that express the potential (the adult). What is growing within the thing, the adult within the child, and is destined to replace it, is the antithesis, representing the potential for something else. Gradually, quantitative changes accumulate in the child, in the programmed direction. There is conflict between the attributes of childhood (the thesis) and the drive to reach the adult stage (the **antithesis**). On the one hand, the developing individual enjoys the lack of responsibility and playfulness of childhood; on the other hand, she or he strives for the independence and privileges of adulthood.[18]

Of course, this conflict is ultimately resolved when a sufficient number and type of quantitative changes have occurred to the point where adulthood becomes dominant. A qualitative change occurs: the passage from child to adult. The child no longer exists or, rather, has been negated by the adult. But the adult still retains within it the characteristics of its previous stage—the child is still within, although the adult is now dominant. The new stage, then, which contains both the vestiges of the old as well as the new, is termed a **synthesis**. A synthesis is a qualitative change; it is also a negation of the previous stage. The synthesis unites the two opposites of the thesis and the antithesis.

Hegel thought that his doctrine of the unity of opposites is demonstrated in nature as well as in human history. In nature it may be exemplified by the theory of colour developed by the German poet, Johann von Goethe (Box 8.2).[19] Nature exists as an indivisible whole and perception strives to reproduce this totality. When we perceive a specific sensation, our retina compensates by generating the opposite, as in a photographic negative. Colours are generated by the interaction of the

---

Box 8.2

In the act which we call seeing, the retina is at one and the same time in different and even opposite states. The greatest brightness, short of dazzling, acts near the greatest darkness. In this state we at once perceive all the intermediate gradations ... and all the varieties of hues. ...

The eye cannot for a moment remain in a particular state determined by the object it looks upon. On the contrary, it is forced to a sort of opposition, which, in contrasting extreme with extreme ... at the same time combines these opposite impressions, and thus ever tends to a whole. ...

It is the universal formula of life which manifests itself in this as in all other cases. When darkness is presented to the eye it demands brightness, and *vice versa*: it shows its vital energy ... precisely by spontaneously tending to an opposite state.

—Goethe, *Theory of Colours* (1840)

opposites, light and darkness. Each colour has an opposite and complementary colour, which 'reciprocally evoke each other' so that 'yellow demands purple; orange, blue; red, green, and *vice versa*'.[20]

The new synthesis, necessarily, does not remain stagnant. Everything changes and new quantitative changes begin to occur immediately, which propel the adult in the direction of old age and ultimately death. The synthesis—the adult—has become a new thesis (what it now *is*). It has a new antithesis (old age) growing within it. Conflict develops between the old (adult) and the new (the incapacities of old age). When the individual reaches old age, it is a realization of the potential of the adult. It is a synthesis because it contains within itself both the changes that have produced the adult as well as the older characteristics of the adolescent and the child, although they recede in importance as new changes accumulate. This is **dialectical** development, in which something assumes a succession of forms, each of which it subsequently transcends.[21]

Dialectical Theory and Social Change

> [W]hat truly exists is, at the same time, an aim that must yet be reached.
> —Georg Simmel, 'The quantitative determinateness of the group' (1917)

The term 'dialectical development' denotes the view that change is progressive and is caused by the conflict of opposites; simply put, the conflict between the thing as it is and the potential inside the thing to be something other than it is. The view that change is inevitable and conflictual, and that the new develops within the old, is the radical 'kernel' in Hegel's dialectical theory, which formed one of the foundations for Marx's theories.

Dialectical theory could also be applied to change in society. Like nature, any given social reality contains within itself a latent 'potentiality striving to realize itself'.[22] Nature exists in 'a perpetually self-repeating cycle' and does not progress over time. Society is unlike nature, Hegel claimed, because human history embodies 'a *real*

capacity for change' towards the better, 'an impulse of *perfectibility*'. Each stage is, by definition, imperfect although less imperfect than the previous stage. But the imperfect 'must not be understood . . . as *only* the imperfect, but as something that involves the very opposite of itself—the so-called perfect—as a germ or impulse.'[23]

Nature is merely cyclical—'the development of the **Idea** in *Space*' through cycles that repeated themselves. History is the spiralling 'development of Spirit in *Time*'.[24] It is not cyclical but ever advancing towards the ultimate, programmed goal, ascending to full self-consciousness. The process by which the inner potential of human society becomes reality is more difficult than in nature, however, because social change is 'mediated by consciousness and will'; that is, humans act in the world to realize their own purposes unaware of any ultimate, divine plan or Idea. Human consciousness is limited to the here and now. Somehow, Spirit must realize itself through the partial and particular actions of conscious human beings who are ignorant of the inner workings of Spirit, of its striving for realization and its ultimate destiny. People act and, unknowingly in the process, Spirit propels human history towards its ultimate goal. Humans are alienated from knowledge of this final goal.

The key achievement of human consciousness was said to be knowledge of freedom, but Hegel did not understood freedom to mean doing whatever you wanted; rather, freedom meant acting on the basis of reason. Reason and freedom did not imply an individual's autonomous choice of any course of action based on his or her personal sense of right or wrong. On the contrary, for Hegel, freedom meant rationally accepting the guidance of existing social institutions and customs, which, in themselves, embodied the fullest expression, at the given time, of human reason. For Hegel, 'The content of what is good or not good, right or not right, is, in ordinary matters of private life, to be determined by the laws and customs of a state.'[25]

Ultimately, human society was evolving along a rational path guided by Spirit or Absolute Mind.

For Hegel, 'reason rules the world, and . . . world history has therefore been rational in its course.'[26] The history of the world is a meaningful progression with a definite and ultimate purpose. Human actions unknowingly help 'realize' an ultimate goal built into the overall plan for society. Above all, this evolutionary progress was directed by world-historical individuals, such as Caesar and Napoleon, who were the agents of the World Spirit acting to help Spirit realize its purpose. Such heroes of an epoch were conscious only of following their own interests and were unaware of 'the general Idea they were unfolding. . . . [T]hey were thinking men, who had an insight into the requirements of the time—*what was ripe for development*', the next, necessary step in the historical sequence. Their action realized 'the very Truth for their age, for their world; the species next in order, so to speak, and which was already formed in the womb of time.'[27]

Others rally around these 'soul-leaders' because they instinctively feel the truth the leader is proclaiming. These heroic individuals may be destructive, but world heroes necessarily sacrifice lesser individuals for the greater good.[28] The Idea works through a special 'cunning of reason' sacrificing its human instruments along the way.[29] Whether any particular strong, passionate, and **charismatic** leader is a world-historical individual who helps realize the next stage of the Idea, or is merely a dangerous criminal or adventurer, depends not merely on whether they 'have willed and accomplished . . . something imagined and projected' but, rather, whether they have accomplished 'something correct and necessary'.[30] Only time could determine whether they were heroes, pushing history forward, Hegel said, or villains vandalizing flower beds: '[S]o mighty a form [as the world-historical individual] must trample down many an innocent flower underfoot—crush to pieces many an object in its path.'[31]

The development of human society, Hegel supposed, was different from the cyclical movement of nature. First, the direction of social evolution was through various stages, each of which was always higher than the one before; that is, in society, social change was progressive. The evolution of society was always upward; each stage was more rational and better than the one before, closer to the ultimate goal of absolute reason.

Second, unlike nature, humans possessed reason. They did not possess ultimate reason; only Spirit or the Absolute Mind knew everything. But humans were able to understand or know (more or less) three things. They were aware of the past; they could understand the present; and they were able to use their imaginations to think about something that did not yet exist—the future. Humans were able to understand that, within the present, there was also potentially something new—the seeds of the new stage for society were already growing in the old. Humans could imagine this potential change.

Humans also possessed the capacity to act on the basis of their reason. In acting in society, humans could try to bring society back to an earlier stage, as the conservative Bonald had hoped to do in France after the Revolution. They could act to try to keep things the way they were, to preserve the status quo, as conservatives generally did, in which case they could be regarded as representing the thesis. Finally, they could try to bring change, to help realize the new stage that, at the moment, was only a potential within the old. By giving humans self-consciousness, Spirit makes the process of its unfolding a difficult and protracted development: 'Spirit is at war with itself.'[32] What actually happened in society was the result of the conflict among these groups of people. Social change occurred, for Hegel, because people caused it to change through their actions.

Nevertheless, for Hegel, the path of social change was still programmed by Spirit. So, when humans struggled and tried to reverse, slow down, or accelerate social change, they were unknowingly pushing society along a general path that had already been determined. Because of the intervention of human reason and human action, the evolution of society was never as neat and uncomplicated as the dialectical changes in nature, which proceeded blindly towards its goal. The actual path of social change was irregular and uncertain, sometimes towards the ultimate goal, sometimes away from it. In the words of the French conservative, Chauteaubriand (1768–1848), some refuse to flow along with the river of destiny, either leaping impetuously ahead or lingering behind:

> Each age is a river that sweeps us along according to the inclination of destinies when we surrender ourselves to them. . . . Some have traversed it impetuously and hurled themselves onto the opposite bank. Others have remained on this side. . . . The two parties shout and insult each other. . . . Thus, the former transport us . . . into imaginary perfections, by making us go beyond our age, the latter keep us behind, refusing to be enlightened and wanting to remain men of the fourteenth century. . . .[33]

Hegel believed, however, that inevitably the evolution of society would be brought on track and lead to the higher, next programmed stage.

Change was slow, developmental, and evolutionary, Hegel said. As society changes slowly over time, traditions evolve and become ever more rational, ever more reasonable. The traditions that existed at any time were the sum total of all past reason. The liberals were right to assume that existing traditions or laws were not as rational as they could be, or would later be, but wrong to conclude they were simply irrational. For Hegel, what is real *is* rational, and what is rational *is* real.

This appears to be a profoundly conservative statement, endorsing the status quo and the existing, anti-liberal Prussian government. Hegel was accused of being a willing spokesman and apologist for absolute power. For Hegel, 'Understanding that which is, is the task of philosophy.'[34] As many critics have objected, this statement denies Hegel's own theory of never-ending change. Hegel, his critics charged, bowed down before existing reality. He had argued that 'theory never marches at the head of reality; it always lags behind.'[35] Arguably, however, since Absolute Mind is embodied in the existing world and ultimately determines the direction of change, the

purpose of theory is not to help determine what *should* be true in the future and guide humanity in its efforts to achieve this end; rather, the purpose of theory is to understand what *is* true in the present. In the hands of Marx, dialectical theory would be given the first, alternative emphasis.[36]

Hegel's Theory of the State

Hegel rejected the liberal view that there was ever a pre-social human being. Human beings were always and everywhere social. Society was not the rational construction of naturally asocial creatures. For Hegel, since love and procreation were natural, the earliest and original form of society was the family. Families combined to form a nation, or a people based on shared language, consciousness, and culture.[37]

In nineteenth-century European society, individuals worked together and competed in the market economy, which Hegel termed **civil society**. Civil society was the realm of individual or private interests that were pursued in capitalist economics. According to McCarney, Hegel recognized two problems that the system of capitalism generated in modern society. One was the tendency to polarize social classes, as great wealth accumulated at one social pole and abject poverty at the other. Hegel's theory could suggest no solution to this problem within the economic system itself. The second tendency was for private interests to gain a monopoly of influence over the government, obliging the state to represent their special interests rather than the general good of everyone.[38]

Part of Hegel's inability to find a solution to the problems of capitalism within the economic sphere was his insistence that the foundation for human freedom was the ownership of private property. Although Hegel believed that everyone 'ought to have property', he believed that it was right that some owned more than others.[39] As Plant argued,[40] Hegel knew that economic forces in modern society were undermining traditional communities and creating in their place a plethora of private, individualistic, and competing interests. The simple society of small owners who produced their own means of subsistence and exchanged any excess for other types of goods had long since disappeared. By Hegel's time, capitalism was an aggressive economic form, the necessary stage that history had reached in its dialectical development.

Although capitalism undermined social unity, as the conservatives had claimed, it also had a positive side. Private property and capitalism formed the indispensable foundation for individual freedom. Private property implied mutual recognition of everyone's right to ownership, which was then written in law.[41] Furthermore, in an exchange economy, an individual's needs had to be met by exchanging goods with others, creating a new type of dependent community. For Hegel, capitalism generated a new form of social order within the agreed-upon laws that regulated property rights and economic exchange.

Yet, as Hegel recognized, modern capitalism was erratic and volatile, analogous to a wild animal that requires 'permanent curbing and control'.[42] Hegel rejected the liberal theory of laissez-faire capitalism. The state must represent the interests of all and control the natural tendency to excessive individualism. Such an interventionist, modern state was being developed in Prussia.[43] The state, Hegel claimed, is an organized political entity that unifies a group of people under a single set of laws, reflecting the highest development of human rationality, self-consciousness, and justice. The state embodies the fullest expression of individual freedom, which supposes a unity between one's actions and the existing social laws and conventions.[44] In Hegel's view, a viable state had to exist above and separate from civil society so that it could represent the interests of the whole, rather than any particular social group. The state was the social institution that most clearly embodied the highest level of human consciousness, reflected in its laws and institutions.

Hegel's complex philosophy, Shirer argues, embraces the idea that the state is the dominant institution in society, having the 'supreme right against the individual, whose supreme duty is to be a member of the State'. For Hegel, long periods of peace corrupt the people: 'War is the great purifier.'

The state accomplishes world-historical deeds and these must take precedence over the 'litany of private virtues—modesty, humility, philanthropy and forbearance'. These virtues may have a place among the life of individuals, but they are not the standards by which the state must be held accountable.[45] Thus, the morality of the state is not the same as the morality of the individual. The needs of the state take precedence over the needs, the happiness, and the rights of the individual.

There was an additional tendency in civil society that Hegel incorporated in his theory. At least since Adam Smith, political economists had recognized the damaging and limiting effects of the modern capitalist division of labour on the individual working person. Modern capitalist labour, Hegel concluded, was 'stupefying, unhealthy and insecure'.[46] Hegel's solution was for individuals to form associations to represent their collective interests in civil society. Civil society was not simply the arena for individual competition, all against all, as liberal theory imagined; rather, groups of people with similar interests joined together to better meet their common objectives. Civil society was split into a number of competing, powerful groups that Hegel called **corporations**. A trade union was a 'corporation'; so, too, was an organization of bankers, as well as organizations formed by industrialists, civil servants, independent crafts workers, and peasant-owners.

The corporations that composed civil society competed with each other in the economic sphere. Hegel believed that each corporation represented a necessary social group—society needed farmers, workers, bankers, soldiers, and so on—but that there was danger to society if one group assumed too much power over the state. An overly powerful corporation would unfairly disadvantage other groups, bringing conflict and disorder. Consequently, society required a third institution, above families and corporations, to regulate these groups and to ensure fair competition so that all the needs of civil society were met. This institution was the state. For Hegel, the state should be distinct from and above any of the corporations, acting as a neutral referee with respect to any single group of corporations while having as its fundamental interest the good of all society. As Plant stresses, Hegel's interventionist state was limited in its role, the better to allow the maximum freedom for the individual. The state's role would include reducing the harmful effects of poverty by fixing a fair price for the necessities of life, reducing commercial conflict by arbitrating disputes, and disseminating useful information.[47]

The state was not to become a corporation unto itself, in which case it would make laws only for the benefit of the government groups; nor was it to be overly influenced by any one corporation. For Hegel, it was difficult to achieve the best form of the state. On the one hand, a monarchy could be independent of the particular individual or corporate interests in civil society and at least theoretically be able to put the interests of the whole nation first. The danger of monarchy was political despotism, although the development of Western political traditions made tyranny unlikely, Hegel thought.

The modern alternative appeared to be direct democracy. Hegel believed the French Revolution had demonstrated that direct, popular democracy was unworkable. Still, Hegel's concern for individual freedom meant that a state must incorporate some form of representative political power, although he rejected universal suffrage—one person, one vote—as so diluted as to be meaningless.[48] For Hegel, the state should include a separation of powers, including a constitutional monarchy and representation from below. Ultimately, what would work was a legislative assembly representing the various corporations, not the individual interests of single people, to mediate between the particular interests in civil society and the universal interest represented by the state.[49]

Overall, however, Hegel was not a practical social reformer. He had no sympathy for those who criticized existing institutions, who rejected the 'is' for an 'ought', even when the present was condemned as unreasonable or unjust. Those who were in 'open revolt against the actual condition of the world' were severely limited in their vision to the here and now and did not understand the Reason that undergirds the whole.[50] Hegel confined his concerns to philosophy and to the present, emphasizing the essential conservatism of his social theory. As Hegel put the case, 'The insight . . . to which . . . philosophy is to lead us, is, that the real world is as it ought to be.'[51]

Hegel's critics complained that by making such statements, he actually supported the Prussian government of his day, which paid his salary as a professor. His theory led to the conclusion that the Prussian state represented the highest stage in the development of society—an apparently static and ultimately nationalistic conclusion. By implying that history had come to an end—having culminated in the present form of the anti-liberal German state—Hegel had contradicted his dialectical theory. From his point of view, the state represented the highest development Reason had achieved on the path to self-consciousness. Marx would later argue that no matter how reasonable the idea of a neutral state above civil society sounded in theory, in practice each state had always been controlled by the economically dominant class and passed laws that expressed the interests of this dominant class against other, subordinate, classes.

For Hegel, theory could understand the stages of development through which society and nature passed. The process itself, however, was uncertain and fraught with conflict and uncertainty. As an individual, Hegel knew his end was certain, though not the precise details through which Spirit realized its purpose. The last stage of his own life must have appeared unprogrammed. In the summer of 1831, a cholera epidemic swept into Berlin from the east. When Hegel died, quickly and unexpectedly in the fall, it was initially attributed to cholera, though Wiedmann argues that Hegel's death was caused by a severe and chronic stomach ailment that had made him ill, periodically, for the last five years of his life.[52]

Hegel was the dominant social theorist in Germany for about a decade after his death in 1831. His followers were soon divided into conservative and radical camps. One tendency was to interpret Hegelianism in spiritual terms, whether Christian or pagan. The Christian Hegelians defined Hegel's Spirit as consistent with God, who existed always and had consciously planned and created the world. In their hands, Hegel's theory became fundamentally deterministic, as humanity fulfilled God's design and would ultimately be merged once again with the deity. The spiritualist view of Hegel's theory was that Spirit existed only in nature and was not conscious of itself, a view consistent with the ancient **pantheism**—spirit existed in everything, from the most humble insect to the great forces of nature. Humans became aware of this pervasive spirituality only through the dialectical development of consciousness. While evolution naturally followed the dance steps of the dialectic, the future was not knowable in the present.

Hegelianism was also interpreted in terms of nationalism. While Hegel clearly believed he knew God's thoughts, the self-consciousness of Spirit was not simply embodied in an individual's mind but, rather, was elaborated over time through the evolution of ideas and the emergence of society, reaching its highest point in the development of the state. As humans became increasingly self-conscious, Hegel reasoned, they developed a sense of their common identity in the nation and constructed an institution—the national state or government—to give expression to this national consciousness. With the development of the state, human consciousness came the closest to Absolute Spirit and, for Hegel, the Prussian state was the closest to this ideal.

Hegel's theory had grown in the soil of German national and cultural pride. Following his death, many of Hegel's followers developed the theme of German nationalism further than had Hegel. German nationalism emerged as an increasingly potent force in the nineteenth and twentieth centuries, fuelled in part by Hegel's paradoxical belief that the state is the fullest expression of human self-consciousness and freedom. In Hegel's social theory, liberalism and nationalism maintained a fragile and sometimes contradictory marriage. The potent combination of German

nationalism and statism would not unfold its full potential until the 1920s and 1930s.

An alternative interpretation of Hegel's legacy emphasized the radical implications of the dialectic, focusing on the inevitability of conflict and change. This interpretation was developed and was expressed by the left, or **Young Hegelians**, many of whom were atheists and revolutionaries. Among the latter group was Ludwig Feuerbach (1804–72), who had been a student in the University of Berlin.

LUDWIG FEUERBACH

'God is merely the projected essence of [humanity].'
—Ludwig Feuerbach, *The Essence of Christianity* (1841)

Feuerbach studied theology and then philosophy, seeking a teaching post in Germany. His career as a university professor was seriously damaged by his atheism, publicly expressed in 1837 and then, more fully, in 1841 in *The Essence of Christianity*.[53] In this, his best-known work, Feuerbach developed a theory of the deity as humanly constructed, a materialist interpretation in contrast to Hegel's idealism.

> The purpose of my writings . . . is: to change men from theologians into anthropologists, from lovers of god into lovers of humanity, from candidates for the afterlife into students of the here and now . . . into free, self-confident citizens of the earth. . . . [F]rom believers into thinkers, from pray-ers into workers . . . from Christians—who . . . are half-angel, half-animal—into men, into whole men.[54]

Feuerbach accepted the viewpoint of philosophical materialism, that an individual's characteristics and mind were determined by and the product of forces operating in his or her environment. *The Essence of Christianity*, in which he elaborated an atheistic interpretation of religion, was the most important application of Feuerbach's materialism. Feuerbach argued that Hegel's view of the relationship between 'Spirit' (a deity or god) and the real world was upside down. For Hegel, Absolute Mind had come first and had then embodied itself in the world—a doctrine consistent with Christian creationism. This **idealism**, Feuerbach believed, was wrong. Rather, Hegel had to be stood on his head because the process was the reverse; that is, humans existed first and the idea of God was a human invention. What is termed knowledge of God, Feuerbach maintains, is humanity's knowledge of itself. '[R]eligion is the solemn unveiling of man's hidden treasures', it is 'the alienation of man from himself'.[55] For Feuerbach, the human image of the Divine Being was only a mirror reflection of the real nature of humanity; that is, 'human nature purified, freed from the imperfections of the human individual, projected into the outside, and therefore viewed and revered as a different and distinct being with a nature of its own.'[56] God is the projected image of the perfect human, and Feuerbach's purpose was to turn the love of God into the love of humanity.[57]

To be consistent with his materialism, according to which the environment causes certain ideas to be formed, Feuerbach had to explain why this particular idea of God had arisen in human consciousness. Religion, he declared, was 'the childlike condition of humanity'.[58] Humans lived in an imperfect world where 'things are not what they ought to be', where people were severely alienated from their true potential. The image they created of a 'god' was simply a reflection of humanity's potential perfection. Religion is essentially the projection of dream images, but not of the unattainable; rather, it is the mirror image of the life that is possible to build on earth. By setting perfection in the spiritual rather than the material world, the belief in the afterlife hindered humanity in its earthly pursuit of the just and wholesome life: 'Religion sacrifices reality to the projected dream.'[59] It was ironic, as novelist Elizabeth Inchbald pointed out, that Christian doctrine held that everyone was equal in the sight of God, but that God was presumed to have ordained inequality on earth (Box 8.3).[60]

What is called revelation or the word of God springs directly from human consciousness. For the ordinary person, moral laws are most effective when they have the force of external compulsion,

---

Box 8.3

Anglican Dean: 'There are in society . . . rich and poor; the poor are born to serve the rich.'
Henry: 'But suppose the poor would not serve them?'

'Then they must starve. . . . Is that a hard condition? or if it were, they will be rewarded in a better world than this.'

'Is there a better world than this?'. . .

'The world to come . . . where we shall go after death; and there no distinction will be made between rich and poor—all persons there will be equal.'

'Aye, now I see what makes it a better world than this. But cannot this world try to be as good as that?'

'In respect to placing all persons on a level, it is utterly impossible—God has ordained it otherwise.'

'How! has God ordained a distinction to be made, and will not make any himself?'

The dean did not proceed in his instructions; he now began to think . . . that the boy was too young, or too weak, to comprehend the subject.

—Elizabeth Inchbald, *Nature and Art* (1796)

when they are perceived as the expression of a divine will. Ordinary people do not perceive any 'universal objective power' merely in their own conscience and rationality; rather, they must project these laws onto a separate, personal, and divine being. In this imaginative process, humanity 'involuntarily objectifies' its 'inner nature and represents it as existing outside of' itself.[61] This tendency of humans to take something of their own creation and then worship it as if it were more powerful than humanity is termed **reification**.

People, however, are not aware that they are doing this. Having unconsciously created a God, they then proceeded to worship this offspring of their own mind. It follows that, when humans are able actually to reach their true potential, it will no longer be necessary to worship an image of their perfect selves. At that point, when alienation ceases, so, too, will religion.

If religion presented a reified image of human potential, how was humanity actually to attain this perfection in the real world? How could the evil conditions of life be overcome and the objective basis for a belief in the supernatural be dissolved? Feuerbach had no practical, no political or economic, answer to the question of actual social change. Instead, he had recourse to the foremost injunction of Christian ethics: universal love. For Feuerbach, humanity is to be loved for the sake of humanity. A person is an object of love because he or she 'is a rational and loving being. This is the moral law of the species, the law of intelligence.' The person who, like Christ, 'rises to the love of the species, to that universal love which alone is adequate to the nature of the species', is a Christian, 'is Christ himself; he does what Christ did.' An individual's love for humanity as a whole must 'become the first and the highest law. . . . This is the highest law of ethics.'[62] In the end, then, Feuerbach became a Christian preacher in the absence of Christianity.

Feuerbach and Marx

Karl Marx, another of the Young Hegelians, was influenced by Feuerbach's materialism and atheistic arguments and, as well, by the view that humans existed in a state of alienation. Marx, however, worked out his own theory, which combined elements of materialism with what he considered to be the radical insights of Hegel. His notes on Feuerbach were collected and published after his death as Marx's *Theses on Feuerbach*.

From one perspective, Marx had argued that Feuerbach, the proponent of materialism, was not materialist enough. Marx's disagreement with Feuerbach was largely about how social change occurs. Like most social theorists, Feuerbach assumed that, having discovered the truth, it was enough to teach the new truth to others who would be able to grasp it. Social change involved a change, first, in the human heart; hence, his injunction to love humanity as a whole. To simplify, Feuerbach's task was to understand the world and share this understanding with others. This was not a complete recipe for social change, Marx believed. In his final and eleventh point (or thesis) on Feuerbach, Marx stated: 'The philosophers have *interpreted* the world, in various ways; the point however is to *change* it.'[63] This oft-quoted epigram is as much a critique of Hegel, who had argued exactly the opposite case, as it is of Feuerbach. Feuerbach's strategy for change was essentially idealistic, Marx argued. People were to be exposed to the truths of their condition by the power of thought and argument. They would be convinced, come to see things differently, then act differently, and change their circumstances in the process. Change originated in ideas and consisted, above all, in changing people's ways of thinking.

Social theories up to then, Marx said, including Feuerbach's, had simply attempted to understand the world. If the goal of social theory was to change the world, Feuerbach's idealism was insufficient. Certainly, Marx agreed, ideas were an important part of the process of social change. To bring change you needed social theory to provide an understanding of the world as it is. But you won't know whether your theory is close to 'truth' unless you actually use it to bring social change, that is, put the theory into revolutionary practice. If the theory fails to bring change or does not bring the desired change, then the theory is seriously flawed. Through a theory of **practice** the objective circumstances of social structure can be connected with someone's subjective understanding. Marx summarized these ideas in his second and third propositions on Feuerbach (Box 8.4).[64]

By 'revolutionary practice' Marx meant that theory is only useful if it guides people in successfully bringing the social change they desire. Once theory is implemented and reality changed, then the theory can be refined and made more accurate. Marx's life work, then, was directed at developing theory and putting it into practice.

According to Marx, both idealism and materialism developed one side of the dialectic of humanity but failed to connect them. As he stated in another context, history is made by active people, a point that Feuerbach's materialism denies. The main problem with any form of determinism is that it treats people as though they are only passive objects, worked upon by external forces over which they have no control. Rather than being *creative* beings, humans are entirely *created* in the deterministic view. In addition, however, people act always on the basis of where they are—their objective reality. They are born into an existing world and have to make choices and take action based on their objective circumstances. People make history, Marx concluded; however, they do not do so from thin air, but only on the basis of the opportunities and constraints presented by real life—not in circumstances of their own choosing. The materialists, including Feuerbach, had left out the creative side of humanity, just as the idealists had ignored the actual structure of social life that is independent of anyone's will and shapes his or her ability to act.

From Hegel the Young Hegelians derived an emphasis on social change: that any given status quo is not going to remain unchanged but is destined to be altered. The seeds of the 'yet-to-be' are planted and grow within the womb of the old. This whole viewpoint contradicts any notion that any given state—in particular the nineteenth-century Prussian state—had reached the final point of social evolution. Ultimately, according to the dialectical outlook, there was no end point other than to be one with Absolute Mind. The second point deriving from Hegel's dialectical theory is that the actual agent of social change is human action—individuals act and bring about social change. Third, the process of social change is conflictual—social conflict is fundamental and even necessary to society; conflict acts as the midwife of the new. These observations indicate the 'radical' kernel of Hegel's thought.

The radical interpretation of Hegelian theory bore the longest-lasting fruit. The relationship between Hegel and Karl Marx has been much debated in social theory. Marx called his theory 'historical materialism', which implies an elaboration

---

Box 8.4

The question whether objective truth can be attributed to human thinking is not a question of theory but is a practical question. In practice man must prove the truth—i.e. the reality and power, the 'this-sidedness' of his thinking. The dispute over the reality or non-reality of thinking which is isolated from practice is a purely scholastic question.

The materialist doctrine that men are products of circumstances and upbringing ... forgets that circumstances are changed precisely by men and that the educator must himself be educated. . . .

The coincidence [coming together] of the changing of circumstances and of human activity can only be conceived and rationally understood as revolutionary practice.

—Karl Marx, *Theses on Feuerbach* (1845)

on Feuerbach, who had turned Hegel on his head. Yet Marx criticized Feuerbach for being overly deterministic, for forgetting that people make history. They are not mere marionettes controlled by environmental forces of which they are barely aware. Hegel had recognized the important role of human action in realizing historical development, though he had ascribed the creative action of social change to world-heroes and traced the evolution of society through the conflict and synthesis of ideas. Marx's closest collaborator, Friedrich Engels, called Marx's theory 'dialectical materialism', by which he meant to convey that Marxism was a synthesis of idealism and materialism, but the latter played the principal role. After Marx's death, historical materialism was interpreted as a form of positivism, a social science that elaborated the laws of historical development and predicted the future. This was the dominant view of Marxism that persisted well into the twentieth century. By the 1920s and 1930s, social theorists in Europe were reinterpreting Marx through the lens of his early, philosophical writings.

KARL MARX

> '[T]he theory of the communists may be summed up in the single sentence: Abolition of private property.'
> —Karl Marx and Friedrich Engels, *The Communist Manifesto* (1848)

Karl Marx (1818–83) lived and wrote entirely in the nineteenth century. The roots of his ideas, though, can be found in the century before, in the Romantic writings of Rousseau, in the rationalism of liberalism and the Enlightenment, and in the upheavals of the French Revolution. For most of the twentieth century, Marx was an important social and political influence. His theories are being revived in the twenty-first century as a potent antidote for the contemporary acquiescence to aggressive capitalism and the accompanying pessimism about human potential.

The son of a Jewish lawyer, Marx was born in a respectable middle-class family. Ideologically, Marx was influenced by his father, who was born

Herschel Levi. A rationalist and a 'perfectibilian',[65] Levi was inspired by the ideals of Voltaire and Rousseau. Out of practical necessity, he converted to Lutheranism in 1817 and adopted the surname Marx. Herschel Marx's beliefs were rooted in the Enlightenment doctrine that humans were born naturally good and equally capable of attaining reason, but were diverted from their goodness by unnatural barriers created by society. Human reason, however, would reveal the truths about the fallacies that held human progress back; reason would expose the priests and the aristocracy as nothing more than the agents behind social evils. In the new, enlightened age, humans would be equal not merely in law but socially and politically.[66] To this liberal, rationalist core of thought that Marx learned at home, his neighbour (and eventual father-in-law), Ludwig von Westphalen, broadened young Marx's intellectual horizons, inspiring a lifelong love of learning. For the young Marx, this meant becoming 'a devoted reader of the new romantic literature'.[67]

As was the case for many sons of the salaried middle class, in 1835 Marx entered the Faculty of Law at the University of Bonn, although he attended a variety of lectures, including discussion of Homer, mythology, poetry, and art. Again, like many middle-class young men, he carried on an active social life, got into debt, duelled, and was arrested at least once for 'disturbing the peace of the night with drunken noise' and riotous behaviour.[68] He preferred art and literature to the study of law and wrote a number of romantic poems. Had these more romantic inclinations remained unchanged, Marx's name would have been erased from history—as would Shakespeare's had he been only an actor.

Marx's life changed dramatically in his second year of university when he transferred to the University of Berlin, at the political and intellectual centre of Germany. Hegel, the contemporary giant of German philosophy, had died a few years before (in 1831) but his legacy dominated intellectual and political debate. Inevitably, Marx was drawn to philosophy and resolved on becoming a scholar and university lecturer. He wrote a dissertation on the debates in Greek philosophy around such fundamental dualisms as free will and determinism, and materialism and idealism. Marx was grappling with the central ideas that still divided philosophers in the nineteenth century. If at this early stage he emphasized the role of human consciousness in bringing social change, Marx was actually working towards a revolutionary synthesis of these philosophical opposites.

He soon found, however, that he would not be able to do this as a university lecturer. He had hoped to get a post at the University of Bonn, but there was no secure academic future for someone with Marx's radical views. Marx turned his hand, instead, to journalism, an insecure way to make a living for his young family. Marx had married Jenny von Westphalen, the daughter of a Prussian official, in 1843 following an engagement that lasted seven years. His poor economic prospects hindered their marriage, but there were also class and religious differences—Jenny's family was aristocratic and Christian. Jenny was a well-educated woman who became closely involved in Marx's writing and politics. She shared a difficult life with her revolutionary husband, spending most of it in exile in London.[69] They had six children. Two daughters did not survive past their first birthdays. A son, Edgar, died of tuberculosis at the age of nine in his father's arms. Three daughters—Jenny, Laura, and Eleanor—survived. After Edgar's death, Marx transferred his keenest affection to his youngest daughter, Eleanor (nicknamed Tussy). He also transferred affections of a less reputable kind to Lenchen Demuth, their housekeeper, who bore a son in 1851. Marx was the father. While Jenny knew of this scandal, she did not divulge it to her daughters. Marx's close friend and collaborator, Friedrich Engels, accepted the role of the illegitimate father to protect the reputation of the Marx household, a role he revealed only on his deathbed.[70]

Marx's infidelity may have been an aberration. His daughters' lives, however, often verged on melodrama. Young Jenny died in 1883, two years after her mother and only a few months before her father. The fate of his last two daughters, Eleanor and Laura, suggests they had learned equal measures of Romanticism and rationalism in the Marx household. Eleanor lived with her English socialist lover, Edward Aveling, both before and after the death in 1892 of his wife. Although Aveling was an unfaithful lover to Eleanor as well, she repeatedly and romantically forgave him. Finally she learned he had married another woman, secretly and under a pseudonym. In despair and humiliation, she and an apparently contrite Aveling agreed to commit suicide together. When the time came, Aveling excused himself, saying he had to conduct some business in town. Eleanor carried on alone. She dressed all in white (in imitation of the suicide of the fictional Emma Bovary), retired to her bedroom, and took prussic acid. Marx's last surviving daughter, Laura, also committed suicide, jointly with her husband, Paul Lafargue, in 1911. In their final note the couple explained they wanted to avoid growing old and senile and becoming a burden on others.[71]

The Young Hegelians

These tragic events would unfold after Marx's death. While he was still engaged to Jenny, writing romantic poems that she alone appreciated and giving up the idea of an academic career, the young Marx found an outlet for his creative talents in philosophy. Serious writing meant that Marx had to deal with the idealistic philosophy of Hegel. There were many aspects of Hegel's doctrine he found very attractive. It was rationalistic, emphasized the interconnectedness of things, focused on the inevitability of change and conflict, and embodied the notion of human perfectibility.

Marx joined the Young Hegelians, who gathered in the lecture halls and taverns of Berlin to debate philosophy. From the many springs that fed Romanticism, the Young Hegelians drew the image of a future, perfectible humanity, freed from the alienation experienced in the world. Feuerbach had argued that, instead of striving to realize their potential in the real world, humans had invented an image of a perfect being—something they called God—and had invented a picture of a harmonious relationship between people and nature—something they called heaven. God and heaven were only real in the sense that they derived from and gave expression to humanity's own potential perfectibility. In short, they were creations of the human imagination and they expressed the degree to which humans were alienated from their potential by the modes of thought they developed to understand the world, particularly religion.

Humanity could overcome its alienation by understanding and criticizing the modes of thought—the social theories—that were part of this alienated existence. The Young Hegelians were engaged in what we would now term 'consciousness-raising', intellectual debate and writing designed to uncover the true relationships between people and the world. It was necessary to expose religion as false idealism and substitute a thoroughgoing materialism. Human emancipation was an intellectual process. What was needed was to understand the world differently and then act on the basis of this new understanding to change social life. Exposing humanity's alienation from its true potential would necessarily lead to overcoming that alienation and achieving that potential.

Since humanity was alienated by virtue of false images, projections, and thoughts, criticism was the tool of liberation—destroy the created, false gods and reveal the true 'god-like' nature of humanity. For Marx, however, criticism was not enough. In fact, criticism alone was bound to fail. For all his proclaimed radical materialism, Marx argued, Feuerbach's conception of social change remained thoroughly idealistic

The fundamental question was this: Why would concrete human beings abandon their illusions and come to believe the truth about their own perfectibility? Marx's materialism led him to the conclusion that 'Life is not determined by consciousness, but consciousness by life'—thinking derived from concrete life experiences.[72] The kind of thinking that would be derived from an alienated existence was precisely the kind of consciousness that humanity actually had, full of illusions, projections, and errors. It was not enough to try to change false ideas; it was necessary to change the real-life conditions that made false ideas necessary, the actual state of existence that continually regenerated them, time after time, despite the best efforts of the critics, or the consciousness-raisers.

Marx concluded that the purpose of philosophy was to change the world. For real social change you needed two things. Certainly there was a role for philosophy (social theory)—a real, materialistic understanding of the world and the relationships between people within it—a theory that would criticize the alienated existence and envisage the future perfectibility of humanity. Marx's theoretical work focused on developing this revolutionary theory. Social theory (philosophy), for Marx, was the 'intellectual weapon of human emancipation. . . . [O]nce the lightning of thought has penetrated deeply into this virgin soil of the people, [they] will emancipate themselves.'[73]

Marx and the Proletariat

Social theory, alone, was not enough. It would be necessary to add action to ideas. Social change required, in addition to theory, a group of people who could grasp the theory, whose life experiences it made comprehensible. Theorists of the past had made the mistake of assuming that some relatively privileged class would be the authors of the new society. Fourier, for example, had expected that his plans for a socialist future would be implemented by small property owners, independent crafts workers, and peasant landowners. But the petty bourgeoisie were more interested in preserving their own property or converting it into large property. At best, they could hope for no more than to turn the clock back to a world where small property owners predominated, a world Marx realized was quickly vanishing.

Robert Owen (1771–1858), the Welsh social reformer and industrialist, on the other hand, did accept that machine industry was here to stay. He directed his appeals for social change to the manufacturing class in the hopes that they would realize the general social benefits to be achieved by co-operative ownership and democracy. But the manufacturing class had their noses to the grindstone of daily commerce and could see no further than their short-term profits. They would reform the capitalist system only when the pressure from below became so strong that they had no choice but to make small concessions to their workers. As for the Young Hegelians, they directed their consciousness-raising to the educated elite.

Marx reasoned, aside from a few exceptional individuals within it (such as Owen), the elite, whether propertied or merely educated, actually benefited materially from the existing society. As a group, they had no real interest in bringing about fundamental social change. In Marx's mind, everyone—even the elite—required liberation from their alienated existence, but not every social group was equally alienated, equally oppressed, equally **exploited** within the existing social order. What was necessary was a social group, a class of people, so alienated, so debased, so oppressed that they *needed* a revolution. It was not a matter of *choosing* to be revolutionary; what mattered was being put in a *material* position where only a revolution could allow them to meet their immediate needs.

In his mid-twenties, Marx identified the industrial **proletariat** (the working class) as this revolutionary subject. As a class of people, the proletariat had nothing. They had lost any independent property they may have owned and were unable to make a living on their own. The working class was forced to agree to accept a wage labour contract in which they sold (perhaps more descriptively rented) their creative energies to a capitalist, who thereafter controlled their productive activities. The proletariat was alienated in all ways possible—from their own property, from control over their working life, from the products they created (which were owned and disposed of by the capitalist). As industrial production proceeded, the proletariat was alienated even from its own creative skills as labour was divided ever more thoroughly until each worker became specialized in only one minute part of a complex productive chain, becoming little more than a machine, a broken spoke in an immense wheel, as Flora Tristan found them during her study of conditions in England (Box 8.5).[74] More than any other human beings, the individual members of the proletariat were alienated from their own human potential.

The alienation of the proletariat was not merely an idea; alienation was the daily reality of a growing proportion of the population. What is more, under the competitive laws of capitalism, the material living conditions of the proletariat were being reduced to the lowest limit. Wages were as low as they could get; working conditions were intolerable; the hours of work were excessively long; all members of the proletarian family, including children, were being forced into wage labour. And then, when it seemed that the life of

---

Box 8.5

Most workers lack clothing, bed, furniture, fuel, wholesome food—even potatoes! They spend from twelve to fourteen hours each day shut up in low-ceilinged rooms where with every breath of foul air they absorb fibres of cotton, wool or flax, or particles of copper, lead or iron. They live suspended between an insufficiency of food and an excess of strong drink; they are all wizened, sickly and emaciated; their bodies are thin and frail, their limbs frail, their complexions frail, their eyes dead. They look as if they all suffer from consumption. It is painful to see the expression on their faces.

—Flora Tristan, 'Factory workers' (1840)

the proletarian was reduced as far as humanly possible, competitive capitalism made matters worse by introducing new technology to reduce labour costs. As new machines were brought in the front door of the expanding factories, workers were being tossed out the back. The results were unemployment and poverty. It was not a poverty that was 'naturally existing', wrote Marx, but a poverty 'artificially produced' by industrial capitalism.[75] The real emancipation of humanity could be carried out, Marx wrote, only by:

> [a] class in civil society that is not a class of civil society, . . . a sphere of society which has a universal character because its sufferings are universal, and which does not claim a *particular redress* because the wrong which is done to it is not a *particular wrong* but *wrong in general*. . . . [A] sphere of society which claims no *traditional* status but only a *human status* . . . which is, in short, a *total loss* of humanity and which can only redeem itself by a *total redemption of humanity*. This, . . . as a particular class, is the *proletariat*.[76]

The emancipation of the proletariat from the existing society is the precondition for the complete emancipation of all of humanity, Marx concluded. For Marx, 'Philosophy is the *head* of this emancipation and the *proletariat* is its *heart*.'[77]

Marx arrived at this position by theorizing. His was a deduction, but it also reflected the growing class conflict he perceived, even in Germany on the threshold of the Industrial Revolution where weavers had initiated working-class revolt in 1844. The poet Heinrich Heine commemorated their struggle, imagining them weaving a death shroud with a 'threefold curse in it' for religious hypocrisy, the miserly rich, and the ignorant patriot (Box 8.6).[78] The fundamental role of the industrial proletariat as the genuine revolutionary class was a position Marx would consistently maintain at the core of his theory. His empirical studies and the subsequent elaborations of his theory served to confirm the revolutionary role of the proletariat.

The Proletariat and Revolution

Two thorny issues that Marx had to confront after proclaiming that the industrial working class would be the authors of their own liberation— and, in the process, emancipate humanity—were these: (1) the question of how the proletariat would develop self-knowledge about their own exploitation and, equally important, understand their own capacity and accept the need to overthrow capitalism; and (2) why the proletariat should, in particular, have this revolutionary role? Were there not groups in society even more oppressed, more down-and-out, than the industrial workers? The first question concerned the relationship between the *material* conditions of the proletariat and its *consciousness*, its understanding of its own conditions. Simply put, the proletariat experienced oppression daily at work, but the actual source of this oppression was, to a degree, hidden from them by virtue of their alienation. They were, by definition, propertyless and were compelled to find employment that would pay a wage. But, in this dependent circumstance, they might come to regard their employment as fortunate rather than as, by itself, a source of their alienation and misery. Capitalism produced an *appearance* of fairness and equality but, in *essence*, capitalism was fundamentally exploitative. In their alienated state, workers could not easily see beyond their daily grind. For Marx, his theory exposed the hidden truths of workers' exploitation, contrary to the mere appearance of fairness and justice, and revealed the inherent potential of the proletariat as both capable of revolutionizing society and as needing a revolution. It was not a matter, to paraphrase Marx, of what any single proletarian thought, or even what the proletariat as a whole may think at any given time; it was a question of what the proletariat *was* and what it would be historically *compelled by circumstances to do*.

How would the head (theory) be combined with the heart (the proletariat) to set off the reaction of a social revolution? Early in his revolutionary career, Marx did not think that this was a

Box 8.6

In somber eyes no tears of grieving;
Grinding their teeth, they sit at their weaving:
'O Germany, at your shroud we sit,
We're weaving a threefold curse in it—
      We're weaving, we're weaving.
'A curse on the god we prayed to, kneeling
With old in our bones, with hunger reeling;
We waited and hoped, in vain persevered,
He scorned us and duped us, mocked and jeered—
      We're weaving, we're weaving.
'A curse on the king of the rich man's nation
Who hardens his heart at our supplication,
Who wrings the last penny out of our hides
And lets us be shot like dogs besides—
      We're weaving, we're weaving.
'A curse on this false fatherland, teeming
With nothing but shame and dirty scheming,
Where every flower is crushed in a day,
Where worms are regaled on rot and decay—
      We're weaving, we're weaving.
'The shuttle flies, the loom creaks loud,
Night and day we weave your shroud—
Old Germany, at your shroud we sit,
We're weaving a threefold curse in it,
      We're weaving, we're weaving.'

—Heinrich Heine, 'The Silesian Weavers' (1844)

particularly difficult combination. The theory would reveal to the proletariat the *real* truth of their oppression and pull aside all the gauze curtains that capitalism had erected between its appearance and its reality. Pushed by the severity of their material oppression, the proletariat would recognize the truth and Marx's theory would then become an actual, material force driving the revolution. It was not a question of telling the truth in general and hoping to convince the world by the logic of the argument; it was not a question of telling the truth to the privileged or the educated, trying to convince them to change their ways in the name of emancipation; rather, it was a truth that only a particular class could, and surely would, recognize as accurately representing their most basic interests. Marx's first task, then, was to develop his theory of the revolutionary role of the proletariat and, at the same time and of equal importance, expose other theories as false. Marx began to assess, criticize, and oppose other theories of social change, revolution, and socialism.

But was the working class the most appropriate candidate to bear the mantle of revolutionary leaders and emancipators of humanity? The deep distrust of the masses held by most intellectuals had a long history. The *philosophes* had placed their trust in the ruling class, expecting them to use their reason and reform society. At the time of the French Revolution, the liberal Girondists represented the propertied bourgeoisie and feared the masses. The Romantics of the 1830s and 1840s were similar—in their eyes the masses were incapable of appreciating the higher civilization that the revolutionary heroes would construct on behalf of the people and in their name. Only the Jacobins had considered themselves the party of the workers, of the urban *sans culottes*, and they had failed to complete the revolutionary transformation; they had failed to bring about *liberté, égalité, fraternité*. The French Revolution had ended with the triumph of the bourgeoisie and, ultimately, in the return of the monarchy. Marx sought to understand why the French Revolution had failed and learn, thereby, what could be done to ensure that the next revolution would succeed. It was necessary that the working class lead the revolution because only they were capable of carrying it through to its logical end—the dissolution of private property and the creation of socialist society.

Was the proletariat, however, the most desperate, the most oppressed, of social classes and, therefore, the most revolutionary? By definition the proletariat consisted of a class of the employed; they had 'nothing to lose but their chains', but these chains were also, in a manner of speaking, lifelines. Workers had employment and were earning wages sufficient at least for bare essentials. Perhaps that made the proletariat relatively fortunate, relatively privileged, when compared with the most down-and-out in society—those who were excluded from the productive system, the beggars, the vagabonds, and the unemployed driven to criminality. They were the ones who genuinely had nothing to lose, who didn't even have any chains to tie them to the status quo. This group, which Marx termed the **lumpenproletariat**, might, therefore, be the most resolute revolutionaries and the ones to whom to direct the message of insurrection.

Among the various socialists active at the time, one charismatic German revolutionary, Weitling, attempted to incite an immediate class war between the rich and the most desperate of the poor, the lumpenproletariat, advocating the use of terror tactics.[79] For Marx, however, this would just be blind rebellion, without any hope of success, and, however brave and desperate, the most oppressed would be unable to bring lasting change to society. Such rebellion was destructive but not creative. Like those involved in the peasant rebellions of the 1300s, the lumpenproletariat had no theory to guide them in the development of the new, socialist society that would replace the existing society. Socialism could be built only by a mass proletarian movement, conscious of its full potential and, therefore, capable of genuine revolution.

Marx's Theoretical and Historical Works

Marx's theory of capitalism and revolution is complex and has been subject to a variety of interpretations. It is convenient to think of Marx's writings as divided into two overlapping periods. In the 1840s Marx developed the core of his theory of historical materialism in response to a variety of other theories, chiefly Hegelianism. Many of the works of this early, or young, or philosophical Marx remained unpublished for decades and did not influence the socialist movement of the pre-1914 period. In the twentieth century, however, especially in the 1920s and 1960s, radical academics rediscovered the early writings of Marx.

The second period is represented by the economic writings of the mature Marx. In these works Marx developed an analysis of the origins, inherent contradictions, and inevitable crisis tendencies of capitalism. This version of Marxism, as a scientific analysis of capitalism and its necessary collapse, was the dominant view of the socialist movement until World War II. This predominantly economic interpretation of Marxism is discussed below. Marx also applied his general theory of historical materialism to the analysis of the major events of his day, as well as to other historical periods and societies. These studies, such as *The Civil War in France* (1871), demonstrated the creativity and usefulness of his general method.

Marx reached intellectual maturity during the 1840s, the culmination of Romanticism and a period of sustained revolutionary ferment in Europe. His view of the world was forged in radical rather than conservative times. Marx worked in the expectation of a victorious socialist revolution. By the time he was 30, in 1848, Marx had developed his distinctive approach to understanding and transforming society. Essential to Marx's method was the combining of theory and practice—theory would guide action and the outcome of this action would then further develop the theory. *The Communist Manifesto*, written by Marx and his long-time collaborator Friedrich Engels on the eve of the 1848 revolution, provides a concise, if oversimplified, statement of Marx's theory at that point in his life. The *Manifesto* itself played no role in the revolutionary movement at that time. What impressed Marx the most, however, was not the revolution itself—it had been widely anticipated—but its outcome: the utter defeat of the working class. In Western Europe, the 1848 revolutions represented a step in the rise of the bourgeoisie, not the proletariat, to power.

The revolution of 1848 had occurred spontaneously, without any well-developed theory or political organization. During the next two decades of Marx's life—the second period of his writing—he dedicated his efforts to overcoming both of these shortcomings. He worked to apply his theory (**historical materialism**) to bourgeois society. In 1867 Marx published *Das Kapital* (*Capital*), his most immediately influential work. Based on extensive historical research, *Capital* is a theory of the origins and characteristics of capitalism, and of the contradictions within capitalism that would inevitably, Marx believed, lead to a revolution, probably in his lifetime. This proletarian revolution would succeed where the 1848 revolutionaries had failed and would give rise to a higher form of social organization: socialism.

Marx realized that his ideas would not be accepted simply on the basis of their truths. There were always two sides to Marx's revolutionary work. Along with his theoretical work, Marx became an active leader in the European revolutionary movement, becoming the most important figure in the First International, an organization of European revolutionary parties. Marx developed his organizational practice in conflict with competing theories and practices. Aside from Marx, the dominant figure influencing the First International was the Russian anarchist, Mikhail Bakunin (1814–76). Anarchism was a direct descendant of early nineteenth-century Romanticism. For Marx, anarchism represented everything that was theoretically and organizationally wrong with the working-class movement at that time, and he and Bakunin carried on an antagonistic and often bitter theoretical and organizational battle.

From Marx's point of view, the **anarchists** had not developed beyond the spontaneous uprisings of 1848. For them, revolution was always imminent, needing only a spark from a dedicated visionary capable of mobilizing the masses into action. In contrast, Marx's economic writings of the 1850s and 1860s were designed to present a scientific analysis of bourgeois society.

HISTORICAL MATERIALISM

Many of Marx's fundamental ideas were written as early as 1845 when Marx and Engels wrote *The German Ideology*, a book they were unable to publish and therefore left 'to the gnawing criticism of the mice'. Human nature was not, for Marx, a fixed thing that remained unchanged throughout the evolution of history. Animals had fixed and unchanging needs. Humans, however, were qualitatively different. They possessed a unique capacity to reason—one of the basic assertions of the Enlightenment. They were able to imagine new desires, new wants that did not yet exist. While being a part of nature, humans were also, to a large degree, above nature. They possessed the potential to control nature and direct it to suit their purposes. Other animals could survive only by slowly adapting themselves to their environment; humans could 'labour', that is, act to change their environment. Thus, humans were separated or alienated from nature, but for Marx that was the precondition for human existence. Moreover, Marx argued, as humans developed new needs and acted on nature (laboured) to transform it, they simultaneously changed their own internal nature. Humans were products of their own societies and human nature was not fixed, but changeable. For Marx, humanity was essentially 'self-created' through labour.[80]

The second initial premise for Marx was that human beings were physical creatures having basic biological needs that had to be met, such as for food and shelter. To understand any society you had to begin by studying how people were organized to satisfy these basic, material needs. Every society had a way to produce and distribute the material necessities of life—an economic system. Understanding the economic system, including its relationships of class and power, was the key to understanding all other parts: 'the anatomy of civil society is to be sought in political economy.'[81]

At the foundation of the economic system were the raw materials provided by nature, such as the land and its resources, and the tools (or technology) humans had developed to help them control and produce useful things. Using Marx's terms, these were the **forces of production**. Over time, human societies had evolved increasingly complex technologies to make a living from nature. Marx classified societies into several stages, from the most undeveloped or primitive to what, for Marx, was the highest form then existing, industrial capitalism. The simplest societies subsisted by hunting and by gathering wild plant foods. Later, with the invention of agriculture, humans took the first decisive step towards the domination of nature. Capitalism, through the Industrial Revolution, had developed the forces of production to their highest point. In the words of *The Communist Manifesto*, the bourgeoisie had played a most revolutionary role by subjecting the forces of nature to human will and creating more powers of production than all previous generations. They cleared whole continents for cultivation and conjured 'whole populations . . . out of the ground'.[82]

Besides the forces of production, in every society humans played different roles in the production and distribution of these useful things created from nature. Marx identified a number of stages in the evolution of society, each of which combined a specific level of technology and a specific type of relationship between different classes of people. These stages Marx defined as distinct **modes of production**. He identified at least five principal modes in European history, linking them in an evolutionary chain.

In the simplest social stage of primitive communism (hunting and gathering), adult members of the society worked and shared equally in the distribution. People produced enough for their subsistence and to enable them to support the next generation, but there was nothing beyond this subsistence level.

The development of agriculture, however, was accompanied by the emergence of unequal social classes: a dominant class now owned and controlled the means of production (the land, resources) and a subordinate class produced their own subsistence and, in addition, also provided the means from which the dominant class could subsist. Societies were now divided into antagonistic social classes and it was the conflict between the dominant, exploiting class and the subordinate, producing class that determined the evolution of history—the transition from one mode of production to the next higher mode. Analyzing the struggle between social classes is the fundamental component of Marxism.

Marx identified two types of agrarian modes of production that had appeared in Europe. The first was the ancient mode of production characterized by the division of society into slave owners and slaves. Over a period of several thousand years, ancient society evolved into a second type of agrarian mode of production, usually termed feudalism. Feudalism emerged in Europe following the fall of the Roman Empire, persisted for about one thousand years, and then began to break down. In was during the period of the dominance of the feudal mode of production that the bourgeoisie had first emerged as a distinct class and developed its own consciousness of its interests. Over time, the capitalists, who represented the next stage of society, grew stronger, fulfilling their historical mission to expand greatly the forces of production and bring into existence the proletariat, who would overthrow capitalism. Marx theorized that capitalism, like every stage before it, would also prove to be transitory and would be replaced by socialism, a higher mode of production.

This was an evolutionary theory of stages through which European society had passed and through which, presumably, all societies would eventually evolve. Each stage, in Hegelian fashion, contained within itself the embryo of the next stage. Each stage would evolve and, then, when it had reached the end point of its possibilities, it would be transformed into the next higher stage. Capitalism in Europe, Marx believed, was in the final stages of conflict, leading inevitably towards a socialist revolution.

An important implication of this theory was that no stage would be transformed into the next higher stage until it had exhausted all its potential. This explained, first, why the 1848 revolutions had failed. Capitalism had not then been ripe for a revolution. The proletariat had not developed to the point where it was ready to overthrow capitalism and create the new society. Second, most countries in the world had not even reached the stage of industrial capitalism. They were still mired in pre-capitalist modes of production.[83] That meant, ironically, that socialists in those societies should help the bourgeoisie come to power so that they could fulfill their historical mission and develop the productive forces. In his concrete, historical studies, Marx had speculated beyond this narrow, theoretical box. He argued that other modes of production had arisen in the Far East. In Russia, he speculated, the transition to socialism might bypass a capitalistic stage, developing directly from a tradition of rural communes. The simplistic stages theory of history, however, became the core of what was called scientific Marxism after his death.

Alienation

The term 'alienation' refers to a separation from a larger whole. Generally, alienation is a negative state and the aim of social change is to reunite the parts with the whole. In Hegel's theory, humanity was alienated from Spirit (God); human society was evolving dialectically in the direction of progressively reducing this alienation. Humans were striving for eventual unity with Spirit, at which point they would cease to be alienated.

For Marx the initial alienation of humanity was the separation of human beings from nature. This resulted from human self-creation and was progressive. Like most nineteenth-century social theorists, Marx accepted this alienation as inevitable. Some naturalists and transcendentalists envisioned alienation from nature as artificial and negative, and believed that it should be overcome only by returning to a state more closely akin with nature. For Marx, however, the development of humanity entailed the conquest of nature rather than the return to a natural state. It was through the domination of nature that humanity's alienation from nature would be overcome.

Other forms of alienation were products of historical development. The most basic of these was the alienation of human beings from each other, brought about by the development of antagonistic social classes following the invention of agriculture. Thereafter, societies were characterized by class conflict. The capitalist mode of production, more than any other, had alienated the majority of humanity to the maximum degree possible. In the earliest stages of the breakdown of feudalism to produce capitalism, the majority of productive workers worked in agriculture, often holding their own pieces of land. The process of capitalist development in England, however, entailed forcing the independent producers off the land, expropriating or alienating them from their **means of production**. Without access to the land—to an independent way to make a living from natural resources—these now unpropertied peasants were forced to become wage labourers, working for the capitalist property owners. It was through this alienation of producers from their means of production that the capitalist class structure developed and the proletariat was created. This form of alienation, moreover, was continually reproduced as capitalist competition forced the smaller owners out of business, to sell off their productive property and, in their turn, to become wage workers. Marx believed that capitalism would eventually destroy the independent petite bourgeoisie altogether, and society would reach its most polarized state of alienation when it was divided between a small minority of wealthy property owners (bourgeoisie) and a large mass of propertyless proletarians. The socialist revolution would return the means of production to the proletarians, eliminating the bourgeoisie.

This was not the only form of alienation under capitalism. As independent producers, the petite bourgeoisie had not only owned the means of production, they had owned their finished product. What they had grown or manufactured, often directly by hand, embodied their skill, knowledge, and ingenuity. It was their property and they disposed of it as they chose within the constraints of the commodities market. Once alienated from the means of production, however, the relationship between the producers and their product was significantly altered. As wage labourers, each producer laboured at creating commodities, continuing to invest the finished goods with his or her talents. Once finished, however, the commodities were the property of the owner. Capitalism alienated producers from ownership of their own work.

As industrial capitalism developed, this simple division of labour described above—between those who produced finished products and the owners—was modified by the introduction of technology. Ever more complex forms of machinery were introduced into the factories, replacing the more complex skilled labour with machines that could be operated by workers with much lower levels of skill. A traditional shoemaker fashioned a shoe out of leather; a wage worker in a shoe factory knew how to operate one machine, which did one small task in the making of a shoe. The wage worker, then, was alienated from the control of the productive process. He or she did not decide what was made, how it was made, what part in the complex division of labour she or he would work, how fast the work was to be done; he or she did not control the techniques and design. Human labour (in modern terms, 'human resources') had been reduced to the level of the machine itself, the most profound alienation of all. Marx and Engels make this point that, for the working class, work loses all its individual character and, hence, all charm for the workers. Each 'becomes an appendage of the machine, and it is only the most simple, most monotonous, and most easily acquired knack, that is required' of them. '[T]hey . . . are daily and hourly enslaved by the machine, by the overlooker, and, above all, by the individual bourgeois manufacturer', a form of petty and embittering despotism that 'proclaims gain to be its end and aim'.[84]

In the end, then, the capitalist mode of production alienated people as far as possible from their own human potential, from the skills and creativity that expressed their human nature. In part, this extreme level of alienation that the majority of people would experience under capitalism made socialism desirable. In Marx's theory, with the final, socialist revolution, the proletariat would assume power in society. For the first time, power would be held by a social class that had no interest in exploiting any other group, a class that had the potential to change society progressively towards eventual equality. In the final stage of communism that would evolve from the socialist mode of production, society would be classless and the alienation of human beings from each other would be resolved.

Marx did not spend much of his time describing this future society. Many of the socialists whose theories Marx had rejected had spent their time constructing, in their own minds, ideal societies. For Marx, socialism would be what the proletariat made it at the time and this could not be foreseen except in certain generalities. In his early writing, however, when Marx did imagine the future society, his writings were tinged with Romantic conceptions:

> In communist society, where nobody has one exclusive sphere of activity but each can become accomplished in any branch he wishes, society regulates the general production and thus makes it possible for me to do one thing today and another tomorrow, to hunt in the morning, fish in the afternoon, rear cattle in the evening, criticize after dinner, just as I have a mind, without ever becoming hunter, fisherman, shepherd or critic.[85]

The State

> The executive of the modern State is but a committee for managing the common affairs of the whole bourgeoisie.
> —Karl Marx and Friedrich Engels,
> *The Communist Manifesto* (1848)

The German Ideology and earlier writing also contained the foundation of Marx's theory of the state. Marx rejected Hegel's theory that the state was a neutral institution operating above the class struggle and working to secure the best interests of the nation as a whole. Marx's views were closer to those of Rousseau. The state was the special creation of the dominant class in the early stage of the ancient mode of production. It was a coercive body designed to expand the interests of the ruling class in foreign conquest and to defend the property owners from attacks by outsiders and from rebellion by those below. Where class divisions existed, a state was a necessary instrument of rule. The state in capitalist society was no different. There existed a ruling class of capitalists who had control over the economic life and the politics of the nation. Laws were passed to meet the needs and interests of the bourgeoisie, regardless of the external form or appearance of the state. It made no difference whether the government was a monarchy, a dictatorship, or democratic in the very limited sense that it could be under bourgeois domination.

Marx's theorizing about the state was affected profoundly by the experience of the Paris Commune of 1871. When the state of Prussia defeated France in a quick war, a conservative provisional government was established in Paris. Working-class Parisians, however, had other ideas. They established an alternative, radical government in the city of Paris with broad, socialist aims, centred on the district of Montmartre. Known as the **Paris Commune**, it represented the first attempt to organize a working-class government. The Commune took such revolutionary measures as organizing the citizens in an armed militia to protect the revolution, and ensuring that the people's representatives would receive a salary no greater than the average worker's pay. The Commune posed in the most concrete way the threat that radical socialism posed for the propertied. With the connivance of the Prussians, the French army was diverted to Paris to suppress the revolution. The attack on the Commune, equally on its men and women, was ferocious.[86] That people are still taught to shrink in horror from the revolutionary Reign of Terror of 1794 while the massacre of the Communards in 1871 is forgotten is a measure of the degree to which history is written by the victors.

The revolution in 1871 was defeated by a French government that still exercised control over the powers of the police and the army. Marx concluded that it was necessary for the proletariat to capture state power completely, wresting all power from the bourgeoisie. Furthermore, Marx believed, the bourgeois state would have to be broken down and rebuilt in its entirety to meet the needs of the proletariat. Based on the experience of the 1871 Paris Commune, it was evident that 'the working class cannot simply lay hold of the ready-made State machinery, and wield it for its own purposes.'[87]

The long-term aim of the proletarian revolution must be the construction of a classless society that would be without a state. In the short run, however, the victorious proletariat would have to construct a new, socialist state. There would still be a need for a state to protect the new society from rebellion of *the former bourgeoisie* and, potentially, from armed invasion by the armies of the international capitalist class. The administrative functions that state bureaucracy handled would be democratized. Marx did not offer any blueprints of how or to what extent a proletarian state would manage the economy and administer services.

While still a state, Marx believed, the proletarian state would be different from all others. For the first time it would be genuinely the state of the majority of the people (the proletariat). But at this early stage of socialism, as one would expect, there would be a need to develop new institutions of all kinds and new relationships between people that were no longer tainted by bourgeois interests. Society would need direction, planning, and security. It would only be after many generations had come and gone, when old ideas and habits such as competition, selfishness, and domination had been progressively eliminated from humanity, that a coercive institution (a state) would gradually cease to be necessary. Over the long range, then, the proletarian state would increasingly become unnecessary, people would become capable of the social self-direction that was part of their human potential, and the state would 'wither away'.

Marx on Class

'The history of all hitherto existing society is the history of **class struggle**.' With these words, written near the beginning of *The Communist Manifesto*, Marx establishes the centrality of class in his theory. It is an exaggeration in two senses. Classes have not always existed; they emerged as a result of historical developments. During the stage of primitive communism, societies were not divided by classes. In addition, class struggle is not the only social relationship that determines the outcome of any specific historical situation. Defining history more abstractly as the progression of stages and modes of production, Marx argued that class struggles are the motor that drives large-scale social and economic development. It follows from this premise that historical forces and events should be interpreted in the light of the role they play in the class struggle.

Beyond **primitive communism**, each mode of production was characterized by a specific class structure. In the ancient mode of production, the most significant class relationship was between the slave owners and the slaves. The slaves produced their own subsistence and, directly, produced an economic surplus that was appropriated by the slave owners and used to support their relative opulence. The exploitation of the slave was direct and obvious—slaves were aware of how much they produced and how little was returned to them for subsistence. Slavery was maintained by brute force and, as well, by the ideology that it was deserved or inevitable for those defeated in war or those who were sold or placed themselves in bondage. Slaves faced the highest degree of oppression of any producing class, and slave revolts were common.

Similarly, under the feudal mode of production, the serfs were aware of their own exploitation in the sense that they laboured to produce their own subsistence and also laboured to produce a surplus for the aristocracy, either by working directly on the overlord's land or by handing over high proportions of the products of their labour. This obviously unequal exchange was justified on religious grounds, by law, by custom, and by the assertion that the producing class received protection and salvation from the upper class and the clergy. Furthermore, under the fief system, serfs had historical rights to a proportion of the production and the right to the perpetual use of the land.

In the capitalist mode of production, two classes again existed in an exploitative relationship: the bourgeoisie and the proletariat. Historically, however, Marx recognized one other important class. The petite bourgeoisie were small independent owners (farmers, crafts workers, merchants) who, like the bourgeoisie, owned their own small property but, unlike the bourgeoisie, worked it themselves and did not hire wage workers. Under the laws of capitalist competition, most small producers and retailers would be forced out of business and sink into the proletariat.

The most significant class relationship was between the property-owning bourgeoisie and the propertyless proletariat. As in every exploitative mode of production, the proletariat produced their own subsistence and, above that, a substantial surplus, which was appropriated by the bourgeoisie. Unlike the other class-based modes of production, however, exploitation within capitalism was less obvious because the workers had agreed to a wage contract that supposedly represented the value of their labour.

Unlike the serfs, proletarians were deprived of any rights over productive property and thus were compelled to seek wage work to subsist. They were free to strike a bargain with any property owner and, at least formally, negotiate the terms of the wage contract. In this apparently free labour contract, the relationship between the wage worker and the capitalist appeared to be formally equal. The two parties agreed that a specific number of hours of work on a specified task were worth a certain wage: it appeared to be an equal exchange and, as the English essayist Carlyle realized, the cash transaction was the sole duty owed the poor by the rich (Box 8.7).[88] Marx recognized, however, that this contract was only a more hidden form through which the producing class laboured to create their own subsistence (their wage) and, over and above that, to produce the goods the capitalist sold for a profit. Marx termed this excess 'surplus value'. Capitalism was no less economically exploitative than the earlier modes of production, although the form of this exploitation was veiled by the appearance of free labour.

Contradictions of Capitalism

Capitalism was a dynamic economic system that survived on the basis of continual growth and change. Fundamentally, this was because it was a competitive system. In the nineteenth century, many owners of production with relatively small and middle-sized businesses competed with each other in the marketplace. Successful competition meant, first, lowering wages. There were limits, however, to how low wages could go with respect to such factors as the supply and demand for labour, the existence of alternative means of livelihood, and the struggle of local groups of workers to meet their interests. A second strategy was to reorganize labour by introducing a division of labour into the manufacturing process that would be more economically productive—although, as Marx made clear, this was more alienating.

The most important way to gain a competitive advantage, however, was by replacing human labour by machinery. Capitalist competition drives technological innovations of certain kinds, particularly those innovations that allow for the more efficient production of commodities. Several consequences follow from this mechanization of

---

Box 8.7

True, it must be owned, we for the present, with our Mammon-Gospel, have come to strange conclusions. We call it a Society; and go about professing openly the totalest separation, isolation. Our life is not a mutual helpfulness; but, rather, cloaked under due laws-of-war, named 'fair competition' and so forth, it is a mutual hostility. We have profoundly forgotten everywhere that *Cash-payment* is not the sole relation of human beings; we think, nothing doubting, that it absolves and liquidates all engagements of man. 'My starving workers?' answers the rich mill owner: 'Did I not hire them fairly in the market? Did I not pay them, to the last sixpence, the sum covenanted for? What have I to do with them more?'—Verily Mammon-worship is a melancholy creed.... 'Am I my brother's keeper?'

—Thomas Carlyle, *Past and Present* (1843)

labour. Much work becomes deskilled as machine operatives are hired to replace highly skilled crafts workers. More easily exploited groups of workers, such as children, women, and migrants, can be hired at lower wages. Furthermore, while there may have been fewer manufacturing plants, factories greatly expanded in size. As businesses went bankrupt, were bought out, or merged with others, capital became concentrated in fewer hands, but in vastly greater amounts.

These developments in capitalism intensified the class struggles between smaller and larger producers and between the capitalist and his or her workforce. More employees worked together in large factories, facing one boss, a situation that helped them to develop a consciousness of their common interests vis-à-vis their employer. The logical and historical consequence of this was the development of trade unions as workers recognized that they were strategically positioned to be able to shut down the economic engine of profit-making, especially since labour was the source of profit. In addition, their numbers were constantly growing; as Shelley had said, 'Ye are many, they are few':[89]

Men of England, heirs of Glory,
Heroes of unwritten story,
Nurslings of one mighty Mother,
Hopes of her, and one another;

Rise, like Lions after slumber,
In unvanquishable number,
Shake your chains to earth like dew
Which in sleep had fall'n on you—
Ye are many—they are few.

What is Freedom?—Ye can tell
That which Slavery is too well—
For its very name has grown
To an echo of your own.
. . .
This is Slavery—savage men,
Or wild beasts within a den,
Would endure not as ye do—
But such ills they never knew.

The **concentration of capital** was helping to create the conditions for the workers' revolution—Marx wrote that capitalism produces, above all, its own gravediggers.

Furthermore, Marx argued that this growth of the productive forces, which was a law of capitalist development (ever more sophisticated technology to increase productivity and profitability), expressed a profound contradiction. Production was becoming more and more social; that is, as each individual worker performed an increasingly smaller part in the overall production process, he or she became, more and more obviously, one cog in a giant enterprise to which (nearly) everyone contributed. Increasingly, individuals were dependent on others for their livelihood and co-operated with them in labour. However, in a contradictory fashion, as work became more co-operative, ownership of the goods produced continued to be in private hands and, in fact, in increasingly fewer private hands. There was a contradiction, then, between the increasingly social nature of the labour process and the increasingly private nature of the appropriation of profits. In this evolution, capitalists were becoming less and less socially necessary. The conditions were being created for the elimination of the capitalist class as entirely parasitic and the self-management of the enterprise by the co-operating workers. The conditions necessary for socialism were being prepared by the capitalist system itself. According to a Hegelian pattern, the characteristics of the new society (socialism) were being prepared by the inevitable developments of the old (capitalism).

Capitalism was the most productive system that humans had yet produced. The chief benefit of capitalism, Marx noted, was that it enormously expanded the productive forces of society and the conquest of nature. A severe contradiction in its productiveness, however, was rooted in the **commodity** form: capitalism produced goods in the form of commodities for sale. Goods can be produced either for use or for exchange. They had a 'use value'—they served a human purpose—and they had an 'exchange value'—humans would want to exchange them for something else. Obviously, anything that had exchange value ought also to have use value; otherwise, why would someone want it? But, Marx argued, capitalism produced for exchange, not primarily for use.

Something produced for exchange must be in demand or it won't be sold. If it can't be sold (exchanged for money), the capitalist won't produce it. Under capitalist conditions, 'demand' means 'effective demand'—consumers must not only have a use for the good, they also have to have the money to purchase it. Poor people may need, or have a use for, decent, low-cost housing, but they don't have the money to pay for it. The demand for low-cost housing is met by slum landlords who can make a profit from renting dilapidated housing for low rent. The homeless don't have the effective demand for even that dismal roof over their heads.

The consequence under capitalism is that the poor do not have their basic human needs met—for decent housing, proper medical care, wholesome food, and so on. The capitalist concentrates on entering the competition to produce goods for the more prosperous consumers, who are able to pay for them. So endless new goods are produced to entice the consuming appetites of the well-heeled, however useless they are in any fundamental sense, while socially important investments in housing, education, medical care, transportation, and so on are neglected. The twentieth-century welfare state would attempt to provide some of these use values, a recognition of the inherently unequal distribution of wealth in capitalism.

Furthermore, in this contradiction between producing goods and having effective demand to purchase them, there appeared another contradiction in the capitalist mode of production. At a society-wide level, where did the money come from to consume all the goods the system was producing? The majority of the population received wages from which they consumed goods; the amount of money in wages was, by definition, less than the selling price of the goods produced. Even if all the wages were spent consuming goods, there would still always be an excess of production over consumption.

This imbalance was one factor Marx believed caused the periodic crises (depressions) of capitalism: the tendency towards **overproduction** (or underconsumption). This argument is summarized in *The Communist Manifesto*: 'Modern bourgeois society . . . [which] has conjured up such gigantic means of production and of exchange, is like the sorcerer, who is no longer able to control the powers of the nether world . . . he has called up by his spells.'[90] If capitalists produced more goods than they could sell, their unsold inventory would grow and goods would overflow their warehouses. Consequently, Marx said, 'there breaks out an epidemic that, in all earlier epochs, would have seemed an absurdity—the epidemic of over-production'—exactly the point made more colourfully by Thomas Carlyle in *Past and Present* (1843).

'Ye miscellaneous, ignoble manufacturing individuals, ye have produced too much! . . . You have produced, produced;—he that seeks your indictment, let him look around. Millions of shirts, and empty pairs of breeches, hang there in judgment against you. We accuse you of over producing. . . . And now there is a glut, and your operatives cannot be fed!'. . .

Too many shirts? Well, that is a novelty, in this intemperate Earth, with its nine-hundred millions of bare backs! . . . I have not in my time heard any stranger speech.[91]

If there was too much supply and not enough effective demand, profits could not be made and there would be no money for investment in making new goods. The result was a commercial crisis during which capitalists had to close down production, lay off workers, and wait for their inventory to be sold off or else destroyed. As factories closed, other businesses found they had too few consumers and they closed, causing a general crisis or depression in the economy. Depressions, however harmful they were to the workers, were not always harmful to the capitalist system, because the inefficient factories were closed for good, the concentration of capital increased, and the conditions gradually brought about a renewed investment in production—an economic upturn.

Capitalist crises can be precipitated by other causes than a tendency to underconsumption. There are also short-term solutions to the problem of an overall lack of effective demand. Capitalists could export their excess production abroad, finding effective demand in other countries by 'the conquest of new markets, and by the more thorough exploitation of the old ones'. From Marx's point of view, the solutions to one crisis merely pave 'the way for more extensive and more destructive crises . . . by diminishing the means whereby crises are prevented'.[92] Once the globe was integrated into a single capitalist market, this solution would have reached an end. Bourgeois society could also temporarily solve a crisis of overproduction by expanding the use of credit, allowing consumers to buy goods in the present on the promise of paying for them later, the origin of the huge debt load individuals and businesses now carry. The government could step in and maintain effective demand by redistributing money to consumers, through unemployment insurance, for example, or by enlarging the role of the government as a consumer of goods by building roads, hospitals, and schools or by expanding the military. The money to pay for this social and military expenditure would come from large bank loans, the origin of the government deficit. This scale of government intervention would not become an important feature of modern capitalism until the welfare state of the mid-twentieth century.

A high level of unemployment was one of the features of a capitalist crisis. In addition, capitalism required a certain level of unemployment to function. Under capitalism, workers' skills also become commodities: they exchange their ability to labour for subsistence through the wage contract. Like all commodities, the price of labour—the wage rate—is affected by such economic factors as supply and demand. When the supply of labour is high and the demand is low, as in a depression, wage rates can be lowered, increasing profit margins. When the demand for labour is high, however, workers can demand better terms in their labour contract, principally, higher wages, thereby reducing profit margins. A degree of unemployment maintains a **reserve army** of labour which can be brought into production when capital has need for it, but which exists also as a permanent oversupply of wage labour, thereby helping to keep wage rates down. Unemployment—and all the distress associated with it—was built into the workings of capitalism. The apparent paradox was that the most productive and technologically advanced economic system in the world had, as its Siamese twin, persistent levels of poverty and unemployment.

As Marx studied these contradictions of capitalism, he theorized that capitalism was evolving in a direction that inevitably created the preconditions for a socialist revolution. Capital was concentrated in fewer and fewer hands. As the petite bourgeoisie gradually disappeared as a middle class, the class structure of capitalist society was increasingly polarized between an increasingly smaller and wealthier ruling class of capitalists and a progressively larger, more exploited, and better organized proletariat. Capitalism itself produced periodic crises that were getting progressively worse. As the forces of production expanded, the potential existed to wipe out poverty and want and to provide everyone with a high standard of living. This potential, however, was squandered by the unequal division of power, resources, and wealth that was endemic to the capitalist system. Eventually, Marx reasoned, capitalism would have run its course. It would be increasingly obvious that a reorganization of society in the interests of the great majority of the producers was possible, desirable, and necessary. Like all exploitative social systems before it, capitalism was destined for the garbage heap of history.

CONCLUSION

The modern doctrines of socialism and communism, which were most clearly articulated by Karl Marx and Friedrich Engels, amalgamated the vision of the Romantic socialists, the rationalism of English liberalism, and the dialectics of German social theory into a new, revolutionary synthesis.

The question of the scientific nature of Marx's theory has given rise to considerable debate since his death. Many of his followers, who claimed to uphold Marx's scientific truths, did not reflect the actual scientific method. Instead, they tended to turn Marx's arguments into dogma, into absolute truths. Scientists, on the contrary, are always tentative about their claims; science as a body of knowledge does not stand still but both grows with new knowledge and undergoes major changes of orientation when new theories are developed that account more accurately for natural observations. As a scientific analysis of society and, particularly, of the capitalist mode of production, which was Marx's specific focus, historical materialism was as much a method as a specific theory.

Marx's theory provided a radical new foundation for the development of social analysis and social revolution. But it was incomplete, sometimes imprecise, and certainly could not provide a prognostication for the future or detail a blueprint of a future communist society. Marxism after Marx would develop in many different directions. In principle, any social science should continue to evolve and change in the light of the actual developments in social life. Nothing is more contrary to science than to turn a theory into a set of absolute truths that must be swallowed whole and are not susceptible to new evidence, to being modified by actual historical practice.

Unfortunately, however, this was precisely what happened to Marx's theory in the hands of many of his followers. The dominant turn-of-the-century interpretation of Marxism, as his theory became known after his death, combined Hegelian evolution and positivist social science. Marxism was assumed to be a theory of history according to which capitalism would follow the logic of its own internal laws to the point of collapse, at which point a proletarian revolution would inevitably occur, moving society into the next, higher, socialist stage. From the perspective of social theory, this one-sided economic version

of Marxism dominated socialist (and sociological) thought and the practice of socialist parties in the decades following Marx's death.

Marx and Engels may have concluded that capitalist society was destined for the landfill, but the trip to this dump would still prove to include many detours and misdirections. As the third millennium began, global capitalism appeared to have buried all its rivals and it was Marxism as a viable social theory that appeared to be threatened with extinction. Tragically, history has a way of repeating itself. As global capitalism has reverted to its laissez-faire roots, the contradictions of capitalism have resurfaced, this time on a global scale. In parallel, Marxism is being reborn. As John Cassidy put the case, 'Many of the contradictions that he [Marx] saw in Victorian capitalism and that were subsequently addressed by reformist governments have begun reappearing in new guises, like mutant viruses.' Marx had predicted 'most of the ramifications' of globalization 'a hundred and fifty years ago'.[93]

In contemporary global capitalism, Cassidy writes, the tendency of capitalism to move towards monopoly has been accelerated. There is 'an unprecedented redistribution of resources from poor to rich'; average real income has stagnated or dropped, while 'profits have soared.' Marx said that profits would increase faster than wages. 'In 1979, sixteen per cent of all the money produced by the corporate sector went to profits and interest; today the figure is twenty-one per cent.'[94] Globalization has been accompanied by 'child labor, corporate tax avoidance, and shuttered American factories', leading some economists to fear 'social disintegration'. Marx would have called it social revolution.

Perhaps most ironic of all, the theorists of contemporary global capitalism perceive their real enemy to be, not the socialists, but the liberal, welfare model of the capitalist state. They oppose (1) government regulations, (2) taxing the rich, (3) government enterprise, and (4) public ownership. Over the last two decades, the capitalist state has attacked and rolled back the ameliorative measures of the welfare state. This welfare version of capitalism, however, had been implemented in the first place to divert capitalism from the dangerous precipice of collapse to which laissez-faire had led it in the Great Depression, and simultaneously to save capitalism from a Marxist revolution. Welfare capitalism has its roots in the kinder, gentler version of liberalism, termed 'social liberalism', developed in nineteenth-century England, the topic of the preceding chapter.

Before social reform could rise to predominance in the West, it had to overcome a resurgence of the older liberal laissez-faire. When the individualistic version of economic liberalism resurfaced in the later nineteenth century, it was buttressed by Darwinism, the latest findings of biological science. Marxism was one widely influential theory to emerge from the mid-nineteenth century. Equally significant for social thought was the theory of evolution advanced by Charles Darwin.

1809 Jean-Baptiste Lamarck (1744–1829) publishes his theory of acquired characteristics.

1853 Joseph de Gobineau (1816–82) publishes his first *Essay on the Inequality of the Human Races*.

1859 Charles Darwin (1809–82) publishes *On the Origin of Species*; his theory of natural selection implicitly suggests that humans share a common ancestor with the great apes.

1877 End of Reconstruction in the US South; army withdraws and 'Jim Crow' era begins.

1879 Opening of Henrik Ibsen's (1828–1906) 'New Woman' play, *A Doll's House*.

1881 Booker T. Washington (1856–1915) becomes principal of the Tuskegee Institute.

1883 German philosopher Friedrich Nietzsche (1844–1900) publishes *Thus Spake Zarathustra*.

1884 Herbert Spencer (1820–1903), social Darwinist, publishes *The Man Versus the State*.

1889 Jane Addams (1860–1935) co-founds Hull-House, part of the Settlement House and American Progressive movements.

1891 Oscar Wilde (1854–1900) publishes his novel *The Picture of Dorian Gray*.

1892 Ida Wells (1862–1931), black journalist and activist, begins anti–lynching campaign.

1893 Émile Durkheim (1858–1917) publishes *The Division of Labour in Society*.

1895 Durkheim publishes *The Rules of Sociological Method*.

1898 Émile Zola (1840–1902) publishes his open letter *J'Accuse*, denouncing official corruption in the Dreyfus case.

1899 W.E.B. Dubois (1868–1963) publishes *The Philadelphia Negro*.

1899 Thorstein Veblen (1857–1929) publishes his caustic *Theory of the Leisure Class*.

1900 American naturalist author Theodore Dreiser (1871–1945) publishes *Sister Carrie*.

1900 Sigmund Freud (1856–1939) publishes his work on *The Interpretation of Dreams*.

1903 Emmeline Pankhurst (1858–1928) founds the Women's Social and Political Union.

1905 Max Weber (1864–1920) publishes *The Protestant Ethic and the Spirit of Capitalism*.

1908 Georg Simmel (1858–1918) publishes *Sociology: Investigations on the Forms of Sociation*.

1909 Establishment of the multiracial National Association for the Advancement of Colored People (NAACP).

1912 Durkheim publishes *The Elementary Forms of the Religious Life*.

1914 Beginning of the First World War (1914–18).

1914 Weber publishes *Economy and Society*.

1915 Opening of D.W. Griffith's (1875–1948) controversial film, *The Birth of a Nation*.

1917 Russian Bolshevik Revolution, led by V.I. Lenin (1870–1924).

1918 British women over the age of 30 win the right to vote; age lowered to 21 in 1928.

1919 German and Hungarian revolutions suppressed.

1920 19th Amendment to US Constitution grants women the right to vote.

1925 American author F. Scott Fitzgerald (1896–1940) publishes *The Great Gatsby*.

1929 Karl Mannheim (1893–1947) publishes *Ideology and Utopia*.

1930 Freud publishes *Civilization and its Discontents*.

1933 Nazi Party under Adolph Hitler seizes power in Germany.

1934 G.H. Mead's (1863–1931) *Mind, Self, and Society* is published.

Part III

FROM CERTAINTY TO DOUBT

Karl Marx had wanted to dedicate the first volume of *Capital* to Charles Darwin, the English biologist and evolutionist. Darwin declined the offer. For Marx, Darwin's immediately controversial *Origin of Species* had revolutionized biological science in much the same way that the theory of *Capital* revolutionized economic theory. Many of the similarities shared by the two theories were common in nineteenth-century thought, such as the evolutionary perspective itself and the doctrine of inevitable progress. In other respects, the theories were opposed. Darwin believed only in slow, gradual, and cumulative change, making his theory compatible with the conservatives rather than with Marx. In Marx's theory, profound historical change emerged from social revolutions. For Darwin, on the contrary, nature never makes leaps.

Chapter Nine attends to the emergence of evolutionary theory in natural science and its application to sociology. The application of the conception of evolution to nature was first formulated, in recent time at least, in the eighteenth century. It was preceded by great changes in the study of geology, which proved that the Earth was far more ancient that previously thought. Evolution occurs only over enormous stretches of time. The first question evolutionists had to answer was by what natural mechanisms evolution proceeded. One popular hypothesis was that there must be some inner spiritual force that propels evolution in a progressively more complex direction. This explanation would continue to influence biological thought and be reflected in social thought well into the twentieth century.

Darwin proposed, in addition, the theory of natural selection. Those members of a species with favourable traits passed them on to many offspring, while those with unfavourable traits died early and left few descendants. Controversial from the start, Darwinism implied that humans were just a more successful animal in nature. This perceived degradation of humanity to the level of the beasts had many implications for society and for social thought. Inevitably, the doctrine of the survival of the fittest was adopted by sociology. When this doctrine was applied to the struggles for dominance in society, within society between human races, and between different nations, the result was social Darwinism.

The ideology known as social Darwinism found a congenial home in the United States, where an aristocracy of monopolists recognized in it a rationalization for their power and wealth. They needed little reassurance on matters of race. The promise of African-American emancipation—the topic of Chapter Twelve—had been snuffed out by a potent combination of legal and illegal racism, leaving theorists to ponder assimilation or black nationalism. More threatening to the white American elite at the time was progressivism, a grassroots movement based in small capitalism rather than in any conception of socialism. When American critics pilloried the robber barons and the 'leisure class', the elite knew to whom they referred.

Darwinism also had a disquieting effect on literature. If life as a whole was not guided by a superior force or spirit, whether supernatural or rational, but was determined merely by randomness and chance, then people were the victims of circumstances and misfortune would be just as likely as good fortune. Applied to literature, this pessimistic viewpoint was expressed in the genre of naturalism.

Other intellectuals drew a similar lesson from Darwin. If humans were merely powerful beasts, then morality was a humbug. Nothing except false, humanly constructed rules and conventions stood in the way of the gratification of one's desires. Life had no purpose other than the maximization of pleasure and experience. The result was decadence, a movement that drew from the individualism of Romanticism and led to a number of modern forms of cultural expression having in common the expression of individual desire. Like the Romantics before them, though exponentially, the decadents lived their rejection of the moral standards of bourgeois society and indulged their desires.

These ideas are pursued in Chapter Thirteen, particularly through the theories of the philosopher, Friedrich Nietzsche. Morality was not only false, said Nietzsche, it had been devised to subdue, control, and stifle the minority of creative individualists who needed to be liberated from the constraints of modern society. Good and evil were purely relative to the standards that those with power declared them to be. The time was coming when the creative minority would throw off the centuries of chains that had bound them, giving rise to a new elite of supermen who would combine reason and passion in a new orgy of creative energy. Some of Nietzsche's perspectives were later developed by Karl Mannheim, one of the last classical sociological theorists whose theory of the sociology of knowledge was influential for the structure of this book.

While the turn-of-the-century world witnessed the attempt to construct sociology as a science, psychology was more rapidly establishing its claims to scientific validity. In Vienna, the Austrian psychiatrist Sigmund Freud was more concerned that primitive, instinctual human energy had to be controlled in order to protect civilization. As essentially superior animals, humanity was dangerous and, if unleashed, people's instinctive

aggression would be more destructive than creative. Freud had, for a man, unprecedented access to women's talk about their sexuality, from which he built an elaborate theoretical structure claiming to explain the normal evolution of psychosexual development and, through deviations from the normal, the genesis of mental disorders.

Nietzsche's elitism and Freud's pessimism about human nature were shaped by a context replete with social rebellion. The socialist movement was active and growing in turn-of-the-century Europe, particularly in Germany. For Nietzsche, both liberalism and its close cousin, socialism, were secularized versions of Christianity—expressions of morality without God. Both sought the impossible. Equality was unachievable and undesirable, since it could only be achieved by lowering the creative and the strong to the level of the mindless and the weak. For Freud, human nature presented socialism with an insurmountable barrier. The most cherished ideals of socialism and liberalism were, at best, mere wish fulfillment. Worse than socialism for Nietzsche, Freud, and a host of others in late Victorian society was the women's movement. The new, independent woman was viewed by them as a perversion of woman's real nature.

By late in the century, psychology permeated social science. Everything people did seemed to be reducible to a psychological state. Comte's dream that sociology would achieve dominance among the social sciences had not been fulfilled. Yet the turn of the century was also the golden age of sociological theory. The French sociologist, Émile Durkheim, whose ideas are discussed in Chapter Ten, was convinced that there was more to society than the individuals who comprised it, and more to the individual then merely personality. By studying suicide, seemingly the most isolated and purely psychological act, Durkheim demonstrated that patterns of suicide helped to explain the causes of self-destruction sociologically. By looking at the factors that bound, to various degrees, individuals to their society, Durkheim explained the rates and the incidence of suicide without recourse to psychology.

Durkheim was the chief founder of sociology in France. He was concerned to show how social forces external to the individual shaped her or his actions. Durkheim's social theory was written in the context of the great challenges of the time—feminism, socialism, and decadence—and was directed, above all, against the individualistic theory of Herbert Spencer.

Max Weber was Durkheim's counterpart in Germany, although the two worked independently of each other. As discussed in Chapter Eleven, Weber developed his sociology in the context of a debate with the legacy of Marxism, opposing in particular the economic determinism that characterized the German socialist movement. Weber's sociology was historical and cross-cultural, but always interested in people's beliefs and values as they influenced their social action. In contrast to Durkheim, then, Weber's sociology included a central role for subjectivity.

Weber never pursued his interest in subjective states in a social psychological direction. Similar to Durkheim, he was concerned with defining and developing the new discipline of sociology. His contemporary, Georg Simmel, took a more individualistic tack, initiating the study of social interaction. Social life and institutions were generated by the interactions of the people who comprised them.

Simmel's social theory fizzled in Germany; in America it found a congenial following. America was the natural home of individualistic social psychology, developed in the early decades of the twentieth century by George Herbert Mead, whose ideas are discussed in Chapter Fourteen. By the mid-twentieth century, the study of the use of symbols in interaction, which resulted in the social construction of institutions (in fact, the construction of each individual's reality), was a significant subdiscipline that challenged the structural analysis of society derived, in part, from Durkheim and Weber. Sociology had been fragmented into a multi-paradigm Humpty Dumpty that contemporary theorists are seeking to piece together again.

9 EVOLUTION AND SOCIOLOGY

Evolution is one of the great ideas of the nineteenth century that shaped the modern world view. The belief that change was slow, gradual, and peaceful was congenial to the **Victorian** mind. Yet, from at least 1859, the year Darwin published *On the Origin of Species*, the word 'evolution' evoked the most vociferous and acrimonious debates in popular as well as intellectual circles. A variety of types of otherwise incompatible social theories, including laissez-faire economics, Marxian socialism, and literary decadence, claimed to be related to Darwinism.

That society had evolved from simple to complex, or through a series of predetermined stages, was a fundamental postulate of a great variety of social theories. Saint-Simon and Comte had hypothesized a law of historical development that society passed through successive stages. The conservatives had fostered an organic image of social functions and an evolutionary view of the history of nations through the slow growth of precedents and traditions. Hegel had imagined a great, cosmic story of universal evolution driven by principles inherent in the world. In conservative theory, evolution justified the existence of social institutions that liberal rationalists had condemned as unjust, unnecessary, and undesirable. Marx had brought the dialectic down to earth, but the notion of 'hidden impulse' still drove his theory of the evolution of history.

It appeared that the ancient analogy that society was like a biological organism had a solid foundation in fact. As sociology emerged in the late nineteenth century, evolution and organicism were adopted as central theoretical concepts. The great intellectual challenge occurred when the principle of evolution was applied to the natural history of the universe and to the origin and development of life on earth. Traditionalists balked because of a threat they perceived to religious dogma. The Victorian age is synchronous with the attack of science on religion. Well into the twentieth century, however, scientists were still disputing the mechanisms underlying evolution. In the context of intellectual and popular controversy, evolution, particularly Darwinism, shaped the imagination of the age.

THE THEORY OF EVOLUTION

As in so many instances, ancient Greek philosophers anticipated the debate between those who claimed that evolution had occurred by chance and those who believed in the immutability of species. According to Aristotle, Empedocles had advocated the theory of random change (Box 9.1).[1] During the earliest period of ancient Greek science, many natural philosophers believed that nature changed over time, old species died out and new ones appeared, and humans 'originally came from the animal kingdom'.[2] Although he believed that the world was ancient, Aristotle claimed that it had neither a beginning in time nor an end and that everything had always existed as it was. According to his anti-evolutionary theory, all species of life were immutable—they had always existed in an unchanged form. Each species could be arranged on a 'great ladder' from the lowest to the highest, with humanity at the top, fixed in position for eternity.

Box 9.1

According to Aristotle, Empedocles had argued that, in the first stage of the formation of living creatures, various parts of animals existed separately and were not at first connected together: 'On the earth many heads sprang up without necks, arms wandered bereft of shoulders, and eyes strayed alone in need of foreheads.' It was a bizarre image. These wandering parts longed to combine with one another so, in a second stage, various limbs and organs 'came together as each happened to meet', entirely by chance. As the body fragments mingled, 'a myriad kind of mortal creatures were brought forth, endowed with all sorts of shapes, a wonder to behold. . . . Many were born with faces and breasts both front and back, oxen with the heads of men, and mixtures partly of men and partly of women's nature, fitted with shadowed [sexual] parts.' Over time, those creatures that were not constituted in a suitable way, such as the 'man-headed oxen', perished. Those whole-natured creatures, which were formed from parts that came together according to a logical formula and satisfied mutual needs, survived and began to reproduce themselves.

Aristotle put an end to this speculation about random evolution. For him, the fact that the parts of every animal fit together showed evidence of divine planning.

—Aristotle, quoted in W. Guthrie, *A History of Greek Philosophy* (1962)

The view of an unchanging, hierarchical universe appeared to be consistent with a literal reading of the Bible and remained the dominant view for the next 2,000 years. By the eighteenth century, just prior to the age of revolution, nature was still represented as Aristotle's **Great Chain of Being**. It was assumed that the Christian deity had created the world and all the species in it in their final form and at one time, in a grand hierarchy stretching from the lowest form of life ascending through numerous rungs until it reached humanity. Each species remained fixed and unchanging, and fit perfectly into its environment. Nature afforded the clearest proof of divine planning.

The ladder of nature originated at the top with God, the most perfect being, and worked its way down through categories of angels, humanity, the animals, and so on. The higher the rung on the ladder, the nearer the being was to perfection. Humanity came about midway on the scale. This model embraced in one conception both the natural and the spiritual orders, since both were viewed as elements within a continuum rather than as opposites. The eighteenth-century English poet, Alexander Pope, captured the idea memorably in *An Essay on Man*:[3]

> Vast chain of Being! which from God began,
> Natures ethereal, human, angel, man,
> Beast, bird, fish, insect, what no eye can see,
> No glass can reach; from Infinite to thee,
> From thee to Nothing.

Following Aristotle's principle of an immutable hierarchy in nature, the Swedish botanist Carl Linnaeus (1707–78) developed a system for classifying nature into classes, orders, genera, and species, giving each species a unique two-part Latin name. The first term in the scientific name represented the genus, the second the species. Humans became *Homo sapiens*, the term *sapiens* implying wisdom and reflecting the Enlightenment principle that humanity's main distinguishing feature was rationality. By giving humanity a genus, Linnaeus was not suggesting that humankind was not a unique creation. Humans were physically part of nature although their ability to reason made them distinct from the animal world and was connected to the supposition they possessed a soul. Linnaeus further subdivided the human species according to race, a classification he based on physical, cultural, and even moral criteria. In 1735 he divided humanity into four races arranged, inevitably, in a hierarchy. Reflecting some of the 'noble savage' beliefs of Rousseau, Linnaeus placed American Natives at the top of the hierarchy, followed in order by Europeans, Asians, and Africans.

Unlike Aristotle, Christian mythology presumed a relatively recent creation. Perhaps the world was created as recently as 4004 BC, a date suggested by Archbishop James Ussher.[4] This date, thought to be consistent with a literal interpretation of the Bible, was an image of life and time that corresponded neatly with the fixed hierarchies of feudalism and with traditional social theory.

As Europeans conquered distant continents and explored what to them had been remote parts of the world, they encountered novel forms of life that began to undermine the concept of Aristotle's static universe. One of the earliest opponents of the assumption of unchanging species was Walter Raleigh, an English pirate, adventurer, and explorer who found time between 1603 and 1616, while in the Tower of London waiting to be beheaded, to write several volumes of a history of the world. Unlike most scientists and philosophers of his day, he had travelled to distant lands, sailed around the globe, and founded a colony in what was then very much a new world. Raleigh's life experiences taught him to doubt the received wisdom of an unchanging nature.

New and amazing species had to be fit somewhere into Linnaeus's system of classification and into Biblical orthodoxy. As the number of species grew, the literal interpretation of the story of Noah's Ark became increasingly implausible. Raleigh had wondered how large a ship it must have been to hold two members of each species on the earth. It was, in fact, inconceivable. Raleigh did not doubt the Biblical Flood, but he concluded that European species must have been carried to the New World where they underwent a gradual transformation of their shape caused by the new

climate, eventually developing new species.[5] Life forms, then, were not immutable; rather, they underwent structural modification over time.

For Linneaus, the diversity of species may be greater than previously thought, but new species could still fit into his hierarchy of unchanging nature. Potentially more troublesome was the existence of fossilized bones and fossil imprints of species embedded into rock—species that appeared to have changed over time or even to have become extinct.

Fossils or *Via Plastica*?

What we now consider fossilized remains from ancient life forms had been known for centuries. As Wendt points out,[6] thousands of frozen mammoth carcasses had been found in Siberia, and their tusks became the source of imported ivory. Fossils of sea creatures had been found in rock quarries thousands of miles from the sea, even on high mountain slopes. The dominant explanation of these phenomena was simply that these were freaks of nature. At the time of creation, a mysterious force—termed **via plastica**—had caused the shape of some rocks to imitate living creatures. They were nothing more than a practical joke of nature. Linnaeus, who accepted the *via plastica* theory, devoted only a single page of his *Systema Naturae* to fossils, classifying them as a form of 'mineral'.[7] According to the novelist John Fowles, in 1857 the marine biologist, Gosse, made an even more ingenious suggestion. When God created Adam, Gosse said, he created at the same time all the fossils that appeared to be of extinct life forms.[8]

The most profound scientific assault on this belief in a fixed, unchanging universe began in France, at the same time that the French Revolution was about to demolish the feudal edifice. Paradoxically, strict censorship laws coexisted in eighteenth-century France with the most radical thought. There were many critical books to be burned and liberal authors to be imprisoned or exiled. Undaunted, the French materialists and atheists of the Enlightenment turned their attention to such potentially heretical subjects as the geological age of the earth and the origins of humanity. Nineteenth-century biologists and geologists continued their empirical inquiry into the origin of the universe, the earth, and life itself. France produced the first modern evolutionists.[9] In Paris, Count Buffon became Linnaeus's chief antagonist. Species were not immutable, Buffon asserted; rather, they changed slowly over time, sometimes improving sometimes degenerating, because of the effects of climate and nutrition. For Buffon, 'Nothing stands still; everything moves.'[10]

The theory of evolution required a prior revolution in knowledge about time and space. Evolution required immense spans of time—millions of years, not merely 6,000 or the 75,000 that Buffon had suggested—and evidence that forms of life had changed significantly over time. Early in the scientific revolution astronomers had perceived the vastness of the universe and the almost incredible number of stars (calculated in 2001 as approximately a million billion). The geologist, Charles Lyell, caused a similar revolution in perspective when he determined in 1830 that the world was ancient in age, millions, not mere thousands of years old. On this new platform of time, biologists erected a new vision of human origin and human nature.

The theory of evolution suggested that humanity, far from being a unique creation, was merely a highly successful animal. Linnaeus had classified human beings as a species, part of the order of primates, a designation they shared with the great apes. As orangutans and chimpanzees were brought from Asia and Africa into Europe and taught simple human-like skills, the distance between the highest animals and humanity appeared to be narrowed further. People speculated whether the great apes could learn to speak. The discovery of tribal societies with Stone Age technologies further narrowed the species gap and fuelled speculation about the existence of species intermediate between apes and humanity that perhaps had resulted from the mating of apes with 'natives'.[11]

Furthermore, the discovery of the actual nature of fossils appeared to demonstrate a large number of extinct species; the mammoth and an ancient type of rhinoceros, for example, had once lived in Europe and northern Asia. The fossil record also demonstrated that species had changed their form considerably over time. These two discoveries were incompatible with the traditional concept of the Chain of Being. Even Linnaeus, at the end of his life, struck out from his *Systema Naturae* the principle that forms of life are immutable—the cornerstone of the Great Chain of Being. By the end of the eighteenth century, some scientists were debating theories to explain how evolution occurred in nature.

JEAN-BAPTISTE LAMARCK

The idea of slow, progressive development—evolution—was already a part of the intellectual landscape before Darwin. The revolution in thinking occurred when the theory of evolution was connected to the generation of life. Life had clearly originated from inanimate matter. The orthodox view considered this generation miraculous, directed by a superior, supernatural will. Each species was a unique creation, unrelated to any other. The complex ways that individual species fit so thoroughly into their different environments seemed to be evidence of planning and creativity.

The eighteenth-century German poet, Goethe, challenged this view in his scientific explorations and implied in his poetry that life had evolved. His imagination ran ahead of scientific theory and the empirical observations that grounded explanation in observation. Even for scientists inclined to accept evolution, there were formidable obstacles. The incomplete fossil record had not yielded clear evidence of one species evolving into another species. This is still subject to serious scientific debate. It was not until the twentieth-century exploration of genetics and the principles underlying inheritance that evolution become the dominant perspective in biological sciences. There was no scientific understanding of how the first spark of life could have originated spontaneously in inert matter. In some contemporary scientific circles, it is held that the original spark of life on earth had an extraterrestrial, though materialistic, origin.

Prior to Darwin, the French scientist Jean Baptiste Lamarck (1744–1829) was the first prominent evolutionist. Lamarck is remembered now more as the scientist who proposed an incorrect explanation for evolution. He ought to be remembered as one of the earliest and most prominent evolutionists, whose ideas proved more compatible with social than biological science. For Lamarck, who published his theory in 1809, the year of Darwin's birth, fossils were direct ancestors of the present forms of life—succeeding generations of a species developed over time and passed on their slightly modified form to their offspring. His views were in direct opposition to the assumption of the immutability of species, a position vigorously defended by the most prominent scientist of Lamarck's day, Georges Cuvier (1769–1832). None of Lamarck's ideas challenged Cuvier more thoroughly than his belief that over a long evolutionary time, a four-legged animal had learned to walk on two legs; its front paws had become hands; the use of its hands had led to an enlarged brain, to speech, to community, and, ultimately, to reason itself—to humanity. The original four-legged animal ancestral to humanity, Lamarck claimed, had been a 'higher ape'.[12]

There appeared to be fossil evidence for different organisms existing at different times, but the central problem in evolution was the scarcity of evidence in the fossil record for actual evolutionary change itself. How did one organism gradually change into another? The main issue of contention was by what means evolution proceeds. How do organisms gradually change their form so that a species changes slowly over time and entirely new species arise?

Lamarck's explanation was twofold. First, he believed that an organism's will or effort was the crucial cause of evolutionary progress. In his view, evolutionary change was purposeful, almost intended by the organism. Second, the mechanism of evolution was use or disuse, what became known as the inheritance of **acquired characteristics**.[13]

According to Lamarck, over the course of its life an animal changed its physical appearance by selective usage. A giraffe stretched its neck slightly

longer reaching for high leaves, thereby acquiring a slightly longer neck than the one with which it was born. It then passed on this acquired characteristic to its offspring, which was born with a slightly enlarged neck. In this way, over generations, the giraffe neck became elongated. Evolution derives from the effort an organism makes to better fit into its environment,[14] as the eyes of the fish in Tolkien's *The Hobbit* grew:

There are strange things living in the pools and lakes in the hearts of mountains: fish whose fathers swam in, goodness only knows how many years ago and never swam out again, while their eyes grew bigger and bigger and bigger from trying to see in the blackness.[15]

Lamarck, along with the rest of the scientific world of the nineteenth century, misunderstood the process of genetic inheritance.

Lamarck's view gradually became popular after his death. Comte argued that human nature was not fixed forever; rather, it was modifiable within very narrow limits. In his view, continuous and uniform activity produced 'an organic improvement which can gradually become fixed in the race, if it has persisted long enough'.[16] Lamarck's idea that an animal's use or disuse of an organ would be inherited by its offspring was widespread and became an important component of Darwin's explanation of evolution. The two evolutionists parted ways on the question of whether there was an underlying purpose behind evolution. Darwin's theory undermined this belief in an overall purpose or meaning in nature.

Lamarck's theory combined a materialist explanation for evolution—the effects on a species of its use or disuse of its organs—and an idealist element, an underlying motive force that pushed evolution forward. That was the only possible way, Lamarck believed, to account for the progress that was evident in evolution. The fundamental idea that subsequent theorists were to draw from Lamarck was the notion that evolution was progressive, that species moved from lower to higher and that it was possible to understand this process as a series of progressively higher stages or types. According to this perspective, humans were more developed in their evolution than dolphins, Caucasians more advanced in evolution than Aborigines, and European culture more advanced than African.

In the absence of some underlying purpose, Lamarck asserted, evolution by chance would be as likely to lead to deterioration as progress. In the long run, when traditional thinkers gave up on the immutability of species, they would turn to Lamarck's theory as being compatible with a form of **creationism**. The fact that each creature fit so well into its environment, they argued, was evidence of planning by a superior intelligence—a deity. Lamarck's model of inheriting acquired characteristics fit the development of human societies, where purposive action could be linked to progressive change, better than it did the natural world for which he had initially intended it. At first, however, the early ideas of evolution were attacked in their entirety. As in social theory generally after the French Revolution, there was also a conservative reaction against the idea of evolution.

THE CONSERVATIVE REACTION

The ideas of the French evolutionists fundamentally challenged traditional Christian beliefs. Just as the ideas of the Enlightenment were declared false and dangerous, the theory of evolution was deemed morally reprehensible. Lamarck was dismissed in England as a French atheist and his revolutionary ideas were shelved.[17] One response among Christians was simply to declare the scientific evidence false and rely on a literal interpretation of the Bible. For most scientists who considered the problem, however, the existence of extinct species exposed in the ancient fossil beds had to be acknowledged and explained.

At first, the new discoveries were made to fit into the old explanation. Having abandoned the *via plastica* theory, traditional thinkers asserted that fossils were evidence of the Biblical Flood. When it was discovered that different fossils appeared to exist in different rock formations—simpler fossils

in more ancient rock, more complex fossils in more recent rock strata—the evidence for slow, evolutionary change was strengthened. For traditional thinkers, however, the inconvenient scientific facts had to be shoehorned into the existing belief system. The succession of extinctions revealed in the fossil record meant to them that there had been multiple floods or other disasters, not just one Great Flood, and that successive catastrophes had been followed by multiple creations.

Generally speaking, the first responses to the existence of facts that contradict a theory are never enough to refute the theory for those with a vested interest in believing it. The first response is to try to fit the new facts into the old theory. This was achieved by the doctrine knows as **catastrophism**, which claimed the Flood of Noah's time was simply the last in a series of catastrophes that had decimated all earlier existing forms of life on the earth after which, time after time, the deity had started life anew, with a new creation and new forms of life. As Wendt outlines the argument of the catastrophists,[18] each layer of rock, from bottom to top, had been created at successively more recent times and each layer contained extinct forms of progressively more advanced life forms. After each catastrophe, God had created a new set of species, more fully developed than the previous, destroyed set. These successive destructions and creations had eventually led to humanity as the highest form.

This new interpretation was consistent with a Christian theology (although not one that assumed the earth had been created, literally, in six days). In the aftermath of the French Revolution and during the conservative reaction, catastrophism became 'widely popular'.[19] The chief theorist of catastrophism was Georges Cuvier. Twenty years before Lamarck's death and just before the evolutionist's total blindness, Cuvier put a premature end to Lamarck's reputation and career. In a confrontation described by Wendt,[20] Cuvier appeared unexpectedly in Lamarck's lecture hall, hurled personal insults, and stalked off to his own lecture hall with Lamarck's students trailing behind. Cuvier then proceeded to use his extensive knowledge of geological time and the fossil record to support his theory of catastrophes. Each fossil, Cuvier claimed, was a unique animal that was created as it was, died unchanged, and did not slowly develop into another form or species.[21] Furthermore, there was clear evidence of mass extinctions in the fossil record—a fact recognized in modern science. Cuvier's knowledge and charisma carried the day. Lamarck felt disgraced. He died penniless and in obscurity to be vindicated post mortem, at least in part, by a new generation of evolutionists.

By the middle of the nineteenth century Charles Darwin had developed an evolutionary theory that eventually put the religious version of catastrophism in the scientific dustbin and Lamarck on the bottom shelf. Darwin's theory of evolution did not appear until 1858, almost 30 years after Lamarck's death, when he and Alfred Wallace independently presented papers expounding the theory of **natural selection**. By that time the public was somewhat better prepared to accept evolution, although not necessarily Darwin's version of it. As Stromberg argued,[22] Darwin contributed both the genius that fit all these pieces into one theory and, as well, spent a lifetime assembling scientific evidence to support his argument.

DARWIN AND NATURAL SELECTION

Over the course of his early scientific career, Darwin made careful observations of numerous species and their environment, particularly between 1831 and 1836, which he spent on a long, scientific sea voyage of discovery aboard the *Beagle*. As a result of his observations, he devised a new theory of evolution, but followed this with more than 20 years of further study and observation before he ventured to publish his discoveries in his *Origin of Species* (1859), one of the most influential books of the century.

Darwin drew his principal insight from the pessimistic liberal, Thomas Malthus, who regarded nature as a struggle for existence that left the strongest and best surviving. In Darwin's mind,

this struggle is not a war of all against all, as in Hobbes's theory; rather, the world is a place where each member of the species strives against the problems of survival posed by nature, struggling to feed itself and procreate in a difficult environment. In the *Origin of Species*, Darwin proposed that natural selection was the actual mechanism of evolution. Each species is represented by numerous individual organisms, which differ one from another, demonstrating a tremendous amount of variation in traits. Some individual members of a species, by chance, have features that give them a slight advantage over other members of their species in the same environment. Each giraffe, for example, is somewhat different from every other. Like people who come in a variety of sizes, each giraffe differed from the others in height, some relatively tall, others relatively short. To use other examples, some cheetahs could run slightly faster than others; some members of a species of moth could blend into their environment more fully than other members, and so on.

In each case, certain individual members of a species were better adapted to their environment than others. Longer-necked giraffes could reach the leaves on the taller trees while short ones were more likely to feed poorly; faster cheetahs were able to catch more antelopes than slower ones; well-camouflaged moths avoided becoming dinner for some other species. Those members of the species that are better adapted will tend to live longer and pass on their beneficial characteristics to their offspring; the disadvantaged will have fewer offspring and their less advantageous traits will disappear in the species. Over time, the species will gradually change until it fits more and more perfectly into its environment. This is the process of natural selection. Adaptation, then, was not the result of an animal's 'efforts' to meet environmental challenges, as Lamarck had proposed, but simply occurred naturally as animals struggled to survive in nature.

When the environment changes, new traits will be selected and the species will change slowly, or evolve, to be increasingly adapted to its new environment. If members of a species migrate to a new habitat such as an island with a distinct environment and are then isolated from breeding with members of the species left behind, then the two separate branches will evolve in different directions, gradually becoming increasingly unlike each other. Eventually they will become two separate species, unable any longer to mate successfully with their former relatives.

Like Lamarck, Darwin did not understand the mechanisms of genetic inheritance, of mutation and sudden leaps in evolution. Not until the twentieth century was the mechanism of genetic inheritance understood, as well as the process of mutation by which an individual member of a species could develop, by chance, a new inheritable trait. For Darwin, the principle of evolution was simple: nature did not make leaps.

The fossil record was also incomplete and had serious gaps, offering little evidence of the actual transformation of one species into another. Nevertheless, Darwin marshalled his facts carefully and produced an explanation that became increasingly accepted in English biology. The contemporary theory of evolution, which is the foundation of the study of biology, has advanced beyond Darwin; nevertheless, natural selection is still regarded as a crucial component of the theory.

While *On the Origin of Species* was immediately controversial, Darwin had only hinted at the place of humanity in this evolutionary scheme—Lamarck had been more direct in his claim that humankind had evolved from a higher ape. At the end of his book, Darwin suggested that, from his theory, 'Light will be thrown on the origin of man and his history.' The publication of Darwin's two later books, *The Descent of Man and Selection in Relation to Sex* (1871) and *The Expression of the Emotions in Man and Animals* (1872), made the connection explicit: like any species, Darwin said, humanity had also evolved from earlier, simpler forms. Darwin rejected the notion that animals were driven by instincts while humans alone possessed a mind and were capable of higher mental functions. Darwin asserted that humans and animals had many behavioural characteristics in common and that animals were capable of actions that demonstrated considerable mental ability.[23]

Darwin had worked out his controversial theory about natural selection and human origins well in advance of publishing them, and ventured to make his view public only with large amounts of observational data as proof. His views about gender and race were less 'heretical'. As a Victorian, Darwin subscribed to the view that men and women had different mental dispositions. Men were more energetic and possessed more inventive genius than women. They were more competitive and, hence, more ambitious and selfish. Women were tenderer and had greater powers of intuition and imitation.[24] On the basis of his research, Darwin contended, biology determined that women were naturally suited for nurturing and caregiving, but not for conflict or leadership. The tendency to draw distinctions between types within a species was contradicted by Darwin's emphasis on variability within a species and the liberal view that human character was shaped, in many respects, by social circumstances and opportunity. Darwin was careful to support the equal education of women and was impressed by the quick ability of individuals from less developed cultures to learn the customs and culture of European society.[25]

Darwin and Victorianism

During Victorian times science and Darwin were not alone in challenging Christian faith. Historical research into the history of the Middle East had cast doubt on the accuracy of the Old and New Testaments and the uniqueness of Christianity.[26] For these new atheists, the term 'gospel truth' was an oxymoron. Then, Darwin's ideas challenged fundamentally many cherished Victorian beliefs. By providing a scientific grounding for the theory of evolution, Darwin helped undermine literalist Christianity. The theory that life arose from random activity and evolved slowly over millions of years was considered to challenge the belief of many Christians that the universe was created by God, that divine intelligence had planned the world and all the variations in it, and that there were ultimate truths and moral standards in the universe. Darwinism challenged the beliefs of both Christians and secular humanists. What was to prevent human beings from acting on their most selfish desires when the future promised nothing more than a cold grave? If we were just one additional kind of animal, then rules about ethics, sexuality, and morality might not be absolute values, but mere human conventions—as represented by the Bloodhound Gang, although the novelist John Fowles makes the same point less brazenly in *The French Lieutenant's Woman* (Box 9.2).[27]

Secular humanism, however, suffered a similar fate. Darwin said that *Homo sapiens* were simply of a species, one kind of animal among others—more successful perhaps, but only by chance. He concluded that the universe had no purpose; there was no particular meaning inherent in life. Life activity was ruled by chance and accident. It appeared that retrogression and extinction were just as likely to occur as progress and success. If this were true, what meaning or purpose was constituted in the existence of life? From the perspective of Darwinism, the answer was: none. There were only the meanings that humans chose to give it. His was a bleak, amoral view of the universe that denied a link between reason and anything invisible;

and it was influential in a variety of intellectual circles, beyond science and into the arts.

There were several responses to Darwin's 'attacks'. The Roman Catholic Church acted officially to list Darwinism and evolution as modern heresies and to reiterate the doctrine of papal infallibility.[28] Darwin's books were added to the list Catholics were forbidden to read, the *Index librorum prohibitorum*.[29] **Fundamentalists** rejected the new evolutionary doctrines no less firmly than did the Roman Catholics by calling emotionally for a commitment to unquestioned faith. Faith in God, one's personal salvation, and the imminence of the second coming of Jesus Christ were considered to be founded on intuitive knowledge. Less dogmatic theologians argued that evolution was simply part of the Divine Plan and was compatible with a deity who had set the world's patterns of evolution in motion. This was the view that Darwin's contemporary, Alfred Wallace, had promoted.

A variety of social attitudes emerged directly from the general pessimism many Victorians drew from Darwinism. One lesson from natural selection appeared to be that everything happened by 'luck', 'fate', or chance. There was no particular order in the universe, therefore universal rules could not be established about good and bad, morality or immorality. Nature was indifferent to

---

Box 9.2

> You and me baby ain't nothing but mammals,
> So let's do it like they do on the Discovery Channel.
>
> —Bloodhound Gang, 'Nothing but Mammals' (2000)

Darwinism, as its shrewder opponents realized, let open the floodgates to something far more serious than the undermining of the Biblical account of the origins of man; its deepest implications lay in the direction of determinism and behaviourism, that is, towards philosophies that reduce morality to a hypocrisy and duty to a straw hut in a hurricane.

—John Fowles, *The French Lieutenant's Woman* (1970)

good intentions. There was no point in planning the future and no point in attempting to reform society. What was destined to come would come, regardless of anyone's efforts. All one could do was to surrender to one's fate. Deep pessimism was the only realistic attitude to adopt.

Decadence was a second possibility. If there was no deity, there need not be absolute rules of morality or altruistic meaning to life. Then what was life for? In the decadent view, life was for pleasure. The only sensible way to live was to experience sensations and maximize your enjoyment. The boundaries of morality, of justice, had been swept away. There was no point in striving to be 'good'. In the place of traditional values was erected the indulgent search for gratification and extreme experience. The only thing worth striving for was sensation and excitement.

These developments were certainly **unintended consequences** of Darwin's doctrines. Pessimism and decadence were given their most direct expression in the arts and in the lifestyle of a minority of turn-of-the-century intellectuals, a new generation of artists, writers, poets, and musicians. Their attitude was marked by the absence of an explicit social theory. Life did not need—in fact, it could not be given—an explanation. It just was. From the point of view of intellectual history, however, this in itself was a kind of theory.

NATURALISM

As the nineteenth century passed from early optimism to the pessimism of the 1890s, realism shaded imperceptibly into **naturalism**, a literary genre that influenced the elitist, anti-democratic culture that would come to dominate the avant-garde of the late nineteenth century. This new line of social theory was indebted to Darwinism. While the realists attempted to reveal the truths of the common person in a spirit of democratic egalitarianism, the naturalists usually focused their art on those who were more marginal or down and out. Naturalist fiction differed from realism in its subject as well as in its sense of the forces that underlie the real. Protagonists were not so much victims

of society, but of fate, of degenerate human nature, or of other circumstances beyond their control or comprehension. Like the realists, the naturalist movement focused on real-life situations, though usually of the seamier kind. The realists had painted peasants in the fields or eating potatoes; they had portrayed workers trudging to or home from work. The naturalists were fascinated by the marginalized of society, the outcast and destitute.

The French writer, Émile Zola, wrote as though he were a scientist uncovering social problems among the underclass of prostitutes, criminals, and social outcasts. The naturalists removed the focus from individual morality. Bourgeois literature and drama had generally been concerned with the struggle between good and evil in people's characters. How you acted in the world was a matter of choice, a test of your inner character and strength, of your virtue and morality. After Darwin, a different image of the human being emerged. Rather than being self-determined, people's characters were shaped by the interplay of forces such as their heredity (the moral traits they had inherited biologically) and their environment. The person resembled a puppet pulled about, tragically or comically, by forces she or he did not understand and could not control.

The English novelist, Thomas Hardy, represents this pessimistic outlook in his writing. It was difficult, thought Hardy, for artists to view nature in quite the same way after Darwinism. Nature had not changed; people's perspective on nature had changed. Birds sang to define and defend their territory; trees struggled for life against odds that threatened to snuff them out; vines grew and strangled the saplings they embraced (Box 9.3).[30] Nature was 'red in tooth and claw', as the poet Alfred Tennyson had claimed in his poem 'In Memoriam', nine years before Darwin's Origin. He named the literary style that celebrated the 'glowing gloom' of chaos 'Zolaism' (for the French writer, Émile Zola).

Hardy's universe was completely indifferent to human endeavours and aspirations to live a moral life. It was a cruel, heartless world, and only people with no higher moral inclinations or

Box 9.3

[A]ll she could see were more trees. . . . At their roots were stemless yellow fungi like lemons and apricots, and tall fungi with more stem than stool. Next were more trees close together, wrestling for existence, their branches disfigured with wounds resulting from their mutual rubbings and blows. It was the struggle between these neighbours that she had heard in the night. Beneath them were the rotting stumps of those of the group that had been vanquished long ago, rising from their mossy setting like black teeth from green gums.

On older trees ... huge lobes of fungi grew like lungs. Here, as everywhere, the Unfulfilled Intention, which makes life what it is, was as obvious as it could be among the depraved crowds of a city slum. The leaf was deformed, the curve was crippled, the taper was interrupted; the lichen ate the vigour of the stalk, and the ivy slowly strangled to death the promising sapling.

—Thomas Hardy, *The Woodlanders* (1887)

refined feelings were suited to it. By no means did survival of the fittest imply that the best succeeded. In contrast, those who strove the hardest to achieve ethical ends faced disappointment and disillusionment. Given the actual state of nature, ruthless and amoral people were the best adapted to their natural and social environments and were the mostly likely to succeed within them. Thus, Hardy's naturalism contracited the social Darwinist assumption that the successful were equal to the 'best'.

Writing in the age of positivism and Darwin, Hardy wrote about characters who were not fully responsible for the outcomes of their actions. Their efforts to direct events in their lives were largely doomed to failure. The human ability to reason paled into insignificance alongside the powers of genetic inheritance, environmental determinism, fate, and nature. If, for Hardy, there was a supreme being or a 'President of the Immortals', as he put it in his novel, *Tess of the D'Urbervilles* (1891), this deity was a malevolent rather than a benevolent force. The combined forces of nature, society, and fate confound human intention at every turn. The would-be hero is inevitably doomed.

A convention of popular Romantic fiction coincides chance with good fortune.[31] In Hardy's naturalism, however, coincidence works to thwart rather than to promote human happiness. In *Tess of the D'Urbervilles*, a tragic chain of circumstances is unleashed when Tess's letter of confession to Angel Clare never reaches her but is accidentally hidden under the doormat.

It was not only the fates, but also social conventions that conspired to destroy Tess. By Victorian standards, Tess was an immoral woman. An early victim of seduction, Tess became a mistress and a criminal. In one sense, her eventual death by hanging represented what Victorian England would have expected as the suitable outcome of such a life. Nevertheless, Hardy's characterization scandalized Victorian propriety. He presented Tess as a victim, as an essentially 'good' woman. Wrong had been done to her by the very conventions of the Victorian society that had determined her fate and then destroyed her.

In the United States, the controversial Theodore Dreiser (1871–1945) exemplified the conscious use of naturalism in fiction. Like Hardy, his heroes, too, challenged the double moral standards of the times. As Pizer argues,[32] realist literature was defended in late nineteenth-century America as being democratic and egalitarian in spirit, as focusing attention on the common person rather than on the aristocratic rich. Realism depicted life as it more generally was, with the warts clearly visible, rather than through the lens of Romantic illusion or wishful thinking. Realism evolved into naturalism in American literature as authors focused on the socially marginal or morally suspect individual, who struggles in an environment of uncontrollable social forces, always subject to the vicissitudes of random chance and fate.

Dreiser had experienced the hardship of poverty and was largely self-educated. At a time when journalists were engaged in harsh social criticism of the new American elite (the 'robber barons') and the hardships and oppression facing working people, Dreiser found work as a newspaper reporter, an occupation that allowed him to develop his writing craft and also brought him into contact with the poverty and social dislocation of the seamier side of turn-of-the century America. His understanding of these social conditions was influenced by his reading of French authors such as Émile Zola and the social Darwinists. Dreiser wrote that reading Herbert Spencer's *Synthetic Philosophy* 'quite blew me to bits intellectually.'[33] Life was a struggle for survival in a new, urban jungle, where human behaviour was dictated by chemical substances in the blood and where the overwhelming tide of human affairs determined people's fate (Box 9.4).[34]

Dreiser's criticism of American capitalism is most biting in *The Financier*, a story about a rapacious 'robber baron'. In this novel, Dreiser reflected both the 'survival of the fittest' mentality of Spencer and, as well, Nietzsche's concept of the 'superhuman' (see below). In Dreiser's view, the problems of American capitalism were caused both by the economic system that promoted fierce competition for the rewards of material success, and by human nature itself, which had not yet evolved sufficiently far from the instinctual beast within humanity. These basic, instinctual desires, when combined with the capitalist culture and ethic of endless competition and consumption, proved a deadly combination. Even achieving success in the American sense did not bring happiness or contentment; in fact, it was incapable of doing so. Ultimately, both the culture of America and the nature of humanity would have to change for social reforms to be truly effective.

In his first novel, *Sister Carrie* (1900), Dreiser told the story of an ordinary young woman, Carrie Meeber, described as 'a fair example of the middle American class—two generations removed from the emigrant'. Self-interest was her guiding characteristic and 'she was . . . ambitious to gain in material things.'[35] As the subtitle of Chapter One asserts, Carrie was 'a waif amid forces' she did

---

Box 9.4

I discovered that all that I had deemed substantial—man's ... very identity save as an infinitesimal speck of energy ... drawn or blown here and there by larger forces in which he moved quite unconsciously as an atom—was questioned and dissolved.... Up to this time there had been in me a blazing and unchecked desire to get on and the feeling that in doing so we did get somewhere. Now in its place was the definite conviction that spiritually one got nowhere ... that one lived and had his being because one had to, and that it was of no import, no more so than that of any bug or rat. Of his ideals, his struggles, deprivations, sorrows as well as joys, it could only be said that they were chemic compulsions—something which for some inexplicable but unimportant reason responded to and resulted from the hope of pleasure and the fear of pain. Man was a mechanism, undevised and uncreated—and a badly and carelessly driven one at that. He was governed by creature desire....

—Theodore Dreiser, *Newspaper Days* (1922)

not comprehend. Like 'The Magnet Attracting', she was moved 'by forces wholly superhuman', becoming one of the numberless crowd of migrants pouring from rural to urban America, a mere 'wisp on the tide'.[36] For Dreiser, as the Darwinists had theorized, humans were dominated by instincts and 'creature desires' more than by reason and free will.

Chasing the American Dream, Carrie was drawn to Chicago, which was rapidly being transformed from a quiet railway junction to a metropolis of extremes. Carrie quickly came to perceive 'how much the city held—wealth, fashion, ease—every adornment for women, and she longed for dress and beauty with a whole heart.'[37] What she found, however, was the dull routine of working-class subsistence as a proletarian machine operative in a shoe factory. Initially forced to board with relatives, she found them tied to an endless round of drudgery and deprivation, the 'grimness of shift and toil'.[38] Carrie's mind was elsewhere; her feelings, especially her desires, ran deeply: 'She longed and longed and longed.'[39]

When Carrie found the means to achieve the material trappings of success, she succeeded not by dint of hard work—the path to upward mobility for women was greatly restricted—but by becoming the mistress of a travelling salesman. Eventually Carrie was able to find prosperity in a slightly more respectable career in the theatre. Dreiser's novel scandalized his audience. *Sister Carrie*—the character as well as the novel as a whole—was deemed amoral because Dreiser was transgressing a socially accepted moral code. Proper values were supposed to lead to success, while those who followed the easy, immoral path inevitably came to bad ends. Carrie's apparent success demonstrated the opposite moral lesson, as had Moll Flanders's picaresque career in Defoe's novel a couple of centuries earlier. Dreiser's naturalism did not knuckle under the moralistic prescriptions of late Victorianism.

Sister Carrie also dealt more overtly with sexuality than was considered proper; although more was implied than described, the reader was left in no doubt about what had transpired. The novel had a stormy history of publication, partly also because of its use of profanities, an important mark of realism in fiction. Many of Dreiser's other works suffered similar problems. Some sexually explicit passages in *Jennie Gerhardt* (1911) and *The 'Genius'* (1915) were edited before publication. Even so, the New York Society for the Suppression of Vice threatened to bring criminal charges for obscenity against the publisher unless the obscenity and blasphemy were expurgated.[40]

The principal 'desire' in Dreiser's novels (and in his personal life) was for sexuality, a literary theme that encountered a social minefield in early twentieth-century America. In his reply to the critics who complained that immoral literature undermined people's virtue, Dreiser accused them of hiding their real motivation: 'The influence of intellectual ignorance and physical and moral greed upon personal virtue produces the chief tragedies of the age, and yet the objection to the discussion of the sex question is so great as to almost prevent the handling of the theme entirely.'[41] In England, where *Sister Carrie* had a more receptive audience, the taboo about describing sexuality in literature was about to be demolished by D.H. Lawrence, although for many decades Lawrence's work would be published in the United States only in expurgated editions.

In their experimentations with more sexually explicit material, many early twentieth-century novelists sought to replicate the artistic freedom that visual artists who had painted nude women and men had so long enjoyed, although they had done so in relatively immobile contexts, similar to still lifes. The graphic depiction of copulation, for example, was generally eschewed except in the underground market for pornography, which proliferated in Victorian times. The overt display of sexuality as a normal part of the visual culture is one of the most obvious differences between the late nineteenth century and the contemporary West. At the beginning of the twentieth century, the boundary between the pornographic underculture and the more elite artistic exploration of sexuality was being breached. In Vienna, Victorian reticence about public discourse on sexuality was being eroded under Sigmund Freud's guidance, as middle-class women were revealing their sexual abuse and their desires on the physician's 'couch'. The attempt to create a new science of 'sexology' stimulated a widespread public discussion of forms of sexuality. As it passed through the psychoanalytic movement initiated by Freud and modern psychological literature, human sexuality became a dominant theme in Western culture. For moralists, the apparent decline in sexual ethics was proof of the decadent consequences of Darwinism.

HERBERT SPENCER AND SOCIAL DARWINISM

Darwin had derived his central conception of natural selection, in part, from the 'survival of the fittest' doctrine of the old laissez-faire liberal, Thomas Malthus. Later liberals returned the favour, utilizing Darwin's theory to justify competitive capitalism and discredit the theories of social liberals and reformers. The application of Darwinian principles to social theory was called **social Darwinism**. By the mid-nineteenth century, the ideas of laissez-faire capitalism were being eclipsed by those who recognized the need for government-sponsored reforms. Liberalism was put on the road to social liberalism by theorists such as Jeremy Bentham, Harriet Taylor, and Florence Nightingale (see Chapter Seven). Darwin, however, vindicated the older, dog-eat-dog vision of social life, the vision of Malthus and, before him, of Hobbes.

Darwin's theory implied that humans competed with each other for survival. In this process, the successful clawed their way to the top of the social pyramid, while the unsuccessful sank to the bottom of the social heap, where the poor, the uneducated, and the unemployed mingled hopelessly. The laws of evolution, in fact, could explain the whole drama of human history: the rise and fall of civilizations; the emergence of Europe as the dominant part of the globe; the inevitability of technical progress that had come with the Industrial Revolution. The equating of success with moral values—the 'best' people being the survivors—

was extrapolated to societies and nations summarized in the phrase 'might makes right'.

Hegel and the conservatives had already applied the principle of evolution to human history. For Hegel, however, it had still been necessary to hypothesize a supernatural Spirit who wrote and directed the script of human progress. Now a theory of history could be devised based on natural laws such as natural selection and the impact of an advanced culture on a backward one. The daunting task of applying the principle of natural evolution to all of human history was addressed by the English sociologist, Herbert Spencer (1820–1903). His doctrine expressed the perspective known as social Darwinism.

Spencer grew to maturity in the early years of triumphant British industrial capitalism, when laissez-faire ideas dominated politics and economics and the British government was busy deregulating the economy. By mid-century, British capitalism was about as free of government interference as it would get and the tide was already turning towards a more socially conscious type of liberal social theory and politics. By that time, Spencer's ideas had been set and he maintained a single-minded defence of economic individualism until his death, long after capitalism had moved from being relatively small-scale and competitive to become large-scale oligopolies. Spencer found himself increasingly out of step with modern society.

Although his father was a schoolmaster, Spencer's formal schooling lasted for only three months. Like Mill, he was home-schooled, being taught science and mathematics by his father and uncle, and became thoroughly agnostic. Joseph Priestley's social ideas were especially influential on young Spencer, MacRea argues. From Priestley, the discoverer of oxygen, Spencer drew a deep antipathy towards all forms of government interference in the liberties of the individual. Like Malthus, Priestley decried any government assistance for the needy or the poor, for victims of disaster or disease. Allow nature to take its course, he recommended, because government always makes things worse.[42] This was as close to any statement of faith that Spencer would whole-heartedly embrace.

Like Darwin and Wallace, Spencer derived the idea of the survival of the fittest from Malthus. Society was inherently competitive, he believed, and from this competition came human progress. The laissez-faire doctrines of free trade, free enterprise, and free competition were the social equivalent of Darwin's natural selection. Since these were the motors of progress, it followed that the proper course for human development was to allow these laws of competition to operate without interference; to do otherwise would only cause harm to society.

For Spencer, the most dangerous shark in the economic environment was the threat of government regulation and the expansion of the power of the state over the individual. For the social liberals, the greatest threat to the well-being of the nation came from the harmful consequences of laissez-faire and the shark-like, rapacious businessmen who became rich on the exposed backs of the labouring poor. Far-sighted liberals perceived the warning of a greater danger on the horizon. Unless workers' grievances were satisfied, they might rise in revolution. Spencer argued that this discontent was the consequence of providing elementary schooling for the working class, another social liberal reform. Educating workers had resulted in increasing their expectations for things that were impossible. They had been fed 'pleasant illusions' that produced only discontent.[43] The real interest of the business class was to protect laissez-faire, not to reform the system.

Government Regulation

Spencer was an absolute opponent of the modern, interventionist state. In 'The new Toryism', Spencer complained, 'Most of those who now pass as [Social] Liberals, are Tories of a new type.'[44] For the last couple of decades, Spencer wrote in 1884, Liberals had changed their tune. In the early years, the movement from freedom to restriction had been easy. Individuals had looked to government to satisfy their grievances and this was appropriate

because the source of the grievance was usually government restriction itself. Under the old-fashioned conservatives (or Tories), the state had exercised a great deal of coercive power over the freedom of individuals. Repealing these restrictive laws removed the obstacles to individual freedom. The Liberals, Spencer said, had increasingly reduced the power of the state and expanded the liberty of individuals in the decades after Napoleon's defeat in 1815. When the East India Company had a legal monopoly of trade with India, the law blocked other businessmen from entering the trade, restricting their freedom. When the government dissolved the monopoly, anyone with sufficient capital could accumulate additional money by trading in the now open Indian economy.

What if the source of the grievance, however, was not in restrictive laws but resulted from the action of individuals themselves? Working people were angered by the long hours and unsafe working conditions they had to endure, by the employment of children in unhealthy occupations, by the adulteration of their food, by the deplorable state of their substandard housing, by the absence of medical attention they could afford—an apparently endless litany of injustices and exploitation. Again, they looked to government to remedy their hardships. But this situation was now entirely different from the past, Spencer argued, and government reform produced harmful consequences for the whole economy.

When the population demanded reforms from government, which necessarily meant adding more restrictions on the freedom of business owners, fundamental weaknesses of the democratic system in an era of universal franchise were exposed. Politicians of whatever party had to pander to the demands of the population in order to win re-election. That meant making promises and then delivering them. Since at least 1860, Spencer complained, Malthus's principle of population growth had been extrapolated to legislation: the government had been exponentially increasing the amount of new legislation restricting the freedom of individuals in the conduct of their businesses. New government rules imposed standards on the conditions of factory work, the production and serving of food and drink, the hours of work, rental housing, the education of children, and so on. To make his point, Spencer lists pages of examples of legal restrictions that, as he deemed a final irony, the rich had to pay for out of their taxes.[45]

What these Christians and social liberals did not realize, Spencer argued, was the ultimate harm caused by their interference. They were caught up in a short-term perspective, relieving this suffering here and that hardship there, while losing sight of the bigger picture. There was much more at stake than mere reforms, however pernicious they were alone. The socialists were pushing the process along, attacking the exploiters on behalf of those they called wage-slaves and intending to bring fundamental social change. The real question, then, was where all these reforms were leading, what kind of social structure was being created in the absence of any foresight by Parliament.[46] Spencer complained that, step by step, government reforms were building big, bureaucratic government: 'The numerous socialistic changes made by Act of Parliament', in addition to others yet to be made, 'will by-and-by all be merged in State-socialism':

> The belief, not only of the socialists but also of those so-called Liberals who are diligently preparing the way for them, is that by due skill an ill-working humanity may be framed into well-working institutions. It is a delusion. The defective nature of citizens will show themselves in the bad acting of whatever social structure they are arranged into. There is no political alchemy by which you can get golden conduct out of leaden instincts.[47]

The future would bring an era of a new form of slavery. For Spencer, a slave was defined as someone who 'labours under coercion to satisfy another's desire.' Slavery is more severe the greater the 'extent to which effort is compulsorily expended for the benefit of another instead of for self-benefit'. It doesn't matter whether the benefit from the labour is received by a slave owner, a private company, or the community as a whole because it is taken from the individual. Under socialism, what one produces is taken by the state and, in return, he or she receives from the 'general store' of goods what the state awards. It is still a form of slavery, Spencer believed, and worse than the kind the socialists said existed under capitalism.[48] By Spencer's definition, even the self-employed were becoming slaves. Government taxation, which takes away part of what someone earns for the benefit of others, is a modern form of slavery. Hence, right-wing theorists in our day who still endorse Spencer's laissez-faire ideology proclaim what they call 'tax freedom day', dividing an individual's annual income into the part that is taxed (the measure of Spencer's definition of slavery) and the part that the individual can spend personally. This approach presumes that taxes are not expended socially to benefit all taxpayers directly or to bring numerous indirect benefits to the wealthiest by sustaining a social system in which vast inequalities are justified and protected.

Spencer did not see the movement towards state capitalism as part of the inevitable evolution of industrialism, as Marxists suggested, or as a necessary element in the development of positivism in Comte's evolutionary theory. For Spencer, big government was contrary to the direction natural evolution would have taken society. The coming of modern state socialism was the result of choices made by politicians, journalists, trade union leaders, and other decision-makers who did not accept the truth, as Spencer put it, that 'miseries are caused by the ill-working of human nature' and therefore are not curable.[49]

Even if state socialism was intended to work for the mutual benefit of all, Spencer continued, by his definition it would still be a mild form of slavery. More importantly, however, it could never be mild. 'The machinery of Communism . . . has to be framed out of existing human nature; and the defects of existing human nature will generate . . . the same evils'. Humanity's love of power, selfishness, injustice, and untruthfulness will inevitably doom any attempt at social reform. Inevitably the leaders of such a society will take whatever measures are necessary to maintain their own supremacy, creating a great tyranny 'under which the mass of the people, controlled by grades of officials, and leading lives that were inspected out-of-doors and in-doors, laboured for the support of the organization which regulated them, and were left with but a bare subsistence for themselves.' Human nature will guarantee this outcome.[50]

The alternative to the slow rise of authoritarianism in liberal democracy or to its fullest expression in modern socialism was to allow the maximum of economic freedom to all persons. Laissez-faire works to the advantage of the great majority. Spencer asks, what causes the existence of overcrowded, slum housing? The fault lies at the doorstep of the legislature, not in the corporate boardroom. Government taxes on bricks and wood make it too expensive to build decent houses for the poor. More importantly, the evil of slum housing is caused by government regulation of rents. When government attempts to make rent affordable, the inevitable result is fewer and worse houses for the poor. Fixed rents allow landlords who own substandard houses to make a reasonable living, perpetuating slum housing; but the rents are not high enough to induce people with money to build slightly better housing, because the rent would be too low for profit-taking. Consequently, only houses for the better off were constructed, while the poor were crowded into the substandard houses that the landlord cannot afford to repair without also raising the rent.[51]

A suitable house for the poor could be constructed; but that would occur only with the deregulation of rents. Spencer realized that rent for better housing would have to be higher, but, he contended, it wasn't that the poor could not afford higher rents; they merely wasted their pay on unnecessary consumption. In short, since all benefits that the poor think they receive from the government actually come from taxing the rich, Spencer complains, if the rich were allowed to use the capital for their private businesses that is otherwise lost to taxes, benefits for all would result.

Social Darwinism

The doctrine of evolution would seem to be incompatible with a belief in a fixed human nature. Spencer admitted that human beings are modifiable to a degree through the use or disuse of their faculties, and that such adaptive changes are inheritable. Over time, 'constitution fits itself to conditions'. Under new conditions, such as in the Americas, 'new national characters are even now being moulded'. Similarly, every law that serves to modify human action will eventually cause 'fresh adjustments of their nature', a 'remoulding of the average character'.[52] In Spencer's sociology, human history was driven by cultural evolution as new characteristics were developed and passed on to future generations—an adaptation of Lamarck's theory of evolution. The culture of society would evolve progressively, then, in the absence of conscious meddling by the state.

Both the prosperous entrepreneur at the top of the social scale and the down-and-out at the bottom, Spencer argued, deserved their fate. The poor had refused work or found it distasteful: 'They are simply good-for-nothings, who in one way or another live on the good-for-somethings.' It is only natural that they should bring unhappiness on themselves and their families; it is the 'normal result of misconduct'. Their suffering is not removable, and it is not the duty of the state to try to remove it. 'To separate pain from ill-doing is to fight against the constitution of things', a law that is found both in religious ethics and in natural science. The religious injunction that those who do not work shall not eat, Spencer argues, 'is simply a Christian enunciation of that universal law of Nature under which life has reached its present height—the law that a creature not energetic enough to maintain itself must die.'[53]

Social activities 'are the aggregate results of the desires of individuals who are severally seeking satisfactions, and ordinarily pursuing the ways which, with their pre-existing habits and thoughts, seem the easiest.' From this it follows that social development was generated, for the most part, 'by men's efforts to achieve their private ends.' All technological innovation, the catalyst of progress, has resulted from individuals pursuing their individual purposes; nothing has been achieved by state intervention other than the preservation of order, which is the sole legitimate purpose of government.[54]

In nature, every organism requires special protection and care while young. Failing to provide for the next generation would doom the species. Once mature, however, the reverse proposition applies. At that point, individuals are either well-endowed or poorly endowed, 'each adult gets benefit in proportion to merit—reward in proportion to desert'; that is, all the necessities to sustain life. In competition with members of its own and antagonistic species, the individual either 'thrives and propagates' or 'dwindles and gets killed off'. Nature provides for multiplication of the superior. If the reverse occurred, the multiplication of the inferior, 'progressive degradation would result' for the species as a whole, which would not hold its place in the struggle for existence. This idea was clearly expressed by Darwin (Box 9.5).[55] Similarly, a society that stands in competition with other societies can only hold its own if it propagates superior, well-endowed individuals. To do otherwise can end only in disaster. Society must be arranged so that rewards are commensurate with the demand for an individual's particular labour.[56] Spencer was worried that

society was slowly declining because the poor and the least fit had more children than the rich, who were supposedly the fittest. Over time, then, the population would deteriorate as undesirable people proliferated. In the bleak **Malthusian** tone, Spencer declared that poverty, starvation, and misery were, in fact, 'far-seeing benevolence'.[57] This survival-of-the-fittest doctrine is the core of social Darwinism as an ideology.

Spencer had staked these claims in his *Social Statics*, published in 1851. Three decades later he declared, 'The beneficial results of the survival of the fittest, prove to be immeasurably greater than' those he had anticipated, a truth that 'is recognized by most cultivated people'. Yet, Spencer bemoaned, 'now more than ever before in the history of the world, [legislators] are . . . doing all they can to further survival of the unfittest!'[58] Spencer's fundamental assumption was that those who are suffering under present arrangements deserve their fate. Sympathy is misplaced when people do not let nature take its course. The unworthy deserve their sufferings, which would come automatically through the struggle for existence. To whom should sympathy be extended? Spencer's answer is: those who are well off. Social reformers make life 'harder for the worthy and inflict on them and their children artificial evils in addition to the natural evils they have to bear!'[59] While most money comes from the 'relatively

---

Box 9.5

With savages, the weak in body or mind are soon eliminated; and those that survive commonly exhibit a vigorous state of health. We civilized men, on the other hand, do our utmost to check the process of elimination; we build asylums for the imbecile, the maimed, and the sick; we institute poor-laws; and our medical men exert their utmost skill to save the life of everyone to the last moment.... Thus the weak members of civilized societies propagate their kind. No one who has attended to the breeding of domestic animals will doubt that this must be highly injurious to the race of man. It is surprising how soon a want of care ... leads to the degeneration of a domestic race; but excepting in the case of man himself, hardly anyone is so ignorant as to allow his worst animals to breed.

—Charles Darwin, *The Descent of Man* (1871)

well-off', the 'virtuous poor' are also made to pay, Spencer claims, to support the 'vicious poor':

> [T]he well-being of existing humanity . . . [is] secured by that same beneficent, though severe discipline, to which . . . creation at large is subject: a discipline which is pitiless in the working out of good , , , which never swerves for the avoidance of partial and temporary suffering. The poverty of the incapable, the distresses that come upon the imprudent, the starvation of the idle, and those shouldering aside of the weak by the strong, which leave so many 'in shallows and in miseries', are the decrees of a large, far-seeing benevolence.
>
> The process *must* be undergone and the sufferings *must* be endured. No power on earth . . . can diminish them one jot.[60]

Evolutionary Sociology

The social liberals and socialists regarded society as a '**plastic** mass', as dough they could shape according to their will. Like the conservatives, Spencer assumed an organic conception of society that he termed scientific—society was like an organism, a living body, with a natural structure having numerous parts all interdependent, each of which had specific functions to perform for the good of the whole.[61] Any action affecting one part of the social whole produces consequences for the other parts.

Spencer contrasted 'artificial' with natural development. The supernatural creation and control of life and society, as well as the practice of government interference in social life, were 'artificial'. Society, as life itself, had evolved naturally 'by changes as insensible as those through which a seed passes into a tree', reaching its present complexity 'slowly and silently'. Society is not the creation of great individuals but has grown naturally to its present form, whatever that may be, and the government of any nation conforms to the average character of its members. A government or powerful individual, such as Cromwell or Napoleon, may artificially attempt to change the arrange-

ments under which people live, but such change is always temporary and sooner or later previous conditions will be restored.[62] Permanent change must be developed slowly; no permanent change results suddenly from without.

Spencer saw society as resembling a living organism in that both size and complexity increase over time and generate a structure of parts that are functionally interdependent. Both exist as a whole, although there is constant replacement of those parts that do not affect the totality. Furthermore, both societies and species of life exist in a variety of forms, a variation explained by the surrounding conditions within which each evolved. Finally, in more complex organisms and in society, 'feeling is monopolized by one class of the vital elements.' In an organism, only a special tissue experiences feeling. In society, while 'all the members are endowed with feeling' and 'the units of a community are all sensitive, they are so in unequal degrees. The classes engaged in laborious occupations are less susceptible, intellectually and emotionally, than the rest; and especially less so than the classes of highest mental culture.'[63]

Spencer seeks analogies between the structure of organisms and the structure of various degrees of societies, from the simplest 'Bushmen' to more complex societies, which progressively develop divisions of labour among their members, as more complex organisms develop functionally different parts. In organisms and in societies, development proceeds 'from the homogeneous to the heterogeneous' and 'from the indefinite to the definite'. The circulation of the blood in a body is parallel to the circulation of commodities in society, providing the middle or merchant class with the vital task of sustaining social life.[64]

Eventually, through the natural processes of cultural evolution, a class distinction emerges between a regulatory and co-ordinating minority and a large class of producers, the two classes growing increasingly apart in function. The former originates in struggle among individuals, through which in primitive societies 'the strongest, most courageous, most sagacious, become rulers and leaders', finally producing a dominant class. As society develops, effective rule demands intelligence more than brute strength and government develops parallel to the nervous system of an organism.[65]

The weakness of a kingship model is that it is likely to be swayed by personal or class interests. So long as the nature of humanity is savage or anti-social, despotic rule—Hobbes's Leviathan—is necessary. Only a 'strong, determined, cruel ruler . . . can repress their explosive natures and keep them from mutual destruction.' The result is the kind of society Spencer calls 'military', which is dominated by a centralized warrior class and directs its energies at defensive and offensive warfare. Over time, however, the old predatory instinct dwindles from lack of use as the changing conditions of social life modify the character of individuals and sympathetic feelings grow. The authority of the ruler diminishes.[66]

In more complex societies, a third, 'trading or middle class' emerges. Society evolves from the military type to the industrial type. Societies that progress further evolve a representative body (Parliament) analogous to the brain that averages 'the interests of the various classes in the community'. A good Parliament, for Spencer, is one in which the interests represented are so sufficiently balanced that legislation allows to any one class only what is consistent with the claims of the other classes.[67] Democracy, Spencer argued in 1857, was 'the best form of government' provided it does not extend beyond its comparatively limited function of maintaining order and protecting the nation from external enemies. Even less intelligent people could understand these limited functions, which did not extend to interfering in the operation of economic laws.[68]

While Spencer approved of Parliament in principle, he had objections to representative government. Many electors do not have the will to elect proper representatives. Shopkeepers vote according to their most prominent patron; in a larger class of voters, small sums of money or the liberal supply of beer is all it takes to secure a vote. Besides a lack of will, most electors lack ability. Higher-class voters are too often

characterized by gross political ignorance while, among the larger, lower class, there exists 'an almost hopeless stupidity'. Spencer quotes from Thomas Carlyle, who defined the people as 'twenty-seven million, mostly fools'. Elected members are really representative of the people who elect them in one sense only, Spencer claimed: 'of the average stupidity'.[69] These representatives then legislate in every aspect of the life of society when they are unequal to understand any part of it. What they lack, in particular, is knowledge of the natural laws of society, a gap his sociology was meant to fill.[70]

The analogy between living organisms and society was not perfect. The essential difference was that, in an organism, the welfare of any part was subservient to the welfare of the whole, which had a single, corporate consciousness. A pain experienced by any part of the organic body is felt by the entire being. The body of society, however, is made of independent living units each with its own consciousness and with individual feelings of pleasure or pain. From this it follows that the welfare of individual citizens cannot be sacrificed to the welfare of the society.[71]

SOCIAL DARWINISM IN AMERICA

The type of sociology that found favour in North America was profoundly affected by the developments in sociological thought in Europe. There were two competing influences on American sociology, one derived from the positivists, Saint-Simon and Comte, and influenced a reformist strain in American social science; the second derived from Herbert Spencer. Both influences rejected the eighteenth-century assumption that society rested on a social contract. Rather, like the conservatives, Comte had focused on the development of a science of society that would emphasize the social structure and its effects on the individuals within it. For the positivists, while a society was obviously made up of individuals, the social structure was more powerful than the individuals who composed it: the whole was greater than the sum of its parts.

More significant than Comte's positivism for the very beginnings of American academic sociology were the ideas of Spencer, whose popularity in US universities extended into the twentieth century. In America, Spencer's ideas on progress, individualism, and the survival of the fittest seemed to express an American ideal or an explanation of the status quo.[72] Spencer's ideas were interpreted and popularized by William Sumner, regarded by some as the father of American sociology. Sumner probably was the most important proponent of social Darwinism in American thought and an outspoken propagandist for the older version of nineteenth-century liberalism.

In Sumner's view, the competitive economy rewarded the virtuous and punished those who were, in his words, 'negligent, shiftless, silly and imprudent'.[73] In this marriage of the Protestant ethic of hard work and sacrifice to natural selection, Sumner eased the consciences of the wealthy and powerful—regarded as 'robber barons' by the social liberals—assuring the rich that the pursuit of profit was beneficial for society as a whole and that they represented the highest stage of ability and morality. Sumner's was an ethic tailored to fit the needs and interests of the wealthy elite.[74]

Sumner's social Darwinism was based on the application of the biological principle of natural selection to society, the correlative of which was that individual intervention ('meddling') would most likely result in negative consequences. It was better to allow social processes to proceed unhindered. Intervention, Sumner argued, could deflect society from the natural and best evolutionary path. People had an unfortunate habit of attempting to help the down-and-out through individual charity or government reform. Like Malthus, Sumner believed that such reforms made conditions worse in the long run, not better. Sumner's only hope, which he regarded as faint, was that people might be convinced through the educational system to allow the natural laws of social evolution to work out freely without intervention, a policy he was convinced would produce the best results for society as a whole. This new application of the old laissez-faire doctrine had the consequence of preserving the existing forms of the social structure—the status quo—and thereby primarily benefiting the dominant classes.

The writings of Spencer and Sumner reflected an interpretation of Darwinism that transformed the outlook of conservatives. Competitive struggle was a natural law and, since society evolved at a glacial pace, reforms that violated the status quo were dysfunctional, or harmful, to society. Edward Youmans, another American sociologist and an early advocate of social Darwinism, argued that:

> the spirit of civilization . . . is pacific, constructive, controlled by reason, and slowly ameliorating and progressive. Coercive and violent measures which aim at great and sudden advantages are sure to prove illusory. . . . [Science shows] that we are born well or born badly and that whoever is ushered into existence at the bottom of the scale can never rise to the top because the weight of the universe is upon him.[75]

In short, social evolution will naturally and slowly move in the direction of making society better—more peaceful, harmonious, and prosperous. Problems will eventually solve themselves. So leave things alone and don't try to intervene with social reforms.

This organic conception of society was highly conservative because it implied that social classes—capital and labour—existed in a natural state of harmony. Consequently, class conflict could result only from incorrect perceptions that failed to recognize this harmony. Labour should co-operate with capital and be satisfied with its place, performing its function within the social whole.

For Spencer, conflict was individualized. The individual failed to fit properly into the social structure, hence individuals were the proper focus of scientific interest. Social science must study those individuals who don't fit in and learn how to intervene successfully to alter their particular, inappropriate habits. This tradition is reflected most clearly in the prominent place most social thinkers gave to education and in their concern with its function of producing good citizens. Social transformation was to be effected by individual character reformation—change people's individual characters and you make them fit properly into society. This view was to have practical consequences in the development of the profession of social work, which was the social science designed to identify individual maladaptations to society and intervene in those cases to help the persons fit in wherever was appropriate for them.

Consistent with the ideologies of competitive capitalism, the interpretation given to the extension of Darwinian natural selection to social evolution meant 'that every established and settled institution is justified, in its setting, as an adaptation'.[76] Whatever social institutions exist inevitably represent the latest and most progressive point reached by social evolution: in brief, what is, is right.

This close correspondence between ideology and the preservation of major social institutions and interests is one of the most important contextual factors in the acceptance into academe of sociology as a discipline. Sociology became an established university discipline as an ideological handmaiden to the rich and powerful. This illustrates a major sociological theme: that in 'determining whether . . . ideas are accepted, truth and logic are less important criteria than suitability to the intellectual needs and preconceptions of social interest.'[77]

While social Darwinism, then, had a relatively brief career in sociology, even in the United States where this theory seemed best suited, its more long-lasting consequence was in modern economics where laissez-faire policies are once again dominant and social Darwinism justifies the elimination of any socially liberal program aimed at ameliorating the conditions of the poor. That there were such liberal programs, however, suggests that alternative ideologies competed with the pontifications of Herbert Spencer. Turn-of-the-century America was also the era of progressivism, of muckraking journalism that exposed the corruption of office and wealth, of a reform movement rooted in a socially conscious Christianity. That side of American intellectual life also was given a sociological face.

IMPERIALISM AND RACISM

The law of the struggle for existence embraced not merely the competition of individuals within a nation, but the conflict of nation against nation and race against race. The European conquest of the world, initiated by Columbus in the fifteenth century and pursued relentlessly by innumerable European traders thereafter, reached its zenith in the nineteenth century. The ideology of the 'White Man's Burden' proclaimed the self-promoting justification that it was necessary to drag the inferior races into civilization. In England, the novelist Rudyard Kipling best exemplifies the promotion of colonial domination and extreme nationalism. In Victorian England, while liberals slowly inched towards social reform, the conservatives drew their strength from patriotism, from the Empire and the new laissez-faire policies that could apparently be justified by social science in its social Darwinist guise.

In this competition between the races, the British nation and what was termed the white race were seen to have emerged triumphant, an outcome that was supposedly indicative of natural superiority. In *A History of the Sciences*, Mason exemplifies this viewpoint by citing the essay, 'On National Life from the Standpoint of Science', written by Karl Pearson in 1900. Pearson believed that racial conflict and hatred were natural, and that doctrines such as Christian brotherly love and Marxist internationalism were unnatural and harmful to the progress of humankind. There has always been, Pearson maintained, 'a struggle of race against race, and nation against nation':

> The man who tells us . . . that he loves the Kaffir [African] as he loves his brother is probably deceiving himself. If he is not, then all we can say is that a nation of such men . . . will not stand for many generations: it cannot survive in the struggle of nations.[78]

In anthropology, the social Darwinists applied the principle of evolution to all of human prehistory, in which it was assumed that one could arrange the so-called 'primitive' societies in a single line of evolution from most to least undeveloped. They assumed that society progressed along an evolutionary path from small, simple, primitive groups to large-scale, complex, and industrial societies. They believed, furthermore, that modern, complex society was better in all respects than more 'primitive' societies—better ethically and morally as well as technically. European society was in all ways superior to other world cultures. This justified what became known as 'social imperialism'—the doctrine that it was both right and inevitable that European nations would come to dominate and control the rest of the world.

Other cultures, by this definition, were backward. Europe would break down these traditional social systems, replace their religions with Christianity, and impose European standards of truth, justice, and government. Europe simply showed the rest of the world the image of its own future. Colonial conquest, cultural destruction, and the subordination of other nations all could be justified as in the best interests of those who were being dominated and colonized. As with the doctrine of the survival of the fittest, the ideological element (the view that an idea serves a vested interest) is obvious here. Not all Western ideologies were equally pernicious. Radical and liberating ideas flowed east and south along with the ethics and ideologies of global capitalism.

Within European social thought, social Darwinism shaped social theory in such fields as anthropology and criminology. These theories were used to justify a new form of imperialism, the conquest and colonialization of less economically industrialized parts of the world, principally at the time in Africa. Social Darwinism had already been extended to legitimate the conquest of weaker by stronger nations. Economist Walter Bagehot argued exactly this point in 1872, claiming that by such conquest 'the best qualities wanted in elementary civilization are propagated and preserved', since 'the most warlike qualities tend principally to the good.'[79]

As European society came to dominate the world from 1492 onward, the conception grew that Europeans—the white race—must be biologically superior to other races. The assumption of racial inferiority/superiority both justified and provided an explanation for the success of Europe in colonizing and enslaving other peoples. Racism is the ideology of superiority based on Darwinian science: since humanity had evolved, so had the different races. Some races, however, were further along the evolutionary ladder. They were biologically superior—more evolved. This idea was 'scientific' in that it turned for justification of its claims to supposed empirical fact, rather than, for example, to religious grounds.

Ideas of racial inferiority had a long history in Europe. Aristotle had believed in the natural inferiority of slaves. In 1735 Linnaeus had attempted to divide humanity into a scientific subclassification with the American Indian representing the 'noble savage'. By 1775, however, as Patterson demonstrates,[80] the standard view had changed. The white race, by then defined as Caucasians, were assumed to be the original type of humanity. From them had diverged, in one direction, the Ethiopians (Africans) and the Malays (South Asians) and, in another direction, the American Indians and the Mongolians (East Asians). Furthermore, by that date it was assumed that the races differed in innate intelligence and that this could be determined from the different sizes and shapes of the heads found among the various races of humanity.[81] Increasingly, then, science was used to define racial inequalities and thereby justify the unequal treatment of the races. Modern racism is based on the use of science to justify these inequalities.

One of the chief inspirations of modern, scientific racism was the French aristocrat, Joseph Arthur de Gobineau (1816–82). In his 1853 work, *Essay on the Inequality of the Human Races*, Gobineau proposed that humanity was divided into distinct races, which were unequal in their natural abilities. The races existed in a natural hierarchy, with Europeans at the top and Africans at the bottom. Gobineau proposed further, however, that one part of the Caucasian racial group, the Aryan or Nordic aristocracy, had the greatest capacity for creativity and development—they were the superior racial group.[82] The Aryans were the natural rulers of humankind and, as Tom Buchanan said in *The Great Gatsby*, had been responsible for the development of civilization (Box 9.6).[83]

Gobineau believed that the mixing of races was causing the Nordic race to degenerate. Having achieved the most highly developed civilization, Europe was slowly declining as the 'blood' of the superior race was diluted through intermarriage. Such **miscegenation** was responsible for the false claims of equality that had led to the French Revolution. On the basis of such purely ideological claims, social Darwinism led logically to the **eugenics** movement, according to which human society could be improved by selective sterilization and breeding. The view that those defined as the weakest should be allowed to die out to prevent them from reproducing was explicit in Malthus, Darwin, and Spencer. Following from Spencer's belief that the 'human stock' was getting worse because society violated the law of natural selection by allowing the poor and unfit to reproduce at a faster rate than the rich and fit, the eugenics movement, founded by Charles Darwin's cousin, Francis Galton, sought to reverse this trend.

Galton was a statistical researcher interested in the principles of heredity. He observed that the offspring of the most talented individuals tended also to be gifted, which he attributed to inheritance; genius was inherited the same way as blue eyes. Consequently, it should be possible, by careful selection of parents, to engineer an improvement in the human stock, as animal breeders were doing for other species. For Galton, natural selection accounted for racial differences in intelligence. Benign climates produced inferior races while more difficult and varied climates, such as in Northern Europe, selected a greater proportion of intelligent people.

In *Hereditary Genius*, Galton devised the term 'eugenics' to mean the science of improving the human genetic pool by encouraging the most intelligent to have children while preventing the weaker from reproducing. According to the eugenics movement, in the world of nature the struggle for survival ensured that the best of any species would survive, while the least well-adapted—the weakest, less active, less energetic—would die or be killed, yielding few offspring. Modern society, however, prevented the struggle for existence from

---

Box 9.6

'Civilization's going to pieces,' broke out Tom violently. 'I've gotten to be a terrible pessimist about things. Have you read "The Rise of the Colored Empires" by this man Goddard?'

'Why, no,' I answered, rather surprised by his tone.

'Well, it's a fine book, and everybody ought to read it. The idea is if we don't look out the white race will be—will be utterly submerged. It's all scientific stuff; it's been proved.'

'Tom's getting very profound,' said Daisy, with an expression of unthoughtful sadness. 'He reads deep books with long words in them. What was that word we—'

'Well, these books are all scientific,' insisted Tom, glancing at her impatiently. 'This fellow has worked out the whole thing. It's up to us, who are the dominant race, to watch out or these other races will have control of things.'

. . .

'This idea is that we're Nordics. I am, you are, and you are, and—' After an infinitesimal hesitation he included Daisy with a slight nod. . . . '—And we've produced all the things that go to make civilization—oh, science and art, and all that. Do you see?'

—F. Scott Fitzgerald, *The Great Gatsby* (1925)

'cleansing' the population. Following Malthus's arguments, Christian charity for the poor as well as humanitarian sentiments helped those with undesirable traits to survive, under the assumption that the poor in society were physically and morally the worst of humanity. Most ominous, to Galton and the eugenics movement, was the tendency for the poor to have more children than the rich.

Over time, then, the positive human traits, supposedly represented by the wealthy, would become less and less common while the disadvantageous traits, passed on by the parents of the poor to their numerous offspring, would increase. The 'national stock' of humanity, then, would degenerate over time. Such changes, the eugenicists supposed, were responsible for the fall of ancient empires and were being allowed to happen in society again. European civilization was doomed to be overwhelmed by mediocrity unless the principles of eugenics were adopted. According to the eugenics movement, people who were mentally defective, disabled, chronically unemployed, or criminal should be sterilized so they could not reproduce. This would lead to a gradual improvement of humanity. Galton's most

immediate influence was in the United States, where concern about the large number of recent immigrants from rural Italy, Russia, and Poland, as well as many Jews, raised fears of racial degeneration. The laws to exclude certain immigrants that were passed in the first third of the twentieth century, in the United States and the Anglo dominions of Australia and Canada, were based on the assumption that science had proven that these ethnic groups were mentally and morally inferior. The concern of the eugenicists with interracial marriages was portrayed critically in the Australian movie, *Rabbit Proof Fence* (Box 9.7).

The use of 'science' to justify racism is not an error merely of the past. In the recent turn-of-the-century conservative climate, arguments have been revived claiming that social inequalities in races are reflections of innate inferiority. Intellectual superiority again is being attributed to some races over others. These ideas are emerging in a society that, officially at least, embraces multiculturalism and human rights. In more explicitly racist societies, such as in apartheid South Africa, the use of science to justify the unequal treatment of races was perpetuated late into the twentieth century.

Box 9.7

Notice, if you will, the half-caste child. And there are ever increasing numbers of them. What is to happen to them?

Are we to allow the creation of an, unwanted, third race? Should the coloured be encouraged to go back to the black, or should they be advanced to white status and absorbed in the white population?

Now, time and again, I am asked by some white man, 'If I marry this coloured person, will our children be black?' And as Chief Protector of Aborigines, it is my responsibility to accept or reject those marriages.

Here is the answer [shows slides]: Three generations; half-blood grandmother, quadroon daughter, octoroon grandson. As you can see in the third generation, or third cross, no trace of native origin is apparent. The continuing infiltration of white blood finally stamps out the black colour. The aborigine has simply been bred out....

[I]f we are to fit and train such children for the future, they cannot be left as they are, and in spite of himself, the native must be helped.

—*Rabbit Proof Fence* (2003), directed by Phillip Noyce, screenplay by Christine Olsen

This theory that blamed the fall of civilization on racial mixing was most popular in Germany. It was propagated by popular figures such as the Romantic German composer, Richard Wagner, whose race theory accepted Gobineau's ideas about the existence of a hierarchy of races and of the superiority of the Nordic (variously, the 'German' or the 'Aryan') race. For Wagner, the success of a race depended on the 'purity' of its 'blood', which must be protected at all costs.[84]

Eugenics had its fullest expression in Germany in the 1930s and 1940s when the Nazi Party adopted the 'final solution' to annihilate Jews, as well as murder Gypsies, the mentally ill, the disabled, chronic criminals, Communists, and others deemed undesirable. At the same time, the Nazis experimented with breeding a super Aryan race, selecting men and women to serve as 'ideal' parents. If a social theory can be evaluated by the extremes to which it has led, social Darwinism, to its discredit, led to the death camps at Auschwitz and Bergen-Belsen.

CONCLUSION

The individualistic emphasis of modern liberalism was influential in social theory, particularly in British and American sociology. Herbert Spencer had latched onto Malthus's phrase 'survival of the fittest' to describe his social theory, a view of the world that was compatible with the Darwinian conception of natural selection. Spencer applied the concept of evolution to society not as Hegel had done, as the progressive working out of a spiritual destiny, but more as Darwin conceived nature: a process with a natural dynamic that, once set in motion, continued under the impetus of its own inertia of motion guided by natural laws. If there was a god, it was better described as nature, fate, and destiny.

Spencer was the unreformed liberal of old, the heir of Malthus and Adam Smith. The ideology of liberalism had changed over the nineteenth century, particularly in the hands of Bentham and the social liberals. In place of the old theory of laissez-faire, the modern liberals stressed social reform and state regulation of the economy. Liberalism had been infused with some of the ideas of the socialists. Spencer combined laissez-faire with the conservative ideas that society resembles an organism composed of unequal parts, all performing necessary functions for its survival, and that society slowly changes over time by a process of peaceful evolution. With Spencer, then, the social theory of laissez-faire—discarded by the liberals—made a comeback as part of modern conservatism.

For Spencer, social evolution was an impersonal process within which circumstances and the environment were all-powerful. According to social Darwinism, Hofstadter argued,[85] social evolutionary development was a predetermined cosmic process 'toward a remote but comfortable **Elysium**'—towards eventual perfection. Social evolution proceeded the same way evolution in nature occurred. It was guided by blind forces that no one could control but, nonetheless, always led to progress—in nature, to species better and better adapted to their environment; in society, to inevitable social progress.

In this sense, Spencer was a theorist of the early Victorian age, the period in nineteenth-century England that was named after the long-reigning Queen Victoria. In social theory Victorianism was equated with the doctrine of progress, the belief that society would inevitably improve over time. The unprecedented growth of industrial capitalism and the success of the British Empire worldwide seemed proof that the future, too, belonged to Britain.

Victorianism also implies strict, middle-class morality and traditional gender roles: sexual repression for women and the double standard for men. The middle of the Victorian age was a trough between two peaks of feminist resistance, the earlier occurring during the age of revolution, and the later becoming part of an end-of-the-century cultural transformation. Despite Darwin's very conventional beliefs about the natural origins of traditional gender roles, the theory of evolution posed the most serious challenge to Victorian morality and convention. Marx had initially intended to dedicate his first volume of *Capital* to Darwin. When applied to society, however, Lamarck's theory—that acquired characteristics are passed on to succeeding generations—is more appropriate than Darwin's model of random variations succeeding or failing according to environmental influences.

The implications of social Darwinism led to a **gradualistic fatalism** in which human intervention to direct the course of social evolution by bringing about social reforms was considered counterproductive, even harmful. It was better to let the laws of social evolution operate blindly, without interference. This was a new, scientific restatement of the old liberal policy of laissez-faire applied to society as a whole, not just the economy.

It is easy to see how this idea was 'ideological'; that is, it was an idea that served a vested interest, in this case, the interest of the new bourgeoisie and successful members of the middle class who had succeeded in the competitive world. It is no wonder that Spencer was the toast of many wealthy and powerful members of the upper classes in Britain and the United States. Spencer was a popular, frequently read author in the last decades of the nineteenth century. His views were particularly well suited to the competitive capitalist system that had developed in the United States. At the turn of the twentieth century, much American sociology was markedly social Darwinist.

The contemporary right-wing policy is, once in power, to limit state interference in the economy, deregulate business, and undermine social programs. Globalization in the twenty-first century is predicated on this belief in the inevitably beneficial effects of the free market. Just as Herbert Spencer challenged the social liberalism of the nineteenth century, so contemporary theorists of capitalist globalization have been successful in whittling away the welfare state, which had been so painfully constructed in the advanced capitalist societies in the twentieth century.

When the middle classes had been revolutionary, culture became increasingly democratic. As realism turned the weapons of literary criticism on the capitalist order itself, the idea of democracy began to lose favour. Democracy had been a powerful idea when the middle class had used it to attack the elitism of the aristocracy. It was a less useful idea when particular interest groups among the common people, including women, demanded more genuine political power. In this fragmented context, social theory became increasingly elitist.

Towards the end of the nineteenth century, social theory had taken a wolfish turn. Theorists expressed a profoundly anti-democratic ideology. The 'masses'—the common people—were now deemed to be incompetent, unintelligent, genetically inferior, and unsuited for political power. Society was a hierarchy (an idea with a long history). At the top was an elite of intelligent, capable, hard-working men who were the real rulers of society. All human progress had come about because of the work of great men—Alexander the Great, Julius Caesar, Napoleon Bonaparte. Late nineteenth-century great men were the barons of business—the Krupps in Germany, the Rockefellers and Melons in the United States. The ideological table was being prepared for the twentieth-century doctrines of fascism and Nazism, with their absolutist leaders and spaniel-like followers.

ÉMILE DURKHEIM

SECOND EMPIRE, PARIS COMMUNE, THIRD REPUBLIC

Louis Napoleon's *coup d'état* in 1851 had snuffed out the short-lived Second Republic and recast France as a Second Empire, although Louis did not cut as regal a figure as his namesake. Seated once more in power, the dominant monarchists and Bonapartists pushed the republicans and the socialists into the background. The conservative sentiments among the landowners and prosperous peasantry were sponsored by the Roman Catholic Church and protected by the army. The bourgeoisie was comfortable under the benign authority of the Empire. As long as executive power took care of French business, capitalist proprietors were content, as French industrialization closed the gap with Germany. Meanwhile, the urban middle-class republicans and the radical Parisian proletariat waited for an opportune moment to resume the struggle for power.

Conditions changed suddenly following France's rapid and humiliating defeat by the Prussian army in 1870, a war that brought down Louis Napoleon. Paris was surrounded by the Prussian army but the invaders were unable to enter the city. A national spirit spread among the Parisian populace, uniting them to resist the foreign aggressor and reviving revolutionary aspirations. In the chaos of war and defeat, a new conservative government was hastily thrust into office under pressure from the Prussian army. Created to negotiate peace terms with Germany, the government was unrepresentative of the swelling spirit of resistance, and French patriots were unwilling to accept peace on the terms offered. In Paris, radical republicans rebelled and established an alternative, revolutionary municipal government called the Commune of Paris. The French government and the political right were determined to suppress this rebellion of radicals and socialists. An informal truce between the Prussian and French governments allowed French troops to enter Paris and, in a week of bloody fighting, the rightists regained control of the city. The army and its reactionary supporters took literally the Communards' defiant slogan, *Vivre libre, ou mourir!* ('Live free, or die!').The massacre of thousands of French citizens by the French army left a deep and lasting imprint on the nation.

Out of the bitter memories and generations-long anger that grew out of the repression of the Paris Commune, a Third Republic was created in France, which lasted until World War I. The political atmosphere was still volatile, as it had been during the Second Republic. Monarchists and Bonapartists attacked the government from the right; on the left, a revolutionary labour movement known as 'syndicalism' kept alive the image of the Commune and the aspirations of the working class. Beneath the surface of political conflict lay fundamental changes in the French economy. While agriculture continued to be backward and dominated by small, conservative, and traditional peasant proprietors, by the 1880s French industry was developing rapidly.[1] As always in periods of industrialization, the French proletariat was refuelled by legions of former peasants who migrated to the new industrial centres, particularly Paris, exchanging the dull monotony of rural poverty for the apparent glitter of urban variety. Social disruption on a grand scale was the inevitable result, causing uprootedness, disorder, and a sense of social estrangement.

The easy Prussian victory had revealed to France's embarrassment her backwardness. The old institutions of French society, which continued to have a strong grip on the population, had failed in the nation's hour of need. None failed more than the Catholic Church, which had spoken for the propertied and for retrograde politics. For republican government and industrial capitalism to be secure it would be necessary to break the back of this traditional order. As a first step, the new republican government sought to lessen the ideological power of the clergy by separating Church and state. The French system of education was the most important target of state intervention because it was top-heavy with clergy and traditionalism. In its place, the government established a state-run, secular system of public education; an important step towards opening all fields, particularly intellectual ones, to persons of talent regardless of class. One scholar who benefited from these republican reforms was Émile Durkheim (1858–1917), who became professor of sociology at the Sorbonne, the prestigious French university, and used his position to define and carve a space for the new academic discipline.

DURKHEIM

Durkheim came from a long line of rabbis in the province of Lorraine, one of the territories over which Germany and France would fight until 1945. Although his family expected him to study Jewish theology and continue the family tradition, Durkheim broke the mould. He was 12 when the Prussian army marched in and annexed Alsace-Lorraine to Germany and when the French army turned its cannons and bayonets on Parisian workers. These were defining moments for a generation of French women and men. Throughout his life Durkheim was a republican and a French nationalist.

Durkheim began teaching philosophy in Parisian schools in 1882, the year the republican

government had wrested control of the educational system from the Catholic Church and began to establish secular state education.[2] Opportunities were opening for talented people who formerly would have been excluded. Durkheim, a scholar from the provinces with a Jewish ethnic background, rose in the new world of secular French education. He was in the right place at the most propitious time. Of the many liberal doctrines Durkheim would embrace, equality of opportunity resonated with his own experience.

The French government's educational reforms coincided neatly with Durkheim's chief intellectual preoccupation—establishing a sound, secular, and scientific foundation for the French moral code. Durkheim believed that the educational system, which transmitted the accumulated cultural heritage from one generation to the next, could be used to institute a just allocation of social positions and inculcate ethical standards. In 1887, Durkheim began teaching social science at the University of Bordeaux. His first major work was *The Divisions of Labour in Society* (1893).

For Durkheim, modern industrial society was undergoing an appalling moral and ethical crisis. The glue that had held traditional society together had dissolved. European society was divided by violent class conflicts, severe inequality, declining morality, and misguided individualism. The old sense of community had been replaced by a feeling of aimlessness. The principal symptom of this crisis was the conflict and disorder in the economic life of society. This was not a new discovery. Spencer had assumed that social conflict was normal and that, through the struggle for existence, the better individuals rose to the top of the social ladder. For Marx, industrial conflict was a rehearsal for the revolution that would overthrow the exploitation at the root of class warfare. In contrast, Durkheim saw the social disorder of his time as a 'sickness'[3] that required a cure.

The Dreyfus Case

From 1893, the year of Durkheim's first major publication, to the end of the century, the dominant issue that threatened to plunge French politics into another civil war was the case of Alfred **Dreyfus**, a captain in the French army. Dreyfus was convicted at courts martial of conspiring to sell military secrets to Germany and was sentenced to life imprisonment in the notorious penal colony of Devil's Island off the coast of French Guinea. To have uprooted a French traitor should have been cause for national celebration. Dreyfus, however, was not guilty. Durkheim played a prominent and public part in the campaign to secure justice for Dreyfus.[4] In Durkheim's view, people had celebrated Dreyfus's conviction because they were seeking a convenient scapegoat for the economic troubles and moral distress of their lives. Dreyfus, a Jew, had been made to bear the burden of the social distress facing France. 'When society undergoes suffering', Durkheim wrote, 'it feels the need to find someone whom it can hold responsible for its sickness, on whom it can avenge its misfortunes, and those against whom public opinion already discriminates are naturally designated for this role.'[5]

As critics of the Dreyfus affair uncovered evidence of a desperate cover-up by the French army, liberals, socialists, and republicans coalesced to defend Dreyfus, along with France's image as the home of liberty. Extreme nationalists and French conservatives accused the left of being unpatriotic. The affair dragged on throughout the 1890s, highlighted by the publication in 1898 of a fervent open letter under the title *J'accuse* (*I accuse*) written by the novelist Émile Zola. The letter named the military officers and public officials who were the real guilty parties responsible for crimes against justice and humanity, and denounced the deliberate cover-up (Box 10.1).[6] French intellectuals have consistently played an important public role in politics, and Zola's letter helped solidify liberal and republican opinion. Zola himself became a *cause célèbre* after he was charged with libel for his accusations, convicted, and sentenced to a year in prison—a punishment he narrowly avoided by fleeing to England. Within a year, however, the actual traitor had confessed, Dreyfus had been pardoned and restored to the army, and Zola was celebrated by many as a morally courageous national hero.

Durkheim played a less flamboyant role than Zola in the defence of Dreyfus. However, Dreyfus, like Durkheim, was Jewish and the affair incited an explosion of virulent anti-Semitism from the French right. Liberals were shocked at the revelation that French racism was so deep, bitter, and violent. Perhaps because of his own ethnic background, Durkheim did not emphasize the racist nature of the affair. Instead, he defended Dreyfus on the universal grounds of human rights. He believed that French Jews, such as himself, were being rapidly assimilated into French society and would soon become invisible as a cultural minority. For Durkheim, the Dreyfus affair was symptomatic of other, deeper, and more structural crises in French society, and it was these Durkheim sought to explain and remedy.

Box 10.1

I am confident . . . the truth is on the march and nothing shall stop it. The Affair is only just beginning, because only now have the positions become crystal clear: on the one hand, the guilty parties, who do not want the truth to be revealed; on the other, the defenders of justice, who will give their lives to see that justice is done. . . . [I]f the truth is buried underground, it swells and grows and becomes so explosive that the day it bursts, it blows everything wide open along with it. Time will tell: we shall see whether we have not prepared, for some later date, the most resounding disaster.

—Émile Zola, *J'Accuse*, 13 January 1898

ANOMIE AND SOCIAL MILIEUX

There is no such thing as society. There are individual men and women, and there are families.

—British Prime Minister Margaret Thatcher (1987)

When Margaret Thatcher claimed that society did not exist, that it was merely an idea that people constructed, she denied the central concept of Durkheim's social theory. For Durkheim, although the social did exist in the mind of individuals, it exhibited the characteristics of an external thing, composing a force outside and coercive upon the individuals who composed it. The problem was that modern society was unhealthy. When a society existed in a healthy state, Durkheim believed, people's actions were guided by a set of moral rules that appeared normal and natural to them. In most of their social life in the family, for example, people's actions were shaped by ethical principles that were widely shared. In modern society, however, this fundamental consensus was being undermined by the absence of ethical principles to guide people's dealings with others. Without stable moral standards of behaviour, social life existed in a state of anomie—an absence of rules. Anomie was caused by the enormous changes in the material life of French society that had proceeded so rapidly they had outstripped the ability of morality to keep pace. 'By nature', Durkheim reasoned, 'we are not inclined to curb ourselves and exercise restraint.' Unless social rules were imposed on individuals by the power of society as a whole, self-interest would dominate. People would be unable to construct a moral, civilized society and 'acquire a taste for altruism, for forgetfulness of self and sacrifice'.[7]

Traditional society had been characterized by a consensus about moral beliefs and actions. The morality that corresponded to this earlier type of society, however, had evaporated along with the traditional social structure that had sustained it. The new structure that was replacing it had not yet had sufficient time to develop new moral standards in place of the old, leaving a vacant spot in human consciousness. 'We need to put a stop to this **anomie**', Durkheim asserted.[8] It was not possible simply to resurrect the older morality that had been irretrievably lost and no longer corresponded to the new social conditions. Nor was it possible simply to improvise a new morality and then impose it on modern society. This would be purely artificial and ineffective. Even the modern state, that massively overgrown instrument of social regulation, was incapable of establishing a new morality for society. It was too remote from the complexities of social life.[9] What was missing was a scientific analysis of society that would effectively diagnose the illness, prescribe the minimally necessary medicine, and cure the patient.

Social Health

The task of social theory was to realize that society was struggling to cure itself; it was slowly moving towards a new equilibrium, a new standard of health consistent with its new conditions of existence. An effective new moral code could emerge only gradually when the conditions for it were ready. The task of sociology was to help establish the modern moral order. It was first necessary to understand the social forces that were either tending towards this new stability or were hindering its evolution. Once social scientists uncovered the impediments to social order, they could seek to remedy them.

The problem of healing society was compounded by the existence of false cures, as the history of medicine had been plagued at an early stage by charlatan doctors and quack elixirs. The sociologist Herbert Spencer had made the mistake of focusing too much on the individual at the expense of society. The socialists had made the opposite error of assuming that society needed to be overturned in a revolution. In the politics of Durkheim's France, the socialist movement was prominent in a variety of forms. When he was studying at the *École Supérieure* in Paris, Durkheim began a lifelong friendship with Jean Jaurès, the future socialist leader.[10] Jaurès's politics were reformist and conciliatory, though they were considerably to the left of Durkheim's mild social criticism. The two were united in their defence of the French Republic against conservatives and reactionary nationalists and, later, in their opposition to war.

Durkheim was passionately opposed to the glorification of class conflict and the violent, revolutionary character of Marxism. His objective was to help create the conditions for social peace without making any fundamental changes in the structure of the status quo. Marx had said that peace and harmony were impossible under capitalism, but his doctrine, Durkheim implied, had 'been rightly reproached with being subversive and revolutionary' and was 'scientific in name only'.[11] Durkheim wanted to prove Marx wrong, both in theory and in practice. The organism of society was ill and his intention was to restore social health. Marx may also have believed that capitalist society was sick and had intended to apply his own cure but, for Durkheim, the socialist revolution was an operation that would kill the patient. In his view, sociology should ignore these theories and 'be neither individualistic, communistic, nor socialistic in the sense commonly given these words.' These doctrines had no scientific value because they were political doctrines that intellectuals intended to impose on society rather than concepts that actually described and interpreted social reality.

According to Durkheim, society is a separate and overarching reality that exists apart from the individuals who comprise it, just as an organism is distinct from its component cells. Society is the sum of the complex relationships into which people are born. Durkheim agreed with Spencer and Comte that society was a natural phenomenon. Humanity had never been without a kind of society. Social life was the result of a spontaneous development rather than deriving from some rational 'plan thought out by the reflective intelligence'.[12] Both Comte and Spencer believed that the existence of society was rooted in the instincts of human nature found in each individual. People were originally drawn together by 'instinctive

forces such as the affinity of blood, attachment to the same soil, the **cult** of their ancestors, [and] a commonality of habits'. Drawn into proximity with others, people were obliged to enter into social relations and co-operate with them. Social bonds tightened and a distinct society was formed, with specific rules and habits and with a single, common consciousness.[13]

Durkheim does not simply reject any notion of human instinct, but he claims that humanity is not merely an addition to animal qualities. Human nature results from what Durkheim terms a 'recasting' of the animal nature that results from losing some animal instincts. A human being is not simply an animal who has certain additional qualities; human nature is 'the result of a sort of recasting of the animal nature'. Not only have humans lost many instincts, as they have learned to adapt to the social environment, but many ideas and sentiments that might be assumed to result naturally are replaced with 'contrary sentiments'. Consequently, 'it is a vain enterprise to seek to infer the mental constitution of the primitive man from that of the higher animals.'[14] In Durkheim's social theory, the attributes characteristic of human nature, including the intellectual and moral culture that gives humanity its distinct character as a species, come from society. Without language, science, art, and moral beliefs, humans would descend to the level of animals. But, Durkheim continues, that is only one side of the relationship because society, in turn, exists only in and through individuals: 'If the idea of society were extinguished in individual minds and the beliefs, traditions and aspirations of the group were no longer felt and shared by the individuals, society would die.' Society 'is real only in so far as it has a place in human consciousness.'[15]

For Durkheim, primitive societies were homogeneous and individuals possessed little in their consciousness that was distinct from the consciousness of everyone else. It was not that primitive societies did not allow individuals to develop an awareness of their separate interests or, as Spencer believed, that individual personality had been suppressed artificially. For Durkheim, 'it is quite simply because at that moment in history' individual personality *did not exist*, an idea that was similarly expressed by the social psychologist, G.H. Mead (Box 10.2).[16] In this view, only in higher societies does **egoism** insinuate itself everywhere and individualism penetrate areas previously closed to it.[17]

Durkheim's sociology, then, inverts Spencer's in which social life was the sum of the various natures of the individuals who comprised it. For Durkheim, what individuals think and feel is 'much more a product of common life than a determining factor in it'. Most states of consciousness, Durkheim asserts, would not have occurred among people who were 'isolated from one another and would have occurred completely differently among people grouped together in a different way.'[18]

The 'Science of Morality'

With this argument, Durkheim reversed the view liberal social theorists held of the relationship between the society and the individual. For them, the chains of society had become so tight they were strangling the natural impulses of the individual. These social scientists, Durkheim said, had not been scientific. They were concerned with what they thought ought to be true rather than with what was true. He intended 'to constitute the science of morality'. Trying to impose an arbitrarily chosen set of moral rules on people would not work. Social scientists needed to discover the actual causes of human behaviour. Only with this knowledge could they successfully guide the process of developing logical rules for future action and concretely implementing them.[19]

Establishing a science of morality would appear to be a contradiction in terms. Science deals with material things, tangible objects that can be measured and manipulated. Morality seemed fundamentally different, consisting of an intangible set of ideas that had existence only in the realm of thought. To be valid, Durkheim reasoned, social science must rest on a solid foundation of fact similar to those natural laws the physical scientists claimed to have discovered. Durkheim agreed with Locke's scientific principle of causality, which claimed that an object's external appearance provided a relatively faithful representation of its reality. Things really were what they appeared to be in the eyes of the majority of observers. As long as all the phenomena of a certain order can be shown to possess characteristics 'identically and without exceptions', it is logical to conclude that they reflect its reality. In his early *Rules of Sociological Method*, Durkheim stated that science begins with sense perceptions and borrows 'the material for its initial definitions directly from perceptual data'. Concepts derived from the scientific method 'adequately express things as they actually are'.[20] In Durkheim's hands, this idea

---

Box 10.2

One difference between primitive human society and civilized human society is that in [the former] the individual self is much more completely determined, with regard to his thinking and his behaviour, by the . . . social group to which he belongs, than he is in [civilization]. In other words, primitive . . . society offers much less scope for individuality—for original, unique, or creative thinking and behaviour on the part of the individual self within it or belonging to it—than does civilized . . . society; and indeed the evolution of civilized human society from [the] primitive . . . has largely . . . resulted from a progressive social liberation of the individual self and is . . . made possible by that liberation.

—G.H. Mead, *Mind, Self and Society* (1934)

was more complex than it sounds. In the natural sciences, the elements that combine to make a compound are not immediately apparent in our perception. If everyday consciousness accurately reflected the way the world actually worked, there would be little need for social science. Scientific analysis must be able to penetrate beneath surface experiences and uncover the real basis of social action, of which individuals may be totally unaware. Thus, in his later study of religion, Durkheim argued that, 'beneath the surface of things . . . external resemblances suppose others which are profound.' Essentially, he believed that no significant moral belief or set of beliefs that persist in society can rest on illusions or lies; they must have a real foundation that gives them their stability, a basis that may not be immediately apparent but can be uncovered through social science.[21]

Methodologically, Durkheim argues that sociology is distinct from philosophy, which is founded on 'a logical concept, a pure possibility, constructed simply by force of thought'. They begin by creating an idea and then illustrate this idea with facts drawn arbitrarily from history to sustain it. Sociology seeks to make generalizations from concrete reality, which can be understood through systematic historical and ethnological observations.[22]

Moral values are not held consistently by societies through time and space. They change throughout the course of history as changes in social structure bring about corresponding changes in morality. 'Moral facts are phenomena like any others', Durkheim argues. They are 'rules for action' that can be observed, described, and classified, and laws that explain them can be uncovered.[23] It may appear that social life is like 'shifting sand', so free, fluid, and fleeting it cannot be grasped by any scientific observer. Nevertheless, there exist collective habits that give rise to rules, regulations, proverbs, conventions, and so on, that exist more or less permanently as an object of study.[24] Durkheim calls these collective habits, these common 'ways of acting, thinking, and feeling', **social facts**. They can be observed and should be treated as the fundamental data of social science. Insofar as social phenomena exhibit regularity and uniformity, 'we must study them objectively as external things, for it is this character that they present to us.'[25]

A social fact has an objective, independent existence external to the individual and his or her individual consciousness. Social facts are social since their source is society as a whole, not in biology or merely in the individual consciousness. It could be argued, for example, that racism is a set of attitudes existing only in the minds of individuals. For the man and woman subject to racial discrimination, however, racism is as much a part of everyday reality as the money in their pockets. Social facts have 'ascendancy over the individual', exercising a coercive power independent of an individual's will[26] and producing, as sociologist Max Weber said, an unalterable order of things (Box 10.3).[27]

Box 10.3

The capitalistic economy of the present day is an immense cosmos into which the individual is born, and which presents itself to him, at least as an individual, as an unalterable order of things in which he must live. It forces the individual, in so far as he is involved in the system of market relationships, to conform to capitalistic rules of action. . . .

Thus the capitalism of to-day, which has come to dominate economic life, educates and selects the economic subjects which it needs through a process of economic survival of the fittest.

—Max Weber, *The Protestant Ethic and the Spirit of Capitalism* (1904)

In the prehistory of social science, Durkheim claims, society appeared to be the product of the ideas people held. As a result, ideas became the subject matter of sociology. Although Comte had declared social phenomena to be natural facts that were subject to laws, thereby implicitly recognizing their character as things, he still focused his study on ideas. Comte and Spencer both had believed that social life was naturally progressive, induced by a tendency inherent in human nature that impelled humanity to forever go beyond 'its achievements either in order to realize itself completely or to increase its happiness'. In neither case was this alleged cause a fact, Durkheim argued. It was merely postulated and constructed by the mind of the theorists. Comte's law of three stages, for example, in which the positive stage was declared to be the final and highest level of social evolution, was entirely arbitrary.[28]

Durkheim stated that social evolution had no preplanned course or necessary series of stages, as in the Hegelian or Marxian dialectic. Although the existing state of society makes certain types of progress possible that would otherwise be precluded, you cannot examine the entrails of the past to predict the predetermined course of the future. You study the present state of society to determine how it had developed to its current stage and to understand what additional changes are possible and desirable. Durkheim termed the given state of any society a '**social milieu**', which was the essential condition of collective existence in the specific time and space. A social milieu represented a social whole, the structure of an existing society, or a social institution. As a social fact, a given social milieu existed apart from, independent of, and coercive upon the individuals who existed within it. If you try to change a society by exerting an external force or by implementing an internal reform, your efforts will be ineffective unless they are consistent with what is possible within the existing social milieu.[29]

In Durkheim's theory, society has a reality of its own different from the sum of all the people who comprise it, since a 'whole is not identical with the sum of its parts.' What matters is the way the parts are put together, the relationships the elements of society have to each other. Social phenomena vary with the way the constituent parts are grouped. This is another way of saying that social phenomena vary according to their social milieu.[30] For Durkheim, there are a variety of social milieux, just as there are a number of different types of biological organisms. In viewing a social organization as a unified milieu, Durkheim conceived society to be like an organism—in author George Eliot's words, 'like that wonderful piece of life, the human body' (Box 10.4).[31] An actually functioning society, then, consists of a variety of parts that are useful to it. These parts 'combine in such a way as to put society in harmony with itself and with the environment external to it.' To explain a social fact we must 'show its function in the establishment of social order.'[32]

If something new develops in society and persists, it must perform some useful function; otherwise it would disappear. To explain this, Durkheim uses a biological as well as an economic analogy. If something isn't useful to society, it is actually harmful because it costs resources to maintain it. It places 'the budget of the organism' in deficit.

The organic model of society had been part of the bedrock of traditional thinking, but it had been largely eclipsed in social theory following the rise of liberalism, which deposed the organic conception of society and substituted a mechanical model based on the Newtonian laws of physics. Society in the liberal conception was thought to be like a machine that was rationally constructed by human beings and susceptible to radical remodelling. Following the biological revolution of the nineteenth century, however, social scientists revived the organic analogy.

Durkeim's Study of Suicide

The view that the social milieu exerted a constraining force on human action was the underpinning of Durkheim's study, *Suicide*, published in 1897. Durkheim's purpose was to establish sociology as a distinct discipline, apart from biology

Box 10.4

[If a man] says that in politics or in any sort of social action he will not care to know what are likely to be the consequences to others besides himself, he ... might as well say that there is no better rule needful for men than that each should tug and rive for what will please him, without caring how that tugging will act on the fine widespread network of society in which he is fast meshed.... None of us are so ignorant as not to know that a society, a nation is held together by ... the dependence of men on each other and the sense they have of a common interest.... [If we forget this] we should be much like sailors cutting away the timbers of our own ship to warm our grog with.... [S]ociety stands before us like that wonderful piece of life, the human body, with all its various parts depending on one another, and with a terrible liability to get wrong because of that delicate dependence.... [Diseases are difficult to diagnose] because the body is made up of so many various parts, all related to each other, or all likely to feel the effect if any one of them goes wrong. It is somewhat the same with our old nations or societies.

—George Eliot, *Felix Holt* (1866)

and psychology, by examining as a social fact a phenomenon that seemed most private and individualistic. He demonstrated that the rate of suicide was determined by a collective reality, by 'real, living, active forces', which are greater than and independent of the individual.[33] The circumstances in which people find themselves vary considerably in the degree to which the individual is integrated into the collective life of society or is relatively isolated and alone. Those who are normally integrated, other things being equal, would be unlikely to take their own lives. Suicide tended to be more common among people who were socially estranged because of the weaker ties binding them to society. Durkheim termed these egoistic suicides. The opposite situation—being excessively identified with the collective life of society—was also associated with a higher suicide rate where individuals would sacrifice themselves for the community, an act termed altruistic suicide.

The suicide rate was also directly affected by the recurring economic crises in society. Some millionaires, when reduced to paupers by a stock market collapse, leap to their deaths from skyscraper windows. Consistent with Durkheim's analysis of the unregulated nature of modern capitalism, many people who were thrust suddenly into greatly different social circumstances—whether sudden poverty or wealth—lost their grip on the moral chains that defined their lives and had a greater propensity for self-destruction, or anomic suicide.[34] In short, Durkheim argued, an individual's social milieu exercised a determining effect on her or his consciousness and actions, including even as lonely an act as suicide.

The Division of Labour

Durkheim grew up in a profoundly religious, moral, and tightly knit community. He understood almost intuitively what it meant to be integrated into a social milieu and to feel the power of controlling forces greater than the individual. When he stepped from the wings onto the larger stage of French society, he encountered a disintegrating social audience suffering from the moral crisis of anomie. Most social critics argued that society was fragmented and lacked cohesion because of the corrosive effects of the modern division of labour, which was hated as much by Romantics as by conservatives. Romantics felt that modern industry debased individuals by dividing their work so finely that they became insignificant cogs in vast enterprises, performing endless repetitions of simple actions that destroyed their human potential. Even where work was not so grossly divided as in the factory system, occupations were nevertheless increasingly specialized and subdivided. Conservatives worried that people were becoming increasingly single-minded about their egotistical self-interest at the expense of any common concerns they had with others or with their society as a whole.

Even social theorists such as Comte, who thought the division of labour was a necessary condition of existence in modern society, believed that it undermined social cohesion. Anomie, then, was modern society's natural state. For Comte, unity had to be imposed by expanding the powers of the government and, as he later believed, through a new Christianity. Durkheim argued, on the contrary, that the division of labour was not the culprit causing the lack of cohesion in society. If the different parts of the labour process were sufficiently linked together, they would regulate themselves. It would take time for this new social harmony to establish itself spontaneously. To make his argument, Durkheim undertook a historical analysis of the division of labour in society.

In the prehistory of human societies, the sexual division was one of the earliest forms of specialization. According to Durkheim's biological model, the path that individuals follow in their growth to maturity reproduces, in abridged form, the evolutionary development of the species. Prior to puberty, boys and girls are roughly identical in strength and ability, reflecting the original physical equality of the two sexes. The female form was the original, common type of the species, Durkheim claimed, from which the male sex gradually diverged. Durkheim believed that prehistoric men and women had been roughly equal in strength: 'woman was not at all the weak creature that she has become as morality has progressed.' Aside from reproduction, the **functions** performed by women were not distinct from male ones and 'the two sexes lead roughly the same kind of existence.' Among some Aboriginal peoples in America and

the South Pacific, Durkheim pointed out, women play a part in political life and actively engage in fighting. 'One of the distinctive attributes of a woman today, that of gentleness, does not originally appear to have been characteristic of her.'[35]

As societies evolved, the sexual division of labour became increasingly specialized. Women withdrew from warfare and public affairs, and their lives came to centre entirely around their families. Among civilized people, Durkheim concluded, 'woman leads an existence entirely different from the man's.' Differences in the functions performed by the two sexes correspond to physical differences. It is not only size, weight, and shape that are dissimilar; 'with the advance of civilization the brain of the two sexes has increasingly developed differently.' Women have been assigned the affective function, and men are superior in the intellectual function. Men, for example, increasingly abandon writing literature in favour of studying science.[36]

The sexual division of labour did not necessarily create a war between the sexes. On the contrary, the separation of social functions is complementary. Women and men need each other more than ever to fulfill social needs that each sex is specifically fitted to perform. The same logic applies to the division of labour as a whole. Each separate, specialized part depends on the others for its means of existence. Durkheim sought to understand the historical process that produced this larger division of labour.

Science proceeds by classifying the great diversity of reality into a manageable number of similar types based on the most essential characteristics. Societies differ one from another according to the nature and the number of the parts that make them up and the way that these parts are combined. As biological organisms are divided into so many species, the various forms of social organization can be classified into a number of 'social species', which are qualitatively distinct types that cannot be placed on a single line of historical development.[37] The concept of the **social species**, Durkheim argues, occupies the space between the philosophical notion that all people possess the same essential characteristics and the historical point of view that each society is unique and that no generalization among societies is possible.

THE SEGMENTAL SOCIAL SPECIES AND MECHANICAL SOLIDARITY

For Durkheim, the simplest society is one that does not include other social types simpler than itself; it is but a single segment. This definition conforms to the Darwinian notion of the 'horde', which is a group composed of more or less identical members of the same species, allowing for age and sexual differentiation. For Durkheim, the horde is a single-segment society and is the seed from which other, more complex social species developed. All more complex societies are aggregates of this original type.[38]

Durkheim's purpose is not to propose a complete or even a preliminary classification of the various social species, but to distinguish between two basic types, the segmented and the organic. A segmented society is composed of a number of similar components that are aggregated and in which the concept of individualism has not developed. People in simple societies are similar to each other and, consequently, do not assert their individualism as the dominant feature of their personalities. Durkheim accepted the notion that primitive people closely resembled each other mentally as well as physically. Lebon's skull measurements, he believed, showed that barbarians had cranial capacities more similar in size than those of modern people, reflecting their similar mentalities. Physical similarities correspond to psychological similarities. Slave traders, for example, believed the character of the slaves they were buying—whether loyal, treacherous, hard-working, or savage—depended on their place of origin, since all people from the same area had similar temperaments. Barbarians possessed little individuality, as Weitz had asserted, and they also looked alike (Box 10.5).[39]

People possess individual personality, but they also express a second consciousness common to the whole of their society. In fact, just as a society is a thing like an organism, a society possesses a distinctive consciousness that exists apart from each individual. People are embedded in a set of rules and understandings that is bigger than they are; that exists outside them and is imposed on them; that existed before they were born and will continue after they are dead. This is the collective consciousness, which Durkheim defines as the 'totality of beliefs and sentiments common to the average members of a society'. The **collective consciousness** represents the highest form of mental life because 'it is the consciousness of the consciousness.' Being external to and above the individual consciousness, it reflects permanent and essential aspects of things and crystallizes them into communicable ideas. It sees from above, and further, embraces all known reality, conceived as the totality.[40]

The collective consciousness forms a determinate system having a life of its own that binds

Box 10.5

Just as the Romans found among the Germans very great similarities, so do the so-called savages produce the same effect upon the civilized European.... [Lack of experience] could hardly produce this consequence if the differences to which the civilized man is accustomed in his native environment were not in reality more considerable than those he encounters among primitive peoples. This saying of Ulloa is well known and often quoted: that he who has seen one native of America has seen them all.

—Theodor Waitz, quoted in Durkheim, *The Division of Labour in Society* (1893)

individuals directly to society.[41] It holds them tightly in its grip and limits them within a concrete and definite social horizon. By these mechanical causes, Durkheim claims, the individual personality is absorbed into the collective personality. The simple society is bound together by **mechanical solidarity**, which forms a rock-solid foundation.[42]

Like the conservatives, Durkheim understood that pre-modern society was held together by irrational factors such as traditions, customs, and religion. Primitive societies were characterized by small group size, homogeneity of circumstances, and less developed individuality. Conformity of morality, thought, and conduct prevailed, Durkheim claims, and the individual was almost submerged in the 'race'. This highly developed intellectual and moral conformity is only rarely found in modern societies,[43] which were being increasingly secularized as religion extended 'over an ever diminishing area of life'.[44] Ironically, Durkheim's theory of religion, elaborated in *The Elementary Forms of the Religious Life* (1912), contributed to the secular understanding of religious phenomena in society.

Elementary Forms of Religion

Religious beliefs and practices were an important, even dominant, element of the collective consciousness of the early and simpler societies. What was the origin of the belief in the existence of a second, spiritual world? When Durkheim published his theory of religious origins in 1912, he had to confront other theories that sought to explain why people in primitive societies developed the idea of a spiritual world parallel to and acting upon the physical world they inhabited. Saying that human nature was naturally religious simply sidestepped the question. Similarly, claiming that religious beliefs reflected people's intuitive understanding of an actually existing spiritual world placed the study of religion outside science. The task of social science was to account for the existence of religious beliefs on its own terms.

No known society, Durkheim argued, was without a religion, so the beginning of the concept could not be traced directly. Instead, Durkheim advanced a novel thesis by asserting that there 'was no given moment when religion began to exist'.[45] For Durkheim, human beings always had lived in some form of society and for just as long had held some form of religious belief. Rather than speculating arbitrarily about how a religious idea might have first arisen, Durkheim proposed a single, well-made experiment, using data from historical observation to analyze and explain the simplest and most primitive religion actually known, that is, the religion found in a society with the simplest social organization. By discovering some of the fundamental elements of an actually existing but primitive religion, Durkheim sought to understand religious phenomena in general.

In Durkheim's view, religion must be based on some fundamental truth. It was axiomatic in sociology, he claimed, that no human institution could have originated through errors or lies. A village **shaman** may claim that his prayers and dances would bring rain, but the untruth of this claim must have been exposed every time the shaman failed to coax drops from the sky. Yet, people's faith persisted. The origin of the faith in the shaman must have had another source. The faithful justify their beliefs with reasons that may be, and generally are, erroneous; but the true reasons do not cease to exist, and it is the duty of science to discover them. For Durkheim, the religious experience is no mere illusion; it has an objective foundation, but the reality may be very different from the ideas that believers have of their religion.

The most rudimentary existing societies, Durkheim believed, were the Aboriginal societies in Australia. Durkheim did not undertake fieldwork in Australia, relying instead on secondary sources from early anthropologists such as Edward Tyler. One of his primary sources was *The Native Tribes of Central Australia* written by biologist Sir Baldwin Spencer, ethnologist Francis Gillen, and anthropologist Sir James G. Frazer. From these sources Durkheim concluded that Aboriginals in Australia lived in a homogeneous society organized on the basis of clans, a form he believed to be the simplest. These Aboriginal peoples practised a religion known as totemism. Since totemism was inseparable from a **clan**-based social organization, Durkheim concluded it was the most elementary religion we can know.[46]

In Durkheim's view, primitive societies were held together by mechanical solidarity for which a shared consciousness was essential to their continued existence. It appeared, however, that the life of the simple clan-based societies made the persistence of a collective consciousness difficult. Clans lacked any effective central authority, they had no territorial consistency, and members were scattered through a number of distinct groups by the rules of marriage. Most of the life of clan members was spent in small family groups, widely separated from others, going through the dull, daily routine of making a living from the land. When they were separated from the group, individual sentiments prevailed, threatening to undermine the collective consciousness. It would require very powerful sentiments to maintain the unity of such a society. In primitive societies, the collective consciousness had a highly religious character. It was easy to see how a shared belief in supernatural forces helped to maintain social solidarity; it was more difficult to understand how the collective consciousness originally conceived a religious world view. In many cases, Durkheim claimed, people admit that God is 'a figment of their imagination'. Yet the idea of God holds tremendous force. Since '[n]othing proceeds from nothing', the force must come from somewhere.[47]

The evolution of humanity and of society has occurred in tandem. Humans have never lived in the absence of a society, which has existed prior to every given generation and will persist after the present one is dead. Members of a society feel united by bonds of blood and by a community of interest and tradition. The existence of society is possible only through the creation of common symbols that allow individuals to develop both their individual consciousness and to communicate their understandings to each other. Verbal language is the most fully developed system of communicable symbols and without it a collective consciousness could not arise. 'Thus social life, in

all its aspects and in every period of its history, is made possible only by a vast symbolism.'[48]

Individual minds act and react with one another. When they assemble together, the members of society relive their companionship, celebrate the mythologies of their hero ancestors, and renew their moral unity. While not necessarily related by common ancestors, members of a clan think of themselves as a single family and recognize kinship duties to one another. Members of the clan feel bound by a common moral authority, by collective understandings, and by shared symbols. They experience this as a feeling of dependence on superior forces existing outside themselves. Being unaware that collective life is the real source of this dependency, they impute the force to a mythological system that they create mentally but assume to be more powerful than they are.

The persistence of the collective consciousness is strengthened by connecting social sentiments with enduring, material objects. In Australia, each clan has a specific name, known as its **totem**, which serves to designate the clan. These totemic objects are usually animals, are often vegetables, and are sometimes inanimate objects such as rain, hail, clouds, the moon, autumn, fire, smoke, and so on. The totem of the clan is the totem of its members. The collective name, the totem, is all that unifies the group during most of its existence when the members are scattered about.[49]

The ordinary life of Aboriginal societies passes through two distinct phases. While most of the time members of the clan are separated into small family groups, periodically the clan is gathered together to celebrate a ceremony. Through these communal gatherings, society is 'periodically made and remade'. When the collective life of people in society reaches a high degree of intensity, it causes what Durkheim calls a 'state of effervescence', which changes people's mental life and awakens religious sentiments. Once brought together, with little capacity for rational control of the passions, Durkheim suggests, primitive people are transported easily to an extraordinary enthusiasm marked by extreme behaviours that feeds on the energy of the group and grows to a frenzy of unrestrained and unheard-of actions. In this 'violent super-excitation of the whole physical and mental life', usually at night under the cover of darkness, taboos are broken, '[m]en exchange wives with each other', and sometimes incestuous unions are 'contracted openly and with impunity'.[50] Vital energies are overexcited, passions more active, sensations stronger—some of these are produced only at this moment. Individuals no longer recognize themselves; they feel transformed. This emotional basis of religious experience persisted in Christian evangelism, as the hysterical prayer meeting described by Frances Trollope in 1832 attests (Box 10.6).[51]

To account for these intense impressions that originate outside themselves, people impute exceptional powers to objects with which they are in close contact. Above the real world where their **profane**, everyday life passes, they construct another in their minds. The sacred is something that people have added to and conceived as existing above the real. In one sense, this other world is purely idealistic; it does not exist except in the mind of the believers. For Durkheim, the 'forma-tion of the ideal world . . . is a natural product of social life.'[52] When society assembles and concentrates itself it causes 'an exaltation of the mental life', which awakens a new life of idealistic conceptions that 'correspond to this new set of psychical forces' added to but placed above everyday existence. An original synthesis of particular consciousnesses results in the creation of a collective consciousness, a synthesis that 'has the effect of disengaging a whole world of sentiments, ideas and images which, once born, obey laws all their own.' Once conceived and shared, these essentially religious ideas evolve, change, and transform themselves in ways that are not determined 'by the conditions of the underlying reality'. This new mental life is so independent that it often creates manifestations that have no utility whatsoever other than pleasure or aesthetics, especially in mythology and ritual.[53]

At the origin of religion is the implicit feeling that the universe is bound together by indefinite, anonymous forces comparable to the physical forces that individuals experienced directly. The object that is the totem of the clan becomes the

---

Box 10.6

The preacher described, with ghastly minuteness, the last feeble fainting moments of human life . . . up to the last loathsome stage of decomposition. . . . [He] made known . . . his description of hell. No image that fire, flame, brimstone, molten lead, or red hot pincers could supply, with flesh, nerves, and sinews quivering under them, were omitted. The perspiration ran in streams from the face of the preacher; his eyes rolled, his lips were covered with foam. . . . And now in every part of the church a movement was perceptible. . . . Young girls arose . . . and several came tottering out, their hands clasped . . . and every limb trembling. . . . the sobs and groans increased to a frightful excess. Young creatures, with features pale and distorted, fell on their knees on the pavement, and soon sunk forward on their faces; the most violent cries and shrieks followed, while from time to time a voice was heard in convulsive accents, exclaiming 'O Lord!', 'O Lord Jesus!', 'Help me, Jesus!' and the like. . . . One young girl, apparently not more than fourteen . . . was as pale as death; her eyes wide open, and perfectly devoid of meaning; her chin and bosom wet with slaver; she had every appearance of idiotism. I saw a priest approach her, he took her delicate hand. 'Jesus is with her! Bless the Lord!' he said, and passed on.

—Frances Trollope, 'A Revival' (1832)

visible representation of both this universal force, which Durkheim calls the totemic principle, and of the clan itself, that is, society.[54]

As a religion, totemism embraces 'the universality of things' and gives 'a complete representation of the world'. For the Australian Aborigines, 'things themselves, everything which is in the universe', are distributed among the clans in a logical way so that the classification of objects is systematic.[55] Only humans possess the intellectual capacity to create a general classification of objects. Humans, then, have constructed the idea of class. In Durkheim's view, the concept of classification—one of the basic categories of the intellect—could not have been constructed without an actual model to suggest it. A classification is an arrangement of related things in a hierarchy 'of subordination and co-ordination, the establishment of which is the object of all classification'. People arranged their knowledge in a hierarchy only after knowing what a hierarchy was, and this concept was 'exclusively a social affair. It is only in society that there are superiors, inferiors and equals.' Humans derived these ideas from society and then projected them into their conception of the natural world.[56] Durkheim believed the development of generalized concepts about the world and the origin of the concept of the sacred—that is, religion—were intimately connected.

He further surmised that the result of this dual life is the emergence of two distinct and separate mental states in the Aboriginal consciousness, the world of profane things and that of **sacred** things. The more intense the experience of collective power, the more likely it is that people would be convinced the sacred and profane realms really exist. For Durkheim, 'Religious force is only the sentiment inspired by the group in its members, but projected outside the consciousnesses that experience them, and objectified . . . fixed upon some object that thus becomes sacred. . . . the sacred character is added to or superimposed upon them.' The superstructure of religious beliefs is built on the material foundation of collective life, the fact that people live together in moral communities.[57]

Society is the real foundation of religion. Religious forces translate how the moral authority of the collective consciousness penetrates and shapes the individual consciousness. '[T]he sacred principle is nothing more nor less than society transfigured and personified.'[58] The ritual actions and the feelings they induce, which in the minds of the believers attach them to their god, simultaneously strengthen the bonds that attach them to their society, of which their god is only a figurative expression. Collective representations can make something sacred, or highly venerated, out of that which, objectively, is the commonest object. What is a flag but a piece of cloth? What confers exceptional value upon a cancelled postage stamp? These powers are purely ideal in that they are conferred on objects by people, yet they are then assumed to be powerful in themselves and capable of determining people's actions as if they were the same as physical forces.[59]

Religion is more, however, than beliefs, the aspect that has been the focus of most intellectual debate. Durkheim considered the reality of religion to be intimately bound up with the actions, or religious rites, that are observed. For Durkheim, society is something that has to be sustained and recreated. If humanity ceased to believe in its gods, then the gods would die; if individuals ceased to believe in and practise their socially induced habits, society would not continue to exist. Behind the apparently irrational practices of religious rites is a 'mental mechanism' that gives them meaning and significance.

The effect of the cult in reality is to recreate society, the 'moral being upon which we depend'. Simultaneously, 'the individual soul is regenerated too, by being dipped again in the source from which its life comes.'[60] The kinship celebrated in the rite is both made and remade in the action, for 'it exists only in so far as it is believed in, and the effect of all these collective demonstrations is to support the beliefs upon which they are founded.'[61] The real significance of the cult is the moral regeneration of the individual and renewal of the unity of society, attaching the individual to the group and the present to the past. The Aboriginals explain their rites as having been originated by their ancestors and faithfully reproduced. The tradition perpetuates the memory of the moral system as well as the cosmology, serving to 'sustain the vitality of these beliefs, to keep them from being effaced from memory and, in turn, to revivify the most essential elements of the collective consciousness.'[62]

Social Evolution: Volume and Dynamic Density

Society might have stagnated once it reached the segmental level of development, where it was bonded by a mighty collective conscience. Durkheim believed there was no inherent motor in the human species causing perpetual progress. What accounts for the dynamic of social evolution and the ever-increasing fragmentation of the division of labour? Durkheim pointed to one crucial factor in social change, the size of the population, although too many people do not cause a society to change as long as there is enough vacant territory into which some may migrate and replicate societies similar to the ones they had left. When these avenues for migration disappear, further increases in the volume of society mean that the population becomes more concentrated. Social change is caused by what Durkheim terms the **dynamic density** of society, which implies physical concentration, but, more importantly, it reflects the number of individuals who are in actual social relationship with each other who also live a common life.[63]

Once societies have grown and become more condensed, 'the struggle for existence becomes more strenuous' in the new conditions of existence. As more people compete with each other in a given territory, it becomes less and less possible to make a living in the old way, from an unspecialized task that is the same as everyone else's. The greater intensity of the struggle makes it necessary for individuals to change their mode of living. They could respond to the struggle for existence in a number of ways, such as by emigrating or turning to crime, or even by suicide. Most people are deflected from these solutions because,

through their life in society, they experience a bond that ties them to their country and they develop sentiments of sympathy for their fellow citizens. Most take the path of least resistance, which is the development of more specialized forms of work within their present society.[64] The more a society grows in membership and the more people are drawn closer together, the more fierce the struggle becomes and the greater the need for further specialization.

Those who are inferior in the new competitive world are forced to give up positions they had hitherto occupied because they can no longer sustain themselves. Consequently, the 'small employer becomes a foreman, the small shopkeeper an employee'. Differences in heredity or environment do not drive social evolution, although once it is set in motion they mark out the furrows along which specialization proceeds. The struggle for existence does not eliminate inferior individuals; rather, Durkheim suggests, this Darwinian spectacle 'is a gentle dénouement.' People with inferior minds or bodies can still find functional niches somewhere in society.[65]

The division of labour proceeds both horizontally, separating work into specialties, as well as vertically, producing differences of power and wealth. Those who triumph in the new conditions within which the struggle is fought take on the specializations of control and domination. For Durkheim, the ultimate inequality was the existence, from birth, of rich and poor, a social fact he calls an external inequality since it does not necessarily reflect an individual's inner worth, talents, or abilities. Although modern society is marked by serious conflict between the haves and have-nots, it does not automatically follow that this great inequality causes violence. Less developed societies were even more unequal, but these inequalities did not threaten social cohesion because people were otherwise tightly bound to their society. In their eyes, society epitomized the beliefs and practices by which they lived. It was the foundation of the moral and religious order, making society appear sacred to them. Social inequalities were not merely tolerable, but seen as natural.

While people in traditional society regarded inequality to be inevitable, people in modern society increasingly regard great inequalities as intolerable and malleable. As the social milieu becomes more complex and unstable, the traditions and conventional beliefs of the old social structure are shaken and become unreliable. The old social equilibrium is broken. Simultaneously, the powers of rationality are developed through which individuals adapt themselves to the more mobile and complex social environment. Social life is rendered more intense 'by extending the horizon of thought and action of each individual'.[66] Restoring a new **social equilibrium** requires an expansion of the function of intelligence. Consistent with Lamarck's theory of evolution, our brain enlarges and our intelligence and sensibility develop as we exercise them more because of the greater fierceness and violence of the struggle of life. Without willing it, all classes become more intelligent, as a comparison of industrial workers with rural, agricultural labourers demonstrates.

Social evolution is not propelled because people feel new needs or desires. That is putting ideas rather than the objective conditions of existence in the driver's seat of social change. 'If we specialize it is not so as to produce more, but to enable us to live in the new conditions of existence created for us.' In short, the conditions of existence change. This necessitates specialization by the laws of competition; existence becomes more difficult and strenuous, which demands new resources that the division of labour supplies. Being forced by the new circumstances to work at more specialized tasks, people develop a greater diversity of tastes and aptitudes as well as skills and knowledge, which make people believe, after it has occurred, that the division of labour was desirable and useful. Equilibrium is re-established at a higher, more progressive level; society is more developed and increasingly specialized. Civilization 'is itself a necessary consequence of the changes occurring in the volume and density of societies.' As individuals seek to maintain their position by specializing more, they work harder and stimulate their faculties excessively. They then

produce a higher culture. So civilization is not a goal that motivates people to achieve more, nor is it a desire prior to its attainment; it is the necessary result of structural change in society. Life is lived more intensely, but this does not necessarily mean it is happier or more moral. People 'go forward because they must.'[67]

THE INDUSTRIAL TYPE OF SOCIETY AND ORGANIC SOLIDARITY

As labour functions become increasingly specialized, the traditional form of solidarity rooted in social similarities is undermined. Comte regarded the division of labour as 'the most essential condition of social life' because it linked people 'with the line of their predecessors . . . and even to the line of their various successors' and, as such, was 'the principal element in social solidarity'. This view reflected the older, conservative model of society as an organic succession of generations. People were dependent on others, Comte realized, but this mutual dependence did not automatically create a common morality and social order.[68]

Durkheim considered the division of labour to be a necessary and positive component of industrial societies and generated a new form of social solidarity. While people were necessarily doing smaller and smaller parts of larger and larger processes, this did not necessarily stunt anyone's potential. A surgeon was highly specialized, but his work was hardly alienating in Marx's sense. Furthermore, as work became more specialized, individuals were no longer self-sufficient. A different kind of glue that arose from mutual need was emerging to bond society together. As people do less and less for themselves, they are increasingly dependent on others for their daily needs— from the food they eat, to the shoes they wear, to the entertainment they crave. This mutual dependency creates a new sense of social togetherness, which Durkheim termed **organic solidarity**. The term expressed what Durkheim felt to be the central paradox of the modern world: that people increasingly become conscious of individual rights and desires while, simultaneously, they become more dependent on a multitude of others for survival.

As occupational functions become more separate, moral diversity increases. The old collective sentiments become increasingly powerless to contain the centrifugal tendencies of the division of labour, which separates people and divides them. The mechanical solidarity that linked individuals together in the simple society had not yet disappeared entirely as a result of social evolution, although over time it became supplemented by organic solidarity, which eventually became the dominant type. Organic solidarity has progressed only as mechanical solidarity has regressed. Like an organism, the internal unity of society is an internal solidarity caused by 'the spontaneous consensus of its parts'.[69] Organic solidarity develops because the division of labour links the various social functions closely together and 'constitutes the establishment of a social and moral order *sui generis*.'[70]

But this process has not yet been consummated. First, the loss of mechanical solidarity was not matched by an equivalent growth of the organic variety. In addition, the nature of organic solidarity, which had to be consistent with modern individualism, was different. In the gap between the loss of the old social bonds and the difficulty in producing the new, the social disease of anomie emerged, reflecting the absence of rules to guide social life. Social evolution had not produced, along with a changed social structure, the complementary set of moral principles suitable for the new condition. A large fault line had appeared between the new structure and the existing moral beliefs and practices, which are difficult to uproot from the hard, heavy soil of the past. The moral dilemma of society, however, went deeper than this. The division of labour produces modern individualism.

Humans are reasoning animals because they are social. As instinct has retreated in human life, 'Consciousness fills the space that instinct leaves free.' A new psychological life, also *sui generis*, arises in society that is freer, 'more complex and more independent of the organs that maintain it'.

In less developed societies, psychological life is identical for all members and individual differences are lost in the midst of overwhelming social similarities. As society evolves and becomes denser, individuality begins to emerge and differences multiply. Each individual now becomes a spontaneous source of activity. Individual personalities are formed and each becomes conscious of itself. Although Durkheim agreed that human psychology was too free and complex to be explained by physical causes, he maintained nevertheless that it was possible to understand consciousness scientifically.[71] For Durkheim, the consciousness of individuals comes from society: 'Most of our states of consciousness would not have occurred among' people who were 'isolated from one another and would have occurred completely differently among people grouped together in a different way.'[72] Individual differences don't precede collective life, Durkheim argues; they derive from it. Individualism, then, is not anti-social. 'It is not the absolute personality of the monad, sufficient unto itself, and able to do without the rest of the world.' Individuality is a product of society and presupposes it.[73]

The person is the product of two forces, said Durkheim; the internal sensations of desire and passion tend to individualize humans. Each body is distinct, each 'forms a special centre about which the collective representations reflect and colour themselves differently.' Each one expresses the same moral and social world of ideas and sentiments 'in its own fashion'. But this individualization is not the essential characteristic of the personality. On the contrary, passion tends to enslave the consciousness. Modern individualism derives more from reason than from the body: 'we are more personal the more we are freed from our senses and able to think and act with concepts', which derive from the collective consciousness, from society.[74]

Society is more tightly bound together the more the individual consciousness overlaps the common consciousness, as it does most thoroughly in simple societies. Second, the more intensely a person feels the collective consciousness, the more it affects his or her choices and the stronger the solidarity. Finally, the more the common beliefs and practices are clear-cut, the less individuals diverge from them and the more consensus there is in society about moral and ethical rules. The more general and indeterminate the rules are, the more individual reflection intervenes and the more centrifugal tendencies (those that cause a force to move away from a central point) multiply—as they do in modern society.

Over time, the common consciousness becomes 'weaker and vaguer', expressing fewer strong and well-defined sentiments. It gradually loses the power to dominate consciousness that it possessed in the beginning. Simultaneously, the individual consciousness throws off the yoke of the collective consciousness and becomes increasingly preponderant,[75] the result of 'an iron law . . . against which it would be absurd to revolt.'[76] While beliefs and practices assume a less religious character, Durkheim noted, the dignity of the individual becomes the object of a type of religious worship, forming, in a manner of speaking, a common faith, which is a key element of the modern collective conscience. The doctrine of individualism, however, does not bind us to society the way the older collective consciousness did. 'Thus it does not constitute a truly social link.'[77]

What prevents social life from collapsing as mechanical solidarity grows weaker is that the division of labour increasingly fulfills the function performed formerly by the older collective consciousness. 'This is mainly what holds together social entities in the higher types of societies.'[78] The more specialized our activity is, the more personal it is, yet we depend more on society for everything else. Each individual has a personality and a sphere of activity that are her or his own, an increasingly free area the collective consciousness cannot regulate. Paradoxically, the 'more extensive this free area is, the stronger the cohesion' that arises from organic solidarity. Society functions more effectively as a whole at the same time that each individual moves in his or her own way. Although our

activity is never completely original and we follow the rules of given occupations, 'this leaves much room for the free play of our initiative.' Like a higher organism, each part of society is increasingly specialized and differentiated, yet the result is the greater unity of the organism.[79] Durkheim summed up his distinctive approach by claiming that the primary function of the division of labour was to produce social solidarity, not its opposite. The economic importance of the division of labour was insignificant compared with its moral effects. It could create 'a feeling of solidarity' like friendship.[80]

For Durkheim, the weakening of the collective consciousness is a normal phenomenon and is not the cause of the great crises in modern society that Durkheim was attempting to understand and prevent. All modern society needed in order to maintain the unity of the whole was the development of organic solidarity. Social crises were caused by the fact that social evolution had not advanced far enough. Some of the necessary conditions for the full existence of organic solidarity were still to be realized. In the meantime, the function of social science was to diagnose the problems of modern society and prescribe remedies consistent with the emergence of organic solidarity. If the division of labour, nevertheless, appeared to bring in its wake many negative social facts, these problems could be modified by conscious intervention once their nature was sufficiently understood.

NORMAL AND ABNORMAL SOCIAL FORMS

Durkheim thought that the 'principal object of all sciences of life . . . is to define and explain the normal state and to distinguish it from' abnormal states. A physician needs to know what makes a healthy body in order to recognize and treat illnesses. What might appear an illness to one might be a sign of health for another. All social theorists distinguish what they define as normal from the abnormal, Durkheim argued, but their distinctions have been based on ideological biases rather than scientific grounds.

Class Conflict

Durkheim considered class conflict to be patho-logical; the socialists thought its absence to be unhealthy. For the socialists, capitalism was a deviation from the normal or desirable state, but it was widely diffused and constantly growing. Spencer had considered the extension of the pow-ers of government to be the 'radical vices of our societies', but both regularly increased as society advanced. If normality is merely a characteristic ideologists can choose to impute to things, reality can be assumed to be whatever we think it is,[81] and social theory has no secure foundation.

This non-scientific approach to society is not merely mistaken, it is socially dangerous. Social-ists, for example, imagine a peaceful and equal future society with plenty for all. But this idealism places the ultimate social goal for humanity so far into the distant future that it discourages some people from doing anything because it is so remote, while it arouses 'others who, in order to draw a little nearer to it, quicken the pace and plunge into revolutions.' Rather than pursuing what appears to be an attractive though remote ideal, people should 'work with steady persever-ance to maintain the normal state' and to help re-establish it when it is threatened. The statesman should be like a physician who prevents illnesses 'by good hygiene' rather than by amputation, and cures those illnesses that appear.[82]

The crucial question was whether the dis-tinction between normal and pathological phe-nomena could be made scientifically. Most social theorists believed that science cannot teach what ought to be. Science observes and explains, but does not judge. It can explain effects, but not determine what ends or even what means should be pursued. What is needed, Durkheim argues, is to find an objective criterion that is 'inherent in the facts themselves, which enables us to distin-guish scientifically' between healthy and morbid social phenomena. Then a theorist will be faithful to the scientific method and still be able to 'throw light on practical problems'.[83]

Normal Defined

Durkheim proposed to define normal by the degree to which a phenomenon was general and widespread in society.[84] If a phenomenon appears in the majority of the individual members of the species, and individual variations occur only within a narrow range, it is the normal or average type. The existence of this normal type is the def-inition of health; hence every deviation from this standard is pathological. Unhealthy variations are exceptional in space and time. They are found only in the minority of cases and do not persist.[85]

In Durkheim's view, phenomena that are the most widespread must, by definition, be healthy and the most advantageous for society. He takes greater frequency as proof of their superiority. Abnormal characteristics are rare because the organism that possesses them has greater difficulty surviving. Once science has established the nor-mal case and the reasons for its existence, it is appropriate to modify individual deviants to con-form to the normal condition.[86] It follows, how-ever, that anything new in society would be unhealthy. Yet societies continually change and evolve in the direction of greater complexity and individuality. What is healthy at one point in time may become unhealthy in the new conditions that are coming into being. Similarly, what is defined as abnormal and deviant may be socially useful, not merely by reinforcing the awareness of the norm, but by introducing an innovation that reflects the new solidarity emerging.

After the conditions of existence of a society have changed, many older beliefs or practices per-sist due to blind habit. In this case, what is gen-eral and, by definition, 'normal' would no longer be useful. To claim that a trait is normal, Durkheim adds, the scientist must show that it is useful to the organism and performs a function necessary to health. It must be shown to be aver-age or common, and to be logically necessary.

To distinguish the normal from the patholog-ical in 'lower cultures' is relatively easy. In the higher societies, which still are evolving and have not run their entire course, 'the sociologist may then be embarrassed in deciding whether a phenomenon is normal or not.' However, the method is simple. First the social scientist will establish 'by observation that a particular fact is general'. Then she or he will investigate the conditions that existed in the past that corresponded to the normal type and determine whether these conditions are the same or have changed. By this reasoning, the weakening of collective sentiments in general and religious ones in particular is normal.[87] Similarly, the present anomic state of economic relations in modern society also is normal because it reflects the absence of regulation.

The Forced and Anomic Divisions of Labour

As modern society evolved, the division of labour had exhibited some pathological, or socially unhealthy, forms of the division of labour. It was pathological, thought Durkheim, for someone to be forced to do a job for which he or she was not suited. He termed this situation the forced division of labour and believed that this social wrong could be fixed under capitalism. The genuinely organic society would have equality of opportunity—all must be free to discover their own talents and every occupation in the job hierarchy must be open to those with the appropriate abilities. Durkheim knew that capitalist society did not work that way. He believed, however, that it could. The educational system must be reformed so that talented people could be discovered and the best people slotted into the jobs most appropriate for them. He had no faith in the social Darwinist notion that competitive capitalism, by itself, would ensure that the best rose to the top while the worst specimens of humanity sank to the bottom.

The division of labour had been organized and regulated in the past through the institution of castes or classes. A caste system, where occupations (functions) are allocated according to set rules, works more or less smoothly because it reflects the actual distribution of abilities among the population. Over a long period of time, he argued, people's inherited abilities corresponded to the positions society assigned them. In a class society, which encourages social mobility, there is often a discrepancy between the social role assigned to a person and his or her natural abilities. The lower classes were often dissatisfied with their lot and aspired to positions prohibited to them. Class warfare had been the result, caused by the way labour was shared out.

In modern society, no particular position is predetermined from birth, although individuals inherit specific tastes and aptitudes, and this causes frustration if they are not taken into account in their daily work. Not only must everyone have a task, it must also be agreeable. Otherwise, only coercion can maintain what would be a troubled solidarity. Normally, Durkheim maintains, an internal and spontaneous harmony will develop between each individual's nature and his or her social function. People are normally happy fulfilling their nature, just as organs are satisfied with the quantity of nourishment they require to fulfill their functions. The division of labour produces solidarity only 'to the degree that it is spontaneous', that is, when people receive status and rewards that are consistent with their abilities and effort.[88] In modern society, the division of labour has not been permitted to follow its spontaneous course. Inequality of wealth prevents the just allocation of talents to specific functions, causing disharmony and jeopardizing organic solidarity.

The problem, Durkheim believed, was not necessarily that social positions and the amount of wealth that corresponded to them were unequal. It was a normal tendency of the division of labour to progressively increase inequality. Yet in modern society, the belief was becoming widespread that there should be greater *equality* among citizens. According to Durkheim's reasoning, by becoming widespread this belief proved itself not to be an illusion but 'must express . . . an aspect of reality.' At first glance this appeared to be paradoxical. Durkheim resolved the contradiction by claiming that people do not commonly mean that individuals should be equal in the conditions of their life. Some people deserved to be in the inferior positions in which they found themselves. The sentiment for equality, he argued, implied only that people should be equal in their chances of acquiring superior positions. Society 'recognizes as unjust an inferiority that is personally not merited' and consequently strives to reduce inequality of opportunity as much as possible by helping the greatly disadvantaged to move up, making 'room for all the deserving'.[89]

While Durkheim did not accept the view that social rewards should be equal, grossly excessive inequality—some people living as billionaires while others starved—was not functional for the smooth running of society. The existence of greatly unequal rewards was another pathological form of the division of labour. Vast inequalities were not simply morally wrong; they caused social conflict and social instability. Durkheim wanted to bring about reforms that would reduce this anomic and socially unhealthy level of inequality.

But, he argued, society did require a considerable degree of inequality. Not all jobs were equally important in society. Some jobs were functionally more crucial than others; people needed higher rewards as incentives for performing these most important tasks. A certain amount of inequality, then, was necessary and socially beneficial. The division of labour should be both horizontal (specialization) and vertical (unequal rewards). The socialists, however, had claimed that unequal rewards led to social conflict, something Durkheim wanted to avoid. Was conflict in capitalism unavoidable? Durkheim did not think so.

In the simple societies, people's ambitions are limited by the strength of the collective consciousness. In a society that is held together by organic solidarity, subversive tendencies emerge when people feel thwarted in their ambitions. The flood tide of discontent grows more violent, Durkheim said, while the dyke of the collective conscious is more frequently breached. Consequently, it is indispensable for the division of labour to be more nearly spontaneous and society should attempt 'to eliminate external inequalities as much as possible'.

Certainly, individuals will always have unequal internal merit and consequently, people will always be placed unequally in society;[90] however, contracts between people that are not based on their social merit are morally invalid.

For Durkheim, 'If one class in society is obliged, in order to live, to secure the acceptance by others of its services, whilst another class can do without them, because of the resources already at its disposal, resources that, however, are not necessarily the result of some social superiority, the latter group can lord it over the former. In other words, there can be no rich and poor by birth without their being unjust contracts.'[91] Paradoxically, the division of labour should be as spontaneous as possible while, simultaneously, society seeks to assist the talented but disadvantaged individuals to rise on the social ladder. From Durkheim's perspective, economists such as Adam Smith deserved credit for first discovering that social life was naturally spontaneous and that any restraint causes it to deviate from this course. But freedom was taken to be an absolute and, by definition, social constraint could only diminish freedom.

While this may be the dominant mode of thinking in liberal society, Durkheim concluded, it was wrong and unscientific. The truth was the reverse of what appeared to be true. Liberty itself, he claimed, is the product of regulation. Rather than being antagonistic to social action, it is its result. Liberty is a conquest by society over nature; it requires an utter reversal of the natural order. Natural physical inequalities and unequal advantages are the very negation of liberty because they forbid some people the freedom to do what they otherwise might wish. Liberty is only realized as humans rise above nature, become social beings, and regulate their social life. In Durkheim's view, the concept of freedom could only arise in a society, that is, in a situation of social constraint. Once the concept of freedom is understood by people, it is indispensable that social action be directed to evening out as much as possible the external inequalities that deny some people the degree of liberty that should be the right of all. Just as ancient people needed a common faith, people in the most advanced societies had a need for justice. The social mission 'is to inject an even greater equity into our social relationships' to ensure the free development of socially useful forces. This is not, Durkheim claimed, some Utopian and unscientific attempt to make social life conform to our idea of what it should be. Working to lessen external inequalities simply anticipates the normal state to come.[92] Durkheim predicted that, as the organized type of society develops, the form of justice represented by equality of opportunity will become still more absolute. Present progress, while considerable, 'gives only a slight idea of what will be accomplished later.'[93]

Social critics, however, complained that the division of labour had been taken to absurd and unhealthy lengths in the factory system. Durkheim was aware that the individual had been reduced to a cog in a machine and called it 'a debasement of human nature'. Comte had earlier noted the unfortunate moral effects of extreme specialization. For Durkheim, providing workers with a wide, general education would not compensate for their overspecialization at work; rather, it would make it increasingly intolerable to them. The division of labour had a built-in mechanism to resolve the problem because workers are in constant contact with others and interact with them. Machines repeat motions but do not perceive the sense of them. Workers know their activity has a meaning and contributes towards a goal they can conceive more or less distinctly. They feel they are of some use; their routine labour is still the activity 'of an intelligent being'.[94]

The function of the educational system is to teach that unequal rewards are both necessary and can be just. Once people are fairly allocated to the various jobs according to their talents, and once the income for any job is determined by the functional importance of the job, it becomes the task of the educational system to convince people that those who were more highly rewarded deserved what they received. The result of this ideological teaching, if effective, would be to help create a society that is still unequal (in terms of rewards and conditions of life), but is socially stable and

not divided by those conflicts that are tearing modern society apart.

Theory of Corporations

Creating a moral consensus in society is a function that can best be performed by a body that is intermediate between the overgrown state and the egotistical individual. The division of labour was in an anomic state because of the absence of regulation. 'A society made up of an extremely large mass of unorganised individuals, which an overgrown state attempts to limit and restrain, constitutes a veritable sociological monstrosity.' Society cannot be left to the fate of innumerable economic decisions that are purely individualistic. Equally wrong would be to seek social harmony by further expanding the role of government. Collective activity is too complex to be expressed by a single state that is remote from the people. If the state is the sole environment for common living, people 'contract out'.[95]

The solution to the dilemma of regulation lies neither in state intervention nor laissez-faire. Spencer had compared the process of digestion and the diffusion of nutrients through the body to the economic system in society that distributes goods and services for individual consumption. The conscious mind doesn't tell the stomach to excrete acids or order the liver to remove impurities; these occur automatically. By analogy, Spencer argues, economic activity also works spontaneously and there is no need in society for any conscious controlling mechanism, such as state intervention. Laissez-faire economics is consistent with organic life. Not exactly, counters Durkheim. He agreed that the state—the social brain—cannot control the daily actions of the economy even if it tries, contrary to what the socialists believe. But this is to misunderstand how both the body and society actually work. While the brain doesn't control digestion, it remains subject to regulation by other bodily organs that excrete chemicals and regulate the metabolism.

The economic system in modern society actually functions quite badly, not like the smooth and harmonious digestion we experience after a good meal. The problem in the economic sphere is that intermediate organs of regulation, like those that work so well in the intestines, have been insufficiently developed by society. Neither the family, religion, nor the state is capable of providing the close-knit moral regulation that modern society requires. The workable solution Durkheim proposes is regulation through the occupational group or corporation, consisting of 'all workers . . . in association, who all cooperate in the same function'. A corporation would provide a strong moral environment for the creation of a new collective personality and consciousness. '[O]ccupational life is almost the whole of life', Durkheim believed. Consequently, a corporate group that was made 'a definite and recognized organ of our public life' would be always present and exert a dominant influence during the most important years of an individual's life, and its control would extend into non-working life. The corporation has everything necessary to give individuals a setting and draw them out of their 'state of moral isolation'.[96]

The presently existing trade unions would not do because they exist in a relationship of warfare with employers. Labour contracts represent the relative power of the parties, not the strength of their moral rights. The two contracting parties only appear to have contradictory interests, leading them to form separate organizations that reflected their different consciousness. Actually, workers need employers to provide them with their means of production as much as employers need to hire workers to make profits, so a mutual, organic need and a basic interest are shared by the two groups. Social stability would be improved by developing a single organization for each industry, representing all occupational groups of workers as well as capitalists. Corporations might even become the foundation of political organization in place of territorial divisions.

The expansion and reform of the role of professional or corporative bodies do not remove the need for other reforms, but it is 'the *sine qua non* of their effectiveness'. Even if inherited wealth ceased and all people began their lives in a state of economic equality, the problem of anomie in

the economic sphere would still exist. Social activities would still need regulation. Durkheim's advice was to begin immediately to institute these corporative reforms and the new moral force that were so desperately needed in society.[97]

In modern society, where 'the collective consciousness is increasingly reduced to the cult of the individual', social reform is necessary to prevent the anti-social effects of excessive egoism. This does not require any Utopian fantasy or excessive state domination. 'It requires us only to be charitable and just towards our fellow-men, to fulfill our task well, to work towards a state where everyone is called to fulfill the function he performs best and will receive a just reward for his efforts.' Such a society is far from being realized and it is a laborious task to erect such a society 'in which each individual will have the place he merits and will be rewarded according to his deserts, where everyone will consequently cooperate spontaneously both for the common good and that of the individual.' Morality must link us 'to something other than ourselves'.[98]

For Durkheim, society in the early twentieth century was undergoing a stage of transition that resulted in 'moral mediocrity'. The great things that had excited the previous generations no longer inspired the present, but there was nothing to replace them: 'the old gods are growing old or already dead, and others are not yet born.' But this state of incertitude and confused agitation could not last forever. A day would come when society would again experience a 'creative effervescence' through which new ideals would arise to guide humanity. The French Revolution had failed to keep alive revolutionary faith, but that did not mean that new symbols would not be created that would be adequate for the future. While no gospel was immortal, humanity was still capable of inventing new ones.[99]

DURKHEIM'S CONSERVATIVE REFORMISM

Durkheim wanted to emancipate sociology from partisan politics without making it a purely theoretical discipline. Although sociology must eschew ideologies in favour of science, after which it can 'silence passions and prejudices', this did not mean that sociologists must have no interest in practical questions. 'Just because everything happens according to laws it does not follow that we have to do nothing.' The social environment establishes the limits to what can be effectively accomplished by conscious social reform.[100]

Sociology was not merely descriptive; it was partly prescriptive because social science can help point out the direction society ought to follow and the avenues we ought to avoid. Rather than let causes produce effects randomly, according to whatever forces move them, they should be guided by reflective thinking. Science must discover the laws of social change and anticipate the changes the new social structure requires to function properly. By examining the existing society, we will discover that reality is not always harmonious, that it possesses contradictions or 'imperfections' that can be remedied.[101]

Hitherto, social scientists such as Comte, Marx, and Spencer had projected an image of an ideal society and then measured the existing society by that yardstick. That made them far too critical and disrespectful of existing social institutions. Durkheim also had an image of a more desirable future in his stated intention to help reduce social anomie within the foundation of that modern industrial society that produced anomie as a normal feature of its evolutionary development. Just as human health is an ideal, so raising social health as closely as possible to perfection is a goal worth pursuing. It is a question of recognizing several potentials that are immediately realizable and of determining the one that is least socially disruptive yet still propels society in the direction that is consistent with a scientific definition of social health—the society without anomie. For Durkheim, 'To seek to realise a higher civilization than that demanded by the nature of the prevailing conditions is to desire to let sickness loose upon the society of which one forms a part. It is not possible to stimulate collective activity excessively, beyond the level determined by the state of the social organism, without compromising its health.'[102] George Eliot called this 'fool's work' or, worse, 'wicked work' (Box 10.7).[103]

Box 10.7

[I]n our society, there are old institutions, and among them the various distinctions and inherited advantages of classes, which have shaped themselves along with all the wonderful slow-growing system of things made up of our laws, our commerce, and our stores of all sorts ... which must be used as they are until new and better have been prepared, or the structure of the old has been gradually altered. But it would be fool's work to batter down [an irrigation] pump only because a better might be made, when you have no machinery ready for a new one; it would be wicked work, if villages lost their crops by it. Now the only safe way by which society can be steadily improved and our worst evils reduced, is not by any attempt to do away directly with the actually existing class distinctions and advantages, as if everybody could have the same sort of work, or lead the same sort of life ... but by the turning of Class Interests into Class Functions or duties. What I mean is that each class should be urged by the surrounding conditions to perform its particular work under the strong pressure of responsibility to the nation at large. . . . But this end will not come by impatience. . . . Still less will it come by mere undoing, or change merely as change. . . . The nature of things in this world has been determined for us beforehand. . . .

—George Eliot, *Felix Holt* (1866)

If anomie is normal and perpetual, nothing can be done; if the conditions that give rise to anomie are normal, but social evolution may be guided in the direction that would reduce this anomie, then the role of the intellectual and sociology in particular is to help society reach a better future. It is not possible or even desirable to duplicate the mechanical solidarity of the simple society because social evolution has emancipated the powers of the individual consciousness; there is no going back. In fact, what is necessary is the further development of each individual. Ideally, each individual would express her or his full uniqueness through the even finer development of the division of labour. Durkheim argues that individuals become ever more autonomous in industrial society as they become increasingly dependent on society. While apparently contradictory, these two movements are resolved by the division of labour.

Durkheim recognized that his 'reasoning is not at all revolutionary.' Rather, it was 'essentially conservative', since it conceived social facts as deterministic rather than arbitrary. The truly radical and dangerous theory regarded society as the result of conscious manipulation, from which it followed that 'in an instant, by a simple dialectical artifice, [social order could] be completely upset!' His science of morality, however, 'imparts to us a prudently conservative disposition of mind.' It teaches us to treat social reality with utmost caution. Morality cannot be modified without affecting all the other existing social facts and the repercussions cannot be worked out in advance. Basically, if a moral fact exists, it must serve a social purpose or correspond to some social need and therefore 'it has a right to our respect.' The goal of intervention is not to construct another morality above the dominant one, but to improve the existing one in a practical manner.[104]

Certainly, some things or sentiments have no utility for society. They may be completely irrational. Nevertheless, they should be allowed to continue because undermining them has the effect of also undermining social cohesion and, consequently, would be prejudicial to society. Irrational customs, therefore, must be protected. Sociologists must treat social institutions 'with respect but without mystic awe, by making us appreciate both their permanent and their ephemeral aspects, their stability and their infinite variability.'[105]

So it is with that form of ephemeral idea known as religion. As long as there is society, religious thought will persist. In Durkheim's conception, however, what is likely to persist is a highly secular form of religion. The defining characteristic of religious thought was an absolute demarcation between the sacred and the profane. Durkheim had argued that even in secular society, certain conceptions and symbols were invested with special respect of an almost sacred character—the national flag, the office of the President, the celebrity. For Durkheim, religion and science differ in degree but not kind. Both pursue the same ends and focus attention on nature, humanity, and society. Religion translates these realities into a shared language that does not differ fundamentally from that employed by science. Both modes of thought connect things to each other, establish relations between them, classify and systematize them. All science does, Durkheim argues, is perfect its method by purging accidental elements, encouraging a spirit of criticism that is absent from religious thought, and developing ways to set aside bias, prejudice, and subjective influences. Science is merely 'a more perfect form of religious thought'. As a result, science has tended to surpass and substitute itself for religion in 'cognitive and intellectual functions'.[106] Science grants religion a right to exist, but not 'its right to dogmatize upon the nature of things and the special competence it claims for itself for knowing man and the world. As a matter of fact, it does not know itself.'[107]

Durkheim is unwilling to follow this secularization to the conclusion that the modern form of thought will be exclusively scientific. Science can explain religion, he asserts, but not take its place. In the future, religion would be more likely to transform itself rather than disappear. There is something eternal in religion. The only conflict between religion and science rests on one point: its speculative function. Speculation cannot be scientific: 'the obscure intuitions of sensation and sentiment too often take the place of logical reasons.'[108] Where science is fragmentary, incomplete, and slow, religion is an impetus to action. A theory that makes men live and act must go beyond science.

CONCLUSION

Durkheim developed his sociology in a complex intellectual environment. He matured intellectually at the end of the nineteenth century, a time when the dominant philosophy was highly subjective and hostile to a science of human action. Durkheim's *Rules of Sociological Method* was sharply attacked by critics who complained that he was 'eliminating the mental element from sociology'.[109] Yet, claimed Durkheim, he was following the steps of psychologists who had been developing the scientific study of the human mind for decades. For Durkheim, psychology focused on the consciousness of individuals, while sociology was concerned with collective consciousness, the group mind: '[E]very time that a social phenomenon is directly explained by a psychological phenomenon, we may be sure that the explanation is false.' The territory in between, social psychology, was as yet undeveloped.[110]

In 1912, Durkheim concluded his study of religion by arguing that, 'in the majority of cases we see the good victorious over evil, life over death, the powers of light over the powers of darkness.' He felt at the time that this positive outcome reflected real life 'because reality is not otherwise'. If, however, the relationship between these contradictory forces were reversed, life would no longer be possible; but, he argued, 'as a matter of fact, it maintains itself and even tends to develop.'[111] Yet, even as Durkheim wrote, the forces he counted on to create a new sense of solidarity in modern society were faltering. Religion

had been in decline throughout the age of science, but an alternative anti-rational sentiment was emerging in modern society. Darwin had simply been the most obvious catalyst of anti-religious sentiments. The division of labour showed no signs of becoming less anomic, less forced, in Durkheim's terms. Alienation was the norm for industrial society and it was growing more profound, not becoming less serious. Social problems were not being solved or even adequately understood by the new engineers trained in sociological methods.

Finally, industrial society was not proving to be inherently peaceful. Comte and Spencer had argued that the new class of industrialists made the most profit when there was the highest level of international trade. The main condition necessary for maximizing international trade was the absence of war. Consequently, the more industry developed and the more industrialists occupied powerful positions in government, the less likely would it be that nations would want to go to war. This logic was, however, simplistic. Warfare might temporarily suppress international trade, affecting profits negatively. But should a nation be victorious in war, the industrialists of that nation would have expanded the territory over which they would control the markets. This would mean even higher long-term profits. In addition, war was good for some businesses.

Industrialists in England, France, Germany, the United States, Italy, and Japan were competing with each other for worldwide markets and to secure access to vital raw materials. They were rapidly dividing the poorer continents of Asia and Africa among themselves, coming into conflict worldwide. Rather than entering an age of peace, the table was being set for the destructive world wars of the first half of the twentieth century. Industrial capitalist society was, by its nature, aggressive and warlike rather than peaceful. The details about where war would begin and which countries would ally with others were simply matters of concrete history. The inevitability of world conflict was rooted deeply in the sociology of industrial capitalism.

Durkheim experienced World War I as a triple tragedy. His initial sentiments, along with his socialist friend, Jaurès, were opposed to war. Jaurès was assassinated for his anti-war politics, a loss Durkheim felt deeply. Once France was unavoidably entangled in the war, Durkheim did his nationalistic duty as a civilian while his son, who was of an age to do his duty in uniform, was killed.

Durkheim never recovered from the psychological trauma of his son's death. He died in 1917, at the age of 58, while the slaughter continued on the Western Front.[112] His hopes for society had been eclipsed by world events. In this sense, the pessimistic German sociologist, Max Weber, had a better grasp of the actual direction that history would take in the first decades of the twentieth century.

MAX WEBER

Émile Durkheim had been optimistic about the ability of social scientists to solve the problems of industrialism. In contrast, German sociologist Max Weber (1864–1920) was pessimistic about the future direction of European society. Although they were contemporaries—Weber was six years younger than Durkheim—the two sociologists wrote from different national traditions. Durkheim developed his theory in relation to French positivism and Spencer's social Darwinism. Weber's German heritage included the idealistic philosophy of Kant and the historical studies of Wilhelm Dilthey, who emphasized the dialectical interaction between people's knowledge and their cultural history. Weber also responded more directly than Durkheim to Marx because the intellectual interests of the two theorists overlapped and the German Marxist party was an influential force in national politics. Marx had analyzed some of the economic elements of alienation in the modern world, Weber argued, but there were other, more profound forms of alienation than those Marx had identified. What was worse, Weber believed, no solution to these social ills was possible.

Max Weber was born in Erfurt, Germany, the first of eight children. His father was a lawyer who came from a family of industrialists and merchants in the textile business. According to Dirk Käsler, the senior Weber was a self-satisfied and uncritically patriotic bourgeois politician, who was content under the authoritarian rule of Bismarck, the German Chancellor. In the home, he was dictatorial, patriarchal, and self-centred. Max Weber's mother, whose family also was politically well connected, was well educated and active in social affairs. Her humanitarian sentiments and pious religious views clashed with the pragmatic and worldly lifestyle of her husband. By the time Max was 12 his parents' mutual hostility was open in their family home, now in Berlin.[1] Some of the ambivalence created in Max Weber by his upbringing is illustrated in the mixed motives of Walter Bidlake, a character in Aldous Huxley's novel, *Point Counter Point*:

> At a distance, theoretically, purity and goodness and refined sensuality were admirable. But in practice and close to they were less appealing. . . . They were low, these sensual feelings; they were ignoble. . . . In his imagination he heard his father's rich and fleshy laugh. Horrible! Walter's whole conscious life had been oriented in opposition to his father, in opposition to the old man's jolly, careless sensuality. Consciously he had always been on the side of his mother, on the side of purity, refinement, the spirit. But his blood was at least half his father's.[2]

At the University of Heidelberg, as a young bourgeois scholar, Weber combined typical student antics in the company of his fraternity brothers with an appreciation for serious study. Weber developed close ties to his mother's family and became increasingly critical of his father's politics and lifestyle. He reoriented his political convictions in sympathy with the political ideals of the Romantic rebels of 1848, the entrepreneurial energy of the active bourgeois class, and the social concerns and religious convictions of his mother.

Although he rejected the extreme German patriotism his father endorsed, Weber undertook compulsory military service in the German army. Surrounded by models of self-discipline, Weber developed his lifelong habits of intensive study and ascetic living.[3]

Much of Weber's emotional and intellectual life was a struggle between extremes as he constructed an independent stand on social questions. As a young man in his early and mid-twenties, while living at home in Berlin, Weber experienced the emotional disintegration of his parents' marriage, which he blamed on his father. His first love was his cousin, Emmy Baumgarten. By 1887, she was suffering from a serious mental illness. Emmy recovered after a lengthy period of hospitalization and maintained a long-lasting friendship with Weber. In 1893, he married his father's great-niece, Marianne Schnitger and, although they became intellectual and moral comrades, their union was not sexually fulfilling. Weber found satisfaction in desire a decade later, not as a husband, but in extramarital affairs.[4] Marianne Weber was a strong and independent woman who was active in women's rights campaigns. After World War I, she became head of the liberal wing of the German women's movement. Max Weber supported the feminist critique of patriarchal dominance in domestic relations, the subject of his last and most bitter confrontation with his father.[5]

By 1890, Weber was voting for the conservatives and developing connections with evangelical Christian reformers. He had a difficult time finding a consistent home for his political and academic ambitions, finding much to oppose in any consistent but one-sided political philosophy. Weber entered the economic and political debates of his day, aligning himself with the social reformers by attacking the powerful *Junker* class in rural eastern Germany. In a public lecture in 1895, Weber demanded that the large semi-feudal estates be broken into smaller landholdings to encourage bourgeois agriculture. Simultaneously, he distanced himself from the left, claiming that the socialists naively confused value judgements with statements of fact. At that time he made his own value stance clear. He was in favour of German

nationalism and supported German imperialism in the language of the social Darwinists. Fifteen years later, however, he would speak out against racist ideologies.[6]

Weber was dogged by political and personal conflicts throughout the 1890s. He maintained contact with Christian social reformers and with socialists, and tried to balance his interests in political activity and academic inquiry. He was appointed to a university chair by the age of 30, the fruits of a reputation for scholarship. As a mature, married, and successful man, Weber condemned his father's oppression of his mother. The resulting break with his father was left unresolved when the older Weber died in 1897. A few months later, Weber began to suffer the symptoms of what would develop into a serious mental breakdown, which forced him to withdraw from lecturing and public controversy. Throughout the remainder of his life, Weber would occasionally suffer from a nervous disorder characterized by exhaustion, anxiety, and an inability to work. He balanced these episodes with other periods during which he maintained a rigorous and productive schedule of academic and political activity.

Weber's lacuna from lecturing, which began after his first nervous attack in 1897, lasted six and a half years, during which time his prodigious study continued. Weber began to develop his distinctive non-naturalistic approach to sociological methodology, which was distinct from the positivist spirit found in Durkheim. Weber pursued the largest of comparative sociological questions: what was distinctive about social developments in the West that had led to its dominant position in the world? While his research was extensively historical, Weber was dissatisfied with a purely historical approach, which examined events in relation to the peculiar and unique circumstances that created them. Rather, sociological analysis had to be addressed to the comparative study of large-scale, socially significant, and generalized phenomena. In 1904, Weber spent five months travelling in the United States, continuing his examination of the connection between Protestantism and the rise of capitalism in Europe and

America. Over the entire decade he worked on his major project, *Economy and Society*, a work that was unfinished at his death and was published under the supervision of Marianne Weber.[7]

Politically, Weber became increasingly estranged from the conservative policies of the Kaiser's regime in Germany—he welcomed the 1905 revolution against the Tsar in Russia—but he was equally alienated from the German Social Democrats, a Marxist party that was still revolutionary in its ideology and rhetoric.[8] When he was active, Weber entered into heated debates about business education and German patriotism. Although he was a captain in the German reserves, he defended the rights of pacifists. In 1913 he spent time in Italy with an anarchistic commune of 'nature children' and vegetarians, an eye-opening experience reinforcing his sense of the value of freedom. Above all, Weber wanted to stand in defence of disinterested scholarship, exposing those who allowed their value judgements to masquerade as objective knowledge. In the highly politicized atmosphere of pre-war Germany, value-free analysis was both unpopular and unrealistic.[9]

Weber was not initially in favour of war, but in 1914 he fell in with the war enthusiasm of the moment, referring to the war as 'great and wonderful'. Characteristically, disillusionment came later. He advocated limiting the German war objectives and, contrary to his previous support of German imperialism, opposed annexing conquests to German territory. In his view, the war was being run by armaments manufacturers and *Junker* landlords. He foresaw that the German policy of unrestricted submarine warfare would bring the United States into the war, causing an escalation that would lead to Germany's defeat. As the war dragged on, Weber became more critical of German policy and began campaigning for a new, people's political order and a post-war constitutional monarchy. He continued the study of world religions and, in 1918, accepted the chair of political economy at the University of Vienna, where he gave a series of lectures on Economy and Society, subtitled 'a positive critique of the materialist conception of history'.[10]

The materialist conception was the theoretical core of the Marxist German Social Democratic Party. Weber was critiquing the dominant interpretation of his time—that Marxism was a version of economic or technological determinism in which people's thoughts and beliefs were relegated to a secondary, derived role. Marx had argued that the purpose of theory was to change the world but, Weber argued, he had understood it one-sidedly. Like Marx, Weber approached political economy within a global and historical perspective, but Weber sought to understand the social, cultural, and political foundations of economic processes. The essence of his critique was that the Marxists paid insufficient attention to the ideological basis of social life, which could be independent of economic factors and contrary to them.

As he pursued these large, historical questions, Weber developed an individualistic methodology that, if only implicitly, undergirded his political economy. Like Durkheim, who wrote *Rules of Sociological Method* and founded a journal to shape the new approach to studying society, Weber consciously promoted the new discipline in Germany. In his *Economy and Society*, Weber systematically established a set of sociological concepts and methodological principles for analyzing society. For Weber, sociology was a science that attempted the interpretive understanding of the causes and consequences of **social action**. An action is anything a human being does that has, for her or him, a subjective meaning. A social action, in addition, must take into account the actions of other people. To pray alone is a meaningful action, but not a social one. Social action was the central subject matter of Weber's sociology.[11]

Weber studied social history from the foundational notion that individuals acted purposively or intentionally. This individualistic method had proved particularly useful in the study of economics, where the price of a good or the likelihood of success or failure in a venture depended on the cumulative effect of a great number of rational, individual choices. In economics, and even more so in sociology, the actual course of human action seldom followed what would be predicted from a pure model of rational choice. People's actions were oriented in a number of ways. The ends they sought may be rational, or emotional, or expressed in some purely idealistic fashion, such as achieving religious salvation. Much human behaviour was not rational and resulted purely from habit or from blindly following custom or tradition. Furthermore, regardless of the original meaning or intent of an individual's actions, they may produce consequences that were neither foreseen nor anticipated.[12]

Economic laws are generalizations of what would most likely occur if people acted rationally with knowledge of all important circumstances. Since the actual course of events is always some distance from this hypothetical or ideal model, economists can compare what actually happened with the rational model and seek to account for the variations. Similarly, the task of sociology is to develop a set of typical models of action that could then be used, interpretively, to explain events. The importance of subjectivity for Weber is to understand how people form common interpretations of their social world that help shape the society in which they live. Weber's analysis of historical epochs consistently focuses on the importance of ideological and political factors in shaping social development. In contrast to a theory that deterministically places the economic factor always in the dominant position, Weber's approach is deliberately **multi-variable**. The beliefs and world views within which people act are often independent of their economic situations and frequently form the preconditions necessary for the existence of specific kinds of economic relations.

THE PREDOMINANCE OF THE WEST

The fundamental question Weber posed in his comparative and **interpretive sociology** was directed towards understanding why Western civilization became predominant in the world, why, in Western civilization only, certain 'cultural phenomena have appeared which' are not merely local or national, but possess 'universal significance and value'. The Western cultural heritage was unique for producing the experimental method as part of the 'rational, systematic, and specialized pursuit of science', the use of rational concepts and systematic methods in the study of politics, the development of a rational jurisprudence, the use of 'rational tone intervals' in music, 'the rational utilization of lines and spatial perspective' in art, 'a rational, written constitution . . . [and] an administration bound to rational rules and laws'. Had he lived a few decades longer, Weber could have added 'rational genocide'. In short, Weber considered Western culture to be distinguished from all others by the predominant place afforded to rationalism in all aspects of life, from art and music to law, science, and government. Furthermore, Weber argued, 'the same is true of the most fateful force in our modern life, capitalism.'[13]

Western global domination was rooted in the Industrial Revolution, barely more than a century old in England and currently underway in Weber's Germany. Industrialism was the product of capitalism, so the source of Western power must be located in the forces that created capitalism. How had capitalism arisen in the West and what was the source of its prodigious ability to transform the globe? Weber wasted little time in critiquing the theory of **economic determinism**—that capitalism was the necessary outcome of an apparently predetermined sequence of historical stages, emerging from and transcending feudalism. Weber's method involved comparing a number of historical and contemporary processes that, while generally similar, differed in the presence or absence of the decisive factor under examination.[14] Modern capitalism entailed the *rational* pursuit of profit that was ever renewed. Only in the modern Western world do rational capitalistic enterprises, which are organized by the principles of free labour and profit-making, provide the majority of consumption goods available in a market society.[15]

This system of rational enterprises was not caused by the emergence of a new attitude of acquisitiveness. From Weber's point of view, 'the economic impulse is universal.'[16] Different societies structure economic self-interest in a variety of ways. 'The impulse to acquisition, pursuit of gain, of money, of the greatest possible amount of money' has existed apart from capitalism and is not its defining characteristic. 'This impulse exists and has existed among waiters . . . prostitutes . . . dishonest officials . . . gamblers and beggars.' Unlimited greed for gain, which Weber calls an irrational impulse, was not identical with modern capitalism, and was not its spirit.[17]

An older form of booty capitalism had existed in all previous civilizations. These early capitalistic adventurers, Weber claimed, sought to acquire plunder directly through violence or else they acquired money as booty through the long-term exploitation of subjects. For Weber, such activities as the marauding expeditions launched by the Vikings were 'economically-oriented action' that used physical force to appropriate goods.[18] This kind of capitalism persisted in the modern world among 'promoters, large-scale speculators . . . and much modern financial capitalism', particularly but not exclusively during wars.[19]

In between the profit-driven but sporadic raid for booty and modern, rational capitalism are found varieties of private profit-making that have a rational character and therefore resemble modern capitalism, such as commercial trade, money-changing, and money-lending. These practices became common all over the world once a money economy had been created.[20] Epochs of antiquity had been shaped by profit-making enterprises where property was an object of trade in a market economy. This was capitalism, Weber agreed; yet everywhere, despite these beginnings, capitalism developed extensively only in the West.[21] To understand the specificity of Western development, Weber analyzed a number of comparative, historical cases, including India, China, and ancient and medieval Europe. Capitalism failed to grow in these societies, Weber said, for specific cultural, social, and political reasons.

India and the Caste System

Foreign and internal trade and the use of credit and usury had existed since ancient times in India, which, Weber said, was a land of commerce.

A politically oriented capitalist trade developed in India about the seventh century BC and for the next thousand years a capitalist market developed and expanded. Rich nobles, who still received money from the land, moved into the cities and accumulated wealth through trade. Urban centres flourished, merchant and craft guilds existed comparable to those of the European Middle Ages, and 'elements of a truly feudal structure existed in most parts of India.' In Indian history, periods of political unity were separated by long periods of political disunity and the existence of numerous competing, warring states. Individual capital was strong whenever petty princes competed among themselves and sought the support and financial backing of the merchants and guild masters. India's social structure 'appears to have stood for a time close to the threshold of European urban development'.[22]

Many of the necessary preconditions for rational capitalism existed in India. Warfare, politics, and finance were subject to rational theorizing. **Tax farming**, state contracting, and trade monopolies developed along lines that paralleled the West. Indian mathematics, justice, and science were well advanced and could have served as a legal foundation for private enterprise. The merchant class was as autonomous legally as medieval European commercial capitalists. Finally, Weber added, 'nowhere is there to be found so little condemnation of and such high regard for wealth.' Yet, Weber realized, no indigenous rational capitalism developed. Instead, Indian religion and social structure, organized in the **caste system**, had obstructed the emergence of a modern, rational economic system.[23]

To understand why Indian society did not develop a modern form of capitalism, it was necessary to analyze the social and political factors that produced economic stability. This led Weber to examine the basis of political authority. He was particularly interested in the factors that compelled subordinate individuals to obey the commands of those above them. If a chief or ruler had the ability to force underlings to obey even if they resisted, she or he exercised naked power, but this was inherently unstable over longer periods of time. A more stable system arises where members of the staff calculate their material advantages and believe their own interests may be satisfied by obeying the chief. Such relationships are vulnerable still because, at any given time, it may be in an individual's interest to break solidarity with the chief rather than maintain it. Custom, or the tendency to obey out of long-standing habit, produced more stability, but it probably would not be enough to ensure obedience.

In the most stable and long-lasting relationship, people are willing to obey because they believe their ruler has a right to give orders. In Weber's terms, the ruler's authority acquires **legitimacy** in the eyes of subordinates when they believe that the social order is valid and they have a duty to obey.[24] The strongest solidarity occurs when a system of authority 'attempts to establish and to cultivate the belief in its "legitimacy"'. Different types of authority rest their claims to legitimacy on distinct grounds. Throughout history, most claims to be obeyed have been accepted on the grounds of tradition and the hereditary status of the person who occupies a position of privileged status: 'legitimacy is claimed on the sanctity of an order which has always existed' and obedience is offered on the basis of the personal authority of the chief, strict moral standards, or religious attitudes.[25]

In small-scale, early societies, chiefs were the most respected among the elders or occupied the dominant, patriarchal position of authority in the family. As the power of the chief expanded, an administrative staff evolved to serve the ruler and govern the territory and villages, which were occupied by those defined as subjects under the control of the rulers. At first, the administrators were personally related to the chief. Over time, the chief increasingly chose advisers, administrators, and military leaders from among his or her most loyal followers. Weber termed this type of political and military structure a form of **patrimonialism**.

In this type of administration, the monarch could stand at the apex of a system of tax farming through which a decentralized network of officials were given the right to collect local taxes in return for regular payments to the royal court. An independent source of wealth would free the monarch from the necessity of borrowing money from the urban guilds and merchants. In many ancient societies, an administrative class could be drawn only from a religious order. In India, the self-interest of the local rulers led them to form an alliance with a group of educated and capable officials whose subsequent dominance of Indian culture and society was fateful for the future course of Indian history. These officials were the **Brahmans**, the superior stratum of a specifically Indian religion that led to the creation of an exceptionally rigid, traditional social structure, which blocked the indigenous development of Indian capitalism.

The Brahmans were the high priests of Hinduism, a religion that believed the laws of the cosmos were inherent in everything and everyone. Hindus believe that a soul lives through a succession of separate existences in a cycle of birth, death, and rebirth. According to the law of **karma**, the soul would be reborn in a situation that was a consequence of her or his actions in previous lives. From Weber's perspective, 'Brahmanical theory served as an unequalled tool to tame the subjects through religion.' You were born in the condition fate has determined for you and that you deserved: 'Rebirth can drag man down into the life of a "worm in the intestine of a dog" but, according to his conduct, it may raise and place him into the womb of a queen'.[26]

The prospect of social mobility through favourable rebirth was accompanied by the other side of the doctrine of karma—the imposition of inviolable rules requiring that each person fulfill the duties of her or his social status during any specific rebirth. With the collusion of the princes, who were thereby secured in their dominant social positions, the Brahmans imposed the caste system according to which society was arranged in a fixed hierarchy of hereditary statuses. Hindus were tied to 'a yoke of rituals unmatched elsewhere in the world' (Box 11.1).[27] In the doctrine of karma, the 'order and rank of the castes is as eternal as the courses of the stars and the difference between the

> **Box 11.1**
>
> As a young boy, Velutha would come ... to the back entrance of the Ayemenem House to deliver the coconuts they had picked from the trees in the compound. Pappachi would not allow Paravans into the house. Nobody would. They were not allowed to touch anything that Touchables touched. ... Mammachi ... could remember a time, in her girlhood, when Paravans were expected to crawl backwards with a broom, sweeping away their footprints so that Brahmins ... would not defile themselves by accidentally stepping into a Paravan's footprint. In Mammachi's time, Paravans, like other Untouchables, were not allowed to walk on public roads, not allowed to cover their upper bodies, not allowed to carry umbrellas. They had to put their hands over their mouths when they spoke, to divert their polluted breath away from those whom they addressed.
>
> —Arundhati Roy, *The God of Small Things* (1997). Copyright © 1997 by Arundhati Roy. Reprinted by permission of Random House Canada.

animal species and the human races. To attempt to overthrow them would be senseless.' To influence your fate positively in the next life, you must strictly fulfill your caste obligations in your present life and shun 'any sacrilegious attempt to move out of' your caste. High aspirations cause people to neglect their caste duties, bringing harm in the present and the future life. As Weber asserts, 'The castes might face one another with bitter hatred. . . . However, as long as the *karma* doctrine remained unshaken, revolutionary ideas or progressivism were inconceivable, particularly as the lowest castes had the most to gain through ritual correctness and were therefore least inclined towards innovation.'[28]

For Weber, the caste system imposed a powerful barrier to the emergence of rational capitalism in India. In part this was caused by the strict requirement that caste members must be separate from each other—inferior castes were unclean. Those who were assigned to some tasks, such as preparing leather from the hides of cattle, an animal sacred to Hindus, were so polluting that, 'By their very presence they infect the air of a room, and so defile food in it that it must be thrown away.'[29] Social solidarity, then, does not develop among citizens of a town or nation but more narrowly, in one specific location in an ever-expanding hierarchy of castes and subcastes that overlapped with ethnic and racial distinctions.

For Weber, the essential barrier the caste system erected against rational capitalism was less its specific and exclusionary practices and more the spirit of the system, which was completely traditionalistic and anti-rational in its effects. Modern industrial capitalism was extremely unlikely to have originated in a caste society since 'strict, traditional ritualism is not conducive to innovations or likely to facilitate the germination of capitalist enterprise.'[30]

China, the Clan, and Bureaucracy

Chinese civilization was equally hostile to rational capitalism, although not on the grounds of religious traditionalism. Weber believed that Chinese people had been recognized for industriousness and hard work and had been intensely acquisitive for a long time. As in India, the germ of capitalist enterprise existed early in Chinese history and persisted throughout the centuries. The history of China also alternated between periods of unification dominated by a succession of strong imperial dynasties interspersed with periods of political disintegration and internal strife. For almost 900 years before the third century BC, a form of feudal monarchy existed in China, during which the classics of Chinese philosophy were written. Among these, the practical and ethical system of Confucianism came to dominate the world view of China's civilization.

The feudal period collapsed in an epoch known as the Warring States Period, which about 220 BC culminated in the establishment by the Qin **dynasty** of a unified and internally pacified, imperial system. From Weber's point of analysis, when left to themselves ancient social systems most often ossified, settling into patterns of tradition and custom that were accepted as legitimate on the grounds that they had always existed. Social change had to come from outside the social system, primarily through foreign conquest—as frequently occurred in the history of India and China.

Social change may result from the dynamic activity of individuals who possess exceptional qualities, often regarded as divine in origin, that seem to set them apart from others. Such individuals possess charisma, which is recognized when followers rally to the cause of the 'chosen ones' offering them personal loyalty despite the fact that they do not possess any traditional status, prestige, or authority. They feel a sense of duty, which is often reinforced by supernatural beliefs, to follow such a leader, a situation Weber defines as **charismatic authority**. Invariably, the charismatic leader challenges the old traditions and imposes new obligations on her or his subordinates. On the basis of charisma, whole dynasties can fall or be created, and new ideologies can sweep away traditional religions and customs.

The exceptional nature of charismatic authority makes it potentially very short-lived. It disrupts everyday economic and social life, particularly among the most committed disciples. Initially, the leader's followers 'live communistically in a community of faith and enthusiasm, on gifts, "booty", or sporadic acquisition.' Only a small minority will devote their lives to this idealistic call. The majority need to make a more stable living. Hence, the followers appropriate for themselves powers of control and economic advantages, and they take steps to regulate recruitment. Once established, these powers and

advantages typically become traditionalized by being made hereditary, as happened in China.[31]

The new social order created by the charismatic leader persists only when it is transformed into a permanent, routine structure. Some fiscal organization is needed for regular collection of taxes or for raising contributions. The officials are differentiated from the taxpayers and the charismatic group becomes transformed into one of the forms of everyday authority, typically decentralized patrimonialism. Weber termed this evolutionary pattern the **routinization of charisma**.

Out of the social change initiated by charisma emerges a new social order that eventually also becomes defined as traditional. In China, the need to re-establish central power was necessitated by the predominance of inland trade and the need for canal construction and dykes to control the annual flooding of China's massive rivers. Regulation on this large scale required central authority, which in periods of unification was organized as a patrimonial state under an imperial system. Three types of patrimonial regimes competed over the centuries for power in China. Administrative posts were initially filled by the emperor's kin or members of the aristocratic families. Very early in history, however, the Chinese developed a more advanced form of patrimonialism in which administrative positions were monopolized by scholars—the mandarins—who were meticulously trained in the rituals and practices of Confucianism. The new imperial authority established a hierarchy of offices giving opportunities for officials of low birth and allowing wealthy commoners to hold official state posts. Weber refers to this process as 'administrative rationalization'. The scholars, who were competing for power with the great families of the early feudal period, formed an 'extra-patrimonial staff' appointed to administrative offices by the emperor. The result was the creation of an imperial **bureaucracy** with open recruitment to office based on examinations and selection by merit rather than by rank or birth.[32] While the mandarins filled an administrative role similar to the Brahmans in India, they lacked the hereditary monopolization of office the caste system gave the Indian elite and the powerful religious foundation that Hinduism provided for the Indian social structure.

The power of the emperors was confined in the **mandarin system** by traditions and customary rules. At times, emperors struck back against the Confucian scholars, even executing many of them, in order to consolidate their position as absolute rulers, a form of power Weber called sultanism. An emperor who ruled as a sultan exercised the maximum amount of power to select advisers and bureaucrats, and ruled as an arbitrary autocrat.[33] The mandarins persistently resisted the imposition of absolute imperial power. Under such tyrannical rulers, taxes were raised beyond traditional limits, labourers were conscripted to work on massive building projects such as the Great Wall, and popular resentment grew into violent rebellion. The outcome was that new dynasties replaced the old. In the long run, Weber said, the final victory always fell into the hands of the scholars because their rational administrative and economic policies were necessary for restoring imperial authority. They were more efficient than either the sultan's eunuchs or the emperor's personal favourites.[34]

Weber argued that the imperial system blocked the extensive development of market capitalism. During the period of warring kingdoms and imperial disintegration, a politically oriented class of merchants and moneylenders prospered. By the time of the Han dynasty (206 BC), millionaires existed. As the imperial system became consolidated, however, this type of capitalism declined because it was linked closely with competition between states. At the same time, pure market capitalism, which required extensive trade, was merely rudimentary.[35]

Under the mandarins, social position was allocated by qualification for office, determined by strict education and examination rather than by wealth. Chinese scholars created a unifying culture, playing a role similar to the Brahmans in India. The educated classes were self-recruiting and not linked necessarily to aristocratic classes or to wealthy merchant families. This status position shaped the mandarin's attitude towards economic policy, generating a culture of disrespect for wealth attained through commercial transactions in a free market. Weber argues that 'Such aversions are common to all bureaucracies.' China did not possess a rising bourgeoisie that was conscious of its power and position with sufficient strength to challenge the power of the patrimonial government.[36]

Capitalistic activity in industry and trade did not lead to modern capitalism. The Chinese economy lacked the legal and societal foundations for capitalism. The best opportunities for accumulating wealth were held by officials who had the right to collect taxes. Under the Chinese system of officialdom, officials used their fortunes to acquire landholdings and to assist their children to obtain educational qualifications for office. Office-holders, in turn, enriched their relatives and opened opportunities for their clan members. Weber says the Chinese elite 'was neither feudal nor bourgeois, but speculated in opportunities for the purely political exploitation of office.'[37] Jung Chang gives a succinct description of mandarin China in her novel, *White Swans* (Box 11.2).[38]

Patrimonialism was only one of the sources that consolidated a traditional, non-rational economic system in China. The role played in India by the caste system was similar to the place in Chinese civilization occupied by the patriarchal clan. Underneath the appearance of central power and a unified bureaucratic officialdom, Chinese society was geographically decentralized. China was divided into provinces under the control of local governors who, at various times, contested with the central Empire for power. The emperor appointed mandarins to provincial posts, but 'real power lay in the hands of unofficial, native subordinates.' The imperial authorities exercised only a very loose control over the rural and urban Chinese who, Weber stated, governed themselves.[39]

The persistent strength of the Chinese community was rooted in the traditional village, which was held together by rigid kinship bonds cemented by a cult of ancestor worship. Imperial authority from above had to compete with the strong cohesion of Chinese clans, which were based on what Weber termed **patriarchal authority**—the will-

Box 11.2

My great-grandfather was the only son, which made him of supreme importance to his family. Only a son could perpetuate the family name. . . . He was sent to a good school. The goal for him was to pass the examinations to become a mandarin, an official, which was the aspiration of most Chinese males at the time. Being an official brought power, and power brought money. Without power and money, no Chinese could feel safe from the depredations of officialdom or random violence. There had never been a proper legal system. Justice was arbitrary, and cruelty was both institutionalized and capricious. An official with power *was* the law. Becoming a mandarin was the only way a child of a non-noble family could escape this cycle of injustice and fear. Yang's father had decided that his son should not follow him into the family business of felt-making, and sacrificed himself and his family to pay for his son's education. . . .

[His wife] came from a family of tanners called Wu. Because her family was not an intellectual one and did not hold any official post, and because she was a girl, she was not given a name at all. Being the second daughter, she was simply called 'Number Two Girl' (*Er-ya-tou*).

—Jung Chang, *White Swans: Three Daughters of China* (1991). Reprinted by permission of Simon & Schuster Adult Publishing Group. Copyright © 1991 by Globalfair Ltd. Reprinted by permission of HarperCollins Publishers Ltd. © Jung Chang 1991.

ingness of the extended family members to grant authority to the predominant, elderly man in the clan. The clan resisted the outside power of state officials, landlords, employers, and any other external superior, and thwarted any movement towards 'the selection of labour on a free market'. In short, the rational bureaucracy was confronted with a resolute and traditional power that 'operated continuously and rested on the most intimate personal associations.'[40]

The power of the clan, which shaped the lives of the majority of Chinese in rural villages, also extended to the cities. Economic life in Chinese cities was not closely regulated by imperial power but, instead, by patriarchal clan authority. The urban economy was controlled by a variety of closely knit occupational associations that determined the life of their members so that 'nowhere was the individual so utterly dependent upon craft and merchant guilds as in Chinese cities.'[41]

Nevertheless, Weber argued, commerce, money changing, and lending practices were propitious for the development of capitalism in China. Capitalist business associations that were organized in communal workshops developed specialized technical and commercial management. By the nineteenth century, residential and economic mobility had increased and choice of occupation had been free for a long time. There were few legal limitations on trade. 'From a purely economic point of view it might appear that a genuine bourgeois, industrial capitalism could have developed from the[se] petty capitalist beginnings.'

Production, however, took place in decentralized domestic households in which the household economy was not separated from production for the market.[42] International trade was minimal and, eventually, China sought to insulate itself from foreign influences by confining trade to a handful of firms operating through the port of Canton. No factories producing mass consumer goods were built because there was no steady market, and no Western-style bourgeoisie emerged. For Weber, this failure resulted from a number of reasons, nearly all of which stemmed from the structure of the political system within which Chinese capitalism existed.[43]

Central authority in China was shaped in part by patrimonial authority, which tended towards arbitrariness and favouritism, and by a powerful bureaucratic class of administrators who worked within a realm of unshakable, sacred tradition. Both elements of the Chinese political system impeded the development of industrial capitalism. In order to be secure in their calculated economic decisions, capitalists need a stable framework of government regulation and laws. Mandarin administration was traditional, revenue collection became the principal spoil available to those in office, and decision-making was oriented to customary ethics rather than legal norms. In Weber's words, 'Capital investment in industry is far too sensitive to such irrational use of authority and too dependent upon the possibility of calculating in advance the steady and rational operation of the state machinery to emerge under a government of this type.'[44]

In sum, rational industrial capitalism was handicapped, 'basically, by the lack of spiritual foundations'. China was ideologically dominated by a class of Confucian officials who combined elements of rational, bureaucratic recruitment and organization with an economic ethos focused on making a personal profit by gaining a political office with the right to collect revenue.[45] The mandarins defended their place in the imperial system on magical grounds, attributing natural and social disasters to violations of the ethical principles of Confucianism, a doctrine that solidified patriarchal and clan rule, erecting a social barrier to the development of rational capitalism.

Ancient Europe and Slavery

From his investigations into ancient history, Weber had discovered that many of the characteristics of modern capitalism had existed at various times and places, but that political and social factors had impeded the indigenous movement towards industrial capitalism. The ancient civilizations that had emerged in Europe and the Near East appeared to provide an even wider framework for capitalism. Partly because of its geographical location around a great inland sea, commercial trade in the ancient world, both local and international, was geographically extensive and profitable. Large cities existed, though they

were centres of consumption more than of production. While the modern proletariat did not exist in antiquity, the capitalistic concept of the employer existed in a developed form. Some artisans were hired as free labourers or worked in joint co-operatives. Although there were no factories of a modern type, Weber found that a large number of skilled workers occasionally were massed in workshops attached to households. In addition, banking practices, such as loans, bank payments, and the charging of interest, were known.[46] Despite preparing some of the disparate ingredients for economic change, the ancient world did not combine them in a system of rational capitalism.

The most distinctive feature of the social structure was slavery, an economic form that persisted to a much greater degree than in any other civilization. Inasmuch as the slave labour force was bought in an open market, agricultural land was an object of trade, and agricultural goods were produced to be sold, ancient agriculture was economically capitalist in character.

The use of slave labour handicapped the development of a rational economic system, Weber maintained. It required a more extensive initial outlay of capital. Reliable cost accounting was difficult because slave capital was 'insecure and subject to unpredictable risks'. Because slave labourers were appropriated by an owner as a form of capital good, they were inefficient and disinterested in the quantity or quality of production. With little incentive to work beyond a necessary minimum, slave labour exhibited a relatively low standard of performance that became customary and could be exceeded only by ruthless methods that threatened to incite rebellion.[47] Slave mortality was high and political upheavals could eliminate the investment. Slave production could only be profitable in conditions of fertile land, 'cheap food, monopoly prices for the products, and low slave prices'.[48] Slave labour was confined to large plantations producing such things as oils and wine or to maintaining herds. The most important type of agriculture was grain production, which required too much individual effort to be productive under a slave regime. Small-scale tenant farming dominated ancient agriculture because it was 'the most remunerative way to exploit landed property'.[49]

There was a free, propertyless group consisting of 'peasants, tenants, hawkers and wage earners'. Political conditions specific to each country shaped the relative importance of free and unfree labour and the manner in which slave labour was subjected to capitalist exploitation. In times of extensive warfare, when the free population was away on campaigns that often lasted for years, slave labour was used more extensively. Military expansion led to an increase in the supply of slaves and furthered their private, capitalistic exploitation, although this factor did not solely determine the degree to which slavery, or capitalism, developed.[50]

In addition to the existence of slaves as a form of capital good, a second peculiarity of Mediterranean capitalism was the extensive use of government contracts. Public finance was the oldest large-scale organization in antiquity. In the late Roman Republic, which lacked a bureaucratic administration equivalent to the Indian Brahmans or the Chinese mandarins, private contractors were used to administer conquered territories and collect tribute, in turn supplying the state with money. Through these arrangements, private contractors exercised some degree of economic control over military and political policy. Because of the unique political structure of the Roman state, capitalism reached its highest point in this period.

City-states, especially republican ones, 'looted subject populations for the benefit of capitalist interests'. Rome subjected the people in the conquered territories to brutal exploitation at the hands of private capital through usurious tax farming, rent squeezes, and slave trading. Tax farming was the most significant form of capital investment.[51]

The conditions in the Roman Republic, soon doomed to fall into the hands of the Emperor, Caesar, were depicted by novelist Arthur Koestler in *The Gladiators*, his account of the slave rebellion in Rome led by Spartacus (Box 11.3).[52] As political power was centralized in the imperial hands, the emperors progressively emancipated themselves from their dependence on private capitalists and the economic needs of the state were met by compulsory contributions of money and labour instead of by competitive contracts. Accordingly, the ancient freedoms of citizens came to an end. Monarchies tended to be more interested in the long-term security of returns than short-term maximization of profits. Hence, royal domains were leased to small tenants, slave farming was replaced by sharecropping, and estates were exploited for rents. State control, monopolies, and bureaucratic regulation excluded private capital and throttled ancient capitalism.

In short, the most important limitation to the development of ancient capitalism arose from the political characteristics of the society. Private capitalists were limited to tax farmers, shopkeepers,

---

Box 11.3

Doomed is the Roman Republic.... Once upon a time Rome was an agricultural state, now the peasantry has been bled empty, the State with it. The world had expanded meanwhile, cheap corn was imported from all lands, farmers had to sell their fields and live on alms.... cheap slave labour was imported from all lands; artisans starved and workmen went abegging. Rome was flooded with corn; it rotted in the granaries; and for the poor there was no bread. Rome was full of working hands, they opened begging or closed to fists; no hands were wanted. The scheme of distribution was at fault, Rome's economic system had not adapted itself to a wider world, it was gradually petrifying....

—Arthur Koestler, *The Gladiators* (1939)

and artisans. Capitalist entrepreneurs, Weber commented, held a precarious social position. Those who lived off the rent received from tenants—the rentiers—were the ideal independent citizens because they were ready to serve in the army when needed. Political theory in ancient society was hostile to the profit motive for political rather than ethical reasons.[53]

WESTERN CAPITALISM

In these ancient societies, non-capitalist forms of exploitation prevailed, such as extracting rents, other fees, and labour services from tenants who worked the land. The great majority of the population was rural. Capitalism implied producing goods to be used as objects of trade and for the accumulation of profits. It was closely associated with the emergence of a distinct class of urban merchants whose livelihood was principally derived from trade. As elsewhere, Weber argues, the engine of economic development is to be found in the political and social conditions prevailing in society. In the case of medieval and early modern Europe, these conditions were propitious for the emergence of capitalism.

Medieval cities in Europe possessed a degree of independence and autonomy that ancient cities either seldom possessed or lost in the course of historical change. On the basis of an independent legal system and an autonomous, rational administration, the town burghers and guild masters erected a set of institutions within which they could pursue their economic interests.[54] These capitalists accumulated wealth independent of the various patrimonial forms of exploitation that shaped the economic system of feudal Europe.

When powerful and centralizing nation-states did develop in late medieval Europe, the cities also lost much of their autonomy. Laws were codified and the adjudication of courts brought the towns under a uniform and centralized legal system. The armed forces also came under the control of the state, replacing the occasional service expected from feudal knights and their retainers with a professional army. Weber calls this process the

separation of the army from the means of warfare. Europe entered into a centuries-long period of warring national states during which the monarchies became increasingly dependent on financial loans from the urban merchant class. This alliance between the state and private capital created great opportunities for the merchant class, out of which emerged, Weber said, the national bourgeoisie in the modern sense of the word. Again, political developments were at the foundation of the development of capitalist enterprise.[55]

Economically, these early Western states moved towards a more rational economy. It was becoming increasingly expensive to run the expanding national governments. The system known as mercantilism, which appeared in England in the beginning of the fourteenth century and was extensively attacked by Adam Smith in the late 1700s, was designed to benefit manufacturing interests, the national government, and even the poor. Exports were encouraged from labour-intensive industries. Mercantilism created monopolies for specific groups. The granting of monopolies under the mercantilist system had the political objective of guaranteeing that a considerable share of the national income would accrue to the state. This political capitalism had more in common with the irrational ancient varieties than with the modern type. Modern capitalism, Weber concluded, did not grow out of mercantilism.

In England, a class of capitalist entrepreneurs had grown up alongside and apart from the monopoly system, and independent of the political administration. In the political struggles that wracked the nation in the 1600s, these small capitalists sided with Parliament against the monarchy and its system of economic privileges, which the government of Oliver Cromwell systematically sought to eliminate. In Weber's words, two types of capitalism faced each other: irrational capitalism 'sustained by fiscal or colonial privileges and public monopolies against capitalism oriented to market opportunities for saleable goods'. By the eighteenth century, the class of industrial entrepreneurs had secured the permanent support of Parliament and mercantilism was gradually dismantled in favour of free trade.[56]

For Weber, however, this fundamental change is not simply a question of class struggle and bourgeois revolution. Additional, non-economic prerequisites made industrial capitalism possible in the West. Modern, Western capitalism is a distinctive form of economic action in which people consciously weigh alternative ends in order to achieve their desires for utilities, whether that involves profitability or acquiring consumption goods through peaceful commerce.[57] From a comparative historical perspective, this rational, self-centred calculation of advantage (**formal rationality**) had become the constant mindset of the whole society. It is sharply distinguishable from the types of action that predominated in antiquity, where people followed customs or traditions, or were swept into irrational social movements that overrode their immediate economic interests. Rational capitalism required a whole cultural shift reflected in a multitude of social and cultural changes as well as economic and political ones. It represented a fundamental change in world views.

Weber enumerated a variety of these social prerequisites of modern capitalism. Capitalism required a legal and administrative system that operated according to fixed, understandable, and uniform laws. Political power had to be oriented to establishing the free market economy, in which people's satisfaction results from their self-interested calculations of exchange. Weber argued that Western religions were advantageous for capitalism. Of all the ancient religions, Christianity was the most opposed to the belief in magic, which, elsewhere, was an entrenched obstacle to the development of a rational view of the world. More specifically, a rational capitalistic establishment uses formal capital accounting to calculate profits and losses through the modern method of double-entry bookkeeping that balances debits and credits.

In rare cases, capitalism in the modern era was based on slave labour. Specifically, this occurred on agricultural plantations in the southern United States, in the Caribbean, and in South America. Basically, however, rational capitalism is based on free labour. Weber realized that this implied

formal or legal freedom—the threat of starvation obliged labourers to seek work for wages. Freedom of labour developed slowly in Europe. Between the tenth and thirteenth centuries, Weber argued, workers tended to exercise ownership over their own means of production, whether constituted as land or as the tools of the artisan. As the market system advanced, however, the property of small owners was progressively expropriated. Autocratic owner/managers possessed large amounts of property that were rationally and efficiently administered. Capitalists controlled credit and the sale of finished products, disciplining labour in households by supplying the raw materials and the tools of production. Later, they developed workshops in which all the non-human means of production became fixed or working capital owned by the capitalists and labour became hired 'hands'. Once begun, this rationalization of economic production spread throughout the industry in a bitter competitive struggle.[58] Eventually, workers were entirely expropriated from the means of making their own independent livelihood. The final step in the transition to capitalism was the mechanization of production. Even management was handed over to an official while the owner became an agent of the banks.[59]

As all these factors coincided in time and place, they still required a final element: 'the rational spirit, the rationalisation of the conduct of life in general and a rationalistic economic ethic'.[60] The spirit of the Indian caste system and of the Chinese bureaucracy had hindered the development of capitalism; the necessary ingredient that the West was able to add was the widespread acceptance of the **spirit of capitalism**. For the source of this essential ingredient, Weber turned to Western religion, specifically to Puritanism.

Capitalism and the Protestant Ethic

In *The Protestant Ethic and the Spirit of Capitalism*, first published in 1904–5, Weber theorized that the rise of capitalism could not be explained simply by analyzing the economic system. For the Marxists, the economic change from feudalism to capitalism had come first. In turn, this change of the 'economic base' had affected other, **super-structural**, changes, such as religious beliefs. Specifically, the Marxists appeared to be assuming that the Protestant Reformation was caused by the development of capitalism.

Weber agreed that there was a connection between rational capitalism and Protestantism. In Northern Europe, the majority of industrial capitalists were Protestants. How can this symbiotic relationship be understood? Weber's analysis in *The Protestant Ethic* approaches the problem by examining the influence of religious ideas on the development of a specific, capitalist economic spirit. Although this appears to reverse the base/superstructure assumption of the Marxists, Weber explicitly denies that he is making such a claim. His study investigates 'only one side of the causal chain'. It was not his 'aim to substitute for a one-sided materialistic an equally one-sided spiritualistic causal interpretation' of history.[61] His later research, as indicated above, offered a more complex analysis of the evolution of capitalism.

Weber held that modern capitalism is associated not just with rationalism, but with a particular form of rationalism—what he termed the 'spirit of capitalism'—that he identifies with devotion to hard work in a specific occupational calling. He asks whose legitimate intellectual child this spirit is. People in the Middle Ages were hostile to this spirit, associating it with the lowest form of greed and avarice. 'By nature', Weber asserts, an individual 'does not . . . wish to earn more and more money, but simply to live as he is accustomed to live and to earn as much as necessary for that purpose.' This traditional attitude hindered the capitalistic attempt to intensify work and increase the productivity of labour. Weber concluded that capitalists needed a powerful, ideological ally to help instill the necessary spirit of working for its own sake.[62]

In the highly competitive world of early commercial capitalism, capitalists could gain a competitive advantage if they were prepared to rationalize their production methods and, simultaneously, reduce their consumption so that as

much capital as possible could be reinvested back into the business. The day of the leisured capitalist, as well as the volatile capitalism of booty and grand speculation, was over. Into its place had stepped the calculating, temperate, and reliable bourgeois. For Weber, 'The **ideal type** of the capitalistic entrepreneur . . . avoids ostentation and unnecessary expenditure, as well as conscious enjoyment of his power, and is embarrassed by the outward signs of the social recognition he receives. His manner of life is . . . distinguished by a certain ascetic tendency. . . . He gets nothing out of his wealth for himself, except the irrational sense of having done his job well.' By calling this portrait an 'ideal type' Weber implied that you are unlikely to encounter such an entrepreneur in real life, but the type describes the combination of characteristics that led to early success in capitalist enterprise.[63]

Where could you find an entrepreneur who would approximate this type? Weber's answer is the crucial point of his thesis. The personal characteristics and world view of the successful entrepreneur paralleled precisely the ethical system promoted by the early Calvinists, particularly the Puritans of England and New England. Puritanism might have seemed an unlikely candidate for the parent of an economic system based on buying, selling, and trying to get rich. Christianity had a long tradition of linking wealth with godlessness. Puritans focused their attention on piety—strict religious observance—and oriented their action to the next world and salvation. Rather than seeking or valuing materialistic rewards and pleasures, they were ascetic in their habits, sober, serious, and hard-working. Nevertheless, Weber found, Puritans were disproportionately active in capitalistic acquisition. Business leaders and capitalists as well as skilled workers and commercial employees were overwhelmingly Protestant.

The fundamental change in ideological perspective originated with Calvin and his doctrine of **predestination**. According to Calvin, since God was all-powerful and all-knowing, he knew in advance what an individual's fate would be. You were either the fortunate recipient of God's grace, which meant you would be saved and spend eternity in heaven, or you were damned. Grace was a gift; it was not something you could earn by doing good works. Weber refers to this doctrine's 'extreme inhumanity' and says that the consequence 'was a feeling of unprecedented inner loneliness of the single individual.' The Puritan rejected all magic from religion, proclaimed 'the corruption of everything pertaining to the flesh', and regarded as negative 'all the sensuous and emotional elements in culture and in religion, because they are of no use toward salvation.'[64]

It might be thought that the belief in predestination would produce a spirit of inactivity or even hedonism. If salvation is the only crucially important aspect of life, but nothing you do in your life will affect your fate positively or negatively, what is the point of being pious, or charitable, or loving towards your neighbour? But in a world view where life after death is a certainty and the need for salvation is paramount, what you do in this life matters a great deal. Puritans, Weber argued, searched for certainty of their salvation, of the state of grace. Finding signs of grace 'became of absolutely dominant importance'. For the Calvinist, there was a connection between a person's faith and her or his conduct in the world; 'faith had to be proved by its objective results . . . by a type of Christian conduct which served to increase the glory of God.'[65] While doing good was useless for attaining salvation, it was indispensable as a sign of grace, because Puritans could not rid themselves of the fear of damnation. The only certainty of grace was 'a fundamental change in the whole meaning of life at every moment and in every action'. The Puritan was to tame his emotions and 'lead an alert, intelligent life', rooting out any spontaneous, impulsive enjoyment.[66] By compelling good Christians to eschew earthly pleasures and lead a simple, ascetic life, Puritanism was intimately connected to one of the elements necessary for success—capitalists needed to save their profits rather than spend them wastefully.

Calvinism also was linked to capitalism through the concept of the **calling**. A calling is a life task, a specific field in which God has called the individual to work. In Calvinism, social life is organized according to God's will. God requires achievement and demands that individuals fulfill the obligations that are imposed on them by their position in the world, all for the greater glory of God. You express your piety not by withdrawing from the world, say, into a monastery, but by becoming active in the world in your calling. Fulfilling your duty in worldly affairs becomes 'the highest form which the moral activity of the individual could assume'.[67] Any calling is equally worthy in the sight of God. This idea of doing one's duty in a calling, Weber pointed out, 'is what is most characteristic of the social ethic of capitalistic culture, and is in a sense the fundamental basis of it. It is an obligation which the individual is supposed to feel and does feel towards the content of his professional activity.' The concept of the calling 'gave the way of life of the new entrepreneur its ethical foundation and justification.'[68]

For Calvin, the importance of the calling is that success in your worldly affairs is a sign of being of the Elect, those predestined to be saved rather than damned. To follow the calling as God would wish is to take advantage of opportunities for profitableness. In the words of the Puritan ideologist, Richard Baxter:

> If God shows you a way you may lawfully get more than in another way (without wrong to your soul or to any other), if you refuse this, and choose the less gainful way, you cross [oppose] one of the ends of your calling, and you refuse to be God's steward, and to accept His gifts and use them for Him when He requireth it: you may labour to be rich for God, though not for the flesh and sin.[69]

In short, it is good to be rich. Wealth is enjoined; it is ethically bad only if the gains are ill-gotten or if it leads to idleness and the sinful enjoyment of life. God detests the seigneur and the nouveaux riches, but appreciates the middle-class, self-made capitalist.

Once someone was converted to Puritan beliefs for whatever reason, if they actually put these principles into practice in their daily lives, then certain consequences followed. Working hard, being thrifty, saving money, and not wasting time or money on frivolous pleasures helped the Puritan feel certain about her or his predestination, but such behaviour also was part of the recipe for success in business. As the businesses of the newly converted Protestants thrived, they made larger profits. The richer they were, the more they could feel secure that God was smiling on them, but also the greater they found the temptations of the body and the flesh. John Wesley, precisely understood this dilemma (Box 11.4).[70] There were few morally acceptable ways to handle this monetary success. What were they to do with the money that was rolling in? They couldn't spend it carelessly or for simple pleasures—that was sinful; they couldn't simply put it under the bed—that demonstrated miserliness and greed; they couldn't even give it away because giving the less fortunate charity induced idleness and sinfulness. The only morally acceptable thing to do with the money was to invest it back in the business, to convert it to capital. As profits were plowed back into the business, it grew larger, more successful, and more profitable; again, the even higher profits had to be accumulated in the business. What was happening was that the Protestant was being converted into an industrial capitalist. The system of capitalism, then, was an unintended consequence of a change in religious beliefs.

The rationalist kind of capitalism that came to predominate in the Western world and that led to the Industrial Revolution derived its spirit from the ethics of Protestantism. Over time, however, the specifically religious motivation eroded. Once the Protestant ethic had been embraced fully by the capitalists, they lost their concern about salvation and the spirit of capitalism became simply the 'common sense' that sober bourgeois gentlemen had exercised to achieve worldly success. In the long run, capitalists lost even the ascetic impulse and gave in to the pursuit of wealth for its own sake and for the satisfaction of an endless array of desires and mundane passions. In Weber's eyes, 'material goods have gained . . . an inexorable power over the lives of men as at no previous period in history', a sentiment that has reached its highest development in the United States, where the pursuit of wealth, once stripped of its religious and ethical meanings, tends to have the character of sport. Modernity is an era of 'Specialists without spirit, sensualists without heart'. Yet, this mere 'nullity imagines that it has attained a level of civilization never before achieved.'[71]

The modern economic order operates like a machine that binds human beings tightly to the technical conditions of mechanical production, determining irresistibly the lives of all who are born into it—perhaps, as Weber concluded, 'until the last ton of fossilized coal is burnt'. Concern for worldly goods should have rested on the ascetic

---

Box 11.4

I fear, wherever riches have increased, the essence of religion has decreased in the same proportion. . . . For religion must necessarily produce both industry and frugality, and these cannot but produce riches. But as riches increase, so will pride, anger, and love of the world in all its branches. . . . For the Methodists in every place grow diligent and frugal; consequently they increase in goods. Hence they disproportionately increase in pride, in anger, in the desire of the flesh, the desire of the eyes, and the pride of life. So, although the form of religion remains, the spirit is swiftly vanishing away. Is there no way to prevent this? . . . . we must exhort all Christians to gain all they can, and to save all they can; that is, in effect, to grow rich.

—Max Weber, quoting John Wesley, The Protestant Ethic (1904)

Calvinist's shoulders like a light cloak, easily tossed aside. 'But fate decreed that the cloak should become an iron cage.'[72]

Rationality and Bureaucracy

Weber's metaphor of the 'iron cage' to represent the modern economic order has been applied to rationality overall, and specifically to rational bureaucracy. Above all, what distinguished traditional from modern society was the dominant role played by rationality. In every Western institution, traditional or customary beliefs and actions had been progressively changed to consciously rational ones. Governments identified social problems and devised rational solutions to them, developing large bureaucracies to administer the ever more complex roles the modern state was expected to play. Business corporations were increasingly organized along rational lines. Even religion was becoming more rational and less traditional. Everywhere tradition was giving way to rational calculation and bureaucratic administration.

Varieties of bureaucracy had existed in antiquity, but they had been bound to economically irrational forms of traditionalism. In modern society, legitimacy based on tradition or charisma had given way to the belief in rational authority. In **legal-rational authority**, people owe obedience to those individuals who have come, by legal and valid means, to occupy specific offices, as philosophers obey railway porters according to playwright George Bernard Shaw (Box 11.5).[73] This type of authority presupposes the existence of a bureaucracy, a hierarchy of offices divided into rational, differentiated functions and filled by qualified personnel chosen by merit. As the need for technical and specialized knowledge is continually increasing, bureaucratic organization has been imposed on a great variety of institutions, from the army to the Church.

The purely bureaucratic type of organization, Weber argues is, from a technical point of view, potentially the most efficient and most rational means of controlling human beings. The capitalistic system has played a major role in the growth of bureaucracy because it is stable and reliable and demands strict discipline, making accurate calculations possible. Bureaucratic administration is the modern form required by organizations in all fields, nowhere more than in the modern Western state. For mass administration, bureaucracy is completely indispensable. The only way to escape the influence of bureaucracy

---

Box 11.5

The government of the world, political, industrial, and domestic has to be carried on mostly by the giving and obeying of orders.... 'Don't argue: do as you are told' has to be said ... practically to everybody. Fortunately most people do not want to argue: they are only too glad to be saved the trouble of thinking for themselves....

Nevertheless, there must be some ground for attaching authority to an order. A child will obey its parents, a soldier his officer, a philosopher a railway porter, and a workman a foreman, all without question, because it is generally accepted that those who give the orders understand what they are about, and are duly authorized and even obliged to give them, and because ... there is not time for lessons and explanations, or for arguments as to their validity. Such obediences are as necessary to the continuous operation of our social system as the revolutions of the earth are to the succession of night and day. But they are not so spontaneous as they seem; they will have to be very carefully arranged and maintained.

—G.B. Shaw, 'Preface', *Saint Joan* (1923)

is to turn the economic clock back and revert to small-scale organization—for Weber, a virtual impossibility.

The proliferation of bureaucracy was not altogether a positive thing, reasoned Weber. His chief complaint, however, was not that bureaucracies were inefficient, binding any action in endless red tape, as Charles Dickens pictured the Circumlocution Office—the going-around-in-circles office (Box 11.6).[74] Modern rationality, for Weber, was double-edged. The modern individual was coming increasingly to live in a world where he or she did not exercise real power but was, instead, dominated by enormous institutions—big government, corporations, professional armies, and even hierarchically structured churches.

Marx had written passionately about the alienation of the modern proletariat, focusing on the forms of alienation that capitalism had brought about in the economic sphere. In modern society, Weber argued, even worse forms of alienation were proliferating. Officials, employees, and workers were equally separated from the means of administration.[75] People were increasingly alienated from exercising any real political power, as modern bureaucratic organizations usurped any influence an individual could exercise.

People were increasingly becoming mere cogs in giant wheels, having less and less influence over the direction of society and even over their own lives. Even worse, as bureaucracies grew, they became ever more permanent features of society, continually reproducing themselves and becoming more swollen in size and influence. They had become the very foundation of social life and it was no longer possible to dispense with them. Bureaucracy was a permanent feature of society. At best, you could hope to direct the officials, but they could never be replaced by a more sensitive, human form of administration. Modern society was increasingly becoming an iron cage that the alienated individuals within it could not hope to change.

SOCIAL STRATIFICATION AND CLASS

The expansion of bureaucracy meant, inevitably, the proliferation of officials, office workers, managers, clerks, and other white-collar workers. Modern capitalism had produced a change in the class structure that had not been addressed adequately by Marx—the creation of a new middle class. Society was not polarizing into two hostile classes because a new class had grown in the middle.

Box 11.6

The Circumlocution Office was ... the most important Department under government. No public business of any kind could possibly be done at any time without the acquiescence of the Circumlocution Office. Its finger was in the largest public pie, and in the smallest public tart. It was equally impossible to do the plainest right and to undo the plainest wrong, without the express authority of the Circumlocution Office. If another Gunpowder plot had been discovered half an hour before the lighting of the match, nobody would have been justified in saving Parliament until there had been half a score of boards, half a bushel of minutes, several sacks of official memoranda, and a family-vaultful of ungrammatical correspondence, on the part of the Circumlocution Office. ...

Numbers of people were lost in the Circumlocution Office. ...

In short, all the business of the country went through the Circumlocution Office, except the business that never came out of it; and its name was Legion.

—Charles Dickens, *Little Dorrit* (1857)

One of the most significant inspirations for the study of **social stratification** in contemporary sociology can be found in the work of Weber. His approach is frequently presented as a three-dimensional hypothesis involving stratification by economic position (class), by prestige or honour (status), and by power, although Weber presented the concepts of 'class, status, and party' as phenomena of the distribution of power. For Weber, while it was likely that an individual who ranked high in any one dimension also ranked highly in the others—those with great wealth also exercised political power and had high prestige—this was not necessarily the case. A village priest, for example, was treated with a great deal of honour while having neither wealth nor political power. Those who had newly acquired vast wealth did not simultaneously acquire power or the prestige that is reserved for families who had been wealthy for generations.

This multi-centred theory of social stratification is generally opposed to Marx's assertion that 'class' (economic position) is the most important dimension of stratification. Weber also analyzed class, a concept Durkheim had avoided. For Weber, individuals could be ranged along a continuum of class situations,[76] which were differentiated according to the kind and amount of wealth and skill an individual possessed. Within this long continuum of different class situations, some groupings possessed relatively similar varieties of goods, received similar income, and had roughly the same degree of wealth. A class was a grouping of individuals with a similar class situation. Although not necessarily identical, members of each class grouping possessed about the same chances in life.

These class groupings were not automatically linked to similar degrees of status (prestige) or power. As such, classes were distinct from the estates of medieval Europe, which tied economic position, prestige, and political power in a single bundle. Class groupings arose directly from the economic order of society and were directly connected to the market relations in a capitalist society. According to Weber, 'Class situation' is ultimately 'market situation'.[77] Classes, strictly speaking, were created by the operations of the market and existed only in capitalist society.

Weber distinguished between objective class situations, which existed whether people were aware of them or not, and social classes where more crystallized groupings of individuals were found who were aware of their class membership. To draw out the distinctions, Weber's class theory distinguished among property classes, commercial classes, and social classes. The first two groupings existed objectively in capitalist society. The last, social class, existed both objectively and in the minds of the people who were in them: people identified themselves as belonging to a specific social class.

Property Classes

Arguably, Weber and Marx started at the same point in the analysis of class. For Weber, the ownership of property and lack of ownership of property form the 'basic category of all class situations'.[78] Marx could have made such a claim. The difference, however, is in what each theorist meant by property. Marx meant productive property, the ownership of the means of production, such as land, factories, mines, and small shops. He asked whether people could make a living using their own productive resources or were property-less and had to hire their labour out to an employer for a wage.

Weber's definition of property was considerably wider than Marx's. Weber claimed that there were different kinds of property, which could be differentiated according to the type of property or services that an individual possesses and brings to the market. Some people do possess property in the form of factories, businesses, mines, shipping companies, and so on. They come to the capitalist market in possession of this property, seeking to hire employees. In the market they encounter the owners of other forms of property and an exchange of property occurs. Other individuals, who do not possess factories, come to the market and encounter owners of factories, in which they can be employed in exchange for their wages. Thus, says Weber, they do possess a kind of property. If they didn't, they would have no business coming to the capitalist market at all. What these individuals own, their property, consists of their skills and their ability to perform work of varying kinds and degrees of complexity.

The differences among the types of property that individuals bring to the market divide them into distinct property classes. Some individuals own the rights over property (stocks, for example) and merely collect income from it. These **rentiers**, Weber claims, are 'positively privileged' and hardly have to come to the market at all. In fact, this small group at the top of the stratification system does not directly take part in any exchange involving the hiring of labour.

At the other extreme of the stratification system, at the bottom, are the declassed paupers who possess neither conventional property (businesses) nor marketable skills they can exchange for a wage. In Weber's terms, the disabled, the vagabonds, and the down-and-out possessed no property, not even the ability to work. This small grouping was the only category of people Weber classified as propertyless. They barely participated in the market and were termed by Weber negatively privileged.

The great majority of the workforce, however, was seen as the owners of types of property that they could exchange in the market. They were a middle property class, Weber said, neither positively nor negatively privileged. Next, Weber distinguished types among these property owners (in his expanded definition).

Commercial and Social Classes

This large, middle property class was itself divided into three commercial classes. At the upper extreme of the property classes were the positively privileged entrepreneurs (capitalists who did not merely live off dividends or rent). These were the industrialists, the entrepreneurs who actively invested and managed their wealth. Unlike the rentiers, they could be said to work. At the bottom

level of the commercial classes was the negatively privileged labourer. These were Marx's classical proletariat, made up of both skilled and unskilled manual workers.

The third type of class Weber identified was **social class**. This was defined as those groupings of class situations within which mobility is relatively easy or typical but between which mobility is more difficult. Gradually, specific classes emerge, which are more substantive and crystallized social groups, having persistence over time and developing a consciousness of common interests. The sense of belonging to a social class permeates the members of the class and helps to shape their interpretations of the world.

In his definition of social classes, which would correspond to actual groupings in society, Weber ignored the declassed and the paupers (the 'underclass' of contemporary theory)—they did not constitute a self-conscious social class. At the top of the stratification system in the upper social class, Weber combined the positively privileged group in the economic class, the rentiers, with the positively privileged group in the commercial class, the entrepreneurs. They identified themselves as members of a single, elite social group, married and interacted within their own group, and had similar life chances. This was Marx's bourgeoisie.

The bottom social class consisted of Marx's proletariat; in Weber's terms, the negatively privileged commercial class. Manual labourers who constituted the working class were becoming self-conscious and increasingly organized in trade unions and political parties.

Finally, Weber defined two separate middle social classes. One of these, consistent with Marx, was the petite bourgeoisie or small, conventional property owners (small business owners). In addition, Weber argued that modern capitalism had produced a new middle class of 'propertyless intelligentsia and specialists'. These were members of the 'middle commercial class' who bring mental skills (their form of property) to the market.[79] This new middle class is objectively part of Marx's 'proletariat' but, argues Weber, this new white-collar class owns a superior type of personal property consisting of different and more highly developed skills; they receive more income and other benefits from the exchange of their property; and they are increasingly coming to see themselves as a distinct class, different from and superior to the manual working class.

In sum, Weber argued that social classes are self-conscious collectivities, which are based on the objective groupings defined by economic and commercial classes. In the sequence of intergenerational mobility, movement was easiest or most typical from the working class and the petite bourgeoisie into the propertyless intelligentsia, who, in turn, had the best chance to move into the positively privileged social class.[80]

Weber recognized that the various classes he identified were unequal. He was also concerned with how the labour market functioned to reproduce these inequalities. For Weber, different individuals have come to possess superior or inferior resources on the market with which they can affect the bargaining outcome. Weber's labour market approach, unlike Marx's, does not distinguish qualitatively between the ownership of capital (defined as 'real' property) and the non-ownership of capital, because the latter possess labouring skills that become their 'property'. The rentier receives her or his due reward for ownership of property, as do the other classes, which can be differentiated simply according to the rights they can command over the distribution of the product. This is a different conception of class inequality from that deriving from the Marxian tradition, which rests on a theory of exploitation, in which those who possess property enter into an unequal and exploitative relationship with productive workers in the capitalist mode of production. While both Marx and Weber stress the importance of property, Marx argued that the basis of class divisions is deeper than the appearances of equal exchange on the market. For Weber, class was a phenomenon that arose from market relations, while property was an issue that concerned only the mobilization of advantages in the market.[81] By this definition, class interests referred to the quantity of goods and services received by labour within the bounds of capitalist relations.

As in his theory generally, Weber makes a subjective factor (class consciousness) a central feature of his class analysis. The strength of Weber's analysis of class lies in the recognition that class is more than a certain number of people in a similar economic relationship, but is also to a greater or lesser degree a social entity that must have continuity over time to sustain a class interest and perspective and to intervene as an organized force in social and political affairs. By examining market relations, Weber is able to draw a close link between subjectivity and objectivity, between the social positions of actors vis-à-vis the market and both their consciousness and action as they attempt to secure these relatively immediate interests. Marx argued that his analysis of exploitation indicated the existence of a disparity between the structural interests of the working class and its immediate, everyday understanding of its position in capitalist society. Weber argued that his theory of social classes accounted for the failure of the white-collar middle class to develop proletarian consciousness. For Marx, the contradiction between the workers' objective position and class consciousness would be resolved in the movement towards socialism. Socialism became a legal movement in Germany late in the nineteenth century, leading Weber to speculate about the effects a planned economy might have.

The Planned Economy and Socialism

> [T]he path of human destiny cannot but appal him who surveys a section of it.
> —Max Weber, *The Protestant Ethic* (1904)

For Marx, the labour contract veiled the exploitation built into what appeared to be an equal contract. In the long run, however, he expected that the everyday consciousness of the working class would become consistent with their deeper structural interests in socialist revolution. How did Weber respond to the Marxist expectation that a socialist revolution would enable the working class to reconstruct society and eliminate social alienation? Weber was familiar with the ideas of the socialists of the Second International. In his view, socialism would mean that the state would become the dominant institution directing the economy.

In any economy, efficiency means a close fit between the production of goods and their consumption. In a market economy, the laws of economics work to balance the two. Through the cumulative effects of individual choices, or consumer demand, capitalists produce what people want or can be convinced to desire. The ability of the economy to satisfy demand provided the system with legitimacy. In a **planned economy**, production would proceed according to a rational central plan that would be developed and implemented by a large bureaucracy. The fit between production and consumption would have to be known beforehand—in Weber's terms, the satisfaction of wants (consumption) would have to be oriented to an established order that was seen as valid or legitimate.[82] This would be a difficult fit to achieve.

Another fundamental contradiction in a planned economy was the tendency to 'weaken the incentive to labour'. Workers in capitalism are disciplined by the threat of unemployment. They are coerced to work hard. In a rationally planned society oriented to meeting people's needs, it would be impossible to fire someone because then his or her dependents also would suffer. Incentives to labour in a planned economy could take the form of material rewards, although this might contradict the goal of greater equality. More importantly, officials in a planned economy might stimulate ideal, altruistic motives to induce greater productivity in the attempt to approximate the level of economic production common to a market economy. New traditions would have to replace modern, rational ones. In addition, planned economies eliminate money, reduce formal rationality, and limit capital accounting—all factors Weber had identified that had prevented the emergence of rational capitalism in other societies. They would introduce into the planned economy unavoidable elements of irrationality, which would become 'important sources of all the problems' that would beset socialist society.[83]

The chaos of the capitalist market would be replaced by a rational economic plan and government regulation and supervision of the economy, and this would lead directly to an increase in the size of the government bureaucracy. For Weber, a specialized bureaucracy would be much more important in a socialist than a capitalist organization, for 'socialism would, in fact, require a still higher degree of formal bureaucratization than capitalism.'[84] Socialism and bureaucracy would feed off each other and grow exponentially: 'The development of bureaucracy greatly favours the levelling of social classes' as a normal tendency, while every levelling 'creates a favourable situation for the development of bureaucracy; for it tends to eliminate class privileges' in appropriating means of administration, authority, and offices by wealth. 'This combination everywhere inevitably foreshadows the development of mass bureaucracy.'[85]

Once created, a bureaucracy becomes a permanent part of a society. A bureaucracy would continue to function in a country even if there was a revolution or a foreign invasion. The only question would be who is to control the existing bureaucratic machinery. External control over a bureaucracy is generally ineffective unless it corresponds to the interests of the bureaucrats themselves. Real control is usually in the hands of technical specialists and trained permanent officials, who are more likely to achieve their ends than the non-specialist superiors.

At least under capitalism, Weber said, there were different layers of bureaucracy, often competing with each other. Under socialism and state ownership of the economy, a single, gigantic bureaucracy would control all economic and political institutions. Socialism would be more completely alienating than capitalism had been. If people in capitalist society were increasingly living in an iron cage from which there was no escape, under socialism people would be enclosed in an even stronger and more confining straitjacket.

In a market economy, people engage in economic activity to provide for their ideal or material interests. No fundamental difference would occur if the economy were organized on a socialist basis unless a dictatorial power was exercised by a central authority. Only then could individual interests be overridden. Any socialist system that allowed consultation would also 'open the door to conflicts of interests' because, even in a socialist system, individuals will compare their income and workload with others and judge both in terms of their own interests. Once again, a new round of conflict of interest and claims to appropriate wealth would become normal. In conclusion, Weber admits: 'It is of course true that economic action which is oriented on purely ideological grounds to the interest of others does exist. But it is even more certain that the mass of men do not act in this way, and it is an induction from experience that they cannot do so and never will.'[86]

CONCLUSION

Weber lived through the 1918–19 revolution in Germany and the short-lived socialist regime in Bavaria. His experiences confirmed his earlier opinions. In post-war Germany, Weber became active in the German Democratic Party, though he was not given any formal position. He remained a constitutional monarchist and a German nationalist, and was not enthusiastic about the republican government established in Weimar.[87] Invited to become one of three German representatives to negotiate the terms of Germany's responsibility for the war and determine the principles of reparations, Weber's name became linked with what the German right wing saw as an unpatriotic stab in the back. The army, the refrain went, had been betrayed by German politicians who surrendered unconditionally while no foreign soldier had set foot on German territory.

In autumn 1918 Weber was in Munich at the time of the German revolution. On 4 November, as the revolution was already underway in Kiel and three days before the socialist, Kurt Eisner, seized power in Bavaria, Weber spoke against secession and railed against 'Playing games with the revolution'. The revolt would end with 'a reaction the likes of which we have never experienced', he stated. 'And the proletariat will have to pay the

price.' These pragmatic remarks offended the left and did not pacify the right. When Weber publicly condemned the light punishment imposed on the assassin who killed Eisner in 1919, conservative youth vented their wrath by demonstrating against him.[88]

Personal tragedy also dogged Weber. His mother died that year and, in the next year, his youngest sister committed suicide. In June 1920, at the age of 56, Weber died also, after falling ill with pneumonia.[89] His life's work was left uncompleted. Marianne Weber published some of his work posthumously and also wrote a biography of her husband's life. By the time of his death Weber's importance to sociology in Germany and the United States had been recognized.

In agreement with Durkheim, the most important distinction Weber drew between types of societies was whether they were pre-industrial (traditional) or industrial (modern). Much of Weber's work was addressed to the question of why modern society developed first in the West. As sociology evolved in the first half of the twentieth century, and as it became a particularly American discipline, these grand questions (with some exceptions) were ignored or were appropriated by marginalized subdisciplines. The comparative and historical spirit of sociology atrophied and what grew in its place was a piecemeal examination of social institutions and processes.

Insofar as sociology retained a theoretical framework, however, Weber's work has been influential in a variety of sociological perspectives. Weber attempted to systematize sociological concepts and develop a language for the analysis of social institutions. His approach was multi-variable, distinguishing among the constitutive elements of social life and interrelating them. Understanding society holistically, Weber avoided imposing a unilateral chain of causation in which some factors are always determining. Given the objective of understanding the functioning of society, this approach is fruitful and compelling. Weber's discussion of social phenomena such as the types of legitimate authority, the characteristics of bureaucracy, the changes in the class structure of modern capitalism, and the potentially independent nature of the processes of social stratification have oriented the approach of many twentieth-century sociologists. In their efforts to understand society, sociologists working in what became known as a conflict perspective interpreted Weber as expanding Marx's analysis into issues Marx had ignored or of which he had been unaware.

Underlying Weber's understanding of social processes is his constant concern with subjectivity, with what social actors intend, the meaning they impute to their actions and those of others, and the consequences of their actions. Subjectivity is the distinguishing feature of the scientific study of humanity. Social structures are not merely objective things like the weather but are meaningfully constructed and are shaped by the ideas people have of them. These conceptions are not necessarily rational—they may not even be primarily rational—but appreciating the values and habits as well as the conscious intentions that mould people's lives is crucial for understanding social phenomena and, in the long run, for successfully changing it.

For Weber, by and large, the focus on subjectivity provided a deeper understanding of the institutional and socially constructed forces that propelled history. He did not take his analysis in the direction of psychology, of contemplating the emergence of an individual's self-conception. Yet Weber's definition of social action as involving the reciprocal interaction of individuals—during which they take into account what they interpret to be the intentions and meanings of others in the interaction—reflected the emergence of a modern social psychology that would be the forerunner of an interpretive and micro-level sociology that would be developed in the twentieth century.

12 PROGRESSIVISM AND EMANCIPATION

In the last two decades of the nineteenth century, American industrial capitalism entered what Rostow called its 'takeoff' stage. In half a century, the United States would become the dominant economic, military, and financial power in the world. Like the rapid industrialization in Germany, which was underway simultaneously, American heavy industry was dominated by a class of powerful 'barons' of industry who converted small and medium-sized enterprises into vast concentrations of capital. With the assistance of a compliant government, powerful capitalists gained **oligopolistic control** over specific branches of the market. Among the new class of American robber barons were J.P. Morgan and Andrew Carnegie (steel) and John D. Rockefeller (oil and banking).[1] Ironically, the giants of American business were celebrating Herbert Spencer and his theory of laissez-faire at precisely the time this ideology no longer described the economic system. Oligopoly was destroying competitive capitalism from within, replacing it with the domination of a few strategically located corporations and a new social and economic elite. The era of the robber baron was also the age of political corruption in the cities, of the use of state power to crush the nascent labour movement, and of the rise of US imperialism as American capital pushed the government into colonial ventures in Cuba and the Philippines.

The social dislocations, urban squalor, growing social inequality, and economic depressions that inevitably come in the wake of the free development of industrial capitalism transformed American society and generated movements of protest. European immigrants brought to the New World ideologies of socialism, anarchism, and trade unionism, which directly challenged the control of capital in industrial centres and resource industries. The distress of the small farmer took on a political expression in an anti-big business and anti-government movement known as 'populism', a rural component of a progressive movement that included demands for urban reforms, anti-trust legislation, and labour rights.

The populist ideology that developed in America towards the end of the nineteenth century, while opposing socialism, recognized the inadequacy of competitive individualism. The small-business mentality served as a well-spring for populist movements of protest against the domination of the big economic and political giants, which threatened the independence of the small owner on the farm and the small business operator in urban America. Jacksonian democracy survived in the ideology of popular consciousness even while the material basis of the ideology was being eroded by industrial capitalism. The populist movement included journalists who exposed the baneful influence of businessmen and their control of corrupt politicians in **muckraking** articles and authors whose naturalism exposed the desperate underside of the sweatshop that drove American capitalism. Through his exposure of the conditions in Chicago meat-packing plants in his novel, *The Jungle* (1906), the socialist Upton Sinclair inspired a demand for government regulation in the meat industry. Jack London's equally radical *People of the Abyss* (1903) dramatically brought to the attention of the public the plight of the London urban underclass.

MELIORISM IN AMERICAN SOCIOLOGY

In this atmosphere of social criticism emerged an academic movement for social reform or **meliorism**. Social Darwinism was consistent with American competitive capitalism, but the complexity of social reality supported an alternative perspective. In addition to its rhetoric of free enterprise, American business was oriented to practical goals and immediately applicable innovations. Herbert Spencer was too abstract and theoretical to fit comfortably in the increasingly pragmatic environment of American social thought. Among the earliest sociologists in the United States were Christian reformers who were concerned about making practical institutional and moral improvements in society. To most sociologists at the turn of the century, Shaskolsky argues, the Spencerian formula of laissez-faire had resulted in a moral decline that might undermine the values of the American republic. If society had progressed in the past it seemed clear to many that this did not happen by simply standing aside and allowing the natural forces to work themselves out.[2] On the contrary, the failure to reform society had enhanced the appeal of the populist and radical movements of the time.

The anti-Spencer generation of sociologists, beginning with Lester Ward, rejected the determinism of social Darwinism and naturalism and the atomistic image of the self-motivated, self-interested individual. Instead, they emphasized the importance of individual choice and the need for social intervention in the interests of reform. The view that the evolution of society was necessarily progressive and automatically produced the greatest good obviously was flawed. As single-tax advocate Henry George argued in opposition to Malthus, 'the injustice of society not the niggardliness of nature, is the cause of want and misery which the current theory attributes to overpopulation.'[3] The laissez-faire approach had resulted in a deterioration of conditions, which could have disastrous consequences for American society. In place of the automatic laws of social evolution, social intervention based on conscious motives of amelioration would be effective and desirable.

Realistic intervention in society had to be based on an understanding built on facts determined on the basis of the rigorous application of the scientific method. Just as on the basis of observation and deduction you could predict physical phenomena, the same kind of success could be achieved in the social realm, although the social sciences were perceived to be in a state of infancy. In America, Karl Mannheim observed, sociology renounced any effort to understand the social totality and instead 'split up into a series of technical problems of social readjustment.'[4] The motivation lying behind the foundation of a scientific study of society came principally from the myriad social problems that were perceived to emanate from industrialization. According to Albion Small, one of the leading sociologists of the day, the 'social movement of modern life . . . is the movement of the common will to find and apply some adjustment of the disturbed relationships and dislodged classes; caused by the most revolutionary force ever introduced into human affairs, except the gospel, viz, the modern industrial system.'[5] While America had progressed enormously in a short time, it was merely material progress that had been accompanied (some said necessarily) by a decline in morality. The amelioration of the evil social conditions to which the lower classes were subject would renew the lost moral basis of American society.

In the lead article in the first edition of the *American Journal of Sociology*, Small distinguished between 'popular sociology' and 'scientific sociology'. The popular version, Small claimed, which entailed mass participation and the more militant aspects of populism, was negative and premature. Populists took precipitous action before all the facts were in. Social reform required, first, the scientific collection and interpretation of facts, a role he assigned to sociologists. The task of social scientists was to develop expert sociological knowledge that could guide the political actions taken by the elite. Sociologists must present their data in a specific form that would 'be the one in which

. . . men of affairs themselves view the facts concerned'.[6] While sociology was divided into 'practical' and 'theoretical' branches, the latter was expected to provide knowledge of the underlying laws in accordance with which practical activity could be carried out.[7] Sociology originated primarily as an applied science.

Lester Ward was one of the important figures of early American sociology. Ward developed much of his sociology in opposition to social Darwinism and laissez-faire individualism. The Darwinian belief that evolution proceeded by blind chance was unacceptable to Ward, who preferred the Lamarckian assumption that evolution involved a conscious striving for the higher. Since social laws are similar to natural laws, then just as we intervene in nature to make improvements, a developed science of sociology would become the basis for similar reformism in society. The essential irony of laissez-faire individualism was that freedom of competition had led to economic concentration, which, in turn, inhibited freedom. Therefore, paradoxically, freedom had to be legislated. According to Hofstadter, Ward claimed that a world run on the principles of sociological intervention 'would distribute its favours according to merit', as the individualists demanded, but it would also meet the reform objective of equality. '[E]qualizing opportunity for all . . . would eliminate advantages now possessed by those with undeserved power, accidental position or wealth, or antisocial cunning.'[8]

As a reformist, Ward was voicing the liberal demand to equalize opportunity so that society could ensure that those whom it rewards most highly actually deserved the stipend. Under the existing circumstances, Ward reasoned, it was wrong to identify the successful with the best. Equal opportunity would create the circumstances in which the successful would be objectively the most virtuous. As the clergyman and social gospel advocate, Washington Gladden, argued, this liberalism did indeed 'go far beyond Mr. Spencer's limits, and yet stop a great way this side of socialism.'[9] The socialists were making the more radical demand for an equalization of conditions, not merely the equalization of opportunity to achieve unequal positions. The reformers did not reject the central tenet that progress results from competition; rather, their efforts were directed to ensuring that competition would actually determine that the best succeeded. Since altruism would not evolve automatically, the early American sociologists believed it 'should be strengthened [as] the best possible answer to the threat of socialism'.[10] According to Howard Odum, Ward put his faith in the technical and artificial. His attempt to reconcile elitism and democracy 'foreshadowed social planning'.[11] An intellectual elite was required to shape society so that it would benefit all its members.[12] This argument would later become the core of Karl Mannheim's reformism.

The melioristic movement involved both alterations in the environment of the disadvantaged as well as attempts at moral uplifting. As the depression years of the 1890s receded and were followed by a prosperous inflationary decade, the objective conditions that had given rise to populism diminished. The change was marked ideologically by the ascendancy of **pragmatism** as the dominant American philosophy. In social science pragmatism meant the piecemeal rationalist approach to social reform operating through legislation that was the hallmark of the **Progressive era**. During this period social work split from sociology and sociologists focused their attention on more general issues. This had the effect of muting what critical aspects sociology did possess in its period of anti-laissez-faire agitation as the professional practitioners became somewhat more removed from social problems. American sociologists 'applied themselves to the task of detecting and dissecting the various social problems that marred the societal scenery', ultimately producing a greatly fragmented discipline.[13] The empiricist tradition, strong in American universities, meant that supposedly neutral facts were to be the final arbiters of scientific questions.

The rise of American sociology was intimately connected with another aspect of the general movement towards social reform. The Darwinian controversy prompted many liberal theologians to attempt to reconcile their beliefs with the latest scientific discoveries, which seemed to gain validity with time. Industrialization was accompanied by fears of the consequences of the growing rationality and decline of some aspects of religious behaviour on the part of the working class. To the more liberal churches it seemed futile in the case of the lower classes to minister to the soul when their conditions of life were not conducive to any interest other than material survival. Therefore, Hofstadter concluded, 'alarmed by the violence of labor conflict . . . [degrading] living conditions, and troubled by the failure of the churches to win an adequate following among urban workers', the progressive churches became a social force 'to make a contribution to solving the new moral problems of industrialism.[14] By looking after their material as well as spiritual needs the churches acted in terms of classic self-preservation.

The Christian message was given an increasingly social interpretation. Inspired by Christian socialism in Britain, the **social gospel** movement was intimately connected to the sociology of the period, partly through common objectives and methods in the realm of social reform, partly through a common ethical and moralistic basis, and partly through individuals, since many early sociologists had some ministerial background. On the one hand, then, sociology retained the religious, moralistic message in its teaching, and, on the other, it was legitimized as a discipline through its connections with Christianity. Like sociology, the social gospel movement attempted to chart a course midway between socialism and extreme individualism.

This middle course defines the Progressive period. The early sociologists accepted as valid the American way of life, an ideological stance in the discipline by no means confined to the forefathers. According to Smith, 'sociology developed within the reform movements created to salvage the capitalist system.' Their anti-laissez-faire ideology expressed their support for the emerging new form of rational capitalism and its accompanying imperialism.[15] Ironically but quite logically, the individualist William Sumner resisted both.

Paradoxically, Sumner, the one sociologist against whom all the liberal sociologists were in reaction, opposed state intervention because he recognized that the state is essentially an instrument of political power that social classes employ to advance their own special interests. The benefits accruing from government intervention were distributed predominantly to members of the social class in control of the state, while the burdens rested disproportionately with members of other classes.[16] Sumner's conservative perspective held a nugget of radicalism.

THORSTEIN VEBLEN

Another prominent Progressive era social theorist, the acerbic Thorstein Veblen (1857–1929), was the son of Norwegian immigrants who had settled in the Midwest. In the radical atmosphere of the 1880s, Veblen progressively abandoned his strict Lutheran upbringing, adopting an outsider's perspective as an agnostic and social critic. He studied Marx as an economist and found more philosophy than science in his work. Veblen saw no future in a proletarian revolution, but was sharply critical of the 'predatory' culture of big business. As a student at Yale University, Veblen's views on social evolution and science were affected by William Sumner's social Darwinism.[17] With wit, sarcasm, and a talent for finding the perfect, deflating phrase, Veblen turned this set of ideas into an iconoclastic attack on the business culture of America. He skewered the financial barons and pinned his hopes for the future on scientists and engineers who, he thought, could harness the dynamism of the machine age for the benefit of society.

Veblen's personal and academic life both were troubled. As a teacher, Veblen mumbled through his lectures, hated marking exams, and dished out identical, average grades to students. His classes had a high dropout rate. His relationships with women were equally unsuccessful, but volatile rather than dull. Married twice, Veblen not only had extramarital affairs but was indiscreet about his infidelities. Max Lerner argues that Veblen was consistently denied an academic career on the grounds of his supposed immorality, but fear of his 'dangerous thoughts' was the underlying reason for his isolation.[18] Veblen's bitter attack on the American university system, *The Higher Learning in America* (1918), gave an inside view of the economic and social forces that pervert scholarship in the interests of preserving the power of the few. His critique is still relevant to the contemporary issue of the privatization of higher education.

As an economist influenced by the small-business mentality of rural populism, Veblen criticized big business, but his early interest in socialism did not make him a Marxist. One of the most common criticisms of Marx's economic theory at the turn of the twentieth century was that the working class was not becoming absolutely poorer. Marx, it was claimed, had expected that workers' wages would be driven down to bare subsistence levels by the laws of competition. Known as the **immiseration thesis**, this was thought to be one of the key motivations that would drive the proletariat into revolt against capitalism. However, as critics of Marx pointed out, in the late nineteenth century the working class in advanced capitalism was becoming materially better off. Especially in countries where trade unions had been able to bargain successfully with employers for higher wage rates and improved working conditions, the proletariat was able to share in the profits of the capitalist system. Their living standards were improving and, far from becoming revolutionary, they were becoming content with the system and with the ability to make improvements in their lives within the capitalist framework.

Veblen conceded that the aphorism about the rich getting richer and the poor poorer was 'farcical' if it meant that working people were worse off than in the past. On the contrary, industrial capitalism had brought about 'the most rapid advance in average wealth and industrial efficiency that the world has seen'. While American workers may be improving their economic lot, Veblen argued in 1891, they were by no means content. The aphorism was true in a different sense because the 'industrious poor' were *comparatively* poorer—

poorer in their own eyes.[19] It was not so much a question of how much better off they were compared with the past, but of comparing themselves with those who were even more prosperous than they were. This argument would be repeated in the 1950s and 1960s, and again at the end of the twentieth century, both periods of capitalist prosperity. For Veblen, this was not a simple matter of the gap between the rich and the poor growing wider so that the poor seemed *comparatively* worse off even if, by absolute standards, they were better off than ever. This was the argument of many Marxists; but it was not Veblen's chief point. To understand Veblen and see how his argument had resonance in the 1950s and 1960s, it is necessary to consider first his theory of instincts and emulation.

Instincts of Work and Emulation

Veblen laid out his explanation in *The Theory of the Leisure Class* (1899), the book for which he is best known. As a late nineteenth-century theorist, Veblen was influenced by the ideas of the social Darwinists and the idea that much of human behaviour was biologically determined. There was an instinctual basis for human behaviour. Nevertheless, instincts operated differently in the animal and human worlds. Among simpler organisms, Veblen argued, an instinct could be conceived as a combination of an internal drive (something the organism was driven to satisfy) plus the predetermined behaviour to accomplish the end or satisfy the drive. Insofar as a migratory bird had an instinct to fly south in the autumn, it experienced both an internal 'drive' to migrate and had programmed into it the behaviours necessary to accomplish this end. It was not a learned behaviour but an instinctual behaviour.

Human instincts, however, were of a different character. Veblen accepted the notion that humans had instincts, but no human instinct operated in the absence of social influence. Certainly humans had drives, biological necessities that needed to be satisfied; however, for anything other than the simplest biological reflexes, humans did not possess, genetically, the programmed actions that would satisfy the drive. Instead, humans had a relatively large measure of choice, of alternative means to satisfy their drives. Various cultures could prescribe different but biologically appropriate actions and socialize offspring to follow these distinct rules of behaviour.

Initially, humanity lived in a peaceable culture in solidarity with their fellows and in competition with nature. In this humble, non-aggressive, and indolent stage, certain fundamental psychological characteristics were selected, including truthfulness, equity, sympathy, and the instinct of creative workmanship. From this early beginning, society passed into a second, predatory phase. The initial human traits, developed over a long historical time, were repressed or diminished through a selection process consistent with the new social structure. The principal struggle was no longer with nature but with other individuals. In the context of the predatory, competitive culture, successful individuals required a different temperament. The predatory character is 'free from scruple, from sympathy, honesty and regard for life' and is characterized by 'ferocity, self-seeking, clannishness, and disingenuousness'. Among the three main genetic types Veblen recognized from the European physiological archetypes, it was among the dolichocephalic-blond type that the predatory character was most fully developed.[20]

The predatory culture persisted in modern capitalism, where the interests of the individual were 'best served by shrewd trading and unscrupulous management'. These traits were increasingly anachronistic in a world where the collective interest required 'honesty, diligence, peacefulness, good-will, [and] an absence of self-seeking'.[21] The modern character had equally an anti-social, predatory side, and a creative, productive side. The era of competition had shaken primitive humanity out of its indolence and lethargy, and infused the human character with energy and ambition. Simultaneously, however, anti-social traits shaped the character of the big capitalist, involved in ownership and acquisition. In the past the capitalist was an active participant in the creation of wealth. The industrial sphere selected the

most positive combination of the old, peaceable traits and the creative impulses of the competitive age. By the late nineteenth century, however, industry was under the shadow of mismanagement by bankers and financiers for whom business was merely a way to make money, not a means of improving life for the community. Increasingly, the capitalist was becoming a parasite on industry, focusing exclusively on making profit through financial dealings. They dominated the economic and social scene, and increasingly influenced politics directly.

The difference between the model industrialist and the parasitical financier, Veblen suggested, resulted from the manifestation of two different drives. The main contradiction in modern society, he believed, was derived from the coexistence of two distinct instincts (or sentiments)—**workmanship** and **emulation**. Among the instinctive drives that humans inherited was an important instinct of workmanship—a fundamental drive towards creativity, efficiency, and accomplishment. The modern industrialist embodied this drive. Workmanship was rooted in an even more basic human instinct, curiosity.[22] For Veblen, this instinct of curiosity lies at the root of all human progress.[23] Driven by the instincts of curiosity and workmanship, human thought creates technologies that are appropriate for the given state of knowledge of a culture. Once created, these technologies shape the beliefs and actions of people in society. People become habituated—socialized—into this set of beliefs and actions, which becomes second nature; the beliefs and actions are assumed to be natural and are followed more or less automatically by people.

This tendency for society to reproduce itself—to pass on unchanged from one generation to the next—is contradicted by the fundamental human drive to create. So no human society stands still, and progress is inevitable. Veblen's theory reflected the nineteenth-century doctrine of automatic progress, which he believed was rooted in a fundamental, biological human drive. Unfortunately, modern industrial society was stripping many people of the opportunity to express their creativity and workmanship in their employment and perverting creativity among a minority of business leaders, whose interests were confined to financial manipulations. These were the parasitical financiers, driven by the instinct for emulation. As sociologist C. Wright Mills commented at mid-century, America was split between those groups of people who performed necessary and productive work, among whom the dominant sentiment was useful craftsmanship and productive work, and the modern businessman, whose sentiments were pecuniary (concerned with money-making) and predatory.[24] In his *Theory of Business Enterprise* (1904), Veblen warned that investment solely for the purpose of profit-making expanded the role of speculation and ignored the social implications of making short-term economic decisions based on what was immediately profitable. The result was a tendency to economic dislocation and unemployment, and the control of production in the interests of the financiers who sacrificed the consumers as well as the long-term interests of the economic system.

While economic and social conditions stifled the instinct of workmanship, the instinct for emulation was being strengthened throughout the society. Although the American working class was better off than ever before, their discontent was rooted in a biological drive found in all humans: the tendency to make invidious comparisons with one's fellows. An invidious comparison is one that tends to look enviously or jealously at the accomplishments or acquisitions of others. What Veblen called the drive for emulation was one of the most important motivations shaping human actions. People judge themselves in comparison to others, and, more importantly, argued Veblen, they strive to be seen and thought of as being *better than* their neighbours.

In earlier societies, people would be personally known to their neighbours and their social standing would also be well known. An individual might strive to be recognized, for example, as a better hunter. In a feudal society, someone might base her or his claim for being better than another on the basis of aristocratic birth. In industrial capitalism, however, a person's worth is measured by how much money he or she has.

As a social evolutionist, Veblen argued that in what we would now call hunting and gathering societies (in his terms, savage cultures), the most basic distinction was between women's and men's work. Men's work (hunting) was more prestigious because it had an element of exploit as opposed to drudgery. Even at that early stage of society, employments were invidiously compared: exploit was honourable and noble; other employments that imply subservience or submission were dishonourable, 'debasing, ignoble'.[25]

At a later stage of social evolution, when technology had been developed to a sufficiently high degree, not all members of society were required to participate in securing the necessary means of subsistence. There was, in fact, a surplus, which could support a few highly privileged individuals and, later, a highly privileged class of people who lived off the surplus provided by the labour of the lower class. This privileged group, Veblen asserted, was essentially a **leisure class** and existed in what he termed a predatory culture. It wasn't that the leisure class didn't work. In particular, they monopolized the right to slaughter, whether it was hunting animals or killing people in warfare. These exploits were defined as honorific. On the other hand, the handling of tools, the labour of subsistence, becomes defined as odious, as beneath the dignity of the leisure class: 'Labour becomes irksome.'[26]

The emergence of a leisure class was intimately connected with the emergence of the concept of private ownership. The earliest form of ownership, Veblen claimed, was the ownership of women and of the products of their industry, and thence proceeded more generally to the ownership of things.[27] The basic instinct at the root of ownership was emulation, 'the strongest and most alert and persistent of the economic motives proper'.[28] The amount of property an individual owned became the measure of success; the more wealth accumulated, the higher the honour. Accumulated wealth, and the power that accompanied it, became the basis of reputability. In fact, as civilization progressed, wealth inherited from ancestors conferred even more prestige than wealth acquired by an individual's own efforts.[29]

Merely possessing wealth or power was insufficient, Veblen argued; rather, 'wealth or power must be put in evidence, for esteem is awarded only on evidence.'[30] Equally important was the abstention from labour, from work that was defined as odious or irksome. The wealthy elite distinguished itself by its leisure and by the cultivation of habits and demeanours that reflected its status and came to define good taste.

The chief complication in modern society is that we live and work in places where we are more or less anonymous. We want the strangers we encounter to treat us with the respect we deserve based on our social position and wealth—we want our claims to a certain amount of prestige to be recognized—but, simply by virtue of being strangers, they are unaware of our actual status. In this situation, Veblen concludes, we have to display our wealth conspicuously. By our demonstration of our 'ability to pay', we 'make a showing' in front of the many people we encounter. In Veblen's words, this conspicuous display of our wealth is 'practically the only means which the average of us have of impressing our

respectability on the many to whom we are personally unknown, but whose transient good opinion we would so gladly enjoy. So it comes about that the appearance of success is very much to be desired, and is even in many cases to be preferred to the substance.' In American fiction, Jay Gatsby, the title character of F. Scott Fitzgerald's novel, is the epitome of the nouveau riche who seeks status among the old, wealthy class by making false claims to gentility and hosting fashionable parties. The two most obvious forms of conspicuous display were the size and type of Gatsby's house and car (Box 12.1).[31]

Conspicuous Consumption

The principal concept Veblen developed to describe this need to impress others and thereby establish an invidious distinction is **conspicuous consumption**. The more anonymous the others who have to be impressed, the more mobile the society, the more necessary it is to display one's social status, which means ostentatiously displaying the opulent goods one can afford.[32] In particular, expenditure on superfluous goods, on things that are unnecessary, is the most honorific:

Box 12.1

Nick Carraway, the narrator of *The Great Gatsby*, rented a small house in West Egg, the less fashionable of two seaside communities on Long Island, 20 miles east of New York City. 'Across the courtesy bay the white palaces of fashionable East Egg glittered along the water.' According to Nick's description, his house was 'squeezed between two huge places that rented for twelve or fifteen thousand a season. The one on my right was a colossal affair by any standard—it was a factual imitation of some Hôtel de Ville in Normandy, with a tower on one side, spanking new under a thin beard of raw ivy, and a marble swimming pool, and more than forty acres of lawn and garden. It was Gatsby's mansion.' The ivy did little to conceal Gatsby's ostentatious, nouveau riche style. His automobile was his other obvious object of conspicuous consumption: 'Everybody had seen it. It was a rich cream color, bright with nickel, swollen here and there in its monstrous length with triumphant hat-boxes and supper-boxes and tool-boxes, and terraced with a labyrinth of wind-shields that mirrored a dozen suns.' The passengers sat 'down behind many layers of glass in a sort of green leather conservatory'.

—F. Scott Fitzgerald, *The Great Gatsby* (1925)

'In order to be reputable it must be wasteful.'[33] Veblen's notion of conspicuous waste was especially pertinent to the standards of increasing consumption—keeping up with the Joneses—that characterized the middle class of 1950s America. Conspicuous consumption was not just a matter of maintaining a certain visible standard of living. On the contrary, the standard of decency by which the leisure class measured its success was 'indefinitely extensible'—it had no limits. In fact, social standards necessitated that every advance in income—every increase in one's pecuniary means —was matched by a corresponding increase in consumption. The motive, again, is emulation; the standards by which each class sets its sights are the standards of the class just above it in the social hierarchy. So a dynamic is set in place from the top to the bottom of the class structure. For Veblen, 'The standards of living of any class, so far as concerns the element of conspicuous waste, is commonly as high as the earning capacity of the class will permit—with a consistent tendency to go higher.'[34]

The conspicuously wasteful and honorific also come to define 'taste' and 'the beautiful'. The costliest, purely ornamental object has the highest prestige value: the vapid Daisy, the purebred dog, the racehorse, even the 'close-cropped lawn'.[35] Historically, Veblen notes, the standards of beauty in women have emphasized the importance of the appearance of idleness: 'the ideal requires delicate and diminutive hands and feet and a slender waist.' Chinese foot-binding and the high-heeled shoe were intended to create the maximum of defined elegance and the minimum of practicality. In Veblen's time, women of the leisure class wore corsets designed to give the impression of an impossibly narrow waist. Veblen caustically comments: 'The corset is, in economic theory, substantially a mutilation, undergone for the purpose of lowering the subject's vitality and rendering her permanently and obviously unfit for work.' Both the husband and the corseted wife gain in reputability as a result of her 'visibly increased expensiveness and infirmity'. In Veblen's words, 'These features, together with the other faults of structure that commonly go with them, go to show that the person so affected is incapable of useful effort and therefore must be supported in idleness by her owner.' An elegant dress, similarly, serves its emulative purpose by being expensive, seldom used or perhaps only once, and is the 'insignia of leisure'. The French (high) heel, the skirt, and the habit of excessively long hair are all incapacitating; each affectation 'obviously makes any, even the simplest and most necessary manual work extremely difficult'.[36]

This culture of consumption is made even more wasteful by the imposition of fashion, according to which practically serviceable goods are rendered obsolete by the changing definitions of good taste. Over time, what was seen as fashionable and desirable becomes, first, old-fashioned, then positively odious as we develop an **aesthetic nausea**. In the twenty-first century, we are quite familiar with the dictates of fashion and the importance of novelty; Veblen, however, was breaking new ground.

The same cannot be said with respect to Veblen's views of women. Being a privileged white male—even if an eccentric one—Veblen was at least ambivalent about the New Woman movement of his day, although he recognized the social contradictions out of which the movement had sprung. Veblen was no practical champion of women's equality. His own relationships with women appear to have been predatory.[37] In some of his writing, however, Veblen recognized arguments in favour of women's superiority and their need for an economic outlet for their talents.

It was precisely among upper-class women that the first wave of feminism broke at the end of the nineteenth century and Veblen addressed the issue explicitly in *The Theory of the Leisure Class*. Among what Veblen believed to be human instincts, pride of place was reserved for what he termed the instinct of workmanship, the creative drive at the heart of human progress. According to Veblen, women's temperament was not only more favourably disposed to peace than the male temperament, but women naturally abhorred futility to a greater degree than men. Despite their existence in the leisure class as symbols of the reputability of their fathers and husbands, 'the women of modern industrial communities show a livelier sense of the discrepancy between the accepted scheme of life and the exigencies of the economic situation.'[38]

The status of women in his time, Veblen claims, derived from a common sense that was created in an earlier stage of social evolution and continued to shape beliefs and attitudes in his day. In this traditional scheme of beliefs, a quality of a woman's life was imputed to a man who stood in some relationship of ownership over the woman. The woman was assigned a social sphere that was ancillary to that of the man. She was to be represented in politics by the head of her household. According to this common sense view:

> It is unfeminine in her to aspire to a self-directing, self-centred life; and our common sense tells us that her direct participation in the affairs of the community, civil or industrial, is a menace to that social order which expresses our habits of thought as they have been formed under the guidance of the traditions of the pecuniary culture. All this fume and froth of 'emancipating women from the slavery of man' and so on, is, to use the chaste and expressive language of Elizabeth Cady Stanton inversely, 'utter rot.' The social relations of the sexes are fixed by nature.[39]

This was the prevailing view of most women as well, who necessarily saw themselves as ancillary to men. Veblen asserted there is a new sentiment that, at the least, this arrangement does not serve 'the more everyday ends of life'. Even upper- and middle-class women, who are otherwise quite conservative, perceive a discrepancy 'between things as they are and things as they should be'. But this discrepancy is most keenly felt by that 'less manageable body of modern women who, by force of youth, education, or temperament', have a vivid sense of grievance against their traditional status. This new woman demands emancipation from this status and, simultaneously, demands the opportunity to 'unfold her life activity' for useful employment.[40]

Women were demanding emancipation from exactly those things in their lives that critics of the New Woman movement believed to be their privileges: women are petted by their husbands, required to consume largely and conspicuously, and barred from useful employment. These were the eternal markings of the un-free, Veblen said. Endowed with an instinct for workmanship that is, perhaps, stronger than a man's, a woman's impulse is 'to live her own life in her own way and to enter the industrial process of the community'.[41] Women have their share of the deeply rooted human propensity to self-direction which is more permanent than the traits selected by the more recent predatory culture. The New Woman movement, then, is a reversion to this more generic human type.

The economic conditions of the existing predatory culture and the selection of human traits consistent with it limited the development and practical success of women's emancipation. Similarly, Veblen believed, there were natural limitations to the ability of certain racial groups to 'enter the industrial process'.

More progressively, Veblen rejected the view that Germans represented a distinct, biological race. On the contrary, the German-speaking population of Europe 'is thoroughly and universally hybrid . . . compounded out of the same racial elements' as the European population generally. Writing in 1915, Veblen was aware of the revolution in biology wrought by the study of genetics, which originated in the work of Gregor Mendel. In contrast to purebred types, hybrids possessed a much greater range of inherited traits and aptitudes, making them stronger and more adaptable. Hybrid human societies are gifted with a greater variety of physical and intellectual tendencies and possibilities. Veblen rejected the core eugenics argument that 'pure blood' is better. On the contrary, genetic mixing made cultures stronger,[42] whereas cultures created by people who were genetically homogeneous, such as tribal societies in Africa, were less adaptable and backward.

AFRICAN-AMERICAN EMANCIPATION

Veblen was born in a society that, in the middle of the nineteenth century, still practised slavery. This was a monstrous affront to human potential. While the emancipation of African Americans was largely a result of their own efforts, the anti-slavery cause that developed during the middle decades of the century had numerous adherents in Europe and the United States. Many of the most active in the abolitionist movement were women, who saw a parallel between the slavery of blacks and their own social inequality and bondage. These women were radicalized by their anti-slavery work and applied the ideological and practical lessons to their own lives. As Hymowitz and Weissman explain,[43] 'women learned to defy public opinion, to organize, petition, raise funds, and persevere', thereby bridging the gap that had been drawn between men's and women's spheres.

Harriet Beecher Stowe, the abolitionist author of *Uncle Tom's Cabin* (1852), challenged slavery on moral grounds (Box 12.2).[44] This often melodramatic anti-slavery novel was a vehicle for exposing the abuses of slave owners and their overseers and for raising public awareness of what Frederick Douglass, the black orator and journalist, had called the 'revolting barbarity and shameless hypocrisy' of slavery. *Uncle Tom's Cabin* declared slavery the antithesis of the Christian ethic of brotherhood. Slave owners professed their religious faith while 'Christians as good or better than they—are lying in the very dust under their feet. They buy 'em and sell 'em, and make trade of their heart's blood, and groans and tears.' For Stowe, the question was not to expose the abuses of slavery, but to realize that slavery 'itself is the essence of all abuse.'[45]

Eventually, it took a bloody war and the expediency of recruiting African Americans to the cause of the North to end slavery in the United States. The American Civil War was not fought principally over the issue of slavery; however, in 1863 President Lincoln issued the Emancipation Proclamation declaring an end to the legal institution of slavery in all parts of the United States that were still in rebellion, a move meant to induce the African-American population to fight against the Confederacy. Two years later, in the Thirteenth Amendment to the US Constitution, it was resolved that, 'Neither slavery nor involuntary servitude . . . shall exist within the United States.' By the Fourteenth Amendment, anyone 'born or naturalized in the United States' was given the right of citizenship, and all citizens were guaranteed 'equal protection of the laws'. By the Fifteenth Amendment, the right to vote could not be denied by a state to any citizen 'on account of race, color, or previous condition of servitude' (though not

Box 12.2

This cursed business, accursed of God and man. . . . [R]un it down to the root and nucleus of the whole, and what is it? Why, because my brother Quashy is ignorant and weak, and I am intelligent and strong,—because I know how, and *can* do it,—therefore, I may steal all he has, keep it, and give him only . . . so much as suits my fancy. Whatever is too hard, too dirty, too disagreeable for me, I may set Quashy to doing. Because I don't like work, Quashy shall work. Because the sun burns me, Quashy shall stay in the sun. Quashy shall earn the money, and I shall spend it. Quashy shall lie down in every puddle, that I may walk over dry-shod. Quashy shall do my will, and not his, all the days of his mortal life. . . . This I take to be what slavery is. . . . Talk of the abuses of slavery! Humbug! The *thing itself* is the essence of all abuse.

—Harriet Beecher Stowe, *Uncle Tom's Cabin* (1852)

gender). At the conclusion of the war approximately four million black citizens were emancipated in the southern states. In 1875, a Civil Rights Act was passed by the federal government, making it illegal to bar African Americans from such public accommodations as hotels, railroad cars, and theatres.[46]

Reconstructing the Colour Line

From the point of view of many white southerners, liberal northerners had allied with southern blacks, forcing integration on the unwilling South and giving African Americans political power. African Americans used their legislative rights to begin the process of democratizing the South. In South Carolina, black legislators outnumbered whites and attempted to remove all racial distinctions from the laws, including the ban on interracial marriages.

In most cases, however, the long-standing relationship of domination and subordination was maintained. Formal freedom did not bring social equality or the economic means to be independent of the white upper class. Few former slaves had the ability to acquire land. As agricultural wage labourers or sharecroppers, the rural black population was not, in general, materially better off following emancipation. For the next dozen years, the northern army occupied the South in a period known as **Reconstruction**, becoming the symbol of integration and racial equality. In 1876–7, in the midst of an economic depression, the federal government withdrew its troops from the South. White southerners lost no time in reinstating social, political, and legal inequality.

Upper-class whites used their political power to pass laws at the state level that enforced segregation of public facilities, known as **Jim Crow** laws. Blacks and whites were required by law to attend separate schools, separate restaurants, hotels, theatres, and parks. Black and white cemeteries were legislated. Since blacks legally were citizens, they had a constitutional right to vote; however, to prevent the black population from exercising their political right, state legislators passed laws that had the effect of restricting those eligible to cast ballots. These included tests of literacy, which blacks would fail more frequently than whites. In Mississippi, an 'understanding clause' was used to restrict the number of black voters. Unscrupulous whites used the clause prejudicially, ruling 'that the ignorant white man does understand the Constitution when it is read to him and that the ignorant black man does not.'[47] These laws were clearly discriminatory in their intent or interpretation. At the time, however, conservative, white males dominated the Supreme Court of the United States. In their view, the American Constitution did not prohibit segregation, and the Supreme Court ruled that these racial laws were within the power of the various state governments to enact. In the view of the Supreme Court, separate facilities were not necessarily unequal.

The ultimate form of repression is violence. The terrorist organization known as the Ku Klux Klan was organized by ex-Confederate officers in 1865 to use vigilante violence to maintain white supremacy in the South in the face of northern occupation and the emancipation of the slaves. The Klan faded during the post-Reconstruction period, when segregation and other forms of discrimination against blacks became written into law and were sanctioned by the Supreme Court, although its sordid history could be followed through the twentieth century. In 1883 the Supreme Court declared the Civil Rights Act unconstitutional. Racism was covered with the fig leaf of the **separate but equal** doctrine: as long as facilities could be said to be equal, it was legal to enforce racial segregation. Jim Crow laws rewrote many aspects of the old slave code back into American law.

It is impossible, however, to resurrect the past. Some things had changed fundamentally. Under Reconstruction and its aftermath, a professional black 'middle class' based on small businesses or connected to the black colleges had emerged in the South. In his study of *The Negro Novel in America*, Robert Bone argues that black authors expressed in their novels the socially conservative perspective of the middle class.[48] Their social objective was assimilation, Bone concludes, and this affected the type of writing they produced. They shared with the white majority the ideology of self-help and social climbing. Their black heroes tried to succeed economically by dint of hard, sober work, following the American Dream. For most blacks, however, social and legal caste barriers kept the American Dream at an insurmountable distance.

Black novelists wrote for the black middle class and for the white upper class they hoped would be their ally in the move towards assimilation. Accordingly, Bone argues, they depicted the southern elite as benevolent and cultured, and endeavoured to show that the black middle class could be equally refined. Middle-class blacks drew lines of demarcation between themselves and poor, uneducated blacks, who, they felt, were holding them down and preventing them from being accepted by the white establishment. The problems of the caste line and Jim Crow were attributed to poor whites, who (the argument went) had the most to gain by keeping blacks in a subordinate place. This 'white trash' made up the hooded horsemen who terrorized the black population during the post-Reconstruction era. The appeal to more liberal white opinion was one of the cornerstones of the assimilationist approach of the leading African-American theorist of the late nineteenth century, Booker T. Washington (1856–1915).

BOOKER T. WASHINGTON

> In all things purely social we can be as separate as the five fingers, and yet one as the hand in all things essential to mutual progress.
> —Booker T. Washington[49]

Washington was born in slavery and, following emancipation, became a model of the self-made person. His first paid employment was in a coal mine, but Washington was ambitious to rise in the social ladder and made his way to the Hampton Institute in Richmond, Virginia, to receive **industrial training**. At Hampton, Washington wrote, he was 'surrounded by an atmosphere of business, Christian influence, and spirit of self-help'. By learning 'thrift, economy, and push', he realized 'what it meant to be a man instead of a piece of property'. Not content to work in a simple, industrial pursuit, Washington resolved to go into the deep, southern black belt and establish an industrial training Institute modelled after Hampton. In Tuskegee, Alabama, Washington began his life work in 1881 'in a small shanty church, with one teacher and thirty students'. By 1899, he claimed, the Tuskegee Institute had grown to 1,000 students and 88 instructors,[50] helping thousands of black men and women obtain occupational skills.

Washington's social theory was worked out during the Jim Crow era in the South. His most radical statement asserted that the disadvantages suffered by African Americans were social and historical in origin, and not the result of innate inferiority. For Washington, 'The Negro is behind the white man because he has not had the same chance, and not from any inherent difference in his nature and desires.' The difference between the two communities was 'not an inherent one, not a racial one, but a difference growing out of unequal opportunities in the past', as anthropologist Franz Boas (1908) pointed out:

> [A]n unbiased estimate of the anthropological evidence so far brought forward does not permit us to countenance the belief in a racial inferiority, which would unfit an individual of the negro race to take part in modern civilization. We do not know of any demand made on the human body or mind in modern life that . . . would be beyond the powers of the Negro.[51]

Washington rejected the argument that African Americans have inherent character traits that would prevent them from reaching a high standard of civilization.[52]

If African Americans lacked industriousness and thrift, the cause was cultural deprivation and child-like ignorance. Africans had actually taken the first steps towards civilization when they entered slavery as pagans and emerged Christians: 'they went into slavery without a language, they came out speaking the proud Anglo-Saxon tongue.' The conditions of enslavement, however, did not inspire the much-needed work ethic. Enslaved for 250 years, they were obliged to work hard 'under circumstances which were calculated not to inspire them with love and respect for labour'. Labour performed 'under constant protest . . . was a badge of degradation'. In contrast, 'the civilized white man did little labor with the hands.'[53]

For Washington, the objectives were to make the eight million black Americans 'self-supporting, intelligent, economical and valuable citizens' and, second, to establish proper relations between them and the whites with whom they lived. Blacks needed 'food, clothing, shelter, education, proper habits, and a settlement of race relations'.[54]

Industrial Training and Politics

Washington believed that the route to secure these necessities was practical, industrial education. Merely acquiring knowledge of literature or science did not make people 'producers, lovers of labour, independent, honest, unselfish, and, above all, good'. Education must reflect the present needs and social condition of the race. African Americans needed an education that would fit them to do well those things they could actually be able to do. Although African Americans should be encouraged to prepare for any station in life, the surest way to do this was first to learn to fill the basic occupations.[55] While some should become professionals, the larger proportion of black Americans should be educated in industrial life rather than reaching for something higher: 'we must stop this stepping business'.[56] In his 1965 autobiography, the militant black leader Malcolm X said he received similar advice from his teacher (Box 12.3).[57]

Industrial education would not replicate the labour of slavery but 'lift labour up out of toil and drudgery into that which is dignified and beautiful.' Eighty per cent of African Americans were dependent on agriculture in some form, yet very few had been educated in agricultural sciences.

Since the roots of their degraded condition were deep, African Americans also needed moral and cultural training for good living and citizenship, the solid foundation for future success.[58] During Reconstruction, Washington argued, there had been too much emphasis on politics, on controlling the vote and on office-holding, encouraged by 'unscrupulous whites' who had not been concerned with the future welfare of black citizens. No effort was expended on preparing the African American 'to become an intelligent, reliable citizen and voter'. It had been a mistake to give the franchise to four million ex-slaves who were ignorant and impoverished. A property qualification should have been imposed on both races that would have excluded most blacks from voting since only about 5 per cent of them owned the land they worked on, but would also exclude most poor, ignorant whites. Most blacks, Washington said, would continue to be disenfranchised for a generation.[59]

Industrial training was also the foundation that would cement the friendship between the races. Southern whites would learn to respect and appreciate an African American who was well-trained and educated: 'There is an unmistakable influence that comes over a white man when he sees a black man living in a two-story brick house that has been paid for. . . . It is the tangible evidence of prosperity.' As more prosperous, educated African Americans appear throughout the South, Washington asserted, 'this race question will disappear.' Once the reputation of the race has changed for whites and they are seen as frugal, skilled, and honest, a great many of the most 'discouraging features of our life will melt away'.[60]

Above all, blacks must resist using violence. 'There is danger that a certain class of impatient extremists among the Negroes, who have little knowledge of the actual conditions in the South, may do the entire race injury by attempting to

---

Box 12.3

Mr. Ostrowski, my English teacher . . . was . . . a natural-born advisor. . . .

I know that he probably meant well in what he happened to advise me that day. . . . It was just in his nature as an American white man. I was one . . . of the school's top students—but all he could see for me was the kind of future 'in your place' that almost all white people see for black people.

He told me, 'Malcolm, you ought to be thinking about a career. Have you been giving it thought?'

The truth is, I hadn't. I never have figured out why I told him, 'Well, yes, sir, I've been thinking I'd like to be a lawyer.' Lansing certainly had no Negro lawyers—no doctors either—in those days, to hold up an image I might have aspired to. All I really knew for certain was that a lawyer didn't wash dishes, as I was doing.

Mr. Ostrowski looked surprised. . . . He kind of half-smiled and said, 'Malcolm, one of life's first needs is for us to be realistic. . . . A lawyer—that's no realistic goal for a nigger. You need to think about something you *can* be. . . . Everybody admires your carpentry shop work. Why don't you plan on carpentry?'. . .

What made it really begin to disturb me was . . . that Mr. Ostrowski had encouraged [white students to do] whatever they had wanted . . .

It was then that I began to change—inside.

—Malcolm X, *Autobiography* (1965)

---

advise their brethren in the South to resort to armed resistance or the use of the torch, in order to secure justice.' Washington criticized the lynching, but believed that 'in most parts of the South there is . . . a very large measure of peace, good will, and mutual helpfulness.'[61]

At a time of heightened racial tension and white violence, when the political gains of the Civil War and Reconstruction were being stripped away, Washington called for a withdrawal from politics. To agitate for social equality was extreme folly. Zinn argues that this message appealed to many blacks and even more whites.[62] Washington was politically astute and opportunistic. He used his influence to obtain money from white businessmen such as Andrew Carnegie and John Rockefeller for the betterment of African Americans—betterment within the terms of trade school education, economic stability, and political neutrality. Wielding considerable power among members of the black community, Washington advised US presidents in their appointment of African Americans to political office. Washington was popular with the white establishment. He was invited to the White House and to Windsor Castle in England. Despite official racial segregation, he travelled in private railway cars and stayed in expensive hotels. In his view, these symbols of his status represented the equal treatment all blacks would receive when they, too, achieved economic success. Washington represented the ambitions and perspective of the black middle class.

When Booker T. Washington died in 1915, the demands for integration were reverberating once again in African-American communities and the Ku Klux Klan was revived to turn back the tide of civil rights demands. It was a period of economic difficulty and increasing competition between whites and blacks, as large numbers of African Americans migrated from the rural South to the cities, where they became low-wage competition for white labourers. Any African American who appeared to be challenging the colour line became a target of Ku Klux Klan violence, many being lynched by angry mobs of whites egged on by Klan members. When 255 people were lynched in the United States in 1892, most of them black, independent journalist Ida Wells (1862–1931) began an anti-lynching campaign that challenged the deepest myths of southern gender politics.

IDA WELLS

Ida Wells was born in Mississippi, the daughter of former slaves. When she was 16, her parents died of yellow fever and Wells was able to find work as a teacher to support her siblings. Working as a teacher and as a journalist in the black press in Memphis, Wells had first attacked lynching in a series of articles published in 1883. The next year she thrust herself directly into the eye of the racial struggle when she refused an order to leave the first-class railway car in which she was travelling and for which she had bought a ticket. Her stature might have appeared frail—she was in her early twenties and less than five feet in height—but she was full of determination and indignation. She resisted the conductor's efforts to dislodge her and it took three men to push her out. Undaunted, Wells then sued the railway company for discrimination.[63] Wells

began a second career as a journalist, becoming the part-owner of the Memphis *Free Speech and Highlight*. The job became full-time when she was fired from her teaching position because of an article she wrote exposing the inferior facilities that existed in the segregated black schools.[64]

Eight years later, in response to the brutal lynching of three prominent Memphis black businessmen, she embarked on a crusade to expose the despicable practice (Box 12.4). Wells approached her indictment of lynching sociologically by conducting a statistical analysis of incidents. She proved that most blacks who were lynched were not accused of rape; most had violated the colour line by competing successfully with white businesses, trying to vote, insulting whites, fighting, or refusing to obey a white man. Of those accused of rape, many were having consensual sexual relations with white women.[65] Wells exposed the myths and hidden truths about the sexually predatory and unchivalrous white southern male. Lynching, whites claimed, was necessary to protect chaste, asexual white women from the naturally aggressive and unrestrained sexual impulses of black men, an ideology rooted in racist assumptions about African Americans. In the history of the South, Wells pointed out, the proclivity to rape was primarily found among white men, as the numbers

---

Box 12.4

Ida Wells provided anecdotal evidence that 'some white women love the company of Afro-American' men. 'There are thousands of such cases throughout the South, with the difference that the Southern white [men] in insatiate fury wreck their vengeance without any intervention of law upon the Afro-Americans who consort with their women.' Among them was Edward Coy, who, according to a Chicago newspaper, 'was burned alive . . . protesting his innocence.' The woman, however, 'was publicly reported and generally known to have been . . . intimate with Coy for more than a year previous.' The woman was 'compelled by threats . . . to make the charge against the victim.' 'A large majority of the "superior" white men prominent in the affair are the reputed fathers of mulatto children. . . . There can be no possible belief that these people were inspired by any consuming zeal to vindicate God's law against miscegenists.

—Ida Wells, 'Southern Horrors: Lynch Law in All Its Phases' (1892)

of mixed-race offspring in the South visibly demonstrated. Their horror over sexual relations between freed blacks and white women were simply projections of their own guilty consciences.[66]

Ida Wells was attacked viciously in the press for bringing into the light of day some of the sordid secrets of southern white society and denying the most comfortable of white prejudices about African Americans. Northern journalists responded in an equally racist way. The slander was personal, racial, and sexual. The building housing her newspaper office was burned to the ground and Wells's life was threatened, but Wells persisted, carrying her campaign to England and across the American continent. In 1895, Wells married Ferdinand Barnett, an activist lawyer and editor of the black newspaper, the *Conservator*. Facing the double burden of motherhood and the life of an active social reformer, Wells carried her nursing children with her on speaking tours.[67] Wells raised the issue of lynching to the forefront of the national consciousness and affected the country's national reputation. Her courage inspired a younger generation of black women to create the national Association for Coloured Women, the first national organization of its type.[68]

The Ku Klux Klan was the ultimate power sustaining the prejudices of white southerners. Racial stereotypes were deeply embedded in the white consciousness, according to which the colour line separated civilization from debasement. Among the most deeply rooted and destructive myths was a projection of white fears of miscegenation—racial mixing and the assumed inability of African-American males to control their sexuality, particularly when white women were involved. This myth was at the root of the most influential motion picture to be produced in the early twentieth century, D.W. Griffith's three-hour silent film, *The Birth of a Nation*. In this epic motion picture, Griffith, a white southerner himself, told the story of the Civil War and Reconstruction from the point of view of the white southerner. *The Birth of a Nation* is a milestone in cinema for technique and storytelling. The dramatic final rescue scene builds tremendous

tension in the audience as Griffith rapidly cuts between scenes of the mob, the victims trapped inside a cabin, and the men riding to the rescue.[69]

Based on the blatantly racist novel, *The Clansman*, by Thomas Dixon, Griffith's movie reflected white, southern stereotypes. Northern opportunists hoping to steal the spoils of war from the devastated South conspire with freed, power-seeking southern blacks to supplant the domination of whites. The predominant southern stereotypes of African Americans pictured them either as loyal, docile 'house slaves' or as buffoons—dim-witted, foolish, fearful, and child-like. The most dangerous schemer is Silas Lynch, a mulatto. Dixon's The Clansman used Lynch to reinforce the myth that the offspring of miscegenation have the worst characteristics of both races. Lynch is a sexual predator, consistent with the white myth of black primitive sexuality, but he is also an intelligent schemer, a trait supposedly derived from his Caucasian background.

When the blonde niece of Ben Cameron, the southern hero, jumps to her death to escape from Gus, a lustful ex-slave, Cameron organizes the Ku Klux Klan to protect white women and save the South. In the dramatic climax to the film, the Klansmen ride to rescue Ben Cameron's fiancé from the grip of Silas Lynch and rescue the Cameron family, besieged in a cabin by a mob of armed blacks. The Klansmen emerge as the heroes of white civilization and womanhood, and white supremacy is restored. At the conclusion of *The Birth of a Nation*, white northerners and white southerners are reunited in their common interest to preserve their Aryan heritage. The social Darwinist fear that the allegedly superior Caucasian race would be morally and intellectually degraded by intermarriage with inferior races was part of the common mythology of the period.

If it is possible to look beyond the racist message to its cinematic style, *The Birth of a Nation* provided a stunning introduction to the power of the cinema and introduced many innovative cinematic techniques. Nothing like it had ever been seen. Much of the audience, however, was moved in more than one way. As filmmaker D.W. Griffith promised, 'Art is always revolutionary . . . always explosive and sensational.'[70] It is impossible to ignore the racist message. Griffith's epic film both reflected and crystallized the southern white's fundamental racism and deeply rooted beliefs in the inferiority and potential dangerousness of African Americans. It also reflected a sense of racial superiority that was widespread in the United States in the early decades of the century. Whites in every state urged the government to pass restrictive immigration laws to keep people of colour out of the country and preserve the 'white heritage'. Not surprisingly, in the twentieth century the movie proved to be popular cinema in Nazi Germany and apartheid South Africa.

The Birth of a Nation played to appreciative white audiences, as much for its racist ideology as for its cinematic originality. In the southern states the movie reinforced the myths about black inferiority and the Reconstruction era.[71] By the early decades of the twentieth century, the African-American population in the United States was by no means concentrated in the South. As the black population migrated north from the cotton belt in search of work in the factories and heavy industries of industrial America, the colour bar travelled with them, sometimes in more subtle forms and sometimes more violently. While African Americans may have physically pulled up their meagre stakes and chased the American Dream north, the legacy of the diaspora and their oppression travelled with them.

So, too, did the spirit of resistance. In opposition to Griffith's *Birth of a Nation*, the National Association for the Advancement of Coloured People (NAACP), founded in 1910, organized picket lines outside the theatres to protest the blatant racism and tried to have the film banned. Agitating around the film provided an opportunity for the NAACP to organize and reinforce black consciousness. Of course, even negative publicity can be beneficial for sales. Partly in response to the vituperation Griffith experienced in 1915, his next project was a \$2 million, four-part film called *Intolerance*, in which he depicted religious freedom and targeted judicial injustice. It flopped at the box office, however, and did nothing to undercut the social damage caused by the popular *Birth of a Nation*.

African-American resistance to murder, segregation, discrimination, and systematic inequality took several forms. One tendency, represented by the boycott of *The Birth of a Nation*, was to work within the legal system to change the laws. A more radical approach was the movement for **black nationalism**. These tendencies can be illustrated by examining briefly the ideas of the most prominent African-American theorist and leader during the early years of the twentieth century, W.E.B. Du Bois (1868–1963).

W.E.B. DU BOIS

Booker T. Washington's most prominent opponent in the black community was the black intellectual, William Du Bois. In Du Bois's view, Washington had compromised with the establishment and was personally reaping the rewards of leading blacks away from the demand for equal political and social rights. Having been born into a middle-class black family in rural Massachusetts did not shelter Du Bois from the racism of his classmates. His consciousness about race began to change in 1903: 'It was in the early days of rollicking boyhood that the revelation first burst upon one, all in a day, as it were.' In his 'wee wooden schoolhouse' the children were exchanging 'gorgeous visiting cards—ten cents a package', when one girl 'refused my card . . . peremptorily, with a glance.' Suddenly aware of his absolute difference, of being 'shut out of their world by a vast veil', the 'shadow swept across me', Du Bois exclaimed. Returning contempt for contempt, rejection for rejection, his first response was to withdraw from their world. For much of his life, Du Bois sought to realize the principle of separate black social development, a form of biculturalism within 'one Nation'.[72]

Being rejected by his white classmates was especially galling because of his multiple talents and competitive spirit. Plunging into the heart of the black belt, Du Bois entered Fisk University in Nashville, Tennessee, in his 'young years of high idealism and infinite faith',[73] where he experienced first-hand the contradictions of the South. Fisk provided Du Bois with a black educational environment that was free of white domination and control, embedded, nevertheless, in the wider world of southern racism.[74] Following his graduation from Fisk, in 1895 Du Bois became the first African American to earn a Ph.D. from Harvard University. He broadened his intellectual horizons, studying for a time at the University of Berlin, where he was influenced by Max Weber.

Du Bois began an extensive sociological study of the black community in Pennsylvania and published *The Philadelphia Negro* in 1899. Recognizing the progressive cultural anthropology of Franz Boas, Du Bois situated the social problems besetting the black community in the culture of racism that was rooted in the history of slavery. Given his experience and research, Du Bois concluded that race was the essential division in American society: 'The problem of the twentieth century is the problem of the color line', he declared.[75]

The problem of race in the United States was complicated by the two meanings that the term 'race' evoked. In 1897, Du Bois believed there were physically only two, perhaps three races, 'great families of human beings'. In history and sociology, however, at least eight distinctly differentiated races and many minor race groups existed. Each shared, though not uniquely, a physical race (both the English and the Teutonic races, for example, were white), but were differentiated socially by 'a common history, common laws and religion, similar habits of thought and a conscious striving together for certain ideals of life'. In the United States, the many white races were successfully assimilating, melting into the common pot of a new nationalism. African Americans, 'not only by birth and by citizenship, but by our political ideals, our language, our religion', were also Americans. Further than that, Du Bois said, their Americanism did not go. They could not and should not be absorbed by white America. They were 'members of a vast historic race' that had much more to contribute to and much to teach other races.[76]

In his essay 'Strivings of the Negro People' (1897), Du Bois described the dilemma of this dualistic black consciousness:

> [T]he Negro is a sort of seventh son, born with a veil, and gifted with second-sight in this American world. . . . It is a peculiar sensation, this double-consciousness, this sense of always looking at one's self through the eyes of others, of measuring one's soul by the tape of a world that looks on in amused contempt and pity. One ever feels his two-ness—an American, a Negro; two souls, two thoughts, two unreconciled strivings; two warring ideals in one dark body, whose dogged strength alone keeps it from being torn asunder.[77]

Was an African American first and foremost an American, having to assimilate into white society and 'bleach his Negro soul in a flood of white Americanism'? Or should blacks identify with Africa and proudly proclaim their distinctive culture? Du Bois focused on race and racial pride, on being both an African American and an American. The racial dimension is fundamental and inescapable in Du Bois's social theory; human brotherhood is only possible on the basis of 'the unifying ideal of race'. Rather than obliterate the black race through assimilation, Du Bois envisaged two world races coexisting, each contributing its unique talents and abilities to the culture of the United States.[78]

The world had yet barely glimpsed the potential greatness of African-American culture buried beneath the prejudice of white society and reflected tragically in black self-deprecation. Du Bois acknowledged the pervasive social problems of black urban life, recognized the heritage of moral iniquity from the past and the degradation to which too many members of his race had sunk. The way out of this cultural wasteland was through race organization, solidarity, and unity— African-American colleges, businesses, newspapers, intellectuals, literature, and art. What is more, he proclaimed, 'Not only is all this necessary for positive advance, it is absolutely imperative for negative defence.'[79]

By proclaiming the need for and then actively helping to create the self-organization of African Americans, Du Bois openly challenged the timid assimilationist strategy of Booker T. Washington. In *Souls of Black Folks*, Du Bois analyzed the American colour line and criticized the failures of Washington's strategy of economic development. In the place of Washington's emphasis on slow, ameliorative, economic prosperity, which was ultimately based on the goodness of the white power structure, Du Bois advocated an attack on social segregation along with support for black economic self-sufficiency.

Du Bois agreed that industrial education was a crucial component of black self-advancement but thought Washington's program stood in the way of even more important components of African-American progress. It was based, first, on the conciliation of the South. Washington's compromise with conservative southerners, which proclaimed that each race could be as socially separate as two fingers, meant acquiescence in the face of social segregation, Jim Crow inequality, and the absence of civil rights. In an era when northern financiers invested heavily in southern plantations and sought racial peace without social change, Washington not only spoke the language of the white South, but out of the northern side of his mouth he voiced 'the speech and thought of triumphant commercialism, and the ideals of material prosperity'.[80]

Black Americans had made considerable economic progress since emancipation. By 1910, 25 per cent of black farmers owned their own land. African Americans held thousands of political offices, had opened several hundred private schools and colleges, and substantially increased their net worth. It was, overall, a 'creditable showing'.[81] Yet, even in an era of economic growth, African Americans had not harvested many of the promised material rewards of industrial education, nor, more importantly, had the social status of the race been raised. A distinct caste system had developed in the country, bringing with it discrimination against anyone with the slightest degree of African ancestry. Black Americans were victimized by the formal structures of the law as well as by an extralegal system that operated outside it.

Penitentiaries were filled with African Americans and, when the shell of legality was ignored, they were oppressed by illegal violence.[82] '[E]very step we have made forward has been greeted by a step backward on the part of the American public in caste intolerance, mob law, and racial hatred.'[83]

The focus on work and money advocated by Washington had overshadowed the higher things of life. From the point of view of African Americans, Du Bois claimed, Washington's program asked black people to give up political power, cease making demands for civil rights, and abandon higher education for black youths. It was impossible, however, to separate political and economic rights. Black workers were handicapped by their legal inequality in the face of white competition and blacks could not develop a sense of self-respect in the face of their legal inferiority. Over the previous 15 years, blacks had been disenfranchised; Jim Crow laws had created 'a distinct status of civil inferiority' for blacks, and investments for the higher education of blacks had been withdrawn. It is clear, Du Bois states, 'that the way for a people to gain their reasonable rights is not by voluntarily throwing them away and insisting that they do not want them; that the way for a people to gain respect is not by continually belittling and ridiculing themselves'; rather blacks must insist 'in season and out of season, that voting is necessary to modern manhood, that color discrimination is barbarism, and that black boys need education as much as white boys.'[84] The poet and novelist, Langston Hughes put it more simply (Box 12.5).[85]

Later, Du Bois realized that the idea of industrial education had failed because it could not keep pace with the rapid changes in industrial technique and in the relationship between capital and labour that had occurred. No longer could the condition of the black 'peasant and artisan' be ameliorated 'simply by learning a trade which is the technique of a passing era'.[86]

Black Nationalism and Socialism

Full of the knowledge of the history of race oppression, Du Bois experienced directly, again

Box 12.5

I wonder how it can be
That Greeks, Germans, Jews,
Italians, Mexicans,
And everybody but me
Down South can ride in the trains,
Streetcars and busses
Without any fusses.
But when I come along—
Pure American—
They got a sign up
For me to ride behind:
COLORED
My folks and my folks' folkses
And their folkses before
Have been here 300 years or more
Yet any foreigner from Polish to Dutch
Rides anywhere he wants to
And is not subject to such
Treatments as my fellow-men give me
In this Land of the Free.
Dixie, you ought to get wise
And be civilized!
And take down that COLORED sign
For Americans to ride behind.

—Langston Hughes, *Simple Speaks His Mind* (1943).
Reprinted by permission of Harold Ober
Associates Incorporated. Copyright © 1950 by
Langston Hughes

and again, the contempt of white people, when even poor white children—chained at an early age to race prejudice—jeered and stuck out their tongues at him. He saw on 'pale white faces' a 'deep and passionate hatred', men who appeared to be gentlemen but who would 'grow livid with anger because a little, silent black woman was sitting by herself' in a railway car. 'In Central Park I have seen the upper lip of a quiet, peaceful man curl back in a tigerish snarl of rage because black folk rode by in a motorcar.' In daily acts of humiliation, whites enforce the dictum: 'I am white and you are nothing', assuming 'that of all the hues of God, white alone is candy to the world child'.[87]

In a brief 1911 article in *The Crisis*, Du Bois poured out a bitter stream of scorn aroused by another act of white barbarism, this time in Coatesville, Pennsylvania, where a white mob had burned down the cabin of a black man accused of manslaughter. What he really was guilty of, Du Bois exclaimed, was the 'crime of crimes': blackness, and 'Blackness must be punished.'[88] As the conflagration raged, the man, a 'scorched and crooked thing, self-wounded and chained to his cot, crawled to the edge of the ash, with a stifled groan, but the brave and sturdy farmers pricked him back with the bloody pitchforks until the deed was done.' The next day, white sightseers toured the remains, 'poked the ashes', and shouted 'with glee' when they found a blackened tooth or some unrecognizable piece of bone. Du Bois concluded, angrily:

> But let every black American gird up his loins. The great day is coming. We have crawled and pleaded for justice and we have been cheerfully spit upon and murdered and burned. We will not endure it forever. If we are to die, in God's name let us perish like men and not like bales of hay.[89]

Du Bois's passionate writing and his explorations of the 'souls of white folks' brought charges that his racist attitude to whites was the equivalent of the white prejudice he denounced. Du Bois acknowledged his prejudices, explaining that they resulted from long experience. He had come to expect racist actions, thoughts, and treatments from the white majority, and usually found what he was looking for. Black hatred of whites was the fruit of white racism: 'no Negro born in America can be expected to be sweet-tempered, charitable, and broad-minded towards white people.'[90] Yet, Du Bois wrote in 1910, above the suffering, anger, and hurt 'surges in me a vast pity . . . for a people imprisoned and enthralled [by their racism], hampered and made miserable for such a cause, for such a fantasy.'[91] The black man tried to be broad-minded, Du Bois said, but 'If he fails, do not lay the fault entirely at his own door. Lay it to the last lynching, or to the last time he was insulted in the theater, or to the last time he went hungry because all available hotels and restaurants were closed against him.'[92]

Du Bois eschewed making an alliance with the white upper class and advocated, instead, creating a broad alliance of progressive people, both middle and working class. African-American workers had the most to gain and very little to lose. In 1905, Du Bois's social activism was directed to the founding of the Niagara Move-

ment, an African-American organization specifically created to demand civil rights, working in opposition to Washington's conciliatory politics. The wider movement for civil rights, however, was a cause that crossed race boundaries. The natural allies of the African-American movement for civil rights were anti-racist whites. Du Bois helped found the multiracial NAACP and then, in 1911, began editing *The Crisis*, a periodical dedicated to extending democratic rights to African Americans. From its founding, white liberals occupied prominent positions in the leadership of the NAACP, the organization that spearheaded the political and social struggles for black equality in the United States. Among African-American leaders who did not attend the initial conference, the most prominent was Booker T. Washington.

The effort to organize black Americans was made difficult by two divergent responses to the plight of their race that were rooted in their dualistic consciousness. They lived a 'double life, with double thoughts . . . double words and double ideals', which tempted African Americans to apparently opposite extremes: pretense and hypocrisy, or radicalism and revolt. In the North, Du Bois argued, the radical form of 'ethical striving' prevailed. When a black American migrates from the South into the great northern industrial cities, Du Bois said, 'he finds himself in a land where he can scarcely earn a decent living amid the harsh competition and the color discrimination.' At the same time, he has access to schooling and political organization, through which he 'is intellectually quickened and awakened'. In this consciousness of contrasts, the tendency is to excess, to embrace remote or impossible ideals that eventually breed disillusion and apathy. In the South, blacks defend themselves with 'the natural defence of the weak against the strong', with 'deception and flattery . . . cajoling and lying . . . overlain by submission and subserviency'.[93]

Du Bois continued to work with the NAACP until after World War II. The NAACP adopted several tactics in its struggle for political and social equality. It was at first dominated by white northerners—from the perspective of conservative white southerners, another example of the combination of southern blacks and interfering white northern liberals that had brought about emancipation and Reconstruction. Consistent with this relatively privileged leadership, the NAACP fought segregation through the US court system. Eventually, however, the leadership would adopt the tactics of civil disobedience and mass demonstrations, as in the civil rights movement of the 1950s and 1960s, led by a new generation of activists such as Martin Luther King Jr.

Du Bois recognized the plight of the poor whites, who were in some ways more disadvantaged than the emerging black middle class and were easily aroused to violence in defence of the colour line. Unlike Washington, whose solution was wedded to capitalism, Du Bois developed an early sympathy for some of the aims of the American socialist movement. In 1913 he claimed that African Americans were readying to extend their struggle beyond 'their own rights', to fight 'in the van of progress . . . for the ideals of the greater world in which they live', including 'the emancipation of women [and] . . . the socialization of wealth'.[94]

The essential dilemma that Du Bois had with American socialism was its blindness towards race discrimination. The socialist movement in the United States was an outgrowth of the labour movement. While most African Americans were labourers, they were excluded from the craft unions on racist grounds. No solidarity existed between white and black workers. Black workers were victims of the white proletariat's 'physical oppression, social ostracism, economic exclusion and personal hatred'.[95] White socialists were ignoring the issue of race in the opportunistic hope of forming an alliance with white southern radicals, for whom the colour bar was inviolable. To black Americans, the socialists dissimulated, claiming that racial problems would be solved later, after the objective of socialism was achieved. The socialists had adopted 'a kind of fatalistic attitude' that assumed socialism was 'coming by a kind of evolution in which active individual effort on their part is hardly necessary.'[96] On the contrary, Du Bois believed, the exclusion of the cause

of black Americans would result in a white industrial aristocracy that, although larger in numbers than any previous social elite, would leave African Americans as 'serfs'. For Du Bois, 'the test of any great movement towards social reform is the Excluded Class', the fate of those the program 'does not propose to benefit'.[97] By that measure, the socialist movement was a failure. The NAACP supported black capitalism, which could not be worse than the status quo and might be open to more democratic control.[98]

Over time, Du Bois became increasingly disillusioned with American capitalism and more radical. As early as 1900 he was actively working for the cause of **pan-Africanism**. He sympathized with the Russian Revolution and, in 1926, toured the USSR, an experience that appeared to show that the clearest path for human progress was socialism. After World War II, Du Bois focused his attention on the black liberation movements among the former colonies in Africa and, more directly, became active in the American peace movement and the Campaign for Nuclear Disarmament. During the Vietnam War, Du Bois abandoned his American citizenship in protest, moving to Ghana in Africa in 1961, where he became a citizen just before his death two years later.

CONCLUSION

Two perspectives in American sociology jostled for dominance at the turn of the twentieth century. Social Darwinism lost out in this competitive struggle to a reform-oriented sociology that branched out into social work and social psychology. The genetic approach gave way to environmentalism in sociology, although it shaped the significant American eugenics movement, which inspired racist legislation and was admired by Adolf Hitler. The two most original sociological thinkers were outsiders, the second-generation Norwegian, Thorstein Veblen, and the black sociologist, W.E.B. Du Bois.

Although he was trained as an economist, Veblen's critical writing did not cause a reorientation of American economic theory. Instead, his more lasting influence was in sociology. Veblen turned his critical eye and biting wit on the culture of capitalism rather than on the class struggle, on the superstructure rather than the productive base of society. Veblen's focus on patterns of consumption, lifestyles, and the meanings behind them provide a foundation for the mid-century critique of American society. Conspicuous consumption, planned obsolescence of style, and the establishment of standards of taste by mass advertising had by then come to define the culture of the great mass of the middle class. Veblen also perceived the increasing dominance of politics by business interests. From the White House to local politics, the business of government was ensuring the prosperity of private business. As competitive capital gave way to oligopolies, the need for federal economic regulation grew. Given the close connection between private interests and public officials, however, state regulation was directed at maximizing the interests of large American capital. In the process, the interests of the midwestern farmer, the industrial worker, and the mass consumer were superseded.

Veblen developed his theory as a critical outsider. In contrast, the other great sociological thinker of the time was a committed activist. Du Bois's sociological method meant immersing himself in the community he studied and working in their interest. He was a leader of the community he researched and his social theory emphasized the importance of the racial divide in American society. Sociologically, Du Bois analyzed the link between the structural conditions of the various social classes that made up the black community and their consciousness. Politically, Du Bois intervened to improve the social conditions of African Americans. Although economic self-sufficiency was the basis of improvement, Du Bois fought simultaneously for political and civil rights. The historical task of the black elite—the talented tenth, he called them—was to lead African Americans to cultural parity with whites, not assimilation.

There were four main political solutions to the race question in the United States. One of these was black nationalism. In its most literal form, this could be achieved by carving a black majority nation out of parts of several geographically connected states. Another suggestion was 'colonizing', moving African Americans to territory in the United States where few people lived. Even assuming that a black separate state could be set up in either of these two fashions, Booker T. Washington argued, it would prove impossible to maintain this geographical segregation. African Americans would seek opportunities in white-dominated territories and, if there was anything of value in the black nation, whites would enter in search of it.[99]

A second form of black separatism involved, as much as possible, separate black economic development. African Americans should own their own businesses, buy and sell to other blacks, and patronize services provided by blacks. This would encourage black pride and African-American culture, provide experience in management and business, and develop independence and self-assertion. As Du Bois became more explicitly socialist, he became less inclined towards separate development. Washington was opposed to separatism and did not endorse a commercial 'buy black' policy. Blacks should patronize the most successful and useful business, regardless of the race of the proprietor, the better to learn business skills.[100]

The third solution was repatriation, going back to Africa. There was a history of ex-slaves returning to the American-sponsored colony of Liberia, and the back-to-Africa movement, under the influence of Marcus Garvey, appeared to be a practical alternative in the 1920s. Du Bois's move to Ghana late in his life was as much an expression of internationalism as the return of a racial son. For Washington, 'The idea was chimerical.' There was no place in Africa, Washington believed, where the conditions of life of black people would be improved. Most of Africa was under European colonial domination and the orientation of the colonizers was to secure the land for themselves by expelling or killing Africans.[101]

The fourth possibility was integration, which appeared to be more possible through northern migration than by remaining in the South. Ironically, blacks escaping the South faced an equally overt form of racism and discrimination from northern whites afraid of the competition of cheap labour and based on their own deep prejudices. For Washington, migration north had proved disastrous for African Americans in the face of white discrimination, even from trade unions. African-American morals deteriorated under the impact of the freedom and temptations of the city, Washington warned, producing vicious habits, ill-health, and criminality. He campaigned to keep African Americans in the rural South where they could make the best living and where their services were of most value to the country. The African American should 'cast down his bucket where he is'.[102] Many did, finding their bucket still empty and the colour barrier difficult to cross. Many more carried their buckets to the southern cities, becoming an urban underclass or creating the nucleus of a small but significant black middle class. Northern migration was the solution that millions of blacks had voted for with their feet.

African Americans became part of the great, industrial proletariat in the newly built American industrial belt. It was not until the 1930s, however, with the rise of industrial unionism, that black workers would find a place in the house of organized labour, and not until the 1950s that a movement for civil rights would unite blacks in the American South.

One of the most significant elements dividing the black movement was the place of whites within it. Allowing white liberals rights of membership in largely African-American groups often meant conceding leadership positions to whites. Assimilation had to be part of the organizational means, not only the goal of the movement. Alternatively, black nationalists tended to prefer black-only organizations for fear that integrated groups would sacrifice the real interests of African Americans to the benefit of whites. Many of the same debates about strategic alternatives for change occurred in the women's movement that also developed in the late nineteenth century.

13

FIN DE SIÈCLE SOCIAL THOUGHT: FEMINISM, DECADENCE, AND PERSPECTIVISM

The idea of political and social equality for women emerged in Western history long before it could be publicly advocated and in advance of any popular movement with the potential to implement such a fundamental social change. The modern expression of the demand that the 'rights of man' be extended to all humanity arose during the era of revolutions, most vociferously during the French Revolution. Mary Wollstonecraft's vindication of the rights of women explicitly applied the principles of the bourgeois revolution to women.

In America, the idea of women's rights was revived in the 1830s and wrapped in the moral cause of abolitionism. Abolitionists who were women, such as Sojourner Truth and Sarah and Angelina Grimké, understood the close connection between the oppression of African Americans and the subjugation of women. Their practical experiences in the movement for black emancipation helped them organize for their own rights. Sarah Grimké argued before an anti-slavery convention that she was pleading not only for the cause of the slave, 'but the cause of a woman as a moral, responsible being'. Men and women were created to be equal and whatever is right for one sex must be right for the other.[1]

This sentiment was shared by few men, even those who fought for the rights of the enslaved. In 1840, at the first international convention of abolitionists, women delegated from the United States were refused official recognition and, instead, were shunted to the side galleries as observers. The experience so radicalized 24-year-old Elizabeth Cady Stanton, Olson notes, that she became active in the women's rights movement:[2] 'My

experience', she wrote, 'all I had read of the legal status of women, and the oppression I saw everywhere, together swept across my soul. . . . [M]y only thought was a public meeting for protest and discussion.'[3] In 1848, Stanton and Susan B. Anthony were the key organizers behind the initial Women's Rights Convention held in Seneca Falls, New York. The Convention passed a statement on women's rights modelled after the American Declaration of Independence. During the Civil War, however, most women were prepared to put their particular demands aside and work for an end to slavery and in support of the war effort.[4]

The interwoven struggles for black emancipation and women's rights became unravelled in the post-Civil War era. The fabric of interests was torn over the right to vote. Both the Fourteenth and the Fifteenth Amendments to the American Constitution endorsed the principle that any male citizen, regardless of race, may vote.

The question of extending the franchise to black men was so divisive that it exposed the major fault lines in the reform movements of the day. Feminists asked: but what about women? Sojourner Truth refused to abandon either cause, which she felt were her spiritual missions. If black men receive their rights and not black women, she protested, black men 'will be masters over the women, and it will be just as bad as it was before.'[5] Male abolitionists, including Frederick Douglass, argued that the correct tactic was to separate the two struggles. The majority sentiment was in favour of the black, male franchise, but did not endorse women's rights. It was better to allow the current amendments to pass and then take up the separate cause of women. This position justified the inaction of progressive men who took a pragmatic stand on the grounds that some good could be accomplished, and masked the entrenched opposition of other men who opposed women's rights on principle. As Olson points out, most black women supported the claims for their race, deferring to men and conceding, temporarily, the setback for their sex.[6] White women, however, perceived that their interests were being sacrificed, once again, for the benefit of men. For some, the correct strategy was to support the constitutional change while continuing to lobby for a further amendment to remove the male monopoly on voting rights. Feminists such as Anthony and Stanton, Olson notes, campaigned to defeat the extension of rights to black men only, thereby objectively joining forces with the conservatives, a standpoint she attributed to their class and racial biases.[7]

Despite these divisions, the cause of women's rights was not eclipsed, although it became for a time more exclusively a white, middle-class movement. Of equal importance, the women's movement promoted moral and social reform as much as political equality. At times these two aims merged; at other times single issues predominated. Even male-initiated movements of various kinds could be turned to the advocacy of women's rights. Historian Carol Smith-Rosenberg argues that while middle-class women did not oppose the American Medical Association's campaign to make abortion illegal, they used the campaign to highlight the problems of 'marital rape, unwanted pregnancies, [and] marriage as legal prostitution'. If women asserted sexual power in the home, they claimed, there would be fewer unwanted pregnancies and, hence, fewer abortions.[8]

Social reform movements of the first half of the nineteenth century were intimately connected to religion. Because woman's nature was held to be essentially chaste, moral, and domestic, 'true women' were the guardians of private and, potentially, of public virtue. In England, this argument had been used to justify extending women's salutary

influence to politics and economics. In America, middle-class women were drawn out of the home into civil society by the moral reform movements rooted in the social gospel and, later, by the demands of the Civil War. They cared for the wounded, helped soldiers' families, and prepared food for hospitals. After the war, the reform ethic persisted and many of these 'true women' continued their crusade to bring virtue into the corrupt and violent world of the industrial city that men had established.[9]

THE 'NEW WOMAN' OF THE 1890S

Those mid-Victorian 'true women' who took their moral causes into the street, the saloon, and the workshop necessarily also carried their concerns into politics. They demanded equal education for their daughters and encouraged their ambition to seek equal employment. These daughters of self-educated women took their personal and political politics well beyond the boundaries accepted by their mothers, opening a sometimes bitter generation gap. The 'New Woman' of the 1880s and 1890s was middle class, educated in the new women's or coed colleges, and defied social conventions by remaining unmarried, working in non-traditional careers, and demanding equal rights with middle-class men. Many of these New Women, Smith-Rosenberg asserts, 'were outspoken feminists, addressing issues of industrial, racial, and sexual justice at home and peace in the world.'[10] In hindsight, this period became known as 'first-wave feminism' to distinguish it from a second period of intense activity in the 1960s and 1970s.

In Britain and the United States, the question of the rights of women and their place in society— the 'woman question'—became a matter of heated public debate as women organized and became active in unprecedented numbers. While, for many British feminists, Queen Victoria was admired as a strong, powerful woman, she was not amused at the emergence of the independent New Woman, voicing her disapproval:

The Queen is most anxious to enlist everyone who can speak or write to join in checking this mad wicked folly of Women's Rights, with all its attendant horrors, on which her poor, feeble sex is bent, forgetting every sense of womanly feeling and propriety.[11]

The women's movement at the time had much wider social objectives than winning the franchise. The rise of militancy among working-class women opened new frontiers for the demands of women, but also divided feminists on class lines. Among the middle class, the debates in the 1890s were about women's sexuality, marriage and domesticity, employment equality, and social reform more generally. Terms such as 'feminist', 'socialist', and 'suffragette' appeared as women attempted to define their movement and debated the types of strategies to employ and the variety of aims to pursue.[12]

The arguments about the degradations of marriage and the domestic enslavement of women, Barbara Caine asserts, became central issues in the feminism of the 1890s. The sufferings women experienced in marriage were the subject of a wide range of literature written by both men and women.[13] Whitney Chadwick argues that Anna Sewell, in her popular novel *Black Beauty* (1877), essentially wrote a feminist tract deploring the cruel oppression of all creatures, not only animals but especially women and the working class.[14] At that time, she claims, few women explored the topic of female sexuality directly; instead, analogies displaced eroticism and allowed 'for expressions of feeling unencumbered by social constraints'.[15] Nevertheless, a radical section of the turn-of-the-century women's movement openly championed free love as an alternative to the confinements and oppressions of bourgeois marriage. This demand resurfaced during the 1920s and again as part of a widespread social movement in the 1960s.

At the centre of the Victorian debate was the image of the middle class 'New Woman'. In Britain as well as the United States, the New Woman experimented with new lifestyles in single-sex institutions, such as the new women's colleges and the settlement houses. They relied on their 'sisters' for emotional support, and they worked together in a great variety of reform movements that did much to shape the Progressive movement in America and the labour movement and reform socialism in Britain.[16] Above all, perhaps, they refused to surrender their personal autonomy by re-entering the domesticity of a bourgeois marriage. In the words of the Norwegian playwright Henrik Ibsen, they refused to be dolls in a doll's house. In the 1890s, Ibsen inflamed the debate about the equality of women in the domestic sphere through his controversial play, *A Doll's House*.

HENRIK IBSEN

Dr Stockman: Rubbish, Catherine! You go home now and take care of the house, and let me take care of society.
—Henrik Ibsen, *Enemy of the People* (1882)

Dr Stockman's traditionalist outburst should not be taken to reflect Ibsen's stand on women's independence. Although Ibsen did not directly advocate women's liberation, his plays *A Doll's House* and *Hedda Gabler* were widely interpreted in the 1890s as advocating the emancipation of women.

According to Fjelde,[17] Ibsen's naturalistic plays reflect 'the social lies and corruptions of the time', making him a Scandinavian Émile Zola.[18] In the era of Darwin, Ibsen said, the presumed stability of the social order had been undermined and humankind had 'gone astray'.[19] In *The Pillars of Society* (1877), Ibsen revealed a backstage of crooked business deals hidden behind public respectability. The corruption of these businessmen (who present themselves as social pillars) was exposed by two characters who were, in contrast, socially disrespectable. Yet, this despised minority represented the real pillars of society—those who acted honestly and with the courage of their convictions. For Ibsen, real heroes were individualists, like himself. They were outsiders from the mainstream who would not give in to the tyranny of a petty, public opinion even at great personal cost and sacrifice.

Ibsen's great play, *A Doll's House*, which was so controversial when it first opened in 1878, heralded a turn in drama towards psychological introspection, a burrowing into the intricacies of intimate relationships. In the view of the English playwright, George Bernard Shaw, *A Doll's House* marked the end of a chapter in human history and the dawning of feminism.[20] The intricate relationship between the heroine, Nora, and her husband, Torvald Helmar, examines the 'modern middle-class conception of marriage' and the 'respective definitions that society allows of a man and a woman'. What was most essential in Torvald's life was his public success and honour. 'No man gives up honor for love', he told his wife. For Nora, on the contrary, the truth of her private feelings is essential, because millions of women have given up honour for love.[21]

A Doll's House was inspired by the real-life tragedy of Laura Kieler, a woman Ibsen knew. Kieler's husband was suffering from a serious illness, for which his doctor prescribed a vacation in Southern Europe, but this was beyond their means. When Laura's husband would not agree to a loan, she borrowed the money from a bank, having it co-signed by a male friend (since women could not transact business), and convinced her husband it was an inheritance. When Laura was unable to make the payments, she forged a bond and was discovered. Because Laura's frantic act had undermined her husband's respectability, he disowned her and Laura had a nervous breakdown; he then committed her to an asylum and divorced her.

A Doll's House follows the story of this unhappy marriage through the characters of Nora and Torvald, a prominent and respectable banker. In the beginning of the play, Nora is treated by Torvald—and sees herself—as a doll, or squirrel-like, anything but an independent human being. For the sake of her ill husband, Nora forges her father's signature in order to obtain a bank loan for the needed trip. When Torvald learns, privately, of his wife's rash act, he hopes to bury the truth, to do anything to preserve the appearance of his public respectability. Torvald does not threaten to disown or divorce Nora because that, too, would be a public disgrace; rather, Nora may continue living in his house (though he would remove the children from her evil influence), but this would be merely to 'save the appearances' of respectability. He says the two will live an empty, hollow, loveless life of hypocrisy. Through eight years of a typical marriage, husband and wife have never had a serious conversation in which each had expressed an independent point of view. When the crisis comes, it is too late to undo the damage. Her husband had never understood her, Nora explains.[22]

Nora realizes that Torvald is willing to sacrifice everything to bow to the tyranny of public opinion. She could simply accept her fate, live under the shelter of Torvald's position, disillusioned perhaps, but going through the motions of marriage for the sake of her children, for her own material comfort, and for the 'honour of her husband'—as a Victorian wife would be expected to do. Ibsen, however, brings the story to a conclusion that shocked his audience. Nora has gradually acquired 'distinctively human attributes' and becomes 'a new-born human self'. In the end, resolved to leave Torvald, Nora announces: 'We're closing our accounts.' For her scandalized Victorian audience, she was wilfully abandoning her sacred duties.

Torvald is beside himself. As Karl Mannheim pointed out, Torvald attempts every means to interpret Nora's behaviour within the frame of reference of the typical marriage.[23] He disparages Nora, calling her 'insane' and 'incompetent', thereby revealing his disrespect for her independent mind. She has 'no right' to walk out, he asserts. Worried about 'what people will say', he turns to religion and morality, claiming that her vows as a wife and mother are 'sacred'. Nora replies: 'I have other duties equally sacred. . . . Duties to myself. . . . [B]efore all else, I'm a human being, no less than you—or anyway, I ought to try to become one.' She leaves, heading towards an uncertain future. As the door slams shut on her life with Torvald, we know she is not coming back.

With this assertion of female independence, Ibsen was understood to have made a bold statement in favour of women's liberation. Nora's assertion of her duties to herself, however, also reflected one of the common criticisms of the New Woman: she was guilty of selfish and immoral behaviour. The irony of this denunciation was not lost on feminists who knew which gender habitually indulged in self-centred and amoral actions. But this ideology was part of a turn-of-the-century backlash that was rooted in the new 'science' of 'sexology'. The sexologists were obsessed with describing and classifying the variety of sexual 'perversions' found in human societies. They defined as pathological the New Woman's rejections of motherhood and relations with men, as well as her close personal relationships with other women, which were sometimes overtly sexual. The New Woman, the sexologists asserted, was necessarily a lesbian; hence she was unnatural and either evil or sick.[24] For the first generation of New Women, sexual relations with men were best avoided. They had their hands full reforming the world that men had created so badly. One of these women was Jane Addams, who, Deegan claims, was the most important woman sociologist of her generation.[25]

JANE ADDAMS

[A]ction is indeed the sole medium of expression for ethics.
—Jane Addams, *Democracy and Social Ethics* (1907)

Born in Illinois in 1860, Addams's mother died when she was a baby. She grew to have deep veneration for her father, John Addams. He was a Quaker, committed to a deeply personal, compassionate, and moral belief system that he instilled in his daughter. His primary lessons were modesty and 'mental integrity', to be true to oneself. One Sunday morning Addams's father had admonished her for wanting to wear her gorgeous new cloak, which was better than any coat the other girls owned. In his view, since the inequality represented by clothing might never be righted, 'it was very stupid to wear the sort of clothes that made it harder to have equality even there.'[26]

John Addams was a small businessman who owned several mills and served in the Illinois Senate. On his death it was said that his reputation was so untarnished he was the only senator who had never been *offered* a bribe. His politics were patriotic and international. He admired Abraham Lincoln and the Italian revolutionary, Giuseppe Mazzini, both of whom, he said, fought oppression in their homelands.[27]

At 17, Addams enrolled in the women's seminary at Rockford. She complained about the missionary atmosphere and the 'dull obtuseness' of the boarding school.[28] To escape this 'humdrum' existence, during one long holiday she and four other young women ingested small quantities of opium to appreciate more sympathetically de Quincy's *Confessions of an English Opium Eater* (1822). Despite this experiment, Addams wrote, 'no mental reorientation took place.'[29]

Typical of a New Woman, Addams sought to realize her personal vision of Christianity in social service rather than through the church. She spent the winter after graduating from Rockford attending the Women's Medical College of Philadelphia. During these years, Addams reflects, she was 'enormously interested in the Positivists'. She believed 'that somewhere in Church or State are a body of authoritative people who will put things to rights as soon as they really know what is wrong.'[30]

Serious bouts of ill health forced Addams to leave the Medical College after one semester, and she spent the next years footloose, travelling twice to Europe. Deegan says she was torn by the competing demands of a sick stepmother, a pursuing suitor, and the desire for a career.[31] After witnessing the 'bitter poverty' of the European slums, especially in East End London, Addams experienced the mental reorientation she had been seeking.[32] She began to question her education and commitment. She may have 'dreamed of self-sacrifice, of succor to the helpless and of tenderness to the unfortunate', but the code of ethics she had been taught emphasized the obligations she owed to her family and not the duty women had to the wider society.[33] Generations of women before them had led active and emotional lives. By being educated more formally, the new generation of women had become overly contemplative. They 'had lost that simple and almost automatic' tendency to action in order to bring relief to the suffering and helplessness. She was overwhelmed 'with a sense of her uselessness'.[34]

The belief that young women should become active in the world rather than fulfill traditional family expectations opened a yawning generation gap between parents and their grown-up daughters. Parents didn't perceive their daughters' desire as 'genuine and dignified'. The ambitious daughter, the parents said, was opposing her will to that of her family 'for selfish . . . willful and self-indulgent' ends.[35] Unlike a son, who was expected to make his way independently in the world, a daughter was regarded 'as a family possession'. Her finishing-school training had made her a symbol 'of her father's protection and prosperity'. The new educational ideas, however, no longer fit this mould. Women's educational experiences had developed their individuality, freed their powers of independent action, and imposed an obligation to become citizens of the world.[36] For most young women, however, the immediate and strong claims of their families overcame the unfocused demands of society. The daughter submitted to her filial duty, though often her 'heart' was 'consumed by vain regrets and desires'. The contradiction lowered her vitality and affected her health. In a final irony, the physician prescribed rest when, 'What she needs is simple, health-giving activity', which involves 'all her faculties'.[37]

There were two contradictory paths, Addams says: 'Breaking the marriage ties as Ibsen's "Nora" did, to obtain a larger self-development, or holding to it as George Eliot's "Romola" did, because of the larger claim of the state and society'. Each of these interests had a sound moral basis and a right to its place in life. Addams was clearly not advocating the weakening (and certainly not the destruction) of the middle-class family, nor the self-assertion of the individual will. Both the

family and the state were 'the highest institutions which the race has evolved'. But both must be reconstructed. Parents must come to feel equally the democratic impulse of the wider social claim. Even the family 'is susceptible of progress' and must become engaged in the community and its social movements.[38]

In the English settlement house, Addams found the institutional model for this family-like engagement. A settlement was a residential and social service centre built in the heart of a poor neighbourhood that brought middle-class reformers committed to social action into the lives of the dispossessed. In Addams's conception, a settlement house would unite young women who needed to learn 'of life from life itself'. Young people who had led 'unnourished, oversensitive lives' would be able to restore the balance 'between their theory and their lives', their 'thought and action'.[39]

In 1889, Addams and Ellen Gates Starr founded Hull-House in Chicago. While it was modelled after Toynbee Hall in East End London, Hull-House was more female-centred, egalitarian, and secular.[40] Within the sheltered subculture of the communal settlement house, women could form mutual lifelong emotional and sensual relations. For 40 years Addams shared her life with Mary Rozet Smith.[41] The House provided a secure physical and emotional foundation for women to become active in social reform as a full-time career.

According to Addams, the settlement movement represented 'the desire to interpret democracy in social terms'. It was also part of a wider humanitarian impulse that attempted to proclaim Christ's message in the life of society itself. The New Testament taught that 'the faith of the fisherman and the slave' had been opposed to the accepted belief that a privileged few might build their well-being on the backs of many. Without universal Christian fellowship, the world would 'slip back into the doctrines of selection and aristocracy'. In the modern, industrial city, the settlement attempted to overcome the overaccumulation of social and educational advantages 'at one end of society and the destitution at the other'.[42]

The women in the settlement house under-took a social mission of education and reform. They helped immigrants assimilate into American culture by offering classes in citizenship, teaching the principles of American institutions, and help-ing bridge the widening gulf between first-gener-ation Europeans and their children. Like its English model, Hull-House was situated in the heart of the large and isolated 'foreign colonies' in Chicago. In a neighbourhood surrounded by more than a dozen ethnic groups, Addams found Ital-ians and Jews at the bottom of the sweatshop labour pool. 'An unscrupulous contractor', she wrote, 'regards no basement as too dark, no stable loft too foul, no rear shanty too provisional, no tenement room too small for his workroom.'[43]

It was inevitable that Hull-House would be drawn into labour reform. The present industrial system, Addams said, prevented the realization of social righteousness as well as social order. Addams became the vice-president of the Women's Trade Union League. Women from Hull-House co-oper-ated with trade unions to investigate industrial conditions and made reform recommendations that were incorporated in the first Illinois Factory Act. They investigated the growing problem of unem-ployment and helped establish labour bureaus.[44] Hull-House women were active in combatting the wretched and inadequate housing of the tenements and prohibiting the sale of cocaine to children. They investigated saloons and infant mortality. They opposed corrupt politicians who handed out jobs and favours as personal patronage. They under-stood that problems such as delinquent youth, property crime, and prostitution had social causes.

Hull-House looked to the state for assistance in alleviating these distressing conditions, but also sought to organize community groups to seek self-help through organization and by raising 'moral sensibility'. Hull-House operated a kitchen, a kindergarten, and an evening school and included programming in the arts. At times, Addams wrote, their stage served as a *'theatre libre'*. She made it available to a Chicago troupe to present the con-troversial drama of Ibsen as well as old French comedies by Molière.[45]

Hull-House, and Addams in particular, quickly became controversial. The 1890s were a volatile period in the political and social life of Chicago. Hull-House operated in an atmosphere of intense, partisan propaganda, a time of march-ing under unfurled banners in support of social change. Beginning in 1890, the Working People's Social Science Club held weekly meetings at the House, though Addams thought they focused too much on abstract principles rather than concrete actions. During his lecture tour of the United States the Russian anarchist, Peter Kropotkin, stayed and spoke at Hull-House. When President McKinley was assassinated by a self-styled anar-chist in 1901, the anarchist community in Chicago was subject to severe repression. Addams and Hull-House intervened to ensure that arrested anarchists were treated fairly under the law, bring-ing opprobrium down on the settlement house and solidifying its left-wing reputation.[46]

During this decade, Addams wrote, Chicago seemed divided into two classes: those who held that 'business is business' and eschewed any notion of social reform, and the radicals who claimed that no reform of the industrial situation would succeed until society as a whole was reor-ganized. Her desire was to build a bridge between these two poles. The employers and the 'favored class' were willing to go only so far to implement what Addams called 'social righteous-ness'. They were 'frightened by democracy' and drew the line at factory legislation that would impose shorter hours and regulate wages.[47] The distrust of the practical man of affairs for the enthusiastic radicals was justified in part, Addams believed, because too often the reformer is in rebellion against the social constraints that limit his individual desires rather than opposing the 'general defects of the system'. The business-man, however, then holds the moral failings of these rebels up to the world as a warning against all 'those who refuse to worship "the god of things as they are"'.[48]

Given her critical attitudes, Addams wrote, it is not surprising that the socialists were con-stantly trying to recruit her. She was disenchanted, however, by their insistence that everyone must accept a single creed. From its very nature, she argued, Hull-House 'can stand for no social or political propaganda. It must . . . [never] lose its flexibility.'[49] Even religious instruction was not given at the House. Addams defined her politics as democratic. More than a sentiment that asserts 'the essential dignity and equality of all', democracy for Addams was a moral rather than an intellectual ideal, and it was rooted in the identification with common people.[50]

In her view, she was a pragmatist. It was impractical and wrong to await justice in the millennium, but it was equally impossible to achieve justice 'by the strong arm of a hero'. Reform was, in large measure, personal and moral, achieved one person at a time. Justice came through the development of broad 'sympathies toward the individual man or woman who crosses our path; one item added to another is the only method by which to build up a conception lofty enough to be of use in the world.' Only a moral appeal, she believed, was universal.[51]

This orientation drew Addams to Tolstoyism. The great Russian novelist, Leo Tolstoy, had decided to live not only among the poor and share what he had with the needy, but to share equally in their hardships. In 1896, Addams visited Tolstoy and his family in their simple cottage in rural Russia. To her consternation, Tolstoy tugged at the long sleeves of her travelling gown, telling her that there was enough cloth in one sleeve to make a dress for a young girl. Didn't she find such a dress 'a "barrier to the people"'? She felt admonished as once she had been by her father when she had wanted to wear a cloak that was better than any other child's. On reflection, Addams found Tolstoy's message 'confused and contradictory'. She admired his 'ability to lift his life to the level of his conscience, to translate his theories into action'. But Tolstoyism was not a model that could be applied widely to the problems of an industrial society. She also found Tolstoy dogmatic. He used his powerful personality to compel people to surrender to his vision rather than exploring their differences.[52]

For Addams, in addition to individual moral reform, it was necessary to carry social action to the level of civic, state, and national politics. The old individualistic ethic of the self-made man, which had been advocated so singularly and proudly by Walt Whitman, who reflected the 'over-developed will of the solitary New Englander', was giving way to a new need for association.[53] The very existence of the nation and the state, Addams argued, depended on the character of its citizens. But industrial conditions operating on their own were forcing workers below the standard of decency. Only state regulation could impose the necessary remedies.[54]

Neither employers nor workers expressed the full interests of society, Addams argued. Consistent with her consensus politics, she believed that two moralities were in conflict. Just as the rights of the family must not be sacrificed to the assertion of individual or social demands, businessmen, philanthropists, and labourers were 'all honest and upright'. Their proposed solutions to social problems reflected their background. The self-made businessman encouraged the poor to work harder; the middle-class charity worker sought to help the few individuals who crossed her path; the workingman saw the problem in class terms.[55] None expressed the full interests of society. Addams wished to find a means of dispute resolution that 'could find quiet and orderly expression in legislative enactment'. The practical and democratic solution, she believed, was a system of arbitration to resolve disputes peaceably and within the bounds of law and order. In her view, if labour disagreements could be submitted to a body representing the interests of society as a whole, division and warfare could be avoided and 'we should have the ideal development of the democratic state.'[56]

Addams's Sociology

Addams's understanding of her society was, at first, implicitly sociological. Her background in the social gospel movement was similar to that of many Progressive reformers and early sociologists.

She was generally opposed to the social Darwinism of Herbert Spencer, though she found the Darwinian idea of evolution, 'thirty years after its publication', still 'had about it a touch of intellectual adventure.' The great variety of points of view reflected in the discussions at Hull-House, Addams suggested, reflected 'the fact that the then new science of sociology had not yet defined its own field.'[57] When the first American department of sociology was founded at the University of Chicago in 1892, Addams developed a symbiotic relationship with the eager, young scholars, such as G.H. Mead and John Dewey, who flocked to Chicago.[58] The methods of first-hand social investigation among the disadvantaged used at Hull-House were sociological and helped shape the way the discipline was conceptualized at the University of Chicago. For Addams, a social perspective comes 'only from contact with social experience'. Like scientific data, 'such contact is the surest corrective of opinions concerning the social order, and concerning efforts . . . for its improvement.'[59] Addams's sociological orientation may be illustrated by her understanding of the Devil-Baby phenomenon at Hull-House (Box 13.1).[60]

The data Addams derived from her direct social experiences challenged the class assumptions of 'the industrial view of life' according to which hard work and self-denial would result in a comfortable and wealthy old age. Her understanding of the point of view of the urban poor came from seeing their world through their eyes. Self-righteous reformers complained that poor men drink, but the unemployed man remembered the help and comradeship he received in the saloons. Poor families sacrificed food in order to pay proper respect to their dead. Young working girls were obliged to spend disproportionate sums of money on decent clothes, which represented their status to the world at large and assisted their social advancement. Addams realized that the struggle for existence, 'which is so much harsher among people near the edge of pauperism, sometimes leaves ugly marks on character'.[61] The poor spend more on 'pleasures and indulging their children out of all proportion to their means'. Some poor people who received charity in the

---

Box 13.1

One day in 1916 at Hull-House, 'three Italian women, with an excited rush through the door, demanded that he [the Devil-Baby] be shown to them.' They had heard a rumour that a woman had given birth to a Devil, which had been taken to Hull-House. They had spoken to others who had seen it. 'No amount of denial convinced them that he was not there, for they knew exactly what he was like, with his cloven hoofs, his pointed ears and diminutive tail; moreover, the Devil-Baby had been able to speak as soon as he was born and was most shockingly profane.' For six weeks, a multitude of people paraded to Hull-House to see the non-existing Devil-Baby. To explain this urban legend phenomenon, Addams did not resort to a psychology of the crowd or of panics. By speaking with the aged and distressed women who came to see the apparition and hearing their explanations for the event, Addams realized that the myth was a metaphor that condemned morally blameworthy men and served 'as a valuable instrument in the business of living'. The Devil-Baby represented a supernatural punishment for domestic sin that was used to tame recalcitrant husbands and fathers. Through such myths women opposed brutality with the 'charm of words', hoping to control their husbands' sexual urges, condemn their profanity, and humble their pride.

—Jane Addams, 'The Devil Baby at Hull-House' (1916)

form of daily necessities also paid 'for a bicycle on the installment plan'. But these expenditures, which seemed irrational by the standards of middle-class charity, reflected the visible world the poor experienced daily and tried to emulate.[62]

The urban industrial environment, however, also provided the means and the motivation for much social mischief. Faced with the dull monotony of factory work, demoralized youth escaped their misery by indulging in the 'petty immoralities' that were stimulated by cheap commercial amusements.[63] Young people, Addams said, feel an instinctive desire for adventure and are highly susceptible to dangerous diversions. The variety of 'coarse and illicit merrymakings' overstimulate their senses; they confuse 'joy with lust, and gaiety with debauchery'. Thousands of young people in every American city had become 'frankly hedonistic'. Addams particularly condemned the five-cent theatres that attracted the young with lurid stories of violence and revenge, filling their minds with absurdities that shaped their moral codes.[64]

Addams's condemnation of the popular culture that was sold to the masses would become a staple of reform rhetoric in the twentieth century. She was optimistic, however, that society could establish moral control over the use of leisure.[65] Municipal parks and recreation facilities, as well as community-based clubs, could raise the cultural standards and, through them, the morality of the people. Nevertheless, Addams did not judge all reform efforts by a middle-class measuring rod. Too often, she complained, when middle-class charity workers first encountered the depredations of life among the poor, they imposed ethical standards from their social world onto the other. Their middle-class preconceptions assumed that the poor chose to act improperly out of ignorance or sinfulness. Charity workers demanded impossible virtues such as temperance, cleanliness, thrift, and religious observance.[66] They failed to appreciate the moral goodness of the poor or understand the choices they were forced to make. Poor people, Addams found, dealt with each other directly and frankly, willingly helping out to their limited abilities. The poor were rightly suspicious

of the charity worker who seemed concerned with imposing the ethical standards of those who did not have to do work with their hands. Financial relief was given with delay and caution, in a calculated manner. The needy, Addams said, 'cannot comprehend why a person whose intellectual perceptions are stronger than his natural impulses, should go into charity work at all. The only man they are accustomed to see whose intellectual perceptions are stronger than his tendencies of heart, is the selfish and avaricious man who is frankly "on the make."'[67]

If her concern is genuine, Addams says, the charity worker eventually discovers 'how incorrigibly bourgeois her standards have been'. The conventions of her class 'fail to fit the bigger, more emotional, and freer lives of working people.' Reformers must constantly correct their work by appreciating the daily experiences of ordinary people and incorporating that experience with their own. Real leaders are part of the life of their community and give 'a social expression to democracy'.[68]

Through her action-oriented sociology, Addams came to appreciate 'the extraordinary pliability of human nature'. There seemed to be no limit to the 'moral capabilities which might unfold under ideal civic and educational conditions'.[69] Many things have to change before this may come to pass. Both the radical and the conservative must co-operate in implementing democracy in all its manifestations. Ambitious plans and experiments are prone to fail. Slow, sane, strenuous progress achieves what is feasible, the best that is possible.[70]

The first two decades at Hull-House were marked by great achievements. Thereafter the reform efforts of the settlement were constrained, first, by World War I. Addams's pacifist views, which she refused to abandon and were expressed in the Woman's Peace Party, led to her social and personal ostracism following America's entry into World War I. In the reactionary political atmosphere that followed the war and the Russian Revolution, Deegan asserts, the US government labelled Addams 'the most dangerous women in America'. She continued her work in the American and women's international peace movements in the 1920s, having a salutary effect on American foreign policy.[71] In the Great Depression of the 1930s, Addams was rehabilitated, becoming active in the New Deal that brought concrete reforms to American capitalism. Her international reputation was cemented four years before her death when she was awarded the Nobel Peace Prize in 1931.[72] Even so, her important contributions to sociology were not recognized until second-wave feminists in the 1960s began to search their genealogy.

FIRST-WAVE FEMINISM

Jane Addams was a suffragist and an officer of the National American Woman Suffrage Association. She would have celebrated, along with her sisters, the achievement of the franchise for women in the United States in 1920.[73] As the foregoing illustrates, however, the women's movement was much deeper and broader than attention to this single issue suggests. The feminist movement was not all of a piece. Women's oppressions were many and various: exclusion from formal politics; denial of rights of property as married women that affected them economically; legal restraints that made divorce difficult; social regulation of their sexuality; and the perpetuation of patriarchal control in the household. Various branches of the women's movement fought against all or only some of these injustices.

Arguably, however, a great deal of the organizing energy of first-wave feminism focused political activity on the single issue of the vote. Many of the most militant feminists put their bodies on the line for this central cause. Among the enduring images of the movement are women chaining themselves to the iron fence outside Parliament, refusing to eat when imprisoned, holding mass rallies, suffering ridicule and ostracism, and deliberately breaking windows and vandalizing property. Intense debates on tactics and ends divided the emancipation movement. Should women campaign in a socially acceptable, genteel manner or be more demonstrative? Should they resist

passively or violently? What was the place of men in the women's movement? The wrongs done to women were not the only oppressions in society. What role should the demands of women play in other social movements for social rights, such as trade unions or socialist politics? Even the political aspirations of first-wave feminists at the turn of the twentieth century reflected a number of different political perspectives, including liberalism, socialism, anarchism, and familialism.

The majority of women who were active in the cause of women's rights acted within the dominant, liberal conception of social life. Then, as now, most women who became active sought reforms within the existing social system. The liberal tradition may be represented by the ideas of Harriet Taylor and John Stuart Mill, who advocated women's political emancipation. Like Wollstonecraft, they extolled women's virtues and argued that they were not the intellectual inferiors of men. For Taylor and Mill, women were to be given full, democratic rights, including the right to divorce and to own property in their own right. Taylor had gone further and demanded equality in employment, an issue that 'New Women' had begun to actualize but was still on the feminist agenda in the 1930s, as Olive Schreiner shows:

> *We take all labour for our province!*
> From the judge's seat to the legislator's chair; from the statesman's closet to the merchant's office; from the chemist's laboratory to the astronomer's tower, there is no post or form of toil for which it is not our intention to attempt to fit ourselves; and there is no closed door we do not intend to force open; and there is not fruit in the garden of knowledge it is not our determination to eat.[74]

The militant tradition of female protest in Britain was revived by feminists such as Emmeline Pankhurst, who organized the Women's Social and Political Union in 1903. Pankhurst distinguished herself by her willingness to defy the law in acts of civil disobedience and, even further, to deliberately damage property. The rights of property, she declared, were more respected in England than the rights of women. Arrested on many occasions, Pankhurst refused to eat and repeatedly had to be released. These tactics were imported into the American women's movement and provided a new feminist spark. After three generations of struggle, women won the vote in England, the United States, and Canada. Women over the age of 30 succeeded in winning the vote in Britain in 1917.

Being able to vote and run for national public office were seen as the first and most necessary steps in bringing about the legal reform of other institutions. Women would use their new political power to bring about a higher moral standard for society. They would have laws passed banning such pernicious causes of social troubles as alcohol, prostitution, and gambling. They fought for these and other causes alongside the battle to be recognized as citizens. In 1917, the year of initial enfranchisement in Britain, the first birth control clinic was established in London.[75]

Despite these successes, radical women claimed that narrowly focusing on reforms and single issues left the deeper structures of capitalist domination and patriarchal conventions untouched. Among these was sexuality. The next generation of New Women, who came into predominance in the early decades of the twentieth century, would flaunt their sexuality openly, especially their heterosexuality. Their social and sexual rebellion reflected the Bohemian lifestyles of a flamboyant and deliberately ostentatious generation of artistic rebels that had arisen in Europe towards the end of the nineteenth century.

FIN DE SIÈCLE DECADENCE

> If man is made
> For pleasure, let him take his fill.
> —Henrik Ibsen, *Peer Gynt* (1867)

For many late nineteenth-century men, represented by Ibsen's character, Peer Gynt, the risk of public condemnation was worth the unbridled pursuit of pleasure. Parallel to social Darwinism, an elitist, decadent culture flourished in the arts

towards the end of the nineteenth century. It was profoundly influenced by the pessimism that appeared to derive from Darwin and the theory of evolution by natural selection. Among the naturalists, such as Zola and Dreiser, the novel represented, at least in part, a potential weapon in the struggle for reform. A much more drastic direction was being taken by intellectuals who rejected the belief that art should have any social purpose at all. Increasingly in **modern art** and literature, artists abandoned the attempt to depict the real in favour of more abstract art forms. It was a movement that was parallel to the development of Romanticism earlier in the century, which had been a reaction against the view of the Age of Reason that art was to instruct. In particular, by the late nineteenth century, there was a return to irrationalism and a new anti-scientific ideology that was particularly repulsed by the idea of a social science.

As Russian novelist Fyodor Dostoyevsky believed, any social science must run aground on the essential facts of human free will, imagination, and individuality. Dostoyevsky warned that science tried to teach man:

> that he never has really had any caprice or will of his own, and that he himself is something of the nature of a piano-key or the stop of an organ, and . . . that everything he does is not done by his willing it, but is done of itself, by the laws of nature. Consequently we have only to discover these laws . . . and man will no longer have to answer for his actions. . . . All human actions will then, of course, be tabulated . . . mathematically, like tables of logarithms . . . in which everything will be so clearly calculated and explained that there will be no more . . . adventures in the world.

But, Dostoyevsky asserted, people do not always act in a rational way to meet their interests:

> What is to be done with the millions of facts that bear witness that men, *consciously*, that is, fully understanding their real interests, have left them in the background and have

rushed headlong on another path, to meet peril and danger, compelled to this course by nobody, and nothing, but, as it were, simply disliking the beaten track, and have obstinately, wilfully, struck out another difficult, absurd way . . . in opposition to the laws of reason, in opposition to his own [material] advantage—in fact, in opposition to everything. [This apparently unreasonable action] shatters every system . . . explaining to mankind their real normal interests.[76]

Shakespeare's Hamlet had made a similar complaint that Guildenstern was trying to play upon him like a flute: 'you would seem to know my stops . . . do you think I am easier to be played on than a pipe?'[77]

Those who abandoned any purpose other than portraying their own subjectivity generally regarded the rejection of reason as part of a more profound social rebellion of the individual against the constraints of society and social convention. Both tendencies were apparent in the development of symbolic art, leading in the twentieth century to surrealism—realistic-style paintings of unrealistic things. This concern with symbols was common to painting and literature, and was associated with a new interest in the psychological, with the mysteries of thought processes. The influence of Freud and the various schools of psychoanalysis were very important in shaping this direction for twentieth-century art and literature.

The new, modern mood was captured in the phrase '*fin de siècle*', which became commonplace in France in the 1890s. Henri Ellenberger argues that the new spirit reflected, initially, a belief that the decadence of aristocratic nineteenth-century civilization replicated the moral decline that had caused the fall of the Roman Empire. The notion that the course of history was following a cycle of degeneration rather than progress reversed Victorian optimism. The reverse image of degeneration was reflected in nineteenth-century psychology, in the belief that people who acted in evil or criminal ways were products of their bad biology— genetic reversion to primitive types of humanity.

The fear of degeneration fuelled the racist doctrine that miscegenation would 'mongrelize' the putatively superior European race. Although the *fin de siècle* mood centred in Paris and Vienna was pessimistic, it was also mystical and erotic. The modern Romantics of the age no longer communed with nature but felt at home in the new urban sprawl and in the search for illicit pleasures in the nighttime world of desire, disorder, and danger.[78]

'Modern' is a slippery concept. As a new age arises to evaluate the existing one, it presents itself as modern relative to the old but, in the sequence of change, what was once modern soon becomes passé. For the early generation of sociologists, 'modern' depicted the world of industrialism that had, over the last three centuries, definitively replaced agricultural society in the West. The modern was coextensive with rationalism, limited democracy, and capitalist enterprise. Not all social theorists celebrated the birth of the modern world. While both outright reactionaries and some Romantic idealists sought to overturn the present in favour of the past, most turn-of-the-century artists staked out a variety of other positions that accepted certain elements of the modern while seeking to transcend what they perceived as the negative in their inheritance. The term 'modernism' is used here more narrowly to refer to the reorientation of social thought that began in the late nineteenth century, based on a widespread turn to subjectivity that would expand in the twentieth century beyond the arts into the social and even the physical sciences.

With the failure of the 1848 revolution, a cloud of disillusionment settled on many artists and writers who abandoned the political causes of the past and embraced, instead, a profoundly subjectivist and potentially nihilist art-for-art's-sake ideology. As in the lifestyle rebellion of the early Romantics, the new **avant-garde** intellectuals adopted an anti-bourgeois stance that rejected the crass materialism, the emphasis on utility over beauty, and the uniformity of the modern capitalist culture. At the same time, the core of the movement's ideology was an extreme individualism that was the defining principle of the bourgeois revolution. In their own eyes, the avant-garde constituted a kind of impoverished aristocracy or cultural elite that rejected the new mass culture, decrying what they saw as the lowering of taste by philistine writers, who sold their serialized stories by the line, and by artists, who mass-produced imitations of famous painting styles.[79]

Many late nineteenth- and early twentieth-century artists and writers adopted an even more exaggerated form of lifestyle rebellion than the Romantics of a century earlier. Late Victorian writers and artists began to explore even more forbidden topics, especially sexuality and eroticism. For the upright middle class, this new style was self-indulgent and decadent, destructive and nihilistic. They cast aspersions widely, to enclose both the most licentious artists and those who explored aesthetic questions of form, technique, and subject. The result was a new high culture produced not for an aristocracy or a prosperous bourgeoisie—in fact, in conscious rejection of both of these groups—but instead for the small, elite, artistic community itself. In this light, the great variety of modern schools of the arts continued the apolitical, art-for-art's-sake movement of the nineteenth century. If the human condition, generally, could not be perfected, alienated artists shifted their attention inside, to the artists' personal expressions and explorations of their art for their own and no one else's satisfaction.

As Rubinstein argued,[80] there was a material foundation for this turn inward, to subjectivity. By the 1850s in France and the 1880s in England, with the exception of the novel, the bourgeois classes no longer had need for serious art. They were no longer willing to pay money to artists who expressed rebellious ideas. The bourgeois was comfortable in his existence, sought mild diversions in mass culture, and rejected the openly critical sentiments of the alienated artists. Since the broad middle classes identified completely with what the artists were most alienated from—bourgeois society itself—their art had only a tiny audience and little monetary support. The artist retreated into Bohemia, into a culture of poverty, into an artistic subculture in Soho, London, or on the Left Bank of the Seine in Paris. Although small, this avant-garde artistic community stretched across Europe, from Ibsen's Norway to Dostoyevsky's Russia. As Stromberg put it, a sense of crisis was felt almost simultaneously all over Europe. At its root was a feeling of utter boredom, a sickness unto death with a 'hideous society'.[81]

For the artistic rebel, critic William Gaunt argued, the 'bourgeois was his enemy not simply because he was, as the great Daumier was representing him in lithographs . . . a creature of greed and craft, of physical and mental ugliness, but still more because the bourgeois had an objection to the arts, and to artists, as performing no useful function he could understand.'[82] When the middle class cut the financial strings, the artist no longer felt any obligations except to art itself and to the small, alienated artistic subculture of which he was a part. The French painter Edgar Degas, for example, claimed that:

> Painting was private life. You practised it for two or three living friends and some who were dead!
>
> The others knew nothing about it and never would know anything and consequently you did not care what they thought.[83]

This attitude of alienation from the laws and conventions of society is elaborated by the English poet, A.E. Housman, in 'Last Poems, XII' (1922):

> The laws of God, the laws of man,
> He may keep that will and can;
> Not I; let God and man decree
> Laws for themselves and not for me;
> And if my ways are not as theirs
> Let them mind their own affairs.
> Their deeds I judge and much condemn,
> Yet when did I make laws for them?
> Please yourself, say I, and they
> Need only look the other way.
> But no, they will not; they must still
> Wrest their neighbour to their will,
> And make me dance as they desire
> With jail and gallows and hell-fire.[84]

The Bohemian lifestyle represented a reprise of the Romantic rebellion of the early nineteenth century and foreshadowed the coming 'modernism' of the twentieth. Art for art's sake was characterized, above all, by a turning inside to the mind, to subjectivity, and away from external reality. Realism and scientific rationality were no longer fashionable attitudes to take among the avant-garde; what the artist intended to convey was what was claimed to be a deeper, subjective reality, an inner vision. This new experimental attitude was found also in painting (impressionism, cubism, expressionism), in music, and in dance. In philosophy, Friedrich Nietzsche, whose ideas are discussed below, epitomized this *fin de siècle* disillusionment with the rationalistic core of modern 'civilization' and promoted a new elitism.

Modernism in the arts is much too complex and contradictory a movement to summarize briefly, even with respect to its social and political implications. Some movements, such as futurism, deliberately sought to destroy the old and usher in the modern world. Other artists and writers sought the security of conventional attitudes and institutions. While generally pursuing the aesthetics of their art and exploring form for its own sake, however, many turn-of-the-century artists tended to advocate a politics of personal liberation and opposition to authoritarianism, whether the latter was bourgeois or socialistic. Anti-authoritarianism and the demand for personal lifestyle liberation from a closed, moralistic community are explicitly political ends, whether pursued through a micro-politics (individual to individual) or through wider social movements. In the first half of the twentieth century, politics intruded to a greater extent into the lives of even the more detached and nihilistic of the artists.

The lifestyle politics of the early Romantics had been pushed underground by the suffocating conventions of Victorian propriety. By the latter part of the nineteenth century, lifestyle rebellion was brought once more to centre stage by members of an artistic community that increasingly influenced intellectual and moral beliefs. The result was contestation. There is no single politics of culture. Cultural forms may reproduce, repudiate, or reflect an attempt to disengage from the social order. Ideas, however, may be subversive. The application of reason to critique social institutions, which had been advocated by liberals and the *philosophes* of early modern society, had undermined traditional authority. The liberation of desire likewise appeared threatening to bourgeois society in the 1880s and 1890s. In the long run, capitalism would prove to be extraordinarily adaptive. Liberated desires now feed the ultra-consumption ethic of contemporary economics. Rather than suppress minority appetites, the contemporary economy stimulates them as markets for specialized products. This gives it a paradoxical character: it is subversive of some social conventions while being ultimately reproductive of private, corporate wealth.

The mainstreaming of multiple sexualities in the twenty-first century is a case in point. The anti-gay backlash that is now widespread globally had a counterpart in the late nineteenth century as part of the discourse of 'sexology'. For the 'sexologists', the great variety of 'unnatural' sexual practices, particularly homosexuality, was proof that society was experiencing genetic degeneration. In the contemporary Western society many political jurisdictions have now conceded that equality of human rights extends to groups who express diverse (although not all) forms of sexuality, but in the late Victorian age the state had been in the forefront of the repression of homosexuality. This may be exemplified by the career of the English dramatist, Oscar Wilde (1854–1900), the writer who, in England, most explicitly called for a 'new hedonism', lived the consequences of his rebellion, and died broken by the powers of the state and social convention.

Oscar Wilde and Decadence

For Wilde, humanity had a natural tendency to fear the passions, those inborn desires that placed people on a level with the animals and appeared to be stronger than the rational, mental ability to control them. Defining the passions as 'savage and animal', society sought to subdue them, tame them by self-torture or starve them into submission by self-denial. But, Wilde believed, if you resist expressing your passions and desires, 'your soul grows sick with longing for the things it has forbidden to itself, with desire for what monstrous laws have made monstrous and unlawful.' As a result, 'We degenerate into hideous puppets, haunted by the memory of the passions of which we were too much afraid, and the exquisite temptations that we had not the courage to yield to.'[85] Instead of this Victorian denial of desire, Wilde advocated the lifestyle known as dandyism. In Wilde's version, dandyism sought to spiritualize the senses and 'assert the absolute modernity of beauty'. The dandy created and lived the new standards of taste and aesthetics that freely sought pleasure and gratified desire. The purpose of this new hedonism, Wilde wrote, 'was to recreate life' in an age of Puritan revival. The ethic of hedonism 'was never to accept any theory or system that would involve the sacrifice of any mode of passionate experience. Its aim, indeed, was to be experience itself. . . . [I]t was to teach' people to concentrate 'upon the moments of a life that is itself but a moment' and make life anew.

Wilde was as notorious for his licentious lifestyle as he was celebrated as a playwright. Born in Dublin, Ireland, Wilde's mother was a poet and active in the nationalistic Young Ireland movement of the 1840s. Although he married conventionally and had two children, Wilde transgressed the sexual conventions of Victorian England by following his sexual impulses into a homosexual relationship with Alfred Douglas, the son of the Marquis of Queensbury. In 1885 a Criminal Law Amendment Act had prohibited consensual 'indecent' relations between men. When the Marquis made the relationship between Wilde and his son public, Wilde sued him for libel; however, Wilde was subsequently charged criminally and convicted in 1895, in a second trial, of 'immoral conduct'.[86] Sentenced to two years penal servitude at hard labour, he finished his sentence at Reading Gaol where 'all, but Lust, / is turned to dust In Humanity's machine.' In his *Ballad of Reading Gaol*,

Wilde realized that:

> The vilest deeds like poison weeds
> Bloom well in prison air:
> It is only what is good in Man
> That wastes and withers there.[87]

Wilde became the 'unmentionable one in England'[88]—the original 'he who must not be named'. Wilde had anticipated in *Lady Windermere's Fan* (1893) the social ostracism and condemnation he experienced:

> *Lady Erlynne*: . . . You don't know what it is to fall into the pit, to be despised, mocked, abandoned, sneered at—to be an outcast! to find the door shut against one, to have to creep in by hideous byways, afraid every moment lest the mask should be stripped from one's face, and all the while to hear the laughter, the horrible laughter of the world, a thing more tragic than all the tears the world has ever shed. You don't know what it is. One pays for one's sin, and then one pays again, and all one's life one pays.[89]

Wilde spent the last few years of his life in France, friendless and in penury. He had rejected and defied social conventions and morality in a very public way, which may account for the severity of the response he elicited. He was condemned because of his sexuality. Victorian formality avoided the open acknowledgement even of heterosexuality. Under the proprieties of Victorianism, of course, lay explicit sexuality and sexual diversity, as well as a culture of lower- and upper-class prostitution and commonplace bourgeois male infidelity. It was a society severely and unnaturally divided between the limelight of apparent public morality and a backstage of private vice. As they peeled away the layers of smug hypocrisy shielding Victorian realities, the novelists and playwrights emerged as early and insightful psychologists. Naturalism and decadence helped to usher in the modernist movement, which had a new dark side of desire and disorder that so horrified such traditional Victorians as

Tennyson. He summarized the new and, in his view, objectionable tendencies in art and literature, referring to them as 'Zolaism' in his poem, 'Locksley Hall, Sixty Years After' (1886):

> Bring the old dark ages back without the
>   faith, without the hope,
> Break the State, the Church, the Throne,
>   and roll their ruins down the slope.
> Authors—essayist, atheist, novelist, realist,
>   rhymester, play your part,
> Paint the mortal shame of nature with the
>   living hues of art.
> Rip your brother's vices open, strip your
>   own foul passions bare;
> Down with Reticence, down with
> Reverence—forward—naked—let them stare
> . . . .
> Set the maiden fancies wallowing in the
>   troughs of Zolaism,—
> Forward, forward, ay, and backward,
>   downward too into the abysm![90]

The turn to subjectivity was not restricted to the arts. Nicholls argues that the philosopher, Nietzsche gave a new twist to to *fin de siècle* social thought by replacing pessimism and rationalism with will. When Nietzsche reduced all previous truth claims to subjectivity, he opened space for at least some individuals to invent their own meanings, redefining the creative 'self as active, dynamic, and confrontational'.[91]

FRIEDRICH NIETZSCHE

[T]here is nothing either good or bad, but thinking makes it so.
—William Shakespeare, *Hamlet*, II, ii

Friedrich Nietzsche (1844–1900) thought most people were as easily led by the nose as donkeys. Only at the pinnacle of humanity are there a handful of superior individuals. Their superiority has less to do with their intellect—their ability to reason—than with their will power, their drive to achieve their ends regardless of others.

Nietzsche was born in 1844 to a nationalistic and religious family in eastern Germany. His father was a Lutheran pastor and his mother was the daughter of a pastor. Nietzsche's biographer, Hollingdale, says that young Nietzsche led a secure and happy childhood and was devoted to his father. When he was four, however, his father's untimely death shattered his young son's life.[92] The family household now consisted, all but one, of women: Nietzsche's mother, sister, grandmother, and two maiden aunts. Nietzsche was never married. It is common to interpret his later misogynistic musings about women as a consequence of a rebellion against his all-female upbringing.

At 14, Nietzsche attended a strict public school, where he indulged in mildly rebellious behaviour including drunkenness. He also began to doubt religion. At the Universities of Bonn and Leipzig, Nietzsche studied philology and theology, quickly abandoning the latter.[93] Reading Schopenhauer's *The World as Will and Idea* (1818) profoundly affected young Nietzsche's view of the world. According to this philosopher of pessimism, beneath our conscious mind lies a deep, vital force that is 'will' or desire. Since the will is essentially evil and causes conflict and suffering, all one can do is strive to deny desire and live an ascetic life.[94] Nietzsche turned the concept of a vital will into an underlying human drive that arose historically and seeks to realize desire and power.

In Sedgwick's view, Nietzsche agrees with Hegel that the world is not simply what it is; rather, it is continually becoming something else. Change is fundamental to life and is produced by the conflict between unequal powers. In the place of Hegel's transcendent Spirit, however, Nietzsche argues that the driving force in the world is an underlying 'will to power'. 'Will' pervades and drives all of existence.[95]

Society, which by definition is power, always possesses a hierarchy of domination and subordination. Nietzsche argued that, in ancient society, the dominant elite had ruled unambiguously, enshrining their claims to power in the aristocratic principle that was recognized in custom and law. Modern society, however, was shaped by a conflict between the existing elite and their subordinates. In their attempt to overturn the natural principle of hierarchy, the masses had made the notion of an aristocracy disrespectable, rooting their slave mentality in the passive ideology of Christianity.[96] For Nietzsche, as MacDonald argues,[97] Christianity had arisen as a slave religion, demanding humility, patience, acceptance, forgiveness, and sacrifice. These were characteristics of followers, of the weak and passive. If at one time Christianity had been a tool of the elite to gain control over the masses, the tables had been turned. By embracing Christianity, the natural leaders had turned themselves into sheep. Christianity had become a tool with which the ignorant masses, perversely, had gained control over the elite. To be proud, strong, creative, domineering was un-Christian. Yet these were the inborn talents of the natural aristocracy. Christianity was a perversion of nature: the last had become first; the lion now lay under the lamb; the meek had inherited the earth.

According to MacDonald,[98] Nietszche connected this reversal of nature to a misinterpretation of Greek civilization that had become popular since the Renaissance. According to the dominant view in the West, Greek culture had achieved greatness because of its emphasis on human reason, on science and rationality. The Greeks had excelled in mathematics, philosophy, astronomy, biology—the rational sciences. The essence of humanity was its ability to reason, symbolized, said Nietzsche, by the image of the god Apollo. Since the Enlightenment, the modern age accepted the view that the capacity for rational thought defined humanity and had reached its peak in the scientific method, which alone could separate truth from falsehood.

There was another side of Greek culture, Nietzsche argued, that the Enlightenment had ignored. Greece was great because it freed human creativity, which was based less on reason and more on a primitive urge to express and explore: a creative urge that was expressed emotionally. This side of Greek culture was represented by the god of wine and music, Dionysius, described by Stromberg as the 'lower-class god of music, tragic drama, and drunken orgies'.[99] Full humanity meant embracing both sides of human nature, striking a balance between reason and sensuality as the ancient Greeks had, and as Mark Rampion, a character in Aldous Huxley's novel, *Point Counter Point*, championed:

> The sane, harmonious, Greek man gets as much as he can of both sets of states. He's not such a fool as to want to kill part of himself. He strikes a balance. It isn't easy, of course; it's even damnably difficult. The forces to be reconciled are intrinsically hostile. The conscious soul resents the activities of the unconscious, physical, instinctive part of the total being. The life of the one is the other's death and vice versa. But the sane man at least tries to strike a balance. The Christians, who weren't sane, told people that they'd got to throw half of themselves in the waste-paper basket. And now the scientists and business men come and tell us that we must throw away half of what the Christians left us. But I don't want to be three-quarters dead. I prefer to be alive, entirely alive. It's time there was a revolt in favour of life and wholeness.[100]

Earlier in the nineteenth century the Romantics and conservatives had already embraced the anti-rationalist proposition that the essence of humanity was irrational. For the conservatives, truth was to be found in the slow development of tradition; for the Romantics, truth was found by looking inward, to one's intuition, to an inner spirituality, which had little to do with organized religion.

Nietzsche took this non-rationality one step further. For Nietzsche, there was no truth. There were only equally false claims to truth. As Sedgwick argues, unlike Descartes and Kant who focused on the self-consciousness of the individual mind, Nietzsche argued that *consciousness itself* needed to be explained. In his view, consciousness rests on a foundation of innate instincts and historical experiences that go back to the beginning of the human species. Philosophy, Nietzsche said, must become historical. Early humanity had constructed a conceptual framework of beliefs that were taken to be objectively true because they had utility for the survival of the species. Over time, these beliefs condensed into fixed habits and conventions, and became thought of as knowledge.[101]

For Nietzsche, the most important of these conventions of knowledge, Sedgwick continues, was the development of language, which is constructed through the interaction of humans and their environment. The result is a shared and habitual set of words and grammar conventions that determines how we see the world and how we understand ourselves within it. These conventions are not arbitrary, but this is not because they correspond to some external and absolute reality. They persist because they have proven useful for human survival. Words and concepts were believed, however, to reflect faithfully an objective, external reality.[102]

On the one hand, this belief in the certainty of perception was an important foundation of human society. On the other hand, it eventually led to the question of whether the conceptions we had of the world were actually true. If it is believed that concepts relate to a fixed reality, and it is also recognized that contradictory concepts have arisen in human society (since more than one belief may have proven useful in helping the species survive), then the question arises, which concept is true? While Nietzsche did not believe there was any such truth, Sedgwick points out, the human search for 'truth' became embedded in human nature.[103]

The scientists had attempted to discredit religion by asserting that the scientific method allowed them to separate truth from falsehood. For Nietzsche, however, belief in the scientific method was simply another form of faith, no worse but certainly no better than any other claims to knowledge. There was no single point from which you could distinguish indisputably one truth claim from another. They were all equally false (except, presumably, the claim that all *other* truth claims are false, but not this claim). There was, however, the

perpetual and underlying will to power. Humans could make true whatever they had the power to make true.

Nietzsche's claim, however, was more sociological than this assertion about universal untruth. The second question was: what did truth claims represent? For Nietzsche, individuals and collections of individuals had vested interests. A truth claim represented what an individual or group wished to believe because it was in their interest to believe it and oblige or trick others into believing it as well. So, there was a connection between the position occupied by a group or individual and the particular perspective they would adopt or truth claim they would espouse.

What society accepted as truth depended on power rather than on verifiable veracity. Truth was what people in power said was true, as Quirrell claims in J.K. Rowling's *Harry Potter and the Philosopher's Stone*:

> A foolish young man I was then, full of ridiculous ideas about good and evil. Lord Voldemort showed me how wrong I was. There is no good and evil, there is only power, and those too weak to see it.[104]

Similarly, Oscar Wilde's character, Robert Chilten, asserts, after he had been seduced by the philosophy of power and the gospel of gold: 'power over other men, power over the world was the one thing worth having, the one supreme pleasure worth knowing, the one joy one never tired of.' Wealth had given him freedom, 'and freedom is everything.'[105]

In the Middle Ages, the Church had been successful in having its world view accepted as truth by most people in society. In the nineteenth and twentieth centuries, when formal religion, for many, had been discredited, scientists and other experts advanced truth claims and had them accepted as legitimate even though, Nietzsche argued, they were no more true than the beliefs they had replaced. Social science was the bigger fraud, but natural science, too, was suspect—confined to the superficial and the temporary.

Superman and Misogyny

I am not a man. I am dynamite.
—Friedrich Nietzsche, *Ecce Homo* (1888)

Since the majority of humanity was intellectually weak and incapable of seeing through the various falsehoods, they were easily led and misled. It could not be otherwise because most people lacked the ability to think critically, to make up their own minds. They sought certainty in a world where certainty was impossible. Sedgwick says that, for Nietzsche, since the foundation of society is long-term habit, individuals conventionally conform to the customs of their social order. The social world is governed by normative rules because humans are, essentially, herd animals. Normally, people assume that the rules of society reflect the way things must be.[106] Most people find security in what they are told by authorities, whether the authority comes from the church, the government, or the scientific elite.

Implicit in this necessary social order, however, is the potential to go beyond it, to critique it and see that society could be other than it is. Society produces a minority of autonomous individuals who are exceptions to the rules and conventions. Only a small, intellectual elite possesses the strength and will power to recognize the absence of absolute truth, and accept that the world is interpreted from numerous vantage points. This, Nietzsche argues, is a recognition of 'perspectivism'. Individuals or groups interpret 'reality' from their own point of view. Each perspective represents the particular interest of the person or group who holds it. Recognizing this does not negate the search for truth because there is a fundamental 'will to truth' even if objectivity is impossible. As Sedgwick argues, for Nietzsche, the attempt to achieve the spirit of objectivity means seeking access to numerous viewpoints: 'The more varied and rich our understanding, the better our knowledge.'[107]

Nietzsche's most important books were written in the decade between 1878 and 1888, the latter date marking the beginning of his celebrity.

By then he had been physically ill for a decade and a half and within another year he would be incurably insane, a condition possibly caused by syphilis. His final collapse occurred dramatically early in 1889. Witnessing a cabbie beating his horse with a whip, Nietzsche rushed over and grabbed the animal's neck. Then he lost consciousness.[108] Although he lived for another decade, the decline of his mental ability was absolute. Nietzsche died in 1900, a prophet of a variety of perspectives in the new century.

In Stromberg's estimation,[109] Nietzsche's views offered 'a manifesto for all the different ones': the spiritual minority, the enemies of the crowd, who 'have the courage to accept life as it is, in all its meaninglessness, just because it is.' While the vast majority of humanity was necessarily tied to conventional routine, in his analysis of the emergence of the aristocratic minority of autonomous, critical individuals, Nietzsche anticipated the emergence of a new human type. The modern elite was represented by an individual who embraced Dionysian creativity, who was 'beyond good and evil', beyond concerns of morality, and capable of acting ruthlessly in the interests of free expression. This human-being-to-be was described by Nietzsche as an *Übermensch*, meaning an above-human or *superman*.

Nietzsche's influence was widespread in early twentieth-century Europe. The anarchist left responded positively to his absolute rebellion against conventional morality and politics. Initially, however, the extreme right admired Nietzsche as much. He despised democracy and socialism, which he saw as modern forms of the Christian slave mentality, and glorified natural inequality. In Fascist hands, the idea of the *Übermensch* (superman) became epitomized in the person of the great leader, in a Mussolini or *der Führer*.

Nietzsche also shared with many *fin de siècle* intellectuals a rejection of the feminine. For the avant-garde, Nicholls argues, women epitomized sentimentality and self-absorption in contrast to the masculine virtues of action, risk, danger, and disorder.[110] In *Beyond Good and Evil*, Nietzsche writes that the emergence of 'self-reliant women

. . . is one of the worst developments of the *ugli-fiction* of Europe.'[111] Nietzsche does not respect femininity, which he regards as natural for women, but he despises even more any attempt by women to move into masculine spheres. Woman may 'seek mastery', says Nietzsche:

But she does not *want* truth. What is truth to woman? From the beginning, nothing has been more alien, repugnant, and hostile to woman than truth—her great art is the lie, her highest concern is mere appearance and beauty.[112]

It is not that women recognize there is no objective truth. They do not embody the 'will to truth', Nietzsche believed.

The issue of men and women is a fundamental problem, therefore, necessary to be correct about, writes Nietzsche. Between the two sexes there is a 'most abysmal antagonism' and a necessary 'hostile tension'.[113] '[T]o dream perhaps of equal rights, equal education, equal claims and obligations—that is a *typical* sign of shallowness, and a thinker who has proved shallow in this dangerous place—shallow in his instinct—may be considered altogether suspicious, even more—betrayed, exposed.' On the other hand, a man 'who has depth, in his spirit . . . must always think of women as *Orientals* do: he must conceive of woman as a possession, as property that can be locked, as something predestined for service and achieving her perfection in that.' Consider his misogynist assertions in *Thus Spake Zarathustra* (1883):

Is it not better to fall into the hands of a murderer, than into the dreams of a lustful woman?

. . .

Verily, my brother, said Zarathustra, it is a treasure that hath been given me: it is a little truth which I carry. . . .

[W]hat is woman for man?

Two different things wanteth the true man: danger and diversion. Therefore wanteth he woman, as the most dangerous plaything. . . .

Let men fear woman when she hateth: for man in his innermost soul is merely evil; woman, however, is mean. . . .

The happiness of man is, 'I will,' The happiness of woman is, 'He will.' . . .

Obey, must the woman, and find a depth for her surface. Surface, is woman's soul, a mobile, stormy film on shallow water.

Man's soul, however, is deep. . . .

Then answered me the old woman. . . . '[N]ow accept a little truth by way of thanks! I am old enough for it!' . . .

'Give me, woman, thy little truth!' said I. And then spake the woman:

'Thou goest to women? Do not forget the whip!'—

Thus spake Zarathustra.[114]

Without doubting Nietzsche's misogyny, it is worth adding that his aphoristic style leaves room for interpretation. In part of the above passage, he doubly distances himself. It is Zarathustra who has spoken, and the last and most objectionable assertion is a quotation from an 'old woman'.

Nietzsche was an outsider except among the aesthetic elite, his kindred spirits and self-conceived supermen. Nietzsche preferred imagination to logic and irrationality to science. His notion of the great individualist and ideas about relations between power, the will, and the *Übermensch* would be used to legitimate a turn to authoritarianism in Europe. Although German Fascists later sought to ridicule and destroy what they called decadent art, their claim to be the intellectual heirs of Nietzsche made them the offspring of the self-proclaimed most decadent.

Nietzsche's philosophy was also influential in twentieth-century social thought. He developed his iconoclastic philosophy from the perspective of the origins and consequences of language, helping to inspire a focus on social linguistics and, coupled with his perspectivism, influencing the turn to postmodernism in the 1980s and 1990s. During the 1920s, when Nietzsche's reputation was tarnished by its link to Fascism, the general notion of multiple perspectives on truth was developed by Karl Mannheim, one of the last of the classical sociological theorists.

KARL MANNHEIM

Karl Mannheim (1893–1947) was Hungarian by birth and, following the rise of Nazism, became English by inclination. He was born in 1893 in Budapest, Hungary. Like Durkheim, who published *The Division of Labour* in that year, Mannheim was Jewish. Ethnic identity would prove fateful for his academic career.

Mannheim began studying at the University of Budapest in 1912, where he followed the typical path of reform-minded students. Many of Mannheim's enduring values were formed during this period. The reformers he associated with were socialists with respect to economic organization, favouring state planning and economic regulation, but they were not revolutionaries. Their aim was to replace the authoritarian Austro-Hungarian regime with a liberal, parliamentary state.

In Budapest, Mannheim was influenced by two strong personalities. One was the liberal reformer Oscar Jászi who was repelled by positivism—the view that the social world is reducible to facts that can be understood and manipulated—and instead sought to raise the moral and aesthetic standards of humanity. Jászi had little faith in the potential of the masses, a doctrine that even many Marxists were beginning to doubt. Consistent with *fin de siècle* theory, social renewal depended on the actions of the intellectual elite. Mannheim endorsed this elitist theory of politics and the goal of promoting 'spiritual renovation' in society.[115]

Mannheim's other inspiration in Budapest was the Marxist, George Lukács. Lukács abandoned the economic core of Marxist theory and returned to Marx's earlier, more philosophical writings to develop a theory of culture. This meant focusing Marxist analysis on the ideological superstructure of society rather than the economic base, a focus that paralleled Mannheim's interests. Lukács's politics, on the other hand, were not to Mannheim's taste. Drawn to the revolutionary theory of Vladimir Lenin and the Russian Bolshevik Party, Lukács straddled the fine line between Leninism and independent Marxist politics. When Hungary erupted in revolution in 1919, Lukács jumped in, becoming Commissar of Education in the radical regime of Bella Kun.[116]

The revolution of March 1919 overthrew the short-lived Hungarian Democratic Republic, which had been set up immediately after World War I. Similar insurrections erupted simultaneously in Germany. Mannheim had supported the Hungarian Republic and remained aloof from Kun's radical Budapest regime. Within months it was overthrown by a counter-revolutionary army of ex-soldiers and peasants, assisted by foreign troops. The new, reactionary government in Hungary was led by a former admiral, Miklos Horthy, who retained dictatorial power for more than two decades, eventually joining the Axis powers in World War II.

From the point of view of Horthy's authoritarian regime, liberals were as bad as radical socialists. Mannheim was forced into exile, settling in Heidelberg, Germany, in 1919. He found progressive German academics divided between the value-free sociology of Max Weber and a form of literary Romanticism that was remote from everyday affairs. He was drawn to Weber's historical analysis, but not his pessimism about the future of society. Mannheim considered himself part of the younger generation who sought to reorient social theory and intervene positively in the political and cultural life of Germany. In the hands of Nietzsche, Simmel, and Weber, however, social theory had become thoroughly relativistic, since, if all truth claims rested on the perspective of those who held them, no values or knowledge claims could be absolute. Social science, from these thinkers, had failed in its goal of providing guidance for society on the path of progress and prosperity. However, Mannheim was unwilling to abandon this goal. Sociology needed a new theory that could account for the diversity of points of view and establish truths that were real though not absolute, and were necessary for 'the planned guidance of people's lives on a sociological basis, and with the aid of psychology'.[117]

Ideology

Few social scientists fully accepted the naive positivism that assumed our perceptions are an accurate representation of the real world and that, on the basis of the accumulation of these perceptions, a theorist could arrive at objective, absolute truth. For the new generation of sociologists, which included Mannheim, even the Newtonian laws of physics were being seen as relatively rather than absolutely true. In the age of Einstein, the world was not what it appeared to be.

In the nineteenth century, scientists believed that the universe was deterministic and everything in it was in principle predictable, once all the relevant laws had been discovered. This view collapsed when Einstein's theory of relativity showed that space and time were not constants. Time appears to run slower near large gravitational objects. Other scientists found it impossible to accurately measure and predict the behaviour of minute particles in the atom. The theory of quantum mechanics, which was formulated in the 1920s and is the basis of most modern technological developments, introduced a greater degree of uncertainty in scientific predictions than even Einstein could accept. Rather than being able to predict accurately a single, determined outcome from a set of factors, scientists following **quantum theory** can make only probability statements: the outcome would be X in a certain number of cases and Y in a certain number of other cases. The inability to predict exactly every instance means that quantum mechanics resembles tossing a die: we know reasonably accurately how often in 100 throws we will get a six, but not whether any given toss will be a six.[118]

Since Comte, sociological positivists had been trying to model social science after the natural sciences. Quantum mechanics contradicted this trend; natural science now appeared similar to the social variety, where we can predict how many people will register in university for any given year, but not whether any specific individual will enrol or decide to travel instead. With the newly discovered principle of uncertainty, modern science undermined theories of determinism that had been applied to society. As Aldous Huxley pointed out, scientific laws were, at least in part, subjective. They were human constructions rather than accurate descriptions of an objective universe (Box 13.2).[119] Behind the nineteenth-century positivists' claim of finding exact, objective knowledge were implicit value judgements. The old beliefs in inevitable progress and simple realism—things were as they appeared to be—were ideas that merely reflected the unproven faith of scientists.[120]

Box 13.2

'But why should the science be obsolete?' asked Lucy. . . .

'. . . he's committed to nineteenth-century materialism. You can't be a true [materialist] without being a mechanist. You've got to believe that the only fundamental realities are space, time and mass, and that all the rest is nonsense, mere illusion. . . . He's sadly worried by Einstein. . . . How furious he gets with old Mach! They're undermining his simple faith. They're telling him that the laws of nature are useful conventions of strictly human manufacture and that space and time and mass themselves, the whole universe of Newton and his successors, are simply our own invention. The idea's as inexpressibly shocking and painful to him as the idea of the non-existence of Jesus would be to a Christian. He's a scientist, but his principles make him fight against any scientific theory that's less than fifty years old.'

—Aldous Huxley, *Point Counter Point* (1928)

Mannheim did not doubt that there was an objective reality—facts did exist. Accordingly, knowledge is influenced by the nature of the object you are examining. Social life would be impossible if people randomly confused one object with another, a knife with a piece of celery, a cliff with a step. But equally, knowledge is subjective and depends on the nature of the knower. For Mannheim, the immediate sensations that humans derive from their perceptions provide only the raw material for knowledge. The rational mind must organize this information into categories and conceptual forms. Following Nietzsche, Mannheim believed that these concepts are derived historically. They are given by the culture and they shape the individual's frame of reference. Every definition embodies the entire system of thought of the thinker who employs it and is guided by his or her political interests and evaluations.[121]

This relativistic understanding of human consciousness was itself the result of a historical process that had undermined the stable, absolutist view of knowledge that characterized feudal Europe. In traditional society, the elite members of the clergy formed a well-defined caste of intellectuals who monopolized the power to interpret the world. The result was a single, dominant conceptual scheme providing the faithful with a unitary world view or **Weltanschauung**. Intellectual debate was structured around a set of principles, which were held to be absolute, were derived from an ultimate authority (God), and could be understood only intuitively. The orderly nature of life was taken for granted and unusual events were defined as arbitrary acts of God. Within these dogmatic assertions, battles over what was true reflected the various positions of power in the Church. Within this magical-religious view of the world, there was no way other than through faith to determine truth or falsity. This uniform world view served a psychological-sociological function by creating a common definition of the situation that united people's experiences, their inner mental life, and their conduct.[122]

Traditional thinking was sociologically true to the extent that it was not contradicted by experience. A world view is not abandoned for purely

theoretical reasons. Ultimately, however, social reality changes and grows incongruent with traditional explanations. When people's experiences change so fundamentally that a gap appears between the novel experiences they have and the traditional mode of thought, a crisis in understanding occurs. From being sociologically true, traditional explanations become false—they no longer function to reinforce the existing world view. Even so, traditional ideas are not easily abandoned. The group that has an interest in perpetuating the old world view continues to propagate it even when social change has swept beyond it. They continue to advocate antiquated theories, values, and norms that distort knowledge. In Mannheim's terms, the traditional interpretation has degenerated into **ideology**, the perspective of a dominant group that is unable to perceive the new facts that have undermined its social dominance. Ideology represents the distorted thinking of those who 'have not yet grown up to the present'.[123]

The medieval clergy had used their socially monopolistic position to inculcate their widely accepted ecclesiastical view of the world. Breaking this monopoly inaugurated the modern era. At first, a new stratum of intellectuals—the Enlightenment *philosophes* and English empiricists—attempted to develop an alternative, but still absolute, doctrine of knowledge founded on the fiction of the self-sufficient individual who possessed, at birth, all the fundamental capacities of humanity. Philosophers such as Kant proposed to study consciousness in itself; not the particular consciousness of individuals in their socio-historical situation, but the absolute truths that any mind could derive from rational thinking. This was a necessary step in the emergence of an adequate theory of knowledge because it focused attention on the role of the human subject in perceiving the world. What we know is not merely an unambiguous mirror in the mind of what is really out there; knowledge is, to some extent, a construction of the mind.

Hegel had added a historical perspective to this subjective view of knowledge. Although he argued that the historical process was guided by a universal world spirit, different forms of consciousness emerged over time, shaping the *Volksgeist* or folk spirit of various nations. Marx developed this approach more thoroughly by arguing that, within a nation, different forms of consciousness emerge, which are shaped by the distinct experiences shared by members of each social class. Human thought processes—the internal structures of consciousness—were identical; yet people in different social situations developed divergent conceptions of the world they all shared.

Mannheim believed that, even in traditional society, the thought processes, concepts, and views of the world of the various estates (nobles, peasants, and so on) were certainly different. Yet, there was no crisis in thought because, in part, all groups shared an identical, ecclesiastical world view. In addition, the perceptions of the oppressed classes did not enter the consciousness of the social elite. The two social spheres were separate.

Once the single *Weltanschauung* had been shattered, however, the conditions under which knowledge is produced changed. Different conceptions of the world emerged and competed with each other. At this point, people became aware of the ideological element in their opponent's thinking: the arguments they made merely expressed their self-interest. They sought to **unmask** the distortions and untruths, the conscious disguises their opponents used to hide their real motivations. In the era of competitive capitalism, with its minimalist ethic of 'let the buyer beware', exposing cheats and charlatans became a matter of common sense and economic survival, as Franz Kafka indicated in his brief meditation 'Unmasking a Confidence Trickster'[124] (Box 13.3). In modern society, we are now constantly aware of 'disguises, sublimations, and refractions', Mannheim noted: '[T]he word **simulacra**, which appeared in the political literature of the sixteenth century, may be regarded as a forerunner of the present attitude.'[125]

This psychological insight into everyday dishonesty, which Mannheim calls the 'particular conception of ideology', is still valued in the modern world. As society changes, however, a sociological form of the unmasking of ideology emerges. When people began to experience rapid social mobility and changed their position in the class structure, different conceptions of the world began to coexist in the mind of a single individual. Rather than being defined simply as conscious lies, it was necessary to understand the different world views as reflecting fundamentally different thought systems, experiences, and interpretations. To unmask an opponent now meant to expose her or his world view. Untruthfulness was rooted in

---

Box 13.3

[The narrator is accosted on the street by a man with whom he was barely acquainted, who] thrust himself unasked upon me for two long hours . . . [until] shame suddenly caught hold of me. . . . The man was a confidence trickster, nothing else. And yet I had been months in the town and thought I knew all about confidence tricksters, how they come slinking out of the side streets by night to meet us with outstretched hands like tavern-keepers, how they haunted the advertisement pillars we stood beside, sliding around them . . . and spying on us with at least one eye. . . . I understood them so well . . . and to them I owed my first inkling of a ruthless hardness which I was now so conscious of, everywhere on earth, that I was even beginning to feel it in myself. How persistently they blocked our way. . . . How they refused to give up, to admit defeat, but kept shooting glances at us. . . . I rubbed my finger tips together to wipe away the disgrace.

—Franz Kafka, 'Unmasking a Confidence Trickster' (1913)

the social situation that gave rise to the distortion. Unlike conscious lies, however, these distortions in thought were often unconscious. For people in distinct social situations, the same facts of experience were perceived through different logical categories, generating conflicting modes of thought. The thinking subject, however, was unaware of the mechanisms underlying this process and the collective-unconscious motives reflected by it.[126]

Dominant groups failed to perceive aspects of the social situation that would undermine their dominance. Mannheim termed this form of distorted thinking, which preserves the status quo, 'ideology'. Among oppressed groups, a diametrically opposed type of thought emerged that Mannheim labelled **Utopia**. Utopian thinking is oriented towards something that doesn't yet exist, but *could* exist in the future. Utopian thinking tends to overturn the present order. Mannheim described the relationship between Utopia and the existing order in terms of Hegelian dialectics (Box 13.4).[127] Since the interest of oppressed groups is to overthrow the social structure, they perceive only those elements of reality critical of society and ignore any aspects that would 'paralyse its desire to change things'. Neither the dominant nor the oppressed group is capable of diagnosing correctly the existing condition of society.[128]

At this point, social theory has reached the stage of absolute relativism. There is no longer any truth; there are only variously situated untruths. Weber's response to this dilemma had been to construct a sociology that would be, as much as possible, value-free—though not in the positivistic sense, which assumed it was actually possible. Instead, Weber argued, sociologists should seek to recognize their biases and attempt to overcome them, thereby getting as close as possible to objective knowledge. Mannheim proposed a different solution. Rather than trying to act as though value judgements could be recognized and put aside, sociologists should develop a theory of knowledge that incorporates evaluations.

The Sociology of Knowledge

> It is a more worthy intellectual task to learn to think dynamically and relationally rather than statically.
> —Karl Mannheim, *Ideology and Utopia* (1929)

The basic principle of Mannheim's approach to the sociology of knowledge is that people's patterns of thought and conduct are predetermined by their social location. For Mannheim, it is not people 'in general who think, or even isolated individuals who do the thinking'; rather, thinking occurs among certain groups of people 'who have developed a particular style of thought in an endless series of responses to certain typical situations

---

Box 13.4

Every age allows to arise (in differently located social groups) those ideas and values in which are contained in condensed form the unrealized and the unfulfilled tendencies which represent the needs of each age. These intellectual elements then become the explosive material for bursting the limits of the existing order, leaving it free to develop in the direction of the next order of existence....

This formulation of dialectical progression, of the situation, and of the contradictions to be found in the realm of thought, should be regarded as nothing more than a formal outline.... The most immediate problem of research is to bring the conceptual scheme and empirical reality into closer contact with one another.

—Karl Mannheim, *Ideology and Utopia* (1929)

characterizing their common position.'[129] The techniques of psychoanalysis pioneered by Freud had penetrated beneath the surface behaviours of the individual to uncover his or her unconscious motivations. Through introspective self-examination, people become visible to themselves. In turn, sociologists were in a position to analyze the knowledge claims of specific groups to reveal the collective-unconscious motivations that undergird them.

The goal of the sociology of knowledge is to diagnose the social situation and become critically aware of the collective-unconscious motivations affecting social action. When we understand the way that social forces unconsciously determine our conduct, we can control our actions rationally and emancipate ourselves as much as possible from these influences. Control of the collective unconscious, Mannheim declared, is the definitive problem of the age.

Mannheim decided that it is impossible to believe that the perspective of any particular group is absolutely true, because there are too many points of view of equal value and prestige, all containing some elements of an existing truth that none could grasp and could never be apprehended in its entirety. Like Nietzsche's perspectivism, striving for objectivity requires access to a variety of viewpoints. Abandoning the objective of a single truth did not mean, for Mannheim, giving up the goal of discovering *approximate* truths that are useful in guiding our actions. The key sociological insight is that all knowledge is intimately bound up with the matrix of interacting social forces that affect the individual. The task of the sociologist is to move from relativism—all claims are equally false—to **relationism**, which seeks to understand the interactions between the social situation of various groups and their thinking.[130]

Stating that knowledge claims are socially located and not absolute leaves open the question of the extent to which these sets of knowledge claims are valid relative to one another. Mannheim supposes that each point of view has an element of truth that reflects something important about the social situation that generated it. The sociologist

can correct the limitations inherent in each 'narrow' point of view by allowing each to clash with its opposite. He imagines that one gets closer to the elusive goal of objectivity by juxtaposing different points of view. As the sociologist's knowledge of 'reality' assimilates more of these divergent positions, this knowledge will transcend the more limited horizon of any particular point of view and become comprehensive and inclusive. The goal is 'the broadest possible extension of our horizon of vision'. For Mannheim, one point of view is more valid than another if it is more comprehensive and, pragmatically, if it provides the most serviceable 'instrument for dealing with life-situations'.[131]

Mannheim divides the social process, which is the subject of sociological analysis, into two components. One is the settled, orderly, and rationalized sphere, which it is possible to analyze more or less completely and is subject to orderly rules of administration. In this sphere, the aim of sociology is to construct a body of general knowledge that is 'knowable by all and communicable to all'.[132] In the hands of Durkheim and Weber, sociology represented an attempt to devise an objectively valid set of truths to describe, define, and classify these structural regularities. Because there is no neutral place to observe society, however, observers also are participants in the conflict of forces. Their modes of thought are bound up with the general political and social currents of their place and time. Even in analyzing this apparently straightforward realm of social facts, it is easy for sociologists to represent unconsciously their own particular experiences as though they were objective categories. In fact, their analysis will necessarily reflect the partial and socially conditioned perspective of their particular social situation. Consequently, those who attempt to employ a non-evaluative approach must continually be self-conscious of 'the social equation in their thinking'.[133]

The second sphere of social history is the political, the realm that produces future action. In the political sphere, tendencies are continuously in flux, forces change, and new forces enter the system. It is possible to imagine a social science that could develop relatively valid generalizations about the first, regular, and repetitive social sphere. It is more difficult to imagine a science of the political, the realm in which people are forced to make decisions and act on them. In the historical and political spheres, Mannheim asserts, 'the voluntaristic element has an essential significance for knowledge.' Politics involves acting, bringing the new into existence. We act as 'knowing subjects' and help to shape 'the process of becoming'. Action is undertaken within a complex matrix that includes our particular interests, our purpose, the evaluations we make of possible alternatives, and our social standpoint and the *Weltanschauung* this entails.[134] Mannheim argues that the sociology of knowledge must be extended to develop an understanding of this political realm of change and uncertainty.

Although all knowledge is inevitably partisan and fragmentary, the recognition of this fact makes possible a science of politics. Each point of view must be complemented by all others. This 'implies the possibility of an integration of many mutually complementary points of view into a comprehensive . . . science of the whole.'[135] In the perception of music, Mannheim says, a melody is 'immediately perceived as a whole and not as the mere sum of the single tones and intervals contained in it.'[136] Aldous Huxley, in his novel *Point Counter Point*, uses the more complex musical concept of 'counterpoint'—in which one melody is superimposed upon a second and different melody to create a complex harmony—to illustrate how individuals with their differences nevertheless compose a complex unity. As all the musical elements are separable, so are contrasting social perspectives; yet all are essential to the wholeness of the composition. Huxley's reference point for the complex relationship between the whole and its parts is Bach's 'Suite in B minor'. However, Huxley, the mystic, perceives the unity of the whole through feelings and intuition, not social science (Box 13.5).[137]

Mannheim, who would grant that the intuitive perception of the whole is suitable for musical composition, finds intuition inadequate for understanding social life. Grasping the structure of the social whole requires painstaking analysis. Intellectual research and analysis can come close to creating the synthesis of the whole from the

---

Box 13.5

In the opening *largo* John Sebastian [Bach] had . . . made a statement: There are grand things in the world, noble things; there are men born kingly; there are real conquerors, intrinsic lords of the earth. But of an earth that is, oh! complex and multitudinous, he had gone on to reflect in the fugal allegro [the counterpoint movement]. [In the opening] You seem to have found the truth; clear, definite, unmistakable, it is announced by the violins; you have it, you triumphantly hold it. But it slips out of your grasp [in the counterpoint] to present itself in a new aspect among the cellos and yet again in terms of [the flute's] vibrating air column. The parts live their separate lives; they touch, their paths cross, they combine for a moment to create a seemingly final and perfected harmony, only to break apart again. Each is always alone and separate and individual. 'I am I,' asserts the violin; 'the world revolves around me.' Round me,' calls the cello, 'Round me,' the flute insists. And all are equally right and equally wrong. . . . [It is] a slow and lovely meditation on the beauty (in spite of squalor and stupidity), the profound goodness (in spite of all the evil), the oneness (in spite of such bewildering diversity) of the world. It is a . . . unity that no intellectual research can discover, that analysis dispels, but of whose reality the spirit is from time to time suddenly and overwhelmingly convinced.

—Aldous Huxley, *Point Counter Point* (1928)

disparate points of view that exist in the matrix of a single socio-historical current. Hegel and Marx, for example, each had attempted to construct a valid synthesis from opposite perspectives. A synthesis is not a question merely of adding all the partial truths into a single, final truth. Since everything is in the process of becoming, any synthesis must be dynamic. Furthermore, Mannheim argues, points of view diverge not just in subject matter, but in how they set the problem and the 'categorical apparatus and principles of organization' they employ.[138] Some social perspectives talk past each other and use concepts that are incompatible. Darwinism and fundamental Christianity had little common ground from which a synthesis could be built.

An axiom in the sociology of knowledge is that the thinking of a group is rooted in its social location. All views are partial. How is a synthesis of the whole possible and who is in a position to do this? A valid synthesis must retain much of the accumulated cultural knowledge derived from previous epochs. In addition, it means assessing the here and now from the perspective of what is no longer necessary in social life and what is not yet possible to achieve. It demands an experimental outlook, sensitive to the dynamic nature of social life and its wholeness. Assuming that such a complex synthesis is possible, Mannheim continues, it is only consistent in the sociology of knowledge 'to suppose that the tendency towards a total synthesis must be embodied in the will of some social group'.[139]

Hypothetically, the further an observer is from a given situation the more possible that he or she will be able to develop a relatively valid (comprehensive and useful) synthesis of different perspectives. The sociologist must become an anthropologist of one's own society. In Mannheim's terms, such a relatively objective outlook can be formulated only by an 'unanchored, *relatively* classless stratum' that is 'not too firmly situated in the social order'. This group was the 'socially unattached intelligentsia'.[140] Unlike medieval intellectuals, who had been confined in their thinking by the interests of the Church,

nineteenth-century intellectuals had become increasingly detached and independent. The result had been 'a wonderful flowering of a free intellectual and cultural life' that was 'free to a very great extent from the class prejudices which previously had always entered into intellectual life'.[141]

Only such a free intellectual stratum could, first, conceive of a relatively objective point of view and, second, strive to create a synthesis of perspectives. While the perspective of intellectuals is determined by their specific background, it is united through the intellectual medium of a common educational heritage, which contains all the contradictory points of view. The uniquely independent social position of intellectuals gives them the ability to adapt to and consciously choose any viewpoint. They are able to become self-conscious of their own social moorings and choose their allegiance. The commoner, Burke, spoke for the aristocracy; Marx was born of the middle class, not the working class.

More importantly, thought Mannheim, intellectuals were in the unique position of being capable of making another and better choice than merely choosing sides in the social conflict. Implicit in the peculiar position of the intelligentsia is a social mission to advocate for the interests of the whole society. Intellectuals have a 'need for total orientation and synthesis'. Ordinary political thinking exaggerates the differences between perspectives. The mission of the intellectuals is to reconcile the variety of perspectives in a dynamic equilibrium that is oriented to the whole of society.[142] By making such political choices, they could 'achieve a synthesis from the most comprehensive and most progressive point of view' that would guide the transformation of social conditions and the individuals within them, providing the opportunity for greater mastery of the world. You are least free when you act under the impact of unknown and unrecognized forces. The sociology of knowledge reveals these unconscious determinants and motivations, and brings them into the realm of 'the controllable, calculable, and objectified'.[143]

Elites and Mass Society

> Figuratively speaking, reconstructing a
> changing society is like replacing the wheels
> of a train while it is in motion, rather than
> rebuilding a house on new foundations.
> —Karl Mannheim, *Man and Society in an Age
> of Reconstruction* (1940)

As Mannheim's image of changing the wheels of a
moving train illustrates,[144] he conceived the
achieving of a greater control over the social world
to be complex and difficult. Ironically, the historical process in Germany was going in a direction
opposite to greater control and calculation. The
portents of the Nazi future were apparent in the
1920s, though Hitler's rise to power was not
inevitable. As a naturalized German who was also
a Jew, Mannheim's reputation in German academe
grew and he was appointed Professor of Sociology
at Frankfurt.

At the time he published *Ideology and Utopia*
in 1929, Fascism had become a fixture of the
German political stage. Once the Nazis had
secured political dominance in Germany, however, Mannheim's career and many of his intellectual hopes collapsed. A Nazi decree of April
1933, aimed to suppress prominent Jews, suspended Mannheim from his academic position.
As Kettler et al. point out, the National Socialists
'cruelly parodied' Mannheim's hope that the sociology of knowledge could achieve a rational,
dynamic equilibrium through a synthesis of conflicting perspectives. The Nazi ideology, instead,
provided a new, emotional, and irrational *Weltanschauung* that was either acquiesced in or hungrily
swallowed by the German masses who blindly
accepted the most barbarous myths about the
world. Once more Mannheim was forced to
migrate, ending his life in exile in England where
he died in 1947.[145]

England was Mannheim's third intellectual
home. The rise of Fascism forced Mannheim to
reconsider his social theory. The intellectuals of the
Nazi regime applied their rational understanding
of society and psychology to destructive ends and

encouraged the worst aspects of human irrationality. In response, Mannheim did not abandon his
theory of knowledge. The predominance of group
irrationality emphasized more powerfully than
before the importance of reason. The ability of the
Nazi elite to control society revealed the crucial
importance of encouraging the power of the civilizing rather than of the destructive elite.
Mannheim realized, however, that insight into the
relativity of ideas and social situations, which had
been the fruit of the sociology of knowledge, had
helped create an atmosphere of discouragement
and resignation. In the face of this uncertainty, liberal intellectuals had abdicated their responsibility
to shape social events (Box 13.6).[146]

While the liberal intellectual elite failed to
shoulder its leadership burden, history confirmed
the power of a directing minority to determine
events, whether for good or ill. In 1940,
Mannheim published in England an expanded
version of a book he had written in the previous
decade in Germany, after he had examined, first-
hand, the point of view of English liberalism. *Man
and Society in an Age of Reconstruction* was a synthesis of two complex and different world views
that coexisted in his consciousness, the fruit of the
sociology of knowledge he had theorized in the
1920s. Following the rise of Fascism, Mannheim
sought to understand the processes that led,
through social disintegration, to the collapse of liberal democracy and the rise of brutal dictatorship.

Sociologically, Fascism was not a gross aberration that 'just grew', like Topsy. Mannheim did
not consider that it was simply rooted in human
instincts of aggression or violence. While humanity comprised innate drives and generalized forms
of neuroses, human nature was essentially plastic;
the decisive factor must be a social structure that
called forth certain tendencies or suppressed others. Fascism was the consequence, though not
necessarily the inevitable consequence, of trends
deeply rooted in liberal, democratic culture.
Understanding modern totalitarianism required
an analysis of group psychology in the era of mass
society. This led Mannheim to the correlation of
character and social structure, to 'how different

Box 13.6

For a time it was healthy to see the limitations of . . . [rational understanding], especially in social affairs. It was healthy to realize that thinking is not powerful if it is severed from the social context and ideas are only strong if they have their social backing, that it is useless to spread ideals that have no real function, and are not woven into the social fabric. But this sociological interpretation of ideas may also lead to complete despair, discouraging the individual from thinking about issues which will definitively become the concern of the day. This discouragement of the intelligentsia which may lead them to too quick a resignation as their proper function as the thinkers and forerunners of a new society, may become even more disastrous in a social setting where more depends on what the leading élites may have in mind than in other periods of history. The theory that thought is socially conditioned and changes in different periods in history is only instructive, if its implications are fully realized and applied to our own age.

—Karl Mannheim, *Man and Society in an Age of Reconstruction* (1940)

social and historical situations fostered different forms of personality'.[147]

Both the social order and human psychology were being thoroughly transformed in the modern world. Liberal capitalism and laissez-faire had collapsed worldwide in the Great Depression, producing anarchy and chaos in political and cultural life. This 'economic maladjustment' could not be understood 'unless its psychological implications and consequences are put into their proper place.'[148] Humans regressed, not to more primitive instincts (as Freud proposed), but to earlier historical stages, particularly militaristic ones. Fascism represented an unstable combination of rational social planning and mass, emotional hysteria. The irrationality reflected the survival of atavistic traits that were primitive and dangerous. Planning, on the other hand, reflected the social structure of the future, although in a distorted way.

With the emergence of mass, industrial society, the structural foundation of Western society had been fundamentally transformed. The old ways of economic and political domination no longer worked, making economic and social planning essential. Fascism meant bad social planning, leading to 'dictatorship, conformity, and barbarism'.[149]

Mannheim's task was to propose a system of democratic planning that would not sacrifice real liberty or abandon democratic self-determination. People automatically assumed planning and totalitarianism were synonymous. Freedom, Mannheim believed, need not be the antithesis of planning and efficiency. It was necessary to examine the conceptions of freedom that had arisen historically and the new conception of freedom that was relevant to the present era.

At the beginning of the 'bourgeois era', freedom meant economic self-determination. Early industrialization had produced a relatively large social elite based on the widespread ownership of small economic holdings. Individual proprietors had to direct their economic actions rationally to fit their self-interest. As Durkheim had said, as the world of individual competition replaced mechanical solidarity, 'for the first time an individual is born' who thinks rationally and takes responsibility for her or his actions. At this stage, people's perspective was limited to their own advantages and the immediate results they could achieve.[150] Mannheim called intelligent thinking 'substantial rationality'.

Industrialization, however, had introduced a second kind of rationality, which Mannheim termed 'functional rationality'. As economic life became increasingly differentiated and complex, human reason was applied to the creation of large, bureaucratic political and economic structures organized along rational lines. More and more individuals employed in these structures were enmeshed in complex webs of regulations and standardized behaviours. Two important consequences followed. First, at least in their working lives, individuals were required to repress their emotions and impulses in order to fit into the hyper-rational bureaucratic structure. This led to a fundamental dissociation of human nature that was expressed in the split between work and leisure activities. Second, the growth of organizational, functional rationality undermined substantial rationality, 'the capacity to act intelligently in a given situation on the basis of one's own insight into the interrelations of events'. Rather than raising the average capacity of individual rationality, industrial society had a paralyzing effect. It deprived the average individual both of the capacity for rational insight and of the feeling of responsibility for her or his actions.[151]

The rise of capitalism initially produced a 'public', a large body of individuals who ran their own affairs and took responsibility for government. Industrialism reversed this trend, fracturing the self-conscious 'public' into an amorphous mass that becomes increasingly incompetent except within its ever-narrowing sphere of work, and a variety of elites who rise to power in different social spheres. As the capacity of the average individual diminishes, industrial society transfers responsibility and intellectual capacity to the elites who direct the bureaucratic structures and the process of rationalization. Elites monopolize positions of social power through the concentration and centralization of capital and because social knowledge and administrative activity become centralized in their hands. Mannheim warned about the equally significant 'concentration of the instruments of military power' that lessened the chance for revolutionary change and also threatened the ability of the masses to express their democratic will.[152]

The counterpart to the emergence of the masses was the creation of an almost caste-like bureaucratic elite that was increasingly isolated and distant from the masses. The modern mass was different in character from the oppressed masses of people in traditional society. Unlike feudal society, in which the common people were excluded from the world of political decision-making, one of the consequences of industrialism had been to draw more and more individuals from historically passive and disadvantaged classes into political action. As soon as the 'intellectually backward masses' entered the political realm, 'their intellectual shortcomings . . . even threaten the élites themselves.'[153] With their rationality stunted, individuals in the modern mass feel caught up in an economic world they are increasingly unable to understand and control. They experience an overwhelming anxiety, and appeal to a strong leader to bring security.

The psychological characteristics of the masses derive from the fractured nature of industrial society. Assuming that humans possess an inborn set of impulses, drives, and emotions, Mannheim argues that the widespread rationalization of everyday life 'means a constant repression of impulses'. These irrational psychic energies and drives are sublimated in mass society in cultural events such as sports and celebrations. More ominously, in democracies where masses dominate, irrationalities enter the political realm where rationality ought to prevail. Members of mass society are 'much more subject to suggestions, uncontrolled outbursts of impulses and psychic regression'.[154] Political elites in a mass society seek to influence the unorganized masses by appealing to emotional and irrational symbols. Unsublimated psychic energies threaten to produce an irrational, emotional outbreak that 'threatens to smash the whole subtle machinery of social life.' What is called mass democracy is a politics of emotions in which mass psychoses actually rule the world. Democracy gives rise to its antithesis and provides the weapons for its own destruction.[155]

The future will be determined by the conflict among small, elite minorities within which the masses will be manipulated, one way or another, by the creative minorities controlling society. In some of these elite groups, primitive traits operate in the absence of any restraint; other groups have developed superior rational and moral capacities and are capable of acting for the whole of society and bearing responsibility for it. Everything depends on which of the groups' outlooks 'will produce the energy, the decisiveness, and the capacity to master the vast social machinery of modern life.'[156]

Mannheim argues that the choice is not between spontaneous freedom and the control of individuals by social forces, but between conscious planning and the unregulated, spontaneous, and unconscious controls that determine everyday action and for which no one appears accountable. The world is dominated by private and vested interests, who wish to use the modern power of the new social techniques, such as propaganda and psychology, to manipulate individuals for their own ends. The powers will not disappear, and they threaten a greater loss of real freedom (the ability of persons to make conscious choices and determine their lives and the future of society) and the substitution of a false sense of freedom that comes with psychological manipulation. This argument would undergird much of the critical social commentary of popular sociology in the 1960s.

Modern society was moving into an era of social planning; the question was what form this planned society would take. Mannheim's *Man and Society in an Age of Reconstruction* attempted to answer this question. The fate of the Western world depended on the self-awareness on the part of the intellectual elite of its historical mission and its acquisition of political influence to direct society through rational planning. These ideas reflected the socio-political context in which Mannheim devised them, principally the rise of Fascism and World War II. A fuller treatment of them requires a more systematic exploration of this context than is provided here.

CONCLUSION

Fin de siècle social thought and capitalist society coexisted in an ambiguity that was deeper than the instinctive opposition of Romanticism to bourgeois philistinism. What the avant-garde rejected, above all, was society itself, the control that social forces of values and morality exerted on individual self-expression. Society limited and inhibited the individual pursuit of desire, the inner drives that were thought to define the nature of the human condition. The individual and society existed in a fundamental contradiction.

The ambivalence was exacerbated by the nature of bourgeois society as it developed at the turn of the century in the era of imperialism abroad and rising living standards at home. Capitalism requires the circulation of capital and commodities, the expanded reproduction of the system. By the 1890s the modern culture of capitalist consumption was in place. Capitalism commodified desires. Everything was for sale; even extreme experiences are now purchased with their specialized equipment, training, and professional support. The culture of modern capitalism exists in a symbiotic relationship with the culture of decadence, by supplying the means for the pursuit of the experience of the moment and even in its courting of potential, sudden death.

The nineteenth-century avant-garde, Nicholls argues, attempted to situate itself outside bourgeois society and in opposition to it. By the 1890s, however, the new generation embraced the modern condition, in which there were no spaces that capitalism had not penetrated, spreading its science, technology, and go-getter mentality. Global imperialism and economic growth at home were connected to a fixation on consumerism and the potentially contradictory notion that liberation could be purchased and desire satisfied or displayed as possibility and titillation.[157]

The ethics of spirituality and anti-materialism shaped alternative perspectives among the Bohemian counterculture. By the 1920s, however, the Bolshevik Revolution in Russia had added a further complication to the ambivalent attitudes of the avant-garde. D.H. Lawrence, for example, condemned in equal measure, and roughly for the same sins, both bourgeois society and Bolshevism. Bolshevism was anti-bourgeois and dynamic, but it was also anti-individualist, an attitude that strikes at the heart of the avant-garde. Any flirtation with Bolshevism could only be historically specific, temporary, and hesitant.

For many artists, the voyage into the unconscious and the imagination was also an escape from reality, a particular form of protest against the status quo. For the artists of alienation, the only liberation from the present is personal, individualistic, spiritual, and subjective. In practice, such liberation is available only to the few, the intellectual elite, who regard themselves as capable of seeing through both the hypocrisy of the present, materialistic culture and the unrealizable pretensions of the social reformers and revolutionaries. These artists were contemptuous of the masses and of the ideology of the masses, of democracy (an impossible illusion), equality (contrary to the laws of nature), and socialism (an absurd combination of both illusions). Friedrich Nietzsche was the most important spokesperson for this late nineteenth-century elitism.

Interpretations of Nietzsche's work have been bipolar in the twentieth century. The political right quickly claimed Nietzsche as a distinguished ancestor. But the end-of-the-century decadents, supposedly the polar opposite of authoritarian Fascism, also declared Nietzsche to be their champion. What both movements held in common was a rejection of many of the central values of Western society, coupled with a fundamentally anti-democratic elitism. While Nietzsche's language is more extreme than Freud's, both were responding to the threat that nineteenth-century men perceived in the emergence of radical political consciousness among women and, in a different form, among proletarian men. For Nietzsche and Freud, a strong, independent, career-minded woman was an ugly and an unnatural sight.

Nietzsche remained an intellectual curiosity, an underground figure, until postmodernism resurrected some of his ideas towards the end of the twentieth century. This is largely because postmodern theorists and Nietzsche had some of the same enemies. Nietzsche had rejected the rationalist legacy of the Enlightenment, all aspects of the scientific method, and the emphasis on human reason, an opposition to the rationalist legacy of Western civilization that has been resurrected by the postmodern turn in social theory.

Nietzsche's relativistic theory of truth influenced the sociological theory that Karl Mannheim developed in the 1920s. Social reality, in Mannheim's view, consists in the mutual relationships among multi-dimensional spheres. History shows that numerous factors interact on one another and that the outcome is always uncertain, with many mutual possibilities coexisting. The far-reaching effects of technological innovation in the military, for example, had upset 'the whole economic order and [had] divert[ed] its course into entirely different channels', changing the class system and producing a new type of mind that paved the way for the modern system of dictatorship.[158] In this dangerous world, the methods of sociology were increasingly of paramount importance. This meant for sociologists a responsibility for developing a theory of the whole within which probable consequences of alternative political choices could be analyzed. The first task of the sociologist is to undertake a qualitative analysis that distinguishes from the chaos of facts the various tendencies and the interplay of social forces. Only then should this complexity be broken down into simpler elements for quantitative analysis.[159]

Writing in the 1930s, in the face of Fascism and, perhaps more importantly, in the emerging tendency for government intervention to smooth out the worst excesses of unregulated capitalism, Mannheim perceived that the direction of social change was towards a mixed economy. With New Deal politics and Keynesian economics, Western democratic governments were moving, more or less, towards the welfare state. Mannheim imagined that, at least in Europe, the social plan likely would predominate and private interests would fit into controlled niches. In America, private economic power would dominate planning. In Europe, where the welfare state developed the furthest, reforming elites were pushed by the democratic sentiments of the masses, who did turn the class struggle into parliamentary and constitutional battles. Sociological understanding planned a very modest role in constructing the modern social formation. In retrospect, his image of the role of the intellectuals in the planned society was Utopian in the earlier sense of being unrealizable. As Mannheim argued, intellectuals can support the dominant ideology of the era or oppose it by highlighting the contradictions and injustices of the present and projecting alternative futures. In fact, many mid- and late twentieth-century sociologists would be more comfortable among the minority groups excluded from political power than in the back rooms of government power.

While Durkheim, Weber, and Mannheim would emerge as the dominant influences in sociology in the first half of the twentieth century, the counterpoint to positivism was developed by theorists who honed in on the subjective or micro side of social life. Just as poet William Blake could 'see a world in a grain of sand', Georg Simmel could connect the totality of society to the most mundane and fortuitous of human actions.[160]

For Simmel, sociological analysis should focus on individuals and then interactions. The emergence of the modern 'self' was an essential characteristic of individualism, which shaped the modern world. Individualism was predicated on freedom and difference and, Simmel argued, necessarily on inequality. From his perspective, society emerged as a complex matrix of social interactions. Simmel analyzed society from the micro rather than the macro perspective, beginning with an understanding of simple, two-person and three-person interactions.

SOCIAL THEORY AND THE MIND

Mannheim's relativism did not lead him to that deep pessimism about the fate of the modern world that had so troubled Weber. Weber's influence in sociology was not confined to his analysis of social structures. His methodological focus had been on the meaningfulness of human action. In the early decades of the twentieth century, sociological analysis took a subjective turn that developed into a distinct paradigm connecting the social and the psychological.

In Weber's view, the sociologist must attempt to attain *verstehen* (understanding), a concept that entailed a conscious appreciation or interpretation of the subjective meaning of another's actions. For Weber, behaviour was social insofar as the actor attached a subjective meaning to it; that is, in orienting action, he or she took into account the behaviour and, presumably, the interpreted subjective meaning of the other social actor.[1] You impute the deeper meaning of the other person, correctly or incorrectly, and orient your action accordingly. While some of these relationships will involve shared meanings, others will not be symmetrical and the interacting parties may not attribute the same subjective meaning to the relationship. Nevertheless, social action always involves some 'mutual orientation in so far as, even though partly or wholly erroneously, one party presumes a particular attitude toward him on the part of the other and orients his action to this expectation.'[2] Social interaction was also the starting point of Georg Simmel's move to an individualistic sociology. The subjectivist turn in sociology foreshadowed by Weber and Simmel developed into a distinct social psychology and micro-

sociology in the twentieth century, particularly in America where theorists preferred the ideological flavour of individualism.

GEORG SIMMEL

In European sociology, the predominant individualist was Georg Simmel (1858–1918). Like Durkheim, Simmel was a secularized Jew; unlike the French sociologist, he was excluded from prestigious university appointments because of his **iconoclasm**. Born in Berlin, Simmel's family baptized him as a Protestant despite their Jewish roots.[3] He studied a broad program at the University of Berlin, especially history, psychology, and philosophy, and then lectured from 1885 to 1914 in meagerly paid or only honorary appointments. Max Weber, who admired his work, attempted unsuccessfully to secure a professorship for Simmel, but he did not receive a chair in philosophy until 1914 at Strasbourg, four years before his death. The appointment was more a question of due recognition than financial need, since Simmel had been provided with an income substantial enough to lead the life of an independent scholar.[4]

Simmel took full advantage of his independence, studying and lecturing on a great variety of intellectual disciplines and developing a reputation as a lively, complex, critical, and negative thinker. His controversial reputation, his connection with socialism, and the anti-Semitism of turn-of-the-century Germany helped exclude Simmel from prestigious university posts and reinforced his situation as an intellectual outsider.[5]

In contrast to his contemporaries, Durkheim and Weber, Simmel did not develop a systematic sociology or methodology. He was criticized for failing to be rigorous, quantitative, and scientific. Instead, Simmel continually crossed the boundaries of social science and philosophy, defending the absence of 'radical clarity of questions and correctness of answers' by arguing that both the infancy of sociology and the 'infinite complexity of social life' meant that a certain measure of intuitive thinking was more valuable, at least initially, than a rigid conceptualization of formulas that would produce only an intellectually sterile social science.[6] Instead of attempting to systematize sociology, Simmel was a brilliant dilettante, adopting numerous perspectives and uncovering the interconnections between diverse objects of study, from the most mundane, such as money, to the most aesthetic, as in the works of Goethe or Rembrandt. Simmel regarded himself, foremost, as a philosopher.[7] Among his earliest intellectual interests was psychology, an established discipline well before sociology in Europe and America. From the 1890s until 1908, Frisby argues, Simmel developed a conceptualization of sociology as an eclectic discipline providing a new standpoint on understanding derived from other disciplines.[8]

Individual and Society

Sociology, with other disciplines dealing with the human mind and actions, faced in the modern world an almost infinite complexity and diversity, not only as regards individuals and groups, but in their interactions. Two exaggerated tendencies, Simmel argued, had appeared in the study of the relationship between individuals and society. From an **atomistic perspective**, the only reality is the individual, who becomes the object of scientific study, by which perspective 'the concept of society evaporates'. Eighteenth-century laissez-faire economic theory and liberal political theory imagined that society emerged as the sum of individual actions. Evolutionary sociology, deriving from Herbert Spencer, posited, on the contrary, an entity known as society that appeared to have an autonomy beyond the activities of the individuals who composed it.[9]

Simmel saw an inherent conflict between the life of society and the lives of its individual members. While society is the fusion of individual interactions, a given society presents itself to the individual as an organ that makes claims on the individual as though it were an alien body—as if it were something more real than the individual. In Simmel's view, society strives to be an organic unit that demands each individual fulfill her or his functions for the benefit of the whole. Yet the individual, also, strives for a specific unity and wholeness, to develop all her or his capacities, not merely those few imposed by the interests of society. The conflict between the individual and society is not rooted in an anti-social human nature, but in the conflict between one egotistical whole (society) that seeks to impose a limited one-sidedness upon one of its parts (the individual), 'which itself strives to be whole'.[10]

The view that the individual strives for wholeness or perfection derived from the Romanticism of Goethe and the philosophy of Nietzsche, for whom the perfection of the individual is an objective value in itself that an individual strives to attain, often irrespective of the person's own happiness. The individual seeks after her or his cravings for the sake of their realization. In this 'working on oneself', no price may be too high, whether sacrifice is demanded from the self or from others.[11]

The concept of the freedom of the individual had its highest development in the eighteenth century in the context of the many and varied restrictions and structural inequalities of the old regime. Theorists such as Smith, Rousseau, and Kant sought to remove these artificial limitations in order for the individual to realize liberty and thereby bring human life back to its natural state. Once put into practice, however, the freedom of the individual results in a self-contradiction unless all are equally strong and privileged. Since this is not the case, freedom leads to the exploitation of the weak by the strong, recreating a power inequality that, like the accumulation of capital, cannot but quickly expand until the freedom of the privileged is at the expense of the loss of freedom of the oppressed. Hence, paradoxically, it is only by removing the freedom to accumulate private property that the greatest barrier to human freedom is removed. Thus, argues Simmel, there is 'a deep antinomy between freedom and equality' that can be resolved only 'if both are dragged down to the negative level of propertylessness and powerlessness'. The only conceivable escape from this dilemma of absolute levelling is in the ethics of altruism—the conscious agreement not to use your inborn gifts, your natural inequality, egotistically for your own benefit. That is what the French revolutionaries understood intuitively, Simmel claimed, when the slogan 'fraternity' was added to 'liberty and equality'.[12]

The eighteenth-century conception of individuality posited a distinction between humanity-in-itself, a constant nature essentially identical in all people, and a differentiated nature—individuality (whatever made individuals unique)—that was external to the self, historical, and accidental. Your individuality was not in your innermost being or self (a more modern view), but resulted from the various experiences of your life—your merely empirically imposed reality. Hence, humans possessed universal, inalienable rights derived from their essential human nature that were common to all. Hence, also, Kant could suggest that a universal and unchangeable ego produces a single objective world that is the same for all individuals. Freedom and equality, then, were assumed to be identical. Once the human mind could be made free of any particular characteristics produced by its given place in the world, and was stripped down to its essential and identical core, then it would be possible to discover the natural laws of humanity and a universal ethics; you could act according to principles that you would generalize to all others.[13]

Freedom or Equality

In the nineteenth century, this Kantian belief in the unity of freedom and equality was split into what Simmel described as two more realistic tendencies: 'equality without freedom, and . . . freedom without equality'. Neither could be attained absolutely, reflecting a sociological ambiguity; both corresponded to great character traits of human nature. The values of one type of person embrace the ideas of equality for all, 'however nebulous and unthinkable in the concrete this idea may be'. For the other type, 'individual differences . . . constitute an ultimate, irreducible' value. These are ultimate values rooted in the different definitions of self rather than being merely rational beliefs.[14] For Simmel, the feeling of equality reflected a collective but unconscious memory of humanity's primitive, undifferentiated state. Socialism, then, was at least in part rooted in 'very obscure, possibly **atavistic-**communistic instincts'.[15] Just as species and societies have differentiated, modern individualism represents a more highly evolved human state.

In the short run, the socialist movement, which is rooted in the politics of class, can successfully equate freedom and equality. For the labourer who faces the hardships of hunger and wage work, a movement towards equality would increase freedom. On the other hand, it was not just the rentier or the capitalist who benefited from the high degree of personal freedom in modern society, which necessarily entails inequality, but the artist and the intellectual as well. Similarly, Simmel pointed out, the women's movement was divided by class interests. Higher-class women seek the skilled employment opportunity in order to secure their independence and demonstrate their abilities. For the woman factory worker, employment represents freedom less than it presents an obstacle to her happiness as a wife and mother.[16]

In the longer run, a socialist society attempting to maximize equality would run aground on the shoals of human nature, on the principles of freedom and imagination that, as novelist Eugene Zamiatin claimed, were opposed to equality and sameness (see the synopsis in Box 14.1).[17] Social differences might be reduced as much as possible, but nothing could eliminate differences in the psychological structure of humanity: individual differences would base their utterly inevitable

Box 14.1

In 1924, the dissident Russian intellectual, Eugene Zamiatin, published a satirical dystopia, *We*, the forerunner of *Brave New World*. Set 1,000 years in the future, the tale recounts the personal journal of D–503, a mathematician in the United State, a totalitarian regime built behind a Great Green Wall. The State claimed to achieve the maximum happiness by imposing the maximum equality, which Zamiatin defined as absolute sameness, the absence of freedom. The principles of Taylorist rationality and Benthamite surveillance were applied to 23 hours of the day, confining freedom and the expression of desire to a fraction of time. D–503, however, was attracted to I–330, a free-spirited woman. Through her, he was exposed to the pleasure, danger, and disorder of free desire, of the 'I' rather than the group conformity of the 'we'. In the ideology of the United State, desire was at the root of freedom and, hence, of unhappiness and inequality. As D–503 wrestles with temptation, State scientists announce they have finally discovered the 'worm in the mind' that is the source of unhappiness: it is imagination. They have found the final cure for the illness of freedom: 'there is a centre for fancy—a miserable little nervous knot in the . . . frontal lobe of the brain. A triple treatment of this knot with X-rays will cure you of fancy.

'*Forever!*

'You are perfect. You are mechanized; the road to one-hundred-percent-happiness is open!'

Now, D–503 has to choose between two potential futures: freedom and desire, or equality and regimentation.

passions of greed and envy, of domination and feeling of oppression, on the slight differences in social position that can never be removed. In addition, there are organizational limitations on the attainment of socialism. Since every society, at least for reasons of technical efficiency, must possess a hierarchy of superordinate and subordinate positions, the only possible kind of equality would be achieved by ensuring that an individual's qualifications corresponded exactly to the position occupied in the hierarchy. However, this is impossible because competence is widely diffused in the population. There are many talented individuals and few superior positions, leaving many individuals personally dissatisfied.[18]

Any association of people in groups, Simmel asserts, necessarily develops a structure of subordination of the many to the few. The group requires leadership because of the essential difference between the mass and the individual. The mass is formed by the individuals that constitute it, but individuals *contribute* different qualities to the common spirit of the group than they *possess* as their private property. Basically, only those qualities can be merged into the group that are common to all. These are the qualities that evolved earliest and are most widespread in the species, by definition, the primitive and inferior and subordinate traits. The mass exists at the lowest common denominator of humanity and therefore violates the individual desire to attain wholeness and perfection. The more complex qualities, which evolved later or developed consciously or unconsciously in society, are not widespread and occur unequally among individuals. These elevate the individual from anything he or she has in common with the masses.[19] Groups, then, require leaders. A synthesis between the opposites of freedom and equality is a logical impossibility.[20]

When social thinkers in the nineteenth century dissolved the assumed unity of freedom and equality, they argued that inequality rather than equality best expressed the essence of society. Once liberated from the chains of traditional authority, social thinkers extended the doctrine of the free individual to emphasize their differences from other individuals—the modern cult of individuality as an absolute value. 'The individual seeks his *self* as if he did not yet have it, and is certain that this self is the only fixed point.' On the one hand, the individual ego may still feel the primitive need for group encouragement and support. 'Or, on the contrary, it may be strong enough to bear the loneliness of its own quality' and hold that the only reason a group exists is to allow an individual to measure his own incomparability and the individuality of his own world by those of the others.

Modern individualism was first elaborated in art, for example in the Romantic writings of Goethe, which, for the first time, 'shows a world which is based exclusively on the individual peculiarities of its protagonists.'[21] Goethe had written that general culture and institutions were mere 'fooleries. Any man's task is to do *something* extraordinarily well, as no other man in his immediate environment can.' It was through Romanticism that individualism reached the common consciousness in the nineteenth century. The Romantic individualist finds his or her identity in what is personally unique.[22] Society, however, requires interactions. For Simmel, the social scene is not constructed by the simple addition of isolated and equal individuals. Society is a relatively objective unity created by a synthesis of the complex, reciprocal, and dynamic interactions of its many parts. For Simmel, individuals 'are the immediate, concrete data of all historical reality.' This mere aggregate of isolated individuals is transformed into particular units by reciprocal interaction.[23] Society is the name given to the sum of the interactions among individuals, which differs according to the number, the character, and the cohesion of the various interactions.[24]

Ultimately, for Simmel, human interactions are based on psychological variables such as motives, drives, and interests, the non-social materials that produce a relatively objective entity known as society. Interaction (or 'sociation' in Simmel's terminology) occurred in its most basic form in face-to-face encounters between individuals, but also appeared in the consciousness of people as objective, impersonal structures that appear to be autonomous. These social formations, however, are the actual product of the interactions that construct them.[25] For Simmel, society emerges from the interaction of individuals, but in the process something new and more complex is constructed that has a more permanent existence.

By conceptualizing society from the bottom up and rooting it in individual psychology and the interaction of these individuals, Simmel was a forerunner of **social psychology** and of the **social interactionist** approach in modern sociology. Simmel's interest in interaction led him to study small group dynamics in dyads, triads, and larger groups, pushing him at times in the direction of social psychology and the distinction between types of personality.

The dyad—closely knit interaction of two people as in sexual or friendship relationships—is distinct behaviourally and morally from membership in the crowd. Crowds heighten impulsiveness and reduce moral restraint. Feeling protected and somehow anonymous when in a group, people may participate in crimes that, if they felt individually responsible, they would shrink from committing. In a crowd, the individual contributes only a fraction towards the outcome of the interaction, minimizing responsibility for the social construction of the whole. The dyad is an opposite social situation because each individual is aware, at most times, that the social construction of the outcome is her or his responsibility. The outcome is a result of the competition or negotiation between the two, and is affected by social factors such as power, prestige, or authority.

The social dynamics of the triad—the interaction of three—adds crucially different elements principally in the possibility of unity and separation. Geometrically, the dyad can be represented by a straight line of communication, back and forth between the two poles. Unity between two is easier to strike and maintain than unity among three. The triad could become a triangle, complicating the negotiated outcome as in the love triangle, which is a staple of comedy and romantic fiction. Like the third wheel on an outing or three children attempting to play together, at any moment one of the three may be defined by the others as an outsider and excluded. The temporary alliance between two can be disrupted by claims of the third for inclusion, or even for replacing one of the favoured individuals in the pair. Each member of the dyad is exclusively dependent on the other for the reciprocation of feelings and sentiments, making it a qualitatively distinct type of relationship. The third party threatens to disrupt this intimacy, resulting in jealousy and competition. In a triad, members can divide and conquer, make alliances or break them.

Adding more members to the group does not substantially change the possibilities of the social dynamics.[26] An intriguing exploration of triadic relationships occurs in Jean-Paul Sartre's play, *No Exit* (1945), which is set in Hell (see Box 14.2 for a brief synopsis).[27]

The *fin de siècle* Bohemians took the Romantic preoccupation with the individual, Fitch argues, and shaped it into the modern search for the authentic, god-like self.[28] The self became an object of adoration, as in Walt Whitman's 'Song of Myself'. When Ibsen's Peer Gynt asks the question, what should a man be? the answer is obvious: '*Himself.*' The Gyntish self is found in:

> The world behind my forehead's arch,
> By force of which I'm no one else
> Than I. . . .

Box 14.2

Three people are confined for eternity in a small room in Hell. Garcin was a soldier who was shot for desertion. Inez was killed in her sleep when her lesbian lover turned on the gas. Estelle died from pneumonia after drowning her infant daughter, conceived out of wedlock. The three soon understand the function of a triad, in Hell: 'each of us will act as torturer of the two others'. First, Inez tries to come on to Estelle and isolate Garcin: 'We two women will have the place to ourselves.' But Estelle rejects Inez because her sole desire is to attract Garcin. Inez realizes she is doubly rejected: It's 'one against two'. Garcin's desires, however, are deeper than sex. He needs someone to sustain his self-image as a man of principle. Thousands may call him a coward, he pleads to Estelle, but, 'If there's someone, just one person, to say quite positively ... I'm brave and decent ... that one person's faith would save me.' But the nymphomaniac Estelle can't give him unconditional respect: 'Coward or hero, it's all one— provided he kisses well,' she replies. So Garcin turns to Inez for self-confirmation, but Inez has no use for him. She plans to divide and conquer. She'll compel Estelle to see Garcin through her eyes, making her despise him, too. This will realign the triad in her favour. In revenge, Garcin can make Inez squeal by caressing Estelle, but Inez is constantly watching them: 'I'm a crowd all by myself', she taunts them. There's no escape—each holds up an inescapable mirror for the other two, creating their reality and self-concept. 'Hell is—other people.'

—Jean-Paul Sartre, *No Exit* (1945). From *No Exit and Three Other Plays* by Jean-Paul Sartre, copyright 1946 by Stuart Gilbert. Copyright renewed 1974 by Maris Agnes Mathilde Gilbert. Copyright 1948, 1949 by Alfred A. Knopf, Inc. Used by permission of Vintage Books, a division of Random House, Inc.

The Gyntish self—it is the host
Of wishes, appetites, desires,—
The Gyntish self, it is the sea
Of fancies, exigencies, claims.
All that, in short, makes *my* breast heave,
And whereby I, as I, exist.[29]

The self is the force pushing the individual to seek fulfillment of the inner appetites and desires. Peer Gynt chases his wishes through a succession of multiple selves, never finding the inner core of his being. For Ibsen, the worship of this god-like self is a disease; it is like shutting oneself in a barrel, hermetically sealed with a self-bung (stopper) and having no thought or mind for others.[30] Such a world, Ibsen suggests in *Peer Gynt*, is essentially a madhouse.[31]

In the Romantic conception of the human soul, the depths of subjectivity were unfathomable by scientific rationality. Embracing irrationalism as a vehicle for truth is different from seeking to understand the irrational. Sigmund Freud, as a physician, regarded himself as a scientist who could investigate and understand the irrational side of humanity in a rational way.

SIGMUND FREUD

Sigmund Freud (1856–1939) distinguished the rational mind, the realm of consciousness, from a second, interior part of the mind of which the individual was unaware. This inner mind—the **unconscious**—required explanation. Freud believed that the unconscious mind had been appreciated for centuries by playwrights and novelists, from the ancient Greeks through Shakespeare, to the novels of Dostoyevsky, making them the earliest investigators of human psychology. Freud's ambition was to place the study of this inner mind on a scientific footing.

Freud was born in Germany in 1856, but spent almost his entire life in Vienna, Austria. Because of his Jewish ethnicity, he was forced into exile following the Nazi occupation of Austria. Although he died in 1939 during the most dangerous days of anti-Semitism, Freud's birth had coincided with the emancipation of the Jews in Germany. Newly mobile geographically and socially in the late 1850s, the Jewish population sought to assimilate into mainstream European culture.[32]

Freud's family migrated to Vienna where they lived an apparently lower middle-class life. Freud was an excellent student and, following a cholera epidemic, resolved to study medicine. He hoped to make a breakthrough discovery in experimental medicine that would establish his reputation and fortune. Marrying his fiancée, Martha Bernays, required financial security and a promise of upward mobility. His initial idea was to discover the medical properties of cocaine. His experimentation, at first on himself, led to a publication announcing the virtues of the drug. When the addictive nature of cocaine became obvious, Freud was forced to build a reputation elsewhere.[33]

Freud and Martha were married in 1886. During the next decade, the couple had six children, while Freud's clinical practice, scientific reputation, and grand ambitions expanded. He delved into the extensive scientific studies of the unconscious mind, hypnosis, obsessions, hysteria (physical symptoms of illness with no obvious physical cause), and phobias (irrational fears).[34] Through his clinical practice with neurotics, Freud developing a distinctive therapeutic method he would call psychoanalysis, a technique of talking therapy—long sessions where the patient recalls past events and describes present fantasies. The method involved bringing repressed memories and feelings to the surface of the conscious mind, systematizing mental processes that occurred spontaneously. In Freud's view, the unconscious broke through unexpectedly into the conscious mind in dreams, in fantasies, in unexpected reactions, in irrational fears, and in sudden and significant turns of phrase that became known as 'Freudian slips'.

During the second half of the 1890s, Freud was his own chief patient, absorbed in the analysis of his own dreams and the search for the root of his own neurotic disorders. In his *Interpretation of Dreams*, published in 1900, Freud examined the way the unconscious mind constructed stories in dreams made up of myths, out-of-context images, and absurd symbols that appeared to have no rational meaning or explanation. For Freud, however, these symbolic expressions could be understood through a type of scientific observation and inquiry with analysis.

Freud said that dreams represented universal patterns of sexual development, such as the competition between a father and his son for the attention of the wife/mother. Childhood feelings had been repressed and could appear to the conscious mind only through the agency of a mental censor that transformed the forbidden sexual content into apparently unrelated symbols, giving dreams their extraordinarily imaginative form. Some symbols in dreams (for example, water, snakes, and falling) had universal meanings. On the other hand, other less generalizable images reflected a person's individual experiences or repressed memories.

Freud believed that the experiences children had in their earlier years were the keys to understanding personality and psychological problems later in life. By having a client describe the images of a dream in detail, and having her/him associate these images with aspects of conscious life, Freud would interpret the dream, explaining what he believed the unconscious mind was expressing. Dream images represented what Freud regarded as universal fears, fantasies, or histories, common to humanity as a whole, or the specific incidents or traumas in an individual's life, particularly those of childhood. In his approach to understanding the human mind, Freud sought to apply a scientific method to the thought of Nietzsche (Box 14.3).[35]

Most of Freud's early patients were middle-class women, who possibly were more prone than men to define their troubles as resulting from some form of personal, mental disturbance. In particular, Freud saw patients who reported suffering from physical ailments that appeared to have no physical cause. In the course of his practice, in which he began to delve into the hitherto forbidden world of female sexuality (an area in which males had been ignorant), Freud was at first surprised to learn that many of these patients revealed having been sexually abused as children. In Freud's early 'seduction theory', this trauma was at the root of their later hysteria and neuroses, which could be cured by recalling the episode, through psychoanalysis and 'free association', to the conscious mind. This theory was consistent with the view he was developing that mental illnesses and neuroses were the result of 'repressed' experiences that had been buried in the subconscious.

But Freud soon began to doubt the veracity of these women's claims. Surely so many of them could not have been abused as children? Discarding his initial belief that his patients were describing actual traumas they had experienced, Freud had recourse to an alternative interpretation: the claims of abuse represented subconscious fantasies that were common to the whole pattern of human psychosexual maturation. This was the beginning of Freud's original psychosexual theory. The reported traumas were part of a universal process of sexual development rather than actual

---

Box 14.3

All instincts that do not discharge themselves outwardly *turn inward*—this is what I call the internalization of man: thus it was that man first developed what was called his 'soul'. The entire inner world, originally as thin as if it were stretched between two membranes, expanded and extended itself, acquired depth, breadth and height in the name of measures as outward discharge was *inhibited*.

—Friedrich Nietzsche, *The Genealogy of Morals* (1887)

events in the lives of young girls or a reflection of the puritanical repression of women's sexuality. Freud came to believe that women who confided to him their histories of childhood sexual abuse were fantasizing; they were verbalizing unconscious longings and wish fulfillment. Of course, today, knowing something of the extent of the sexual abuse of women universally in societies, his disbelief constitutes a further form of abuse, and a trait that calls into question his abilities as a 'scientific' observer and 'objective' analyst.

Freud developed his theory of the mind over several decades. Consistent with the scientific views of his time, he believed that innate instincts and drives undergirded the behaviour both of animals and of humans. According to the biological sciences, humans were born with a number of instinctive urges that had a survival function for the species. For Freud, the repository of instinctual urges deep in the subconscious mind of humanity was termed the **id** ('it'). The infant was entirely self-centred, impulsive, and demanding. One way the id was understood by Freud was in terms of the **pleasure principle**—the demand by the body to have its needs met immediately. In trying to meet these needs, the infant encounters the physical world around it, which does not immediately gratify its desires. The **ego** develops in an attempt to mediate between this external reality and the pleasure principle driving the organism from inside.

Soon, however, society intervenes to demand that these urges be tamed and controlled. The infant could not always eat when hungry. At first, the infant could urinate whenever she or he felt the urge. Soon, however, parents teach the social rules about controlling your biological urges. Parents are primarily responsible for developing the third element of the mind, the **superego** (or conscience). The superego is the accumulated and sometimes unconscious knowledge of social rules, mores, and taboos that the child learns not to violate. At first, the rules are external, imposed on the child by adult authorities. As the superego develops, however, they become ingrained, internalized in the individual; they become part of her or his

personality. The creation of a superego takes place by about age seven, although it is a process that may not be completed or, on the other hand, can be too thoroughly completed.

Instinctual urges, then, have to be controlled, or repressed. The desires are still present, but in many cases the conscious mind has been trained not to perceive them; as Nietzsche claimed, their discharge is inhibited. Instead, instinctual urges are buried in the unconscious, whence they emerge spontaneously in a myriad of ways.

Sexual desire was among the most powerful of the instincts. Children were instinctually sexual beings. Sexual desire was present at birth and, soon afterwards, male infants develop sexual desires for their mothers and express sexual jealousy towards their fathers. This is the Oedipus complex that earned Freud so much opposition at the time because, as Thomas Mann said, it 'relentlessly destroyed all faith in . . . the innocence of the suckling babe.'[36]

Unconscious childhood sexuality is part of what Freud theorized as the normal path of psychosexual development. The infant experiences his or her sexual feelings first about the mouth, through breast-feeding—the oral stage of development. This is followed by a fascination with defecation—the anal stage (from about 18 months to three years). Next, the child reaches the phallic stage of development characterized by recognition of the genitalia and by, for example, masturbation.

The root of normal sexuality as well as all the adult sexual 'perversions' can be found in childhood. For normal development, the child has to learn to redirect sexual energies away from the self (narcissism) towards the appropriate other. There is a point where the focus of sexual energy is on the same sex; normal development, however, demands that the object of sexual attraction become a member of the other sex. The genital stage begins at puberty and is characterized by an interest in heterosexual intercourse. Heterosexual sexuality, then, is the normal and natural outcome of sexual development. Other forms of sexual expression are unnatural and unhealthy. If anything interferes with this normal developmental process, the individual could become fixated at an earlier stage, continuing behaviour inappropriately into adulthood. Homosexuality, along with a number of other sexual practices, such as oral or anal sex, adult masturbation, masochism, sadism, and narcissism, were essentially illnesses cause by arrested sexual development. Presumably, then, they could be cured and, for improved psychological health, they should be cured.

Minor psychological disturbances were neuroses, but more serious psychological problems—psychoses (schizophrenia, manic depression)—were seen as symptoms of repressed severe psychological traumas. Thomas Mann put this more dramatically. Two opposing instincts clashed: 'the compulsive force of love' (libido) and those 'psychical corrective . . . instincts tending to conformability and regularity'. The latter, chastity, apparently triumphed and love 'was suppressed, held in darkness and chains, by fear, conventionality, aversion'. But this was merely 'a pyrrhic victory', for 'love thus suppressed was not dead; it lived, it laboured after fulfillment in the darkest and secretest depths of the being. It would break through the ban of chastity', emerging unrecognizably in 'the form of illness. Symptoms of disease are nothing but a disguised manifestation of the power of love.'[37]

Freud's solution or cure was to have the patient find words to express these supposed repressed experiences, dredged up from the unconscious to the conscious mind. Once the patient could be brought to describe the experience that was at the root of the problem, then it could be discussed or understood rationally and the phobia or hysteria could disappear. If the experience involved some disturbance in the normal path of **psychosexual development**, then the patient could be cured through helping her/him understand what was normal and how her/his experiences had caused deviation from this route. This entailed lengthy sessions, often over a period of years, where the patients talked about their past, remembering childhood experiences, recounting parenting practices and their relationships with their mother and father. This method

became known as psychoanalysis and is popularly portrayed with the patient reclining on a couch while the analyst takes notes.

Basically, Freud's psychoanalytical method was to have a patient tell his or her own biography. Then, Freud, or another therapist using Freud's theory of psychosexual development, would reinterpret the patient's past experiences from the point of view of Freudian theory. Ultimately, Freud's theory was far less scientific than he believed. For some, Freudianism has been largely discredited for the reason that none of his views on the symbolic meanings of the unconscious could be scientifically proven or disproved. Freud built a grand theoretical structure based on clinical experience and his own imagination. In his systematic, psychosexual theories, he constructed an elaborate modern mythology with no solid foundation, which could be accepted on faith or not at all. However, his efforts to unlock the subconscious spurred further efforts to understand the secrets of human personality. In addition to the schools of psychoanalysis Freud initiated or inspired through opposition to his views, his influence resurfaced in the complex work of Jacques Lacan (1901–81) and, partly through his influence, in the late twentieth century among postmodernists.

Once conceived, Freud applied his theory widely. He continued to interpret literature in terms of his psychosexual categories. Beneath the behaviour of crowds and panics he detected the influence of libido, an eros that bound followers to leaders. In *The Future of an Illusion* (1927) Freud called religion a universal neurosis.[38] For Freud, religious beliefs were essentially illusions misinterpreting humanity's unconscious desires as if they represented a deeper, spiritual reality and truth—a profound irony when one considers that his own theorizing amounted to a system of belief. At the dawn of civilization, Freud said, humans lived in a terrifying world and experienced a need for consolation and for understanding. The first step was to impose a human personality on the impersonality of nature, to people the unknown with beings who were essentially like humans. By doing so, humans were no longer absolutely defenceless in the face of the power of the unknown: 'We can apply the same methods against these violent supermen outside that we employ on our own society; we can try to adjure them, to appease them, to bribe them, and, by so influencing them, we may rob them of part of their power.'[39]

In Freud's view, faith in the fantastic and the spiritual was being undermined rapidly by science. The world was becoming demystified. He believed that religion was destined to disappear from human culture when humanity finally gave up this last of its childish illusions. Reason and experience undermine religious claims. In the end, the only religion that could survive the onslaught of rationalism would be a 'purified' doctrine consisting of a belief in a higher Being who cannot be defined 'and whose purposes cannot be discerned', but such a belief system would offer humanity no consolation for its woes or compensation for its unhappiness.[40] Religion was a kind of neurosis that needed a scientific cure. Nevertheless, if humanity was largely unreasonable, as Freud's instinctual theory claimed, then they would always be susceptible to religious illusions based on scientifically unfalsifiable beliefs. It has been argued that Freud's explanation of the unconscious mind hid an equally insecure foundation, despite Freud's scientific pretensions, and was accepted on the basis of its internal logic and apparent clinical success. Beyond any scientific claims, Freudian terminology has entered the **language**: we 'recognize' phallic symbols, discuss sexual frigidity, ridicule penis envy, and refer to sexual energy as libido.

D.H. Lawrence was among the earliest English novelists whose writing reflects the new theories of instinctual, sexual energy. He develops the Oedipal theme in his novel *Sons and Lovers* (1913). In Lawrence's view, mothers love their sons passionately, as if the umbilical cord had never been severed. When Mrs Morel and her son walk down the street they feel 'the excitement of lovers having an adventure together'. Her son 'was like her knight who wore her favour in the battle.' Mrs Morel had no life of her own and lived through her sons, as if their lives were her own. She could

feel she had put a man in two great centres of industry; 'these men would work out what *she* wanted; they were derived from her, and their works also would be hers.' When Mrs Morel was dying of cancer, her son Paul kissed her again and stroked the hair from her temples, gently, tenderly, as if she were a lover.

Paul doesn't fulfill the classic tale of Oedipus, however; he doesn't kill his father. On the contrary, in the face of his mother's suffering, he crushes morphia pills and puts them in her milk, killing his mother but also a part of himself.[41] The intentional murder of his mother is also liberating for Paul since a mother's love is stifling and subtly domineering, which arises from the dependency entailed in living your life through others. For Lawrence, men must dissolve the maternal bond in order to establish their essential selves in relation to the wider world.

Critics in the women's movement have long argued that Freud's theories are particularly misogynistic—a criticism they extend to D.H. Lawrence. Freud offers a supposedly scientific justification for women's second-class status. In his view,[42] when girls discover that their genitals are different from boys, they develop a castration complex, believing that they once possessed and then lost a penis. Freud hypothesized that women invented clothing out of shame to hide their lack of male genitalia.[43] Girls notice not only the difference in anatomy but, Freud believed, understand its 'significance' as well. Because of a boy's 'obviously superior equipment', girls feel wronged and develop 'penis envy'. For women, normal psychosexual development leads them to desire a baby as a substitute for the longed-for penis. In the words of Nietzsche, 'everything in woman hath one solution—it is called pregnancy.'[44]

In Freud's presumption of a normal pattern of development, a girl believes that her mother had also been castrated and, in rejection of her, turns her sexuality towards her father. Unconsciously, she wishes to be impregnated by him: 'a baby takes the place of a penis in accordance with an ancient symbolic equivalence.'[45] The desire for children is part of a woman's normal development and is necessary for preserving the species. Furthermore, the belief about having been castrated leads women, in the course of their normal psychological development, to an acceptance of their instinctive passivity, from which follow the other characteristics of normal femininity.

Some women, however, respond to this penis envy abnormally and develop a wish to have, for example, an intellectual profession for which, as a woman, Freud believes she is biologically unsuited. By some constitutional factor, some women do not assert their natural passivity but cling to masculinity as an abnormal form of the desire for a penis. While this explains, for Freud, the supposed pathology underlying the motivation of the unnatural women who wants to have a career—the New Women of the 1890s—this 'masculinity complex' may also end in female homosexuality.[46]

Freud had accepted at face value all the old prejudices about women (as Wollstonecraft would have put it) and simply put a modern, pseudo-scientific spin on them. Thus, while Freud's psychoanalytic theories have been discarded by the majority of psychologists, these long-standing prejudices have not been undermined, always reappearing in new guises. Freudian theory as Freud had developed it was influential well into the twentieth century. It is perhaps fitting, since the earliest psychoanalysts were novelists and playwrights, that Freudian symbols had their most permanent expression in modern literature, where the questions of sexuality and aggressiveness have been prominently debated.

The life instinct—libido or sexual energy—and the instinct of aggression can also be found reflected in Lawrence's *Sons and Lovers*. The protagonist of the novel, Paul Morel, is having an affair with Baxter Dawes's wife. Dawes initiates a fight with his rival, which quickly develops into a primeval struggle for survival. As Lawrence describes the fight, the reasoning human is temporarily overpowered as instinct takes control of the body:

Pure instinct brought his hands to the man's neck, and before Dawes, in frenzy and agony, could wrench him free, he had got his fists twisted in the scarf and his knuckles dug in the throat of the other man. He was a pure instinct, without reason or feeling. His body, hard and wonderful in itself, cleaved against the struggling body of the other man; not a muscle in him relaxed. He was quite unconscious; only his body had taken upon itself to kill this other man. For himself, he had neither feeling nor reason. He pressed hard against his adversary, his body adjusting itself to his one pure purpose of choking the other man ... silent, intent, unchanging. . . .

Then suddenly he relaxed, full of wonder and misgiving. Dawes had been yielding. Morel felt his body flame with pain, and he realised what he was doing; he was all bewildered.[47]

Morel's conscious mind finally was able to take control. After the fight, the bond between the two men grew stronger, Lawrence said, because they had fought: '[T]hey had met in a naked extremity of hate, and it was a bond. At any rate, the elemental man in each had met.' Afterwards, the two men 'were afraid of the naked selves they had been', an unconscious recognition of the sadomasochistic emotion they had repressed.[48] The closest thing to this aggressive or death instinct is sexuality, Lawrence suggests, describing Morel's other primeval desire in very similar terms:

'Don't "but" me,' he said, kissing her quickly, as a fire ran through him.

She submitted, and was silent.

It was true as he said. As a rule, when he started love-making, the emotion was strong enough to carry with it everything—reason, soul, blood—in a great sweep. . . . Gradually the little criticisms, the little sensations, were lost, thought also went, everything borne along in one flood. He became, not a man with a mind, but a great instinct. His hands were like creatures, living; his limbs, his body, were all life and consciousness, subject to no will of his, but living in themselves.[49]

The Individual versus Civilization

For Freud, the individual and society existed in a powerful contradiction; in his view, 'every individual is virtually an enemy of civilization.' As Morel's fight with Dawes is intended to demonstrate, destructive and anti-social tendencies exist in all humanity. Living in society demands of people that they renounce their instinctual pleasure-seeking and confine their desires within the boundaries that society erects. But the great masses of people 'are lazy and unintelligent'. They are unwilling to surrender their desires and incapable of understanding a reasonable argument. Consequently, to exist at all society requires that a conscious minority 'who possess superior insight into the necessities of life' would acquire power and use coercion to impose social order on the 'resisting majority'. This fact of history is not rooted in culture, Freud argues, and cannot be altered by changing social arrangements, as some social theorists had postulated.[50]

Just as Freud turned his theory into an explanation of the history of an individual, so, too, he believed that psychological processes undergird human history. In *Civilization and Its Discontents*, which Freud wrote after the hysterical and pathological destructiveness of World War I—the collective insanity of a whole civilization—Freud pronounced his verdict on humanity. In Freud's Hobbesian formulation, society emerges when a majority of people establish a power over and against individuals, coercing individuals to limit their pursuit of their satisfactions or pleasures, in Freud's terms, to sacrifice their instincts. In civilization, people have 'exchanged a portion of' their 'happiness for a portion of security'. Liberty is an original and natural, though undesirable, human condition. The continuing demand for freedom is directed against the restrictions of society or 'against civilization altogether'.[51]

The drama of history is to be understood as the struggle of two opposites, represented by Eros, or the instinct of life, and Death, or the instinct of destruction. If sexuality was the dominant instinct in the development of the individual and the preservation of the species, hardly less important was the instinct for aggression. War, competition, inequality, and jealousy all were expressions of humanity's innate aggressiveness. Civilization is a process driven by the erotic instinct (love) but, step by step, it is opposed by humanity's 'natural aggressive instinct, the hostility of each against all and of all against each'.[52] This is a fundamental truth about humanity that the social reformers disavow. For Freud, human beings:

> are not gentle creatures who want to be loved, and who at the most can defend themselves if they are attacked; they are, on the contrary, creatures among whose instinctual endowments is to be reckoned a powerful share of aggressiveness. As a result, their neighbour is for them not only a potential helper or sexual object, but also someone who tempts them to satisfy their aggressiveness on him, to exploit his capacity for work without recompense, to use him sexually without his consent, to seize his possessions, to humiliate him, to cause him pain, to torture, and to kill him. *Homo homini lupus*. Who, in the face of all the evidence in his own life and of history, will have the courage to dispute this assertion?[53]

Novelist Joseph Conrad would not dispute Freud's assertion. His character Marlow penetrated into the heart of Africa along the course of a mighty river, from the coast into the deep interior, and from civilization to the primeval past. Marlow followed the trail of the enigmatic Kurtz, who had ventured into Africa with altruistic sentiments to do good, but instead stepped over the edge and reverted to savagery in a primitive regression to mother earth: '[T]he wilderness . . . seemed to draw him to its pitiless breast by the awakening of forgotten and brutal instincts, by the memory of gratified and monstrous passions.' Kurtz discovered the truth, Conrad concludes, that the 'heart of darkness' is in the soul of mankind with its 'strange commingling of desire and hate', so that, with his last words, Kurtz achieved that supreme moment of complete knowledge . . .'The horror! The horror!'[54]

For Marlow, 'Going up that river was like travelling back to the earliest beginnings of the world, when vegetation rioted on the earth and the big trees were kings.' Feeling cut off from all he had ever known, 'in another existence perhaps', Marlow discovered the darkness within the human soul (Box 14.4).[55]

In Freud's language, humans are wolves to their own species. When the superego is unable to control the aggressive instinct, it 'manifests itself spontaneously and reveals man as savage beasts to whom consideration towards his own kind is something alien.' Any objective consideration of the many atrocities that have been committed throughout history, 'even, indeed, the horrors of the recent World War . . . will have to bow humbly before the truth of this view.'[56]

The aggressive instinct continually menaces the existence of civilized life, which defends itself from destruction by erecting barriers to the uninhibited expression of instinctual energy. Reason is not enough because 'instinctual passions are stronger than reasonable interests.' So the ethical ideal 'to love one's neighbour as oneself' is entirely at variance with 'the original nature of humanity'.[57] The target of this argument about the existence of an 'instinct' for aggression is, quite explicitly, socialism. The socialists, Freud argues, say that humankind is essentially good but the institution of private property has corrupted his nature. If wealth were shared in common, the needs of all would be satisfied and the hostility of one against another would disappear. This belief, Freud concludes, is simply an untenable illusion. Socialism represents the displacement of the illusion of religion from heaven to earth. But, he argues, aggressiveness is not rooted in private property; on the contrary, private property itself is rooted in human instinct. Humans are born physically and intellectually unequal and the instinct for aggression is a tool they use in their struggle for existence. Even if private property were abolished, the instinct of aggression would continue to exert its influence over sexual relations. Should sexual life be made

---

Box 14.4

We penetrated deeper and deeper into the heart of darkness. The roll of drums was heard in the distance. We were wanderers on a prehistoric earth, on an earth that wore the aspect of an unknown planet. We could have fancied ourselves the first of men taking possession of an accursed inheritance, to be subdued at the cost of profound anguish and of excessive toil. Occasionally the steamboat passed villagers with their hands clapping, bodies swaying, and eyes rolling; they were on the edge of a black and incomprehensible frenzy. They glided like phantoms, through incomprehensible surroundings, We could not understand . . . because we were travelling in the light of first ages, of those ages that are gone, leaving hardly a sign—and no memories. The earth was unshackled, monstrous and free. It was unearthly, and the men were—No, they were not inhuman. It would come slowly to one. They howled and leaped, and spun, and made horrid faces; but what thrilled you was just the thought of their humanity—like yours—the thought of your remote kinship with the wild and passionate uproar. Ugly. Yes, it was ugly enough; but if you were man enough you would admit to yourself that there was in you just the faintest trace of a response to the terrible frankness of that noise, a dim suspicion of there being a meaning in it which you—you so remote from the night of first ages—could comprehend. And why not? The mind of man is capable of anything—because everything is in it, all the past as well as all the future.

—Joseph Conrad, *Heart of Darkness* (1902)

completely free and the family abolished as well, Freud agreed that no one could foresee the paths that society would then take. Nevertheless, he asserted, in whatever form society would exist, aggressiveness would reappear because it was an 'indestructible feature of human nature'.[58]

Freud agreed that modern civilization demands that men control their sexual as well as their aggressive instincts, but claimed that they are extremely discontented in the process. They have sacrificed some of their freedom and primitive happiness for some degree of security (an image reminiscent of Hobbes's social contract). But, in the final analysis, the problems of modern society are rooted in human nature, in universal and persistent human impulses. Consequently, we have to 'familiarize ourselves with the idea' that there are problems at the heart of civilization 'which will not yield to any attempt at reform'.[59]

AMERICAN PRAGMATISM AND SOCIAL THEORY

In the United States, however, and not in Germany, this individualistic interpretation of society took root and was developed in the work of social psychologists in the early decades of the twentieth century. Among the early influences on American social psychology and, later, on symbolic interactionism was the work of Charles Cooley (1864–1929). Cooley was concerned with the development among individual human beings of a consciousness of self. The sense an individual has of her or his self emerges through interactions with others. After his encounter with the arrogant Estella, young Pip in Dickens's *Great Expectations* adopts the point of view of his tormentor, and his actions reinforce the new identification (Box 14.5).[60] For Cooley, social interaction is a complex process during which individuals imagine how they are perceived and judged by others and then develop a sense of themselves from these imaginings. The sense of self evolves from a complex interplay involving how others act towards us, how we interpret the meanings behind their actions, and then how we feel and think about ourselves. Cooley termed this process 'the looking-glass self'—you are what your social mirror tells you.

Not all interactions, thought Cooley, have equal consequences in shaping our emerging conception of our self. In particular, our interactions in primary groups (face-to-face encounters with people who matter in our lives) are fundamental in the evolution of our sense of self. It doesn't matter so much if a neighbour down the street thinks badly of you; but it does if your spouse comes to the same conclusion.

Box 14.5

'He calls the knaves, Jacks, this boy!' said Estella with disdain, before our first game was out. 'And what coarse hands he has! And what thick boots!'

I had never thought of being ashamed of my hands before; but I began to consider them a very indifferent pair. Her contempt for me was so strong that it became infectious, and I caught it.

She won the game, and I dealt. I misdealt, as was only natural when I knew she was lying in wait for me to do wrong, and she denounced me for a stupid, clumsy labouring-boy. . . .

I took the opportunity . . . to look at my coarse hands and my common boots. My opinion of these accessories was not favourable. They had never troubled me before, but they troubled me now, as vulgar appendages.

—Charles Dickens, *Great Expectations* (1860–1)

Cooley's ideas about the social nature of psychological phenomena would have their deepest impact at the University of Chicago, where an intellectual generation would establish the interactionist approach to understanding human behaviour. Social psychology emerged in an environment dominated by a practical philosophy and its psychological offshoot in behaviourism.

In the early twentieth century, when sociology was being established in American universities, a specifically indigenous philosophy known as pragmatism was shaping American thought. Philosophically, the new doctrine adopted a realist stance according to which reality exists, in itself, independent of thought and shapes thinking. The pragmatists bracketed European speculative philosophy concerned with the nature of being and focused attention on matters that had practical application to events. Pragmatism reflected the pressing needs of American society to get things done in the face of rapid industrialization and the need to assimilate a variety of recent immigrants. According to Max Weber, pragmatism is linked to the earlier social philosophy of utilitarianism, in which something is a virtue only as it is useful to the individual. Its value does not lie in being true or genuine. The question is whether it 'accomplishes the end in view'. This is equally true of 'strict utilitarianism' as for pragmatism.[61]

The pragmatists imposed this doctrine of utility on questions of truth. The search for ultimate truths was considered fruitless; science revealed truths, but these were only tentative and subject to change. The important factor was to determine what worked; success was the measure of validity, which, at any time, was purely a relative concept. For the psychologist, William James, what was true was whatever conferred benefits. The truth of religious views, for example, were not to be measured by the standards either of rationalist science or speculative theology, but simply on whether they were practically useful for the individual—if God did not exist, it would be necessary to invent the idea of God. Pragmatists confined their attention to the immediately perceivable.

Just as truths were tentative and relative, consciousness was always a response to immediate experience in the light of remembrances from the past. Because experiences were cumulative, no two experiences could be identical, in the sense that you are never the same person you were even moments ago. Consciousness is essentially a train of thought that is reflective and ever-changing—it is what William James called a 'stream of consciousness'. This term, later used to describe a literary style developed by such novelists such as Virginia Woolf and Marcel Proust, described an uninterrupted flow of thoughts, feelings, and impressions in the mind of a single character that replicates the non-linear way that people think.

In America, the home of pragmatism was Chicago, Carl Sandburg's stormy and brawling metropolis—the 'Hog Butcher for the World'. Situated on the invisible line separating the cultivated East from the wild, unpredictable West, Chicago was the centre of the meat-packing industry searingly depicted in Upton Sinclair's *The Jungle* and the city to which Sister Carrie migrated in search of her fortune. It was also an intellectual Mecca for a number of eager and bright social scientists and philosophers in the early decades of the twentieth century, including John Dewey, Robert Park, W.I. Thomas, and George Herbert Mead (1863–1931).

G.H. MEAD

What this psychology is seeking to do is to get control; it is not seeking to settle metaphysical questions.
—G.H. Mead, *Mind, Self and Society* (1934)

George Herbert Mead was an influential philosopher and social psychologist who taught at the University of Chicago from 1893 until his death in 1931. Similar to many American intellectuals of the period, Mead studied philosophy abroad, principally in Germany. Today it is difficult to conceive how far Europe was from America in distance and outlook. Transatlantic crossings were comparatively long. More importantly for an American, studying philosophy in Europe was like stepping into a stuffy and crowded office, filled with uncomfortable furniture, shuttered windows, and scholars whose minds floated somewhere above the real world.

Returning to the hustle of America and Chicago, where action counted more than words, it is understandable that Mead, like most American intellectuals, abandoned the European metaphysical school of philosophy with its concern for essences, consciousness, and the unfathomable mind. Nietzsche had similarly abandoned these metaphysical questions in his turn to an anthropological philosophy. Mead was attracted to two more practical, non-speculative, and empirically oriented movements that had a decidedly American stamp: **pragmatism** and **behaviourism**.

Chicago was the intellectual home of pragmatism, which oriented Mead to the study of things that could be observed and had some practical application. The most practical use for philosophy, he believed, was in psychology, the science of understanding human actions. At the time, American psychology was dominated by an empirical, non-philosophical approach known as behaviourism. The behaviourists were interested in the observable actions of an organism, whether an animal or a human, and the conditions that caused this action. By considering action a form of behaviour, the psychologists stated flatly that they were uninterested in any process that might be going on inside the brain that could not be observed—brain scans were a long time in the future—so it was better to study what could be empirically verified.

John Watson was the most prominent behavioural psychologist of the time. He was studying the process known as conditioning, by which some signal could become a stimulus for an organism, calling for a specific response. If you rang a bell every time you fed a dog, you could make the dog salivate by ringing the bell even if you withheld the food. Children could be taught to be afraid of specific stimuli. From Watson's point of view, complex behaviours were largely the accumulated result of simple stimulus-response conditioning. Behaviourism became a dominant paradigm in American psychology in the middle decades of the twentieth century when it was applied to the modification of human behaviour, providing a quicker cure for some mental disturbances than lengthy sessions on the psychoanalyst's couch. The use of conditioning to deter anti-social behaviour is strikingly portrayed in Anthony Burgess's novel *A Clockwork Orange*, in which the ultra-violent Alex is conditioned to associate scenes of violence with overwhelming nausea.[62]

Behavioural psychology, Mead says, had the practical virtue of ignoring the metaphysical complications of Western philosophy, which had established a series of useless dualisms: the psychical against the physical, mind against body, consciousness against matter. Watson had realized that this type of thinking led into a blind alley, but simply ignoring introspection and assuming that everything could be explained by conditioning through stimulus and response was inadequate. Following Watson, Mead considered his work to be a form of behaviourism, but he distinguished what he termed social behaviourism from the individual type that Watson practised. Watson approached the study of animals by focusing on their observable and objective behaviour. When this was extrapolated to human beings, it meant studying their actions—what they did—and ignoring what they thought. This pragmatic orientation ignored subjectivity—the meaning that actions had for the behaving person. For Mead, an adequate behaviourism must focus on the process through which our responses take place.

The behaviourists, Mead argued, had attempted to deny the existence of a mind or consciousness because introspective philosophy had placed the mind beyond scientific explanation. In doing so, however, Watson had gone too far. The mind exists and, although you cannot reduce it to pure behaviour, it can be explained in terms of behaviour. Mead was one with Watson in 'sidestepping the question as to just what consciousness is' since it is not psychological. The question was: where does this thought process take place? In Mead's words, 'You can explain the child's fear of the white rat by conditioning its reflexes, but you cannot explain the conduct of Mr. Watson in conditioning that stated reflex by means of a set of conditioned reflexes, unless you set up a super-Watson to condition his reflexes.'[63]

Mead's point of departure is that experience is to be understood from the standpoint of society, in particular, from the standpoint that communication is an essential foundation of the social order. That approach is social behaviourism. To focus on communication meant a concern for language, which was not a result of the need of an individual to express his or her inner meanings but arose in the context of group co-operation, which took place through signals and gestures. The acts of individuals are involved in larger, social contexts extending beyond themselves and that implicate other members of the group. While Mead's approach is from the standpoint of the individual, the crucial question is 'the effect that the social group has in the determination of the experience and conduct of the individual members'.[64]

For social behaviourism (or **social psychology**), the whole, which is society, exists prior to the part, which is the individual; consequently, 'the part is explained in terms of the whole, not the whole in terms of the part or parts.' This makes the process sound as linear as individual behaviourism, which proceeds from a stimulus to a specific response. Mead's model, however, was more complicated and dialectical: 'The social act . . . must be taken as a dynamic whole—as something going on—a complex organic process implied by each individual stimulus and response involved in it.'[65]

Social psychology starts with observable social acts, which, in a complex chain of social actions, constitute the social process itself. Social psychology tries to 'state the experiences of the individual in terms of the conditions under which they arise',[66] in relation to the social conditions under which these experiences occur. When these acts are analyzed, it can be seen that they have an inner and an outer phase. While the outer phase is the observable action itself, part of the act is not apparent in behaviour and is not observed. The special interest of social psychology is to explain this inner phase

and its relationship to the social context that created it. This meant understanding things the individual behaviourists had ignored: the mind, the individual's self, and his or her self-consciousness.

Mind and Self

While an act may be undertaken by a single individual, it becomes a social act when more than one person is involved. The simplest social act is a **gesture**, which is the part of the social act that serves as a stimulus to the other participant in the situation. In the interaction of two dogs preparing to fight one another, there occurs 'a conversation of gestures' through which one animal produces a stimulus in the form of growls or barred teeth, and the other responds to these gestures in some fashion. Each response becomes a stimulus for the counter-response of the other in a succession of actions—stimuli and responses—which are all part of the organization of the ongoing act. In a dog fight, or even a boxing match between humans, the gestures are not meaningfully significant because they are not usually thought through or deliberated upon but are more instinctive.[67]

While humans may engage in such a simple conversation of gestures, it is more likely that a human gesture has a conscious meaning. When the gesture means a specific idea to the individual presenting it and the act arouses the same idea in the mind of the other individual, then the gesture has become a significant symbol, the basis of language. A symbol elicits the same meaning from all other members of the language group, allowing them to mutually adjust their behaviour. In Mead's terms, each of the individuals carrying on the social interaction is able to take into consideration the attitude that the other is taking of him or herself. Essentially, this means that the individual has begun to think.[68]

Mead points out the importance of the mutually shared meaning—of a person's being able to impute a meaning to the mind of another that is the same as one's own—by referring to the intellectual breakthrough made by the blind and deaf

Helen Keller when her teacher was first able to help her realize that things had names and shared meanings. In 1887, Anne Sullivan, Keller's teacher, brought a doll to help her learn to associate language with objects. She spelled the letters of 'doll' in Keller's hand, who first regarded it as fingerplay but was ultimately successful in making the letters correctly. This pure behaviour was not a meaningful act, however. It was an act of pure imitation. Keller wrote in her autobiography: 'I did not know that I was spelling a word or even that words existed; I was simply making my fingers go in monkey-like imitation.'[69] In this 'uncomprehending way' she learned to imitate the spelling of a number of words but without conceptually connecting the spelling to a thing with a name. Keller said she had no thoughts because she had no words, only 'wordless sensation'.

A eureka moment came when Sullivan, who had been unsuccessfully trying to teach Keller to distinguish the spelling for 'water' from that for 'mug', took her outside to the water pump. As water poured over Keller's hand, Sullivan spelled 'water' in her other hand, several times. Describing the response in a letter dated 5 April 1887, Sullivan wrote:

> something very important has happened. Helen has taken the second great step in her education. She has learned that *everything has a name, and that the manual alphabet is the key to everything she wants to know*. . . . The word [water] coming so close upon the sensation of cold water rushing over her hand seemed to startle her. She dropped the mug and stood as one transfixed. A new light came into her face. She spelled 'water' several times. Then she dropped to the ground and asked for its name and pointed to the pump and the trellis, and suddenly turning around she asked for my name. . . . All the way back to the house she was highly excited, and learned the name of every object she touched.[70]

Here is Keller's own description of the breakthrough from her autobiography, *The Story of My Life*:

I stood still, my whole attention fixed upon the motions of her fingers. Suddenly I felt a misty consciousness as of something forgotten— a thrill of returning thought; and somehow the mystery of language was revealed to me. I knew then that 'w-a-t-e-r' meant the wonderful cool something that was flowing over my hand. That living word awakened my soul, gave it light, hope, joy, set it free!

[Keller learned that every object had a specific name] and each name gave birth to a new thought. . . . [E]very object that I touched seemed to quiver with life. That was because I saw everything with the strange, new sight that had come to me.

[That summer] I did nothing but explore with my hands and learn the name of every object that I touched; and the more I handled things and learned their names and uses, the more joyous and confident grew my sense of kinship with the rest of the world.[71]

The gesture that is vocal, Mead said, has a unique significance, particularly in language where sounds are used as meaningful symbols. When we vocalize, we hear exactly the same thing as the other hears, whereas only the other can see our facial expression. The sound of one's own voice serves as a stimulus to the speaker as much as it does for the listener. The same meanings are elicited in both parties. Your stimulus not only calls forth a response from another, but it becomes a stimulus calling for a similar response from yourself, since you can imagine how others would respond to it. The bully whose actions cause fear in his victim simultaneously arouses in himself the same attitude. Should the victim turn the tables and call the bully's bluff, his own attitude is revealed to be fear.[72] In Mead's view, through mutual social interaction, we more or less unconsciously see ourselves the way others see us and regard ourselves as others do. This causes us to react to our own gestures and communication. Recognizing anger in our voice, for example, we might act to control it. We are able to put ourselves in the position of the other person and see what she sees, feel what she feels. For Mead, 'It involves . . . an arousal in the individual himself of the response which he is calling out in the other individual, a **taking of the role of the other**, a tendency to act as the other person acts.'[73]

Mind arises when individuals are aware of their relation to the process as a whole and to all the individuals involved in it, including themselves. 'We must regard mind, then, as arising and developing within the social process, within the empirical matrix of social interactions.' Your response is modified by your awareness of the meanings in the interaction and its **reflexive** effect back on you. For Mead, 'It is by means of reflexiveness—the turning-back of the experience of the individual upon him or herself—that the whole social process is brought into the experience of the individuals involved in it.' For Mead, 'it is by such means, which enable the individual to take the attitude of the other toward himself, that the individual is able consciously to adjust himself to that process, and to modify the resultant of that process in any given social act in terms of his adjustment to it. Reflexiveness, then, is the essential condition, within the social process, for the development of mind.'[74]

The **self** develops through interaction; 'it is not initially there, at birth, but arises in the process of social experience and activity' in relation to the process as a whole and the other individuals in the process. The self becomes 'an object to itself', distinguishing the self from other objects and even its own body.[75] In order to engage in rational conduct, which means to deliberate about which stimuli requires a response and what response to make, individuals must be able to take an objective and impersonal attitude towards themselves. That is, an individual must, experientially, get outside him or herself. Individuals become objects to themselves when, in the context of interaction, they are able to take the attitudes of other individuals towards them. This is possible only through communication, i.e., through significant symbols. Society is possible only because people respond in similar ways to specific objects. 'Those attitudes . . . must be there on the part of all.'[76]

The self is essentially a social structure that arises in social experience. An individual, however, will enter any number of experiences. While Mead asserts that there is a unified self that has a reference to the community in which it belongs, this self may be broken up. We relate differently to different people, being one self to one person and someone different to another. 'We divide ourselves up in all sorts of different selves in relation to our acquaintances. . . . There are all sorts of different selves. . . . A multiple personality is in a certain sense normal.' Besides there being a social process as a whole and therefore a complete self that reflects this unity and structure, this unitary self is constituted by various elementary selves.[77] In literature, this sense of multiple selves is reflected in the image of an onion, which can be peeled to reveal successive layers. The difficulty with this image, as playwright Henrik Ibsen's Peer Gynt found out, is that when you peel off the last layer, there really is no centre, no fundamental and unchangeable core to the self. The self is not a thing in itself but a relationship with the external world and with other mutually constituting selves (Box 14.6).[78]

For Mead, the self is created through the process of social interaction. 'Selves can exist only in definite relationships to other selves.' All of the processes involved in the generation of the mind, discussed above, are necessarily implicated in the creation of the self, which is a mental product. Mead illustrates the process through which a self is constructed by distinguishing between play and games. In play, a child takes different roles, reflecting the response she or he has to a set of stimuli that would be similar for others. In a game, however, the child who takes one role must be ready to take the role of the others involved. Successful game-playing requires knowledge of what others will do, that is, 'the child must have the attitude of all the others involved in the game.'[79]

There are two stages in the full development of the self. In the first stage, the individual's self is formed by the particular attitudes others have of him or her that are reciprocated in interaction with them—Cooley's 'looking-glass self'. The second

---

Box 14.6

No Kaiser are you; you are nought but an onion.
   I'm going to peel you now, my good Peer!
   You won't escape either by begging or howling.
   Takes an onion and strips off one coat after another.
   There lies the outermost layer, all torn; . . .
   [Peer peels off several layers, each symbolic of one of the various roles he has played in
his life.] *Pulls off several layers at once.*
   What an enormous number of swathings!
   Is not the kernel soon coming to light?
   Pulls the whole onion to pieces.
   I'm blest if it is! To the innermost centre,
   It's nothing but swathings—each smaller and smaller.—
   Nature is witty!
   Throws the fragments away.

—Henrik Ibsen, *Peer Gynt* (1867)

---

stage results from the fact that all the individuals in a social relationship have a common attitude towards their shared activity.[80] You are able to generalize the individual attitudes of all the members engaged in the same social process and take these attitudes as your own. 'The very universality and impersonality of thought and reason is from the behaviorist standpoint the result of the given individual taking the attitudes of others towards himself, and of his finally crystallizing all these particular attitudes into a single attitude or standpoint which may be called that of the "**generalized other**."'[81] By taking the generalized attitude of the organized social group, the complete self is constituted. As children learn to function in an organized whole through games, they become self-conscious members of the society to which they belong.

The *I* and the *Me*

The meeting of two personalities is like the contact of two chemical substances: if there is any reaction both are transformed.
—Carl Jung, *Modern Man in Search of a Soul* (1933)

The personality as it appears in social experience is constituted as a whole that is separable into two parts or phases. Even though there are numerous selves, all are constituted by social experience in relation to the attitudes of others and, in particular, of the generalized other. When you act, you always act as part of that wider social whole. To this point, then, the self is merely 'a definite organization of the community there in our own attitudes, and calling for a response'.[82] Mead refers to this aspect of the self as a 'me'—the set of attitudes that others have that you assume yourself. The 'me' is constituted by the attitudes of others, making the individual conventional and habitual. It is necessary because the individual must be a member of a community.

The other part of the whole self Mead terms an 'I'. The 'me' sets the situation in which the 'I' responds. In the chain of stimuli and responses that make up social interaction, there is a point where a stimulus has appeared and the response has not yet been elicited. This is the moment of creativity, of uncertainty, when more than one response is possible and the individual exercises some control over the interactive process. This flashpoint, when the actual behaviour is still uncertain, unprogrammed, and potentially novel, is the moment of the 'I'. The 'I' is apparent only before the response is activated, at which point it passes immediately into a 'me'[83] because all social action involves our understanding of others and their mutual understanding of us.

The concept of the 'I' was important for Mead because, without an 'I', there would be only a pro-grammed response, a conditioned reflex that can never elicit surprises or novel behaviour. The response of the 'I' may create a new situation. One may assert 'himself over against others and insist that they take a different attitude toward himself', thereby creating something new that was not pre-viously present in experience.[84] Once a response occurs and the act passes from the moment of being a potentiality to being an actuality, it cannot be withdrawn. Whatever the response, it was a reflection of the situation, one's understanding of the attitude of others and of one's own attitude to one's response, making it always a reflection of the 'me'. Mead wants to capture both the regularity of social intercourse, which is essential for the self and for the community that the interaction con-stitutes, and the potential for uncertainty and change with which every situation and response are pregnant.

Mead illustrates the distinction by considering a politician who proposes and pursues a project of some benefit to the community. His hypothetical politician has the attitude of the community in himself and knows how the community reacts to the proposal. He reacts to his own proposal in a way that is consistent with the community: 'he feels with it. He has a set of organized attitudes which are those of the community.' His self is socially gen-erated and sustained. The potential novelty, the 'I', is in his proposal: 'His own contribution, the "I" in this case, is a project of reorganization, a project which he brings forward to the community as it is reflected in himself.' As a result of that specific response, he is not the same person he was: 'There has now arisen a new social situation as a result of the project which he is presenting.' The procedure takes place in his experience and in the experience of the community and 'He is successful to the degree that the final "me" reflects the attitude of all the community.'[85]

Some individuals are more 'me' than 'I'. Con-ventional people are hardly distinguishable from their neighbours. Other individuals react to the organized community in an attempt to express themselves. These are people who have a 'definite personality' and respond to the organized attitude of the community 'in a way which makes a signif-icant difference.'[86] It is easy to point to specific individuals—Mead suggests Einstein—whose actions made a considerable difference. Such examples are the extreme expression of a constant process of change that usually proceeds imper-ceptibly. In the attitude of the modern artist, who deliberately seeks to break away from convention, 'the element of novelty is carried to the limit.'[87] The possibilities of the 'I' are the most fascinating part of our experience because novelty arises and important values are expressed. We are continu-ally seeking the realization of this self.

Once we respond, the action modifies the social situation, our own attitude, and the atti-tude of others. We may look back on it with pride or mortification. The 'I' becomes part of our memory: 'It is in memory that the "I" is constantly present in experience.' We identify ourselves with the 'I'.[88] Mead sometimes refers to the 'I' as an 'ego'. There is a constant demand to realize one's self through some form of superiority over oth-ers. When misfortunes happen to others, we laugh, which is how the 'I' responds. It is a naive attitude as opposed to the sophisticated attitude of the 'me'. Our sense of superiority is magnified when we identify our self with the group and is especially aggravated in patriotism. 'We all believe that the group we are in is superior to other groups.'[89]

Society

Human society could not exist in the absence of minds and selves; but minds and selves exist only within and emerge from the social process. Since both mutually condition the other, the social process must have evolved over time from a rudimentary beginning in lower stages of development. In the insect world, where a variety of functions are necessary for the survival of the species—like drones and queen bees—structurally different members of the species have evolved that are especially equipped to perform specific functions. In human society, with the exception of the structural and functional differentiation of sex and the physiological process of maturation, there is practically no physiological distinction. Consequently, the organization of individuals has to have a different basis.[90]

Mead minimized individual differences, contending that humans are for the most part identical and there are no essential differences in intelligence between the sexes. Whence came social organization? Mead rejects the individualist theory of social organization derived from early liberal theory. According to the social contract theory, human societies have arisen from fully self-conscious individuals living in a primitive state of equality. Contract theory assumed that people were initially selves in the absence of society and then interacted with others to form society. Mead's argument suggests the reverse: the social organism would have to be there first: 'The self is not something that exists first and then enters into relationship with others. . . . It is a process in which the individual is continually adjusting himself in advance to the situation to which he belongs, and reacting back on it.' This thinking and conscious adjustment 'becomes then a part of the whole social process and makes a much more highly organized society possible.'[91]

Physiologically, the origin of the social is in the relation between children and parents common to all mammals. There are, minimally, gestures but not at first a conversation of gestures. Nevertheless, there we find the beginning of communication. Conflict also exists between individuals, and these at first are mere dogfights. Out of the two processes of co-operation and competition, significant communication—language—arises.

Equally important for development of human intelligence was the use of the hand to manipulate objects. When this action was connected with speech, a powerful combination resulted through which intelligence evolved along with the evolution of the human mind within which a self could develop. Even among lower animals, the raw materials of mind develop. Higher mammals have evolved a certain level of social structure or society and communicate through gestures. In humanity the mind and society evolved together, each mutually conditioning the other. Social organization developed along with the evolution of communication and intelligent manipulation of the world, producing a society and simultaneously constituting a sense of self among individuals. For Mead, 'the complex phases of society have arisen out of the organization which the appearance of the self made possible.' So the self arises out of co-operation and mutual defence and attack. Given this existence of this self, there is 'the possibility of the further development of the society on this self-conscious basis'.[92]

The key process here is the ability of individuals to take the role of the other, through which they can assess their own actions, direct the process of communication, and exercise control over their own responses. It is this control over the process of communication that carries co-operative activity farther. Individuals are able to govern their conduct self-consciously and critically with reference to the other members of the social group as a whole. '[S]elf-criticism is essentially social criticism, and behavior controlled by self-criticism is essentially behavior controlled socially.' Social control is not opposed to the individual and aimed at crushing individuality; it is, 'on the contrary, actually constitutive of and inextricably associated with that individuality'.[93]

The two essential developments of society, which presuppose the existence of communication, are religion, founded on co-operation, and economic exchange, which is carried out because the person with a surplus is able to put himself in the position of the person without, and vice versa. These social processes are universal, as is the later development of democracy. Mead realized that, historically, some groups subjugated others and established relations of domination and subordination. He argued that this was an advance over treating them merely as enemies to be destroyed, because subordinating them 'signifies the expression of self-consciousness reached of one's self in others.'[94] He did not address the question as to whether structured social inequality affects the degree to which an individual can develop an independent sense of self.

While society constitutes the self of the individuals who comprise it, social reality is also changed through the responses of the many 'I's', either profoundly by a creative genius or imperceptibly by the rest of us. Social interaction, then, constructs the reality within which experience occurs. For Mead, through the process of interacting symbolically with others, language can do more than simply signify an object that is already present—pointing to that existing chair or banana peel. The use of symbolic language can constitute an object or a concept that had never been constituted before. These newly created concepts or objects would not exist except within the context of the social relationships that generated them. Mead calls these objects that result from social interaction the elements of common sense; they are the objects that constitute 'the daily environment in which we live'.[95] The significant symbol always presupposes a shared universe of discourse and meaning, constituted by a group of individuals who are participating in a common social process of experience and behaviour.

For Mead, meanings are to be stated in terms of attitudes that are part of the complexities of social stimuli-responses. Consciousness refers to the total organic process, which consists of the attitudes of response and the adjustments the organism makes within the complex environment: '[T]hese attitudes determine the environment. Dividing a situation into an environment and an organism is ambiguous because, ultimately, they constitute a whole: the organism determines the environment as fully as the environment determines the organs.'[96] Mead's ideas would be developed later in a theory of sociology known as social constructionism.

CONCLUSION

At the turn of the century, social thought was embarking on a subjective turn that would be expressed in a variety of contexts, including social theory. The Austrian psychoanalyst, Sigmund Freud, was a pioneer in his attempt to understand the world of the unconscious mind in a rational and, he claimed, scientific way. The school of psychoanalysis remains in his debt. After Freud, the discussion of sexuality was not something to be shunned in conversation. Freud's ideas were equally influential in the arts, where the attempt to depict the unconscious, conceived as the inner reality of humanity, borrowed heavily from Freudian insights. Freudian symbolism appeared in painting, the theatre, and in literature, for example, in the novels of D.H. Lawrence.

In sociology, the micro or social psychological paradigm was foreshadowed in Europe by the individualistic writings of Georg Simmel.. Simmel examined everyday forms of interaction, such as tea parties, fashion, and ritual secrets. All the forms of interaction were purposive; they were 'social games' even to the extent that, in Simmel's view, people actually 'play' society.[97] This insight was pregnant with the future of social psychology. With Simmel, a considerable change in sociological perspective occurs in the claim that individual interactions 'alone produce society'. To borrow a metaphor from Feuerbach, it seems to turn structural sociology on its head. Society and the social structures that comprise it are, in actuality, only the sum of individual interactions. The appropriate locus of sociology, then, shifts away from the study of macro structures, such as economy and class, to the study of the processes underlying the interaction of individuals.

One of the fundamental questions posed by the development of micro-level sociology was the connection between everyday practices and the social structure of society as a whole. Macro-level sociology had focused solely on the latter and either ignored the dynamics of individual interaction or assumed that structural processes were the determining elements. For Simmel, society as a whole could be conceived as an aggregate of micro actions: the whole was equal to the sum of its parts. The American psychologist, G.H. Mead, proposed a complex interrelationship between interaction and society.

Mead asserted that the distinctive aspects of humanity were the mind, consciousness, and the self. Humans both responded to things impulsively (non-reflectively) and also had the ability to reason, to reflect on their impulsive actions, and to alter them to better fit circumstances. People were born into a pre-existing world of symbols that they acquired through socialization; the self initially emerged much as Cooley had suggested. But people quickly learned to interpret others' meanings and negotiate with them to achieve their objectives. Individuals approached each social situation with a particular definition of the situation (a concept developed by Mead's colleague, W.I. Thomas).

One's definition of a situation was not necessarily identical to the definitions of others. In the context of interaction, shared meanings emerge and social life becomes possible as a series of negotiations and compromises. In social psychology, beginning with the interactions of individuals, it is possible to conceive the development of social structures that were greater then the sum of the parts that composed them. In twentieth-century sociology, this dynamic social constructionist view of society would compete with a structural paradigm, deriving from Marx, Durkheim, and Weber. Towards the end of the twentieth century, the theoretical problem in sociology was to conceptualize both elements of action and structure in a comprehensive single paradigm.

CONCLUSION

In 1924, the great German novelist Thomas Mann (1875–1955) published his Nobel Prize-winning novel of ideas, *The Magic Mountain*. Mann used the novel to debate the Western intellectual tradition at a time when that heritage seemed to have spawned the worst excesses of barbarism. In 1914, in company with the majority of intellectuals of the time, Mann had responded patriotically to his nation's call by enlisting to fight in World War I. Disillusion soon followed. The war, he wrote, generated a 'crisis [that] shattered its way through life and consciousness and left a deep chasm behind.'[1] Mann subsequently re-evaluated his politics in response to the cataclysm of war and the subsequent rise of fascism.

The Magic Mountain presents an extended debate between the ideas of classical Enlightenment and Romantic mysticism. The protagonist, Hans Castorp, ascends the Alps to a sanatorium to visit his ailing cousin, a Prussian lieutenant. His stay is prolonged for seven years, partly through ennui and partly as a patient because of a tubercular spot on his lung. From the vantage point of his mountain, Hans Castorp is introduced to the humanistic ideals of the Enlightenment, which are rational, austere, and progressive, but also cold, lifeless, mechanical, and bourgeois. He falls romantically and absurdly in love, experiencing a hopeless passion worthy of Goethe's Werther. In the hands of a decadent, he is introduced to the bacchanal indulgences of drink and food.

Above all, his mind is the subject of a prolonged and unresolved debate between a rationalist and a vitalist. Trying to find his way through this confusing duality, Hans Castorp concludes that rational analysis 'as an instrument of enlightenment and civilization is good, in so far as it shatters absurd convictions, acts as a solvent upon natural prejudices, and undermines authority; good, in other words, in that it sets free, refines, humanizes, makes slaves ripe for freedom.' But, he thinks, analysis 'is bad, very bad, in so far as it stands in the way of action, cannot shape the vital forces, maims life at its roots.'[2] As the representatives of these two opposed life philosophies duel each other, figuratively and literally, Mann implies that rationalism neither can nor should attempt to destroy mysticism, but that anti-rationalism (and decadence) has at its core a self-destructive, though nevertheless still human, impulse.

Hans Castorp's intellectual conundrum is resolved by committing himself to decisive action. In August 1914 he descends from his mountain retreat and enlists in the Kaiser's army to promote the imperialist ambitions of the German elite in the Great War. His fate is uncertain, though the author holds out little hope that, unlike Thomas Mann who survived the war, Hans Castorp will escape becoming cannon fodder.

THE MAKING OF SOCIAL THEORY

The Magic Mountain never resolves the intellectual dilemma between rationalism and subjectivism. The same can be said of the macro-level social issues that are the subject of this more pedantic and restricted narrative on the making of social theory. I have argued here that classical social theories deal with macro-level issues such as the transition from traditional to modern, the rise of capitalism, the state, social inequality, order, change, freedom, and equality. Throughout the book, chains of social theory have been identified and followed through a variety of permutations, even transmogrifications. The classical liberalism of laissez-faire evolved into social liberalism and, from there, to the welfare state, while anti-liberal Toryism morphed into neo-conservatism, which now imposes corporate laissez-faire globally.

Typically, these social theories perceived the rational and the emotional, the objective and the subjective, to exist in an indissoluble duality. Some types of social thought privileged one over the other. Enlightenment rationalism squared off against Romantic subjectivism; social science against *fin-de-siècle* decadence. A few social theorists attempted to resolve the issue by conflating one side of the dualism within the terms of the other. Materialism considers mind to be another arrangement of matter, explicable ultimately by the laws of biochemistry and physics. Arguably, for Hegel, the mental and physical worlds expressed equally the transcendental self-unfolding of Spirit. More commonly, the dialectical approach does not resolve the duality so much as devise a complex model of interactions and mutual conditioning, although in concrete applications one of the elements predominates. For Marx, consciousness presupposes being. For Simmel, social reality emerges from the matrix of individual actions.

The nineteenth century bequeathed a wide range of social theories to the twentieth. The dominant perspective combined an ideology of private ownership with increasingly centralized economic and political power based on ever-new generations of technology and a mass society ethic of ever-expanding consumption. In this world of materialism and anti-intellectual pragmatism, sociology represented an orientation of social reform that, in its classical form, responded to the crises caused by industrialization by analyzing the disjunctions in the social formation that had resulted from rapid change in certain parts of society and relative lag in others. At no time was social science able to close this gap.

In contrast to the high expectations of its founders, sociology did not become the handmaid of politicians, guiding social change in a progressively reformist direction. This unrealized dream of the positivists was echoed in the 1930s by Mannheim's social planning model. While sociology was increasingly marginalized in the universities and turned to the analysis of minorities and marginalized groups, more practical disciplines had greater social and political consequences. Economic principles guided state intervention and, later, deregulation in the twentieth century, while social work and psychology sought to help individuals compensate for the inadequacies of modern capitalism or to help them adjust to the complex and ambiguous demands of mass, industrial society. The dominant ideologies of the early twentieth century were nationalism, imperialism, social Darwinism, and a new conservatism that threatened cherished Western, liberal values.

The nineteenth century was sandwiched between two wars. It began effectively in 1815 following the defeat of Napoleon and ended in 1914 on the battlefields of World War I. Many people at the dawn of the twentieth century had felt that a cataclysmic event was coming, some anticipating impending doom and others hoping for a harbinger of a new sort of future. There had been very few pacifists in 1914, even among intellectuals—Jane Addams was a prominent exception. There were many more in 1918, particularly in the victorious European nations. In Germany, militarism survived the war and fed a new generation of humiliated, deprived, and resentful German patriots. Thomas Mann would recover from his early war enthusiasm and anti-democratic sentiments, eventually being driven out of Germany by the rise of fascism like so many other intellectual Jews, such as Mannheim and Freud.

War in Europe had been predictable as a result of the imperial competition for global power. The nineteenth century bequeathed to the next the scramble for empire that was particularly desperate among the newly industrialized powers of Germany, Japan, and Italy. Through these conflicts, the United States would achieve a position of unbridled power. World War I was the outcome of the struggle between rival states in the interests of national capitalism, but the groundswell of war enthusiasm reflected a dominant ideology in Europe that was widespread. Of all the ideologies that developed in the nineteenth century, the most potent and popular force was nationalism. For people who defined themselves as a nation but were under the imperial heel of a great power—the Serbs under the Austrians, the Irish under the English, the Poles under first one and then another neighbour—national aspirations promised liberation and self-determination. For the old imperial powers and, even more, for the newly emerging ones, nationalism meant patriotism, the celebration of power and domination, cultural pre-eminence, and intellectual superiority.

Social Darwinist precepts reinforced the imperial standpoint. Science, the racists argued, had proven the racial superiority of the white (particularly the so-called Aryan) race, the bearer of civilization and progress. Western imperialism abroad was in the interests of the inferior races who had to be helped, despite themselves, and brought to civilization. It was the white man's burden. It was the responsibility of the whole white race to prevent its degeneration through interbreeding with inferior people. Globally, whites were becoming an increasingly small minority; within the nations of the West they risked the loss of their superiority and, in the process, of the civilization they had achieved. From social Darwinism grew the eugenics movement, which shaped immigration policies and social intervention in the settler nations well into the twentieth century. In Germany, eugenics took an especially virulent form.

Among the threatened values of the West, the most cherished was individual freedom. In economics, liberalism meant the freedom of the owners of capital to pursue their interests as they saw fit because that would ensure the good of the nation and, therefore, of everyone within the nation. Economic progress was guaranteed if the government restricted to the minimum its interference in the business sector, although there were some abuses that required legal remedies. The goal of the state was to protect citizens at home, to advance the interests of the nation (and its wealthiest members) abroad, and to otherwise leave well enough alone.

Political liberalism was more suspect at the beginning of the twentieth century. Majority rule had to be balanced by a healthy and powerful propertied minority with a voice in government at least equal to its stake in the economy. Morality had to be strictly guarded by the churches and the educational system. The routine observance of religious duties helped maintain virtuous behaviour, whether or not religious beliefs were deep or sincerely held. The moral precepts of Victorian propriety were good for society in this best-of-all-possible worlds. It was not, however, even apparently good for a variety of social groups, leading to the production of a number of critical theories and ideologies.

CRITICAL SOCIAL THOUGHT

Beneath this caricature of the dominant ideology, society was fractured by numerous alternative ideologies and world views. Socialism persisted as a strong current threatening the established institutions of Church and state, family and property, upon which the dominant view rested. Temporarily shattered by the abandonment of internationalism in 1914, socialism emerged from the war reinvigorated and radicalized by the success of the Russian Revolution. It persisted as a vision of an alternative future and a practical experiment around the globe for most of the twentieth century.

In the industrialized West, Marxist predictions about the collapse of capitalism never seemed closer to reality than in the 1930s. When the capitalist economic system crashed in the Great Depression, serious flaws were revealed in what had seemed to be a natural and successful national capitalism. It appeared that laissez-faire finally had run into a blind alley. The impulse towards government-sponsored economic reform, which had emerged tentatively in the Victorian age, now began to come into its own. The liberal ideology that dominated much of the next five decades constructed the welfare state, although it was more rudimentary in the United States than in other developed capitalist nations.

In European social thought, the end of the nineteenth century has become synonymous with cultural decadence, a variant of Romanticism that the twentieth century also inherited in major doses. The moral relativism of the decadents drew from Darwin the lesson that the only sensible response to a meaningless world was hedonism and self-expression. A movement that was primarily expressed in literature and the arts, Romanticism presented itself as the instinctive enemy of bourgeois society and, potentially, of any society whatsoever. Although the Romantics shared with the socialists many of the criticisms of modern society, they believed their antipathy was more profound since it rested on a cult of the individual. Romantics rejected the materialism and morality of bourgeois society, but in periods of pessimism they tended to abandon any hope of social revolution or reform. The only genuine change that was possible was in the individual. Romanticism was rooted in subjectivity and the search for meaning within the self.

At the turn of the twentieth century, Romantic subjectivity shaped the countercultural lifestyle of artists, students, and hangers-on in the Bohemian ghettos of Paris, London, New York, and Berlin that attracted disaffected intellectuals. For them, desire was an object to pursue rather than an impulse to subdue. The Bohemians felt morally superior in their material inferiority and heightened experience. Similar individualistic lifestyle rebellions would flash in the 1920s and the 1960s.

The turn to subjectivity and individualism was reflected academically by reversing scientific instruments. While nineteenth-century sociologists had used a social telescope to examine the larger structures of social organization, turn-of-the-century psychologists and behaviourists employed a social microscope to look inside the mind. Freud uncovered the unconscious springs of action, providing symbols and metaphors for a century of psychologically penetrating literature and a growth industry for psychiatric practitioners. Freud's analysis of social relationships in the family—although not necessarily the instinctual basis he postulated as their foundation—provided fruitful if controversial opportunities for the mating of psychoanalysis and social theory. In the United States, George Herbert Mead abandoned the study of consciousness. Instead he analyzed the creation of the self in mutual interaction, helping to form a micro-sociology that focused on symbolic interaction and opposed the structuralism of both mainstream and radical sociology.

The strength and diversity of the alternative conceptions of society and the countercultures that had been carried over into the twentieth century provided sociological evidence that society was fractured by a plethora of social problems and inequalities. The sense of disorder and crisis tortured the minds of social reformers and social scientists. When Durkheim wrote about anomie and the lack of moral regulation in France, he was influenced by more than the absence of economic regulations between the self-interest of individuals and the excessive power of the modern state. He was also responding to the relativism of decadent morality, the challenge of feminism to patriarchal authority, and the threat of the radical socialist movement to economic stability.

Contemporary radicalism has splintered into a multitude of social movements based on the great variety of inequalities that divide modern societies and have given rise to versions of social movement theory still being debated. Among these, the women's movement has emerged as a global force. Feminist thinking had appeared among favourably placed women throughout the early modern age, though it was often marginalized, trivialized, or temporarily sidetracked. Revolution had awakened the rebellious inclinations of several generations of women in the eighteenth and nineteenth centuries, giving rise to a first-wave feminist movement that gained momentum in the new century. While it became broader, the women's movement also became shallower in its goals. When the goal was limited to the franchise, many women were not willing to compromise their tactics. As the campaign for suffrage became more determined and militant, it elicited an alarming amount of state violence until women gradually won political and civil rights. Following this victory a minority of women remained committed to the larger goals of social equality in employment, in the home, in the bedroom, and in society at large. At mid-century a second wave of feminism would crest, threatening the walls of patriarchal power.

In the United States, the legacy of the colour line was maintained in the twentieth century. Jim Crow had been given Supreme Court protection and extralegal violence worsened. The migration of African Americans north into the industrial heartland changed the national demographics and the colour line was fractured into numerous local versions. Although black workers initially faced institutional racism, by the 1930s the new and more militant industrial unions welcomed all workers into the house of labour, black as well as white. By the 1950s, when the civil rights movement gained momentum, a heritage of black nationalism and black culture had evolved to act as a springboard for racial pride and social activism.

A narrative of twentieth-century social thought would be as diverse as the multicultural nations that have proliferated through globalization. At the beginning of the twenty-first century, a feeling of déjà vu permeates social thought. The hopeful expectations of international socialism, black nationalism, and feminist revolution have been eclipsed by global capitalism, the deepening of racial inequalities within and between nations, and resurgent traditionalism. The intellectual disillusionment that has resulted breeds contempt for the whole legacy of Western scientific thought since the Enlightenment and the turn to rationality. Contemporary postmodern theories, which have emerged in this context, return social thought to the relativity of knowledge and truth that modern science had tried to resolve and pragmatism simply bracketed and put aside. It is an exciting if confusing period for sociology and social theory, characterized by multiple competing paradigms. Just as the Romantic conservatives could not turn the clock back to the pre-industrial age, globalization is an established fact. The contemporary struggle is over the nature, direction, and ultimate ends of the global transformation that is underway. In the end, the analysis of contemporary social theory will have to address the question whether a great deal of theorizing has slipped away from the legitimate enterprises that dominated social thought in the classical period: the effort to understand social life as a whole and change it for the better.

Appendix A CONTROVERSIES AND RESOURCES

CHAPTER ONE
TRADITIONAL SOCIETY:
REASON AND DESIRE UNDER WRAPS

Controversies

Chapter One provides a background picture of traditional European society on the eve of transition to the modern world. Was 'reason' a corrosive acid that dissolved traditional thinking; or is reason necessarily contrary to faith and social custom? The chapter illustrates the dovetailing of changes in economic practice and economic ideology. Did one precede the other? Did the existence of one dominant ideological force—the Catholic Church—inhibit social critique? Aquinas was thought to have settled social and economic questions; rather, it could be claimed, he did more to undermine traditional society than shore it up. Is society naturally hierarchical and does it function like an organism?

Resources

- Hugh Trevor-Roper's *The Rise of Christian Europe* (London, 1965) provides an introduction to the early medieval Renaissance and reform movements in the Catholic Church that were smothered by natural and social causes, including the Black Death. It is well illustrated and lively.
- A more detailed account of the sometimes tortuous history of the Catholic Church is provided by A.F. Thomson, *The Western Church in the Middle Ages* (Oxford, 1998).
- Information about the role of women in society at the time of the Crusades can be found in Susan B. Edgington and Sarah Lambert, eds, *Gendering the Crusades* (Cardiff, 2001). Selections examine the role of women in relation to the Crusade movement, for

example, warriors and hostages. It combines literature, history, and social analysis.
- My source for details on the life of Aquinas is Anthony Kenny, *Aquinas* (Oxford, 1980).
- The trend towards cultural studies in the humanities is reflected in Tom Shippey with Martin Arnold, eds, *Film and Fiction: Reviewing the Middle Ages* (Woodbridge, Suffolk, 2003). While examining literature, past and present, the book also analyzes the image of medieval society in modern film.
- Information on many Church-related subjects can be found on-line at the Catholic Encyclopedia. It offers, for example, a detailed overview of Aquinas's life and a summary of his, mainly theological, writings. See: <www.newadvent.org/cathen/14663b.htm>.
- The same source provides information on Abelard's life and accomplishments. See: <www.newadvent.org/cathen/14371a.htm>.
- Further information on the star-crossed lovers, Abelard and Heloise, their letters and history together, can be found at: <www.aug.edu/langlitcom/humanitiesHBK/handbook_htm/heloise&abelard.htm>.
- The site <www.fordham.edu/halsall/women/womensbook.html> has information on women in medieval Europe, also focusing on 'Great Women' in the Middle Ages.
- An interesting site on medieval Italy that focuses on the *Decameron*, a set of 100 medieval tales written during the onset of the plague, is: <www.brown.edu/Departments/Italian_Studies/dweb/society/>. It includes descriptions of medieval Italian society, trade routes, the plague, and includes a search function.
- The Dictionary of Critical Sociology is useful as a general on-line resource. It appears at <www.public.iastate.edu/~rmazur/dictionary/a.html>, on the home page of Robert E. Mazur, Iowa State University.

CHAPTER TWO
THE REVOLUTION IN NATURAL AND SOCIAL SCIENCE

Controversies

Chapter Two, on the revolution in natural and social science, begins with the natural scientific revolution. The main theme of the chapter is the transition from the traditional world view, described in Chapter One, to a modern view based on reason and science, and the application of these principles to understand society. Liberal social theory emerged in conscious opposition to the main institutions and ideologies of traditional society. Why was early science seen as threatening to traditional society? What is meant by a Hobbesian view of human nature? Has this view been vindicated by history? Why is Locke, but not Hobbes, regarded as an essentially bourgeois theorist? Locke's theory of knowledge would appear to be fundamentally sociological. Does knowledge come from sense experience? Is the idea of a social contract a sociological way to describe the origins of society?

Resources

- A concise introduction to the ideas of the early liberals, as well as those of Aquinas and other social thinkers discussed below, can be found in Hans Fink, *Social Philosophy* (London, 1981).
- The most interesting account of Locke, which analyzes the great liberal thinker in terms of the ideology of commerce and race, is Edward Andrew, *Shylock's Rights: A Grammar of Lockian Claim* (Toronto, 1988). This brilliant book situates Locke in his historical context.
- The radical English movements inspired by the rise of liberalism and a history of Bible socialism were the Levellers and the Diggers in England, who represented the left wing of the English revolution. Andre Sharpe's *The English Levellers* (Cambridge, 1998) provides some details on their social and political programs. Sociologically, they represent the interests of the rural petite bourgeoisie, who were being dispossessed by early commercial capitalism.
- Whitney Chadwick's *Women, Art, and Society* (New York, 1990) explores women's art through the modern era. It is a useful resource for many of the topics of this book. In particular, it discusses the sociological relevance of the themes of women's paintings during the Italian Renaissance. A woman's perspective is reflected in their choice of subject.
- John Rogers, *The Matter of Revolution: Science, Poetry, and Politics in the Age of Milton* (Ithaca, NY, 1996), is philosophical and carefully argued; it also connects natural science theory with literature.
- A comprehensive site for information about history, including early modern history, is the Internet History Sourcebooks Project edited by Paul Halsall: <www.fordham.edu/halsall/sbook.html>. The site provides a resource guide, including a link to various medieval studies.
- The on-line Stanford Encyclopedia of Philosophy has an extensive list of political and social theorists, including Bacon and Locke, as well as bibliographies and links to additional sites. The address <http://plato.stanford.edu/entries/hobbes-moral/> provides an overview of Hobbes's moral and political theory.
- The Public Broadcasting Service (PBS) series *Nova* includes a site with information on scientific history. Their page: <www.pbs.org/wgbh/nova/galileo/science.htmlPBS.org> on Galileo includes a summary of his life and an assessment of his place in science, including his erroneous theory of the tides.
- The World Civilizations home page also includes a summary of important figures and discoveries in the scientific revolution: <www.wsu.edu:8080/~dee/ENLIGHT/SCIREV.HTM>.
- On the Diggers, <www.british-civil-wars.co.uk/index.htm> opens the English Civil War site, containing a link to a discussion of the Levellers and the Diggers, including an overview of the movements and the main ideas of figures such as Winstanley. It provides bibliographical details. Part of a project on early modern English history, it includes a list of suggested sites for further information.

CHAPTER THREE
REASON AND REBELLION

Controversies

Hobbes and Locke developed the theory of political liberalism; classical economic liberalism appeared somewhat later. This chapter summarizes the laissez-faire theory associated with the Scottish political economist, Adam Smith, and the social critiques developed to resist the encroachment of capitalism into the traditional economy. Did the economic position of England make it likely that the theory of laissez-faire would strike roots in the nation? Would laissez-faire economics benefit everyone in the society? Consider the radical implications of liberal social theory in relation to the aristocracy. Was slavery reasonable or unreasonable; were liberal principles compatible or incompatible with slavery? Were women better off or worse off in the liberal revolution? In times of change, do critics tend to look forward or back?

Resources

- Thomas C. Patterson's *Inventing Western Civilization* (New York, 1997) is a short, critical examination of the ways in which European social theory created an image of the non-Western as the 'other'. He examines both negative and positive constructions of race and culture.
- An important source for analysis and excerpts from primary sources of theorists who were women is Lynn McDonald, *Women Theorists on Society and Politics* (Waterloo, Ont., 1998). A woman's standpoint emerges early in social theory. This book traces the history of ideas to the early modern period and through the liberal revolutions of the eighteenth century.
- Joyce MacDonald's *Women and Race in Early Modern Texts* (Cambridge, 2002) reflects the close connection that theorist drew between the oppression of women and the oppression of Africans.
- Literature reflects as well as shapes cultural attitudes to minorities, as *The Black Presence in English Literature* (Dover, NH, 1985), the collection of essays edited by David Dabydeen, illustrates.
- The role played by blacks in rebellion is the theme of Gary B. Nash's *Race and Revolution* (Madison, Wis., 1990).
- A source called Lucidcafe <www.lucidcafe.com/library/categoryindex.html> includes a site for information on Adam Smith, as well as additional Web sites and links to texts. It is found at: <www.lucidcafe.com/library/96jun/smith.html>.
- An additional source for full texts from a great variety of authors, including social theorists, is <www.bartleby.com/index.html>, which include Daniel Defoe: <www.bartleby.com/219/index.html#1>. The site: <http://cepa.newschool.edu/het/profiles/defoe.htm> offers a brief biography of Defoe and links to other resources.
- An African-American perspective on Thomas Jefferson in relation to the question of slavery is found at: <http://afroamhistory.about.com/library/bljefferson_slavery.htm>.
- A useful site to explore the issue of abolitionism and the work of prominent abolitionists, continuing into contemporary society, is: <http://afgen.com/slave1.html>. It includes links to resources such as Douglass's Fourth of July speech.
- A general site for links to information on a range of writers is: <www.kirjasto.sci.fi/indeksi.htm#s>; this includes a biography of Jonathan Swift as well as a bibliography of his works:<www.kirjasto.sci.fi/jswift.htm>.
- For a detailed study of *Gulliver's Travels*, see: <www.enotes.com/gullivers-travels/>.

CHAPTER FOUR
ROUSSEAU, RIGHTS, AND REVOLUTION

Controversies

The Enlightenment shared many ideological precepts with the liberal ideas that had developed in England. The *philosophes* critiqued traditional institutions, principally the Church, on the grounds they were unreasonable. While many *philosophes* believed Enlightened monarchs should change society from above, their ideas enflamed the middle and working classes. The French Revolution was the tangible result. Was Rousseau a typical Enlightenment *philosophe*? Arguably, Rousseau's ideas gave rise to a variety of social theories, some diametrically opposed to others. Was the Enlightenment a progressive theory with respect to the status and consciousness of women and racial minorities? In the French Revolution, was revolutionary practice consistent with revolutionary ideology? Can it be claimed, as the French revolutionaries did, that the more things change, the more they stay the same? How can we evaluate the radicalism of Wollstonecraft's social theory? Was Austen a liberal or conservative theorist?

Resources

- A useful and relatively brief account of the events and significance of the French Revolution, through its more or less revolutionary phases, can be found in Peter McPhee's *The French Revolution, 1789–1799* (Oxford, 2002).
- Gisela Bock's *Women in European History* (Oxford, 2002), while covering more ground than is the focus

of this chapter, begins at the beginning by addressing Christine de Pisan's question: 'What are women?' Women were challenging the boundaries of their socially defined natural sphere.

- Margaret Hunt et al., in *Women and the Enlightenment* (New York, 1984), examine the cultural shift in women's life and perspectives beginning with the scientific revolution and the age of Enlightenment, and also women's response to it. They discuss the intellectual emancipation of women, including Astell's ambivalent Anglicanism.
- Another useful source for this period is Carla Hesse's *The Other Enlightenment: How French Women Became Modern* (Princeton, NJ, 2001).
- Sheila Rowbotham's *Women, Resistance, and Revolution* (London, 1972) is an older but important account of the ideologies about women and their responses, particularly through the socialist and revolutionary movements of the eighteenth and nineteenth centuries.
- *The Legacy of Rousseau*, edited by Clifford Orwin and Nathan Tarcov (Chicago, 1997), links Rousseau's ideas to a host of successive theorists and movements, including the French Revolution and nationalism, and examines the effects of his views on ethnicity and difference.
- The Rousseau Association has posted a site on the revolutionary French thinker, including a great variety of links, even to his music: <www.wabash.edu/rousseau/>.
- A site organized under the title the Radical Academy includes links to many social theorists, including Rousseau. The main page can be found at: <http://radicalacademy.com/philclassicindex.htm>.
- The French Revolution may be explored through the site: <http://chnm.gmu.edu/revolution/about.html>. This site is maintained by the Center for History and New Media, George Mason University. It includes a revealing series of images.
- Another source for primary documents on the Revolution is: <www.fordham.edu/halsall/mod/modsbook13.html>.
- Olympe de Gouges's Declaration of the Rights of Women is accessible at: <www.fordham.edu/halsall/mod/1791degouge1.html>.
- Social Science History and Social Science Links, found at:<www.mdx.ac.uk/www/study/linkssh.htm>, includes a brief biography of Olympe de Gouges as well as a host of other social theorists—it is a general site.

- Another general site, The History Guide: Lectures on Modern European Intellectual History, includes links to Mary Wollstonecraft and *A Vindication of the Rights of Woman*. It presents an overview of Mary Wollstonecraft's life and how events affected her work and analyzes *A Vindication*, and also includes a page on William Godwin, Mary Wollstonecraft's partner and an original anarchist, as well as links to texts by Godwin: <http://womenshistory.about.com/library/bio/blwollstonecraft.htm>.

CHAPTER FIVE
THE CONSERVATIVE REACTION AND ROMANTICISM

Controversies

After the French Revolution, society and social theory took a step backward. Arguably, conservatism responded negatively to the Enlightenment and liberalism and revived some of the main elements of traditional social theory. The specific ideas of conservative thinking in France and Britain differed in ways that reflected the social and political history of the two nations. Romanticism shared with the conservatives a fundamental critique of liberalism and the *philosophes* while also rejecting key conservative principles. What distinguishes social liberalism, Romanticism, and pure Romanticism? How can we account for the Romantic movement, in its ideological and practical aspects, sociologically? What key ideas emerge from conservative and Romantic thought that may be regarded as foundation concepts of classical social theory?

Resources

- In Chapter Two of his *The Extreme Right in France, 1789 to Le Pen* (London, 2002), Peter Davies details the events of the counter-revolution of 1789–1830. He analyzes the *émigré* population and presents an overview of de Maistre's doctrine. In addition, Davies traces the resurgence of the right into the 1890s and then the twentieth century.
- Anne Mellor's *Romanticism and Gender* (New York, 1993) is a wonderful book that contrasts the aesthetics of the male Romantics, which she defines as an act of colonization, and the tendency for women in the Romantic age to challenge the male claim of a monopoly on rationality.

- Elizabeth Fay's *A Feminist Introduction to Romanticism* (Malden, Mass., 1998) discusses the rise of the cult of sensibility in early Romanticism, the question of emotion versus reason in, for example, the work of Jane Austen, and examines the role of women as heroines in Gothic fiction.
- Romanticism was expressed in the movement of the Utopian socialists, the topic of Chapter One in Vincent Geoghegan's *Utopianism and Marxism* (New York, 1987), which offers an overview of the ideas of Saint-Simon, Robert Owen, and Charles Fourier. The main argument in the book is the necessity of a 'Utopian' dimension in Marxism.
- The fundamental theme of Chapter Five—that Romanticism had evolved from a concern with social reform to an individual subjectivity—is suggested in Michael Löwy and Robert Sayre's *Romanticism against the Tide of Modernity* (Durham, NC, 2001). They discover that Romanticism occurs in a range of socio-political positions between left and right. It was rooted not so much in class but more comprehensively in the destructive effects of capitalist industrialization.
- A biography of Edmund Burke along with a timeline of important writings and speeches, including a number of quotations from his work, can be found at: <www.blupete.com/Literature/Biographies/Philosophy/Burke.htm>.
- The Encyclopedia of 1848 Revolutions, which can be found at: <www.ohiou.edu/~Chastain/contents.htm>, contains links to a great variety of topics relating to nineteenth-century radicalism in France, including information on Victor Hugo, Auguste Blanqui, and popular culture.
- The page dedicated to Joseph de Maistre, which is situated at the University of Manitoba, contains a brief biography, annotated commentary on his major works, and links to related sites: <www.umanitoba.ca/faculties/arts/history/links/maistre/maistre.html>.
- 'The Romantic Movement in British Literature', by Roger Blackwell Bailey, provides a general link to resources and specific links to 25 English Romantics, including de Quincy and Jane Austen, although not the Brontës. See: <www.accd.edu/sac/english/bailey/engroman.htm>. The Critical Poet site also provides links to the major British Romantic poets: <www.gymnasium-meschede.de/projekte/romantik/background.htm>.
- Links to the main figures of American literary Romanticism can be found at: <http://en.wikipedia.org/wiki/Romanticism#American_Romanticism>; it includes Whitman and Thoreau.
- The place of Victor Hugo's *Hernani* in the rise of French Romanticism is discussed in the theatre history site, which also has links to printed sources: <www.theatrehistory.com/french/romanticism001.html>.
- The on-line ArtCyclopedia is a comprehensive source for information and visual examples of art, including Romanticism, a movement that is defined negatively as essentially anti-classicism:<www.artcyclopedia.com/history/romanticism.html>.

CHAPTER SIX
POSITIVISM AND DEMOCRACY

Controversies

Neither conservatism in its original form nor Romanticism succeeded in becoming the dominant perspective of modern society. On the contrary, the age of science was really only beginning. Inevitably, then, a more rigorous attempt to apply the principles of empirical science to society soon followed. Saint-Simon was influenced by both the Enlightenment tradition, with its emphasis on science and reason, and the conservative understanding that society had to be understood as a whole. His early sociology looked backward to the conservative focus on the irrational underpinnings of society. Is society essentially an irrational construction? Is a secular religion, such as envisaged by Saint-Simon or Comte, possible? Are there laws of society analogous to the laws of nature? What difference would it make if there were or were not such laws? If Comte is the father of sociology, then who are the grandparents? Is positivism inevitably reformist? Is democracy inevitably a tyranny of the majority? Did Tocqueville's analysis of American democracy reflect an aristocratic or a bourgeois, middle-class perspective? Were Tocqueville's views racist? What contributions did Martineau make to social thought?

Resources

- Mary Pickering's *Auguste Comte: An Intellectual Biography* (Cambridge, 1993) provides a biographical introduction to Comte and an overview of the evolution of his ideas from positivist to religious visionary.
- In a brief introduction to Comte's positivism, which contrasted so sharply with the chaos of his private

life, Anthony Giddens, *In Defence of Sociology* (Cambridge, 1996), discusses the idea of a natural science of society and distinguishes the conditions for the creation of social knowledge from the production of knowledge in the natural sciences.

- Pierre Manent's analysis of *Tocqueville, in Tocqueville and the Nature of Democracy* (Lanham, Md, 1996), summarizes his critique of dogmatic democracy, which leads to uniformity and state power, and his position as a 'friend' of democracy, concerned with maintaining freedom in the face of tyranny.

- In his chapter 'Thoreau and the Natural Environment' in *The Cambridge Companion to Henry David Thoreau* (Cambridge, 1995) edited by Joel Myerson, Lawrence Buell presents Thoreau as the first American environmentalist, tracing his development from transcendentalism, through the pristine simplicity of Walden Pond, to a recognition of the importance of the conservation of nature.

- In the fourth chapter of her book *Harriet Martineau: The Poetics of Moralism* (Aldershot, Hants, 1995), Shelagh Hunter traces the development of Martineau's work and ideas in relation to her biography through *Society in America* and afterwards. In her interpretation, Martineau's Christian principles remained constant as Martineau evolved towards Comte's positivism while eschewing his 'New Religion'.

- In *The Woman and the Hour: Harriet Martineau and Victorian Ideologies* (Toronto, 2002), Caroline Roberts puts Martineau's views on a wider social and ideological canvas.

- One of the best sources for information on classical sociologists is the Dead Sociologists Index. The site for Auguste Comte is: <www2.pfeiffer.edu/~lridener/DSS/INDEX.HTML#comte>.

- The History of Economic Thought Web site contains links to hundreds of economic and social theorists, including Saint-Simon, from the following page: <http://cepa.newschool.edu/~het/alphabet.htm#slet>. On that page are links to writings and other resources, including a site called Marxists.org.

- A detailed source on Martineau's life and background, from a Dead Sociologists' link, is: <www2.pfeiffer.edu/~lridener/DSS/Martineau/MARTINP2.HTML>.

- Biographical information, links to other resources, passages from *Democracy in America*, can be found at a site maintained for Tocqueville: <www.tocqueville.org/>.

- A useful site to gain access to many linked pages on the life and works of Henry David Thoreau can be found at: <www.transcendentalists.com/1thorea.html>, including the usual gamut of works, e-text links, commentary, and biography.

CHAPTER SEVEN
SOCIAL LIBERALISM

Controversies

Saint-Simon and Comte moved from a laissez-faire perspective to an increasingly interventionist stance on social questions as their thinking evolved. In England, laissez-faire was a main plank in the dominant liberalism. Arguably, however, the social effects of wide economic freedom made state intervention increasingly necessary. Unlike Comte, Mill was a reluctant reformer. How wide a feminist perspective did J.S. Mill and Harriet Taylor Mill embrace? What were the strongest arguments in favour of the abolition of slavery? It was widely argued that the position of women in the nineteenth century was similar to that of slaves. Was this a perceptive analogy or an exaggeration? Does literature play an ideological role in society, or do people simply consume culture that fits their preconceptions?

Resources

- A discussion of the dialectics of freedom and control in J.S. Mill's social theory is given in Joseph Hamburger, *John Stuart Mill on Liberty and Control* (Princeton, NJ, 1999). The main theme is the necessity to protect individuals from the tyranny of state power, while approving of informal social controls of those with superior natures over their inferiors.

- An interesting argument about the move to realism is made by Isobel Grundy in 'Against Beauty', published in Shirley Neuman and Glennis Stephenson, eds, *ReImagining Women* (Toronto, 1993). She argues that, in realist fiction, women's appearance was depicted more realistically (warts and all) rather than as idealized beauty. In *Nothing But Freedom: Emancipation and Its Legacy* (Baton Rouge, La., 1983), Eric Foner compares the aftermath of abolition in the British and French Caribbean and in the US. The period of Reconstruction appears, in this view, in a more positive light.

- Lynn McDonald's edited collection of essays, *Florence Nightingale on Society and Politics* (Waterloo, Ont., 2003), presents the depth and variety of Nightingale's work in philosophy, science, education, and literature.

Nightingale was a pioneer in social reform and an advocate of the expansion of the role of government in health care and disease prevention.

- The tragic trajectory of the career of the social reformer and labour leader, Flora Tristan, is presented briefly in *The Odyssey of Flora Tristan* (New York, 1988), by Laura Strumingher. It focuses both on her personal troubles and her efforts to intervene on key social issues.
- The Bentham Project, on-line, from the University College, London, is the best spot to begin researching Bentham, including utilitarianism and his Panopticon project: <www.ucl.ac.uk/Bentham-Project/>. See the Classical Utilitarian Site for more resources: <www.la.utexas.edu/cuws/>.
- The Victorian Web provides a brief description and then links to authors, including Dickens, who wrote in the social problems genre: <www.victorianweb.org/genre/problem.html>.
- The Victorian Women Writers Project connects the browser with resources on many nineteenth-century authors, including Harriet Taylor Mill and Harriet Martineau: <www.indiana.edu/~letrs/vwwp/vwwplib.pl?>.
- The on-line address: <www.utilitarianism.com/jsmill.htm> opens a page on John Stuart Mill, including links to *On Liberty* and *Utilitarianism*. The Spartacus school hyper-linked site for Mill is: <www.spartacus.schoolnet.co.uk/PRmill.htm>. See also: <http://65.107.211.206/philosophy/mill/millov.html>, from the University Scholars Programme Project.
- The Norton Anthology of English Literature, on-line, provides resources and links to the important periods of English literature, including the woman question. See: <www.wwnorton.com/nael/victorian/topic_2/welcome.htm>. *Jane Eyre* is cited as an example of the portrayal of the 'new woman' in the novel.
- A site for connections to other resources on Victorianism: <www.gfy.ku.dk/~ams/sh/victorian.html>. You can chase a link to other pages of links, such as an index of resources on the emancipation of women: <www.spartacus.schoolnet.co.uk/resource.htm>.

CHAPTER EIGHT
HEGEL, FEUERBACH, AND MARX

Controversies

German social theory took its own path, on which Romanticism travelled more than Enlightenment

rationality. Many strands of thought combined to produce Hegel's theory, which seems to be a synthesis of reason and spirituality. Is it compatible with Christianity? Is 'dialectical' just a fancy word for 'multi-dimensional', or does it mean something else? Did Feuerbach turn Hegel on his head? Did Marx? Marxism was an attempt at a grand synthesis of the positive aspects of liberalism, political economy, and the Enlightenment. Was Marx's analysis of the potential of the proletariat founded in reality or Romantic illusion? Are the ideas Marx expounded in his critique of Feuerbach contradicted by the positivist interpretation of his major writings? Why did a proletarian revolution fail to materialize in the industrialized West? Why did Marx have such a profound influence in the twentieth century? Are Marx's ideas still relevant in the era of globalization?

Resources

- Interest in Hegel in social theory tends to wax and wane depending on whether society seems on the verge of social change or, as now, when a dominant hegemony prevails and most intellectuals focus on social criticism. Herbert Marcuse's exposition of Hegelian theory, including its roots and its relevance for modern society, which he published as *Reason and Revolution* (New York, 1954), is still a useful source for examining the theory of dialectics and its relevance for Marx.
- The most comprehensive, recent study of Marx's theory of revolution, interpreted from the perspective of revolutionary, non-dogmatic, and non-authoritarian socialism, can be found in the several volumes of Hal Draper's *Marx's Theory of Revolution* (New York, 1990).
- A biography, which connects a theorist's life and times with her or his thought and work, is an excellent way to approach a social theorist. The story of Eleanor Marx's life is replete with detail about Marx and the socialist movement as well as Eleanor's contributions to theory and practical work. See Yvonne Kapp, *Eleanor Marx* (New York, 1977), vol. 1 of which covers the period up to 1883, the death of Eleanor's father.
- The most direct way to approach Marx's ideas is to read *The Communist Manifesto* (Harmondsworth, Middlesex, 1967). Since Marxism is a movement aimed at the common person, a variety of popular summaries have been written to attract people to the movement.
- A more comprehensive source for Marx's ideas that emphasizes the early, more philosophical Marx is

David McLellan, *The Thought of Karl Marx* (London, 1980). Arranged chronologically, this work provides selections from a variety of Marx's writings and places the ideas in context.

- Ellen Meiksins Wood's *Democracy against Capitalism* (Cambridge, 1995) offers a reinterpretation of Marxism as a revolutionary project for the age of globalization. Wood offers a critique of modern capitalism and imperialism and incorporates issues of gender and race in her class argument. Similarly, Ellen Meiksins Wood et al., eds, *Rising from the Ashes: Labor in the Age of 'Global Capitalism'* (New York, 1998), indicates the relevance of Marxist analysis for the contemporary age.

- There are many Internet sites on aspects of Marxism. One of the most comprehensive sites, because it has numerous links to other sources, is: <www.marxists.org/glossary/>, the Encyclopedia of Marxism. It has a useful summary of Marx's main ideas, complete with links to other sources.

- The site: <www.hewett.norfolk.sch.uk/curric/soc/theory.htm> provides a resource base organized as a map of sociological theory. The Marxism page from this map offers simple explanations, sometimes with diagrams to assist explanation:<www.hewett.norfolk.sch.uk/curric/soc/MARX/Marx1.htm>.

- A link to provide access to Marx's writings can be found at: <http://eserver.org/marx/>.

- Information about Marx's feminist and socialist daughter, Eleanor Marx, can be found at: <www.marxists.org/archive/eleanor-marx/>, including a link to a biographical sketch by E.P. Thompson.

- The text of David Riazanov's *Karl Marx and Friedrich Engels, An Introduction to Their Lives and Work* can be accessed at: <http://csf.colorado.edu/psn/marx/Other/Riazanov/Archive/1927Marx/>.

CHAPTER NINE
EVOLUTION AND SOCIOLOGY

Controversies

Since the conservative historicists, it has been commonplace to understand society in terms of a progressive evolution through inevitable stages. As with the scientific revolution generally, the development of concepts for understanding the natural world were applied to the study of society. Darwin is the principal figure in the study of evolution. When his theory of natural selection was applied to society and humanity, a tidal wave of consequences followed. Science seemed poised to overthrow religion and realize the positivist dream of complete social knowledge. Besides its direct application through Herbert Spencer, Darwin's theory influenced a host of end-of-the-century social thinkers, from naturalism in writers of literature to Freudianism in psychoanalytic theorists.

What difference does it make if we analyze society in terms of a biological analogy? Is Lamarckism more relevant to sociology than Darwinism? Darwin and religious traditionalism seemed fundamentally at odds in the nineteenth century. Did Darwinism have more effect on conceptions of humanism than on religion? To what extent is human behaviour controlled by blind, uncontrollable forces? What differences result from adopting a deterministic or fatalistic theory of human action rooted in biology rather than in the environment? Was social Darwinism liberal or conservative in its implications? What has kept social Darwinist views alive into the present? Does difference imply inequality, or are the two principles compatible?

Resources

- Peter Dale's *In Pursuit of Scientific Culture* (Madison, Wis., 1989) contrasts scientific positivism, originating with Comte, and Romanticism, focusing particularly on the Darwinian phase of positivism. He discusses the expression of positivism in English literature, in the works of Eliot and Hardy.

- The fascinating history of the emergence of the concept of evolution and its struggle for pre-eminence is detailed in Loren Eiseley's *Darwin's Century* (New York, 1961). Eiseley discusses Darwin's antecedents and also comments on the weaknesses in Darwin's own thesis that caused him doubt.

- *Social Darwinism in American Thought* (Boston, 1955) is the subject of Richard Hofstadter's study. Besides examining the ideas of such key figures as sociologist Graham Sumner, Hofstadter considers the forces that both welcomed and resisted the Darwinian application to questions of society.

- Darwinian ideas resurface periodically in social thought. Currently, they influence a perspective in social science known as socio-biology. Kevin A. Laland and Gillian R. Brown point out that there are fundamental biological determinants of human behaviour, as discussed in their *Sense and Nonsense: Evolutionary Perspectives on Human Behaviour*

(Oxford, 2002). However, they challenge the more ideological claims of modern socio-biologists.

- The question about the degree to which human behaviour can be controlled by the environment, and the potential effect of this on human freedom, is interestingly addressed by B.F. Skinner, the American psychologist, in his novel, *Walden Two* (New York, 1948).
- A biography of Lamarck and a discussion of his scientific thought can be found at: <www.ucmp.berkeley.edu/history/lamarck.html>. See also: <www.english.upenn.edu/~jlynch/Frank/People/lamarck.html>.
- Darwin's main ideas are summarized on: <http://bioweb.cs.earlham.edu/9-12/evolution/HTML/theory.html>. The LucidCafe page on Darwin, <www2.lucidcafe.com/lucidcafe/library/96feb/darwin.html>, contains links to related Web sites and e-texts of Darwin.
- Darwin's principal popularizer in England was Thomas Huxley, about whom information can be found at <www.ucmp.berkeley.edu/history/thuxley.html>. For more information, see the Huxley File at Clark University: <http://aleph0.clarku.edu/huxley/>.
- The Image Archive on the American eugenics movement is a resource-rich site, at: <www.eugenicsarchive.org/>. It includes a brief but useful discussion of the social origins of eugenics. Eugenics Watch, at <www.eugenics-watch.com/roots/>, provides detailed information on the roots of the movement, with a discussion of abortion.
- The Dead Sociologists link to Herbert Spencer is a good place to begin on-line investigation: <www2.pfeiffer.edu/~lridener/DSS/INDEX.HTML#spencer>. The Victorian Web, which includes the site: <http://65.107.211.206/philosophy/spencer.html> on Herbert Spencer, is a resource for the period as a whole.

CHAPTER TEN
ÉMILE DURKHEIM

Controversies

Durkheim is a link in a long chain of social thought stretching back through Comte to the conservatives, and past them to traditional social theory. While holding liberal principles, he reacted negatively to the excessive individualism of turn-of-the-century social thought and to the growing socialist movement. If you treat things in society as though they were social facts, do you gain more than you lose? Is such a perspective inherently conservative—tending to preserve the status quo? For Durkheim, is society founded on material factors or on consciousness? What are the implications of the view that religion is essentially a projection of social relationships on the question as to whether religion will become fully secularized? Is Durkheim a critic of capitalism or an apologist for capitalism? What were Durkheim's main contributions to the development of modern sociology?

Resources

- In his *Politics, Sociology and Social Theory* (Stanford, Calif., 1995), Anthony Giddens interprets Durkheim's politics as attempting to synthesize elements from irrational conservatism and socialism. In his discussion of Durkheim's individualism, Giddens points out that, despite his emphasis on social facts, Durkheim makes an argument for the importance of the acting subject in creating social reality.
- Durkheim was an assimilated Jew. The position of Jews in early twentieth-century France is discussed in Pierre Birnbaum's study, *Anti-Semitism in France* (Oxford, 1992), which situates one element of Durkheim's intellectual context—the rise of an anti-Semitic movement in France at the end of the nineteenth century. Chapter One establishes the meaning of anti-Semitism and makes a case for the need for comparative, historical analysis, stressing the distinguishing features of this ideology over time.
- The Dreyfus affair was an important context within which Durkheim developed his social theory. Eric Cahn's *The Dreyfus Affair in French Society and Politics* (New York, 1996) goes beyond an account of the events and personalities in the case to consider its effects on different segments of French society and the nature of the wide coalition of forces that emerged in the movement.
- Durkheim drew important information from the writings of social anthropologists, a discipline that was expanding in the late nineteenth century. An account of this early anthropology is found in Paul Erickson and Liam Murphy's *A History of Anthropological Theory* (Peterborough, Ont., 1998), which traces the origins of the social science from antiquity to Darwin and discusses the role that Durkheim played in influencing the theoretical foundations of French structural anthropology.

- As for many of the theorists discussed in this book, the most accessible orientation to the life and work of an author can be found in the series on 'Key Sociologists'. In this series is Kenneth Thompson's *Émile Durkheim* (New York, 1982), which combines biographical information with a summary and brief examination of his main texts.
- *Durkheim Today* (New York, 2002), edited by W. Pickering, includes an initial chapter by Kenneth Thompson that raises such issues as Durkheim's Jewish identity and his views on and relations with women.
- Chapter Ten of Sue Stedman-Jones's *Reflections on the Interpretation of Durkheim in the Sociological Tradition* (New York, 2002), edited by W.S.F. Pickering, notes how often Durkheim's work has been interpreted negatively, though in different terms at different times: as deterministic, as metaphysical positivism, and as conservatism.
- The Jewish virtual library provides a site on anti-Semitism, <www.jewishvirtuallibrary.org/jsource/antisem.html>, that includes a link to the Dreyfus affair: <www.jewishvirtuallibrary.org/jsource/anti-semitism/Dreyfus.html>.
- The site: <http://ssr1.uchicago.edu/PRELIMS/Theory/durkheim.html> gives a summary of many of Durkheim's key ideas and conceptions in the analysis of sociology, such as the division of labour in society.
- The Durkheim pages, maintained at the University of Illinois in Urbana, include a timeline, a glossary, and summaries of Durkheim's main works. See: <www.relst.uiuc.edu/durkheim/>.
- The Émile Durkheim Archive also provides a great deal of information, including links to his core ideas, with quotations and explanations:<http://durkheim.itgo.com/main.html>. For example, the discussion on Durkheim's text about the sociology of suicide is found at: <http://durkheim.itgo.com/suicide.html>.
- See <www.hewett.norfolk.sch.uk/curric/soc/DURKHEIM/Durk.htm> for the Durkheim page link from the general sociological map.

CHAPTER ELEVEN
MAX WEBER

Controversies

Weber was Durkheim's contemporary, though he developed sociology from a different national background. In the context of a large and influential socialist and labour movement, Weber had to confront the legacy of Marx more directly. Weber's approach to sociology was influenced by German historicism, leading him to take a large-scale, historical approach to the fundamental questions of his day. Even more than Durkheim, Weber focused on the role of ideas in shaping society, although not in the absence of the social context from which they derived. Ideas were not merely superstructures, although the consequences of social action were often unintended. Weber attempted to develop a systematic conceptual scheme for understanding society.

In Weber's view, why did the West excel relative to the East? Compared to the positivist interpretation of Marx that dominated German Marxism, Weber's theory was multi-dimensional. Were Weber's differences with Marx more profound than this? Why did sociology, as it developed in the twentieth century, prefer Weber's analysis of class and power to Marx's? What elements in modern society made Weber pessimistic about the future? From the summary of Weber's perspective on society and history outlined in Chapter Eleven, what concepts of his are useful for understanding contemporary society?

Resources

- Anthony Giddens, in Chapter One of his *Politics, Sociology and Social Theory* (Stanford, Calif., 1995), provides a comprehensive and contextualized overview of the evolution of Weber's politics from right to left, as his broad sympathies with reform (echoing the concerns of Marx) were tempered by the pessimism of the other dominant nineteenth-century thinker, Nietzsche.
- The link between Protestantism and the rise of capitalism has been one of the most controversial aspects of the debate on Weber's social thought. In this connection, the historian R.H. Tawney's older text, *Religion and the Rise of Capitalism* (New York, 1954 [1926]), still provides a balanced view of the elective affinity between religious and economic change.
- Norbert Wiley's 'Introduction' to his edited book, *The Marx-Weber Debate* (Newbury Park, Calif., 1987), summarizes many of the points of contention and seeks to find some common ground where Marx and Weber's ideas intersect. The essays that follow offer a variety of points of view on these issues.
- Max Weber's methodological principles are important in their own right. *Max Weber's Methodology: The*

Unification of the Cultural and Social Sciences (Cambridge, Mass., 1997) by Fritz Ringer presents a historical understanding of Weber's ideas relative to his intellectual field. To the contention that Weber's work is neither Marxist nor idealist, Ringer adds that he offers neither interpretive (empathetic) nor causal (positivist) explanations.

- In *Democracy against Capitalism: Renewing Historical Materialism* (Cambridge, 1995) Ellen Meiksins Wood, one of the more perceptive contemporary Marxists, argues that when Weber rejected Marx's belief in the human potential for emancipation, he was left to choose between despair and the inevitability of capitalism and bureaucracy, or the celebration of it. He chose the former.
- The first chapter of Peter Wagner's *A History and Theory of Social Science* (London, 2001), 'Classical Sociology and the First Crisis of Modernism', places the emergence of classical social theory (including Weber) in the context of nineteenth-century rationalism and traces the disintegration of this classical, holistic vision in the early twentieth century in the face of what he terms 'scientification and discipline segregation'.
- One of the best sources for information on most of the important sociologists discussed in this text is <www2.pfeiffer.edu/~lridener/DSS/INDEX.HTML>, the Dead Sociologists Index, including Weber: <www2.pfeiffer.edu/~lridener/DSS/INDEX.HTML#weber>.
- Criticisms of Weber's thesis on the Protestant ethic and the spirit of capitalism are summarized and discussed by Sandra Pierotti at the following location: <www.ecs.gatech.edu/support/sandra/paper.html>. She discusses several critics who dispute Weber's interpretation of Calvinism. R.H. Tawney argued that the direction of causal influence was the reverse of what Weber had found.
- The site: <http://ssr1.uchicago.edu/PRELIMS/Theory/weber.html> gives a summary of many of Weber's ideas and conceptions in the analysis of sociology.
- Another useful Max Weber home page, by Frank W. Elwell of Rogers State University, is accessed at: <www.faculty.rsu.edu/~felwell/Theorists/Weber/Whome.htm>. It includes a discussion of the relationship between Marx and Weber.
- Max Weber's approach to the study of religion is discussed in the site: <http://religions.myztek.com/holbrook/weber.htm>. It includes links to other (such as Marx and Freud) theorists' approaches to religion.

CHAPTER TWELVE
PROGRESSIVISM AND EMANCIPATION

Controversies

European social theories, as represented by such figures as Durkheim and Weber, were slow to make their way into American sociology. At first, the dominating figure was Spencer, but despite his ideological affinity with American capitalism, theorizing on such a grand scale was out of character for the United States. The dominant perspectives were more practical and pragmatic. An indigenous form of social liberalism, consisting of Christian-inspired reformism and a social work impulse, inspired many early American sociologists in their attempt to ameliorate conditions for the victims of American industrialization. Among the rural class of small property owners, a political movement known as Progressivism sought to reverse the tide of power that was shifting to eastern trusts and banks. As the Chicago School of sociologists focused attention on the conflict between traditionalism and modernism in the new immigrant communities, African Americans identified the colour line as the essential division in American society.

What were the sociological and cultural foundations of meliorism? Did Veblen critique America as an outsider more than as an insider? Veblen's *Theory of the Leisure Class* was popular again in the latter half of the twentieth century. How is it relevant to an understanding of modern capitalism? Why was Booker T. Washington celebrated by both white and black Americans at the turn of the century? Is there a difference between the work of a sociologist and the work of an investigative journalist? Were the tactics for social change adopted by Du Bois more or less effective than Washington's? Were there significant parallels between the movements for black civil rights and women's emancipation?

Resources

- Dorothy Schneider and Carl Schneider's *American Women in the Progressive Era* (New York, 1993) examines issues such as the movement into paid employment, the efforts of women to control their sexuality, the suffragette movement, and pacifism among women in World War I.
- Carroll Smith-Rosenberg's *Disorderly Conduct* (New York, 1986) is a collection of essays tracing the development of dissent among American women

from Jacksonian democracy through the Progressive era. It discusses the dismissive psychological arguments advanced by men in the face of women's anger and activism.

- In Chapter Three of *Cultural Consumption and Everyday Life* (London, 1999), by John Storey, the contributions of Veblen and Simmel are debated in relation to such topics as the dynamics of fashion and identity through consumption. These ideas are traced forward to the later twentieth-century thought of Pierre Bourdieu.

- The early chapters of Lee D. Baker's *From Savage to Negro: Anthropology and the Constitution of Race, 1896–1954* (Berkeley, Calif., 1998) focus attention on the construction of race, for example, through social Darwinism. Chapter Three, on American popular culture, discusses topics such as black nationalism and the political implications of popular views on race and culture. It discusses how popular periodicals influenced middle-class conceptions of race.

- Volume One of *The Classical Tradition in American Sociology* (Thousand Oaks, Calif., 1997), edited by Jeffrey Alexander et al., is a collection of period pieces that reflect the concerns of American sociologists during the early era of the foundation of sociology as an academic discipline.

- Herbert Storing's edited anthology, *What Country Have I?* (New York, 1970), includes writings on politics and society by black Americans, from Augustus Washington to the work of Du Bois and on to the Black Power movement of the later twentieth century. Lynne Olson, *Freedom's Daughters: The Unsung Heroines of the Civil Rights Movement from 1830 to 1970*, does a similar service for the writings of black American women.

- The Radical Academy on-line provides information on important sociological figures, including Thorstein Veblen. See: <http://radicalacademy.com/amphilosophy8a.htm#veblen>. This site links to: <www.mnc.net/norway/veblen.html>, which contains additional hyper-links relating to Veblen.

- Another site useful for Veblen references is: <http://villa.lakes.com/eltechno/TVcorhis.html>. It includes a link to the centennial reassessment of Veblen's theory of conspicuous consumption.

- A source for resources on the Progressive Era in the United States, created by Robert Bannister of Swarthmore College, can be found at: <www.swarthmore.edu/SocSci/rbannis1/Progs/>. It includes a link to on-line public documents. The site <http://cvip.fresno.com/~jsh33/prog.html> gives a number of useful links to events during the Progressive era, as well as central individuals, such as Emma Goldman. See: <http://sunsite.berkeley.edu/Goldman/Exhibition/>.

- A guide to Booker T. Washington on-line, compiled by Bennie J. McRae Jr, is found at: <www.coax.net/people/lwf/bt_wash.htm>. A brief biography of Washington appears at: <http://docsouth.unc.edu/washington/bio.html>.

- The Spartacus site is another general resource for a variety of individuals and movements, including Ida Wells, accessed at: <www.spartacus.schoolnet.co.uk/FWWwells.htm>. It includes excerpts from some of her writings.

- A useful orientation to W.E.B. Du Bois can be found at: <www.duboislc.org/html/DuBoisBio.html>, 'A Biographical Sketch By Gerald C. Hynes'. It includes a link to the Du Bois home page, at: <www.duboislc.org/index.html>.

- The site: <www.bartleby.com/61/catpages/Sociology.html> gives a comprehensive on-line glossary, defining sociological terms and indicating their pronunciation and etymology

Chapter Thirteen
Fin De Siècle Social Thought: Feminism, Decadence, and Perspectivism

Controversies

Romanticism was the response of intellectuals in the eighteenth and nineteenth centuries who resisted the application of scientific principles to the study—and the remaking—of society. Primarily, Romantics embraced the individualist core of liberal theory and resisted the claims of society generally. Nineteenth-century science threatened more effective control and social intervention. In response, turn-of-the-century intellectuals adopted an even more extreme rejection of the claims of rationality and indulged in artistic and lifestyle movements that rejected all bourgeois conventions except liberty. The 'New Woman', at least in her more radical demands, sought a deeper sexual equality than the right to vote for a parliamentary representative. The transgressive 'dandy' applied the principles to a wider sexual freedom. Social thought was ripe for reorientation.

In social philosophy, Nietzsche emphasized the elements of emotion and will. Why would the point of view known as perspectivism have an ambivalent effect on social science? What were the political implications of Nietzsche's social theory? In psychology, Karl Mannheim, whose sociology of knowledge adapted classical sociology (Marx and Weber) to the age of perspectivism, is discussed in Chapter Thirteen. In the decade of Fascism, state socialism, and capitalist depression, Mannheim sought to create a third, middle path between the extremes of totalitarianism and laissez-faire. Does Mannheim abandon the search for truth? Considering the role of sociology, what links Mannheim with Comte? Is Mannheim's plan for reconstruction of society Utopian in the old-fashioned sense?

Resources

- *Victorian Sexual Dissidence* (Chicago, 1999), edited by Richard Dallamora, examines such topics as spinsters, the dandy, the image of the male body, the adolescent boy as a figure of female-female desire, and the association of homosexuality with the birth of ideas and human creativity.
- David Owen's scholarly *Nietzsche, Politics, and Modernity* (Thousand Oaks, Calif., 1995) introduces Nietzsche's theory briefly in relation to liberalism, discusses his perspectivism, which attacks the idea that knowledge can be disinterested, and distinguishes Nietzsche's 'will to power' from Hobbes and social Darwinism.
- While psychoanalysis in the hands of Freud is anti-feminist, Karen Horney distinguished herself as a feminist and psychoanalyst. See Marcia Westkott, *The Feminist Legacy of Karen Horney* (New Haven, 1986)
- Barbara Winslow's *Sylvia Pankhurst: Sexual Politics and Political Activism* (New York, 1996) introduces the British women's movement through a biography of Pankhurst, the suffragette and socialist feminist who tried to inject feminist language into the workers' movement.
- Chapter One, 'Historical Precedents', of Jennifer Somerville's *Feminism and the Family* (New York, 2000) traces briefly the history of patriarchal thinking in aristocratic, Enlightenment, and bourgeois forms in the context of debates about the woman question and the suffrage movement.
- Bryan Palmer provides an account of the emergence of a consciousness about eroticism and sexual difference in 'Nights of Leather and Lace', a chapter in his *Cultures of Darkness* (New York, 2000). This book of cultural history is an excellent source for understanding private and clandestine rebellions.

- Chapter Two, 'From Wilde to Wild', in Brian McNair, *Striptease Culture* (London, 2002), examines issues of feminism and sexuality and compares end-of-the-century movements of the nineteenth and twentieth centuries. The surface similarities (such as backlash politics) mask substantial progress in the intervening century.
- An introduction to the decadents can be found at <www.jahsonic.com/Decadents.html>. The link to 'Symbolism' provides hyperlinks to a variety of individuals, movements, and ideas. The page on Salome: <www.jahsonic.com/Salome.html>, for example, indicates the significance of this image of the decapitating seductress for end-of-the-century thought.
- From the same source, the page on Sigmund Freud, <www.jahsonic.com/Freud.html>, summarizes a few key ideas, links Freud backwards to de Sade and forward to contemporary theory, and annotates several useful print sources.
- C. George Boeree's page on Personality Theories: Sigmund Freud—<www.ship.edu/~cgboeree/freud.html>—summarizes the most important of Freudian concepts, such as transference, sublimation, and reaction formation. It recommends *The Psychopathology of Everyday Life*, Freud's favourite of his works.
- The site: <www.fns.org.uk/index.htm> claims affiliation to the Friedrich Nietzsche Society. The Philosophy Pages project provides a list of primary and secondary sources, with some links, for the works of Nietzsche: <www.philosophypages.com/ph/niet.htm>. Another source that discusses Nietzsche's ideas in relation to the philosophy of existentialism is located at: <www.dividingline.com/private/Philosophy/Philosophers/Nietz/NLife.shtml>.
- The site: <www.tasc.ac.uk/depart/media/staff/ls/Modules/Theory/Mannheim.htm> provides a brief biographical sketch of Karl Mannheim, lists his main writings, and recommends some (mostly older) sources.

CHAPTER FOURTEEN
SOCIAL THEORY AND THE MIND

Controversies

Sigmund Freud initiated an attempt to understand the deeper instinctual and unconscious motivations scientifically, providing an ideological foundation for the modern emphasis on sexuality. Is Freudian theory more ideological than scientific? In sociology, the outsider, Georg Simmel, appeared to turn the discipline on its head. What difference does it make if you understand society as the creation of acting individuals rather than as a pre-existing structure?

Freud took part in the nineteenth-century reorientation to human psychology. While Europeans tended towards a more holistic approach to the human psyche, American individualism shaped an experimental psychology that focused on behaviour. The synthesis of these approaches produced a social psychology that, in the hands of theorists such as Cooley and Mead, examined the social processes through which individuals develop a sense of self. In Europe, the chaos of early twentieth-century war, reconstruction, revolution, and extreme reaction affected the generation of sociologists who matured in the early decades of the century. Is there a connection between the demands of American society and pragmatism and behaviourism? Does social science advance further by ignoring or analyzing the phenomenon of 'mind'? In social psychology, is mind a construction of society, or vice versa?

Resources

- An important general source for most of the primary thinkers discussed in this book is Terry Kandal's *The Woman Question in Classical Sociological Theory* (Miami, 1988). Kandal reviews the theoretical treatment of women and the women's movement by 13 male social theorists. The first four chapters cover the ideas of thinkers from Mill to Mannheim.
- In the 'Introduction' to his *Modernist Writing and Reactionary Politics* (Cambridge, 2001), Charles Ferrall discusses a number of prominent, early twentieth-century writers, including Eliot, Pound, Lawrence, and Conrad, who reflected a conservative intellectual orientation. They advanced an aesthetic modernism while rejecting liberalism, democracy, progress, and industrialism. This was part of the English context to which Mannheim responded.
- Philip Morgan's *Fascism in Europe, 1919–1945* (London, 2003) examines the roots of Fascism in the turn-of-the-century counterculture and the psychology of crowd behaviour (Chapter One). Also sociologically relevant is Chapter Six, which examines the phenomenon of Fascism in its appeal to the 'people' rather than to a class.
- In her book, *Distorting Mirrors: Visions of the Crowd in Late Nineteenth-Century France* (New Haven, 1981), Susanna Barrows examines the accounts of social scientists on crowd behaviour, including emotional contagion, hypnosis, and criminal anthropology. In Chapter Seven, she discusses the role Le Bon played in popularizing the view.
- Tom Goff, in Chapter One of *Marx and Mead* (Boston, 1980), critiques the sociology of knowledge as being circular, and then develops an analysis that attempts to link Marx's theory of praxis and Mead's social psychology to create a dialectical synthesis of these apparently contradictory thinkers.
- The site <www.trinity.edu/mkearl/knowledg.html> explores the question of how we know truth. Interestingly presented and multi-disciplinary, the discussion includes sociological topics such as the social construction of reality and a wide range of sociological thinkers (Thomas and Garfinkel, for example).
- The site: <www.pragmatism.org/>, called the Pragmatism Cybrary, is a comprehensive resource for additional links; for example, it contains a link to Charles Peirce, the founder of American pragmatism, John Dewey, and William James.
- An interesting link is to <http://theliterarylink.com/metaphors.html>, that demonstrates how much of everyday thinking (about topics such as war or economics) is done in terms of metaphors: 'concepts we live by'.
- In many cases the best place to begin is an Internet encyclopedia, such as the Encyclopedia of Philosophy, which contains an item on G.H. Mead: <www.iep.utm.edu/m/mead.htm>. It contains details of his life and outlines the ideas of his major works.
- An explanation of the concept 'definition of the situation' as developed in an excerpt from W.I. Thomas appears at: <www2.fmg.uva.nl/sociosite/topics/texts/thomas.html>.
- A useful source is the Mead project at Brock University. See: <http://spartan.ac.brocku.ca/~lward/>. It includes links to other related sociological thinkers, such as Cooley.
- The Sociology in Switzerland page, Simmel On-Line, is a comprehensive first page to search information on Simmel: <http://socio.ch/sim/index_sim.htm>. It includes biographical information, texts in English, and a discussion of the significance of Simmel's works.
- Overall, useful bibliographical information (primary sources) on dozens of well-known sociologists can be found at <www2.fmg.uva.nl/sociosite/topics/sociologists.html>.

a priori
Conclusion derived from deduction that is based on an assumption, not on experience or perception.

abolitionists
Individuals opposed to the practice of slavery and demanding emancipation of slaves.

acquired characteristics
Traits that an organism develops over the course of its life; Lamarck believed these traits could be inherited.

aesthetics
Artistic principles focusing on beauty; concern for what is beautiful or in good taste.

aesthetic nausea
As fashions become old and new ones appear, the older ones become repulsive to some persons.

alienated
The state of not having realized one's full potential; separated from the mainstream or from something essential to the quality of life.

anarchists
Revolutionaries who challenge all authority as oppressive and demand a society with no governance.

anomie
Durkheim's term for the condition of modern society in which there were too few moral regulations as guides.

anti-Semitism
Actions and beliefs aimed at the oppression of Jews.

antithesis
For Hegel, the potential inherent in a thing that is striving to realize itself; contradicts a thesis.

aristocratic culture
Belief that an aristocracy—the social elite—creates the highest development of morality and civilization.

art-for-art's-sake
Movement in the arts focusing on the style or form of the art and not produced for any other social purpose.

artifice
Use of deceitful means to secure a goal; typically employed by subordinates such as slaves and children.

assimilated
The condition of a minority merging with the dominant group, thereby losing its distinctive social characteristics.

atavistic
In evolutionary theory, the appearance in later generations of traits generally bred out of the species.

atomistic perspective
View in sociology that society was created by the separate actions of individual humans.

avant-garde
The latest style in art; in advance of the usual; progressive, leading-edge ideas, especially of an artistic movement.

backstage
The area of human conduct that is private and usually hidden; a term from the dramaturgical social analysis of Erving Goffman.

back-to-Africa
Proposal to have African Americans migrate to Africa as supposed solution to racial strife in the US.

behaviourism
Study of the observable actions of an animal or human without consideration to mental processes.

beyond the pale
Beyond the boundaries of polite society; 'pale' refers to the initial part of Ireland conquered by the English.

Bible Communism
The belief that Christianity initially entailed social equality and the sharing of private property.

black nationalism
Movement to create, within US territory, a black majority nation; also refers to separate development in US.

bracketing
To put aside a controversial point or argument and proceed to argue without considering it.

Brahmans
The superior caste in India, consisting of priests and intellectuals.

bureaucracy
Hierarchical structure of governmental administration with offices often rationally and competitively organized.

Byronic
Heroes depicted by Byron who were tall, dark, handsome, melancholy, moody, and frequently doomed.

calling
Calvin's doctrine that God intends each person to work in a certain field; secular success can give glory to God.

caste system
Structure of Indian society in which an individual is born into a rigid, unchangeable hierarchy of status.

catastrophism
Belief that God has recreated life many times, each time except the last having destroyed it, e.g., by flood.

charisma
Special powers of an exceptional individual who attracts others to obey by force of personality.

charismatic
Possession of special qualities by an individual that attract others to follow and obey.

charismatic authority
Power of a leader because of the tendency of his followers to obey based on leader's special characteristics or claimed divinity.

Chartists
Working-class movement in 1840s England demanding political reforms and the vote for working men.

Civil Code
Napoleon's code, which established laws for social life; it particularly reinstated patriarchal rule.

civil disobedience
Practice of disobeying unjust laws and enduring the legal consequences in order to expose their injustice.

civil society
The realm of the state beneath its governance in which private interests compete.

clan
A subset of a tribe; has its own symbols and rules of action to which in-group members are beholden.

class struggle
The central dynamic Marx identifies as the motor that pushes historical progress.

collective consciousness
For Durkheim, the totality of beliefs and sentiments common to the average members of a society.

colonization
The conquest of territory by a dominant nation; in philosophy or criticism, act of taking over another's claims or rights.

colour line
The often visible social barrier erected to segregate blacks from whites in the US.

commercial capitalism
The practice of buying and selling consumption goods on an open market.

commodity
A good produced for the purpose of exchanging it for another good or for money.

Commonwealth
Republican government formed in England under control of Parliament and Oliver Cromwell.

concentration of capital
Tendency for capitalist businesses to grow progressively larger and less competitive over time.

concubinage
Sexuality demanded from women placed in oppressive conditions, such as slavery.

conservatism
Political doctrine supportive of the existing social and political arrangements.

conspicuous consumption
Visible display of expensive consumer goods to claim prestige from anonymous others.

Conspiracy of the Equals
Jacobin-inspired conspiracy in 1797 to bring the Revolution back to the path of radicalism.

constitutional monarchy
Government with a separation of powers, including a monarch whose powers are limited by law.

contingent
Dependent on specific circumstances; true only at specific times and places.

corporations
Organizations of people who share a fundamental common interest, such as all being engaged in one industry.

coup d'état
Quick, military takeover of a government by force.

creationism
Doctrine that the world and life on it resulted from the act of a supernatural power; opposed to evolutionism.

cult
For Durkheim, a simple tribal religion; a set of collectively shared, elementary religious beliefs.

customs
Conventional behaviours, followed by habit and derived from tradition; a form of non-rational behaviour.

de facto
That which exists in fact, regardless of whether it should or whether it exists legally.

decadence
In a meaningless, Darwinian universe, the rejection of all standards except those of pleasure and experience.

deductive reasoning
Method of arriving at conclusions solely through the process of logical thought.

Deist
Follower of Deism, the belief that God created the world and the laws of nature but left it to work on its own.

despotism
Arbitrary rule of a single monarch, either tyrannical or enlightened.

dialectical
For Hegel, the process of change through which a thing develops, driven by a conflict of opposites within it.

dissenting
Opposing established doctrines and customs, whether in religion or society generally.

Dreyfus
French captain falsely accused of spying for Germany; major late nineteenth-century scandal.

duality
Philosophical view that reality is divided into two, independent and opposite principles; e.g., mind and body.

dynamic density
Degree to which people in society are brought into close contact and relationship; partly related to number.

dynasty
An unbroken line of hereditary monarchs or emperors, marking a historical era.

dystopia
Depiction of a future society that is usually dominated by a tyrannical state and oppressive technology; opposite of Utopia.

economic determinism
View, attributed to Marx, that capitalism was the necessary outcome of a predetermined sequence of economic stages.

economic protectionism
Use of government power to protect national industry, usually by taxing imports.

ego
That part of the mind that represents self-consciousness and mediates between desire and action.

egoism
Tendency to put the interests of the individual above society; exclusive focus on self-interest.

Elysium
In Greek mythology, a supernatural place of ultimate and final happiness; resting place of heroes.

emancipation
The granting of full rights of citizenship and freedom, as in the abolition of slavery or the liberation of women.

émigrés
Usually upper-class individuals who flee to another country during a revolution in their homeland.

empirical method
To employ observation and experiment to derive knowledge from sense experience; inductive knowledge.

emulation
For Veblen, an innate drive in humans to compare oneself to others and attempt to be better than they are.

Enlightenment
Era in which theorists emphasized the dominant position of reason in the conduct of human affairs.

estates
Social categories into which people are born and, by custom, remain for their lifetime.

eugenics
Movement aimed at preventing the birth of those deemed inferior and encouraging the procreation of those deemed superior.

evangelicalism
Movement associated with basic Christian teachings, strict Biblical, as opposed to traditional, interpretations, and emotional preaching.

evolution
Doctrine of slow, peaceful, gradual change, first applied to social development and later to biology.

exploited
For Marx, the condition of not receiving the full value of the goods to which you devote your labour.

expressionism
Artistic style focusing on the depiction of the inner, emotional state of the artist.

feminist standpoint
Analyzing society from the point of view of women, focusing on women's strengths and men's oppressive behaviours.

feral child
Child who is abandoned or isolated from society and is unsocialized; wild and natural like an animal.

feudal society
Social structure in which grants of land are made to inferiors in return for rent and services.

First Reich
The first period of German unification under Charlemagne in the ninth century.

forces of production
For Marx, the combination of the material necessities required to produce goods, such as technology.

formal rationality
Tendency to calculate rationally the best means to attain a desired end.

free enterprise
The right to pursue opportunities for private profit without state restriction or interference.

Freemasons
Members of a male secret society designed for mutual assistance and bound together by mystical symbols.

function
A purpose that a part of society fulfills to maintain the health of the social organism.

fundamentalist
Person who believes in the absolute certainty of religious truths and a literal interpretation of scripture.

gender politics
Drawing attention to issues of women and power, in public and private spheres.

general will
Rousseau's belief that people are bound to obey mutually agreed-upon rules for the benefit of all.

generalized other
The understanding one has of the average meaning that others attribute to a common activity.

genre
A particular mode of artistic expression within a medium; for example, within literature (or the cinema), a western or mystery.

gesture
For Mead, a primary action that serves as a direct stimulus for another's response.

Girondins
Revolutionaries in France who were anti-clerical, anti-aristocratic, and liberal; less radical than Jacobins.

Gothic
An ornate, spiritual style characteristic of the Middle Ages; in the novel, suggesting horror and magic.

gradualistic fatalism
Belief that human society is outside the conscious control of humanity and that intervention makes things worse.

Great Chain of Being
Hierarchical arrangement of life from simple to complex, fixed eternally by God or nature.

heresy
Ideas defined as false and dangerous to true belief.

hierarchy
An unequal structure consisting of a graduated series of steps differentiated from higher to lower.

historical materialism
Marx's term for his theory of social organization and historical change.

human nature
Inborn characteristics thought to be common to all of humanity.

hysteria
Psychological symptoms thought to be the external expression of a hidden psychic trauma.

iconoclasm
Tendency to be critical and to undermine what are held to be sacred objects or symbols.

id
The name Freud gave to the idea of instinctual drives that are innate and motivate individuals.

Idea
For Hegel, analogous to Spirit; the force striving to realize itself through historical development.

ideal type
A model of a phenomenon specifying only essential elements; hence unlikely to be found in reality.

idealism
In philosophy, the doctrine that mind is prior to matter and constitutes matter; opposite to materialism.

ideology
For Mannheim, the motivating concepts of a dominant group that justify and reinforce its position.

immiseration thesis
An idea, attributed to Marx, that the proletariat would become absolutely poorer over time.

impressionism
Artistic style founded on viewer's perception of light and colour rather than traditional, realistic drawing.

individualism
Doctrine asserting the primary importance of the individual person and his or her universal, human rights.

inductive reasoning
The use of rational thought, combined with experimentation and observation of particular instances, to infer a general law.

industrial capitalism
Private ownership of industry characterized by large factories, Investment in technology, and high output.

industrial style
Nineteenth-century prose published serially in journals and paid for by the line; often quick and unpolished.

industrial training
Booker T. Washington's scheme for educating blacks in mechanical occupations, but avoiding political activism.

interpretive sociology
Approach to sociology that focuses on the meaning that people have for their actions.

invisible hand
Adam Smith's laissez-faire doctrine that an unrestrained capitalist economy would inevitably benefit all.

Jacksonian democracy
A grassroots democratic movement seeking reduced state power and founded on small property.

Jacobins
Most radical faction in the French Revolution; claimed to speak for the Parisian workers.

Jim Crow
Laws establishing and enforcing the practices of racial segregation in the US South.

Junkers
Class of aristocratic landowners and army officers concentrated in eastern Germany.

karma
Hindu doctrine that the soul is continually reborn; the status of a rebirth is a function of behaviour in past lives.

labelling theory
Theory that people come to imitate the behaviours that others have expected them to possess.

labour theory of value
The value of a commodity is equal to the amount of labour expended on it.

laissez-faire
Economic doctrine asserting the maximum freedom of the business class to trade without restriction.

language
Complex, meaningful verbal symbols developed and used for communication and interaction.

legal-rational authority
Modern system in which people obey because the office individuals occupy gives them power to decide.

legitimacy
Belief held by people that a set of arrangements, such as authority, deserves their obedience.

leisure class
Predatory elite persons in society who live off the labour of others and who define their prestige by not working.

Leviathan
From Hobbes, a single, sovereign power in society; an authoritarian state.

liberalism
Social doctrine stressing the political and economic rights of the individual.

lifestyle
View, especially of the Romantics, that you should express your ideals in daily life.

lumpenproletariat
For Marx, those potentially of the working class who were excluded from production; vagabonds, thieves.

Malthusian
Reference to Malthus's theory that society would be better off if the fittest alone were allowed to propagate.

Malthusianism
Doctrine that overpopulation is inevitable because human population grows exponentially whereas food supplies increase arithmetically.

mandarin system
In China, the dominance in administration of bureaucratic scholars selected by examination.

materialism
Belief that nothing exists other than matter, so knowledge derives from perceptions of the real world.

means of production
The physical requirements for the production of goods, such as land, tools, buildings, etc.

mechanical solidarity
Durkheim's term for the forces that bind simple societies, made up of identical parts.

melioristic
Reformist; changes to society that alleviate the most serious effects of social inequality and poverty.

melodramatic
Writing style characterized by simple plots, good overcoming evil, stereotyped characters, and sentimentality.

mercantilism
Economic theory creating a national economy through trade monopolies and hoarding of gold.

metaphysics
Branch of philosophy dealing with abstract concepts such as existence, essence, and knowledge.

miscegenation
Production of offspring from racially different parents.

modern art
Turn-of-twentieth-century movement to focus art on issues of form—style, colour, design—not on content.

modes of production
Distinct stages in the progressive development of human society consisting of specific forms of production.

monotheism
Belief in the existence of a single, all-powerful God; opposed to polytheism, the belief in many gods.

muckraking
Type of journalism that exposes corruption and scandal in high places.

multi-variable
Argument that a social phenomenon can be best accounted for by examining many causes.

narcissism
The love of the self to the exclusion of others.

National Assembly
The body of elected representatives of the people of France, established in the Revolution.

natural law
Principles of ethics and morality common to all humanity deriving from God or nature.

natural philosophy
An older term for the study of the natural sciences such as biology and astronomy.

natural selection
Theory that evolution proceeded gradually as members of a species most suited to their environment survived.

naturalism
Movement in literature and art to depict nature and society realistically and in great detail, often viewing the margins of society, the outcast and underclass, as victims.

necromancer
One who exercises the occult practice of attempting to contact the dead to forecast the future.

negation
For Hegel, the process of change when a thing becomes what had been only a potential; a qualitative change.

neo-classicism
Application of standards of reason to artistic and literary production based on Greek and Roman models.

nihilistic
Tendency, often in artistic expression, to believe that nothing has any value; nothing matters.

Nonconformist
Member of non-Anglican Protestant denomination in England; rejects established, state religion.

nouveaux riches
Persons of recently acquired wealth; sometimes scorned by aristocratic, long-established, moneyed families.

oligopolistic control
Economic competition in a branch of industry reduced to a few dominant, colluding corporations.

optimism
Belief that all will turn out well; opposite of pessimism.

organic conception of society
Belief that society is like a body, consisting of parts that perform different functions for the whole.

organic solidarity
Durkheim's term for the mutual forces that bind complex societies, with a great division of labour.

overproduction
A tendency in capitalist society to produce more goods than the potential market can buy; under-consumption.

pan-Africanism
Movement to unite the nations and peoples of Africa into one great confederation or nation.

pantheism
Belief that God, or spirit, is diffused throughout material existence; everything has a spiritual dimension.

Paris Commune
A type of socialist government formed in Paris in 1871 that was suppressed by the French army.

patriarchal authority
Giving obedience to the dominant, usually elderly, male in a clan or extended family.

patriarchy
The rule of the dominant male in the family; more generally, male dominance in society.

patrimonialism
A social system dominated by an aristocracy and based on the inheritance of position and property.

perspectivism
For Nietzsche, the view that all truth claims are equally relative and all express the will to power of a group.

philistines
Members of bourgeois society whose goals and values never rise above the mundane acquisition of goods.

philosophes
The critical social theorists of the Enlightenment, especially in France.

philosophical radicals
The followers of utilitarianism, Bentham's scheme to maximize the well-being of the majority.

planned economy
An economic system in a socialist society in which production and consumption are organized by the state.

plastic
Capable of being shaped or moulded into different forms; belief that human nature is modifiable.

pleasure principle
Fundamental human drive to satisfy desires immediately; becomes repressed in adulthood.

pogrom
The systematic repression, murder, and expropriation of Jews.

political economy
The scientific study of society, later broken into the disciplines of politics, economics, and sociology.

popular democracy
Rule by the masses; in liberal theory, universal suffrage giving all people political power.

positivism
The theory that laws determining human society could be discovered, similar to the laws of physical science.

practice
For Marx, the need to see how theory works in the empirical world in order to evaluate its accuracy.

pragmatism
American movement in philosophy that judged ideas by their practical use; 'truth' was what worked, for now.

praxis
For Marx, the combination of theory and practice, thinking and doing.

predestination
Calvin's doctrine that God knows every person's ultimate fate and that good works cannot win salvation.

prejudices

Beliefs held by custom in the absence of reason; often used for negative stereotypes imposed on minorities.

primitive communism

Marx's term for the earliest type of human society marked by a low productive level and social equality.

profane

The opposite of sacred; that which is ordinary and has nothing spiritual about it.

Progressivism

Late nineteenth-century middle-class American movement of social reform directed against big capital and big government.

proletariat

Marx's term for the industrial working class.

Protestant ethic

As defined by Weber, the ethical practices of Calvinists, such as hard work, abstinence from pleasure, and frugality.

providentially

Put into place by the actions of a Supreme Being; Providence: one's fate as determined by God.

psychosexual development

Freud's theory that there was a normal path of development of sexual maturity leading to heterosexuality.

Puritans

Protestant followers of Calvin, who believed in strict morality and hard work.

Quakers

Adherents of Protestant denomination notable for its progressive stand on social issues such as equality, the abolition of slavery, and pacifism.

qualitative change

For Hegel, the change in a thing from one stage to a higher, more developed stage; a negation.

quantitative changes

For Hegel, the gradual accumulation of small changes within a thing as it develops its potential.

quantum theory

Model of physical science according to which a given outcome may be probable, but is not determined.

rationalism

Doctrine that truth can be discovered through the powers of the human mind.

reactionary

Extreme conservative who, usually following a revolution, wishes to bring back previous social conditions.

realism

Artistic movement in which the artist attempts to depict nature or social conditions as they are.

Reconstruction

Post-Civil War era in US South; time of emancipation of slaves and of legal equality; ended about 1877.

reflexive

The reaction upon an actor following the action and an elicited response by another.

Reformation

Split in the Christian Church separating Protestant reformers from Roman Catholicism.

reification

Tendency to take something humanly created and worship it as if had power over people.

Reign of Terror

Arbitrary use of the guillotine to silence opponents of the French Revolution; associated with the Jacobins.

relationism

For Mannheim, understanding the interactions between the social situations of various groups and their thinking.

Renaissance

The rediscovery of the knowledge of the ancient world that elevated confidence in human potential

rentiers

Property owners who did not work and lived on the revenue from their holdings.

reserve army

For Marx, the unemployed in capitalist society who can be called in and out of work as capitalism demands.

revelation

Belief that God has revealed certain truths to humanity

Rights of Man

Famous Declaration of the French Revolution; enshrined revolutionary values of liberty, equality, fraternity.

robber barons

The elite of late nineteenth-century American businessmen who enriched themselves by all means available.

Romantic conservatives
Writers and artists who glorified the Middle Ages and developed escapist, romance fiction.

Romanticism
Artistic movement focusing on subjective experience, emotions, and intuition rather than on rationality.

routinization of charisma
Process by which an extraordinary set of social institutions gradually becomes normalized and domesticated.

sacred
Pertaining to God; opposite of profane; what is special and revered as if it possessed power.

sadism
Sexual pleasure derived from inflicting pain on others; named after the cruel sexuality depicted in the writings of the Marquis de Sade.

Saint-Simonism
Movement inspired by the ideas of Saint-Simon, particularly his plan for a new Christian religion.

sans culottes
Ordinary French workingmen and Republican citizens who wore trousers rather than knee breeches.

skeptical
To doubt, especially to doubt the truth claims of accepted doctrines and beliefs.

secular
Reference to that aspect of society not concerned with the spiritual or otherworldly.

secularization
Tendency for aspects of society to become regarded as profane rather than sacred; the decrease in religious interest, especially in industrial society.

seditious
Tending to undermine established, legitimate authority; acts of treason.

sensibility
Understanding derived from sympathetic feelings and intuition; thought to characterize females.

separate but equal
Argument that while facilities for blacks and whites in the South were segregated, they were otherwise equal.

separation of powers
Political power should be divided among executive, legislative, and judicial branches, not centralized.

sexual liberation
Permitting women to control their own sexual acts and their bodies.

sexual licence
Absolute freedom of the individual to pursue sexual desires.

shaman
A role played by persons in simple societies based on a claim of a special attribute to understand or influence spirits.

simulacra
Shadowy likenesses of something.

social action
For Weber, anything a human being does that has, for her or him, a subjective meaning.

social class
For Weber, groupings of people occupying economic positions that remain stable in terms of membership.

social contract
The rational agreement among humans to establish a single authority and hence society.

social Darwinism
Application of natural selection to human society; competition allows 'the best' to rise and 'the worst' to fail.

social equilibrium
In the organic model of society, state at which the parts of society work harmoniously together.

social facts
Collective habits, common ways of acting, thinking, and feeling, that are real in their consequences.

social gospel
Movement within Protestant Christianity aimed at reforming social conditions for the poor in this world.

social liberalism
Doctrine that government intervention was necessary to reform social conditions and protect minorities.

social milieu
For Durkheim, a social whole, the structure of an existing society or social institution.

social psychology
According to Mead, the study of the individual self in its dependence on the social group.

social realism
Realism in literature with an aim to expose social wrongs and incite reform.

social rights
Belief that people have the right to economic well-being in housing, employment, health care, etc.

social romanticism
Romantic expression in art, literature that combined Romantic elements with social criticism for the purpose of social reform.

social species
Durkheim's term for the different general types of societies that have essential elements in common.

social statics
The study of the structure of society; in particular, the relation of the parts to the maintenance of the whole.

social stratification
View that society is unequally organized along dimensions of power, prestige, and wealth.

socialism
A communal type of social organization, usually without private property, designed to equalize social life.

sociology
The science of society founded by Comte to understand the law-like generalizations governing human life.

Spirit
For Hegel, the ultimate universal force, analogous to an absolute deity, which drives the process of change.

spirit of capitalism
For Weber, the practice of hard work and plowing profits back into a business; parallels Protestant ethic.

stages
Specific epochs of social evolution through which society evolves in a predetermined fashion.

state of nature
Conditions in which the earliest humans supposedly lived, without society, government, or laws.

status quo
Presently existing conditions; things as they are, often assumed to be as things ought to be.

storm and stress
German literary movement (*Sturm und Drang*) emphasizing individual rebellion, introspection, national identity.

subjectivity
Focus on ideas and feelings derived from an individual mind; ideas are personal and relative, not objective.

sui generis
Unique; constituting a particular social order that exists independently.

superego
That part of the mind that represents the rules of society that have been internalized by the individual.

superman
Nietzsche's description of the coming elite of men who combine willpower, creativity, and energy.

superstructure
Marx's theory that economic factors determined other aspects of society as a base supports a building.

symbol
For Mead, a gesture that conveys a meaning shared by all parties to the interaction.

symbolic interactionism
Perspective in sociology focusing on how tentative social structures are created through daily action.

symbolism
Artistic style using indirect symbols to express or suggest ideas or emotions.

synthesis
The result of a qualitative change or negation; becomes the new thesis.

taking the role of the other
Ability of an individual, when interacting, to place himself in the position of the other.

tax farming
Decentralizing the right to collect taxes, passed to the ruler, by allowing the 'farmer' to retain a proportion.

thesis
For Hegel, the existing state of a thing, what it is at a specific stage; contains within it an antithesis.

Tories
Traditional conservatives in England advocating paternal concern for the poor and opposing laissez-faire.

totem
An object, usually an animal, that stands as the symbol of a clan group in a tribal society.

transcendentalism
Belief that the divine spirit exists in all of creation; a naturalistic philosophy opposed to rationalism

transgressive
The act of defying conventions by doing the opposite of what is customary; commonplace rebellion.

two nations
Disraeli's description of England as dangerously divided between the rich and the poor.

tyranny
Government that is cruel and arbitrary, whether from a single ruler (autocrat) or other form of rule.

tyranny of the majority
Tendency of the majority in a democracy to oppress the minority.

unconscious mind
For Freud, that part of the mind that contains irrational drives and repressed memories; revealed in dreams and slips of the tongue.

unintended consequences
Results of social action that were neither foreseen nor, usually, desired.

unmask
For Mannheim, to reveal the distortions and untruths behind an opponent's arguments or world view.

usury
Charging interest on a loan; seen in traditional Christianity as a sin.

utilitarianism
Doctrine that the aim of policy should be to achieve the maximum happiness for the maximum number.

Utopian
A term used by Mannheim to describe the vision of an oppressed group that is seeking to induce social change.

Utopian communities
Small-scale, egalitarian communities, often founded in America, to recreate society on particular idealistic principles, after Sir Thomas More's *Utopia* (1516), which described the ideal city-state.

verstehen
Weber's term for the ability of an individual to subjectively appreciate another's point of view.

via plastica
Supposedly mysterious force of nature causing certain rocks to resemble organisms; now called 'fossils'.

Victorian
Description of characteristics of nineteenth-century English society, such as rigid morality, prudishness, etc.

Volksgeist
Each nation was characterized by a unique spirit providing every nationality with a different character.

Weltanschauung
The all-encompassing world view characteristic of a particular group.

Westernizers
In Russia, those who advocated changing Russian customs and laws in accordance with Western models.

white supremacism
Racist doctrine according to which the white race is superior to others and deserves to dominate them.

woman question
In socialist theory, whether women should struggle for class revolution or for their own liberation.

workhouse
Institution in which the poor, orphans, homeless, and destitute were confined and put to hard labour.

workmanship
For Veblen, an innate drive in humanity to succeed, create, and accomplish things through individual effort.

Young Germany
Literary movement of liberal writers in Germany inspired by the 1830 revolution in France.

Young Hegelians
Left-wing followers of Hegel such as Feuerbach and Marx; developed Hegel's theory in a radical direction.

NOTES

PREFACE

1. Émile Durkheim, *The Elementary Forms of the Religious Life*, trans. J.W. Swain (London: Allen & Unwin, 1964 [1912]), 237.
2. Ibid., 94.
3. Thomas Mann, *The Magic Mountain* (New York: Alfred A. Knopf, 1961 [1924]), 32.
4. Karl Mannheim, *Man and Society in an Age of Reconstruction* (New York: Harcourt Brace, 1940), 210.
5. Durkheim, *Elementary Forms*, 237.

CHAPTER ONE

1. John Marenbon, *Early Mediaeval Philosophy (480–1150)*, 2nd edn (New York: Routledge, 1988), 82.
2. David Nicholas, *The Evolution of the Medieval World* (New York: Longman, 1992), 321.
3. Ibid., 112.
4. Marenbon, *Early Mediaeval Philosophy*, 82.
5. Jill N. Claster, *The Medieval Experience: 300–1400* (New York: New York University Press, 1992), 155.
6. A.F. Thomson, *The Western Church in the Middle Ages* (New York: Oxford University Press, 1998), 49–50.
7. Mark Twain, *A Connecticut Yankee in King Arthur's Court* (Berkeley: University of California Press, 1983), 109–10.
8. Karl Mannheim, *Man and Society in an Age of Reconstruction* (New York: Harcourt Brace, 1940), 272.
9. Thomson, *The Western Church*, 141.
10. D.J.B. Hawkins, *A Sketch of Medieval Philosophy* (Westport, Conn.: Greenwood Press, 1972), 46.
11. Jeffrey Burton Russell, *A History of Medieval Christianity: Prophecy and Order* (New York: Thomas Y. Crowell, 1968), 176.
12. Quoted in Anne Fremantle, *Age of Faith* (New York: Time Inc., 1965), 95.
13. Marenbon, *Mediaeval Philosophy*, p. 158. Marenbon notes that the Christian was 'more perceptive and logically acute' in the debate (p. 158).

14. Hawkins, *A Sketch of Medieval Philosophy*, 48.
15. Excerpt from Abelard's *Confession* [c. 1135], 187–91, in Charles T. Davis, ed., *Western Awakening: Sources of Medieval History*, vol. 2 (New York: Appleton-Century-Crofts, 1967), 188–9.
16. Hawkins, *A Sketch of Medieval Philosophy*, 47.
17. Michael Kesterton, 'A college girl undone by her professor', *Globe and Mail*, 20 May 2000, A18.
18. Ibid.
19. John H. Mundy, *Europe in the High Middle Ages, 1150–1309* (London: Longman, 1973), 208.
20. Thomas C. Patterson, *Inventing Western Civilization* (New York: Monthly Review Press, 1997), 106.
21. Mundy, *Europe in the High Middle Ages*, 209.
22. Whitney Chadwick, *Women, Art, and Society* (London: Thames and Hudson, 1990), 30.
23. Lynn McDonald, 'Early theorists', in McDonald, ed., *Women Theorists on Society and Politics* (Waterloo, Ont.: Wilfrid Laurier University Press, 1998), 9.
24. Quoted ibid., 11–12.
25. Chadwick, *Women, Art, and Society*, 56.
26. Nicholas, *The Evolution of the Medieval World*, 429–31.
27. Rosamond McKitterick, *The Early Middle Ages* (Oxford: Oxford University Press, 2001), 70–1, 88.
28. Sheila Rowbotham, *Women, Resistance and Revolution* (Harmondsworth, Middlesex: Penguin Books, 1972), 19.
29. William Shakespeare, *Othello*, IV, iii, *The Collected Works of William Shakespeare*, ed. Hardin Craig (Glencoe, Ill.: Scott Foresman, 1961), 973–4.
30. Mundy, *Europe in the High Middle Ages*, 215–19.
31. Esther Fuchs, *Sexual Politics in the Biblical Narrative* (London: Sheffield Academic Press, 2003), 11.
32. André LaCocque, *The Feminine Unconventional: Four Subversive Figures in Israel's Tradition* (Minneapolis: Fortress Press, 1990), 32.
33. Humbert of Romans, quoted in Mundy, *Europe in the High Middle Ages*, 221.
34. Mundy, *Europe in the High Middle Ages*, 211.
35. Claster, *The Medieval Experience*, 223–4.

36. Rowbotham, *Resistance and Revolution*, 19–20.
37. Thomson, *The Western Church*, 142–3.
38. Claster, *The Medieval Experience*, 338.
39. Hugh Trevor-Roper, *The Rise of Christian Europe* (London: Thames and Hudson, 1965), 169.
40. Anthony Kenny, *Aquinas* (Oxford: Oxford University Press 1980), 12.
41. Ibid., 2. Kenny is quoting from Aquinas's earliest biographer.
42. Ibid., 2–4.
43. Thomas Aquinas, *The Summa of Theology*, 30–83, in Paul E. Sigmund, ed., *St. Thomas Aquinas on Politics and Ethics* (New York: W.W. Norton, 1988), 41.
44. Even the heavens were structured hierarchically; in fact, 'in every hierarchy of the angels there are orders that are differentiated according to their various functions and actions and duties.' Aquinas, *Theology*, 41.
45. Kenny, *Aquinas*, 10.
46. Aquinas, *Theology*, 38–9.
47. Ibid., 41.
48. Ibid., 39.
49. Jakob Grimm and Wilhelm Grimm, *The Complete Grimm Brothers' Fairy Tales* (New York: Avenel Books, 1981), 664–6.
50. Matthew, 19:17–23. This is the famous 'eye of a needle' passage (v. 24).
51. Grimm and Grimm, *Fairy Tales*, 664.
52. 'Where we have not sinned we are equal.' Aquinas, *Theology*, 37.
53. Ibid., 39.
54. Augustine, quoted in Eugène Portalie, SJ, *Guide to the Thought of Saint Augustine* (Chicago: Henry Regnery, 1960), 115.
55. Aquinas, *The Summa Against the Gentiles*, 3–11, in Sigmund, ed., *St. Thomas Aquinas*, 3.
56. 'Such conclusions do not have the force of proofs, but are either doubtful opinions or sophistries.' Ibid., 4–5.
57. Ibid., 13.
58. Aquinas, *Theology*, 38.
59. Ibid., 37–8.
60. Chadwick, *Women, Art, and Society*, 48.
61. Portalie, *Guide to the Thought of Saint Augustine*, 215.
62. Aquinas, *Theology*, 40.
63. Ibid., 79–80.
64. Ibid., 71.
65. Ibid., 52.
66. Ibid., 72.
67. Ibid., 52.
68. Ibid., 73. In his novel, *The Magic Mountain* (New York: Alfred A. Knopf, 1961 [1924]), Thomas Mann provides a succinct summary of the traditional, Christian objections to private property, commercial activity, interest, and supply and demand: 'every rich man was either a thief or the heir of a thief' (p. 403).
69. Edward Andrew, *Shylock's Rights: Grammar of Lockian Claims* (Toronto: University of Toronto Press, 1988), 27–8. While commerce was unnatural for Aristotle, 'Plundering foreigners at war and hunting natural slaves were, in Aristotle's view, more just and honourable occupations' (p. 28).
70. Max Weber, *The Protestant Ethic and the Spirit of Capitalism* (New York: Charles Scribner, 1958 [1904]), 107.
71. Aquinas, *Theology*, 74.
72. Ibid., 72.
73. Ibid., 74.
74. Karl Mannheim, *Ideology and Utopia* (London: Routledge & Kegan Paul, 1936 [1929]), 85.
75. Aquinas, *Theology*, 75.
76. Ibid., 75–6.
77. Walter Ullmann, 'The new orientation', in Paul E. Sigmund, ed., *St. Thomas Aquinas on Politics and Ethics* (New York: W.W. Norton, 1988), 118–19.
78. Aquinas, *On Kingship*, 14–29, in Sigmund, *St. Thomas Aquinas*, 26.
79. Ibid., 18–24.
80. Aquinas, *Theology*, 59.
81. Aquinas, *On Kingship*, 24.
82. Paul E. Sigmund, 'Introduction', in Sigmund, ed., *Aquinas on Politics and Ethics*, xvi.
83. Ibid.; Kenny, *Aquinas*, 26.
84. Dante Alighieri, *The Divine Comedy* (New York: W.W. Norton, 1970), 3.
85. Ibid., 20–6, 35, 47.
86. Ibid., 601.
87. Trevor-Roper, *The Rise of Christian Europe*, 173.
88. David Hume, excerpt from *History of England*, xv–xxiii, cited in Robert Southey, *Wat Tyler* (Oxford: Oxford University Press, 1989 [1794]), xviii.

CHAPTER TWO

1. Whitney Chadwick, *Women, Art, and Society* (London: Thames and Hudson, 1990), 63–5.

2. Ibid., 59.

3. Stephen F. Mason, A History of the Sciences (New York: Collier, 1962), 59.

4. Bertolt Brecht, Galileo (New York: Grove Press, 1966), 73

5. Mason, History of the Sciences.

6. Brecht, Galileo, 48–9.

7. Mason, History of the Sciences, 162.

8. Thomas C. Patterson, Inventing Western Civilization (New York: Monthly Review Press, 1997), 34.

9. Ibid., 35.

10. Maria Mies, Capitalism and Accumulation on a World Scale (London: Zed Books, 1986), 87.

11. Annette T. Rubinstein, The Great Tradition in English Literature: From Shakespeare to Shaw, vol. 1 (New York: Monthly Review Press, 1969), 107–8.

12. Robert Hendrickson, Book of Literary Anecdotes (New York: Wordsworth Reference, 1990), 198.

13. Peter Richardson, 'Base metal to gold', CAM (Cambridge Alumni Magazine) no. 33, Easter Term, 18.

14. Ibid., 18, 16.

15. Mary Shelley, Frankenstein, or the Modern Prometheus (New York: Oxford University Press, 1993 [1818]), 30–1.

16. Quoted in Richardson, 'Base metal', 17.

17. By not assuming an interventionist deity in his theory, Novack notes, Bacon divorced 'philosophy from theology and reason from faith'. George Novack, Empiricism and Its Evolution (New York: Merit, 1968), 17.

18. Alan Ryan, 'Hobbes' political philosophy', in Tom Sorell, ed., The Cambridge Companion to Hobbes (Cambridge: Cambridge University Press, 1996), 208.

19. Noel Malcolm, 'A Summary Biography of Hobbes', in Sorell, ed., Cambridge Companion to Hobbes, 14–17.

20. Christopher Hill, Puritanism and Revolution (Manchester: Panther History, 1968), 268.

21. Malcolm, 'Summary Biography', 27–8.

22. Ibid., 32.

23. Thomas Hobbes, Leviathan, ed. C.B. MacPherson (Harmondsworth: Penguin, 1968 [1651]), 712.

24. C.B. MacPherson, 'Introduction', in Hobbes, Leviathan, 21.

25. Malcolm, 'Summary Biography', 35–6.

26. MacPherson, 'Introduction', 18–19.

27. Ibid., 27–9.

28. Hobbes, Leviathan, 81–3.

29. Ibid., 118–20.

30. Ibid., 127–30.

31. Ibid., 150.

32. Ibid.

33. Ibid., 150–2.

34. Ibid., 189–90.

35. Ibid., 188.

36. Ibid., 209.

37. Ibid., 183–5.

38. Ibid., 211. 'The inequallity that now is, has bin introduced by the Lawes civill.'

39. Ibid., 183–5, 161.

40. Ibid., 183–5.

41. Ibid., 161.

42. Ibid., 185–6.

43. Ibid., 187–8.

44. Ibid., 209.

45. Ibid., 169.

46. Ibid., 223.

47. Ibid., 190.

48. Ibid., 192. Hobbes uses the term 'covenant', by which he means the promise to carry out a contractual obligation at some future time (p. 193).

49. Ibid., 196, 161–2. 'In a state of nature, the only possible mutual fear is fear of an invisible power, a god; hence, promises are accompanied by an oath to strengthen the other's belief in them' (pp. 200–1).

50. Niccolò Machiavelli, The Prince, ed. Mark Musa (New York: St Martin's Press, 1964 [1532]), 137, 139.

51. Hobbes, Leviathan, 201–2.

52. Ibid., 227–8. Humanity, which is the work of nature, constructs an 'Artificiall Man' in the form of a state. The state has an 'Artificiall Soul', which is sovereignty, that gives 'life and motion to the whole' political body consisting of various parts 'made, set together, and united'. Ibid., 81–3.

53. Ibid., 231. Speaking of the right to punish, which belongs solely to the sovereign in society, Hobbes says: 'the subjects do not give the Sovereign that right; but onley in laying down theirs, strengthened him to use his own, . . . so that it was not given, but left to him, and to him onely' (p. 354).

54. Ibid., 232–6, 372–3.

55. Ibid., 241–5

56. Ibid., 225–6.

57. Ibid., 264.

58. Ibid., 239–41.

59. Ibid., 272.
60. Ibid., 376.
61. Hill, *Puritanism and Revolution*, 284–5.
62. Hobbes, *Leviathan*, 313.
63. Ibid., 297. Hobbes complained that many preachers and lawyers who spoke against the sovereign power of the king 'had their education' at the universities. The universities 'season' their students with a 'subtile liquor . . . against the Civill Authority' (pp. 384–5).
64. Ibid., 380.
65. Ibid., 360–1.
66. Ibid., 370.
67. Hill, *Puritanism and Revolution*, 276–8.
68. Ibid., 280.
69. This phrase Rogers cites from Milton's epic poem, *Paradise Lost*. See John Rogers, *The Matter of Revolution: Science, Poetry, and Politics in the Age of Milton* (Ithaca, NY: Cornell University Press, 1996).
70. Ibid., 187–9.
71. William Golding, *The Lord of the Flies* (Harmondsworth, Middlesex: Penguin, 1964 [1954]). This book is commonly used in the high school English curriculum. William Golding was awarded the Nobel Prize for literature in 1983.
72. Hobbes, *Leviathan*, 717–18.
73. Mason, *History of the Sciences*.
74. John Milton, *Paradise Lost and Selected Poetry and Prose* (New York: Holt, Rinehart & Winston, 1966), 349.
75. Hill, *Puritanism and Revolution*, 274.
76. Crane Brinton, *The Anatomy of Revolution* (New York: Vintage, 1965), 165.
77. Gerrard Winstanley, *The Law of Freedom in a Platform* (New York: Schocken, 1973), 59–60.
78. Rogers, *The Matter of Revolution*, 178–9.
79. Margaret Cavendish, quoted ibid., 182.
80. Cavendish, quoted ibid., 182–3.
81. Cavendish, quoted ibid., 187.
82. MacPherson, 'Introduction', 53–7.
83. J.R. Milton, 'Locke's life and times', in Vere Chappell, ed., *The Cambridge Companion to Locke* (Cambridge: Cambridge University Press, 1994), 5.
84. Ibid., 5–7.
85. Ibid., 9.
86. John Locke, Excerpt from *An Essay on Human Understanding*, in *The Locke Reader*, ed. John W. Yolton (Cambridge: Cambridge University Press, 1977), 130.
87. Ibid., 72–3.
88. Quoted in Roger Woolhouse, 'Locke's theory of knowledge', in Chappell, ed., *Companion to Locke*, 147.
89. These natural laws were still thought to derive from a deity, although if interpreted simply as laws of nature, they could be adapted to secular interpretations, as they would be later by Charles Darwin.
90. John Locke, *Two Treatises of Government*, ed. Peter Laslett (Cambridge: Cambridge University Press, 1988), Treatise II, 269.
91. Ibid., 271.
92. Ibid., 280.
93. Ibid., 271.
94. Ibid., 286–8.
95. Ibid., 290.
96. Ibid., 291.
97. Ibid., 290–1. 'And hence subduing or cultivating the Earth, and having Dominion, we see are joyned together. The one gave Title to the other. So that God, by commanding to subdue, gave Authority so far to *appropriate*. And the Condition of Humane Life, requires Labour and Materials to work on, necessarily introduces *private Possessions*' (p. 292).
98. Ibid., 292–3.
99. Ibid., 295.
100. Ibid., 302.
101. Ibid., 295.
102. Richard Ashcraft, 'Locke's Political Philosophy', in Chappell, ed., *Companion to Locke*, 248.
103. Peter Laslett, *The World We Have Lost* (London: Methuen, 1965), 107–8.
104. Ibid., 109.
105. Locke, *Two Treatises*, II, 350–1.
106. Ibid., 275.
107. Ibid., 232–3.
108. Ibid., 325–6, 356.
109. Ibid., 366–7.
110. Edward Andrew, *Shylock's Rights: A Grammar of Lockian Claims* (Toronto: University of Toronto Press, 1988), 115.
111. Hans Aarsleff, 'Locke's influence', in Chappell, ed., *Companion to Locke*, 259.
112. Laslett, *The World We Have Lost*, 111.
113. Richard Ashcraft, *Revolutionary Politics and Locke's Two Treatises of Government* (Princeton, NJ: Princeton University Press, 1986), 145–9.
114. Locke, *Two Treatises*, II, 373.

115. Ashcraft, *Revolutionary Politics*, 578–9.
116. Andrew, *Shylock's Rights*, 62.
117. Ashcraft, 'Locke's Political Philosophy', 244.
118. Howard Zinn, *A People's History of the United States* (New York: Harper Perennial, 1995), 73–4.
119. Andrew, *Shylock's Rights*, 62–3.
120. Patterson, *Inventing Western Civilization*, 93.
121. Ibid., 107–8.
122. Ibid., 108.

CHAPTER THREE

1. Adam Smith, *An Inquiry into the Wealth of Nations* (New York: Putman, 1877 [1776]), 333.
2. Ibid., 335, 359–61.
3. Ibid., 485–6.
4. Ibid., 27.
5. Daniel Defoe, *Robinson Crusoe* (Harmondsworth, Middlesex: Penguin, 1965 [1719]), 243.
6. Smith, *Wealth of Nations*, 38.
7. Ibid., 53.
8. Ibid., 65.
9. Ibid., 270–1.
10. Ibid., 269.
11. Ibid.
12. Charles Dickens, *A Tale of Two Cities* (Toronto: Copp Clark, 1935 [1859]), 99.
13. Smith, *Wealth of Nations*, 264–6.
14. Smith, *Wealth of Nations*, 334, 340.
15. Ibid., 524.
16. Ibid., 421–2.
17. Ibid., 353.
18. Ibid., 336.
19. Ibid., 347.
20. Ibid., 570–1.
21. Charles Dickens, *A Christmas Carol* (London: Folio Press, 1970 [1843]), 16.
22. Smith, *Wealth of Nations*, 673.
23. Ibid., 673, 674.
24. Ibid., 352.
25. Ibid., 354.
26. Ibid., 75.
27. Ibid., 21.
28. Ibid., 20. Smith's example was the 'very trifling manufacture' of pins whereby 10 workers could produce 48,000 pins in a day by a detailed and minute division of the labouring process, while a single worker 'could not . . . have made twenty, perhaps not one pin in a day.'

29. Thomas Malthus, quoted in Donald Winch, *Malthus* (Oxford: Oxford University Press, 1987), 19.
30. Ibid., 19.
31. William Blake, quoted in Annette Rubinstein, *The Great Tradition in English Literature* (New York: Monthly Review Press, 1969), 401.
32. Thomas Mann, *The Magic Mountain* (New York: Alfred A. Knopf, 1961 [1924]), 199.
33. David Dabydeen, 'Eighteenth-century English literature on commerce and slavery', in Dabydeen, ed., *The Black Presence in English Literature* (Manchester: University of Manchester Press, 1985), 30–1.
34. Alexander Pope, 'An Essay on Man', in Pat Rogers, ed., *Oxford Authors: Alexander Pope* (Oxford: Oxford University Press, 1993), 280.
35. Daniel Defoe, 1725, quoted in Rubinstein, *The Great Tradition*, 284.
36. Ibid., 251–87.
37. Karl Marx, *Capital*, vol. 1 (New York: International Publishers, 1967), 76.
38. Defoe, *Robinson Crusoe*, 175.
39. Quoted in Peter Earle, *The World of Defoe* (New York: Athenaeum, 1977), 263.
40. George Anderson and William Buckler, *The Literature of England: An Anthology and a History* (Glenview, Ill.: Scott, Foresman, 1967), 563, 565, 566.
41. Jonathan Swift [1724] quoted in Rubinstein, *The Great Tradition*, 233.
42. Jonathan Swift, *Gulliver's Travels* (Boston: Houghton Mifflin, 1960 [1726]), 128.
43. Ibid., 148–50. What might result from such disjointed writing may be suggested by the lyrics of the Beatles' 'Come Together' or Cream's 'White Room'.
44. Ibid., 193–200.
45. Ibid., 209, 200, 208.
46. Karl Mannheim, *Ideology and Utopia: An Introduction to the Sociology of Knowledge* (London: Routledge & Kegan Paul, 1936 [1929]), 198.
47. René Descartes, 'Discourse on the method', in Enrique Chávez-Arvizo, *Descartes: Key Philosophical Writings* (Ware, UK: Wordsworth Classics, 1997), 72.
48. Ibid., 71–2.
49. Alfred Tennyson, 'The Higher Pantheism', in J.H. Buckley, ed., *Poems of Tennyson* (Boston: Houghton Mifflin, 1958), 352.

50. Descartes, 'Discourse', 91–2; René Descartes, 'Meditations on the first philosophy', in Chávez-Arvizo, *Descartes*, 140.

51. Ibid., 92.

52. Ibid., 85.

53. Friedrich Engels, *Socialism: Utopian and Scientific* (New York: Progress Publishers, 1972), 31.

54. Herbert Wendt, *In Search of Adam* (New York: Collier, 1963), 95.

55. Quoted ibid.

56. Ibid., 99.

57. Ibid.

58. Pope, 'Essay on Man', 298.

59. Voltaire, *Candide or Optimism* (New York: Appleton-Century-Crofts, 1946 [1759]), 7, 72.

60. Ibid., 7, 17, 42, 63.

61. Ibid., 2, 63.

62. Ibid., 113–14.

63. Howard Zinn, *A People's History of the United States* (New York: Harper Perennial, 1997), 69–70.

64. Thomas Paine, *Common Sense* (Harmondsworth, Middlesex: Penguin, 1986), 65.

65. Edward Andrew, *Shylock's Rights: A Grammar of Lockian Claims* (Toronto: University of Toronto Press, 1988), 138.

66. Zinn, *People's History of the United States*, 98.

67. John Locke, *Two Treatises of Government*, Treatise II, ed. Peter Laslett (Cambridge: Cambridge University Press, 1988), 321.

68. R. Howard Bloch, *Medieval Misogyny and the Invention of Western Romantic Love* (Chicago: University of Chicago Press, 1991), 27–8.

69. Ibid., 27–33.

70. Christine de Pisan, quoted in Lynn McDonald, ed., *Women Theorists on Society and Politics* (Waterloo, Ont.: Wilfrid Laurier University Press, 1998), 11.

71. Maria Mies, *Patriarchy and Accumulation on a World Scale* (London: Zed Books, 1986), 78–83.

72. Rubinstein, *The Great Tradition*, 216.

73. Addison, quoted ibid., 217.

74. Mary Astell quoted in McDonald, ed., *Women Theorists*, 18–19.

75. Sheila Rowbotham, *Women, Resistance, and Revolution* (Harmondsworth, Middlesex: Penguin Books, 1972), 17.

76. Daniel Defoe, 1698, quoted in Rubinstein, *The Great Tradition*, 155.

77. Thomas Jefferson, letter to Anne Willing Bingham, Paris, 11 May 1788, in *Thomas Jefferson: Writings* (New York: Library of America Literary Classics, 1984), 922–3.

78. McDonald, ed., *Women Theorists*, 41–5.

79. Ibid., 40.

80. Astell, quoted ibid., 18–19.

81. Ibid., 20–1.

82. Ibid.

83. Sophia, quoted ibid., 40.

84. Carol Hymowitz and Michaele Weissman, *A History of Women in America* (Toronto: Bantam Books, 1978), 30–5.

85. Ibid., 36.

86. Ibid.

87. Locke, *Two Treatises on Government*, II, 322–3. Dabydeen claims that Daniel Defoe had written against slavery as early as 1702. Dabydeen, 'Literature on commerce', 38.

88. Quoted in Rubinstein, *The Great Tradition*, 319.

89. Ibid., 319–20.

90. Dabydeen, 'Literature on Commerce', 28.

91. Ibid., 27, citing Eric Williams, *Capitalism and Slavery* (Chapel Hill: University of North Carolina Press, 1944), 52.

92. Defoe, *Robinson Crusoe*, 199.

93. Ibid., 177–9.

94. Ibid., 177–8.

95. Ibid., 212.

96. Dabydeen, 'Literature on Commerce', 28–9.

97. Smith, *Wealth of Nations*, 308.

98. Ibid.

99. Ibid.

100. Gary B. Nash, *Race and Revolution* (Madison, Wis.: Madison House, 1990), 15.

101. Ibid., 14–15.

102. Ibid., 9.

103. Ibid., 11–12.

104. Phyllis Wheatley quoted ibid., 58.

105. Ibid., 25.

106. Ibid., 177.

107. Benjamin Banneker, 'A letter . . . to the Secretary of State', ibid., 178.

108. Ibid., 180.

109. Ibid., 177.

110. Ibid., 17–18.

111. Frederick Douglass, 'Fourth of July Oration' (1852), in H.J. Storing, ed., *What Country Have I?* (New York: St Martin's Press, 1970), 34–5.

112. Nash, *Race and Revolution*, 36–42.

113. Ibid., 46.

114. Ibid , 49–50.
115. Dabydeen, 'Literature on Commerce', 34–5.
116. Jeanne-Marie Roland, quoted in McDonald, ed., *Women Theorists*, 99.
117. Mann, *The Magic Mountain*, 98.

CHAPTER FOUR

1. John R. Gillis, *The Development of European Society, 1770–1870* (New York: University Press of America, 1983), 224.
2. George Anderson and William Buckler, eds, *The Literature of England: An Anthology and a History* (Glenview, Ill.: Scott, Foresman, 1967), 425–8.
3. Whitney Chadwick, *Women, Art, and Society* (London: Thames and Hudson, 1990), 128–9.
4. Emmet Kennedy, *A Cultural History of the French Revolution* (New Haven: Yale University Press, 1989), 84–6.
5. Ibid., 84.
6. Gillis, *Development of European Society*, 224–5.
7. Peter Gay, 'Introduction', in Peter Gay, ed., *Jean-Jacques Rousseau: The Basic Political Writings* (Indianapolis: Hackett, 1987), ix.
8. Tracy B. Strong, *Jean-Jacques Rousseau: The Politics of the Ordinary* (Thousand Oaks, Calif.: Sage, 1994), 4–5.
9. Rousseau, quoted ibid., 5.
10. Gay, 'Introduction', x; Strong, *Rousseau*, 6; Lynn McDonald, ed., *Women Theorists on Society and Politics* (Waterloo, Ont.: Wilfrid Laurier University Press, 1998), 110.
11. Jean-Jacques Rousseau, *Discourse on the Sciences and the Arts*, in Gay, ed., *Rousseau*, 1, 2.
12. Gay, 'Introduction', xi.
13. Rousseau, quoted in Strong, *Rousseau*, 6.
14. Strong, *Rousseau*, 7.
15. Jean-Jacques Rousseau, *Discourse on the Origin and Foundations of Inequality Among Men*, in Gay, ed., *Rousseau*, 33.
16. Rousseau, *Foundations of Inequality*, 35, 55. Rousseau believed that humanity's 'impulse of compassion' extends beyond other people to all 'sentient creatures', which gives all animals 'at least . . . the right not to be needlessly mistreated' by people (p. 36).
17. Ibid., 38–9.
18. Ibid., 40, 42, 46. Just as animals degenerate as a result of domestication, humans experience the same: 'in becoming habituated to the ways of society and a slave, he becomes weak, fearful, and servile; his soft and effeminate lifestyle completes the enervation of both his strength and his courage' (p. 43).
19. Ibid., 44–5, 46, 48.
20. Ibid., 56–7. In sum, 'There was neither education nor progress; generations were multiplied to no purpose. Since each one always began from the same point, centuries went by with all the crudeness of the first ages; the species was already old, and man remained ever a child' (p. 57).
21. Ibid., 61.
22. Ibid., 46.
23. Ibid., 47, 61.
24. Rousseau, *On the Social Contract, or Principles of Political Right*, in Gay, ed., *Rousseau*, 142.
25. Rousseau, *Foundations of Inequality*, 62–3.
26. Ibid., 64.
27. Ibid.
28. Ibid., 65.
29. Rousseau, 'Discourse on the Origin and Foundation of Inequality Among Men', in Victor Gourevitch, ed., *The Discourses and Other Early Political Writings* (Cambridge: Cambridge University Press, 1997), 161.
30. Rousseau, *Foundations of Inequality*, 68, 67.
31. Ibid., 68.
32. Ibid., 76, 70.
33. Rousseau, *Social Contract*, 193.
34. Rousseau, *Foundations of Inequality*, 78.
35. Rousseau, *Social Contract*, 148.
36. Rousseau, *Foundations of Inequality*, 72–3.
37. Rousseau, *Social Contract*, 170–1, 152.
38. Ibid., 177, 150.
39. Ibid., 150–1.
40. Ibid., 155–6.
41. Ibid., 217–18.
42. Ibid., 180.
43. Jean-Jacques Rousseau, *Émile*, William Boyd, ed., *The Emile of Jean-Jacques Rousseau* (New York: Columbia University, 1963), 15–16, 18.
44. Ibid., 20–1, 33.
45. Ibid., 35–7.
46. Ibid., 38, 51, 39.
47. Ibid., 44–5.
48. Ibid., 93, 97, 103.
49. Ibid., 106–10, 120.
50. Ibid., 130–4.

51. Rousseau, *Foundations of Inequality*, 56; *Émile*, 135.
52. Rousseau, *Émile*, 133.
53. Ibid., 131–2.
54. Rousseau, *Foundations of Inequality*, 56.
55. Rousseau, *Émile*, 13, 147.
56. Ibid., 134–5.
57. Ibid., 135.
58. Ibid., 137–8, 149.
59. Ibid., 139–40.
60. Chadwick, *Women, Art, and Society*, 137–8.
61. Rousseau, *Émile*, 149–51.
62. Ibid., 153, 157.
63. Strong, *Rousseau*, 7.
64. Jack R. Censer and Lynn Hunt, *Liberty, Equality, Fraternity: Exploring the French Revolution* (Philadelphia: University of Pennsylvania Press, 2001), 3.
65. Robert Southey, 'Song', in *Wat Tyler*, Act II (Oxford: Woodstock Books, 1989 [1794]), 23–4.
66. Rousseau, *Social Contract*, 197.
67. Carla Hesse, *The Other Enlightenment: How French Women Became Modern* (Princeton, NJ: Princeton University Press, 2001), 20.
68. William Wordsworth, 'The Prelude, Book VI, Cambridge and the Alps' (1805), 'To a Friend, Composed Near Calais' (1802), in *The Oxford Authors: William Wordsworth* (Oxford: Oxford University Press, 1984), 459, 282.
69. Roland Stromberg, *An Intellectual History of Modern Europe*, 2nd edn (Englewood Cliffs, NJ: Prentice-Hall, 1975), 203.
70. Gustave Flaubert, *Madame Bovary* (New York: Signet, 1964), 91–2.
71. Roland Stromberg, *European Intellectual History Since 1789*, 6th edn (Englewood Cliffs, NJ: Prentice-Hall, 1994), 204. 'Robespierre wished to build a stadium holding twelve thousand people to allow the crowd to watch the legislators.'
72. Ibid., 19.
73. Hesse, *The Other Enlightenment*, 7–9.
74. Quoted in Jonathan Wordsworth, 'Introduction', in Wordsworth, ed., *Helen Maria Williams: Poems 1786* (Oxford: Woodstock Books, 1994).
75. Mark Twain, *A Connecticut Yankee in King Arthur's Court* (Berkeley: University of California Press, 1983), 111–12. The English historian Catherine Macaulay had made a similar observation in 1790 about the early reports of violence in France: 'I do not indeed exactly know how much blood has been spilled in France, . . . but by all the general accounts that have been transmitted to us, the history of monarchies will point out as many sufferers who have fallen in *one hour* to the *rage* and *outrageous pride* of kingly despots.' Quoted in McDonald, ed., *Women Theorists*, 60.
76. Censer and Hunt, *Liberty, Equality, Fraternity*, 148.
77. Karl Mannheim, *Man and Society in an Age of Reconstruction* (New York: Harcourt Brace, 1940), 222.
78. Chadwick, *Women, Art, and Society*, 63–4.
79. Ibid., 93–7.
80. Ibid., 92.
81. William Shakespeare, *Julius Caesar*, II, i, *The Complete Works of William Shakespeare*, ed. Hardin Craig, (Glenview, Ill., Scott Foresman, 1961), 780.
82. Ibid., *Macbeth*, I, v, 1050.
83. Phyllis Mack, 'Women and the Enlightenment: Introduction', in Margaret Hunt, Margaret Jacob, Phyllis Mack, and Ruth Perry, *Women and the Enlightenment* (New York: Haworth Press, 1984), 8, 6.
84. Catherine Macaulay, quoted in McDonald, ed., *Women Theorists*, 49, 57.
85. Macaulay, quoted ibid., 58.
86. Ibid., 53.
87. Chadwick, *Women, Art, and Society*, 134–7.
88. Censer and Hunt, *Liberty, Equality, Fraternity*, 57.
89. Ibid., 59.
90. Quoted in Sheila Rowbotham, *Women, Resistance, and Revolution* (Harmondsworth, Middlesex: Penguin Books, 1972), 39.
91. Censer and Hunt, *Liberty, Equality, Fraternity*, 80–1.
92. Rowbotham, *Resistance and Revolution*, 38.
93. Hesse, *The Other Enlightenment*, 112.
94. Censer and Hunt, *Liberty, Equality, Fraternity*, 147.
95. Marie-Jeanne Roland, quoted in McDonald, ed., *Women Theorists*, 100.
96. Darline Levy, Harriet Applewhite, and Mary Johnson, eds, *Women in Revolutionary Paris, 1789–1795* (Urbana: University of Illinois Press, 1980), 87–96.
97. Olympe de Gouges, 'Declaration of the Rights of Women', Postscript, 1791, ibid., 94.
98. Thomas C. Patterson, *Inventing Western Civilization* (New York: Monthly Review Press, 1997), 106.
99. Hesse, *The Other Enlightenment*, 81–2, 140.
100. Censer and Hunt, *Liberty, Equality, Fraternity*, 90.

101. Hesse, *The Other Enlightenment*, 146.

102. McDonald, ed., *Women Theorists*, 107.

103. Censer and Hunt, *Liberty, Equality, Fraternity*, 178.

104. McDonald, ed., *Women Theorists*, 108, 114–15, 120–1.

105. Anne Mellor, *Romanticism and Gender* (New York: Routledge, 1993), 39.

106. Janet Todd, 'Introduction', in Todd, ed., *Mary Wollstonecraft: Political Writings* (Toronto: University of Toronto Press, 1993), viii–ix.

107. Mary Wollstonecraft, *A Vindication of the Rights of Men*, in Todd, ed., *Mary Wollstonecraft*, 52, 13.

108. Ibid., 12, 27, 30.

109. Ibid., 59, 61, 16.

110. Ibid., 230–1, 77, 237.

111. Ibid., 60–1.

112. Todd, 'Introduction', xxii–xxiii, xxxii.

113. Rowbotham, *Resistance and Revolution*, 44.

114. Mary Wollstonecraft, *Vindication of the Rights of Women*, in Todd, ed., *Mary Wollstonecraft*, 69–72.

115. Ibid., 75, 77.

116. Ibid., 232.

117. Ibid., 77.

118. Ibid., 235–6, 238, 237.

119. Ibid., 140.

120. Ibid., 47–8.

121. Ibid., 88.

122. Ibid., 115–16, 106.

123. Ibid., 92.

124. Mellor, *Romanticism and Gender*, 34.

125. Wollstonecraft, *Vindication of the Rights of Women*, 204–26.

126. Ibid., 132, 151, 102–3, 272, 204.

127. Ibid., 119.

128. Mellor, *Romanticism and Gender*, 40.

129. Ibid.

130. Ibid., 45–9.

131. Loraine Fletcher, 'Four Jacobin Women', in John Lucas, ed., *Writing and Radicalism* (London: Longman, 1996), 115.

132. Ibid., 113.

133. Ibid., 115–16.

134. Jane Austen, *Persuasion* (Peterborough, Ont.: Broadview Press, 1998 [1818]), 171.

135. Ibid., 161.

136. Ibid., 48.

137. Ibid., 149.

138. Jane Austen, *Mansfield Park* (Peterborough, Ont.: Broadview Press, 2001 [1814]), 214. That Thomas Bertram owned an estate in Antigua was established in the second paragraph of the book.

139. John Sutherland, 'Where does Sir Thomas' wealth come from?', in John Sutherland, *Is Heathcliff a Murderer?* (New York: Oxford University Press, 1996), 8. In the TV mini-series version of *Persuasion*, the link between slavery and the standard of living, which Fanny shared, was made explicit in the dialogue, as was the link between the ownership of slaves and the patriarchal control of women in England.

140. Austen, *Mansfield Park*, 208, 304, 289.

141. Ibid., 35.

142. Ibid., 42.

143. Austen, *Persuasion*, 178.

144. Austen, *Mansfield Park*, 106, 232, 361, 289, 299.

145. Ibid., 323–4.

146. 'A lion can raise a mouse; a mouse is still a mouse.' Sal Maggio (played by Christopher Walken), in the film *Kangaroo Jack* (2003), directed by David McNally, screenplay by Scott Rosenberg and Steve Bing.

147. Austen, *Mansfield Park*, 418.

148. Austen, *Persuasion*, 103.

149. Ibid., 130.

150. Ibid., 243.

151. Quoted in Mellor, *Romanticism and Gender*, 55.

152. Jane Austen, *Pride and Prejudice* (New York: Airmont Books, 1962), 94, 95–6.

153. Ibid., 96.

154. Ibid., 97.

155. Ibid., 299.

CHAPTER FIVE

1. Quoted in Howard Zinn, *A People's History of the United States* (New York: Harper Perennial, 1995), 70.

2. Quoted ibid., 95.

3. Robert Southey, *Wat Tyler* (Oxford: Woodstock Books, 1989 [1794]).

4. The English philosopher, Bertrand Russell, remarked caustically that 'in his youth Wordsworth sympathized with the French revolution, went to France, wrote good poetry, and had a natural [out of wedlock] daughter. At this period he was called "bad". Then he became "good," abandoned his daughter, adopted "correct" [conservative] principles, and wrote bad poetry.' Quoted in

Robert Hendrickson, *The Wordsworth Book of Literary Anecdotes* (New York: Wordsworth Reference, 1997), 307.

5. Manfred Kuehn, *Kant: A Biography* (Cambridge: Cambridge University Press, 2001), 26

6. Ibid., 33.

7. Ibid., 45.

8. Ibid., 89, 105.

9. Roger Scruton, *Kant* (New York: Oxford University Press, 1982), 4–5.

10. Richard Rorty, 'Habermas and Lyotard on Post-Modernity', in James Farganis, ed., *Readings in Social Theory: The Classical Tradition to Post-Modernism*, 3rd edn (Toronto: McGraw-Hill, 2000), 436. (Originally published in *Praxis International* 4, 1 [Apr. 1984]: 32–44.)

11. Émile Durkheim, *The Elementary Forms of the Religious Life*, trans. J.W. Swain (London: Allen & Unwin, 1964), 9, 14.

12. Ibid., 13, 11.

13. Ibid., 14–15.

14. For Durkheim, divine reason is not empirically verifiable and, being immutable, it is incapable of explaining the 'incessant variability' of 'the categories of human thought' that are, essentially, collective representations dependent on how groups' mental states are socially founded and organized (ibid., 15–17).

15. Ibid., 445.

16. Kuehn, *Kant*, 338.

17. Ibid., 342.

18. Ibid., 366, 372, 374–6.

19. Ibid., 298–9.

20. Ibid., 309.

21. Ibid., 116, 33.

22. Ibid., 400.

23. Carla Hesse, *The Other Enlightenment: How French Women Became Modern* (Princeton, NJ: Princeton University Press, 2001), 120. For the materialists, woman's natural weakness was physiological—women were incapable of deriving general, abstract principles from specific, particular experiences. Both Kant and the materialists accepted the ancient duality that women differed essentially from men in their more limited mental capacity.

24. Kuehn, *Kant*, 405; emphasis in original.

25. Ibid., 421.

26. Georg Simmel, 'Individual and Society in Eighteenth and Nineteenth-Century Views of Life', in

Kurt H. Wolff, ed., *The Sociology of Georg Simmel*, (Glencoe, Ill.: Free Press, 1950), 69.

27. Hesse, *The Other Enlightenment*, 105–6.

28. Jacques Godechot, *The Counter-Revolution: Doctrine and Action, 1789–1804* (Princeton, NJ: Princeton University Press, 1971), 82, 96.

29. Ibid., 87.

30. Ibid., 87–9, 96–7

31. Ibid., 93.

32. Ibid., 90–4, 97–100.

33. F.P. Lock, *Burke's Reflections on the Revolution in France* (London: Allen & Unwin, 1985), 28.

34. Ibid.

35. Edmund Burke, *Reflections on the Revolution in France*, ed. William Todd (New York: Rinehart, 1959), 85–6. See Thomas C. Patterson, *Inventing Western Civilization* (New York: Monthly Review Press, 1997), 102.

36. Burke, *Reflections*, 96.

37. Ibid., 39. For Burke, nature teaches us to revere individuals 'on account of their age' and 'on account of those from whom they are descended' (p. 40).

38. Ibid., 105.

39. Ibid., 104–5.

40. Burke, quoted in Edward Andrew, *Shylock's Rights: A Grammar of Lockian Claims* (Toronto: University of Toronto Press, 1988), 165.

41. Burke, *Reflections*, 59.

42. Ibid., 153.

43. Ibid., 13–16, 67–8.

44. Ibid., 28, 21, 23–4.

45. Ibid., 169–70.

46. Ibid., 44–5, 99, 171–2, 91–3.

47. Ibid., 208.

48. Ibid., 37–9.

49. Ibid., 169–70.

50. Burke, quoted in Andrew, *Shylock's Rights*, 159–60.

51. Eric Hobsbawm, *The Age of Revolution, 1789–1848* (New York: Mentor, 1962), 291.

52. Alfred, Lord Tennyson, 'You ask me why', in *Poems of Tennyson*, ed. J.H. Buckley (Boston: Houghton Mifflin, 1958), 85.

53. Burke, *Reflections*, 34–9.

54. 'There is more sagacity in thy body than in the best wisdom.' Friedrich Nietzsche, *Thus Spake Zarathustra* (New York: Modern Library, 1917 [1883]), 51.

55. Burke, *Reflections*, 109–10.

56. Ibid., 117–19. 'He who gave our nature to be per-fected by our virtue, willed also the necessary means of its perfection—He willed therefore the state' (p. 119).

57. Frank O'Gorman, *Edmund Burke: His Political Philosophy* (Bloomington: Indiana University Press, 1973), 14.

58. Burke, *Reflections*, 57–8.

59. Ibid., 43.

60. Ibid., 58. Burke proved his point that only the leisured become learned by quoting *Ecclesiasticus*, ch. xxxviii: 'How can he get wisdom that holdeth the plough . . . that driveth oxen; and is occupied in their labours; and whose talk is of bullocks?' [verses 24, 25]. 'They shall not be sought for in public counsel' [verse 33]. Ibid., 58 n.

61. Ibid., 70, 74.

62. Emmet Kennedy, *A Cultural History of the French Revolution* (New Haven: Yale University Press, 1989), 105–6.

63. Heinrich Heine, 'Germany, A Winter's Tale', *The Complete Poems: A Modern English Version*, ed. Hal Draper (Boston: Suhrkamp/Insel, 1982), 487–8.

64. Roland Stromberg, *An Intellectual History of Modern Europe*, 2nd edn (Englewood Cliffs, NJ: Prentice-Hall, 1975), 230.

65. Kennedy, *A Cultural History*, 107.

66. Eugene H. Peterson, *Subversive Spirituality* (Grand Rapids, Mich.: W.B. Eerdmans, 1997), 3.

67. Stromberg, *An Intellectual History*, 230.

68. Johann Wolfgang von Goethe, *The Sorrows of Young Werther* (New York: Lovell, Coryell & Co, 1882 [1774]), 48.

69. Ibid., 28.

70. Martin Swales, *Goethe: The Sorrows of Young Werther* (Cambridge: Cambridge University Press, 1987), 94.

71. Nicholas Boyle, *Goethe: The Poet and the Age* (Oxford: Oxford University Press, 1991), 174–5. In Leipzig, Germany, theologians successfully lobbied the city council to make it an offence to sell a copy of Goethe's novel and also to wear the Werther costume. Swales, *Goethe*, 97.

72. Mary Shelley, *Frankenstein, or the Modern Prometheus*, (Peterborough, Ont.: Broadview Press, 1994 [1818]), 155–6.

73. Goethe, *Sorrows*, 11.

74. Gustave Flaubert, *Modame Bovary* (New York: Signet, 1964 [1857]), 95.

75. Ibid., 148.

76. Ibid., 148–50.

77. Ibid.

78. Morse Peckham, *Victorian Revolutionaries: Reflections on Some Heroes of a Culture Crisis* (New York: George Braziller, 1970), 236.

79. Kennedy, *A Cultural History*, 136–7, 106.

80. Geoffrey Gorer, *The Life and Ideas of the Marquis de Sade* (Westport, Conn.: Greenwood Press, 1962).

81. Peter Weiss, *Marat/Sade* (London: Calder and Boyars, 1965), 56–7.

82. Gorer, *Marquis de Sade*, 49.

83. Weiss, *Marat/Sade*, 42, 49.

84. Philippe Seminet, *Sade in His Own Name* (New York: Peter Lang, 2003), 8.

85. Aldous Huxley, *Brave New World* (Harmondsworth, UK: Penguin, 1963 [1932]), 10.

86. John Gillis, *The Development of European Society, 1770–1870* (Washington: University Press of America, 1983), 227.

87. George Gordon, Lord Byron, 'Sonnet on Chillon', in G. Anderson and W. Buckler, eds, *The Literature of England* (Glencoe, Ill.: Scott Foresman, 1967), 745.

88. Byron, *Childe Harold's Pilgrimage*, canto 3, stanza 23, in Anderson and Buckler, eds, *Literature of England*, 747.

89. Anne Mellor, *Romanticism and Gender* (New York: Routledge, 1993), 23.

90. Ibid., 23.

91. Ibid., 23–4.

92. Ibid., 24, 29.

93. Prometheus, in Greek mythology, was the creator of men, who were made to stand upright in the image of the gods. Later, he stole fire for their use, for which Zeus punished him.

94. Shelley, *Frankenstein*, 214, 23, 34.

95. Ibid., 38–9.

96. Ibid., 39–40, 189.

97. Ibid., 188.

98. Ibid., 138–9. This is hardly a feminist sentiment.

99. Ibid., 165.

100. Ibid., 181, 183.

101. Mellor, *Romanticism and Gender*, 23–4.

102. William Blake, 'Holy Thursday' [1789], in Mason, ed., *The Oxford Authors: William Blake*, 269.

103. William Blake, quoted in Annette Rubinstein, *The Great Tradition in English Literature: From*

Shakespeare to Shaw (New York: Monthly Review Press, 1969), 396.

104. John Sutherland, 'How does Victor make his monsters?', in Sutherland, *Is Heathcliff a Murderer?* (New York: Oxford University Press, 1996), 32.

105. Percy Shelley, 'Song to the Men of England', *The Poetical Works of Percy Bysshe Shelley* (London: Henry Frowde, 1908), 568.

106. Quoted in Robert Hendrickson, *The Wordsworth Book of Literary Anecdotes* (New York: Wordsworth Editions, 1997), 244–5.

107. Sheila Rowbotham, *Women, Resistance, and Revolution* (Harmondsworth, UK: Penguin, 1972), 246.

108. Hendrickson, *Wordsworth Book of Literary Anecdotes*, 246.

109. Quoted in Rubinstein, *The Great Tradition in English Literature*, 554.

110. Charles Morazé, *The Triumph of the Middle Classes* (Garden City, NY: Anchor Books, 1968), 165–6.

111. Hesse, *The Other Enlightenment*, 147.

112. Morazé, *Triumph of the Middle Classes*, 170–82.

113. Gillis, *The Development of European Society*, 227.

114. Heinrich Heine, 'For the Cause' [1842], *The Complete Poems*, 400.

115. A. Sailes, P. Cazaubon, and B. Guerrey, 'The "black-devil" fit for the Pantheon', *Guardian Weekly*, 26 Dec. 2002–1 Jan. 2003, 19.

116. C. Simon, 'Family of genius descended from a slave', *Guardian Weekly*, 26 Dec. 2002–1 Jan. 2003, 19. In 2001, the French government honoured Alexandre Dumas by removing his remains to the Pantheon in Paris, the tomb of France's most respected artists and authors, and apologized for the humiliation Dumas had received. The honour was also a political statement of toleration in the face of a new upsurge of racism in France.

117. Gillis, *The Development of European Society*, 230.

118. John Keats, 'Ode on a Grecian Urn', *Selected Poetry* (New York: Oxford University Press, 1996), 178.

119. Flaubert, *Madame Bovary*, 57, 58, 111. The year before he wrote *Madame Bovary*, Flaubert travelled extensively in Egypt.

120. E.J. Hobsbawm, *The Age of Revolution, 1789–1848* (New York: Mentor, 1962), 307.

121. Ibid.

122. Anthony Esler, *Bombs, Beards, and Barricades: 150 Years of Youth in Revolt* (New York: Stein and Day, 1971), 302.

123. Stromberg, *An Intellectual History*, 237.

124. Karl Mannheim, *Ideology and Utopia* (London: Routledge & Kegan Paul, 1936 [1929]), 148.

125. Karl Mannheim, *Man and Society in an Age of Reconstruction* (New York, Harcourt Brace, 1940), 241.

CHAPTER SIX

1. Edmund Wilson, *To the Finland Station: A Study in the Writing and Acting of History* (Garden City, NY: Doubleday, 1953), 1–3.

2. Felix Markham, 'Introduction', in Markham, ed., *Henri de Saint-Simon: Social Organization, The Science of Man, and Other Writings* (New York: Harper and Row, 1964), xii.

3. Keith Taylor, 'Introduction', in Taylor, ed., *Henri Saint-Simon: Selected Writings on Science, Industry and Social Organization* (New York: Holmes and Meier, 1975), 13–18.

4. Ibid., 18–20.

5. Mary Pickering, *Auguste Comte: An Intellectual Biography*, vol. 1 (Cambridge: Cambridge University Press, 1993), 84.

6. Taylor, 'Introduction', 18–23.

7. Ibid., 24–9.

8. Henri de Saint-Simon, 'Introduction to the scientific studies of the 19th century', in Taylor, ed., *Saint-Simon: Selected Writings*, 93–8. Italicized in original.

9. Henri de Saint-Simon, 'Industry', in Ghita Ionescu, ed., *The Political Thought of Saint-Simon* (Oxford: Oxford University Press, 1976), 104.

10. Henri de Saint-Simon, 'On the reorganization of European society', in Ionescu, ed., *The Political Thought*, 85.

11. Ibid., 84–6.

12. Markham, 'Introduction', xxi.

13. Saint-Simon, 'Industry', 104, 121.

14. Ibid., 99, 116–17.

15. Henri de Saint-Simon, 'New Christianity', in Ionescu, ed., *The Political Thought*, 211.

16. Henri de Saint-Simon, 'On the industrial system', in Ionescu, ed., *The Political Thought*, 178.

17. Saint-Simon, 'Industry', 99–101.

18. Henri de Saint-Simon, 'Second letter', *L'Industrie*, in Taylor, ed., *Saint-Simon: Selected Writings*, 163–4.

19. Saint-Simon, 'New Christianity', in Markham, ed., *Saint-Simon: Social Organization*, 109, 111.

20. Henri de Saint-Simon, 'Fragments on social organization', in Taylor, ed., *Saint-Simon: Selected Writings*, 269–71.

21. Heinrich Heine, 'Germany: A Winter's Tale', in Hal Draper, ed., *The Complete Poems: A Modern English Version* (Boston: Suhrkamp/Insel, 1982), 484–5.

22. Saint-Simon, 'Fragments', 262–5.

23. Ibid.

24. Saint-Simon, 'New Christianity', in Markham, ed., *Saint-Simon: Social Organization*, 105.

25. Saint-Simon, 'New Christianity', in Ionescu, ed., *The Political Thought*, 213.

26. Saint-Simon, 'Fragments', 166.

27. Henri de Saint-Simon, 'On the replacement of government by administration', in Taylor, ed., *Saint-Simon: Selected Writings*, 208–9.

28. Saint-Simon, 'Industry', 115.

29. Saint-Simon, 'New Christianity', in Markham, ed., *Saint-Simon: Social Organization*, 99, 107.

30. Ibid., 104.

31. Saint-Simon, 'New Christianity', in Ionescu, ed., *The Political Thought*, 210.

32. Henri de Saint-Simon, 'Introduction to the Scientific Studies of the Nineteenth Century (1808)', in Markham, ed., *Saint-Simon: Social Organization*, 20.

33. Saint Simon, 'New Christianity', in Ionescu, ed., *The Political Thought*, 211.

34. Saint-Simon, 'New Christianity', in Markham, ed., *Saint-Simon: Social Organization*, 113.

35. Saint-Simon, 'Introduction to the Scientific Studies', in Markham, ed., *Saint-Simon: Social Organization*, 49–54.

36. Enfantin, quoted in Markham, 'Introduction', xxxviii.

37. George Lichtheim, *A Short History of Socialism* (New York: Praeger, 1970), 44.

38. Pickering, *Auguste Comte*, 3–4.

39. Ibid., 20–30.

40. Stanislav Andreski, 'Introduction: Comte's place in the history of sociology', in Andreski, ed., *The Essential Comte* (London: Croom Helm, 1974), 7–8.

41. Pickering, *Auguste Comte*, 315–22.

42. Ibid., 326–7.

43. Ibid., 385–92.

44. Ibid., 542–60.

45. Andreski, 'Introduction: Comte's place', 8–9.

46. Comte, 'Positive Philosophy', in Andreski, ed., *The Essential Comte*, 19–27.

47. Ibid., 37–8, 125–6, 128, 132–3.

48. Ibid., 37–8, 125–6, 128, 135, 144. Rousseau's belief that the state of nature was superior to the civilized state was the metaphysical form of the theological dogma about the 'fall of man', through which people worship the past and see society as decadent (p. 151).

49. Ibid., 127, 129, 147.

50. Ibid., 157–8.

51. Ibid., 149, 154. Social statics confirms the observation of French and German theorists that 'there is a constant and necessary solidarity of political power and civil power, which means . . . that the predominant social forces become in the end also the ruling forces' (p. 152).

52. Ibid., 155–6.

53. Ibid., 172–3, 163–4, 175.

54. Ibid., 176–7, 226.

55. Ibid., 192.

56. Ibid., 226–7.

57. Gustave Flaubert, *Sentimental Education* (London: J.M. Dent, 1941 [1869]), 129.

58. Valerie Pichanick, *Harriet Martineau: The Woman and Her Work* (Ann Arbor: University of Michigan Press, 1980), 3–4.

59. Ibid., 7–10, 105–6.

60. Ibid., 21, 55, 63.

61. Ibid., 76.

62. Ibid., 80.

63. Ibid., 193–7.

64. Harriet Martineau, *Society in America*, vol. 1 (London: Saunders and Otley, 1837), 90. Martineau noted 'the awful hypocrisy of an Alabama law which fined masters five hundred dollars for teaching slaves to read, and only two hundred dollars for torturing them' (p. 88).

65. Harriet Martineau, 'Martyr age of the United States', in Lynn McDonald, ed., *Women Theorists on Society and Politics* (Waterloo, Ont.: Wilfrid Laurier University Press, 1998), 141.

66. Martineau, *Society in America*, I, 196.

67. Harriet Martineau, '*Daily News* 13 August 1862', in McDonald, ed., *Women Theorists*, 145.

68. Ibid.

69. Harriet Martineau, 'The negro race in America', ibid., 146–7.

70. Martineau, '*Daily News* 2 July 1864', ibid., 161.

71. McDonald, *Women Theorists*, 158–9.

72. Ibid., 167.

73. Martineau, *Society in America*, I, 200.

74. Gayle Graham Yates, ed., *Harriet Martineau on Women* (New Brunswick, NJ: Rutgers University Press, 1985), 129.

75. Martineau, 1834, quoted ibid., 134.

76. Ibid., 129.

77. Pichanick, *Harriet Martineau*, 225–3.

78. Alexis de Tocqueville, *Democracy in America*, vol. 1 (New York: Vintage Books, 1945 [1835]), 3, 6, 14, 129.

79. Ibid., 8, 12.

80. Ibid., 45, 28–30.

81. Ibid., 30–45.

82. Ibid., 31, 49, 184.

83. Ibid., 53–4, 299–305.

84. Ibid., 47–54.

85. Ibid., 314–19, 337.

86. Ibid., 56. This argument would be developed by Georg Simmel.

87. Ibid. '[T]here is a kind of aristocratic refinement and an air of grandeur in the depravity of the great' (p. 235).

88. Ibid., 246–9.

89. Ibid., 212.

90. Ibid., 208.

91. Ibid., 187.

92. Ibid., 257–72.

93. Stendhal, *The Red and the Black* (Toronto: John C. Winston, 1949 [1830]), 4.

94. Henrik Ibsen, 'An Enemy of the People', *Two Plays* (London: Methuen, 1984 [1882]), 192–5.

95. Tocqueville, *Democracy in America*, I, 269–70, 279.

96. Ibid., 180–2. 'Parties are a necessary evil in free governments' (p. 181).

97. Ibid., 273.

98. Ibid., 273–6.

99. Ibid., 344.

100. Ibid., 257, 344.

101. Ibid., 345, 24.

102. Ibid., 351–2.

103. Ibid., 356, 346–7.

104. Ibid., 354, 366, 369.

105. Ibid., 370, 344–6.

106. Ibid., 375–9, 394.

107. Ibid., 371–2.

108. Ibid., 373–4.

109. Ibid., 388–93.

110. Ibid., 391–2.

111. Ibid., 326.

112. Eric J. Sundquist, 'Introduction: The Country of the Blue', in Sundquist, ed., *American Realism: New Essays* (Baltimore: Johns Hopkins University Press, 1982), 5.

113. Henry David Thoreau, 'Civil Disobedience', in Richard Dillman, ed., *The Major Essays of Henry David Thoreau* (Albany, NY: Whitson, 2001), 48.

114. Ibid., 48.

115. Ibid., 51.

116. Ibid., 53.

117. Ibid., 56–7.

CHAPTER SEVEN

1. Richard D. Altick, *Victorian People and Ideas* (New York: Norton, 1973), 117–18.

2. William Thomas, *Mill* (Oxford: Oxford University Press, 1985), 11.

3. Charles Dickens, *Hard Times* (New York: New American Library, 1961 [1854]), 11, 16–17.

4. Ibid., 12.

5. Ibid., 120.

6. Ibid.

7. Ibid., 11.

8. Ibid., 76.

9. Benjamin Disraeli, *Sybil, or the Two Nations* (Harmondsworth, UK: Penguin Books, 1980 [1846]), 96.

10. Altick, *Victorian People*, 87.

11. In the United States, social upheavals were more easily displaced by further western expansion and war with Mexico.

12. Altick, *Victorian People*, 144.

13. Ibid., 23, 138.

14. Thomas Carlyle, *Past and Present* (New York: Everyman's Library, 1969 [1843]), 172–3.

15. Oscar Wilde, *The Picture of Dorian Grey, The Writings of Oscar Wilde* (New York: Oxford University Press, 1989 [1891]), 71.

16. Oscar Wilde satirized the upper-class fear of the radical consequences that must follow educating the masses in 'The Importance of Being Ernest', *Writings*, 493.

17. Smith's laissez-faire economic theory resurfaced at the end of the nineteenth century in the social Darwinism of Herbert Spencer and Graham Sumner, and again in the late twentieth-century revival of neo-liberalism by Margaret Thatcher, Ronald

Reagan, and Brian Mulroney. What was once 'liberal' became 'conservative'.

18. Thomas, *Mill*, 2–3.

19. Ibid., 3.

20. Gertrude Himmelfarb, *Victorian Minds: A Study of Intellectuals in Crisis and of Ideologies in Transition* (New York: Harper & Row, 1968), 116–18.

21. John Stuart Mill, 'Bentham', in Albert William Levi, ed., *The Six Great Humanistic Essays of John Stuart Mill* (New York: Washington Square Press, 1963), 28–9. For Mill, Bentham was the 'questioner of things established' (p. 28).

22. Ibid., 43.

23. Dickens, *Hard Times*, 13.

24. Ibid., 63.

25. Mill, 'Bentham', 52.

26. John Stuart Mill, 'Coleridge', in Levi, ed., *Six Great Humanistic Essays*, 89–91.

27. Thomas, *Mill*, 19.

28. Mill, 'Bentham', 61–3.

29. Mill, 'Coleridge', 110–11.

30. Himmelfarb, *Victorian Minds*, 146–7.

31. Sulamith Firestone, *The Dialectic of Sex: The Case for Feminist Revolution* (St Albans, Hertfordshire: Paladin, 1973), 24.

32. Sheila Rowbotham, *Women, Resistance, and Revolution* (Harmondsworth, UK: Penguin Books, 1972), 46.

33. Gail Tulloch, *Mill on Sexual Equality* (Hemel Hempstead: Harvester, 1989), 77.

34. Alice S. Rossi, 'Sentiment and Intellect: The Story of John Stuart Mill and Harriet Taylor Mill', in Rossi, ed., *Essays on Sex Equality: John Stuart Mill and Harriet Taylor Mill* (Chicago: University of Chicago Press, 1970), 56.

35. Himmelfarb, *Victorian Minds*, 140–1. This is the interpretation of the modern laissez-faire propagandist F.A. Hayek.

36. Mill, 'Coleridge', 114–15.

37. John Stuart Mill, 'On liberty', in Levi, ed., *Six Great Humanistic Essays*, 127–31.

38. Ibid., 218.

39. Ibid., 135–9.

40. Alfred Tennyson, 'You ask me why', in *Poems of Tennyson*, ed. J.H. Buckley (Boston: Houghton Mifflin, 1958), 85.

41. Mill, 'On liberty', 180.

42. Ibid., 212.

43. Ibid., 219.

44. Ibid., 219–20.

45. Ibid., 230.

46. Ibid., 206.

47. Ibid., 214.

48. Ibid., 230–1.

49. Ibid., 234–7. 'The mischief begins when, instead of calling forth the activity and power of individuals and bodies, it [the state] substitutes its own activity for theirs' (p. 240).

50. Ibid., 238.

51. The social theory of Robert Owen's socialism, the co-operative movement he inspired, and trade unionism are not discussed in this volume.

52. Barbara Caine, *English Feminism, 1780–1980* (New York: Oxford University Press, 1997), 14–15.

53. Altick, *Victorian People*, 53–4. The first two quotations were from the poet, Alfred Tennyson.

54. Oscar Wilde, 'Dorian Grey', 83. Men, on the other hand, represented the triumph of 'mind over morals'.

55. Altick, *Victorian People*, 54.

56. Florence Nightingale, 'East-End Distress', in Lynn McDonald, ed., *Women Theorists on Society and Politics* (Waterloo, Ont.: Wilfrid Laurier University Press, 1998), 169.

57. Whitney Chadwick, *Women, Art, and Society* (London: Thames and Hudson, 1990), 166.

58. Quoted in Altick, *Victorian People*, 54.

59. Caine, *English Feminism*, 56.

60. Ibid., 82–4.

61. Ibid., 88–9.

62. Ibid., 98–9.

63. Florence Nightingale, 'Draft Note 1 July 1865', in McDonald, ed., *Women Theorists*, 172–3; ibid., 167.

64. Florence Nightingale, 'East-End Distress', 169

65. Ibid.; McDonald, ed., *Women Theorists*, 167.

66. McDonald, ed., *Women Theorists*, p. 173.

67. Rossi, 'Sentiment and Intellect', 20–1.

68. John Stuart Mill, 'The Subjection of Women', in Rossi, ed., *Essays on Sex Equality*, 160.

69. Himmelfarb, *Victorian Minds*, 135–40, 144–5.

70. Rossi, 'Sentiment and Intellect', 22–3.

71. Quoted in Harriet Taylor Mill, 'Enfranchisement of Women', in Rossi, ed., *Essays on Sex Equality*, 94.

72. Mill, 'Subjection of Women', 138, 149, 190–1.

73. Taylor Mill, 'Enfranchisement of Women', 100–1.

74. Ibid., 95–6. John Stuart Mill in *The Subjection of Women* commented 'that wives are in general no better treated than slaves; but no slave is a slave

to the same lengths, and in so full a sense of the word, as a wife is' (p. 159).

75. Taylor Mill, 'Enfranchisement of Women', 108–9.

76. Mill, 'Subjection of Women', 136.

77. Taylor Mill, 'Enfranchisement of Women', 113–14. Mill argued that servitude that was short of brutalization was less corrupting for the slave than the slave owner, since unrestrained power caused the most damage to individual character. Mill, 'Subjection of Women', 213.

78. Taylor Mill, 'Enfranchisement of Women', 120, 114–15.

79. Ibid., 114, 117. She adds that 'no other inferior castes that we have heard of have been taught to regard their degradation as their honour' (p. 118).

80. Helen Taylor [1867] quoted in Gillian Beer, *George Eliot* (Bloomington: Indiana University Press, 1986), 153.

81. Helen Taylor, 'Personal representation', in McDonald, ed., *Women Theorists*, 206–7.

82. McDonald, ed., *Women Theorists*, 203.

83. Taylor Mill, 'Enfranchisement of Women', 119; Mill, 'Subjection of Women', 153.

84. H.W. Janson and A.F. Janson, *The History of Art* (Englewood Cliffs, NJ: Prentice-Hall, 1995), 702.

85. Clarence Darrow, in Donald Pizer, ed., *Documents of American Realism and Naturalism* (Carbondale: Southern Illinois University Press, 1998), 141. Darrow (1857–1938) was the best-known progressive lawyer in the United States. He defended the Haymarket anarchists, socialists Eugene Debs and Big Bill Haywood, as well as John Scopes in the famous Tennessee 'monkey trial' (1925). Scopes had been charged with teaching evolution in a public school.

86. George Eliot, quoted in Beer, *George Eliot*, 35.

87. George Eliot, *Middlemarch* (New York: Signet, 1964 [1871–2]), 10.

88. Quoted in Frank Kermode, 'Afterword' to Geroge Eliot's *Middlemarch* (New York: New American Library, 1964), 814.

89. George Eliot, *Felix Holt, the Radical* (Oxford: Clarendon Press, 1980 [1866]), 20, 101.

90. Dickens, *Hard Times*, 122.

91. During Victorian times, animals were similarly depicted as the victims of unjust circumstances and evil intentions, most memorably in the novel *Black Beauty*, by Anna Sewell.

92. Dickens, *Hard Times*, 142.

93. Ibid., 165.

94. Ibid., 141–6.

CHAPTER EIGHT

1. William L. Shirer, *The Rise and Fall of the Third Reich: A History of Nazi Germany* (Greenwich, Conn.: Fawcett Publications, 1962), 135–6.

2. Charles Morazé, *The Triumph of the Middle Classes* (Garden City, NY: Anchor Books, 1968), 182–5.

3. Sophie de Condorcet, quoted in Lynn McDonald, ed., *Women Theorists on Society and Politics*, Waterloo, Ont.: Wilfrid Laurier University Press, 1998), 126.

4. Jacques Godechot, *The Counter-Revolution: Doctrine and Action, 1789–1804* (Princeton, NJ: Princeton University Press, 1971), 103–5.

5. Shirer, *Rise and Fall*, 143.

6. Quoted ibid., 138–9.

7. Martin Swales, *Goethe: The Sorrows of Young Werther* (Cambridge: Cambridge University Press, 1987), 3.

8. Heinrich Heine, Preface to 'Germany: A Winter's Tale', *The Complete Poems: A Modern English Version*, ed. Hal Draper (Boston: Suhrkamp/Insel, 1982), 482.

9. Franz Wiedmann, *Hegel: An Illustrated Biography* (New York: Pegasus, 1968), 9–21.

10. Hegel, quoted ibid., 38.

11. Ibid., 20–40.

12. Ibid., 56–7.

13. McCarney argues that Hegel's idealism is a form of 'realism' in that Hegel 'is committed to the existence of a reality that is fully independent of what is known or believed about it by consciousness.' Joseph McCarney, *Hegel on History* (New York: Routledge, 2000), 34.

14. Wiedmann, *Hegel*, 50.

15. McCarney, *Hegel on History*, 52–3.

16. G.W.F Hegel, *Philosophy of History* (New York: Collier, 1900 [1822–30]), 62.

17. Ibid., 62, 106.

18. As Alice Cooper put it: 'I'm a boy and I'm a man / I'm eighteen and I don't know what I want / . . . / I got a baby's brain and an old man's heart'. From 'I'm Eighteen', *A Fistful of Alice*.

19. Johann von Goethe, *Theory of Colors* (Cambridge, Mass.: MIT Press, 1970 [1840]), 5, 13, 15.

20. Ibid., 5, 13, 15, 21.
21. Hegel, *Philosophy of History*, 116.
22. Ibid., 105.
23. Ibid., 108.
24. Ibid., 125.
25. Hegel, quoted in McCarney, *Hegel on History*, 73.
26. Hegel, quoted ibid., 24.
27. Hegel, *Philosophy of History*, 76–7. While 'the deeds they perform, appear as their own creations . . . they have right on their side . . . they know what the truth of their time and their world is. . . . [W]hatever they do is right.' Hegel, quoted in Wiedmann, *Hegel*, 80–1.
28. Hegel, quoted ibid.
29. Hegel, quoted in McCarney, *Hegel on History*, 108, 109.
30. Hegel, quoted ibid., 116.
31. Hegel, *Philosophy of History*, 79–80.
32. Ibid., 106.
33. Francois de Chautebriand (1797), quoted in Jacques Godechot, *The Counter-Revolution, Doctrine and Action, 1789–1894* (Princeton, NJ: Princeton University Press, 1981), 127.
34. Wiedmann, *Hegel*, 78.
35. Quoted ibid., 80.
36. McCarney, *Hegel on History*, 96–9. For McCarney, Hegel's meaning was that the rational *becomes* actual rather than that the actual *is* rational. The statement is identified with constant change, hence providing a foundation for a radical rather than a conservative interpretation.
37. Ibid., 140–1. The most rapid development of a people comes from ethnic diversity, providing the material for conflict, difference, and progress. Far from being racially 'pure', Hegel pointed out, the Germans were ethnically diverse and shaped by non-German religion, culture, and laws. Hegel opposed the emerging theory of the racial superiority of the so-called Aryan race (pp. 140–2). The German *nation* or state may be superior, but there was no such entity as a German *race*.
38. Ibid., 181–3.
39. Ibid., 187–9.
40. Raymond Plant, 'Economic and Social Integration in Hegel's Political Philosophy', in Donald Philip Verene, ed., *Hegel's Social and Political Thought* (Atlantic Highlands, NJ: Humanities Press, 1980), 63–6.
41. Ibid., 73.
42. Hegel, quoted ibid., 75.
43. Ibid., 75–6.
44. McCarney, *Hegel on History*, 157–9.
45. Hegel, quoted in Shirer, *Rise and Fall*, 144.
46. Hegel, quoted in Plant, 'Hegel's Political Philosophy', 79.
47. Ibid., 78.
48. W. Ver Eecke, 'Relation between Economics and Politics in Hegel', in Verene, ed., *Hegel's Thought*, 96.
49. Ibid., 97; Plant, 'Hegel's Political Philosophy', 78, 81.
50. Hegel, *Philosophy of History*, 83–4.
51. Ibid., 84.
52. Wiedmann, *Hegel*, 107–8.
53. E. Graham Waring, 'Introduction', in Ludwig Feuerbach, *The Essence of Christianity* (1841), eds Waring and F.W. Strothman (New York: Frederick Ungar, 1957), iii–iv.
54. Quoted in Wiedmann, *Hegel*, 119–20.
55. Feuerbach, *Essence of Christianity*, 11, 18.
56. Ibid., 12.
57. Feuerbach, quoted in Wiedmann, *Hegel*, 119–120.
58. Feuerbach, *Essence of Christianity*, 11.
59. Ibid., 46–9.
60. Elizabeth Inchbald, *Nature and Art* (Oxford: Woodstock Books, 1994 [1796]), 77–9.
61. Feuerbach, *Essence of Christianity*, 58–9.
62. Ibid., 63, 65.
63. Karl Marx, *Theses on Feuerbach*, in Frederick Engels, *Ludwig Feuerbach and the Outcome of Classical German Philosophy* (New York: International Publishers, 1941), 85.
64. Ibid., 82–3.
65. Isaiah Berlin, *Karl Marx: His Life and Environment* (New York: Oxford University Press, 1963), 30.
66. Ibid., 27–8.
67. Ibid., 32.
68. David McLellan, *The Thought of Karl Marx* (London: Macmillan, 1971), 3; Berlin, *Karl Marx*, 33.
69. Oscar J. Hammen, *The Red '48ers* (New York: Charles Scribner, 1969), 189.
70. Jerrold Seigel, *Marx's Fate: The Shape of a Life* (Princeton, NJ: Princeton University Press, 1978), 275–7.
71. Ronald Florence, *Marx's Daughters* (New York: Dial Press, 1975), 73, 76–7. In Émile Durkheim's terms, Eleanor's suicide was 'anomic' while Laura's was 'altruistic'.

72. Karl Marx, 'German Ideology', in T.B. Bottomore, ed., *Karl Marx: Selected Writings in Sociology and Social Philosophy* (New York: McGraw-Hill, 1964), 75.

73. Marx (1844), in Bottomore, ed., *Karl Marx: Selected Writings*, 183.

74. Flora Tristan, 'Factory workers' (1840), quoted in McDonald, ed., *Women Theorists*, 135.

75. Karl Marx, 'Toward the Critique of Hegel's Philosophy of Right' (1844), in Lewis Feuer, ed., *Marx and Engels: Basic Writings on Politics and Philosophy* (Garden City, NY: Anchor Books, 1959), 265.

76. Marx (1844) in Bottomore, ed., *Karl Marx: Selected Writings*, 182.

77. Ibid., 183.

78. Heinrich Heine, 'The Silesian Weavers', in Draper, ed., *The Complete Poems*, 544.

79. Berlin, *Karl Marx*, 111.

80. K. Marx and F. Engels, 'The German Ideology' (1845), in Feuer, ed., *Marx and Engels*, 253–4.

81. Karl Marx, 'Preface to A Contribution to the Critique of Political Economy', in Bottomore, ed., *Karl Marx: Selected Writings*, 51.

82. K. Marx and F. Engels, 'The Communist Manifesto' (1848), in Feuer, ed., *Marx and Engels*, 12.

83. Marx analyzed modes of production other than the stages identified here, such as the Asiatic mode, which was characterized by powerful tendencies to stagnate and remain unchanged.

84. Ibid., 14.

85. Marx and Engels, *The German Ideology*, quoted in McLellan, *Thought of Karl Marx*, 217.

86. F. Engels, 'Introduction' to Karl Marx, *The Civil War in France* (Peking: Foreign Languages Press, 1979 [1891]), 4.

87. Marx, *Civil War in France*, 64.

88. Thomas Carlyle, *Past and Present* (New York: Dutton, 1960 [1843]), 141.

89. Percy Shelley, 'The Mask of Anarchy', *The Poetical Works of Percy Bysshe Shelley* (London: Henry Frowde, 1908), 337–8.

90. Marx and Engels, 'Communist Manifesto', 12–13.

91. Carlyle, *Past and Present*, 165.

92. Marx and Engels, 'Communist Manifesto', 13.

93. John Cassidy 'The Next Thinker: The Return of Karl Marx', *The New Yorker* (20 and 27 Oct. 1997): 20.

94. Ibid., 27.

CHAPTER NINE

1. Aristotle, quoted in W. Guthrie, *A History of Greek Philosophy* (Cambridge: Cambridge University Press, 1962), 201–4. I am indebted to Susan Haley for bringing this ancient debate to my attention.

2. Herbert Wendt, *In Search of Adam* (New York: Collier, 1963), 40.

3. In G. Anderson and W. Buckler, *The Literature of England* (Glenview, Ill.: Scott, Foresman, 1967), 551.

4. Loren Eiseley, *Darwin's Century* (New York: Anchor Books, 1961), 61. Altick claims that a later theologian pinpointed the time more precisely as 9 a.m., 23 October, 4004 BC. Richard D. Altick, *Victorian People and Ideas* (New York: Norton, 1973), 99.

5. Wendt, *In Search of Adam*, 40–1.

6. Ibid.

7. Ibid., 18. This theory was proposed by the Arab scholar Ibn-Sina, known in Europe as Avicenna (980–1037), who, like Aristotle, believed that nature had no history.

8. John Fowles, *The French Lieutenant's Woman* (New York: Signet, 1970), 131n. Fowles comments that this 'must surely rank as the most incomprehensible cover-up operation ever attributed to divinity' (pp. 131–2n).

9. Eiseley, *Darwin's Century*, 10.

10. Wendt, *In Search of Adam*, 82.

11. Ibid.

12. Ibid., 187–8.

13. Lucille B. Ritvo, *Darwin's Influence on Freud: A Tale of Two Sciences* (New Haven: Yale University Press, 1990), 49–50.

14. Eiseley, *Darwin's Century*, 49.

15. J.R.R.Tolkien, *The Hobbit* (London: Unwin Paperbacks, 1975 [1937]), 76.

16. Auguste Comte, 'Positive Philosophy', in Stanislav Andreski, ed., *The Essential Comte* (London: Croom Helm, 1974), 169.

17. Eiseley, *Darwin's Century*, 54–5.

18. Wendt, *In Search of Adam*.

19. Eiseley, *Darwin's Century*, 69.

20. Wendt, *In Search of Adam*.

21. Ibid., 188–92.

22. Roland Stromberg, *An Intellectual History of Modern Europe*, 2nd edn (Englewood Cliffs, NJ: Prentice-Hall, 1975).

23. Kevin A. Laland and Gillian R. Brown, *Sense and Nonsense: Evolutionary Perspectives on Human Behaviour* (New York: Oxford University Press, 2002), 34.

24. Ibid., 34–5.

25. Ibid., 35–6.

26. Roland Stromberg, *European Intellectual History Since 1789*, 6th edn (Englewood Cliffs, NJ: Prentice-Hall, 1994), 122–3.

27. Fowles, *French Lieutenant's Woman*, 99.

28. Stromberg, *European Intellectual History*, 123.

29. The *Index*, first created by Pope Pius IV in 1559, listed books that were deemed to be dangerous to Christian faith and morality.

30. Thomas Hardy *The Woodlanders* (London: Macmillan, 1963 [1887]), 59, 376.

31. It is also a conventional Hollywood plot device.

32. Donald Pizer, *Documents of American Realism and Naturalism* (Carbondale: Southern Illinois University Press, 1998), 4.

33. Theodore Dreiser, *Newspaper Days* (Philadelphia: Pennsylvania University Press, 1991 [1922]), 610.

34. Ibid., 610–11.

35. Theodore Dreiser, *Sister Carrie* (New York: Harper and Row, 1965 [1900]), 4.

36. Ibid., 26.

37. Ibid., 23.

38. Ibid., 11.

39. Ibid., 108.

40. Donald Pizer, *The Novels of Theodore Dreiser: A Critical Study* (Minneapolis: University of Minnesota Press, 1976), 142.

41. Theodore Dreiser, 'True Art Speaks Plainly', in Pizer, *Documents*, 180.

42. Donald MacRea, 'Introduction', in MacRea, ed., *Herbert Spencer: The Man versus the State* (Harmondsworth, Middlesex: Penguin Books, 1969), 15.

43. Herbert Spencer, 'The coming slavery', in MacRea, ed., *Herbert Spencer*, 96–7.

44. Herbert Spencer, 'The new Toryism', ibid., 63.

45. Ibid., 71–7.

46. Spencer, 'The coming slavery', 91.

47. Ibid., 110.

48. Ibid., 100–1.

49. Ibid., 106.

50. Ibid., 108–10.

51. Herbert Spencer, 'The sins of legislators', in MacRea, ed., *Herbert Spencer*, 120. Spencer quotes from his 1850 book, *Social Statics*, where he had originally made this argument.

52. Ibid., 133.

53. Spencer, 'The coming slavery', 82–3. Spencer realizes his attempt to define charity as un-Christian is contrary to what most Christians believe, and he is mystified that Christians seem disinclined to accept this 'truth' (p. 83).

54. Spencer, 'Sins of legislators', 133–5.

55. Charles Darwin, *The Descent of Man and Selection in Relation to Sex* (New York: Appleton, 1898 [1871]), 136.

56. Spencer, 'Sins of legislators', 136–8.

57. Herbert Spencer, quoting from *Social Statics* (1851), ibid., 138–9.

58. Spencer, 'Sins of legislators', 141.

59. Ibid., 144. '[I]s it not cruel to increase the sufferings of the better that the sufferings of the worse may be decreased?' (p. 146).

60. Ibid., 146.

61. Ibid., 147.

62. Herbert Spencer, 'The social organization', in MacRea, ed., *Herbert Spencer*, 195–8.

63. Ibid., 205.

64. Ibid., 214–15.

65. Ibid., 225.

66. Herbert Spencer, 'Representative government —What is it good for?', in MacRea, ed., *Herbert Spencer*, 261.

67. Spencer, 'Social organization', 229.

68. Spencer, 'Representative government', 265–8.

69. Ibid., 242–3, 249.

70. Ibid., 249–51.

71. Spencer, 'Social organization', 204–5.

72. T.B. Bottomore, *Critics of Society: Radical Thought in North America* (London: George Allen & Unwin, 1967), 24.

73. Quoted in Richard Hofstadter, *Social Darwinism in American Thought* (Boston: Beacon Press, 1955), 10.

74. Leon Shaskolsky, 'The Development of Sociological Theory in America: A Sociology of Knowledge Interpretation', in Larry T. Reynolds and Janice L. Reynolds, eds, *The Sociology of Sociology* (New York: David McKay, 1970), 10.

75. Youmans, quoted in Hofstadter, *Social Darwinism*, 47.

76. Galloway Keller, quoted ibid., 157.

77. Galloway Keller, quoted ibid., 204.

78. Stephen F. Mason, *A History of the Sciences* (New York: Collier, 1962), 423.

79. Quoted ibid., 422–3.

80. Thomas C. Patterson, *Inventing Western Civilization* (New York: Monthly Review Press, 1997).
81. Ibid., 109.
82. Hans Kohn, *The Twentieth Century: A Mid-way Account of the Western World* (New York: Macmillan, 1949), 134.
83. Fitzgerald's purpose, of course, is to reveal the vapidity of the characters he portrays and, thus, to denigrate their ideals.
84. Kohn, *Twentieth Century*, 135.
85. Hofstadter, *Social Darwinism*, 125.

CHAPTER TEN

1. Charles Morazé, *The Triumph of the Middle Classes* (Garden City, NY: Anchor Books, 1968), 485.
2. Steve Fenton, *Durkheim and Modern Social Theory* (Cambridge: Cambridge University Press, 1984), 11.
3. Émile Durkheim, *The Division of Labour in Society* (New York: Free Press, 1984 [1893]), 339.
4. Fenton, *Durkheim*, 118–19.
5. Durkheim, quoted ibid., 119.
6. Émile Zola, 'Letter to M. Félix Faure, President of the Republic', in Zola, *The Dreyfus Affair: 'J'accuse' and Other Writings*, ed. Alain Pagès (New Haven: Yale University Press, 1996 [1898]), 52.
7. Durkheim, *Division of Labour*, xxxii, xxxiv.
8. Ibid., 340.
9. Ibid., 339, liv.
10. Fenton, *Durkheim*, 11.
11. Émile Durkheim, *The Rules of Sociological Method* (New York: Free Press, 1964 [1895], 142; Durkheim, *Division of Labour*, xxviii.
12. Durkheim, *Division of Labour*, 150–1.
13. Ibid., 219–20.
14. Emile Durkheim, *The Elementary Forms of the Religious Life*, trans. J.W. Swain (London: Allen & Unwin, 1964 [1912], 66.
15. Ibid., 359.
16. G.H. Mead, *Mind, Self and Society* (Chicago: University of Chicago Press, 1934), 221.
17. Durkheim, *Division of Labour*, 142–6.
18. Ibid., 286, 276, 287. Unlike Spencer, who derives society from the nature of the individuals that comprise it, 'it is indeed rather the form of the whole that determines that of the parts' (p. 287).
19. Durkheim, *Rules of Sociological Method*, 26, xxxix–xl; Durkheim, *Division of Labour*, xxv.

Durkheim said he was writing in a period of 'renascent mysticism' and, instead, proposed restoring faith in human reason (*Rules of Sociological Method*, xl).
20. Durkheim, *Rules of Sociological Method*, 23, 43. For Durkheim, the 'simple truth' is that 'our ideas of physical things are derived from these things themselves and express them more or less exactly' (p. 23). Durkheim said that it was necessary to assume a certain attitude to mental representations, examine them objectively from the outside; in short, to treat them as though they were things (ibid., 123).
21. Durkheim, *Elementary Forms*, 5.
22. Ibid., 4.
23. Durkheim, *Division of Labour*, xxv–xxvi.
24. Durkheim, *Rules of Sociological Method*, 45–6.
25. Ibid., 2, 27–8. 'The first and most fundamental rule is: *consider social facts as things*' (p. 14).
26. Ibid., 3, 10, 2, 4, 30, 10, 6. Durkheim qualifies this by agreeing that all constraint is not normal; only that derived from intellectual or moral superiority is normal. 'But that which one individual exercises over another because he is stronger or wealthier, especially if this wealth does not express his social value, is abnormal and can only be maintained by violence' (p. 123n).
27. Max Weber, *The Protestant Ethic and the Spirit of Capitalism* (New York, 1958 [1904]), 54–5.
28. Durkheim, *Rules of Sociological Method*, 19, 117–19.
29. Ibid., 117–21.
30. Ibid., 102, 112. In different, organic language, Durkheim claimed that 'the facts of social morphology are of the same nature as physiological phenomena.'
31. George Eliot, *Felix Holt, the Radical* (Oxford: Clarendon Press, 1980 [1866], 414–15.
32. Durkheim, *Rules of Sociological Method*, 97.
33. Émile Durkheim, *Suicide: A Study in Sociology* (New York: Free Press, 1951 [1897]), 38–9.
34. Ibid., 209–16, 221, 241–6.
35. Durkheim, *Division of Labour*, 18–19.
36. Ibid., 20–1.
37. Durkheim, *Rules of Sociological Method*, 77–8.
38. Ibid., 82–3.
39. Durkheim, *Division of Labour*, 88–9.
40. Durkheim, *Elementary Forms*, 444.
41. Durkheim, *Division of Labour*, 61, 38–9. The collective consciousness is 'totally different from the

consciousness of an individual although it is only realized in individuals. It is the psychological type of society' (p. 38).

42. Ibid., 242, 131. Spencer's axiom was that '"a society . . . is formed only when . . . there is cooperation."' Durkheim asserts 'this alleged axiom is the opposite of the truth.' Rather, Comte was correct when he had asserted: '"co-operation, far from being able to produce a society, supposes necessarily its spontaneous establishment beforehand."' (Ibid., 219.)

43. Durkheim, *Elementary Forms*, 5–6.

44. Durkheim, *Division of Labour*, 119.

45. Durkheim, *Elementary Forms*, 8.

46. Ibid., 96, 167.

47. Durkheim, *Division of Labour*, 119.

48. Durkheim, *Elementary Forms*, 231.

49. Ibid., 102–4, 233.

50. Ibid., 214–16.

51. Frances Trollope, *Domestic Manners of the Americans* (London: Routledge, 1927), 64–7. I first encountered this excerpt in Lewis Coser, ed., *Sociology Through Literature* (Englewood Cliffs, NJ: Prentice-Hall, 1963).

52. Durkheim, *Elementary Forms*, 422.

53. Ibid., 424.

54. Ibid., 200, 206.

55. Ibid., 141.

56. Ibid., 147–8.

57. Ibid., 229, 272. The 'world of representations in which social life passes is superimposed upon its material substratum, far from arising from it', contrary to the view of historical materialism (p. 272).

58. Ibid., 359.

59. Ibid., 227–8.

60. Ibid., 349.

61. Ibid., 358.

62. Ibid., 375.

63. Durkheim, *Division of Labour*, 113–14, 203–5.

64. Durkheim, *Rules of Sociological Method*, 92–3; Durkheim, *Division of Labour*, 208.

65. Durkheim, *Division of Labour*, 211–13, 201.

66. Durkheim, *Rules of Sociological Method*, 96, 115.

67. Ibid., 93; Durkheim, *Division of Labour*, 216–17, 276.

68. Durkheim, *Division of Labour*, 23, 295–6.

69. Ibid., 296–7.

70. Ibid., 21.

71. Ibid., 284–6.

72. Ibid., 286–7. 'Society does not find ready-made in individual consciousness the bases on which it rests; it makes them for itself' (p. 287).

73. Ibid., 217–21.

74. Durkheim, *Elementary Forms*, 270–2.

75. Durkheim, *Division of Labour*, 121. 'Individualism and free thinking are of no recent date. . . . They are a phenomenon that has no fixed starting point' but have developed throughout history, though not in a linear way (p. 121).

76. Ibid., 122. In Durkheim's terms, the 'average intensity and degree of determinateness . . . diminish' (p. 117).

77. Ibid., 118, 122. If individualism is the 'exclusive basis' of a theorist's 'moral doctrine', they may 'justly [be] reproached with effecting the dissolution of society'.

78. Ibid., 122–3.

79. Ibid., 85.

80. Ibid., 17.

81. Durkheim, *Rules of Sociological Method*, 73–4.

82. Ibid., 75.

83. Ibid., 47–9.

84. Ibid., 75. For Durkheim, 'the generality of phenomena must be taken as the criterion of the normality.'

85. Ibid., 55–7. No institution, practice, or moral standard is good or bad for all social types, and 'the corresponding phases of their evolution' have to be considered (pp. 56–7).

86. Ibid., 58–60. Some phenomena may not be useful but are 'necessarily implied in the nature of being'. Thus the pains of parturition are normal since they are part of the 'conditions of existence of the species'.

87. Ibid., 60–2, 62n.

88. Durkheim, *Division of Labour*, 312. Even then, caste sentiments survive in prejudice and favouritism (p. 313).

89. Ibid., 314.

90. Ibid., 318.

91. Ibid., 319.

92. Ibid., 321–2.

93. Ibid., 315–16.

94. Ibid., 306–8.

95. Ibid., lv, xxxiv–xxxv.

96. Durkheim, *Suicide*, 378–9.

97. Durkheim, *Division of Labour*, lv–lvii.

98. Ibid., 338–9.

99. Durkheim, *Elementary Forms*, 227–8.

100. Durkheim, *Rules of Sociological Method*, 146; Durkheim, *Division of Labour*, 279.
101. Durkheim, *Division of Labour*, xxvi–xxvii.
102. Ibid., 279.
103. George Eliot, 'Address to Working Men, By Felix Holt', *Felix Holt*, Appendix C, 416–17.
104. Durkheim, *Rules of Sociological Method*, xxxviii–xxxix; Durkheim, *Division of Labour*, xxvii–xxix.
105. Durkheim, *Division of Labour*, 62; Durkheim, *Rules of Sociological Method*, 143.
106. Durkheim, *Elementary Forms*, 429.
107. Ibid., 430.
108. Ibid., 431.
109. Durkheim, 'Author's preface' to *Rules of Sociological Method*, xli.
110. Durkheim, *Rules of Sociological Method*, 104.
111. Durkheim, *Elementary Forms*, 421.
112. Fenton, *Durkheim*, 17.

CHAPTER ELEVEN

1. Dirk Käsler, *Max Weber: An Introduction to His Life and Work* (Chicago: University of Chicago Press, 1988), 1–3.
2. Aldous Huxley, *Point Counter Point* (Harmondsworth, Middlesex: Penguin, 1969), 15.
3. Käsler, *Max Weber*, 4–5.
4. Ibid., 3, 5–8.
5. Ibid., 16–17, 22.
6. Ibid., 6, 9, 17.
7. Ibid., 13, 17.
8. Ibid., 14.
9. Ibid., 16–18.
10. Ibid., 19–20.
11. Max Weber, *The Theory of Social and Economic Organization*, ed. Talcott Parsons (New York: Free Press, 1964 [1920]), 88.
12. Ibid., 113–15.
13. Max Weber, *The Protestant Ethic and the Spirit of Capitalism* (New York: Charles Scribner, 1958 [1904–5]), 13–17. Andreski translates 'fateful' as 'significant'.
14. Weber, *Theory*, 97.
15. Ibid., 279–80.
16. Max Weber, *Max Weber on Capitalism, Bureaucracy and Religion*, ed. Stanislav Andreski (London: Allen and Unwin, 1983), 129.
17. Weber, *Protestant Ethic*, 17.
18. Weber, *Theory*, 159–60.
19. Weber, *Protestant Ethic*, 20–1.
20. Weber, *Theory*, 279.
21. Weber, *Capitalism*, 41.
22. Ibid., 85, 91–101.
23. Ibid., 85–6, 106.
24. Weber, *Theory*, 124, 382.
25. Ibid., 325–8, 341.
26. Weber, *Capitalism*, 104, 108.
27. Ibid., 88; Arundhati Roy, *The God of Small Things* (Toronto: Random House, 1997), 70–1.
28. Weber, *Capitalism*, 107–8.
29. Ibid., 88.
30. Ibid., 106–7.
31. Weber, *Theory*, 367–8.
32. Weber, *Capitalism*, 67, 71; Weber, *Theory*, 377.
33. Weber, *Theory*, 347.
34. Weber, *Capitalism*, 69.
35. Ibid., 76.
36. Ibid., 74.
37. Ibid., 76.
38. Jung Chang, *White Swans* (New York: Anchor Books, 1991), 22.
39. Weber, *Capitalism*, 69–71, 62.
40. Ibid., 76–9.
41. Ibid., 60–2.
42. Weber, *Theory*, 264.
43. Ibid., 166, 261; Weber, *Capitalism*, 80–2.
44. Weber, *Capitalism*, 82–4.
45. Ibid., 84.
46. Ibid., 33–9.
47. Ibid., 45; Weber, *Theory*, 237.
48. Weber, *Capitalism*, 43–6.
49. Ibid., 49.
50. Ibid., 48, 51.
51. Ibid., 55, 54.
52. Arthur Koestler, *The Gladiators* (London: Hutchinson, 1965 [1939]), 14.
53. Weber, *Capitalism*, 57–8.
54. Weber, *Theory*, 353.
55. Weber, *Capitalism*, 149.
56. Ibid., 157.
57. Weber, *Theory*, 158–9.
58. Weber, *Protestant Ethic*, 67–8.
59. Weber, *Theory*, 247–59.
60. Weber, *Capitalism*, 128.
61. Weber, *Protestant Ethic*, 27, 183.
62. Ibid., 56–62.
63. Ibid., 67–71.
64. Ibid., 103–5.

65. Ibid., 110, 114.
66. Ibid., 115, 118, 119.
67. Ibid., 80.
68. Ibid., 75.
69. Baxter, quoted ibid., 162.
70. Ibid., 175; Weber's emphasis.
71. Ibid., 181–2.
72. Ibid., 181.
73. G.B. Shaw, 'Preface' to *Saint Joan* (London: Longmans, 1957), 41–2.
74. Charles Dickens, *Little Dorrit* (Harmondsworth, Middlesex: Penguin, 1967 [1857]), 145–7.
75. Weber, *Theory*, 338–9.
76. Max Weber, *Economy and Society: An Outline of Interpretive Sociology* (New York: Bedminster Press, 1968 [1922]), 302.
77. Weber, *Theory*.
78. Ibid., 182.
79. Many later twentieth-century neo-Marxists compiled a similar list of classes, and while some disputed the existence of a 'new middle class', all sought to include the large white-collar grouping explicitly in the analysis.
80. Weber, *Economy and Society*, 305.
81. Anthony Giddens, *The Class Structure of the Advanced Societies* (London: Hutchinson, 1977), 204.
82. Weber, *Theory*, 213.
83. Ibid., 214–15.
84. Ibid., 338–9.
85. Ibid., 340.
86. Ibid., 319–20.
87. Käsler, *Max Weber*, 20–2.
88. Ibid., 21, 23.
89. Ibid., 23.

CHAPTER TWELVE

1. Gustavus Myers, *History of the Great American Fortunes* (New York: Modern Library, 1936).
2. Leon Shaskolsky, 'The Development of Sociological Theory in America: A Sociology of Knowledge Interpretation', in Larry T. Reynolds and Janice L. Reynolds, eds, *The Sociology of Sociology* (New York: David McKay, 1970), 11.
3. Quoted in Hofstadter, *Social Darwinism*, 112.
4. Karl Mannheim, *Ideology and Utopia* (London: Routledge & Kegan Paul, 1936 [1929]), 228.
5. Graham Taylor, quoted in Albion W. Small, 'The Era of Sociology', *American Journal of Sociology* 1, 1 (July 1895): 3.
6. Ibid., 14.
7. Howard Odum, *American Sociology: The Story of Sociology in the United States through 1950* (New York: Longmans, Green, 1951), 62.
8. Hofstadter, *Social Darwinism*, 83.
9. Washington Gladden, quoted in Richard Hofstadter, *Social Darwinism in American Thought* (Boston: Beacon Press, 1955), 105.
10. Ibid., 100.
11. Odum, *American Sociology*, 81–2.
12. Shaskolsky, 'Development of Sociological Theory', 11; Hofstadter, *Social Darwinism*, 83.
13. Shaskolsky, 'Development of Sociological Theory', 12–13.
14. Hofstadter, *Social Darwinism*, 18.
15. Dusky Lee Smith, 'Sociology and the Rise of Corporate Capitalism', in Reynolds and Reynolds, eds, *Sociology of Sociology*, 68–84.
16. Roscoe C. Hinkle and Gisela J. Hinkle, *The Development of Modern Sociology: Its Nature and Growth in the United States* (New York: Random House, 1974), 13.
17. Max Lerner, 'Introduction' to *The Portable Veblen* (New York: Viking, 1969), 3–4.
18. Ibid., 8–10, 17.
19. Veblen, 'Some Neglected Points in the Theory of Socialism' (1891), in Lerner, ed., *The Portable Veblen*.
20. Thorstein Veblen, *The Theory of the Leisure Class* (New York: New American Library, 1953 [1899]), 151–2.
21. Ibid., 154.
22. David Seckler, *Thorstein Veblen and the Institutionalists* (Boulder: University of Colorado Press, 1975), 58.
23. Ibid., 58–63.
24. C. Wright Mills, 'Introduction' to Veblen, *Leisure Class*, xii.
25. Veblen, *Leisure Class*, 28.
26. Ibid., 31.
27. Ibid., 34.
28. Ibid., 85.
29. Ibid., 37.
30. Ibid., 42.
31. F. Scott Fitzgerald, *The Great Gatsby* (New York: Scribner, 1953 [1925]), 5, 64.

32. Veblen, *Leisure Class*, 72.
33. Ibid., 77.
34. Ibid., 86.
35. Ibid., 99.
36. Ibid., 121, 107.
37. Mills, 'Introduction', ix.
38. Veblen, *Leisure Class*, 229.
39. Ibid., 230.
40. Ibid., 231–2.
41. Ibid., 232.
42. Thorstein Veblen, 'Races and Peoples', in Lerner, ed., *The Portable Veblen*, 301, 304–5.
43. Carol Hymowitz and Michaele Weissman, *A History of Women in America* (Toronto: Bantam Books, 1978), 79.
44. Harriet Beecher Stowe, *Uncle Tom's Cabin* (New York: New American Library, 1966 [1852]), 242.
45. Ibid., 209, 242.
46. Howard Zinn, *A People's History of the United States* (New York: Harper, 1995), 193–4.
47. Booker T. Washington, *The Future of the American Negro* (New York: Negro University Press, 1969 [1899]), 212.
48. Robert Bone, *The Negro Novel in America* (New Haven: Yale University Press, 1965).
49. Quoted in Herbert J. Storing, ed., *What Country Have I? Political Writings by Black Americans* (New York: St Martin's Press, 1970), 93.
50. Washington, *Future of the American Negro*, 107–8.
51. Franz Boas, quoted in W.E.B. Du Bois, 'Race Friction between Black and White' (1908), in Meyer Weinberg, ed., *W.E.B. Du Bois: A Reader* (New York: Harper & Row, 1970), 203.
52. Washington, *Future of the American Negro*, 26, 31–2, 167, 168.
53. Ibid., 24, 3–4, 85, 86.
54. Ibid., 5, 110.
55. Ibid., 27, 18, 68–9. 'The Negro has the right to study law; but success will come to the race sooner if he produces intelligent, thrifty farmers, mechanics, and housekeepers to support the lawyers.'
56. Ibid., 73, 96, 98.
57. Malcolm X, *The Autobiography of Malcolm X* (New York: Grove Press, 1965), 36–7.
58. Washington, *Future of the American Negro*, 34, 35. Washington ridiculed girls who could locate Peking on a globe, but could not 'locate on an actual dinner table the proper place for the carving knife and fork or the meat and vegetables' (p. 51).
59. Ibid., 38, 11–13, 144–6.
60. Ibid., 83, 85, 101, 102, 103, 100. 'It is not in the province of human nature' that an intelligent, prosperous, and virtuous man, whatever his race, 'shall very long be denied proper respect and consideration' (p. 176).
61. Ibid., 205, 207.
62. Zinn, *People's History*, 203–4.
63. Lynne Olson, *Freedom's Daughters: The Unsung Heroines of the Civil Rights Movement from 1830 to 1970* (Toronto: Simon & Schuster, 2002), 33–5.
64. Kay Broschart, 'Ida B. Wells-Barnett', in Mary Jo Deegan, ed., *Women in Sociology: A Bio-Bibliographical Sourcebook* (New York: Greenwood, 1991), 433.
65. Ida Wells, 'Southern Horrors', *Selected Works of Ida B. Wells-Barnett* (New York: Oxford University Press, 1991), 21, 24–5.
66. Olson, *Freedom's Daughters*, 36–41.
67. Broschart, 'Ida B. Wells-Barnett', 434.
68. Olson, *Freedom's Daughters*, 45.
69. The same technique is employed, for example, in the movie *Payback* (2000), starring Mel Gibson.
70. D.W. Griffith, quoted by Leon Litwack, 'The Birth of a Nation', in Mark C. Carnes, ed., *Past Imperfect: History According to the Movies* (New York: Henry Holt, 1996), 141.
71. Ibid., 136.
72. W.E.B. Du Bois, 'Strivings of the Negro People' (1897), in Weinberg, ed., *A Reader*, 19. Du Bois writes: 'The sky was bluest when I could beat my mates at examination time, or beat them at a foot race, or even beat their stringy heads' (p. 19).
73. W.E.B. Du Bois, 'Fisk' (*Crisis*, 1924), in Weinberg, ed., *A Reader*, 172.
74. W.E.B. Du Bois, 'The Negro College' (1933), in Weinberg, ed., *A Reader*, 178.
75. Quoted in Meyer Weinberg, 'Introduction', in Weinberg, ed., *A Reader*, xv.
76. W.E.B. Du Bois, 'The Conservation of Races' (1897), in Storing, ed., *What Country Have I?*, 78–9, 82.
77. Du Bois, 'Strivings of the Negro People', 20.
78. Ibid., 20, 25.
79. Du Bois, 'Conservation of Races', 83.
80. Du Bois, 'On Mr. Booker T. Washington and Others', in Weinberg, ed., *A Reader*, 93.
81. W.E.B. Du Bois, 'The Social Effects of Emancipation' (1913), in Weinberg, ed., *A Reader*, 72–4.

82. Ibid., 75–8.
83. Du Bois, 'Negro College', 178.
84. Du Bois, 'On Mr. Booker T. Washington', 97–9.
85. Langston Hughes, *Simple Speaks His Mind* (Mattituck, NY: Aronian Press, 1976), 44–5.
86. Du Bois, 'Negro College', 180.
87. W.E.B. Du Bois, 'The Souls of White Folk' (1910), in Weinberg, ed., *A Reader*, 303, 300, 299.
88. W.E.B. Du Bois, 'Triumph' (1911), in Weinberg, ed., *A Reader*, 307.
89. Ibid., 308.
90. W.E.B. Du Bois, 'Prejudice' (1927), in Weinberg, ed., *A Reader*, 326–7.
91. Du Bois, 'Souls of White Folk', 301.
92. Du Bois, 'Prejudice', 327.
93. W.E.B. Du Bois, 'The Religion of the American Negro' (1900), in Weinberg, ed., *A Reader*, 211–13.
94. Du Bois, 'Social Effects of Emancipation', 74.
95. W.E.B. Du Bois, 'Socialism and the Negro Problem' (1913), in Weinberg, ed., *A Reader*, 337–40.
96. W.E.B. Du Bois, 'The Class Struggle' (1921), in Weinberg, ed., *A Reader*, 341.
97. Du Bois, 'Socialism and the Negro Problem', 338–9.
98. Du Bois, 'Class Struggle', 342–3.
99. Washington, *Future of the American Negro*, 158–9.
100. Ibid., 180.
101. Ibid., 201, 160. Washington quotes 'Old King Cetewayo', who said: 'First come missionary, then come rum, then come traders, then come army', and English imperialist Cecil Rhodes, who expressed the 'prevailing sentiment': 'I would rather have land than "niggers"' (p. 160).
102. Ibid., 166, 165, 202, 189, 193, 226.

CHAPTER THIRTEEN

1. Quoted in Lynne Olson, *Freedom's Daughters: The Unsung Heroines of the Civil Rights Movement from 1830 to 1970* (New York: Simon & Schuster, 2001), 28.
2. Ibid., 30.
3. Quoted in Howard Zinn, *A People's History of the United States, 1492–Present* (New York: Harper Perennial, 1995), 121.
4. Shulamith Firestone, *The Dialectic of Sex: The Case for Feminist Revolution* (St Albans, Vt.: Paladin, 1973), 24.
5. Quoted in Olson, *Freedom's Daughters*, 32.
6. Ibid., 31.
7. Ibid.
8. Carol Smith-Rosenberg, *Disorderly Conduct: Visions of Gender in Victorian America* (New York: Oxford University Press, 1985), 243.
9. Ibid., 173.
10. Ibid., 176–7.
11. Queen Victoria, quoted in Richard D. Altick, *Victorian People and Ideas* (New York: Norton, 1973), 58.
12. Barbara Caine, *English Feminism: 1780–1980* (New York: Oxford University Press, 1997), 144–6.
13. Ibid., 136–9.
14. Whitney Chadwick, *Women, Art, and Society* (London: Thames and Hudson, 1990), 185–6.
15. Ibid., 177.
16. Smith-Rosenberg, *Disorderly Conduct*, 253–5.
17. Rolf Fjelde, 'Foreword' to Henrik Ibsen, *Four Major Plays* (New York: Signet, 1965).
18. Ibid., xi.
19. Ibsen quoted ibid., xix.
20. Shaw quoted ibid., xxv.
21. H. Ibsen, *A Doll's House* (1879), in *Four Major Plays* (New York: Signet, 1965), 112.
22. Ibid., 109.
23. Karl Mannheim, *Man and Society in an Age of Reconstruction* (New York: Harcourt Brace, 1940), 302.
24. Smith-Rosenberg, *Disorderly Conduct*, 265.
25. Mary Jo Deegan, 'Jane Addams (1860–1935)', in Deegan, ed., *Women in Sociology: A Bio-Biographical Sourcebook* (New York: Greenwood Press, 1991), 37.
26. Jane Addams, *Twenty Years at Hull-House, with Autobiographical Notes* (New York: Macmillan, 1916), 11, 7, 15, 14.
27. Ibid., 32–3, 21–2.
28. Ibid., 43–4, 54. Addams left the Seminary in the summer of 1881, returning one year later to become one of the first four BA graduates of the recently chartered Rockford College. Her first financial gift to Rockford was one thousand dollars, with the stipulation that it be used to purchase scientific books (pp. 62–4).
29. Ibid., 46. A young teacher brought into their confidence confiscated the remaining powder as well as the illicit copy of de Quincy, and administered an emetic.
30. Ibid., 81–2.

31. Deegan, 'Jane Addams', 38.

32. Addams, *Twenty Years at Hull-House*, 65–9.

33. Jane Addams, *Democracy and Social Ethics* (New York: Macmillan, 1907), 90, 100–1.

34. Ibid., 73. She wrote: We had been 'lumbering our minds with literature that only served to cloud the really vital situation spread before our eyes' (70–1). 'I was certainly much disillusioned at this time as to the effects of intellectual pursuits upon moral development.' Addams, *Twenty Years at Hull-House*, 77, 118.

35. Addams, *Democracy and Social Ethics*, 73–4.

36. Ibid., 82–5

37. Ibid., 86–7.

38. Ibid., 76–8.

39. Addams, *Twenty Years at Hull-House*, 36, 85, 115. Truth was to be put to the ultimate test: 'the conduct it dictates or inspires' (p. 85).

40. Deegan, 'Jane Addams', 38.

41. Sara M. Evans, *Born for Liberty: A History of Women in America* (New York: Free Press, 1989), 180.

42. Addams, *Twenty Years at Hull-House*, 79, 123–6. These ideals spring from the social gospel movement.

43. Ibid., 415, 99.

44. Ibid., 221.

45. Ibid., 357, 394.

46. Ibid., 402–7.

47. Addams, *Democracy and Social Ethics*, 165, 225.

48. Addams, *Twenty Years at Hull-House*, 183–4.

49. Ibid., 125–6. Addams sensed 'that shedding of blood which is sure to occur when men forget how complicated life is and insist on reducing it to logical dogmas' (p. 75).

50. Addams, *Democracy and Social Ethics*, 6–8.

51. Addams, *Twenty Years at Hull-House*, 58; Jane Addams, *The Excellent Becomes the Permanent* (New York: Macmillan 1970 [1932]), 45.

52. Addams, *Twenty Years at Hull-House*, 260–73. 'Fanaticism is engendered only when men, finding no contradiction to their theories, at last believe that the very universe lends itself as an exemplification of one point of view' (p. 179).

53. Ibid., 360. '[O]ur very democracy so long presupposed that each citizen could care for himself that we are slow to develop a sense of social obligation' (p. 368).

54. Ibid., 229. This argument, Addams noted, was condemned as socialism; yet it was exactly this reasoning that led to the 10-hour Bill that had been confirmed by the Supreme Court of the United States.

55. Addams, *Democracy and Social Ethics*, 170.

56. Ibid., 171–2. '[T]hat which may appear as a choice between virtue and vice is really but a choice between virtue and virtue.' (p. 172).

57. Addams, *Twenty Years at Hull-House*, 62, 182.

58. Deegan, 'Jane Addams', 39.

59. Addams, *Democracy and Social Ethics*, 7.

60. Jane Addams, 'The Devil Baby at Hull-House', in Joyce Carol Oates, ed., *The Best American Essays of the Century* (Boston: Houghton Mifflin, 2000), 75, 81–3.

61. Addams, *Democracy and Social Ethics*, 31–5, 44.

62. Ibid., 51–6.

63. Jane Addams, *The Spirit of Youth and the City Streets* (New York: Macmillan, 1957 [1909]), 131, 107.

64. Ibid., 7, 159, 30, 79–80.

65. Addams, *The Excellent Becomes the Permanent*, 8.

66. Addams, *Democracy and Social Ethics*, 27–8.

67. Ibid., 19–23.

68. Ibid., 38, 176–7, 224.

69. Addams, *Twenty Years at Hull-House*, 452.

70. Addams, *Democracy and Social Ethics*, 151–3, 116.

71. Glenna Matthews, *The Rise of Public Women* (New York: Oxford, 1992), 181.

72. Deegan, 'Jane Addams', 40.

73. Ibid.

74. Olive Schreiner, quoted in Vera Brittain, *Testament of Youth* (Glasgow: Fontana, 1978), 41

75. Caine, *English Feminism*, xv.

76. Fyodor Dostoyevsky, *Notes from Underground* (New York: Dell, 1960 [1864]), 41–5.

77. William Shakespeare, *Hamlet*, III, ii.

78. Henri F. Ellenberger, *The Discovery of the Unconscious: The History and Evolution of Dynamic Psychology* (New York: Basic Books, 1970), 280–3.

79. Peter Nicholls, *Modernisms: A Literary Guide* (Berkeley: University of California Press, 1995), 6–16.

80. Annette Rubinstein, *The Great Tradition in English Literature: From Shakespeare to Shaw* (New York: Monthly Review Press, 1969), 848 ff.

81. Roland Stromberg, *European Intellectual History Since 1789*, 6th edn (Englewood Cliffs, NJ: Prentice-Hall, 1994), 139.

82. Gaunt, quoted in Rubinstein, *Great Tradition*, 849.

83. Degas, quoted ibid.

84. A.E. Housman, 'Last Poems, XII', in *Collected Poems and Selected Prose* (London: Allen Lane, 1988), 109.

85. Oscar Wilde, 'The Picture of Dorian Grey', in *The Writings of Oscar Wilde* (Oxford: Oxford University Press, 1989), 65, 62.

86. 'Two Loves', the infamous Douglas sonnet used against Wilde at his trial, ends: 'I am the Love that dare not speak its name.' Isobel Murray, 'Introduction', *The Writings of Oscar Wilde*, xv.

87. Oscar Wilde, 'The Ballad of Reading Gaol', in *Writings*, 564.

88. Rubinstein, *Great Tradition*, 854.

89. Oscar Wilde, 'Lady Windemere's Fan', in *Writings*, 367.

90. J.H. Buckley, ed., *Poems of Tennyson* (Boston: Houghton Mifflin, 1958), 508–10.

91. Nicholls, *Modernisms*, 73.

92. R.J. Hollingdale, *Nietzsche: The Man and His Philosophy*, rev. edn (Cambridge: Cambridge University Press, 1999), 5–8.

93. Ibid., 20–1, 31.

94. Ibid., 71–2.

95. Peter Sedgwick, *Descartes to Derrida: An Introduction to European Philosophy* (Oxford: Blackwell, 2001), 261.

96. Ibid., 259–60.

97. John MacDonald, 'Frederick Nietzsche', in MacDonald, *Architects of Modern Thought* (Toronto: CBC, 1959).

98. Ibid.

99. Stromberg, *European Intellectual History*, 151.

100. Aldous Huxley, *Point Counter Point* (Harmondsworth, Middlesex: Penguin, 1969 [1928]), 122–3.

101. Sedgwick, *Descartes to Derrida*, 68–74.

102. Ibid., 71–4.

103. Ibid., 75.

104. J.K. Rowling, *Harry Potter and the Philosopher's Stone* (Markham, Ont.: Scholastic, 1997), 211.

105. Oscar Wilde, 'An Ideal Husband' (1899), *Writings*, 419–20.

106. Sedgwick, *Descartes to Derrida*, 262.

107. Ibid., 77.

108. Hollingdale, *Nietzsche*, 194, 237.

109. Ibid., 151–3.

110. Nicholls, *Modernisms*, 77.

111. Quoted in B. Roszak and T. Roszak, eds, *Masculine/Feminine* (New York: Harper and Row, 1969), 4.

112. Quoted ibid.

113. Quoted ibid., 6.

114. Friedrich Nietzsche, *Thus Spake Zarathustra* (New York: Modern Library, 1917 [1883]), 69, 79–81.

115. David Kettler, Volker Meja, and Nico Stehr, *Karl Mannheim* (London: Tavistock, 1984), 19, 40. The goal of spiritual regeneration was inspired by the Russian novelist, Dostoyevsky.

116. Ibid., 37.

117. Karl Mannheim, *Man and Society in an Age of Reconstruction* (New York: Harcourt Brace, 1940), 222.

118. Stephen W. Hawking, *A Brief History of Time* (Toronto: Bantam, 1988), 32, 55–6. Einstein could not accept the principle that there was an element of randomness in nature. He declared flatly, 'God does not play dice' (p. 56).

119. Huxley, *Point Counter Point*, 158.

120. Karl Mannheim, *Ideology and Utopia: An Introduction to the Sociology of Knowledge* (London: Routledge & Kegan Paul, 1936 [1929]), 79–80.

121. Ibid., 91, 77, 177, 245.

122. Ibid., 9, 83, 10, 19.

123. Ibid., 85–9, 36.

124. Franz Kafka, *The Penal Colony: Stories and Short Pieces* (New York: Schocken, 1961), 26–7.

125. Mannheim, *Ideology and Utopia*, 57n.

126. Ibid., 51, 91.

127. Ibid., 179–80.

128. Ibid., 36.

129. Ibid., 3.

130. Ibid., 75, 83.

131. Ibid., 266–7, 94–5, 271, 268.

132. Ibid., 100–10, 149.

133. Ibid., 103–4, 166–7.

134. Ibid., 168, 125.

135. Ibid., 132. Mannheim analyzes five general modes of political thought and locates the social position each represents: bureaucratic conservatism, conservative historicism, liberal democratic bourgeois thought, the socialist-communist conception, and Fascism (pp. 105–27).

136. Mannheim, *Man and Society*, 184.

137. Huxley, *Point Counter Point*, 29–30.

138. Mannheim, *Ideology and Utopia*, 134–6.

139. Ibid., 136.

140. Ibid., 137.

141. Mannheim, *Man and Society*, 101.

142. Mannheim, *Ideology and Utopia*, 140–3, 152. Mannheim notes that not all have chosen to accept

this mission. Given their essentially middle position, some intellectuals have tried to remain unattached and indifferent to the social process—the movement of art for art's sake, for example. Others have voluntarily affiliated with one of the antagonistic classes, becoming apologists for the dominant class or spokespersons for the oppressed (p. 140).

143. Ibid., 163–4, 169.
144. Mannheim, *Man and Society*, 12.
145. Kettler et al., *Mannheim*, 75, 11.
146. Mannheim, *Man and Society*, 365–6.
147. Ibid., 121–3, 147–8.
148. Ibid., 141.
149. Ibid., 6.
150. Ibid., 59, 68–9.
151. Ibid., 58.
152. Ibid., 47–8.
153. Ibid., 44, 46. Irrational is not automatically negative; it can drive one to a rational end, 'creates cultural values through sublimation', and 'heightens the joy of living' when it does not threaten the social order (p. 62).
154. Ibid., 60.
155. Ibid., 98, 61, 45, 63.
156. Ibid., 75.
157. Nicholls, *Modernisms*, 79–80. In 'Dorian Grey', Oscar Wilde's decadent character, Lord Henry, advises Dorian: 'You must have a cigarette. The cigarette is the perfect type of a perfect pleasure. It is exquisite, and it leaves one unsatisfied. What more can one want?' (p. 107). Putting the consumer ethic differently, Wilde added: 'we live in an age when unnecessary things are our only necessities' (p. 117).
158. Mannheim, *Man and Society*, 183, 243.
159. Ibid., 185. 'The forced imposition of mathematical and mensurative methods has gradually led to a situation in which certain sciences no longer ask what is worth knowing but regard as worth knowing only what is measurable.'
160. Kurt H. Wolff, *The Sociology of Georg Simmel* (Glencoe, Ill.: Free Press, 1950), 40–1.

CHAPTER FOURTEEN

1. Max Weber, *The Theory of Social and Economic Organization*, ed. Talcott Parsons (New York: Free Press, 1964 [1920]), 88.
2. Ibid., 88, 118–19.
3. Kurt H. Wolff, 'Introduction', in *The Sociology of Georg Simmel* (Glencoe, Ill.: Free Press, 1950), xviii, xlii n. 6.
4. Ibid., xviii.
5. David Frisby, *Georg Simmel* (London: Tavistock, 1984), 27.
6. Wolff, 'Introduction', xlvi n. 32, xlix n. 46.
7. Frisby, *Simmel*, 25.
8. Ibid., 48.
9. Ibid., 49.
10. Ibid., 58–9.
11. Wolff, *Simmel*, 61–2.
12. Ibid., 64–7.
13. Ibid., 69–72.
14. Ibid., 73–4.
15. Ibid., 79.
16. Ibid., 74–5.
17. Eugene Zamiatin, *We* (New York: Dutton, 1952 [1924]), 167.
18. Wolff, *Simmel*, 75–6.
19. Ibid., 28–9.
20. Ibid., 77–8.
21. Ibid., 78–9.
22. Ibid., 80, 82.
23. Ibid., 40–1.
24. Frisby, *Simmel*, 50.
25. Ibid., 62–3.
26. Wolff, *Simmel*.
27. Jean-Paul Sartre, *No Exit and Three Other Plays* (New York: Vintage, 1960), 18, 42, 39, 40, 46–7.
28. Robert Fitch, *Odyssey of the Self-Centred Self* (London: Allen & Unwin, 1962), 35–6.
29. Henrik Ibsen, *Peer Gynt*, Act IV, sc. I (1867), in *The Works of Henrik Ibsen* (Boston: Charles Lauriat, 1911), 176–7.
30. Ibid., IV, xiii, 229.
31. Fitch, *Odyssey of the Self-Centred Self*, 64.
32. Henri F. Ellenberger, *The Discovery of the Unconscious: The History and Evolution of Dynamic Psychology* (New York: Basic Books, 1970), 420–2.
33. Ibid., 428–41.
34. Ibid., 444.
35. Nietzsche, quoted in Nicholls, *Modernisms*, 91; Nietzsche's emphasis.
36. Thomas Mann, *The Magic Mountain* (New York: Alfred A. Knopf, 1961 [1924]), 127.
37. Ibid., 128.
38. Ellenberger, *Discovery of the Unconscious*, 525–7.

39. Sigmund Freud, 'The future of an illusion', in James Strachey, ed., *Sigmund Freud: Complete Psychological Works*, vol. 21 (London: Hogarth Press, 1961), 16–17.

40. Ibid., 54.

41. D.H. Lawrence, *Sons and Lovers* (New York: Viking, 1958 [1913]), 37, 92, 79, 101, 113, 407.

42. Sigmund Freud, 'Anatomy is Destiny', in Roszak and Roszak, eds, *Masculine/Feminine*, 19–29

43. Ellenberger, *Discovery of the Unconscious*, 529.

44. Friedrich Nietzsche, *Thus Spake Zarathustra* (New York: Modern Library, 1917 [1883]), 80.

45. Freud, 'Anatomy is Destiny', 24.

46. Ibid., 26.

47. Lawrence, *Sons and Lovers*, 379.

48. Ibid., 379–82.

49. Ibid., 363.

50. Freud, 'The future of an illusion', 6–8.

51. Sigmund Freud, 'Civilization and its discontents', in Strachey, ed., *Sigmund Freud*, 93–4, 115.

52. Ibid., 122.

53. Ibid., 111.

54. Joseph Conrad, *Heart of Darkness* (Toronto: Signet Classics, 1967 [1910]), 143, 149, 147.

55. Ibid., 102, 103, 105–6.

56. Freud, 'Civilization', 112.

57. Ibid.

58. Ibid., 112–14.

59. Ibid., 115.

60. Charles Dickens, *Great Expectations* (New York: Airmont, 1965 [1860–1]), 54–5.

61. Max Weber, *The Protestant Ethic and the Spirit of Capitalism* (New York: Charles Scribner, 1958 [1904]), 52.

62. Burgess demonstrates the inhumanity of this type of forced conditioning but, ultimately, Alex loses the essence of what makes him an individual personality along with his desire to kill tramps. For Burgess, as for Freud, our propensity for violence is an essential element in the human psyche. Anthony Burgess, *A Clockwork Orange* (Harmondsworth, Middlesex: Penguin, 1972).

63. George H. Mead, *Mind, Self and Society: From the Point of View of a Social Behaviorist* (Chicago: University of Chicago Press, 1934), 106.

64. Ibid., 7.

65. Ibid.

66. Ibid., 39.

67. Ibid., 42–4.

68. Ibid., 45–7.

69. Helen Keller, *The Story of My Life* (New York: Random House, Inc., 1902), 35.

70. Ibid., 256–7. Keller's first 'great leap' was learning obedience (p. 252).

71. Ibid., 36–7.

72. Mead, *Mind, Self and Society*, 65–6.

73. Ibid., 73.

74. Ibid., 133–4.

75. Ibid., 135–7.

76. Ibid., 138–9, 161.

77. Ibid., 140–4.

78. Ibsen, *Peer Gynt* (1867), 276. In the animated movie *Shrek* (2001, directed by Andrew Adamson and Vicky Jenson), the title character tries to explain that 'there's a lot more to Ogres than people think.' Ogres are like onions, he says, because they have 'Layers. Onions have layers; Ogres have layers.' Shrek, however, is unable to articulate the metaphor beyond this point.

79. Mead, *Mind, Self and Society*, 164, 149–51, 154.

80. Ibid., 158.

81. Ibid., 90.

82. Ibid., 178.

83. Ibid., 277.

84. Ibid., 196.

85. Ibid., 187.

86. Ibid., 197, 200.

87. Ibid., 202, 209.

88. Ibid., 174–5.

89. Ibid., 199, 205–7.

90. Ibid., 227–31.

91. Ibid., 233, 182.

92. Ibid., 237–9.

93. Ibid., 254–5.

94. Ibid., 284.

95. Ibid., 79.

96. Ibid., 128–9.

97. Wolff, *Simmel*, 40–1.

CHAPTER FIFTEEN

1. Thomas Mann, *The Magic Mountain* (New York: Alfred A. Knopf, 1961 [1924]), v.

2. Ibid., 222.

INDEX